MUSICAL EVENTS

MUSICAL EVENTS

A Chronicle, 1983-1986

ANDREW PORTER

GRAFTON BOOKS

A Division of the Collins Publishing Group

LONDON GLASGOW
TORONTO SYDNEY AUCKLAND

Grafton Books
A Division of the Collins Publishing Group
8 Grafton Street, London W1X 3LA

First published in the USA by Summit Books,
A Division of Simon & Schuster, Inc., 1989

Published in Great Britain by Grafton Books 1990

These essays first appeared in *The New Yorker*
Copyright © Andrew Porter 1983, 1984, 1985, 1986, 1989

British Library Cataloguing in Publication Data
Porter, Andrew
Musical events: a chronicle, 1983-1986.
1. Western music
I. Title
781.68

ISBN 0-246-13312-0

Printed in Great Britain by
Hartnolls Ltd, Bodmin, Cornwall

Again,
for William Shawn,
with respect, gratitude, and affection

CONTENTS

INTRODUCTION

THIS collection, another survey of three years' musical events, is intended to reflect the wide range of the musical adventures that were offered in an age at once busily creative and eager—probably more eager than any previous age—to explore and enjoy the music of all ages. It begins with an account of a new Bayreuth production of *The Nibelung's Ring,* a century after Wagner's death, and ends with a cheering audience at the close of a Tanglewood new-music week. The lyric dramas considered reach from the thirteenth-century musical comedy *Robin et Marion* to new operas by Karlheinz Stockhausen (*Thursday,* from the seven-day cycle-in-progress *Light*) and by Harrison Birtwistle (*The Mask of Orpheus*), both of which summoned most of the means that contemporary music commands in a demonstration of music's power to affect our lives. Orpheus, throughout the centuries—for Monteverdi, Gluck, Stravinsky, Kurt Weill, Birtwistle, Elliott Carter, Hans Werner Henze, and many another composer—has been an exemplification of that power. Mozart called him Tamino, Wagner called him Tannhäuser, and Stockhausen calls him Michael.

George Frideric Handel is a recurrent figure in these pages. The season 1984–85 saw the tercentenary of his birth (on February 23, 1685) and brought many Handel performances. In the following seasons they continued: Handel's greatness, once discovered, was not forgotten. "Discovered" may seem a strange word to apply to so celebrated a composer, but the extent and variety of his achievement had not been widely recognized while only a few of his operas and only his most famous oratorios were performed with any frequency. There are reviews here of the operas *Alcina, Ariodante, Giulio Cesare, Imeneo, Rinaldo, Serse, Teseo,* and *Tolomeo*; of the oratorios *Athalia, Belshazzar, The Choice of Hercules, Deborah, Hercules, Israel in Egypt, Judas Maccabaeus, Samson, Semele,* and *Solomon*; of the serenatas *Aci, Galatea, e Polifemo* and *Acis and Galatea*; and of the ode *Alexander's Feast.* I considered collecting them into a single "Handel" section but decided that it made sense to let them punctuate the chronicle of what else was happening during these years. In many different ways, Handel provided a touchstone. In troubled times, his music was a model of sanity, clarity, and certainty, of fluency combined with freshness of invention. He lived before Goethe, the writer who has left the greatest mark on music, but much of his subject matter was drawn—even if at first or second remove—from

9

literature that has shaped the Western imagination: the Greek dramatists, the Bible, Ovid, Ariosto and Tasso, Racine, Milton. His much discussed practice of "borrowing"—from his own earlier compositions and quite as often from the compositions of others—and his bold developments and transformations of the borrowed material make him a type at once of "continuity" and of "progress": two things often considered in these reviews. There is the continuity of musical history, the influence of composer upon composer, and the continuing influence of masterpieces in interpretations by generation after generation of performers. On the other hand, there are the discoveries: the musical inventions of a Carter, Boulez, or Stockhausen, new ways of thinking, new forms, new kinds of sound; discoveries of older music previously unheard by modern audiences; discoveries about older music and its modern performance that are made both in the concert hall and in the study.

In Boston, at the Early Music Festival, Nicholas McGegan presented Handel's *Teseo* in as close an approach as the circumstances allowed to the musical and theatrical practices of the composer's day. In Purchase, at the PepsiCo Summerfare festival, Peter Sellars set Handel's *Giulio Cesare* in a contemporary Near-Eastern capital. Both shows were revelatory. They had in common a blazing belief in Handel's theatrical power, his ability to speak directly to modern audiences. And both were uncut—in strong contrast to cut-and-shuffle presentations of *Rinaldo* at the Met and *Alcina* at the City Opera which are also reviewed here. No hard-liner, I am ready to be stirred by both historical and updated interpretations. These years witnessed "director's opera," at its best and its worst, growing ever more dominant—especially in the European houses, where people began to wonder whether ever again they would see a *Barbiere* or a *Carmen* set in Seville, a *Norma* without rifles and tanks, a *Ring* in which Loge did not carry a briefcase and the *Financial Times*. In this country, the San Francisco *Ring* was brought to completion. (Loge carried the *Wall Street Journal*, but Froh carried a lyre.) In Castle Hill and then Purchase, Sellars, with *Così fan tutte*, embarked on a Mozart-Da Ponte "cycle" that has been both acclaimed and deplored. The Juilliard staged a bloody *Traviata* in which Violetta's cherished letter served her as a Kleenex. Several operatic productions by famous men of the theatre—Peter Hall, Peter Brook, Peter Stein, Peter Sellars, Andrei Serban, Liviu Ciulei, in retrospect Erwin Piscator—are considered here.

Without prejudice, I hope. Each on its merits. As I write this introduction, an editorial credo by Patrick J. Smith, the new editor of *Opera News* (the magazine of the Metropolitan Opera Guild), appears. One of its clauses is, "New approaches to production, despite numerous outrageous instances, have been and will be the lifeblood of the future of opera." Mr. Smith instances Sellars's 1988 production of *Tannhäuser*, for the Lyric Opera of Chicago, as a model. When a composer and his director are at odds, I tend to side with the former. There are operas that can benefit from wholesale directorial distortion, revision, and rewriting, but not many—and they are generally operas that might as well be left unrevived. Wagner's famous imperative "Macht Neues!" (often cited by directors who strain for novelty) was uttered as a rebuke to those who sought by tinkering and revisions to bring new life to an old work: better to start afresh with something else. In the Chicago *Tannhäuser*—whose scenes were set in a

10

Miami motel, the Crystal Cathedral, and an airport lounge—the composer and the director were not at odds. The show held listeners intent on Wagner's opera and inspired its singers to uncommonly eloquent performances. (My enthusiastic review of it belongs to a later collection.) "New approaches," however, can also be new in their bold, uncompromising search for another kind of originality—an attempt to recreate the original work in every attainable detail. The venture of reintegrating *was die Mode frech getheilt*—breaching the barriers that custom and convention may have erected between the original force of a composition and its present-day reception as a familiar classic—can take different forms.

And not only in the opera house. Not all music is opera, even if most music, for nearly four centuries, has been. During the three seasons here considered, Handel was a touchstone in other ways. Some of the Handel performances were given with "original instruments," others with modern instruments played in a "modern" manner, and others with modern instruments bowed, blown, and fingered with an awareness of eighteenth-century phrasing and articulation. That is another concern of our day. It affects audiences' response not only to what was once called "early music" but to Beethoven, Rossini, Schubert, Berlioz, Schumann. In the closing decade of the twentieth century, Verdi, Wagner, Brahms, Debussy, Mahler, even the earlier works of Schoenberg and of Richard Strauss have become "early music"—some of it apparently calling for the sounds of instruments different from those in our modern orchestras, some, perhaps, for such less radical restorations as gut strings and the platform placements of the composer's day. But instruments—though their sound is very important in making sense of the music written for them—do not play themselves. Far more is involved: technique (portamento, for one thing), understanding, feeling, identification. There is a chapter here about the renewed attention to the metronome markings that Beethoven attached to his works. More and more conductors are striving to match them, and on instruments kin to those of Beethoven's day they can more convincingly be achieved. Yet no one who in his youth thrilled to Furtwängler's performances of Beethoven symphonies with the Vienna Philharmonic now scorns all that they offered because they moved at tempi different from those that Beethoven specified. Today—provided that other things, such as the merits of the pianist, are equal—I prefer to hear Mozart's, Beethoven's, Schubert's piano music played on modern replicas of instruments of the composers' time than on modern Steinway replicas of late-nineteenth-century instruments. Similarly with string quartets and symphonies. But other things seldom are equal. I hope that these pages reflect mixed feelings—individual, particularized, varying, and inconsistent responses. A critic tries to be more curious than censorious; cognizant of practical constraints; enthusiastic whenever he can be; generous toward honest endeavor even while impatient of pretension.

During these three years, my own awareness of practical constraints and the ways that they can affect particular performances was sharpened by some extra-critical activity. The Seattle Opera invited me to stage Verdi's *La forza del destino*; Indiana University, in Bloomington, to stage Handel's *Tamerlano*; and

11

Carnegie Hall to "semistage"—to add some dramatic element to—its concert presentations of *Orlando* and *Semele*. And from Shakespeare's play I fashioned a libretto for John Eaton's opera *The Tempest*. There are those who hold that critics should keep themselves aloof from any personal contact with artists, and those who hold that the more practical knowledge and experience of their subject critics can acquire, the better. Peter Brook has a good passage about critics, playwrights, and performers in *The Empty Space*. He writes of "our shared aim," "our common task," and continues:

> The more a critic becomes an insider, the better. I see nothing but good in a critic's plunging into our lives, meeting actors, talking, discussing, watching, intervening. I would welcome his putting his hands on the medium and attempting to work it himself. Certainly, there is a tiny social problem—how does a critic talk to someone he has just damned in print? Momentary awkwardnesses may arise—but it is ludicrous to think that it is this that deprives some critics of a vital contact with the work of which they are a part. The embarrassment on his side and ours can easily be lived down and certainly a closer relationship with the work will in no way put the critic into the position of connivance with the people he has got to know.

The list of critic-composers who have publicly assessed compositions by their colleagues, rivals, friends, and foes and performances by artists who also performed (or failed to perform) their works is long. It includes Schumann, Berlioz, William Henry Fry, Hugo Wolf, Debussy, Dukas, Reyer, Deems Taylor, Havergal Brian, Virgil Thomson, Elliott Carter. When Rossini's *Stabat mater* appeared, Wagner sent off a scathing review of it to the *Neue Zeitschrift*, and J. W. Davison—long the critic of the London *Times* and married to the well-known pianist Arabella Goddard—ventured into "practical criticism" by publishing a jolly set of *Bologna Quadrilles;* they were based on the *Stabat mater* themes. Henry F. Chorley translated *Faust* for Gounod and wrote the words for Valentin's aria, "Even bravest heart may swell," which was added to *Faust* in England. In this country, Henry Krehbiel, the critic of the *Tribune* from 1880 to 1923, devised *Mozart and Salieri* for the American première of *Der Schauspieldirektor*—an ingenious version amplified by music from other Mozart operas. W. J. Henderson, an admirable critic, famous as having reviewed the Met for longer than anyone else (his career began in 1870, when he was a schoolboy, and lasted to 1937), wrote the libretto for Walter Damrosch's *Cyrano de Bergerac*, which was produced at the Met in 1913, with Frances Alda, Riccardo Martin, and Pasquale Amato. (Krehbiel gave it a cool review.)

In Seattle, where the company owns a replica of the scenery that Carlo Ferrario designed for the Scala première of *Forza*, in 1869, I gained first-hand experience of the painted-canvas décor that Verdi knew. It allows swift, open-stage changes of scene; as late as *Aida*, Verdi wrote music continuous through the scene changes, and the curtain did not fall during an act. We knew about this kind of scenery in theory; in Seattle I discovered how it worked in practice. On the other hand, someone who had often in print deplored cuts that distort a composer's original structure was compelled to trim the long score to bring it within the company's orchestral budget. In Bloomington, *Tamerlano*—

accompanied by modern instruments, and enacted, at my request, in stark, simple Appiesque spaces—was also abridged. Insofar as that represented not taxing young singers beyond their effective resources, it seemed to me justified. Insofar as it represented not challenging at length an audience unaccustomed to Handel opera, I had qualms. I remembered Winton Dean's stern sentences in *Handel and the Opera Seria*: "Opera by its very nature is a gigantic series of compromises, and its realization in performance may involve further adjustments between the ideal and the practicable. . . . But a compromise between what a great composer desires (provided it is practicable) and what we happen to be accustomed to is not a valid artistic operation." My share in the Carnegie performances—which were uncut—was concerned with "presentation." Handel himself was a pioneer and master of concert-platform theatre. In a great series of dramatic oratorios, he wrote musical dramas (his own term for some of them) that dispense with costumes and scenery, dramas in which the scenes change more swiftly even than Verdi's—in the twinkling of a harpsichord cadence. But *Orlando* is an opera, and *Semele*, although it was first presented "after the manner of an oratorio," was composed to an opera libretto by Congreve. Concert-platform drama is important in New York and is being taken up increasingly by the European companies. Concert performances expand the repertory, and they allow important singers to be heard in works that the big companies cannot afford to stage. (Without Eve Queler's Opera Orchestra and its concert performances, New York would not have heard Gabriela Benačková or Smetana's *Libuše*; without Carnegie's own series, Frederica von Stade as Massenet's Chérubin.) The small companies, often working in school auditoriums, church halls, or churches, matter, too. There are accounts in these pages of—I pick five works at random—John Christian Bach's *Amadis de Gaule*, Donizetti's *Giovedì grasso*, *Gianni di Parigi*, and *Gemma di Vergy*, and Franchetti's *Germania*, which were revived by enterprising small companies.

The book is not all about opera, though much of it is. Most great composers—the exceptions are few—spent most of their time setting words to music, for the church, the theatre, or the concert room. A recurrent concern here is the importance of using the words as well as the notes for communication: if Orpheus when first he struck his lyre and raised his voice had been incomprehensible, he would have moved men's souls less potently. Still, the trees, stones, and beasts that heard him, and were moved, were responding, no doubt, to the force and eloquence of pure sound. And I am not unresponsive to the sounds and structures of symphonies, string quartets, and sonatas. Prominent among the works without words which appeared in these years were Boulez's *Répons* and *Dérive*, Carter's *Penthode*, Peter Maxwell Davies's Third Symphony, Lutoslawski's Third Symphony, and big new piano concertos by Milton Babbitt, Charles Wuorinen, and Peter Lieberson. Carter's *In Sleep, in Thunder* and Michael Tippett's *The Mask of Time* were among the works that used words but were not operas. Some of the younger composers who came to prominence were Michael Torke, Susan Blaustein, Tod Machover, George Benjamin, Hans Abrahamsen, and Kamran Ince. The quatercentenary of Heinrich Schütz's birth was celebrated, and the tercentenary not only of Handel's but of Johann Sebastian Bach's and Domenico Scarlatti's. Bruckner and Jean Barraqué, Nicolas Gombert and Philip

13

Glass, Haydn and John Harbison, Lully, Ligeti, and Lieberson, Massenet, Martinů, and Donald Martino mingle in these Handel-punctuated pages.

The reviews were written when William Shawn was still the editor of *The New Yorker*. He gave me freedom, trust, encouragement—and plenty of space. His enforced departure from the magazine, at the hest of its new owner, is still mourned by those who worked there while Mr. Shawn was its editor. Eleanor Gould Packard's acute reading of what we write remains; my desk copy of *Fowler* bulges with her precise, entertaining exegeses of points that she first raised in galley margins. My particular editor in these years was Susan Moritz, who has now left to cultivate if not her own garden, at any rate the gardens of others. It was a weekly pleasure to discuss with her not just writing about music but music itself. Martin Baron and his team of checkers continue to save me from misspelling names, misdating, misquoting. At Summit Books, Ileene Smith and Alane Mason have been patient with an author who finds it hard to meet deadlines. Patrick Dillon brought operatic and phonographic lore to his reading of the manuscript. The index was compiled by Jerold Ordansky and Sydney Wolfe Cohen.

New York
May 1989

PART
I

1983 – 1984

Music Visible

August 29, 1983

Wagner's various attempts to explain in words what *The Nibelung's Ring*—conceived in 1848, and brought to performance only in 1876—might mean are confused and contradictory. In an 1856 letter, the composer told August Röckel that "something quite different came into being from what I had originally planned," for "during the execution—in fact, even in the planning—I was unconsciously following a different, much deeper view of things" and "unwittingly, instead of one phase in the evolution of the world, was seeing the very essence of the world, in every imaginable phase." As composition proceeded, there were further developments. *The Ring* became at once a world history, starting with man's first polluting attempts to harness nature to his uses; a contemporary parable about capitalism and its attendant evils; and a dramatic image, apt for Jungian exposition, of the human psyche. From its inception, it had also been an adventurous narrative—a splendid old tale of gods, giants, men, and dwarfs, of magic, murder, and love, taking place in grandly picturesque Rhine scenery. The deeper meanings are carried more by the music—a sixteen-hour score of unparalleled richness, splendor, and formal intricacy—than by the words and the actions. (*Ring* commentators and *Ring* directors have often dwelt too partially on the latter ingredients, but exciting new studies of the music have started to appear.) To anyone who asks me what *The Ring* means, I say, "Listen first to the Furtwängler and the Reginald Goodall recordings." But that's only a beginning. The work is completed in the theatre, where, as Wagner said, "it is the performers who play the essential artistic part," while the composer's contribution is judged by the extent to which he has been able to inspire the drama enacted before us. "By drama, I mean not the dramatic poem or text but the drama we see taking place before our eyes, the visible counterpart of the music." In a famous phrase, he described his music dramas as "deeds of music made visible." In Bayreuth, he built a theatre where music and drama could work together in perfect balance.

Bayreuth's latest production of *The Ring*—its "British *Ring*," conducted by Sir Georg Solti, directed by Sir Peter Hall, and designed by William Dudley—has been criticized, not unfairly, for technical inefficiency, for blandness in the enactment of what should be vividly dramatic encounters, and for some undistinguished singing. It has also been criticized, but less fairly, for failing to embody a "conception." Operatic directors with "conceptions" in the form of reinterpretations, distortions, partial glosses, or misconceptions are a curse of our day. Bayreuth also presented this summer a ridiculous *Tristan,* directed by Jean-Pierre Ponnelle, in which Isolde, Mark, and Melot did not come to Kareol except as figments of Tristan's fevered delirium. From 1976 to 1980, it presented a *Ring* of sorts—its "French *Ring*," directed by Patrice Chéreau and conducted by Pierre Boulez—in which the huge myth dwindled to an allegory of economic history in the last century; untrue to the music and untrue to the text, it was enlivened by keen family scenes and some amusing anachronisms. Most modern productions of *The Ring* have treated it as Wotan's tragedy: Wotan's well-intentioned dream of social justice doomed (in anti-Wotan versions) by his greed for personal power or (in versions sensitive to the nobility of Wotan's music) by the criminal compromises the god has made—flaws in the foundation on which he seeks to build. "Valhalla is Wall Street," Wieland Wagner once declared. A new director can say "Wotan is Stalin" or "Wotan is Reagan" or "Wotan is Mrs. Thatcher" and, by suppressing or altering what does not fit his thesis, make some trenchant, and even accurate, points. Hall avoided specificity—thereby increasing applicability—and attempted to stage a "complete" *Ring*. In a preliminary note, he wrote:

> Naturally, I am interested in the political side of *The Ring*, but I think this has been so emphasized in recent years that the sensual side—not only the sexuality of Siegmund and Sieglinde, but the pure love of Brünnhilde—has been overlooked. I have concentrated on the complete narrative story of *The Ring*, and that is complex and contradictory. It can, and perhaps should, mean different things to each individual who sees it. In his polemical and absorbing *Ring* in 1976, for instance, Patrice Chéreau told us that the revolution is coming, but the *Ring* does not say that to me at all. The revolution fails, and what the *Ring* tells me is that life goes on, seasoned by some forgiveness, some humanity, and some love.... In Wagner's text and music, I find a classical story of the conflict between power and love; of how heroic love eventually redeems characters who have been corrupted by power.

Among other things, Hall hoped to restore to Siegfried his due importance. (As Carl Dahlhaus remarks in *Richard Wagner's Music Dramas,* "the thesis that Siegfried's drama is only a corollary of Wotan's tragedy may appear illuminating at first but comes to grief on the theatrical fact that Siegfried's drama occupies the tetralogy's two longest parts.") He professed fidelity to the text and promised to be "as faithful as possible" to the stage directions. For the first time in over thirty years of *Ring*-going, I saw Fricka arrive in a ram-drawn chariot and saw Brünnhilde leap onto a horse and ride into a blazing pyre.

Hall's initial plan was right, but in its execution there was many a slip. He and Solti had taken the risk of engaging several artists new to their roles. The Siegfried they worked with, Reiner Goldberg, withdrew from *Götterdämmerung* some weeks before the opening and from *Siegfried* after the dress rehearsal. The deputy was Manfred Jung, an accurate, reliable, energetic, but charmless hero, without chivalry of appearance or manner—blunt-featured and blunt in his interpretation. He made it possible for the show to get on but left a hole in the drama. The Wotan, Siegmund Nimsgern, fell out halfway through the cycle. In *Das Rheingold* and *Die Walküre,* Nimsgern had been uncommanding but not unpromising: the voice was generally firm and full, although the narrative was begun in a buzzy monotone. Then his indisposition was announced, and in *Siegfried* Bent Norup stood in for him. The phrase is apt: Norup stood onstage and sang in the notes, none too steadily; he was no Wotan. The third principal, Hildegard Behrens, a new Brünnhilde, was more successful, but she has been overpraised. Her voice is not a heroic soprano; it lacks the power, the amplitude, the glory that a Brünnhilde needs. Like many modern singers, she produced notes rather than lines; she should work with Goodall. But the sound was clear and always audible, and she is an attractive, arresting, and intelligent actress.

A shortage of Wagnerian singers, except basses, tends to blight any *Ring* today, and Hall cannot be blamed for that. (San Francisco's half-*Ring* in May was, by and large, better sung than the Bayreuth cycle.) But other, less forgivable things went wrong. Hall, it was reported, does not yet command German, and so there could hardly have been detailed rehearsals such as Cosima held when she explained and demonstrated to her cast that Alberich and Hagen must pronounce consonants differently from Wotan and Siegfried. There was a lack of sharp verbal characterization in the declamation. And some of the stage clumsiness was ascribed to imperfect communication between the director and his German crew. The men inside the dragon could be heard shouting instructions to one another. When Mime's corpse was bundled into the cave, those in the upper part of the house then saw it get up and walk off into the wings, and did not restrain their mirth. One does not expect such things at Bayreuth. At a press conference, Hall declared that the rehearsal time had been too short to prepare the *Ring* he wanted—the excuse did not go down well—and asked us to suspend judgment until next year's revival. No doubt the time was short for a director whose ideas, as Hall himself put it, "do not really take shape until he works with people on the stage." But much of that time had plainly been spent on unnecessarily—and sometimes ineffectively—elaborate scenic devices.

At curtain rise, the stage was filled with a tank of water in which three stark-naked Rhinemaidens were swimming while they sang. (Lucky Rhinemaidens! In the auditorium, we sweltered.) We observed them in an angled mirror intended to make the surface of the water seem vertical. But since they emerged from their tank to enact the encounters with Alberich, awkwardly, on a narrow front-stage track, there was little Rhine-bed illusion—less than in the old Covent Garden production of 1949 (my first *Ring*), when the maidens "swam" gracefully on invisible wires and before our eyes could dart from Alberich's embrace up to the watery heights. Moreover, in that old set—designed in 1934 by Gabriel Volkoff—we saw the strong flow of the river, an image that Wagner prescribed, and a needed one. Not in this décor.

Covent Garden's third and fourth postwar *Ring* productions were both mounted on intricate, costly pieces of machinery that could be put through eye-catching maneuvers. Bayreuth's "British *Ring*" followed suit. Dudley had designed a huge, stage-spanning reversible platform (inspired, he said, partly by the white shape in Turner's "Snowstorm: Hannibal and His Army Crossing the Alps," partly by the airfoil curve of a jetliner's wing), hydraulically powered, able to swivel, to soar, to loop the loop; and Hall seemed to have been carried away by his gigantic toy. Sometimes he set it moving in midscene, to merely distracting effect. In the last scene of *Siegfried,* Brünnhilde was strapped to its underside, and it slowly spun around to reveal her. In the Ride of the Valkyries, it hovered like a silver spaceship, high above the stage, with Gerhilde, Ortlinde, Waltraute, and Schwertleite perched on it, seat-belted. To that turbulent music, filled with excitable motion, it made a slow, stately landing, and the Valkyries unbuckled. At the end of the act, it took off again, with Brünnhilde aboard, gently steaming at its center on what looked like a giant hotplate. There was no rampart of flame around her.

Thoughts about Wagnerian staging seem to move in cycles. It was Cosima in the nineteenth century—although it could well have been Wieland in the twentieth—who said of *Tristan* that "we must banish everything that is merely conventional, everything realistic," and of *Die Meistersinger* that "the so-called liveliness and naturalness of the chorus, the stereotyped exchanges of glances and gestures, I consider bad, a debased form of realism." In advance, Hall enunciated precepts close to those that Emil Preetorius, Winifred Wagner's designer in the thirties, set out in his *Wagner: Bild und Vision:*

> For his penetratingly descriptive music, Wagner needs a certain nearness to nature, which should not, however, be naturalistic in the literal sense. Thunder and lightning, rainbow, river, and moonlight, flickering flames, scudding clouds . . . all these must be depicted clearly and with a certain power of illusion; the horse Grane . . . and the dragon cannot simply be ignored. . . . Wagner needs these natural elements.

But in practice Hall and Dudley, in several scenes that were bare where Wagner called for forest and crag, parted company with Preetorius, who continued, "On no account may one simplify or stylize at will, or be diverted into mere suggestiveness, or get involved in the abstract." The new *Ring* was a puzzling mixture of literalness—the real water (there was more of it in *Siegfried* and *Götterdämmerung*)—and bleak, ineffective abstraction. The absence of grassy banks and rocky seats led to much sitting, kneeling, and lying on the bare floor, all of which looked stagy. There was evidently some idea of sharply distinguishing the world of men from a *Star Wars* realm of the gods; it is an idea untrue to the *Ring* topography and to its natural imagery. The realism was often halfhearted. Siegfried brought on a forest bear, but it remained coyly upstage and did not advance to chase Mime about, as Wagner's boisterous stage direction requires. Act III of *Götterdämmerung* opened in a pretty birch glade, where the naked, comely Rhinemaidens looked like Lucas Cranach Graces but the birch trees did not convincingly join the ground from which they were supposed to be growing. Hunding lived in a hobbit house, a roomy burrow beneath an ash tree. Three seats were placed in readiness around his table: Siegmund was evidently expected to supper. When the door flew open and moonlight streamed in, the effect was magical—or would have been had everything happened on cue. But then, as if in deference to bad modern tradition, the house itself disappeared around the lovers, and by exaggeration Wagner's careful imagery was spoiled. When Brünnhilde ordered the vassals to bring stout logs for Siegfried's pyre, they came on carrying dainty green fronds. Against black backcloths, scene after scene was wreathed in monotonous, depressing stage fog; one began to wonder if Bayreuth's steam machine had sprung a leak.

Hall began *Siegfried,* Act III, with a striking and original scene: Wotan's visit to Erda where she lived cocooned amid the roots of the World Ash Tree. But since both words and music tell of Wotan's employing mighty spells to summon a reluctant Erda away from her subterranean dreams and up to the world's surface, this was a transgression against the text, an irrelevant image. So was the presentation of the solemn, majestic goddess as a lusty young sexpot. The ram-drawn chariot, motionless atop a moving black box, looked rather silly. The dragon was feeble; I've seen dragons—Volkoff's among them—compared with which Dudley's was a puny blindworm. But the horse in the final scene was fine. In the first, 1876 *Ring,* Wagner banished Grane—played by Ludwig of Bavaria's stallion Cocotte—from the Annunciation of Death passage, as being a distraction. But the last, long speech of the cycle is addressed to a horse, and Cocotte was led on to listen to it. In Hall's *Ring,* Miss Behrens mounted a hobbyhorse; seen in silhouette amid the smoky glare at the back of the stage, it reared up realistically and charged into the fire. What followed was less successful. Wagner—who "himself was by no means certain what his own work meant," says Dahlhaus—tried various summings up and in the end set none of them, leaving the orchestral and scenic peroration to carry his "meaning." While under Schopenhauer's influence, he had spoken (in that letter to Röckel) of "recognizing the nothingness" of the world. The next year, he abandoned *The Ring,* after the second act of *Siegfried.* But a year later he told Mathilde Wesendonk of having discovered "a saving way ... that no philosopher, especially not Schopenhauer, has ever recognized: not an abstract love of mankind but real love, the love that blossoms from sexual love." He composed *Tristan* and then *Die Meistersinger*—passed, as it were, from a yearning for love-in-death to a joyful affirmation of life—and then, twelve years after he had set *The Ring* aside, and now with Cosima beside him, returned to the cycle and to the love of Brünnhilde and Siegfried. The final stage directions tell of men and women watching in agitation the fiery destruction of the old gods; the Redemption by Love motif pours from the orchestra. It is a deed of music difficult to make visible. Some directors return to the opening scene of the cycle—primeval order restored—and others suggest the dawn of a brave new world. Both solutions seem glib. Hall's final tableau—the flying platform once again, now apparently scorched and blistered—seemed inadequate.

Dudley's costumes were generally poor. The Valkyries wore black tights and shimmering black tunics. Brünnhilde changed into a white nightdress for *Götterdämmerung.* Loge was all in black, with a braid of fiercely hennaed hair down his back. Siegmund sported torn golden jeans. Siegfried went on wearing his forest romper suit at his wedding and on the royal hunt. The giants were enormous, but papier-mâché heads and clumsy papier-mâché hands made them inexpressive, and one could hardly believe in them as skillful builders.

So much goes into *The Ring* that it needs a book to describe a production fully. (Books have been written about the Wieland and the Chéreau productions, and one is being written about Hall's.) In brief, one might say that this *Ring* foundered on an unhappy combination of missing principals; ill-conceived and, as it turned out, impractically ambitious designs; and, on Hall's part, overconfidence, misjudgment, and, perhaps, inexperience. (The last is an odd word to use of him, but how else can one account for bungled stagecraft in a theatre famous for its technical efficiency?) Solti's conducting did not save the production. We keep saying hopefully that he seems to be mellowing, broadening, deepening, but in fact this *Ring* was much like his Covent Garden cycles twenty years ago. He excels in smoky, sulfurous passages such as the start of *Siegfried,* Act II. He sentimentalizes tender episodes, and he trivializes excited passages by charging through them. The great Wagner conductors inspire their singers and then seem to accompany them. With Solti, nothing sounds natural for long. He often begins an act well and then starts worrying at the music—pushing, nudging, jabbing, driving, or else dragging. Instead of glorying in the warm, broad, blended Bayreuth sound, he tried to turn it into Solti sound—hard-edged, forcible, clear, strident at climaxes—and to this end he removed a large section of the "blending screen" Wagner installed over the orchestra. *Das Rheingold* began not with a mysterious, magical resonance welling up from the depths but with a plain double-bass E-flat; and throughout I was conscious, as never before in Bayreuth, of individual instrumentalists bowing, blowing, or banging away.

Jeannine Altmeyer's Sieglinde was bright-toned and true, not quite warm enough in feeling; when Siegmund drew the sword from the tree she gave a vulgar scream unwritten by Wagner. Siegfried Jerusalem's Siegmund was agreeably romantic. Doris Soffel's Fricka had authority of bearing but not of voice. Josephine Barstow's Gutrune was mannered, unnatural. Norup's Gunther was a wobbly cipher. Jung's Loge was unlyrical. Peter Haage's Mime was spry but lacked tone. Hermann Becht's Alberich was powerful, and there was a splendid series of good basses: Manfred Schenk (Fasolt), Dieter Schweikart (Fafner), Matthias Hölle (Hunding), and Aage Haugland (Hagen).

Among the books about the Boulez-Chéreau Ring *are those by Jean-Jacques Nattiez (subtitled "essai sur l'infidélité"), Uwe Faerber ("a critical examination of the tetralogy which marked the 100th anniversary of the Bayreuth Festival"), and Elisabeth Pfluger-Bouillon. Stephen Fay's* The Ring: Anatomy of an Opera *(1984) is a journalistic account of the Solti-Hall production in rehearsals and performance. Solti did not return to conduct its revivals.*

HIGH FESTIVAL

September 12, 1983

IN July 1882, Wagner completed *Parsifal* by bringing it to performance in the theatre for which it had been composed, and a month later—at the last performance in the run of sixteen—he conducted the final scene himself, taking over the baton from Hermann Levi at (the chronicles are precise) bar 23 of the transformation music. A few months later, he died, aged sixty-nine. On his last night, he and Cosima spoke at supper with their children about the ocean and its denizens—they had been reading *Undine*—and, before that, about prisons and punishments, such as the treadmill, as being institutions for the protection of private property. Three nights earlier, Wagner had dreamed of his mother as a young, elegant woman, and, the night after that, of Wilhelmine Schröder-Devrient, whose inspired performance as Beethoven's Leonore, he wrote in *Mein Leben,* determined his decision to become a musician. "All the womenfolk in my life," he told Cosima, "pass before me." (Around this time, he also dreamed of receiving letters from Mathilde Wesendonk and, perhaps, Friederike Meyer, which he left unopened lest Cosima be jealous.) The dreams of his penultimate night are unrecorded, but during it he got up to look for his checkbook, failed to find it, and was disturbed. On his last night, before retiring he embraced Cosima tenderly and said, "Once in five thousand years things work out right!" He played to her the Rhinemaidens' lament at the end of *Das Rheingold*—"False and base those who rejoice on high"—and said, "To think I understood that so clearly at the time!" Once in bed, he added, "I'm fond of them, these humble creatures of the deep, these yearning ones." And with those words Cosima's diary ends. Her daughter Daniela added a brief postscript, recalling among Papa's last observations his ever-increasing admiration for Aeschylus and his distress that men could be so cruel to animals.

About fifty years ago, it was reckoned that more books had been written about Wagner than about anyone else except Christ and Napoleon; and each month continues to bring new volumes about him and his works. The most important publication of recent years has been of Cosima's diaries; they appeared in German in 1976–77—a handy paperback edition is now available—and then in English translation. They tell one of the world's great love stories, and they provide an intimate daily record of Wagner's thoughts, conversations, memories, dreams, reading during the years when he completed the composition of *The Ring,* built Bayreuth, produced *The Ring* there, and composed and produced *Parsifal.* On page after page, they throw new shafts of light on his music dramas: on the significance of particular moments, on deep underlying themes. Hans-Jürgen Syberberg's *Parsifal* film, with its dense networks of imagery and rich allusiveness, gives some idea of the linked complexities of the intellectual life revealed in Cosima's diaries. It is enthralling, but not a model for theatre directors to follow. In the theatre, the aim should probably be clarity, not further embellishment—but not simplification, either—of works already so rich.

In Cosima's account of Wagner's last days, his varied concerns—political, emotional, musical, literary, financial, humane—pass in review. His lifework was not yet finished. *Parsifal* was composed, and Bayreuth was built, but there had been only two Bayreuth festivals: *The Ring* in 1876, and *Parsifal* in 1882. His widow, his son, his son's widow, and then, in 1951, when Bayreuth reopened after the war, his grandsons took up the task of bringing all his operas from *The Flying Dutchman* on to performance there, and of establishing Bayreuth as an annual theatre festival whose high seriousness would draw serious-minded people from all over the world. In Wagner's centenary year, the Bayreuth Festival seems more important than ever. Statesmen, philosophers, poets, musicians, and magnates were there in an audience that also contained many

23

passionately concerned (and frequently vociferous) young people. The performances often left much to be desired. But, as Bernard Shaw, that stern critic of much he saw and heard on the Green Hill, once remarked, whatever shortcomings of execution one may encounter, one never regrets making the journey to Bayreuth.

This year, besides the new *Ring*, there were revivals of *Die Meistersinger von Nürnberg, Tristan und Isolde*, and *Parsifal. Meistersinger* is a 1981 production by Wolfgang Wagner—his second and Bayreuth's fifth since the war. Wieland and Wolfgang have both practiced *Entdeutschungspolitik*—a policy of deliberate de-Germanization, in contrast to the nationalist manifestations of their mother's regime, which led to much misunderstanding of Wagner. All Bayreuth program books now carry on the cover, in three languages, a sentence from Wagner's "Art and Revolution": "Whereas the Greek work of art expressed the spirit of a splendid nation, the work of art of the future is intended to express the spirit of free people irrespective of all national boundaries; the national element in it must be no more than an ornament, an added individual charm, not a confining boundary." The declaration was brought into prominence at Wieland's 1963 *Meistersinger* production, and Sachs sang his eulogy of "die heil'ge deutsche Kunst" not as bombastic assertion but, faithful to Wagner's markings, with gentle, unassertive pride. It has been done that way ever since. Wolfgang's new production is good-humored, jolly, and comfortable to a fault. *Meistersinger* is not all nostalgia, picturesque crooked alleys filled with the scent of elder and linden, and lovely melodies. There is a streak of underlying violence running through all human history, as Sachs observes in his famous "Wahn" monologue—present even in his dear Nuremberg, and ever to be guarded against with all the resources of love and art. Walther draws his sword to carve a way to his desires; Sachs quietly and firmly opposes him. The violence should not be overstated, as perhaps it was in Wieland's 1963 production. But if it is ignored, as in Wolfgang's new production, if there is no pain at all in the drama, the opera loses some of its richness. Peace and happiness are not lightly won. *Meistersinger* is a warning as well as a joyous celebration. Wolfgang gave us a comedy of Eva and her three suitors—all three of them young and handsome. Beckmesser, not Sachs, was allotted the pantomime at the end of Act I—in defiance of Wagner's score. At the end of Act III, Sachs took the laurel wreath from his brow and went up to Beckmesser (who in this version had stayed behind after his discomfiture, to hear what Walther made of the Prize Song), and it looked as if he were going to award Beckmesser the crown. Instead, he clapped him on the shoulder in friendly fashion and hung the crown on the Mastersinger shield. While the populace acclaimed their beloved Sachs, he gracelessly sloped off into the wings. It's possible human behavior—but it's not what the music tells us. Wolfgang invites us to hear with an ironic ear Wagner's totally unironic C-major rejoicing.

Half-timbered Nuremberg was replaced by stone buildings, crisp and new-looking. Old Nuremberg was certainly new once, but *Meistersinger* décor should, I believe, reflect the picturesque archaism that is a deliberate element of Wagner's score. Bernd Weikl, the Sachs, was in fine voice, even if the notion of legato singing seems never to have crossed his mind. Hermann Prey was an entertaining and pleasant Beckmesser. Siegfried Jerusalem was a tall, romantic Walther, whose tenor, however, did not run freely into the higher reaches of the role. Mari Anne Häggander's Eva was competent but colorless. Graham Clark was a loud—not a sweet, winning—David. Manfred Schenk's Pogner was firmly sung but lacked personality. The outstanding bass belonged to Matthias Hölle, the nightwatchman; his eleven-o'clock call, which Wagner wanted sung "with gently quavering voice," rang out with the same grandeur and beauty as had the ten o'clock. The cast (all but the Vogelgesang) has been held intact for three years. The performance ran very smoothly, but there was a slight feeling of routine about it—routine pepped up, not convincingly, by exaggerated "reactions," such as Cosima once deplored ("the so-called liveliness and naturalness of the chorus, the stereotyped exchanges of glances and gestures"). Horst Stein was a solid, rather coarse-grained conductor.

Tristan is a 1981 production by Jean-Pierre Ponnelle. Ponnelle, in his usual search for striking novelties, such as made his *Flying Dutchman,* his *Rigoletto,* his *Falstaff* so distasteful and ineffective, rides roughshod over the opera and manages to destroy its most dramatic moments (the drinking of the potion, for example). His set for Act I is a tease. The ship is formalized; its stern rises as a tree trunk, and its gunwales suggest the ramparts of Kareol. But it proves not to be a unit set after all. Act II is realistic-romantic: an immense, stage-spanning leafy tree, with twisted rugose trunk; mossy banks; a pool of real water in which the lovers dabble their hands and gaze at their reflections. It is played upon by a stunning light show in golds, browns, blues, and silver. Act III is not the Kareol castle garden but a bare rocky islet in a tinsel sea. Here Tristan, watched over by Kurwenal and the shepherd, dies in delirium, imagining that Isolde has returned to him and sung him a Liebestod. The shepherd pipes the *alte Weise* over him like a snake charmer and pipes his jolly tune at Kurwenal's bidding. (Where is the real Isolde meanwhile? Has she settled down as King Mark's wife? Wagner's drama is resolved; Ponnelle's is not.) In Act I, at curtain rise Isolde kneels on the deck in shift and tall crown, a huge cloak spread in a circle around her. (Kneeling is the new cliché at Bayreuth: Sieglinde and Siegmund, Brünnhilde and Siegfried, Kundry and—more appropriately—Parsifal seem to sing most of their music kneeling, and very stagy it looks.) During Isolde's narration, Tristan, behind a gauze screen, mimes the action she describes. Later, they drink simultaneously from a large bowl—with comic effect, for the potion, had there been any, would have slopped out between their mouths.

Johanna Meier, so promising an Isolde a few years ago, and hailed in this production in 1981, was sadly unsteady. Much trouble had evidently been taken to turn Spas Wenkoff into a presentable Tristan. He was accurate. His notes and his words were clear. He acted passably. But his timbre is thick, and his presence prosaic. Hermann Becht's Kurwenal was bawled. Hanna Schwarz's Brangäne was strained and off-pitch. The best singing came from Matti Salminen, a sonorous, if slightly plain, Mark. Daniel Barenboim's conducting was emotional, episodic, short-spanned, and the orchestra was often too assertive. The Liebestod was accompanied as if to obliterate Miss Meier's faltering voice.

The *Parsifal,* directed by Götz Friedrich and designed by Andreas Reinhardt, was new last year. It is set in a giant tower—the walls a series of arcades, tier upon tier—which has been laid on its side: we look through its base, as it were, past a narrowing perspective of arches on their sides, to a top open to the sky except in the first Grail scene. I'm not sure what it "means," but it makes an arresting frame, packed with visual incident, and within it the individual scenes are well designed. The flower garden has the colorful exuberance of Paul von Joukowsky's sketch for the first *Parsifal;* the Good Friday meadow glows and burgeons with a soft radiance (very unlike the glitzy lighting effects in Ponnelle's *Tristan* grove); the Grail hall is noble and imposing. The production has its oddities: Klingsor summons his knights through an intercom, and they prove to be robots; Kundry indulges in some mannered business with bolts of blue cloth. But otherwise it is a solemn, essentially accurate, and beautiful staging, superlatively well lit. Friedrich's interpretative gloss at the end bears thought: women gather and join the knights as Parsifal elevates the Grail; like Tamino, he initiates the closed brotherhood into less restrictive rites.

Moreover, *Parsifal* was the only opera this year that sounded like an authentic Bayreuth performance. James Levine's reading was broad, long-breathed, unhurried, energetic without febrility. The orchestral playing was full, warm, and beautiful. In the title role, Peter Hofmann, an uneven performer, was at his best—not brattish, as he has been in New York, but young, clear, incisive in the first act, noble in the second, and gravely moving in the third. Leonie Rysanek's command of the stage and of the extraordinary character of Kundry was complete; her singing was uneven. There were three first-rate basses in Hans Sotin (a lyrical Gurnemanz), Salminen (a majestic Titurel), and Hölle (second knight). Simon Estes's Amfortas was perhaps a shade overrhetorical, and Franz Mazura's Klingsor was vivid but almost overdone.

For thirteen years, I'd not been back to Bayreuth, where I was once an almost annual pilgrim, and had relied instead on memories of Wieland's productions, of Astrid Varnay's Brünnhilde and Isolde and Hans Hotter's Wotan and Sachs, of Hans Knappertsbusch's conducting for Wagnerian nourishment. The chop and change of later casts (no dependable truly heroic soprano has emerged since Birgit Nilsson sang her last Bayreuth Brünnhilde, in 1967, and no evident successor as Siegfried to Wolfgang Windgassen, who did the part most years from 1953 to 1967), and the prevalence of lightweight conductors provided small inducement to return. Radio relays tended to confirm what one feared about the musical level. The emphasis seemed to be on novel, startling, "shocking" inscenation, on succès de scandale. (Wieland had many new ideas, and some of them were startling, but in his productions he put the emphasis where Wagner insisted it should be—on individual singers inspired to give great performances.) One can't live on memories alone. Although this year *The Ring* was fumbled, *Meistersinger* reduced to a romp, and *Tristan* travestied, Bayreuth cast its wonted spell all the same. *Parsifal* was Wieland's greatest production. It was done from 1951 to 1973. Again and again, I marvelled at it. The new *Parsifal,* richly decked where Wieland's had been magically plain, was scarcely less wonderful.

Melodious Albion

LONDON in August offered a feast of music. At the Albert Hall, the BBC's Proms were in full swing—the world's greatest music festival; fifty-seven concerts this year, with not a dull program among them. Across the Thames, in the second half of the month, South Bank Summer Music, a Greater London Council festival, directed by Simon Rattle, provided rival attractions—twenty-one delectable concerts and recitals. For ten days, Glyndebourne was still on, and at mid-month the English National Opera season opened. The BBC's year-round "festival" on Radio 3—music from the concert halls, opera houses, radio stations, and recording studios of the world, carefully chosen and presented, intelligently introduced and discussed—allowed ears, at least, to visit some of the out-of-London festivals. A broadcast from Edinburgh of a Zemlinsky operatic double bill there was thoughtfully delayed so as not to clash with an interesting Prom.

At the Proms, I heard the European première of Elliott Carter's Triple Duo, a BBC commission. The Fires of London played it still more brilliantly and buoyantly than they had at its première, at Symphony Space in April. A week later, there was another Fires performance of it, from a BBC studio, and I enjoyed Carter's glittering, urgent, yet amiable discourse even more while listening at home, in close-up, with a few rapt friends. The Albert Hall holds some six thousand people; in the better seats its acoustics are warm and clear; and to be one of the intent, enthusiastic Prom audience is a special and stimulating adventure. But over the air one often hears details in better balance. All the Proms are broadcast nationally, and many of them internationally. In my days as a London critic, I would set the tape recorder before leaving for the hall, and then come back to compare distant and intimate views of a new work. But separate, complementary performances—one projected to an audience and scaled to the hall, the other polished to studio precision—are even more revealing.

Peter Maxwell Davies's new Sinfonietta Concertante had similar twinned performances—a Prom première and, two days later, a studio broadcast, both given by the Academy of St. Martin-in-the-Fields, conducted by Neville Marriner. It is the first of three concertante works for chamber orchestra, steps toward a possible concerto. The second of them, *Into the Labyrinth,* with solo tenor, a powerful and eventful piece, had its première at the St. Magnus Festival in June. (James Conlon conducted.) The third, a Sinfonia Accademica, is due next month in Edinburgh. The Sinfonia Concertante is a thirty-two-minute, three-movement classical composition, for wind quintet (flute, oboe, clarinet, bassoon, and horn),

27

strings, and timpani. The Sinfonia Concertante ascribed to Mozart, K. 297b, is a predecessor. The piece is audibly thematic and is audibly in—or at least "on"—F, or else in D minor. (I hear the former, but the composer's program note calls D minor the home tonality.) It is a lyrical, beautiful, and zestful composition, graceful in form, with virtuoso, often playful solo parts, which perhaps only the clarinettist, Antony Pay, did full justice to.

David Lumsdaine's *Hagoromo,* another BBC commission, also had both Prom and studio performances, three days apart, given by the BBC Symphony, conducted by Elgar Howarth. Lumsdaine, born in 1931, is an Australian who has worked in Britain for thirty years. *Hagoromo,* first done at IRCAM six years ago, takes its title from the Noh play about an angel who, having had her feathered robe restored to her by two fishermen, dances for them and in her dancing reveals to them the beauty of the world. It is a long (thirty-four-minute) series of slowly developing dances. The composer's program note includes a catalogue, part of which is:

> a robe of feathers, definite, precise, shifting, blending, dense, transparent, a rainbow—
> a wilderness in the spring, a forest of wildflowers, birdsong, the flight of butterflies . . .
> pines by the sea, sunlight on water . . .
> the folds of time, the harmony of a single flute, the melody of a bell . . .

The music is sensuously beautiful, richly scored for a large orchestra. Each of the three movements starts from a slow, gentle "gesture." Melodies spread gradually through the orchestra, moving against sheets of glinting color—shimmering, iridescent backgrounds. New, strong ideas interrupt their progress, and when they resume they are subtly altered.

It is rash to generalize about British contemporary music on the basis of a dozen new pieces heard in the space of three weeks. Yet several of them had things in common which set them apart from, on the one hand, the earlier British music on the programs—Holst, Vaughan Williams (his lovely *Lark Ascending,* an apt prelude to Lumsdaine's larger hymning of beauty), Britten (his bold Opus 1, the Schoenberg-influenced Sinfonietta, composed when he was eighteen, and *Les Illuminations*), Tippett (the generously lyrical Second Symphony, Stravinsky-influenced), early Davies (the Expressionist *Revelation and Fall*)—and, on the other hand, any of the modish international styles. And, after a New York season rich in rewarding new music, I'll venture the generalization that in London I heard more new compositions that were sustained, long-breathed, large in scale, not jittery, not fragmented in texture. (I'm talking about real new music, not the large-scale, nostalgic Simple Simonries of, in their different ways, Rochberg, Del Tredici, and the minimalists.) Messiaen seems to be a living influence in London, as he hardly is in New York. (*Des Canyons aux étoiles* has been much played by the young orchestras.) There was a Messiaenic paean of joyous, clustered birdsong in *Hagoromo.* Giles Swayne's *Cry,* given at the Proms four days later, is dedicated to Messiaen.

Cry, whatever one thinks of it, is a memorable composition. It is a ninety-minute piece, commissioned by the BBC for the BBC Singers—twenty-eight soloists, who in this work, standing in a wide arc, sing, unaccompanied, each into an individual microphone. Their voices are amplified, electronically mixed and at times modified, and fed into seven loudspeakers around the hall, so that the piece will (as the preface to the score directs) "completely envelop its listeners, creating a sound-world which surrounds them on all sides, and which sets the entire air-space and the building itself in vibration." There are seven movements: void, light, darkness; sky; sea, dry land, vegetation; sun, moon, stars; creatures of the air and water; creatures of the dry land; rest. Swayne has aimed at nothing less than creating a musical analogue of the world as God created it; he describes his piece as "a song of gratitude, praise, hope and (above all) love for the world which formed us and gives us life, and of which we are the temporary and doubtful guardians." Where *Cry* ends, one might say—on the first morning of the world—*Das Rheingold* begins (but a semitone higher). The composer, disclaiming "subjective impressions" and "expression" ("*Cry* is, I hope, no more 'expressive' than a tree or tiger"), sought to create "a world of sound, constructed (like the real world) according to complex mathematical laws and processes." There is no text. The singers sing, cry, shout, patter, whisper syllables chosen for their sonic values, but in the sixth movement their "a da me va" shapes itself into the names of our first parents, and "a ni ma" at the start and end of the seventh adds another verbal element to the "pure" sound. Elsewhere—such is the potency of language—utterances of "sa-me-la," "mana mala," "lalino" begin to sound like words in an unknown tongue. African ritual chant, with its ability to stir European listeners, is one source of this deliberately eclectic and direct composition. Stockhausen must be another. Shining common chords, laid out across four octaves, represent light. There are passages of whalesong and birdsong. The "scoring," brilliant and inventive, amounts to not less than a new kind of orchestra. In 1980, *Cry* was broadcast and then publicly performed in St. John's, Smith Square, a resonant baroque church, now a concert hall that sounds often to new music. Last year, the Netherlands Chamber Choir took it round Holland. The Prom audience cheered it. I confess that, while admiring its scope, ambition, and stunning array of new sounds—and the prowess of the BBC Singers, conducted by John Poole—I grew restive during stretches of what seemed like "minimalist" protraction. [*A recording of* Cry, *on the BBC Artium label, appeared in 1985.*]

Swayne, born in 1946, is one of several British composers who have come to prominence in the last decade. Another is Colin Matthews, also born in 1946, who was represented at the Proms by his eighteen-minute *Night Music,* a dusky, questing, gravely satisfying composition. It was played by the City of London Sinfonia, conducted by Richard Hickox. Paul Griffiths, that fluent chronicler of twentieth-century music, wrote earlier this year that "the generation of English composers born around 1950 is rapidly becoming recognized as something quite exceptional," a "brilliant group." I missed the Piano Concerto of Dominic Muldowney (born in 1952), a Prom commission, but heard and enjoyed *Cimmerian Nocturne,* by Philip Grange (born in 1956), and *The Ring of Eternity,* by Robert Saxton (born in 1953). Each lasts about fifteen minutes. The Nocturne—a Fires commission, first played at the 1980 St. Magnus Festival—is a journey to the heart of darkness (Grange owns the Conrad influence) and an almost painfully keen piece of chamber music. Saxton's work starts from contemplation of Vaughan's metaphysical conceit:

> *I saw Eternity the other night*
> *Like a great* Ring *of pure and endless light* . . .
> *And round beneath it, Time* . . .
> *Like a vast shadow mov'd, in which the world*
> *And all her train were hurl'd.*

Saxton set the poem at the age of eleven (the next year his first opera was performed in London) and again five years later. His new tone poem skillfully forges and at length fuses opposed images of shining calm and shadowy turmoil. It was played by the Northern Sinfonia, conducted by the composer Oliver Knussen (born in 1952).

Let me punctuate this Dodo-like recital ("all must have prizes") with another generalization: that British composers, numerous and prolific, are now composing—constructing, scoring, handling the materials by which their visions can be shared—with exceptional confidence and skill. None of the pieces I heard was awkwardly made or gracelessly written. None was trendy, formulary, or arid. The reasons for that are probably linked: the number of performers (London alone has five full-time symphonies—against New York's one—and several chamber orchestras); the number of performances—not just premières—at which composers hear their own and one another's works; the BBC's bounteous commissions and propagation; education (for three years Swayne was composer-in-residence of the London borough of Hounslow, teaching not "music appreciation" but music-making in junior and secondary schools); and an evident public interest in living composers and their works. Every concert I went to was well attended; so were the preconcert talks. In newspapers and magazines I read six introductory articles to Carter's Triple Duo and, later, a dozen intelligent reviews of it. New music gets published, and scores are readily on sale. The circumstances of concertgoing are agreeable. The Albert Hall, once its hellhole of a box office is passed, is a Victorian delight. The Socialist Greater London Council, helped by glorious weather, has made the South Bank—three concert halls, three theatres, three cinemas, and an art gallery in full swing—a happy place. Its Thames-side terraces, gardens, restaurants, cafés, and bookshops were thronged all day long, and after the concerts people stayed on to discuss what they had heard and felt. (I don't know what it's like in winter, but next season's BBC/London Sinfonietta programs there are dazzling.) Moreover, there seems to be a happy realization that composing, performing, and listening to new music is an important human activity, and also that, while not all new works can be masterpieces, there is no call to dismiss those that aren't with brief, bored indifference or scorn.

Knussen is a composer with a remarkable ear for colors, spacing, and placing. His *Music for a Puppet Court,* a small, exquisite suite for double chamber orchestra, had its première on the South Bank, at a London Sinfonietta concert conducted by Rattle. Three days later, I caught up with Robin Holloway's song cycle *Women in War,* for two sopranos, two mezzos, and piano. It was composed last year—the year Mrs. Thatcher took Britain to war—to a commission from the Arts Council for a companion piece of Janáček's *Diary of One Who Disappeared,* which is for tenor with four small parts for women. The Songmakers' Almanac—a pool of lieder singers, directed by the pianist Graham Johnson, from which song recitals have flowed back into the concert mainstream—took the double bill through the country on the Council's Contemporary Music Network. In the half-hour, three-movement cycle—its text an anthology of First World War writings—the mood changes from enthusiasm ("Sister Susie's sewing shirts for soldiers") to mourning and then to bitterness and anger ("The young men of the world are condemned to death. They have been called up to die for the crimes of their fathers"). It is a powerful and disturbing piece, made with the compound of fluency, generous instinct, and precise musical inspiration which distinguishes Holloway's work. Under the general title "War and Peace," the Songmakers gave five recitals, including cycles by Poulenc, Britten, and Ned Rorem. In the Network's nine touring programs for next season, there is a new work by Colin Matthews and a piquant Sinfonietta double bill: Carter's *In Sleep, in Thunder* and H. K. Gruber's *Frankenstein!!*

I must not leave the impression that nothing but British music was played. At the Proms, Klaus Tennstedt conducted a searing Mahler Sixth, and Janet Baker and William Lewis sang a disappointing, earthbound *Song of the Earth.* The festival included plenty of Mozart (five symphonies, five concertos), Beethoven, Brahms, Bruckner. Abbado conducted the lustrous European Community Youth Orchestra in Wagner, Schumann, Webern, and Strauss. Andrew Litton conducted a bright Bernstein-Copland-Gershwin program. Philip Fowke, an excellent pianist, new to me, played Strauss's *Burleske* and Weber's Konzertstück with warmth and elegance—deputizing for Claudio Arrau, who'd been stung by a bee. Ligeti's *Clocks and Clouds* was winningly done by the London Sinfonietta, conducted by Howarth, and Shostakovich's Fourteenth Symphony had a superb soprano soloist in Felicity Palmer. Poles were prominent: music by Chopin, Szymanowski, and Tadeusz Baird; Penderecki, Lutoslawski, and Andrzej Panufnik on hand to conduct their own works. On the South Bank, along with Mozart, Haydn, Brahms, Berg, an H. K. Gruber première, there was much Janáček; and all Sibelius's symphonies were conducted by Rattle, with the City of Birmingham Symphony. I heard the last Sibelius concert—Nos. 5, 6, and 7—and was spellbound. Sibelius seems new again, and what Constant Lambert wrote a half-century ago, at the close of *Music Ho!,* seems true again:

> The glamour of the anarchist and the mystery of the sphinx have begun to pall. . . . The modern composer has now to consolidate the reckless and fascinating experiments of the pre-war pioneers while avoiding the dog-Latin classicism of the post-war pasticheurs. He must make a synthesis of the present varied elements. . . . There is nothing in music which has really lost its meaning, no device of rhythm, no harmonic combination which the composer of vision cannot reanimate. The music of the future . . . will not be of the type that can be labelled "the new This" or "the new That." It will not truckle to topicality . . . nor will it lose itself in a dream world of forgotten loves and vanished days.

And Sibelius, Lambert declared, while offering no material for the plagiarist, pointed more surely than Schoenberg ("despite his powerful imagination and unique genius") toward "a world of thought which is free from the paralysing alternatives of escape or submission."

Rattle, who is now twenty-eight, goes from strength to strength. He must be the best thing that has happened in British conducting since Beecham. He inspires players and elates audiences, holding them intent on every line, every color, every turn of the argument. Summer Music began with a concert performance of Janáček's *Osud,* which Rattle conducted with the Sinfonietta. It was an evening of blazing beauty and excitement. More of that later: amid such lively concert activity, opera—for once—took second place and must be left to a second report.

SUMMER SAMPLING

September 26, 1983

JANÁČEK'S fourth opera, *Osud (Fate),* composed in 1905, after *Jenůfa,* has been much neglected. Even in Janáček-thirsty Britain—where there have been isolated performances of the early *Šárka* and *The Beginning of a Romance,* and the six other pieces have been played in repertory—*Osud* has had only a BBC studio production, in 1972, and the concert performance that opened London's South Bank Summer Music. The latter roused its audience (which included the directors of several opera companies) to such a peak of enthusiasm that a stage production cannot be far off.

Not without reason, the libretto—drafted by the composer in prose and sent in installments to a twenty-year-old schoolmistress to be turned into "Push-kinesque verse"—has hitherto been found daunting. Desmond Shawe-Taylor, in a famous pioneering article on Janáček (*Proceedings of the Royal Musical Association,* 1958–59), suggested a British analogue to its action. Transported to America, it could run:

> Imagine Horatio Parker explaining to his composition class at Yale that the subject of his new opera derives from an amorous episode that took place many years before at Saratoga Springs. As the climax of the story is reached, there is a nasty storm over the Green, and poor Parker falls unconscious into the arms of his illegitimate son, now one of his pupils. Between them, the storm and recollected emotion have been too much for the old boy.

That corresponds to Act III, which at the opera's first performance (Brno, 1958) and in the BBC production was divided into two, and framed Acts I and II, making them flashbacks. Act I takes place at Luchačovice Spa. There are lively, glittering crowd scenes. The composer Živný and the beautiful Míla meet, and her first words to him when they are alone—"Have you come for your child?"—epitomize the laconic style of a libretto in which much is left unex-

32

plained. Act II is a domestic scene. Míla and Živný's son plays and prattles. Živný tears some pages from the score of the opera he has written about Míla, for now he feels he was unjust to her. At the end of the act, Míla's mother, who has gone mad, throws herself from the balcony, taking Míla with her.

The Janáček operas that first conquered the world were *Jenůfa* and *Kát'a Kabanová,* whose plots are realistic and romantic. But now that *Mr. Brouček,* the *Vixen, Makropulos,* and *The House of the Dead,* whose dramaturgy is altogether unconventional, are widely performed, there seems no reason successful productions of *Osud* should not follow. The lines of the libretto may read naïvely, but the music is wonderful, and in thrilling fashion it lays bare the characters' thoughts and feelings. Under Simon Rattle's inspired direction, the music leaped, danced, and dazzled in the spa scenes; was now tender, now searing in Živný's monologues; and held its listeners spellbound. The London Sinfonietta filled every sharp-cut phrase with color and with quick, keen emotion. There was an excellent cast, led by Philip Langridge as Živný, Eilene Hannan as Míla, and Felicity Palmer as the mother.

The English National Opera season opened with a blunt, heavy revival of its 1976 *Don Giovanni* and continued with a revival of last year's already celebrated *Rigoletto*—Jonathan Miller's version, "set in Little Italy, the part of New York under the control of the Mafia, in the 1950s," which has been very successful with the public. On the whole, I prefer Verdi's version. (The show comes to the Metropolitan in June, and comment on it can wait till then.) At a public dress rehearsal, I saw David Blake's *Toussaint,* a colorful, ambitious, and arresting grand opera, commissioned by the English National, and first performed in 1977. I praised it that year [*Music of Three More Seasons,* pp. 22–25], and this year admired again both the work and the prowess of the company.

At the National Theatre, there was a fizzy *Guys and Dolls,* done with a crispness and scenic bravura to make the *Rigoletto* chorus work seem lame and some recent Broadway revivals (*On Your Toes,* for one) seem dowdy. Opera was represented at the Proms by Rameau's *Hippolyte et Aricie* and Rossini's *La Cenerentola.* The account of Rameau's passionate drama was disappointingly tame and cool but was distinguished by John Aler's freshly sung Hippolytus and Enid Hartle's trenchant Oenone. The *Cenerentola,* from Glyndebourne, was at times carelessly sung and far too broad but was distinguished by Kathleen Kuhlmann's piquant, fluent, and accurate heroine.

Buxton is a Derbyshire spa town—its waters famous since Roman times—with a fine eighteenth-century crescent, by John Carr of York; a grand nineteenth-century hotel, by Henry Currey; and a delightful Edwardian ivory-and-gold opera house, holding nine hundred, by Frank Matcham, whose "sumptuous interior" (Pevsner) was restored in 1979. The splendors of Chatsworth and the romance of Haddon Hall lie close at hand. The country around is beautiful. Buxton is a good festival place, and since 1979 it has had a summer festival, devised by the conductor Anthony Hose and the stage director Malcolm Fraser. Most years, there has been a festival "theme" figure: Walter Scott (represented operatically by *Lucia*), Shakespeare (Berlioz's *Béatrice* and Thomas's *Hamlet*), and David

Garrick (*Il matrimonio segreto*) in earlier years, and this year Boccaccio. The *Decameron* was read aloud—a tale on the hour for ten days. An exhibition included glowing Victorian images of *Decameron* scenes by way of Dryden, Keats, and Tennyson. Boccaccian divertissements brought settings by Italian madrigalists and Tennyson's tushery play *The Falcon*. The operas were Vivaldi's *Griselda* and Gounod's *La Colombe*.

Vivaldi—as the Dallas production of his *Orlando furioso,* three years ago, made plain [*Musical Events: 1980–1983,* pp. 78–82]—is an opera composer underrated and underperformed. His *Griselda* is a bewitching score: a chain of exquisitely beautiful arias, attractively varied in temper, delicately and subtly accompanied, which ravish the ear by their melodic felicity. The story of Griselda, patiently enduring abominable treatment from her husband, ends the *Decameron*. It's an equivocal tale and—like much in Boccaccio—was evidently meant to be so. Petrarch, Chaucer, Hans Sachs, Lope de Vega, and many others made versions of it. Vivaldi used the much-set Apostolo Zeno libretto, touched up for him by Goldoni. It is a satisfactory and moving drama, and a more than adequate framework for the lovely music. The Buxton singers—led by Cynthia Buchan as Griselda and John Mitchinson as her husband—were not baroque virtuosi, but they sang with a fresh, warm, honest response to the melodies and the emotions.

La Colombe is a Boccaccio tale by way of La Fontaine, with all sting removed from the story by Gounod's librettists, Jules Barbier and Michel Carré. In the original, Federico, having nothing else to offer his beloved to eat, roasts his prize falcon; in La Fontaine, the bird is a dove; and in the opera the dove's life is spared after all. *La Colombe,* written for Baden-Baden in 1860 and revived by Diaghilev at Monte Carlo in 1924, is a trifle—a deft and pretty one, gracefully composed. The "punk" setting devised for it in Buxton was grotesquely inappropriate, but its charm survived.

Each year, Buxton also puts on a children's opera. Herbert Chappell's *James and the Giant Peach,* after the scary story by Roald Dahl, has an eclectic, clever score—in the manner, roughly, of Bernstein's *Mass*—and was done with great freshness, naturalness, and zest by its young cast.

Mauricio Kagel's music-theatre piece *Mare Nostrum* was composed for the 1975 Berlin Festival. Since then, several German houses have taken it up. It had its British première this month, at the Institute of Contemporary Art, in London, in a very skillful new English translation by John Patrick Thomas: "Excuse, o pue-blic. We mate many mistates of talking. We are survivors what was lovingly stuck together, the remaindereds. . . . We tell you travels we did. . . ." The piece is subtitled "discovery, pacification, and conversion of the Mediterranean by a tribe from the Amazon." It's a ninety-minute episode in Kagel's long, lively questioning of our listening habits—his long exploration of the understandings, half-understandings, and misunderstandings that can result when we encounter music of other ages or other cultures. This ICA production, based on Hanover's, was directed by Peter Beat Wyrsch, the director of the Pocket Opera in Nuremberg. (It brought Marschner's *Der Vampyr* to the Edinburgh Festival fringe a few years ago, and a surrealist *La Wally* to the Vale of Glamorgan Festival.) A hexagonal blue paddling pool represents the Mediterranean. Around it sit six elegantly clad instrumentalists (flute, oboe, guitar, harp, cello, percussion). A baritone, who is also the narrator, represents the leader of the Amazonian colonists. A countertenor plays the inhabitants of the various countries. Portugal, Spain, France, Italy, Greece, Turkey, and Israel are "subdued" in turn, and the work ends with a "belly dance of death" in the pool and a "primeval scream" from the conqueror.

It's a work easy to grow impatient with at a first encounter—to dismiss as babyish, old-hat avant-gardism. I was tempted to do so, but found that the piece went on nagging at me and demanded to be seen and heard again. At a second encounter, its brief, brilliant inventions fell into place within a coherent whole. Both baritone and countertenor are required to play on a wide variety of Latin-American instruments, and Kagel puts both their shapes and their timbres to highly effective symbolic use. Two American singers active in Germany—Lorenz Minth the baritone, Mr. Thomas the countertenor—gave stunning performances, as singers, speakers, actors, mimes, and instrumentalists. The six young players, conducted by David Sawer, played their music and their occasional roles in the action with high accomplishment. *Mare Nostrum* is not merely a warning against too easy acceptance of the traditional fare offered by opera houses and concert halls but also a fascinating music-theatre adventure in its own right.

Swan of Pesaro

October 10, 1983

Pesaro, a seaside town, on the Adriatic between Rimini and Ancona, enters musical history early in the fifteenth century, when Guillaume Dufay composed motets for the Malatesta family. It opened its opera house, the Teatro del Sole, in 1637, with a production of Giovanni Ondedei's *Asmondo*. In 1792, the Swan of Pesaro, Gioachino Rossini, was born, son of the town trumpeter. In 1818, the Teatro del Sole was rebuilt, as the Teatro Nuovo, and opened with *La gazza ladra,* directed by Rossini himself. In 1854, it was renovated and was renamed the Teatro Rossini. In 1930, it was damaged by an earthquake; restored, it reopened with *William Tell.* In 1980, it was refurbished, and since then it has been the seat of an annual Rossini Opera Festival. The Teatro Rossini is an attractive, traditional, horseshoe-shaped neoclassical house. Like the New York State Theater, it has five tiers, but, unlike the State Theater, it holds not close on three thousand people but about nine hundred. It has fine acoustics. It is intimate yet not at all poky. It enables listeners to hear Rossini's operas, comic or serious, with the kind of rapture that Stendhal described, hanging on each word, inflection, glance, and orchestral subtlety. Both stage and orchestra pit are a shade small, however, to do justice to the grandeur of Rossini's grandest operas.

Rossini left a large part of his fortune—a sum estimated at twenty billion modern lire—to his native city for the establishment of a musical conservatory there. A splendid Liceo came into being; among its directors have been the composers Mascagni, Zandonai, and Alfano. The Liceo houses the Fondazione Rossini, which administers the composer's bequest, supports a Center for Rossini Studies, and has embarked on a critical edition of Rossini's works. The foundation collaborates with the Pesaro Comune in presenting the opera festival, and the operas are performed in newly edited texts. The repertory so far has been: in 1980, *La gazza ladra* and *L'inganno felice;* in 1981, *L'italiana in Algeri, La donna del lago,* and *Gazza;* in 1982, *Edipo a Colono* (a play with incidental music), *Tancredi,* and *L'italiana;* and this year *Il turco in Italia, Mosè in Egitto,* and *La donna del lago.* This summer, each opera had a run of four or five performances, and then there was a week's gap before the next appeared— an inconvenient arrangement for visitors who hoped to see more than one show. I saw *Mosè,* a key work in the Rossini canon.

Rossini composed this *azione tragico-sacra* for Lenten performance in Naples in 1818. The following year, he added to it its most famous number, "Dal tuo stellato soglio," the Israelites' prayer before the crossing of the Red Sea. Stendhal, an untrustworthy historian, declares that it was inserted to distract attention from some ludicrously inept scenic management for the parting of the waters, which the previous year had roused the audience to gales of laughter. After the new prayer, he says, "people stood up in their boxes and leaned out over the balconies, shouting to crack the vault of heaven: *bello! bello! o che bello!*" It was even reported that some forty attacks of nervous fever or convulsions on the part of young women were directly traceable to the effect of the composition. At a Crystal Palace concert in 1892, Bernard Shaw "so wanted to hear it again that after a careful look round to see that none of my brother-critics were watching me I wore away about an eighth of an inch from the ferrule of my umbrella in abetting an *encore.*" In 1827, Rossini revised and expanded *Mosè in Egitto* as *Moïse et Pharaon,* for the Paris Opéra. In this form, usually in Italian translation, the work has had most of its modern revivals. But five years ago the Sacred Music Society of America gave a splendid concert performance, in Avery Fisher Hall, of *Mosè* [*Music of Three More Seasons,* pp. 154–56], and three years later the opera was produced in Lisbon. Last year, a good recording appeared, on Philips, with June Anderson as its heroine and Ruggero Raimondi in the title role. The concert performance and the recording made clear, and the Pesaro production confirmed, that although the finest music of *Mosè* is retained in the much-praised—and justly praised—*Moïse,* the earlier opera is not an inferior work, only a different one.

Eighteen years ago, when the Welsh National Opera brought a production of *Moïse* to Sadler's Wells, I studied the two scores and discovered that the standard twentieth-century commentaries on Rossini were inadequate. At that time, it was an accepted fact of musical history that in his three French grand operas—*La Siège de Corinthe, Moïse,* and *Guillaume Tell*—Rossini reformed opera seria in ways that might be summarized as: a broader construction of numbers, with extended and audacious harmonic schemes; a larger and more "symphonic" role for the orchestra; a more important role for the chorus; and a new simplicity and directness of vocal utterance. These things were acclaimed when the Paris operas appeared and have been made much of ever since. The observations are true. When converting *Mosè* into *Moïse,* Rossini removed three "regular" (cavatina plus cabaletta) arias, two conventional concerted strettos, and a poor, brief chorus; he added an overture, three extended ensemble scenes, and one dramatic, unconventional aria. But close comparison revealed that in his Neapolitan serious operas Rossini was no mere "cynic amused"— Francis Toye's phrase in his pioneering Rossini biography—but already an operatic reformer with a feeling for music-drama of the kind we praise in Handel's dramatic oratorios, in Gluck, in mature Verdi. Charges levelled at him in his lifetime, of being too learned, too complicated, too Mozartian—in a word, too "German"—no longer seemed absurd, although what was then disparaged we hail now as high virtue. In Italy, the composer compromised and sometimes fell back on formulae, it is true. In Paris, where he had financial security, a stable company, a good orchestra, and plenty of rehearsal time, he carried out with determination and consistency reforms already begun in the Naples operas. And in the process, one might add, something of his earlier bravura and zestful brilliance was lost. Now that Rossini becomes better known as the composer of more than *Il barbiere di Siviglia,* a fuller view of his serious operatic achievements is finding general acceptance. Philip Gossett proclaims it in the New Grove.

The eighteenth-century tragedy, by Francesco Ringhieri, on which Andrea Leone Tottola based the libretto of *Mosè* was entitled *L'Osiride.* The love of Osiris, Pharaoh's firstborn, and the Hebrew maiden Elcia is set against the events of Exodus. The latter called forth Rossini's grandest, richest music—starting with a wonderful, winding C-minor theme during the Plague of Darkness, plunging into still darker keys, blazing at last into C major as Moses restores light. But the love music is also arresting and beautiful. In *Moïse,* the solo music becomes less important, and the individual characters—all except Moses himself, thrown into greater prominence as the leader of his people—are less vivid. Choral pieces, dances, and divertissements are added, and, as Gossett has remarked, "the balance between the personal and the public, so carefully controlled in the original, is lost." Some of Rossini's finest inspirations appear in both operas; they shine even more brightly, I think, in the setting for which they were first conceived.

Mosè was composed for contrasted pairs of sopranos, tenors, and basses. Elcia, Isabella Colbran's role, is a heavier, more dramatic part than Amaltea, Pharaoh's consort. Osiris, Andrea Nozzari's role, exploits "heroic" tenor virtuosity through a range from G at the bottom of the bass staff to tenor high C; Aaron, Moses' brother, provides a lighter foil. Moses needs the weighty grandeur of a majestic basso profondo, while Pharaoh (a role often taken by baritones) needs the flexible, fiery brilliance of a basso cantante. Pesaro had assembled a strong cast. The Elcia was Cecilia Gasdia, a twenty-three-year-old soprano who has been in the news lately. (Last year, she stepped in for Caballé at the Scala *Anna Bolena;* in Florence she has sung Bellini's Juliet, Anne in the Ken Russell *Rake's Progress,* and Nannetta in the Giulini *Falstaff.*) She has a clear, attractive timbre, with a gleam in it, accurate musical instincts, and a pleasing stage personality. Daniela Dessì, the Amaltea, had a great success with a beautiful aria, borrowed from the early *Ciro in Babilonia,* that Rossini included in 1818 but dropped in 1819.

37

Rockwell Blake, the Osiris (he also took the part in the Lisbon production), is not much of an actor, but he negotiates Rossini's heroic-tenor music, through all its huge span and with all its intricacies, more deftly than anyone else around and does so in a manner both virile and graceful. Giuseppe Fallisi, the Aaron, was pleasant but unremarkable; it is a small part. Simone Alaimo, the Pharaoh, had a firm, bright high bass and a dramatic presence. Boris Martinovich, the Moses, was not quite so clean of focus, and he seemed rather less than magisterial; his unhappy costume, a sleeveless white shift, was no help.

One of the glories of *Mosè* is the rich, adventurous, subtle orchestral writing. It even includes—on double-basses, at the death of Osiris—those snap pizzicatos the invention of which is commonly ascribed to Bartók. Rossini uses the same orchestra (less one trumpet) that Wagner used in *Die Meistersinger* fifty years later, and in addition a banda turca and an onstage brass band sixteen strong. The Sacred Music Society performance brought us the score in full splendor, jingling johnny and all. The Pesaro forces were smaller: the London Sinfonietta, fifty-three strong for the occasion, had been engaged, and its playing was bright, clean, and sensitive. (Andrew Marriner's long, lovingly phrased clarinet solo deserves special mention.) Claudio Scimone, who had prepared the edition, conducted. He is a champion of the original *Mosè* (he also conducted the Lisbon production and the recording), and he showed much feeling for the forms, the colors, and the long line of the piece. But he was a shade metronomic, unwilling to phrase with rubato as well as by accent and volume. He sometimes held the singers to the beat in places where they needed time to mold their lines expressively. His "no mid-scene applause, if you please, but straight on into the next number" approach struck a somewhat modern, unauthentic note. It was all a little too brisk, perhaps, but with a briskness born of belief in the power of Rossini's music. The general effect was shapely.

Pier Luigi Pizzi, both director and designer of the show, provided a simple, sober, and effective staging. A constructed set of movable stepped ramps and floats seemed opulently crusted with lapis lazuli. The Egyptian cohorts were gleaming in gold. The Jews were in spotless white, looking as if they'd never built a pyramid in their lives—looking, indeed, rather like an assembly of nurses and orderlies. There was plain blocking for the chorus—the Prague Philharmonic Choir, in excellent voice—with moves more decorative for a posse of lithe Egyptian warrior-pages. The Red Sea was all too evidently pieces of cloth agitated by people beneath them. There's a good deal to be said for simple, formal modern productions of Rossini—not fussy, not extravagant, focussed on the essentials of Rossini's greatness. This serious, well-balanced presentation— like Philadelphia's admirable 1981 production of *Moïse*—musically and scenically seized on the serious, noble aspects of the work and rendered them with conviction, yet did not neglect the charm and the sheer excitement of individual vocal virtuosity. It belonged to another and better world than, say, that of Houston's *Donna del lago,* in 1981, where a romantic and carefully constructed opera was reduced to twiddles, tunes, and spectacular vocalism in a decorative frame. All the same, Pesaro might be an ideal place to essay sometime a Rossini production in the manner of Rossini's day, with painted scenery, settings of varied depth, house lights up, and the orchestra not sunk into an anachronistic modern pit—not a "museum" reconstruction, abuses and all, but one aimed at what the composer might recognize as a superior realization of all that he had hoped for, achieved in his own terms.

Massimilla Doni, the heroine of a Balzac story that contains an eloquent account of the opera, was moved by *Mosè* to exclaim, "You German masters, Handel, Bach, yea Beethoven himself, on your knees, behold the queen of the arts, behold Italy triumphant!" She went too far, perhaps. But after both the Sacred Music Society and the Pesaro performances it was easy to understand her enthusiasm.

NOT MAGIC BUT THE HUMAN HEART

October 17, 1983

THE City Opera's presentation of Puccini's *Turandot*—the second production of a season reduced to eight weeks by the orchestra strike—was noisy, coarse, and brutal, but it was not ineffective. Judith Telep-Ehrlich, the Turandot, has a powerful and vigorous soprano. The night I went (the third performance), it was announced that she was suffering from the flu but would sing all the same. She did not, in the usual phrase, crave the audience's indulgence; nor did she need to. The role seemed to hold no terrors for her. Her tone wobbled at the start but soon grew firmer. Her singing was strong and unflagging. It was a performance without subtlety, without delicacy, without the charm and fascination that some performers have brought to the part. It was straightforward, loud, and assured. Jon Fredric West's Calaf can be described in similar terms. There was nothing romantic or aristocratic about this prince; he was a thickset tenor crying the music with the full force of his lungs, lustily and accurately. Joseph Kerman tells us, in *Opera as Drama,* that *Turandot* is a depraved opera whose music is "consistently, throughout, of café-music banality." I've often thought otherwise, beguiled by the chinoiserie glint and attractiveness of the score, and moved, too, by the urgent lyricism with which Reginald Goodall and Rudolf Kempe used to conduct it at Covent Garden. The moral of the opera is blunt and unpleasing: that a frigid, domineering woman becomes, once raped, submissive and loving. The matching bluntness of characterization can to some extent be concealed by a chivalrous Calaf who makes lust seem a metaphor for poetic quest and by a Turandot who suggests unconscious fears and repressed sensuality beneath her icy, man-hating sadism. The myth of the apparently impregnable yet irresistible woman and the hero who must win her or perish in the attempt takes many forms, has wide applicability, and underlies some good works of art. As Kerman says, "Nobody would deny that dramatic potential can be found in this tale." But, he continues, Puccini did not find it, and "there is simply no insight into any emotions that might possibly be imagined in any of the situations, to say nothing of an imaginative binding conception." The City Opera artists—students of *Opera as Drama,* perhaps—evidently abjured as dishonest the usual attempts to present *Turandot* as a serious work of art, to cast visual and tonal glamour over it, and to enrich the characters with psychological nuances. Beni Montresor's scenery and costumes, retained from the company's 1975 production, are gaudy.

39

(His sets are oddly shallow, with cruelly steep staircases; the painted front gauze had a rent and a darn in it.) Jack Eddleman's new staging is commonplace, except when pepped up with shows of somersaults and cartwheels from a team of tumbler-acrobats. Christopher Keene's conducting is energetic, unsentimental, and unmagical, and little attention is paid to such indications as *pp* and *più piano possibile*. But, in its plain, loud way, the performance is a success. The chorus (which has a new chorusmaster, Joseph Colaneri) sings admirably.

Some Puccini biographers make much of the fact that the composer himself "perished in the attempt," unable to melt his ice-girt princess. He died in Brussels, in 1924, with the final duet of *Turandot* unwritten. Three years earlier, he had already begun to quail before this scene on which, he said in a letter to Giuseppe Adami, one of the two librettists, "all that is decisive, vivid, and dramatic in the opera must converge." A new *Götterdämmerung* finale, crossed with *Die Frau ohne Schatten,* seems to have been his aim: "It must be a great duet. These two almost superhuman beings are transformed by love into human beings, and love takes possession of all on the stage in a great orchestral peroration." But a simpler reading of the evidence is that *Turandot* remained unfinished chiefly because Puccini's librettists were tardy. (Throughout musical history, librettists have lagged behind the composers they should be serving.) Not until a few days before he entered the Brussels clinic were the lines for the final duet completed to his satisfaction. He looked forward to composing them as soon as his treatment was done.

Franco Alfano, with Puccini's sketches to guide him, completed *Turandot,* and the opera was published with his ending. At the first performance, in 1926, Toscanini laid down his baton where Puccini had laid down his pen. In subsequent performances, he conducted an abridged and revised version of the Alfano scene—the familiar text of the second and subsequent *Turandot* scores. Sometimes—but unhappily—it is still further abridged in performance by the omission of Turandot's "Del primo pianto," an aria within the duet. The City Opera, however, performs what is billed as the world stage première of the original ending. There are early recordings of "Del primo pianto" by the first German Turandots—Lotte Lehmann, Anna Roselle, Mafalda Salvatini—which include passages of the original version and suggest that at least in Germany and Austria it was once sung. With this ending, the roles become even more taxing. In the space of three measures (at the phrase "Più grande vittoria non volere"), the fuller "Del primo pianto" elicits two more high B-flats, one pianissimo and one fortissimo, and a long fortissimo high C from the soprano. When the Turandot is up to them (as Miss Telep-Ehrlich was), they add excitement and passion to the piece. Further (but ad-libitum) B-flats, B's, and C's for the lovers ring out in octaves over the final chorus.

If modern Turandots sang as lyrically as Lehmann, Roselle, and Salvatini did, in full, shining, unforced tones, and if modern Calafs took, say, the mellifluous Beniamino Gigli, whom Puccini asked for as his interpreter, as a model (Gigli recorded "Nessun dorma" but never sang the role), and if all concentrated on pronouncing the words so that listeners could follow and respond emotionally to every one of them, modern audiences might gain a different idea of Puccini's opera.

Of *Alcina,* the last and richest of Handel's five "magic" operas, Charles Burney wrote, in 1788, "Upon the whole, if any one of Handel's dramatic works should be brought on the stage, *entire,* without a change or mixture of airs from his other operas, it seems as if this would well sustain such a revival." And, after *Giulio Cesare, Alcina* has probably been the Handel opera most often performed in our day. London has seen four modern productions, two of them with Joan Sutherland as the heroine, and two of them in Covent Garden, where *Alcina* was first performed, in 1735. Dallas staged it in 1960, with Miss Sutherland. There was a concert performance in Carnegie Hall in 1974, with Cristina Deutekom. And now the City Opera has put on a production—a production of sorts, but one that shows little understanding of Handelian opera in general or of the particular qualities of *Alcina.* None of these revivals used the *entire* score. At the City Opera, seven of the twenty-six arias are omitted, and four more are abridged to their first sections only. But a Handelian's quarrel is less with the edition—by comparison with the City Opera's travesty of *Giulio Cesare* or with the *Rinaldo* that threatens at the Met, it is a marvel of rectitude—than with the failure to reveal the dramatic merits of the piece.

A quarter-century ago, the failure could have been forgiven. Those dramatic merits have been a discovery of our day, and increasing experience of Handel's operas in the theatre has changed the common view of them. In 1957, when *Alcina* was about to have its first London production in more than two centuries, Winton Dean wrote, in a program note: *"Alcina* is still a singer's opera, depending both musically and dramatically on the treatment of the solo voice and scarcely at all on the plot. . . . To us these disguised identities, jealousies and amorous cross-currents may appear absurdly stilted, if not incomprehensible. They are best regarded as pure fantasy. *Alcina* makes no claim to be anything else." But nine years—and three productions—later, Dean wrote, in his *Handel and the Opera Seria,* of "music of exceptional psychological subtlety." *Alcina,* he says, "is not an opera in which various characters happen to fall in love; it is an opera about the nature of love itself, as revealed in their actions. Its theme is not magic but the human heart. The music and the drama interlock throughout." An opera about the nature of love itself, something to set beside *Poppea, Figaro's Wedding, Così, Tristan!* I doubt whether anyone encountering *Alcina* for the first time in the City Opera staging could have perceived that. The director, Andrei Serban, and his designer, Mr. Montresor, reduced the dramatic metaphors of Alcina's enchanted isle to a disco divertissement, in black and white and mirrors, and larded the action with cuteness and touches of low comedy. There was no suggestion of the place where, in the words of Sir John Harington's *Orlando Furioso* translation,

> *Divers groves there were, of dainty shade,*
> *Of palme, or orange trees, of cedars tall,*
> *Of sundrie fruites and flowers that never fade.*

There was no contrast between the *luogo deserto* of the opening scene and the voluptuous paradise conjured up by Alcina's spells, no "verdant meadows," no frame for the great central portrait of a woman at first happy in her love, then incredulous when she is scorned, menacing and entreating in turn, finally heartbroken. Alcina, as Dean rightly observes, is a tragic heroine: "She has the stature of a queen, the passion of a woman in love, the evil glitter of a sorceress, and the pathos of pride brought low, for she can command everything except the love of the man she wants." Her progress is traced in six great arias, two in each act. At the City Opera, the force of the fourth of them, the second-act finale, "Ombre pallide," after Alcina has called in vain on her spirits and been answered only with silence, was lessened by its transference to the start of Act III. Ruggiero's "Verdi prati," in E major, his tender farewell to enchantments that he can relinquish only with a pang, and Alcina's "Ombre pallide," in E minor, form a planned sequence that should not be broken. Alcina's fifth aria, "Ma quando tornerai," when, like Venus in *Tannhäuser,* she rounds on her departing lover with mingled threat and entreaty, was omitted. So was Ruggiero's most interesting aria, "Mi lusinga il dolce affetto," in Act II, when his conscience begins to stir.

There is no single right way of performing Handel's operas today. *Orlando,* the first of the three Ariosto operas that he brought out in 1733–35, has triumphed recently in Peter Sellars's modern production, in Cambridge, and in Nicholas McGegan's eighteenth-century production, in St. Louis [*Musical Events: 1980–1983,* pp. 196–99 and 403–6]. The two shows had in common that they were entire and that they observed Handel's stage directions, respected his scenic divisions, sequences, and contrasts, and showed complete faith in his dramatic genius. The Serban *Alcina* is an old-fashioned show executed in the old belief that Handel was a quaint fellow whose operas contain glorious music but are not really dramatic.

The music *is* glorious. One's disappointment that the opera as a whole was not being taken seriously—that the Cambridge and St. Louis lessons remain unlearned in New York—was tempered by delight in hearing the score again. Carol Vaness, the heroine, looks beautiful and sings the music in full, rich tones—sometimes too vibrantly rich for stylistic comfort. D'Anna Fortunato, the Ruggiero, is a Handelian of crisp accomplishment. The others are capable. Raymond Leppard conducts. He loves the music, it is clear, but both his rhythms and the timbre and style of the orchestra are somewhat soggy. The recitatives are delivered slowly, in full voice, with pauses between phrases, and with protracted cadences. The opera is sung in Italian; a bilingual libretto was on sale.

The Metropolitan Opera's centenary season began with a revival of *Les Troyens*—an unready, underrehearsed, but not unpromising account of Berlioz's great opera. The company's repertory system, essentially unchanged in a hundred years, precludes the single-minded attention to one opera at a time which many European houses can now afford. In opening week, revivals of *La Fille du régiment, La forza del destino,* and *La Bohème* all went on as well, and an artistic price must be paid for such proliferation. In any case, opening night at the Met is as much a social as a musical event, and I'll hold a review until I have seen the production again, by which time the artists should have entered their roles more thoroughly.

La Fille du régiment is a heavy-handed production—a lusty romp—that Covent Garden put on for Joan Sutherland and Luciano Pavarotti in 1966. It was not liked, and with undisguised relief the company sold the show off to the Met.

Dame Joan is a jolly girl. The joke here is that she throws herself, voice, body, and soul, into a role—Marie, the pert, sparkly little vivandière of the Famous Twenty-first—to which she is ill suited. Times are strange when sopranos whom nature seems to have meant for Marie—Renata Scotto, Mirella Freni—tackle Lady Macbeth and Aida while Dame Joan, who has been our unrivalled Alcina, Semiramis, and Lucrezia Borgia, essays Donizetti's soubrette role. Her voice still functions beautifully; in the lesson scene she did astonishing, delicate, and brilliant things. Tonio was sung by Alfredo Kraus, a suave vocal stylist but no comedian. Richard Bonynge conducted.

Forza was put on with a lineup of big names—Grace Bumbry, José Carreras, Renato Bruson, Nicolai Ghiaurov, Renato Capecchi—but it was an unworthy, an almost meaningless, representation of Verdi's drama. Miss Bumbry, who was in poor voice, sang in an overemphatic manner. Mr. Carreras—who could surely be a winning Tonio—belted monotonously, except in the duet "Solenne in quest'ora." Mr. Bruson belted, too, and forced his loudest notes off pitch. Mr. Ghiaurov and Mr. Capecchi both sounded worn; the latter's Melitone had flashes of wit, but the role—composed for Achille De Bassini, a celebrated Macbeth—lies high for him. The Preziosilla, Isola Jones, was inadequate. If there was any line or purpose in John Dexter's direction, I missed it; his staging seemed limited to rough "blocking" of the chorus while the soloists wandered at will. James Levine conducted.

Ta Ta Ta Ta Ta . . . Dear Maelzel

October 24, 1983

When a work of Beethoven's was performed, his first question was always "How were the tempi?," according to his biographer Anton Schindler: "Every other consideration seemed to be of secondary importance." In December 1826, the composer wrote to his publishers, B. Schott's Sons, asking them not to bring out the Missa Solemnis until he had sent them the metronome markings for it. "In our century, such indications are certainly necessary. Moreover, I have received letters from Berlin telling me that the first performance of the [Ninth] Symphony was received with enthusiastic applause, which I ascribe largely to the metronome markings. We can scarcely have *tempi ordinari* anymore, since the ideas of unfettered genius must be respected." Beethoven had long been a champion of tempo indications more precise than the conventional Italian designations allegro, allegro ma non troppo, allegro assai, etc. In 1812 or 1813, he met J. N. Maelzel, whose metronome was still in the future but who had already invented a graduated ticktock device for setting tempo. Beethoven endorsed it eagerly, as we learn from letters and from an article in the *Wiener Vaterländische Blätter:* "Herr Beethoven looks upon this invention as a welcome means with which to secure the performance of his brilliant compositions everywhere at the tempi conceived by him, which to his regret have so often been misunderstood."

Maelzel began manufacture of his metronomes in 1816, and Beethoven soon acquired one. He urged their "universal use and distribution." Henceforth, he said, he would attach Italian descriptive terms to a composition only to indicate its "spirit," and provide metronome markings to define its tempo, which is "more like the body." He published Maelzel Metronome figures for the first eight symphonies, the first eleven string quartets, and the septet. He published the "Hammerklavier" sonata, in 1819, with M.M. markings. "Metronome highly necessary," he jotted down in 1825 apropos of a passage in Opus 132. The evidence of his continuing trust in the metronome should be stressed, for at least two reasons. First, Schindler, who thought that he alone held the secrets to true Beethoven performance, sought to discredit the markings, claiming that the composer himself had in later life disowned them, and buttressing the assertion with forged entries in the Beethoven conversation books. (The famous canon "Ta ta ta ta ta ... lieber Maelzel," on the Allegretto theme of the Eighth Symphony, may well be another Schindler forgery.) Second, surprisingly few of Beethoven's metronome markings are observed by Beethoven performers. When there is consensus that about half of them are impossibly fast, and a few of them impossibly slow, something has gone wrong. Was it Beethoven's metronome, his employment of it, or his perception of tempo? Or is it present-day interpretation?

The extent of the divergence between markings and interpretation was startlingly revealed by Peter Stadlen in an article in *Soundings* (1982). He undertook a survey of the nine symphonies as performed on record by eight conductors; of the eleven string quartets as performed by six quartets; of the "Hammerklavier" as played by seven pianists; and of the septet as played by four ensembles. And he determined that of the hundred and thirty-six Beethoven M.M. markings involved, only seventy are observed in at least one of the performances. Of the remaining sixty-six markings, sixty-two are faster than in any recording and four are slower.

Was Beethoven's metronome at fault? It seems unlikely. When it went wrong, he had it repaired (as letters of 1819 and 1825 attest). Stadlen worked with metronomes of Beethoven's day and found that they are pretty precise; if anything, they go just a shade too fast—which would result in readings too slow, not (as in most cases) too fast. He tried slowing a metronome down by oiling it with green olive oil adulterated with dust and allowed to oxidize—the most unsuitable lubricant, the British Museum Clock Room told him, that Beethoven could have got hold of in Vienna—and it still kept time. In any case, metronomes that beat too slow also beat erratically, in a way that no musician can fail to notice. So he sought other explanations. He found that the instrument's calibrating scale can be misread by parallax: looking up at a metronome, as from a keyboard, one can read too low a mark on its scale; standing above it and looking down, one too high. But this was still not enough in itself to account for the wider divergences between the markings and their usual execution. Stadlen added the factor of "acoustical delusion." Slow music, he says, sounds slower when played on the piano than on strings. And while Beethoven was nearly deaf by 1817, "it is quite conceivable that after a long career as a pianist, his fingers had retained sufficient keyboard sensitivity to compensate instinctively, in such passages, by playing them a little faster while he was determining the tempo of a symphony or quartet at the keyboard." (Another possible acoustical delusion,

44

surely—one Stadlen does not consider—is that when "performing" a piece in one's mind one is apt to set a slightly faster tempo than at a live performance with instruments.) At any rate, by combining (with a delicacy that this summary of his careful work does no justice to) the factors of possible small mechanical error, possible parallax, and possible acoustical delusion, Stadlen determined that sixty of Beethoven's "absurdly fast" figures can be adjusted to be brought within "the realm of the possible." Of the four figures that are "too slow"—all four in the Ninth Symphony—he ascribes one to parallax, one to clerical error, and one to a compound of both. The fourth—the prestissimo at half note = 132—he considers to be correct, "and the usually adopted faster tempo ... certainly wrong."

Another view is possible, although it takes courage to maintain it against the massed, mutually supportive evidence that Stadlen has collected from so many great musicians, Schnabel, Weingartner, Toscanini, and Furtwängler among them: that Beethoven meant exactly what he wrote, and that our performing traditions are wrong. Benjamin Zander, the conductor of the Boston Philharmonic, argues this case in an essay, "Beethoven's Ninth Symphony and the Metronome," which was distributed to the audience for the performance of the Ninth—an "argument in sound"—that he and the orchestra gave in Carnegie Hall last week.

Tempo and timing matter very much in the Ninth. Its opening, as Tovey says, has been "a radiating point for all subsequent experiments for enlarging the time-scale of music." Beethoven's 1826 letter is testimony to the importance he gave to the metronome markings. But Stadlen's tables reveal that of the sixteen markings in the score Beethoven sent to Berlin, only seven are accepted by one or more of the eight conductors in his survey—who are Weingartner, in 1935, and, from the quarter-century 1952 to 1977, Furtwängler, Toscanini, Erich Kleiber, Walter, Szell, Kempe, and Karajan (twice). Eight markings are unanimously rejected—four as too fast, four as too slow. (One marking, the finale's brief reminiscence of the opening—allegro ma non troppo, quarter note = 88—is, for some reason, unsurveyed.)

For many years, various scores of the Ninth were bedevilled by misprints that clouded discussion of the tempi. The most significant were whole note (instead of half note) = 116 at the trio of the scherzo, and dotted half note = 96 (instead of 66) at the start of the finale. Back in 1922, the composer C. V. Stanford had pointed out the first error (in a letter to the London *Times*), yet in 1966 Pierre Boulez essayed the resultant double-speed reading, endeavoring to make one bar of the trio equal to a bar of the scherzo. It's much too fast a tempo; but Beethoven's marking—Stadlen's eight conductors agree—is too slow. (The slowest performance, Furtwängler's, gets down only to 138.) Several conductors pay lip service to the composer's equation of a trio bar with a scherzo half bar; none of the eight surveyed practice it, however. Mr. Zander did, with an almost altogether satisfactory and convincing result. (I say "almost" because it is a long movement to hear at a single pulse.) As for the 96 of the finale: Weingartner worked from a score with this reading and declared it (in his handbook on the performance of the symphonies) too fast for the recitative, though not for the fanfares. The 96 is a simple misprint introduced by the Schott engraver (who

45

was on page 96 at the time). Most conductors remain close to Beethoven's 66.

There were various other little puzzles about the figures. About twenty years ago, I tried to clear them up by consulting, in the German State Library, the pages of the conversation book for the day—September 27, 1826—on which Beethoven and his nephew Karl established the speeds for the symphony. (I had learned of the pages' existence from a passing footnote in Alexander Thayer's biography which no Beethoven scholar—despite all the controversy about the markings—seemed to have followed up. In fact, Stadlen was already at work on them, and in an important *Music and Letters* article in 1967 he published the pages in facsimile, along with the letter to Schott—slightly misrepresented in Emily Anderson's edition of the letters—in which Karl set out the M.M. markings he and his uncle had arrived at.) I compared the pages with the Berlin score (now in the same library) into which Karl had that day entered the markings. And the figures that Beethoven had decided on—however "impossible" they may seem to his modern interpreters—were no longer in doubt. Most of the figures are in Karl's hand, and a few (I think) are in Beethoven's. The pair worked in haste: the next day they were leaving Vienna for a stay in Gneixendorf, and they wanted to have the Berlin copy—a luxuriously bound presentation volume for Kaiser Friedrich Wilhelm III, to whom the symphony is dedicated—ready for dispatch. But their work was careful, and they checked. The last entry (in Karl's hand) reads, "You took it faster than 126./132/ That's how we did it this morning." And *"Wohin?"*—"Where must I enter it?"—Karl asks against the half note = 80 tempo for the "Joy" theme. He entered it in the Berlin copy at the first sounding of the theme, on the woodwinds, at bar 77 (which is marked allegro moderato in some modern scores—Stadlen follows suit—but is allegro assai in the Berlin copy). He did not reenter the indication—but some modern scores do—when at bar 92 the cellos and basses take up the theme (marked allegro assai in the Berlin copy, but with a pencilled alteration to allegro moderato). All the surveyed conductors then slacken the pace when the singers, led by the baritone, take up the "Joy" theme: Weingartner drops from 100 to 72, Furtwängler from 80 to 54. But Mr. Zander delivered all three statements at Beethoven's half note = 80, and his triple affirmation made excellent sense.

At the alla marcia, Mr. Zander adopted Beethoven's dotted quarter note = 84, and it sounded fine. Both Stadlen and Erich Leinsdorf, in his *The Composer's Advocate,* suggest that the dotted quarter note is a mistake for a dotted half note, which would give a tempo twice as fast; but Leinsdorf's "simple conclusion that in some early copy the half note got some ink into its center and became thereby a quarter note" is invalidated by unblotched, unequivocal quarter notes in Karl's hand. Karl was not immune to scribal error, it is true: in the Berlin score and the Schott letter he gives the scherzo unit as half note = 116, where only a *dotted* half note is possible; and in the allegro energico of the finale he omits in the Berlin score—but not in the conversation book or the letter—the dot that his half note = 84 requires. His penmanship is immaculate to the point of omitting even necessary spots.

In the prestissimo, Mr. Zander was faithful to Beethoven's half note = 132, which Weingartner deemed "impossible ... in this passage of boundless enthusiasm" and increased to 152. (The slowest here of Stadlen's conductors,

Toscanini, sets 144, though he drops to Beethoven's mark by the fifteenth bar; Karajan and Szell both adopt 168.) In sum, of the eight disputed M.M. markings in the symphony—those unobserved by any of Stadlen's conductors—Mr. Zander, I reckoned, was faithful to six: the "fast" andante of the slow movement and the "Joy" statement; the "slow" trio, alla marcia, allegro energico, and prestissimo. In the adagio molto, he was much faster than anyone else, though not quite as fast as Beethoven's quarter note = 60. For the first movement, marked quarter note = 88, he adopted the 76 recommended by Weingartner and practiced by Toscanini and Walter.

Stadlen left it "to future investigations to draw comparisons between metro-nomized movements that resemble one another structurally or poetically." Mr. Zander, in his essay, notes that the only other adagio molto in 4/4 that Beethoven "metronomized' (nine years earlier), the slow movement of the second Razumovsky, bears the same "too fast" figure—quarter note = 60—as the adagio molto of the Ninth, and opens with a theme of similar gait and character. Coincidence? Zander argues that the half notes of both themes are indeed "very slow" at Beethoven's tempo—so slow as to be, at 30, right off the metronome's scale. So "body" (M.M.) and "spirit" (the Italian phrase), he says in effect, are not opposed. But in Stadlen's tables only the Budapest Quartet, in 1951, approaches the Razumovsky marking, and most conductors take the symphony movement at half speed. Arguments about tempo remain abstract until they are put to the test of performance. But I'm not ready, yet, to assess Mr. Zander's Ninth Symphony properly. For one thing, since student days I've been under the influence of a Furtwängler Ninth that—the phrase is trite but true—changed my life, and Furtwängler represents in excelsis the inspired, free, slow-movements-slower, fast-movements-faster approach that has given Beethoven's metronome a bad name. (As a "corrective," I turn to the irresistible Toscanini recording, which treats the markings less extremely but hardly less freely.) For another, alerted by Mr. Zander's essay, I went to Carnegie Hall with a modern, electronic metro-nome in hand, and full attention—surrender—to the music was inhibited by glances at the instrument's winking light. On the conductor's part, too, there must have been an awareness that the performance was also a demonstration, a making of points. Moreover, I was slightly disappointed by the playing of the Boston Philharmonic, about which I've heard good things, and which I have admired (on tape) in Mahler.

Stadlen, starting from the presumption that half Beethoven's metronome markings—despite his championship of the device—belie his intentions, sought and found explanations of why this should be. Mr. Zander, believing that Beethoven intended what he wrote, sought to realize *all* Beethoven's markings for the Ninth, not just half of them. His performance, I understand, may be recorded. I hope it is. The points were well and clearly made, but one would need to hear more performances at these speeds before one could find them proved; the weight of familiarity, of years of being stirred by great interpretations at the traditional tempi, is not lightly shed. One would like to hear the other symphonies treated in this way; they contain twenty-one metronome markings faster than any adopted by Stadlen's interpreters. The string quartets contain thirty-four. Other factors need study, too. What effect may our modern, louder instruments, richer-toned playing techniques, and larger concert halls have had upon tempi? All Stadlen's surveyed pianists play the "Hammerklavier" on a modern concert grand, not on a hammerklavier. These matters are not minutiae, for if Mr. Zander is right we have been hearing the music of the greatest composer only in misrepresentation.

This article produced much correspondence. In the last few years there has been considerable "practical research"—in the form of performances—into the metronome markings for the symphonies: by, among others, David Zinman with the Baltimore Symphony and, on period instruments, Roger Norrington and the London Classical Players, Christopher Hogwood and the Academy of Ancient Music, and Frans Brüggen and the Orchestra of the Eighteenth Century. Richard Taruskin writes trenchantly about several of the period-instrument recordings in "Beethoven Symphonies: The New Antiquity" (Opus, October 1987).

IMAGES OF EXUBERANT BEAUTY

October 31, 1983

MICHAEL TIPPETT's first opera, *The Midsummer Marriage*—a lyrical celebration of love and joy—had its American première this month, in San Francisco. The opera tells of the changing seasons, of nature's endless dance, of the starry heaven and the fruitful earth, and of a young man and a young woman held apart for a while by differing idealisms but joined at last after a mutual sacrifice by which each is enriched. It is a contemporary work that has things in common with *The Magic Flute* and with *The Woman Without a Shadow*. Its profuse, beautiful imagery—musical, visual, and verbal—gladdens the senses and stirs the mind. Tippett, in his essay "Poets in a Barren Age," sought to define a composer's task:

To create images from the depths of the imagination and to give them form.... Images of the past, shapes of the future. Images of vigour for a decadent period, images of calm for one too violent. Images of reconciliation for worlds torn by division. And in an age of mediocrity and shattered dreams, images of abounding, generous, exuberant beauty.

The Midsummer Marriage, composed in 1946–52 and first performed in 1955, at Covent Garden, reflects the bright years when Britain strove to create a new, juster society. Britten's *Spring Symphony* (1949) is another work of the time. The dream, as Tippett observed in that essay, is ever and again shattered. His later works, like Britten's, grew darker. In the Third Symphony (1970–72), he sounded the harsh, questioning fanfares of Beethoven's Ninth and answered them not with shouts of "Joy!" and pealing D-major proclamations of universal brotherhood but with qualified consolation. He sang the blues. In his opera *The*

Ice Break (1973–76), when Hannah's song of healing, a blues transfigured, rises through a city murked by intolerance and brutality, there shines what he has called "a momentary vision of a possibility." There are shadows, dangers, and a death in *The Midsummer Marriage,* but its main song is of fruitfulness and joy.

At the first production, some were bothered by Tippett's dramaturgy, for he had embodied his realistic story—the age-old comedy plot of a marriage delayed both by misunderstandings and by parental opposition—in a scenario where the imaginings and emotional adventures of the characters are given theatrical shape. The poetic metaphors by which we describe and investigate experience take on visual and sonic form; Jungian dreams are enacted. Jenifer, in flight from Mark's embrace, finds herself at the foot of a staircase leading to heaven and, as if it were the most natural thing in the world for her to do, ascends it and passes out of our sight. Gates leading deep into the warm, pulsing earth open to receive Mark. The San Francisco production, directed by John Copley and designed by Robin Don, is the fourth I have seen, and it is the most successful, for it proceeds with utter naturalness, passing effortlessly between "real life" and scenic metaphor. Solos, choral scenes, and dances are blended in a single, spellbinding adventure. I feel unsure of the anthropomorphic elements in the décor: the imagined "temple" in the woods is an Ozymandian shattered visage, and the gates into the earth are represented by an enormous plaster hand, two of whose fingers swivel upward to admit entrance. But the feeling of a dappled glade where enchantments may happen, one whose aspect can suddenly change, is skillfully created by shapes in perforated metal, exquisitely colored, and very skillfully lit (by Thomas Munn). Terry Gilbert's choreography is fearless, beautiful, sensuous, and sensitive to all Tippett's intended imagery. The dancers are good, and Strephon, their leader, played by Jamie Cohen, is outstanding. The chorus—a regular glory of the San Francisco company—is superb. (Dancers and chorus become principals in this opera.) The orchestra, enjoying some of the loveliest nature music ever written, plays with great eloquence. The work, the company's press release says, "was given more than the routine number of rehearsals," and one can well believe it.

As Jenifer, a role created by Joan Sutherland, Mary Jane Johnson sang brightly and truly. Mark, a role created by Richard Lewis, needs fresher, freer tones than Dennis Bailey's, but his characterization was right. Sheri Greenawald and Ryland Davies were deft as the Papagena and Papageno couple, Bella and Jack. Raimund Herincx, who has often played King Fisher, Jenifer's father (it was his Covent Garden début role, in 1968), gave a wonderfully strong and rounded performance. Kevin Langan, a notable Sarastro, made a grave, commanding priest of the temple. David Agler's conducting was clear, controlled, and shapely: I missed just a touch of the excited, passionate advocacy Colin Davis and Richard Armstrong bring to the score. The expert individual contributions came together in a single, inspired presentation of Tippett's inspiring opera. I've never admired Mr. Copley's work more.

The other opera played while I was in San Francisco was *La traviata*—a careful restaging of the piece, by Matthew Farruggio, in Toni Businger's undistinguished but workable décor. It had musical freshness and dramatic urgency, for Richard Bradshaw, its conductor, is a musician with a sure feeling for unwritten but essential rubato—the ebb and flow of musical phrases which Verdi's music needs. An engaging Alfredo, Alberto Cupido, and a subtle, powerful Germont, Leo Nucci, shared his perceptions. The Violetta, Winifred Faix Brown, was a shade less stylish, but she is an able and accomplished singer. The comprimari—and especially Nancy Gustafson, the Flora—were all of them young artists of merit. The orchestra played well. The preludes were movingly shaped. The chorus, again, was outstanding; and the words of its Spanish divertissement could be heard.

On the day of my return to the Met *Troyens,* Placido Domingo's decision to abandon the role of Aeneas was announced. Tatiana Troyanos, the intended Cassandra, was ill and was replaced by an understudy. So of the three principals billed only Jessye Norman, the Dido, appeared. She was remarkable. On the opening night of the season, Miss Norman, at her Met début, had sung Cassandra. Eleven years ago, she made her Covent Garden début in the same role, without much success: "This seemed so glaring a piece of vocal and dramatic miscasting that I cannot begin to understand the thinking that led to it," said the editor of *Opera.* She has majesty and dignity, but there is a softness of grain in her timbre which deprived the heroic virgin's cries of their cutting edge, and she is hardly an impetuous performer. Dido suits her far better. She was warm, regal in manner, opulent of voice; and in the great final sequence of duet, monologue, air, suicide scene, and imprecation she found a new passion and intensity, both as a singer and as an actress. I have known Didos more moving but none more imposing. Wagner's Elisabeth and Mozart's Countess were among Miss Norman's early roles. Lately, she has been singing classical parts: Purcell's Dido (in Philadelphia), Gluck's Alcestis (recorded on the Orfeo label), Rameau's Phaedra (at the Aix festival). In this *Troyens,* her often somewhat generalized, always vastly impressive monumental grandeur became incandescent. She was volatile, as Berlioz's music is—savage and alarming in her wrath, full-hearted and elegiac in her farewell to Carthage, unrestrained and searing in the wordless outburst of grief above stabbing woodwind chords.

On the opening night, Miss Troyanos was Dido, and Mr. Domingo was Aeneas. Both were accurate but not yet fully commanding. The love duet sounded careful, the duet of parting inhibited. At my second performance, William Lewis was Aeneas. His tones were dull and dry until he reached the fifth-act aria, which rang out convincingly. The Troy acts went for little; they could probably with advantage have been omitted, since Gwynn Cornell, the stand-in Cassandra, was unsteady and inadequate. (There's a lot to be said for performing "Troy" and "Carthage" on consecutive evenings—or as matinée and evening performances on a Saturday. *Les Troyens,* which lasts five hours in the Met's two-intermission presentation, is one work, as Berlioz insisted. So is *The Ring.* And Berlioz's drama is powerful enough to carry an audience through a dinner intermission, or even a day's.)

The Met production depends on its principals. It is not a committed, visionary presentation of Berlioz's epic which seems to transcend the individual contributions. The décor, by Peter Wexler, is that of ten years ago, slightly reworked, and it makes no attempt to match the colors, the picturesqueness, the Virgilian romance of the score. The prompt box serves as Achilles' tomb. There is no Trojan Horse. The Royal Hunt and Storm is unstaged. No warm, fragrant, enchanted Mediterranean night embowers the throbbing strains of the septet and the love duet. The wardrobe is meagre: Dido attends the municipal prize-giving, the garden party, and the funeral rite always in the same dull dress; the dancers—whether Egyptian dancing girls or Nubian slaves—all wear white shifts or tights. (Their ballet scarcely bears watching and could well be omitted.) All in all, the show looks—except for the numbers of choristers and supers— like a *Troyens* run up on the cheap and, worse, assembled without imagination or any excited, specific response to Virgil and to Berlioz. Fabrizio Melano's staging is little more than a concert performance in costume—one set on a platform spacious enough to allow the soloists room to move about if they choose to. At the start of the opera, shrill woodwinds and cornets depict the reckless high spirits of the populace—soldiers, civilians, women, and children— as after ten pent years of siege they rush out onto the plain. The stage directions are specific: left, in the distance, the Trojan citadel; right, the stream Simois, with great Achilles' tomb on its bank; three piping shepherds atop the tomb; Mount Ida in the background. Another stage direction calls for dancing to begin five measures before the curtain rises, so that a scene of wild activity, matched to the hectic music, will greet the spectators' eyes. At the Met, the chorus maintains a serried oratorio formation, in a dark, drab scene. And so on throughout the evening.

James Levine's conducting is capable, energetic, and not insensitive, but it misses the special quality, easier to recognize than to define, that distinguishes the true Berlioz interpreter. It took fire, I thought, only when at my second performance Dido was singing. Miss Norman's Dido needs Jon Vickers's Aeneas, but Mr. Vickers's Met assignments this season are Peter Grimes (more of that later) and Florestan.

Riccardo Muti, the conductor of the Philadelphia Orchestra, declared recently that a concert performance may well provide a more honest account of an opera than some of today's fancy productions do. (He opened the Scala season last December conducting what seems to have been a perverse inscenation of *Ernani.*) He has also said that an orchestra that confines itself to the symphonic repertory misses out on some of the best music. Since American opera companies prove unable to offer men like Muti, Abbado, Solti, and Carlos Kleiber conditions that they find acceptable, they conduct staged operas only in Europe. [*Mr. Kleiber came to the Met, at last, in 1988.*] But this month Muti and the Philadelphia gave a concert presentation of Verdi's *Macbeth,* in Philadelphia's Academy of Music and then in Carnegie Hall, that was more dramatic than just about any stage production of the piece I'd seen since Glyndebourne's in 1952. This concert version was on a huge scale. In 1847, before the Florence première, Verdi asked for eighteen witches—three covens of six apiece—and he had a full chorus of forty-eight. Muti had about ninety witches, a full chorus of a hundred and eighty-five (the Westminster Symphonic Choir, in excellent form), and an orchestra of over a hundred. He used the revised version of the opera, which in 1865 was mounted at the Théâtre-Lyrique as a spectacular show to rival Meyerbeer's *L'Africaine* at the Opéra.

None of Verdi's operas was more carefully composed or before its première more carefully rehearsed than *Macbeth*. He exhorted his singers again and again to concentrate on serving the playwright rather than the composer: "Study well the dramatic situation and the words; the music will come by itself." But that music had to be rendered with careful observance of the frequent dynamic contrasts, of instructions such as "pensieroso," "voce soffocata," "cupo," "con orrore," and of the precise phrasing indications. Singers could then be trusted to employ dramatic rubato and to devise their own cadenzas—except in the few places that carry an express prohibition of the wonted embellishments. Verdi said he "endeavored to compose music tied to the text." In 1875, when he was in Vienna to conduct the Requiem and a journalist asked him his opinion of Wagner, he replied tactfully and then added, "I, too, have attempted the fusion of music and drama—in *Macbeth*."

Muti's *come scritto* approach to nineteenth-century scores—a literatim, notatim rendering in all places of the printed text which, as *Opera News* puts it this month, "sometimes borders on the comic"—is unscholarly, unstylish, and, I've found in the past, often undramatic. But in this *Macbeth* he gave his singers and his players rather more room to breathe and express themselves, the words, and the music than I've ever heard him give before. Not quite enough, it is true. (Yet at one point I actually found myself missing the old bandmasterly Muti, who would have invested the jerky dotted rhythms of the final chorus with more snap.) His scrupulous attention to the expression marks brought rich rewards. The murder duet was largely whispered, except in those phrases marked to be sung in full voice. Such an approach requires a faithful edition, one that, for example, shows (as modern scores do not) the composer's subtle, striking differences of articulation in the two verses of Lady Macbeth's drinking song: the first time, a sustained F and a bold slur up the octave on the words "nasca il diletto"; a detached and more emphatic delivery the second time, as Lady Macbeth seeks to enforce merriment on a company perturbed by the royal host's behavior.

The orchestral playing was delicate, opulent, gleaming. The accompaniment to the cutthroats' chorus—one of Verdi's boldest inventions—was splendidly sinister. The invocation of undines and sylphides was a lilting delight. The witches sounded just as Verdi (following A. W. Schlegel, whose famous commentary influenced the composer's thinking about the play) said they should: exalted and prophetic in their oracular moments, coarse and gossipy when cackling among themselves. As Lady Macbeth, Elizabeth Connell made her New York début. A celebrated Ortrud and Amneris, she has become a dramatic soprano with fire and flash in her voice, and her presence is vivid. Renato Bruson was the Macbeth. His performance was serious and strong until, as the evening progressed, he began to push the climaxes too hard and force his notes off pitch. Then the tragic hero turned into a baritone trying to display his voice. Luis Lima was a brave Macduff. Simon Estes was a full-toned Banquo, but one who, especially in recitative, tended to sing in stiffly metronomic note values, uninflected by the sense and shape of the words.

When singers and orchestra are together on a platform, the balance between them is possibly closer to what it was in the theatres of Verdi's day than it is when the orchestra is sunk into an anachronistic modern pit. And ensemble is certainly more easily achieved. Balance and ensemble were excellent in this performance. Muti is a master of color and texture. He plans to go on doing concert operas. It was good to hear a Verdi score so carefully rehearsed, so lustrously played, and so lovingly conducted.

TERRORS AND TRAGEDIES

November 7, 1983

BRITTEN's chamber operas are often performed in America. This season, his three grand operas are more prominent than usual. To represent contemporary opera—works composed in the last half-century—in the centenary season, the Met has chosen *Peter Grimes* and *Billy Budd,* along with Poulenc's *Dialogues of the Carmelites. Gloriana* comes to the Met—and to San Antonio—in June, brought by the English National Opera. There is another *Grimes* due, in Houston, in January, and another, in Los Angeles, brought by the Royal Opera, Covent Garden, during the Olympics.

Peter Grimes, which appeared at Sadler's Wells in June 1945, a month after the ending of the war in Europe, was hailed with enthusiasm. Desmond Shawe-Taylor discerned in Britten "a fresh hope, not only for English, but for European opera." Some British critics tempered their praise. Edmund Wilson had no reservations and placed Britten with the "relatively few composers of the first rank who had a natural gift for the theatre: Mozart, Mussorgsky, Verdi, Wagner, the Bizet of *Carmen.*" The opera—he wrote in some pages that are eloquent about the music and its aims—

> seizes upon you, possesses you, keeps you riveted to your seat during the action and keyed up during the intermissions, and drops you, purged and exhausted, at the end. . . . I do not remember ever to have seen, at any performance of opera, an audience so steadily intent, so petrified and held in suspense, as the audience of *Peter Grimes.*

The Met production dates from 1967. It was directed by Tyrone Guthrie and designed by Tanya Moiseiwitsch, and has the nostalgic interest, to English eyes, of being close to the 1947 Covent Garden production by the same team. (At Covent Garden, the décor was modified when, in 1953, John Cranko took over the stage direction.) In that production, which included six members of the original Sadler's Wells cast, I first got to know the opera. But nostalgia is the least of the emotions stirred by a powerful performance of *Peter Grimes*. With passing years, its freshness, its dramatic force, its richness of musical structure, and its illumination of private and public behavior seem ever to grow. In 1947, Wilson praised Britten's success "in harmonizing, through *Peter Grimes,* the harsh helpless emotions of wartime," in speaking for "the blind anguish, the hateful rancors and the will to destruction of these horrible years." Decades later, Philip Brett, compiler and in large part author of the Cambridge Opera Handbook devoted to *Grimes*, finds it "a musical drama of particular relevance to our present age, and one that may well reveal further levels of meaning to future generations." His book contains valuable new material about the genesis of the opera, sensitive new thoughts about its significances, and some of the best previous writing about it. (The Shawe-Taylor and Wilson accounts of the première are reprinted.) Further commentary, an iconography of productions from Moscow to San Francisco, and the libretto appear in the English National/Royal Opera *Opera Guide* devoted to *Grimes* and *Gloriana*.

The Met revival was conducted by John Pritchard in an assured, masterly fashion. The orchestral playing was not inspired (how can it be when the company must churn out seven opera performances a week, week after week, with the five-hour *Troyens* as one of them?), but it was of good quality. Jon Vickers in the title role was inspired. Grimes comprises within himself three men—victim, destroyer, and poetic dreamer—who in *Billy Budd* are separate. Mr. Vickers embodies the blundering, tormented tragedy in a way that leaves ordinary operatic impersonation behind. It is an alarming, disturbing performance. His voice, his features, his demeanor are distorted, transfigured. He has one of the few voices that can set the enormous Met ringing. The intensity of his utterance informs equally the quiet, almost whispered passages—strange, wild thoughts overheard—that make his portrayal so vivid. It is an unwieldy voice, but as it strains upward into the higher notes of the part the very effort becomes eloquent. As Siegmund, Tristan, and Parsifal, as Florestan, as Don Carlos and Radamès, as both Handel's and Saint-Saëns's Samson, Mr. Vickers will be remembered by all who have heard him. His Grimes is perhaps the most remarkable of all.

Elisabeth Söderström made her début in the new Met as Ellen Orford. (She last sang in the old house nineteen years ago, as the Composer in *Ariadne*.) She gave a beautifully judged, tenderly exact performance. But the house was large for it; one had to focus in, as it were, to appreciate her fine-drawn line. Thomas Stewart's bluff Balstrode was admirable. Many of the other characters—Auntie, Mrs. Sedley, Ned, the Rector—overplayed, verged on florid caricature. Jerome Hines, who has been singing Swallow at the Met for thirty-five years, still mispronounces "quietus." (Not a mere British quibble—a glance at Webster would put him right.) For that matter, I wish Mr. Vickers would now restore the original text in the places where Guthrie, for the 1967 Met production, tinkered with it. When Ellen asks this Grimes where the youngster got the ugly bruise on his neck, he replies, "How should I know?," which is weak and imprecise for the composer's "Out of the hurly-burly." Guthrie's production, now in the care of Bodo Igesz, seemed somewhat underrehearsed. Not Grimes, Ellen, or Balstrode but most of the others signalled to the audience when they would be singing next by slewing eyes out of the action to watch for Sir John's or the prompter's cue. It seems to me a mistake to set the mad scene not in the Borough street, with "Peter alone by his boat in the changeful light of a cloud-swept moon," but in a nowhere-world, with Peter adrift, knee-deep, in a swirl of stage steam. *Grimes* is a realistic opera. The contrast between familiar things (and the real shouting of the distant mob and the boom of the foghorn) and Peter's nightmare is stronger without stagy trimmings. Mr. Vickers's searing performance has no need of them.

The Met opened on October 22, 1883, with a performance of *Faust,* Christine Nilsson the Marguerite. It celebrated the centenary with an eight-and-a-half-hour concert—three and a half hours in the afternoon, five that night—given by a company such as can never have been assembled before. David Hockney's *Tirésias* quayside, the *Arabella* ballroom, the Latin Quarter set of *La Bohème,* and Chagall's *Magic Flute* décor housed the event. The list of singers would fill a column or more: among just the most eminent sopranos and tenors, there were Birgit Nilsson, Joan Sutherland, Montserrat Caballé, Leontyne Price, Martina Arroyo, Grace Bumbry, Elisabeth Söderström, Katia Ricciarelli, Kiri Te Kanawa, and Jessye Norman; and Placido Domingo, Luciano Pavarotti, José Carreras, Alfredo Kraus, James McCracken, Nicolai Gedda, and Jess Thomas. Roberta Peters, Anna Moffo, Régine Crespin, Regina Resnik (the Met's first Ellen Orford), Robert Merrill, Italo Tajo were on the bill. It was a celebration of past, present, and future. During the last lap, Zinka Milanov, Bidú Sayão, Erna Berger, Eleanor Steber, Jarmila Novotna, Risë Stevens, Ramon Vinay sat in state on the stage. Not only international stars but also the house regulars and comprimari performed. Members of the Young Artists Program (notably Gail Dubinbaum, a bright Isabella in the first-act *Italiana* finale) were also on display. The orchestra had its solo spot in a *Leonore* No. 3 lovingly, fervently conducted by Leonard Bernstein. The chorus, conducted by its chorus master, David Stivender, sang the glowing Hymn to the Sun that opens Mascagni's *Iris.* The ballet had a high old time wiggling and leaping through the *Samson* bacchanale.

Such jamborees can be a trial. This one was joyful, and it was also, both in its peaks and on the plain, of uncommon interest to an observer of present-day singing. The high point was provided by Miss Nilsson, who, after a tremendous delivery of Isolde's Narration and Curse, sang an unaccompanied Swedish folk song—Christine Nilsson's favorite encore—with clear, bright freshness of sound, swift, glittering high arpeggios, power to set mountaintops resounding, and delicate, subtle art. At sixty-five, she remains matchless. Miss Sutherland, who is fifty-seven, sang Semiramide's "Bel raggio" with effortless brilliance. But there were younger singers who had sacrificed bloom, sweetness, and purity of tone to volume and power, who were once limpid and melting and have now become harder in timbre and unsteady on loud high notes. Legato was often in short supply. We heard a bumpy account of Gremin's aria, in *Onegin,* and a *détaché* account of the Dutchman's "Wie aus der Ferne," which Wagner marked "con portamento." But from Miss Arroyo, in an *Aida* duet, and from Lucine Amara, in a *Gioconda* duet, we heard pure, flowing, unforced, beautiful sound, welling as if from an open throat; and from Cornell MacNeil, in "Nemico della patria," from *Chénier,* a baritone line that was clear, steady, unpushed, but strong.

At a Y recital last week, the New Arts Trio (Rebecca Penneys, piano; Piotr Janowski, violin; and Steven Doane, cello), the winner of the 1980 Naumburg Award for Chamber Music, played John Eaton's Piano Trio. It is a brief (about eight-minute), intense piece, charged with keen emotion, and composed "in memoriam Mario Cristini." Cristini was one of the last masters of painted scenic perspective in the opera house. Eaton's program note, telling how the music of the trio began to stir as he sat alone on the veranda of Cristini's house above Lake Trasimene, overlooking the silvery, limpid expanse, suggests a scene. Through sounds telling of stillness and quiet stirring, the violin and the cello begin to sing melodies of urgent, lyrical grief. Eaton has an ability like Janáček's to write lines that etch themselves directly on the emotions; and no composer is less problematical in his command of quarter tones that can "bend" familiar pitches to create utterances of new poignancy and can blend into subtly affecting new harmonies. The singing falls silent at last. The trio ends in a silvery stillness now radiant.

This is a rare and beautiful composition, and it was played by the New Arts with a rare command of timbres and of poetic timing. The recital began with an account of Beethoven's "Geister" Trio which was clearly laid out but, I thought, a little plain in its confident—almost overconfident—execution. Miss Penneys's passagework ran a shade too fluently—or, to put it another way, figuration that should be expressive tended to become mere passagework. "Keine Passagen!," Clara Schumann would cry to her pupils—"Why hurry over beautiful things?" Brahms's C-minor Trio was more amply enjoyed. This is the piece of which Clara said, "No other of Johannes's works has so completely transported me." With big tone, supple phrasing, energy, and a romantic ensemble in which individualism and teamwork were balanced, the players responded to the "sustained genius of passion, strength of thought, charm, and expressiveness" that Clara admired.

I received a friendly, amusing letter from Mr. Hines, explaining that the educated pronunciation of "quietus" was not unknown to him but that, in the character of Swallow, he had deliberately mispronounced the word: the pompous local lawyer was using a grand term he had not quite mastered. I replied that since there were five flourishing playhouses in Crabbe's Borough, Swallow must often have heard a Hamlet—Garrick, perhaps—declare what a man might with a bare bodkin make; and that in any case his characterizing point—lost on me, who dislike the creeping modern Italianization of standard British and American pronunciations—was likely to be generally lost in an age when the Deity is more often than not referred to as a "dayity."

Fatal Error of Misguided Love

November 14, 1983

HANDEL'S musical drama *Hercules* has been called "the highest peak of late baroque music drama" (Paul Henry Lang), "perhaps Handel's greatest achievement" (Henry Prunières), "the culmination of the Handelian musical drama, and indeed one might say of the whole musical theatre before Gluck" (Romain Rolland). Winton Dean collects the judgments at the start of the *Hercules* chapter in his book on the dramatic oratorios, and endorses them: "These are no exaggerations." He himself calls *Hercules* a "work of supreme genius" and a "great dramatic masterpiece" that "should be in the repertory of half the opera houses of Europe." But opera houses have been slow to take it up. There was a production at La Scala in 1958–59, grandly cast: Jerome Hines in the title role, Fedora Barbieri as Dejanira, Elisabeth Schwarzkopf as Iole, Franco Corelli as Hyllus, and Ettore Bastianini (an octave too low) as Lichas. In London, its staging has been left to the short annual seasons of the Handel Opera Society, which has produced it three times, between 1956 and 1979. *Hercules* apparently awaits an American stage première. Last week in Merkin Hall, the Sine Nomine Singers and the Philip Levin Baroque Ensemble, conducted by Harry Saltzman, gave a modest but successful concert performance—one that could arouse, or confirm, enthusiasm for the piece but did something less than justice to its grandeur and its dramatic force.

Dejanira is one of the great mezzo-soprano roles. (The Met should stage a production of *Hercules* for Marilyn Horne.) We meet her in the palace at Trachis, lamenting her long-absent lord—"indulging grief," as Lichas puts it. ("A musical drama" is Handel's designation of the work; it was performed in his day oratorio-fashion, but the score and the libretto—like those of his other dramatic oratorios—contain stage directions.) Rich, chromatic accompanied recitatives set the scene; all is sombre, magnificent. There is excess in the large, proud leaps of Dejanira's grieving line, excess in the hectic floridity and sharp dynamic contrasts with which she greets the news of Hercules' return. Hercules brings in his train the captive princess Iole; Dejanira's jealousy is aroused, and the evil emotion poisons her surcharged love. (There is open borrowing from *Othello* in Thomas Broughton's libretto.) With bitter scorn and malice, she rounds on her husband, in "Resign thy club." (Monica Sinclair's spitfire account of the air was once famous.) Her "Cease, ruler of the day, to rise" is a precursor of Lady Macbeth's "La luce langue." As the "last expedient of despairing love," she sends her husband a robe steeped in Nessus' blood; the dying centaur—pierced by Hercules' arrow—had told her it could revive the flame of passion. Instead, it burns Hercules' flesh from his bones. Near-mad with remorse and guilty grief,

Dejanira sings a scena some of which, Hugo Leichtentritt remarked, might have been written note for note by Verdi.

The other characters are firmly, if less vividly, limned. Hercules is bluff, a little boastful, powerfully moving in his tortured death scene. Hyllus, his son, is a chivalrous young prince, and the innocent Iole is a gentle, courteous princess; they suggest an earlier Idamantes and Ilia. Lichas, merely a herald with some recitative announcements in Handel's original plan, gained six airs when the popular actress Mrs. Cibber joined the cast, before the first performance. They are redundant to the drama—Handel dropped Lichas altogether in his revivals—but two of them are fine. Mr. Saltzman retained both, and also the slightly vapid "Constant lovers" (an air to the effect that an occasional tiff adds spice to love—unworthy comment on Dejanira's plight). With mid-act commentary, the chorus sharpens and drives home the dramatic points—its "Jealousy!" is a stunning intervention—and as a Trachinian crowd it closes the three acts with a riotous musette (celebrating the hero's return), a lilting gavotte (looking forward to the restoration of nuptial harmony), and a ceremonial minuet (greeting Hercules' elevation to Olympus). The librettist drew on both Ovid and Sophocles; Dean goes so far as to declare that "in all respects except the poetry—which is not required in a libretto, since the music supplies it—Broughton's version is immeasurably superior" to Sophocles' *Women of Trachis.*

In Berlin in 1936, *Hercules* had an open-air production with a chorus of a thousand. Back in 1895, in Mainz, there had been an attempt to return to the smaller forces of Handel's day: *Hercules* was given with a chorus of a hundred and sixty and an orchestra of eighty, and *The Musical Times* called it "this very modest demonstration." By Victorian—if not by Hanoverian or present-day—standards, it was modest. Mr. Saltzman had a chorus of twenty-six and a band of twenty-one. Handel's own complement varied: he probably had more singers, and his soloists joined in the choruses; he usually had a larger orchestra. But Mr. Saltzman's consort matched the size of the hall. Handel's oratorio soloists were stage-trained. Mr. Saltzman's were not theatrical enough—lines such as "I burn, tormenting fire consumes me" and "Chain me, ye furies, to your iron beds, And lash my guilty ghost with whips of scorpion" can hardly be too strikingly declaimed—but they had begun to shake off "oratorio" blandness. Sometimes one wanted still more attention to the text—to its punctuation, syntax, and sentiments. (For example, the Hyllus, Frank Hoffmeister, omitted the comma in "By honour, love and duty led," and the line was hard to follow.) By and large, the execution was more dramatic than that of *Theodora,* last year's Sine Nomine presentation. Marianna Busching, the Dejanira, made much of the heroine's mad scene. Julianne Baird was a sweet, pure Iole. Jan Opalach was a polished but slightly inhibited Hercules. Jeffrey Dooley sang Lichas' music with such keen, precise art that the inclusion of "Constant lovers" was welcome. The choral singing was alert, distinct in counterpoint, and deft in the cross-accentuations where Handel's verbal stresses break free of bar lines.

Offenbach's *La Périchole,* last week, was the first of the three opéras comiques that Carnegie Hall is putting on this season, with Frederica von Stade their heroine or (in Massenet's *Chérubin*) hero. It was a happy performance. I never saw the Met production, which in 1957 had Patrice Munsel, and in 1970 Teresa Stratas, in the title role; *La Périchole* has meant for me delectable recordings of its airs by Maggie Teyte and by Jennie Tourel. Miss von Stade was quite different from both, and no less bewitching. Her timbre was seductive, her timing exquisite. Delicately, with distinction, she used the music to flirt with every man in the hall, as Hortense Schneider, the first Périchole, must have done. Offenbach's opéra bouffe, first staged in 1868, dates from a time when he was moving from high-spirited comedy spiced with satire toward romance; Miss von Stade boldly stressed the languors and tenderness of the music without losing its sparkle. In recent years, she has done some disappointing, dullish things; her Périchole was as vivacious, bright, and subtle as the Cherubino, ten years ago, that first made me love her.

Neil Rosenshein was a likable, full-voiced Piquillo, but he should cultivate a lighter, more forward delivery, with crisper words, for his French repertory. Renato Capecchi played the Viceroy with wit, with relish that was —just—not too thickly spread. In the large, able supporting cast, John Fryatt's sharp-cut Don Pedro was outstanding. The opera was fully acted by the soloists, on the left half of the Carnegie platform. (The orchestra was stationed on the right.) The director, Bliss Hebert, was also the perpetrator of an ambitious, unstylish, wordy linking narration, in English, which was delivered with deadly cuteness by Madeline Kahn. (The plainer narrative of the RCA recording—in which, however, Régine Crespin makes heavy weather of the title role—is more acceptable.) The chorus—the Orpheon Chorale, in dapper voice—stood across the back. The anonymous orchestra, trimly conducted by Mario Bernardi, seemed rather large; although it didn't drown the singers, Offenbach seems to call for a leaner, less "symphonic" sound.

Ralph Shapey's Quartet for oboe, violin, viola, and cello was composed in 1952 but—"through a series of circumstances concerning the difficulty of the composition," Shapey says in a program note—remained unheard until last week, when James Ostryniec and members of the Alard String Quartet played it in Merkin Hall. It is a brief (about ten-minute), lively, attractive work in three movements. The first of them is beguiling—linear, airy in texture, made of linked, lapped strands of exuberant melody. The central movement, a scherzo in 5/16, treads a maze of light, dancing rhythms. The finale bears a more defiant aspect: with scratchy harmonies and uncompromising gestures it seems to challenge a listener to like it. The challenge, however, is easily met. Mr. Ostryniec and the Alard played the work as if delighting in its rhythmic intricacy and difficult, buoyant lines. The concert began with Otto Luening's *Legend,* for oboe and strings (1951), an agreeable, unmemorable piece—here a little romantic, there neoclassical—by this protean composer. Prokofiev's First String Quartet (1930) and Arthur Bliss's Oboe Quintet (1927) completed the bill.

The Alard is an expert group. It plays in tune, with full, pleasing tone. Its lines are well balanced, its ensemble is precise. But there was something missing. In the Prokofiev, I thought it was wit, quirkiness, liveliness of individual articulation. Prokofiev's quartet can be captivating; it is, in a keen, bright performance by the

Sequoia String Quartet on Nonesuch. The Bliss, a faded score, needs ardent championship today if it is to seem worth doing. Leon Goossens had the knack of piping its pastoral strophes and jigging finale in a way that held the attention; Mr. Ostryniec was a shade too suave, and all the players shared a reluctance to drop below a well-nourished mezzo forte. It was a slightly disappointing concert. In the familiar works, specific characterization was subordinated to general smoothness of execution, to long line even in places where short, punctuated lines are needed, and to homogenized excellence of tone quality. The Alard is not always like this: I recommend a Leonarda record that couples its thoughtful accounts of Karel Husa's adventurous First Quartet and Priaulx Rainier's Quartet, the strong, delicate early work (1939) that made her name. Rainier's *Quanta,* for oboe and string trio, might have been a stronger and apter choice than the Bliss quintet for this twentieth-century program.

SOMETHING BORROWED, SOMETHING NEW

November 28, 1983

MERKIN HALL'S concert series On Original Instruments opened last week with an evening of chamber music: Beethoven's Opus 5 cello sonatas, Haydn's cantata *Arianna a Naxos,* and songs by Johann Friedrich Reichardt and Schubert. The singer was Judith Nelson, the cellist Anner Bylsma, and the pianist Malcolm Bilson. Mr. Bylsma played a "classical" cello. Its bold, grave tones were stronger than those of the five-stringed baroque cello he had played two days earlier, at the Maryland Handel Festival, but were less assertive and less richly resonant than those of a full-throated, floor-anchored modern instrument, with its steel-wound strings. They perfectly matched the sweet, clear singing of Mr. Bilson's fortepiano, a reproduction of the Walter instrument that Mozart owned. Beethoven's sonatas, dating from 1796, are brave, surprising compositions that leap into the next century, and they sounded newly fresh when played—with ardent fancy—on instruments kin to those Jean-Pierre Duport and Beethoven must have used at the first performance, in Berlin, at Frederick William II's court.

Reichardt, formerly Frederick the Great's and then his nephew's Kapellmeister, had been dismissed from his post, for republican sympathies, and was managing salt mines in Halle at the time of Beethoven's Berlin visit. This prolific composer—Grove tells of about fifteen hundred songs and lists over thirty operas—has a place in music history secured by the friendships he pursued with the great musicians and writers of his day, his copious musical journalism, his wide-ranging enthusiasms, and his influence on Schubert. (Today, the music of his daughter Louise, who became a Hamburg choral director and the organizer of a Handel festival, is likelier to find ready revival; there are attractive songs by her recorded on the Leonarda label.) Goethe called Reichardt "the first to make my lyrical work known to the world through music," and Miss Nelson sang two of the Goethe settings. Reichardt's "Kennst du das Land" has been overshadowed by later, greater, more emotional versions. Although some have claimed that the simple strophic treatment is well matched to the artless Mignon, the description, in *Wilhelm Meister,* of Mignon's own performance makes it clear that she essayed a complicated and even rhetorical song. The merry prattle of "Der Edelknabe und die Müllerin" is musicked in Reichardt's happiest vein, and Miss Nelson delivered it with pretty wit. From Schubert she chose Ellen's songs from *The Lady of the Lake*—"Soldier, rest!," "Huntsman, rest!," and "Ave Maria"—doing them in the German translation that Schubert used. (Scott's verses need adjusting to fit the music, but it would make sense in America to sing them in English.) Picturesquely, Schubert made the piano part a soft, distant tracery of the rude sounds—armor's clang, war steeds' champing, trump and pibroch, bugles calling reveille—that Ellen assures soldier and huntsman they will hear no more. On the fortepiano—which also permits vigorous, vivid playing such as on a modern grand must be subdued lest the singer be drowned—the effect was exquisite. Miss Nelson and Mr. Bilson were in perfect balance. Her tone is pure and true, her line delicately spun: after the "Ave Maria" one could echo Scott's

> *What melting voice attends the strings?*
> *'Tis Ellen, or an angel, sings.*

But her feeling for words is still not bright enough. Haydn's Ariadne needs to cry recitative with pronunciation and pacing more dramatic than Miss Nelson allowed her. The arias were beautifully shaped, but after the cantata one could not quite echo a critic of Pacchiarotti's London performances of the piece, in 1791: "Every fibre was touched by the captivating energies of the passion."

Deborah (1733), the second of Handel's English oratorios, is rarely performed, although much of its music is known in other contexts: it was in large part assembled from earlier compositions—notably Coronation anthems, Chandos anthems, and the Brockes Passion. Winton Dean, in his book on the oratorios, passes a severe judgment:

> *Deborah* is a failure. The subject was an unhappy choice; it was poorly handled by the librettist; Handel was not yet at ease with the new form to which he had unwittingly given birth; and he put little effort into the music, which is largely a pasticcio.

In 1732, an unstaged production of Handel's sacred drama *Esther,* at the King's Theatre, had been unexpectedly successful. *Deborah* followed, and then *Athalia.* Samuel Humphreys provided new verses needed for the amplified *Esther,* and the librettos of *Deborah* and *Athalia.* The first and third oratorios are based on strong plays by Racine; *Deborah* is hardly a drama at all but, rather, a narrative of battle preparations, carnage, and triumph. Jael, the hymned heroine, "blessed above women," has been likened in character to Clytemnestra and Lady

Macbeth. Barak, says Dean, "is a muscular tough, Deborah a sententious headmistress with the gift of prognostication—a most repulsive mixture." The piece fails, he argues, not just because its plot and principals are unpleasing but because it lacks "a great central theme and the clash of human personality," which were "the prime sources of Handel's inspiration." He is right, of course, unless one can accept an Israelite victory over the Canaanites ("Hills of slain Load the wide extended plain") as a great theme in itself and can approve Jael's most unchristian behavior—what Milton called her "inhospitable guile." The fugitive Sisera came to her tent "flaming with thirst, and anguish in his look." She took him in and gave him refreshment. He fell asleep.

> *The workman's hammer and a nail I seiz'd,*
> *And, whilst his limbs in deep repose he eas'd,*
> *I thro' his bursting temples forc'd the wound,*
> *And riveted the tyrant to the ground.*

Ildebrando Pizzetti, in his noble second opera, *Dèbora e Jaéle* (it awaits an American première), adds psychological depth to the simple story: at Deborah's insistence, Jael deploys her beauty to ensnare the Canaanite general; but she and Sisera fall in love, and, like E. M. Forster, she discovers that love, pity, and compassion are forces stronger than patriotism, revenge, and religious duty. She does kill him, but only to save him from the Israelites' fury and lest he believe she may have betrayed him. To Deborah's question "Did you hear the voice of the Lord?" she retorts, "Not of your God, of another whom you know not." The plaudits of her people ring hollow in her ears. Humphreys, however, left the tale on the Old Testament level; and Handel's humane sympathies, which often transfigured the plain text of both oratorios and operas, worked but intermittently. His Sisera, proposing diplomatic negotiation as preferable to bloodshed, sings in reasonable, admirable tones; and Barak's gloat over Sisera's death, "Low at her feet he bow'd," is set as a dignified exequy—so much so that Hermann Abert was moved to remark, in 1926: "Before the body of the slain his resentment is silent, and he lowers his spear, so to say, before the dead man, and thinks of him with humane sympathy. Now this is not English, but German, behavior." Handel's concern with human behavior, with national crises and individuals' reactions to them, makes his oratorios ever topical. But German nationalist criticism of the cosmopolitan composer, an Englishman by choice, makes odd reading. Of Jael's air "O the pleasure my soul is possessing," Alfred Heuss wrote, in 1931:

> The murder is committed in a horrible manner; no German would have done it: Humphreys, the English librettist, gives it extravagant praise. If Englishmen did not then, and do not now, see the point of those harmonies (which is to show how utterly a German abhors such barbarities) it is because they have no physical or mental ears.

Dean, from whom the quotations are culled, remarks that Humphreys simply followed the Bible and that Handel simply had copied out, for Jael, an air from the early Italian oratorio *Il trionfo del tempo,* in which Pleasure sings to Beauty, "You swore never to leave me." It should be added that the harmonies—acerb sevenths in a two-part texture—are disconcerting even today: listeners look twice at their scores to ascertain that Handel really wrote the sounds they hear.

Deborah was done last week as the climax of the third Maryland Handel Festival, which was held on the College Park campus of the University of Maryland and in Library of Congress auditoriums. It was an exhilarating and successful performance, given in the spacious university chapel, a neo-Georgian temple undedicated to any particular god. The program book contained an enlarged, excellently legible reproduction of the 1733 libretto, with its spare but necessary stage directions. The band—the Smithsonian Chamber Players, twenty-seven strong—played from photocopies of parts prepared for Handel's friend Charles Jennens, and played on eighteenth-century instruments or copies thereof. The chorus carries the burden of the oratorio; the University of Maryland Chorus, directed by Paul Traver, was an expert body—fresh, strong and athletic in tone, crisp in articulation, quick in response to the emotions of the text. Mr. Traver, who conducted, had the gift both of "presenting" each number as something special and wonderful and of shaping long, balanced spans. This *Deborah* moved more surely, more variously than last year's *Esther,* without gaps in the narrative.

The solo parts were composed for Handel's operatic troupe. René Jacobs, as Barak, Senesino's role, was the outstanding Maryland soloist. Earlier, he had given a public master class in the delivery of baroque vocal music. The rest of the cast, one felt, might profitably have attended this demonstration of the way attention to words, to variety of recitative speeds, to accent, contrast, and phrase can convert bland "oratorio" singing into lively dramatic utterance. His own performance was bright and forward in tone, sharp-cut, arresting, surprising. Miss Nelson, the Jael, was aptly startling in the murder narrative quoted above (a shock seemed to run round the chapel) but elsewhere a shade bland, though always true and musical. Robert Petillo, in a cadet role, revealed an incisive, firmly focussed tenor and a feeling for words; he was equally impressive, at an earlier concert, as a tenor soloist in the ninth Chandos anthem. The title role—written for Anna Strada, Handel's prima donna of the thirties, his Adelaide, Angelica, Arianna, and Alcina; Berenice; Cleofide and Clio; Deborah; Esther and Elmira; Fulvia; Galatea—seemed miscast. Linda Mabbs's voice did not flow evenly or easily; the upper range was tense and unsuitably vibrant. Jan Opalach, the Abinoam, has a fine, fluent baritone of pleasing quality and would be an admirable Handelian if he brought phrases forward onto the lips and revelled in distinct vowel colors; his pronunciation tended to be of the kind parodied by Plunket Greene in *Interpretation in Song,* which turns the first line of *Paradise Lost* into "Arv mahn's farst desorbairdyurnce ahnd tha frurt." Beverly Benso was a trenchant Sisera but almost overdid the assumption of masculinity.

By Dean standards—those that place Handel's *Saul* beside the *Oresteia* and *King Lear,* and his *Hercules* above Sophocles' *Women of Trachis*—*Deborah* can hardly be defended. But no one has ever denied that it is a feast of stirring, magnificent music. The Maryland performance showed it to be that and more: an animated, grand-scale, coherent realization of the Song of Deborah (Judges 5), partly epic narrative, partly paean.

The ninth Chandos anthem and the third concerto of Opus 3, played at the first festival concert, provided foretastes of *Deborah* music in other contexts. The theme of the festival's scholarly symposia was Handel's habit of borrowing and "recycling" passages of both his own and other men's music. The matter has excited detective work, charges, and defenses from Handel's day to this. The borrowings vary from brief, striking ideas to entire movements. Examining the evidence can throw fascinating light on the way his musical mind worked: Donald Burrows's paper on the making of the Anthem on the Peace (1749)—tracing false starts, fresh starts, and jigsaw-puzzle connections between fragments of quite different works which lock to form a new, convincing whole—showed it. To the theft charge, Handel's advocates plead, first, that it was common and accepted practice (yet he seems to have pilfered far more frequently than most of his contemporaries) and, second, that—in a metaphor used by Johann Mattheson, who recognized a tune of his own in Handel's *Agrippina*—the composer repaid loans with interest, by making more of the ideas concerned than their inventors had done. (Anthony Hicks, in a paper provocatively entitled "Diamonds into Pebbles," suggested that of not all Handel's reworkings of his own music can this be said.) The case will not rest so long as every year brings further instances of Handel's borrowings to light. Even his most famous melody, "Ombra mai fu," the start of *Serse*, has been shown to grow from Bononcini's setting of the same libretto. The most disturbing Maryland paper was John Roberts's "Handel's Borrowings from Keiser." Handel's indebtedness to Reinhard Keiser, the director of the Hamburg opera during Handel's Hamburg years, has long been recognized: it was pointed out in his lifetime by the critic J. A. Scheibe; in 1902, Chrysander printed Keiser's *Octavia* as a supplementary volume to his complete Handel edition. But the tally of borrowings from Keiser which Mr. Roberts had amassed—and that from just the relatively few of Keiser's numerous operas which survive—goes well beyond anything known before. ("O ruddier than the cherry" turns up all but note for note in Keiser's *Janus*.) One rubs one's eyes—if only to blur a picture that forms of young Handel setting out from Hamburg with his head, perhaps his bags, stuffed with the hit tunes he has heard there; winning Italian triumphs by serving them up in cantata, oratorio, and opera; and discovering a "method" that continues to serve him well for the rest of his career.

It is not the whole picture. ("O ruddier than the cherry" is in Keiser only an ostinato bass; it took original genius to make it the melody and add the piping obbligato above it.) One need not start thinking of Handel as merely the Great Arranger. But with each large new revelation of his indebtedness the outlines of the old picture of him must shift slightly. I will hesitate before again calling him one of the great melodic inventors of all time. With eagerness, and some apprehension, one awaits the new catalogue of Handel borrowings on which Mr. Roberts is engaged.

MANNERS, VIRTUE, FREEDOM, POWER

December 12, 1983

MILTON BABBITT's piano music is some of the most vivid and attractive of our day: exhilarating and rewarding to hear, and, to judge by the committed, enthusiastic performances given by the latest generation of young virtuosos—pianists such as Alan Feinberg, Robert Taub, Aleck Karis—exhilarating and rewarding to play. Babbitt's *Canonical Form,* a thirteen-minute piano piece of uncommon brilliance, fascination, and charm, had its first performance last month at an Alice Tully Hall recital, played by Mr. Taub, for whom it was composed. It is a set of twice twelve variations—if "variations" is the right term for the musical paragraphs, defined by pauses and, often, cadences, into which it falls. The cogent discourse is set out in lines of elegant spareness and clarity. Each paragraph is shapely; successive paragraphs take up striking points previously made, a matter for new observations trenchant, thoughtful, or witty. The piano writing, never dense, is largely in two parts; even when a hand may fall upon two or three notes at once they often make the effect of a single complex sound within a linear two-part progression. The piece ranges the full keyboard. Some episodes colonize a particular region; others command airy, Berlioz-like spans from fundamentals to distant overtones. There are more consonances, more allusions to traditional triads, than usual. I don't pretend to understand in detail the structural basis of the work. (The composer's program note tells us that "there is a 'canonical series form' that is structurally centric in that the lines, individually and conjointly, instantiate it and refer to it.") But the ear made sense of it—delighted in the progress, the proportions, the control of tension and repose, the sureness of gestures, the brief, bright riffs. One listened as if to a new Goldberg Variations—to a composition in which contrapuntal science, imaginative fancy, and an intelligence alert to the timbres, the resonances, and the finger-determined figurations of the instrument conspire.

Under Mr. Taub's fingers, *Canonical Form* sounded wonderful. He played a new American Steinway (No. CD 237), made this year—a warm, clear, full-toned instrument, strong but not aggressive in forte, delicate but not glassy in pianissimo. His recital began with Beethoven's "Tempest" Sonata and continued with a Brahms group: two Intermezzi from Opus 118 and the C-sharp-minor Capriccio of Opus 76. After the Babbitt, there was Chopin's B-minor Sonata. All were given exceptionally fine, satisfying performances in which large structure and incidental detail, easefulness and energy, musical argument and tonal seductiveness were ideally balanced. Even in a city where each week seems to bring forward new pianistic talent, Mr. Taub is outstanding. He combined intellectual force with grace, untrammelled virtuosity with poetic instinct. As encores, he played two Liszt pieces: a magical *Frühlingsnacht* (the Schumann song transfigured) and a captivating *Campanella*. Mr. Taub's prowess can be admired on two records. CRI SD 461 contains Babbitt's Three Compositions (1947), Seymour Shifrin's *Responses,* and Bartók's and Leon Kirchner's piano sonatas; the recorded sound is a shade hard and bright, but the playing is superb. Harmonia Mundi HM 5133 contains Schumann's *Davidsbündler-Tänze, Frühlingsnacht,* and the Liszt *Rigoletto* paraphrase; it was recorded on the same piano that Mr. Taub used in the Tully recital and does justice to both the eloquence and the tonal beauty of his performances. [*See p. 523 for a later, all-Babbitt recital by Mr. Taub.*]

I was away when Babbitt's *Paraphrases,* for nine winds and piano, had its première, given by Parnassus in March 1980. Parnassus's latest record, CRI SD 499, provides a chance of catching up. The disc also has Donald Martino's *Strata,* for bass clarinet, and Anthony Korf's *A Farewell,* for twenty winds and percussion. But *Paraphrases* is harder going than *Canonical Form,* being in Babbitt's "bitty," or ejaculatory, manner, which makes both lines and pulse hard to determine. Parnassus, directed by Mr. Korf, is now in its tenth season and continues its adventurous policy of presenting works newly composed for it, works new to New York, and loving, carefully rehearsed, vividly executed performances of twentieth-century "classics." Let me pay belated tribute to its gleaming, impassioned, yet disciplined account, in Merkin Hall earlier this year, of Boulez's *Le Marteau sans maître.* The first Parnassus concert this season, again in Merkin, came to a climax with a finely poised, very well balanced performance of Schoenberg's Suite, Opus 29. Dance and dialectic went hand in hand, and the textural hurdles set up by the combination of three clarinets, string trio, and piano were deftly cleared. The concert opened with the American première of Tristan Keuris's Eight Miniatures (1980), for clarinet, mandolin, guitar, marimba, viola, and double-bass—a small, exquisite composition by this attractive Dutch composer. The principal new work was Joel Feigin's Six Poems of William Carlos Williams, for tenor (Gregory Mercer) and an ensemble of eleven players. The poems are a sequence built on observations of trees and flowers. Feigin has overset them, I think: Williams's terse, precise imagery is subjected to expressionist expansion in a way that seemed too violent, gaudy, and exuberant.

Susan Blaustein, whose Sextet (for flute, clarinet, violin, cello, piano and percussion), commissioned by Robert Black's New York New Music Ensemble, had its first performance at the Ensemble's concert in Carnegie Recital Hall last month, writes program notes on her compositions so copious, persuasive, and informative that they leave listeners with little more to do than assess the results against her clearly formulated intentions. She ponders the past and analyzes its productions. Her *Ricercate* for string quartet, introduced at a Group for Contemporary Music concert last year, was inspired by the procedures of Schoenberg's First Quartet; while writing the Sextet she was, she says, "alternately haunted and inspired by certain pieces from the Romantic chamber-music literature," and the work is the outcome of "grappling with nineteenth-century notions of identity, line, form, and return." Both pieces are products of an orderly, intelligent mind; they are soundly and sensitively made; they are substantial and impressive compositions. "Well made" is sometimes employed as an epithet of disdain—but better a well-made play, or sextet, or whatever, than an ill-made one! Of the new works I hear on the critic's round, perhaps only one in ten gets mentioned, sooner or later, in these pages, because for some reason or other it has remained with me. Blaustein's Sextet has. In the program note, she writes that she was "intrigued by the magical power of the long, arching melodic line in that music of the nineteenth century that tells a story with such compelling sweep that it need not end up where it began in order to satisfy our desire for closure." And there are long, compelling lines in the Sextet. But my enthusiasm for it, as must be clear, was tempered: by a feeling that we were being offered commentary, executed with masterly craftsmanship. I suspect that a listener who had not read the program note might share the feeling. The work seemed more intelligent than inspired. But it left me curious to hear it again. In any case, capable musical commentary has an honorable place—as literary criticism has beside literature. On technical grounds one could fault only the central movement, a would-be scherzo, for failing to establish its 3/8 pulse early enough; by the ear it was easily scanned as a slow movement with episodes of rapid figuration.

The concert began with Charles Wuorinen's scoring (1962), for four players, of six pieces from the Glogau Songbook (c. 1480)—a light, attractive, century-spanning suite. There followed Thomas Barker's *10/22 (R-681.7)*, for solo vibraphone—horrid instrument when out on its own—which was based on the composer's notion that data discovered in ballistics research "could be transferred into a musical environment." Then there was Peter Maxwell Davies's *Stedman Caters* (1958, revised in 1968), for flute, clarinet, violin, cello, harpsichord, and percussion, which was based on campanological change-ringing formulas. It is in effect a small concerto for solo percussion with chamber accompaniment. Daniel Druckman, the Ensemble's percussionist, is a showy performer, but not even his skill and flamboyance could save *Caters* from seeming one of Davies's less lovable works. Henry Brant's *Ice Age* (1954), for percussion, piano, and clarinet, was arresting. Here, and again in the Blaustein, the Ensemble's pianist, Mr. Feinberg, made every phrase he played sound important.

The Recital Hall has been redecorated in gray and cream, and a new, wider staircase leads up to it. The ventilation system must be tackled next; at this concert the place was an airless little oven.

Ernani, Verdi's fifth opera and first essay in high romantic drama, is still an exciting piece when it is performed with spirit, when vocal bravura is wedded to dramatic conviction. The Metropolitan's new production—the first of the two new productions that, along with a *Rinaldo* from Ottawa, mark its centenary season—was a tame and vapid affair. On the opening night, something seemed to be happening only while Sherrill Milnes, in the central role—Charles I of Spain, elected Roman Emperor in the course of Act III—was onstage. Mr. Milnes began in uncertain voice but then recovered, and there was some emotion and some majesty in his portrayal. The others—Leona Mitchell (Elvira), Luciano

Pavarotti (Ernani), and Ruggero Raimondi (Silva)—were dramatic ciphers. In the remarkable trio that constitutes the last act, they stood in a row, as if lined up before microphones in a recording studio. One forgives singers who can't act if by their singing they bring the drama to life. These singers didn't.

Verdi's letters written during the genesis of *Ernani* reveal how clearly, before a line of the libretto or a note of the score had been set down, the composer "saw" his musical numbers take shape on a stage, in front of an audience. Joseph Kerman, in his "Notes on an Early Verdi Opera" (*Soundings,* 1973), writes of the young Verdi's "extraordinary insight into dramatic essentials on the grandest level" and his "iron determination to project drama in music." The analyses of two passages—Charles's soliloquy before Charlemagne's tomb, and the final trio—show Verdi devising operatic analogues for big effects in Victor Hugo's drama, and the graphicness of the forms he found leads Kerman to observations like "In making stage designs for *Ernani,* one should elevate the tomb of Charlemagne or do something else to assure that Carlo's entrance into it is as impressive visually as it is musically." The Met production fails because Pier Luigi Samaritani, its director and designer, seems not to have "seen" the music at all—either its large structures or its action-linked details. (This Charles slunk unobtrusively through a little side door set into the base of an equestrian statue of Charlemagne, to lurk there as if in a cupboard.) The action meandered through towering, mannered, rather vulgar sets—they suggested shop-window displays inflated—that dwarfed the singers. James Levine charged through the score with coarse, insistent energy.

A verse of the baritone's "Vieni meco" was cut. The controversial bass cabaletta "Infin che un brando vindice" was included. The tenor-bass duet that should close Act II was replaced by the insert-aria "Odi il voto, o grande Iddio," which Verdi composed, at Rossini's request, for the tenor Nicola Ivanoff. It has a good andante and a trumpery cabaletta. Julian Budden, in *The Operas of Verdi,* remarked that by its inclusion "dramatic values are completely overthrown," since "there is no attempt to sustain the momentum of the scene." But in this particular production such things hardly mattered; the scene had no momentum. And it was interesting to hear the aria in context. Pavarotti has recorded it, along with Verdi's other insert-arias for tenor, on a CBS disc.

In 1983, the authorship of the cabaletta "Infin che un brando vindice" (which incorporates a passage of Nabucco's Act IV cabaletta) was still in doubt. The piece does not appear in the autograph or the early scores of Ernani. It was first published in an 1851 Boosey vocal score; Ricordi published it in 1855 as a cabaletta "eseguita da [not 'composta per'] Marini." The famous bass Ignazio Marini, Verdi's first Oberto, introduced the cabaletta at an 1844 Scala revival of Ernani (and a critic of the time blamed him for doing so). It had been plausibly suggested that the composer-compiler of the number was Donizetti, who supervised the Vienna première of Ernani, given a few months before the Scala revival, and also with Marini; Verdi had asked Donizetti to undertake "any necessary revisions" for the Vienna cast.

But in 1984 Roger Parker turned up the libretto of an 1842 Barcelona production of Oberto in which Marini sang an added cavatina with a cabaletta to very nearly the same words ("Ma fin che un brando vindice"), and a review that describes the piece as "espressamente scritto dal ... maestro Verdi." (See Verdi Newsletter No. 12, 1984.) The following year, Verdi's authorship of the cabaletta was confirmed when Sotheby's put on sale a letter from Verdi to Marini, dated November 15, 1841, containing the text of this insert aria. (See Sotheby's catalogue for the sale of May 9, 1985, item 218, with a facsimile of the first page.) Julian Budden calls the number "a thoroughly undistinguished piece."

MUSICA PER DRAMMA

December 19, 1983

AT a time when vicious spirals of mounting cost and narrowing repertory coil ever more tightly around our big opera companies, and when the Met can put on something as childish and clumsy as its new production of *Ernani,* the endeavors to create musical drama on a smaller scale—shows physically smaller but musically and dramatically adventurous, properly rehearsed, intelligent and imaginative in conception and in execution—become ever more important. Three such shows this season have been the Kentucky Opera's production of Benjamin Britten's *The Turn of the Screw* (1954), a full-length chamber opera for six singers and thirteen players, in the fourteen-hundred-seat Macauley Theatre, in Louisville; the Boston Shakespeare Company's production of Peter Maxwell Davies's *The Lighthouse* (1980), an eighty-five-minute chamber opera for three singers and twelve players, in the company's four-hundred-seat Boston theatre; and *La Tragédie de Carmen* (1981), Peter Brook's potted version of Bizet's *Carmen,* a full-scale opéra comique reduced to eighty minutes for four singers, three actors, and fourteen players, which is running in the eleven-hundred-seat Vivian Beaumont Theatre at Lincoln Center.

In the latest number of *Opera,* devoted to summer festivals, *The Turn of the Screw* is the work most often reviewed: four new productions last summer, in Munich (a staging shared with Cologne), Aldeburgh, Batignano, and Santa Fe. Britten composed it—like *The Rape of Lucretia, Albert Herring, Death in Venice*—in part through dissatisfaction with regular opera-house conditions, but it has become a repertory piece with companies the world over. It is time to drop the old remark that Puccini's *Turandot* (1926) is the most recent opera to have won wide public acceptance. *The Turn of the Screw,* like *Peter Grimes,* seems to draw full and enthusiastic houses wherever it is played. It did so in Louisville. Like all successful and satisfying operas, it works on many different levels. For listeners who know their Yeats, the emphatic refrain of the ghosts' colloquy, "The ceremony of innocence is drowned," must chime with what they read in the morning papers:

Things fall apart; the centre cannot hold;
Mere anarchy is loosed upon the world,
The blood-dimmed tide is loosed, and everywhere
The ceremony of innocence is drowned;
The best lack all conviction, while the worst
Are full of passionate intensity.

It is a heavy charge for Henry James's ghost story (and subtle psychological study), written for *Collier's,* to carry. But Britten's opera transcends its source, and its music explores responsibility, guilt, self-doubt, the conflict between erotic attraction and cool reason, and the struggle against evil in ways that listeners instinctively respond to. James wrote the Governess's story. During the opera, we feel with and through her but also share Peter Quint's confidence in his seductive powers, Miss Jessel's anguish and despair, the corrupted children's fascination with the evil, the housekeeper's reluctance to admit that anything is wrong. Turning from emotion to analysis, we discern a strong, lucid musical structure: a prologue and two spans of eight scenes linked by a theme and fifteen variations. The theme is a twelve-note row—a chain of ascending fourths (or descending fifths) starting on A and sounding the two whole-tone scales—contained in a tonal framework. The first seven scenes (and their preceding variations) spell an A, B, C, D, E, F, G of music's fundamentals. The last variation and scene of Act I and the first of Act II are in A-flat; the tonality of succeeding variations and scenes traces a chromatic descent and return to A. But there is nothing schematic in the working; the music flows as if impelled by the events of the narrative.

The Kentucky performance, conducted by Robert Bernhardt, directed by Nicholas Muni, and designed by Jeffrey Beecroft, was sensitive, accurate, and powerfully moving. The instrumentalists were eloquent. The musical and dramatic pacing was sure. Simply and effectively, the décor suggested country-house comfort and security that throw the horrors into relief. The cast—Glenn Siebert (a brilliantly precise Quint), Edith Davis (a brave, shining young Governess), Sam Jensen (an assured little Miles), Sharon Schuster-Craig (a vivid Miss Jessel), Carol Bober (the Housekeeper), and Ariel Rubstein (Flora)—was admirable. All the performances were detailed, and Mr. Muni's command of stage imagery was sure.

The Lighthouse, Davies's latest opera, first seen at the Edinburgh Festival, is an imaginative construction based on a real-life mystery. In 1900, a supply ship visiting the Flannan Isles lighthouse, in the Outer Hebrides, found the place deserted: everything in order, but no trace of the three keepers, and nothing to show what might have happened to them. The prologue is set in an Edinburgh courtroom—with flashbacks to the ship and to the steps leading to the lighthouse—where three officers (tenor, baritone, and bass), questioned by a solo horn at the back of the auditorium, give an uneasy, discordant account of their visit to the place. Then, in the lighthouse, its three keepers (the same singers) eat supper, play cards—a game of crib, but shot through with tarot resonances—and sing songs. Blazes, the baritone in a ballad accompanied by fiddle, banjo, and bones, tells of a brutal Glasgow childhood: he bashed an old woman to death, and his father was hanged for the murder. Sandy, the tenor, accompanied by cello and out-of-tune piano, sings a sentimental ditty about his golden-haired, blue-eyed youthful love. Arthur, the bass, accompanied by winds and tambourine, sings a blood-and-thunder revivalist hymn. The fog rolls in. The sea rises. Arthur starts the foghorn, singing to himself, aloft in the lightroom, "The cry of the Beast across the sleeping world. One night, that cry will be answered, from the deep." Confinement and tedium have driven the men mad. Their songs have released repressed guilts, which pour to the surface. Blazes sees the old woman and his dead parents return to claim him. Sandy sees the golden-haired boy, long since dead, whom he loved and betrayed. Arthur returns from the lightroom crying that the Beast is called out from his grave deep below the tide. Mutually heightened hysteria seizes on the three of them, and as the lights of the approaching ship grow brighter and brighter, dazzling both them and the audience, they bellow a hymn of crazy defiance at the approaching Beast. A shattering climax—and then things are suddenly quiet again. The three officers are there: "We had to defend ourselves, God help us. . . . They were crazed, run amok, unnatural, daemonic beasts. . . . Explanations will be difficult." There is a coda, in a lighthouse now unmanned, its functioning made automatic. Three keepers, "obscure and phantasmal," sit at supper, and the same conversation begins, but it is lost in an orchestra-crescendo reiteration of the motif "The lighthouse is now automatic"—the statement that closes the prologue. (On the day of the opera's first performance, the real Flannan Isles light stopped working, and a helicopter had to take a crew out to restart it.)

The Lighthouse is a startling and shocking piece of theatre. It is melodramatic—and far more than that. Beneath the exciting narrative and the brilliant sound effects is a taut and shapely score, richly and carefully wrought. Peter Sellars, the director of the Boston production, remarks in a program note that the "most exhilarating and terrifying moments are driven by a Stravinskian precision and resource within a tightly organized structure." David Hoose, its conductor, remarks in another note that "we might most fruitfully approach it first as a piece of music." It was hard to make such a first approach, even though Mr. Sellars gave most of the stage to the orchestra and set the raised structure representing the lighthouse behind it: the surface of the drama proved too vivid. I went again, prepared now for the stunning effects of both the composer and the director, and determined, so far as possible, just to listen. What happened was that I, so to speak, saw with my ears, heard with my eyes. Davies is a most theatrical composer, Mr. Sellars a most musical director, and this was a production—like Mr. Sellars's of Handel's *Orlando* two years ago—in which every move, whether made by the singers or by the actors, whether made on the stage or in musical space, played its part in creating a musical drama. (Only some stilted semaphoring in the mad scene seemed to me ill devised.) This is what opera should be, what both Verdi and Wagner strove for. It is rare to find it achieved on so consistently inspired a level. Director, conductor, lighting designer, a band of first-rate young players, and three subtle, skillful singers—Michael Brown

71

(Sandy), Sanford Sylvan (Blazes), and Kenneth Bell (Arthur)—formed an alert, living ensemble. Lucky Bostonians, I felt, able to go again and again! The piece had a run of eighteen performances.

Luigi Dallapiccola, in a diary note on a *Rigoletto* in which the designer and the director had been prominent but less than sensitive to the score, quoted Busoni's remark (as a dictum that too many directors forget) "Only with a pure, substantial score can an opera outlast its brief existence on the stage and attain the rank of an artistic monument." *The Turn of the Screw* is such a score. First hearings and perusals of *The Lighthouse* suggest that it is another.

The first sentence I wrote in *The New Yorker* was "The dramatic force of Bizet's *Carmen,* an opéra comique done very often, and seldom very well, is most potently released in a small theatre, by a cast of actors who share the language of the audience." (My own first *Carmen*—Tyrone Guthrie's Sadler's Wells production, Anna Pollak its heroine—left an indelible mark.) I was reviewing the Met's 1972 production, planned by Goeran Gentele and executed by Bodo Igesz, and distinguished by a threefold attempt to make the piece fresh again: the spoken dialogue of the original was restored; passages of Bizet's music which had been cut before the première were reinstated; and the "Mérimée perspective," which has Don José at the center of the drama, was observed. In Peter Brook's version, at least one of the cut passages—Carmen's mocking reprise of José's "Je souffre de partir"—is reinstated, and the "Mérimée perspective" is observed. The theatre, by American opera-house standards, is small, and the singers don't push. But they sing in French, which makes the show an exotic, irrational entertainment, and the spoken dialogue is—except for a few phrases—omitted. The original *Carmen* was a drama partly spoken and partly sung. This is "Gems from *Carmen*"—a string of musical highlights with the ensembles and choruses either omitted or played as soundtrack to action. The music of the Smoke Chorus becomes the accompaniment to Carmen's lewd pantomime with a cigar, and that of the Quarrel Chorus to a catfight between Carmen and Micaëla. So far as I know, a large-scale structural analysis of *Carmen,* of the kind that Mozart's, Wagner's, Verdi's, and Britten's operas receive, has not yet appeared. No doubt it will (and it should take into account the careful balancing of speech and song); the work is evidently an integrated masterpiece. The Brook reduction, however, with the music shuffled and reorchestrated for palm-court ensemble by Marius Constant, is no such thing. Forms, sonorities, contrasts, large relationships are scrapped. There is no reason a masterpiece should not be robbed, even with violence, in order to generate something wonderful and new. Brook's great *Orghast* successfully included a long stretch of Aeschylus' *The Persians*. But *La Tragédie de Carmen* resembles the mini-operas, scaled-down versions of the real thing, that cadet companies take round to schools—only it was more carefully, more thoughtfully, more expertly performed. If only all the care and all the publicity had been spent on a Brook production at the Beaumont of *The Lighthouse, The Turn of the Screw, Death in Venice* . . .

BEGINNINGS

DURING the three years between the production of *Die Entführung aus dem Serail,* in July 1782, and the beginning of work on *Le nozze di Figaro,* Mozart made several false starts on comic operas and composed several numbers for insertion in the comic operas of others. In February 1783, he told his father he was working on a German translation of Goldoni's *Servant of Two Masters.* (K. 433 and K. 435 may have been intended for it.) In May, he said he had perused more than a hundred Italian librettos and found none of them usable: so many changes would be needed that it would be simpler to begin with a new one—and would the Abbé Varesco (the librettist of *Idomeneo*) be prepared to undertake it? Varesco produced an idea for *L'oca del Cairo.* Mozart said he quite liked it, adding that "in opera the music is the most important thing" and so Varesco should be prepared "to alter and refashion as much and as often as I wish, and not follow his own ideas." By December, most of the first act was composed. Then came a stream of demands for plot changes; and in February 1784, Mozart laid *The Goose of Cairo* aside. He had also begun work on another opera, *Lo sposo deluso, ossia La rivalità di tre donne per un solo amante.* Just when and why he abandoned it is not known. There seems to have been a year or more of operatic inactivity (the start of another comic opera, *Il regno delle Amazoni,* once dated 1783, and then 1784, has been shifted to the end of 1785); 1784 and early 1785 were rich years for piano concertos. Then came the sudden miracle of *Figaro.*

The miracle seems all the greater and more sudden when we listen to *L'oca del Cairo, Lo sposo deluso,* and the insert numbers, for although they are near in time to *Figaro* they are nearer in manner and matter to the early *La finta giardiniera.* The music, however, is well worth hearing. Much of it has been recorded, but it deserves to be heard in context. That's difficult. Who will hand-on-heart urge a revival of, say, Anfossi's *Il curioso indiscreto* so that we can enjoy in context the three arias Mozart composed for its 1783 Vienna production—two of them for his first love and then sister-in-law, Aloysia Lange, and one for his first Belmonte, Valentin Adamberger? Well, I will. Such Anfossi as I know is not contemptible. It's tuneful. It's mildly adventurous. It's not nothing. There is a score of *Il curioso indiscreto,* Grove says, handily available in the Boston Public Library, and there are scores in Paris and in Naples. And I'll wager that a campus performance of the Anfossi-Mozart *Curioso*—put into English, and put on with spirit and in style by the musicology and conservatory branches of a university, working together—will please its public. No harm if the main revelation is that Mozart rises mountain-high above his prolific and more popular contemporaries; it helps us to hear why he does. So it proved when Siena's Accademia Chigiana put on, in 1975, a composite *La villanella rapita,* with contributions by seven composers, including Mozart's of a quartet and a trio that were small peaks among very agreeable and interestingly varied foothills.

When performed out of context, Mozart's dramatic music is diminished. A proof of that is the pasticcio *Don Pedros Heimkehr,* a modern attempt to string together, along a new libretto, numbers that Mozart composed for *L'oca del Cairo, Lo sposo deluso,* and the operas of others. Far more successful is the version of *Lo sposo deluso* devised and directed by Joseph LoSchiavo, which was put on this month by the Opera Shop of the Vineyard Theatre, on East Twenty-sixth Street. (The theatre is supported by New York State vineyards and serves their wines at its bar.) There survives a manuscript libretto of *The Bridegroom Deluded,* annotated by Mozart with the names of his intended cast. (New Grove, following Alfred Einstein, credits the text to Da Ponte, but neither Mozart's letters nor the verses themselves seem to me to warrant the ascription.) Mr. LoSchiavo kept, in simplified form, the original plot but brought forward the happy ending (young lovers united; the elderly would-be bridegroom, an earlier Don Pasquale, reconciled and offering his blessing) to the end of Act I. Mozart never got round to Act II. He composed an overture that leads into the opening quartet; a soprano and a tenor aria, both set down only in skeleton score (vocal line, bass, and a few instrumental indications); and a fully scored trio. There is music here meant for the first singers of Figaro (as the deluded *sposo*), Susanna (as Eugenia, the principal *donna*), and Constanze (as Bettina). The best numbers are the entrance aria, in high heroic style, for the haughty Eugenia, outraged by the inadequacy of her welcome, and the trio—described by Einstein as "at once passionate and comic, brief and dramatic"—which has links with both *Idomeneo* and *Figaro.* The third rival of the subtitle, Metilde, "a virtuosa of song and dance," would have been played by the first Blonde, but Mozart wrote no music for her, alas, and so Mr. LoSchiavo omitted her. He added an aria for Bettina, "Chi sa, chi sa," written for the first Dorabella to sing in a Martín opera; and a second aria for Eugenia, "Ah, non lasciarmi, no," which, although it is rather a grand affair, to lines from Metastasio's *Didone abbandonata,* composed as a concert piece for the first Ilia, did not sound inappropriate in a scene where Eugenia pretends to be a stern, majestic wraith haled from Hades. The wonderful comic aria "Un bacio di mano," composed for insertion in Anfossi's *Le gelosie fortunate,* and so "symphonic" that some of it then went into the "Jupiter" Symphony, was refashioned to provide a finale. *Lo sposo deluso*—all but "Ah, non lasciarmi"—was sung in English, with spoken dialogue in place of the (uncomposed) recitative. The accompaniment was reduced—or, in the "skeleton" passages, amplified—for a trio of piano, violin, and cello. The opera was preceded by a little recital of chamber music by Mozart, his father, his son, and his London friend John Christian Bach—none too stylishly played.

The Mozart bill was done in alternation with Donizetti's *Il giovedi grasso, o Il nuovo Pourceaugnac,* a merry one-act, eight-character farsa, based on a comédie-vaudeville by Scribe. Ernest, "a bright young man who pretends to be stupid," has been promised the hand of Nina, the pretty daughter of a crusty colonel, but she's in love with Theodore, her father's adjutant, "an extremely shy, irresolute young officer." Their friend Captain Sigismondo thinks of a plan to prevent the match. "Have you seen Molière's comedy *M. de Pourceaugnac?*" "Of course." "Well, today let's reenact it, and get this country bumpkin Ernest so confused that he'll go away." Events don't follow the Molière scenario. Ernest, well aware of what's happening, turns the tables on and discomfits the plotters but, being a sterling fellow, first makes sure that Nina and Theodore are plighted. Ernest was composed for the great Rubini, Sigismondo for the great Lablache. The score consists of a quintet introduzione, three arias, a duet that becomes a trio, another duet, and the finale. It is a delightful, well-composed piece, if not quite on the level of *Betly,* the Vineyard's previous Donizetti production. The musical numbers were—for no good reason—sung in Italian or, occasionally, Neapolitan: although the piece is set on the outskirts of Paris, Sigismondo and his servant Cola come from Naples, and they address one another in almost impenetrable dialect. The dialogue was replaced by an English narrative written by Mr. LoSchiavo (who again directed) and pleasantly delivered, in character, by the Cola, Louis Dall'Ava. The opera, accompanied by a trio of piano, flute, and bassoon, was preceded by a recital of Donizetti chamber music—salon stuff, flimsier than the string quartets of his Bergamo years.

Both *The Bridegroom Deluded* and *Shrove Thursday* were modestly but attractively performed by artists who showed some wit and some character. The best of them were Birgit Djupedal Fioravante, the Eugenia, and David Kellett, the Ernest. But nearly all of them sang too loud at times. In the tiny theatre, made for light, easy, effortless singing—crisply delivered parlando patter, floating headnotes of melting sweetness, a natural flow of limpid, unforced tone, gracefully spun decorations—there was no need for them to push and strain, no need for the tensions that led at climaxes to bulging veins and jaws tensed until they juddered, to *violence* where *douceur* was called for. (In Rubini's day, tenors did not take full voice above high A. Domenico Donzelli, the first Pollio in *Norma,* went into falsetto above G—a falsetto, he told Bellini, "employed with art and with power.") Perhaps the troupe should engage Joan Morris as vocal coach. Miriam Charney, who had made the instrumental reductions, conducted neatly. Mr. LoSchiavo and Sally Locke, the set designer, laid out the action deftly in the angle of the L-shaped theatre—an agreeable place, conducive to enjoyment. One soon forgot the occasional clonk of pipes and whirr of heating fans. The operas came across.

The Washington Opera has grown: from a company that three years ago played four operas four times each to one that is giving an eleven-week season with six performances a week. There are seven productions, three of them in the Opera House at Kennedy Center, which is large but not enormous, and four in the Terrace Theatre, which holds 475 people. One of the four was Handel's *Semele,* first staged there in 1980 and now revived in essentially the same décor, for ten performances. *Semele* is a radiant, tender masterpiece in which pangs, passion, wit, and sensual delight are mingled. At the hands of professional companies, it sometimes fares ill: the English National Opera larded it with excrescent jokiness; Covent Garden swamped it in lavish décor. The Washington staging, by Roman Terleckyj, was sometimes feeble—there were clumsy attempts to give the singers "something to do"—but was not offensive. Zack Brown's sets and most of his costumes were attractive. The women of the cast sang and acted well. The tenor sang well. And the musical direction was in the sure Handelian hands of Nicholas McGegan, whose rhythms were buoyant but never pushed, and who had done much to get the modern instrumentalists to play with eighteenth-century grace and lightness. (There were several baroque bows in the pit.) Musically, the show was not on the level of the *Orlando* Mr. McGegan directed at Washington University, in St. Louis, earlier this year. It hardly could be. There expert baroque players were led from the harpsichord and were ranged close to the singers they accompanied. In Washington, the players were down in a deep, deep pit—the Terrace Theatre seems not to have been designed for pre-Wagnerian opera—whence they could not see the stage. Continuo cello and harpsichord, it is true, were perched on high pedestals; but the cellist and the harpsichordist were immodest players, and instead of accompanying Semele's "Oh sleep" and "My racking thoughts" they turned them, and much of the recitative, into cello-and-harpsichord duos, with a vibrant bass line, tunes and twiddles above, and, as it were, an optional added part for the singer. It was as odd to see the continuo-accompanied airs conducted as it would be to see a conductor at a lieder recital, keeping the singer and her accompanist in time.

I must not exaggerate. This *Semele* was for the most part well played—and far more stylishly played than most big-company Handel is. In the title role, Elizabeth Knighton was excellently clear, fluent, and true. Her notes and her passages were cleanly defined. "Oh sleep" was delicately and exquisitely sensuous. She understood the character, and she knew how to sing recitative— defined by Congreve, in the Argument Introductory to *Semele,* as "that Stile in Musick . . . not confin'd to the strict Observation of *Time* and *Measure*" but "only a more tuneable speaking." The two basses, John Fiorito and Eric Halfvarson, maintained a Victorian recitative style—slow, measured, with ral-len-tan-do closes. Marta Senn, in the twin roles of Ino and Juno, looked lustrous, sounded lustrous, declaimed (in a Spanish-accented English as piquant as Conchita Supervia's) with energy, and sang lightly and pleasingly except when, in cadenzas, she ran up to some unseemly, blowsy top notes. Sheryl Woods, the Iris, was charming. Rockwell Blake, the Jupiter, was poised, polished, virtuoso in divisions—an artist who held listeners intent on his phrasing and brought the house down with his "Where'er you walk." Melvin Earl-Brown, the Athamas, who was allowed only the first of his three arias, sang it deftly. The score was skillfully, not savagely, shortened, but more was omitted than need have been. The intermissions were too long—a small theatre empties and refills more swiftly than a large. If they had been trimmed, more music could have been included without making a later curtain. A four-dollar, sixteen-page libretto was on sale, abridged to include only what was performed. It omitted Congreve's preface and any reference to the verses by Pope and by Congreve added for Handel's setting, and was typographically crude: every line pushed hard left, without distinction between recitative and air or chorus. In the performance, the heroine's name was consistently mispronounced, to rhyme with Emma Mae, and her sister Ino was referred to as if she were the once-famous fruit salt.

As Christmas approaches, a flood of the Eastertide oratorio *Messiah* rises in New York. One may almost resent it—insofar as it keeps attention off the other great Handel oratorios—but can hardly resist it: *Messiah* is so consistently moving and beautiful. From the dozens of New York *Messiah*s I chose a Musica Sacra performance given, in Avery Fisher Hall, by a crack professional choir and orchestra (twenty-nine voices, twenty-six players), with eminent soloists versed, as Handel's were, in opera. It was conducted by Richard Westenburg. The choral singing was nonpareil—light, lithe, fresh in timbre, firm in definition. Three of the soloists—the soprano Arleen Augér, the alto Paul Esswood, and the bass Julien Robbins—were ideal, with effortless, fluent, steady voices, forward words, and supple, sensitive phrasing. The tenor, David Gordon, was a little behind them; his focus was less precise. Mr. Westenburg's reading brought its surprises, some of them questionable (a slowed-down central section of "Rejoice greatly"), others vivid (bursts of mocking musical laughter along the divisions of "He trusted in God," primed by the words, "laugh him to scorn"). The soloists' decorations were apt, interesting, and not excessive. (Sometimes the fiddles echoed them with an aplomb to rouse a suspicion that the "spontaneous" variants had been pencilled into their parts.) Nothing was routined or heavy, and the conductor's claim, in a program note, that transparency need mean no loss of power, and stylistic correctness no loss in depth of expression, was proved. In America, the Georgian and Victorian custom of standing to hear the "Hallelujah" chorus is still observed; but the soloists ought to join in, not stand there like mute footmen.

SONGS WITH A MIND

January 2, 1984

ELLIOTT CARTER's seventy-fifth birthday has been widely celebrated, on both sides of the Atlantic. On the day itself, December 11, his three latest compositions were played at a Speculum Musicae concert at the 92nd Street Y: the song cycle *In Sleep, in Thunder* (1981), receiving its first performance in this country; the Triple Duo (1983); and *Changes* (1983), a guitar solo, which had its first performance. They were preceded by the First String Quartet (1951)—the work, written without regard for the difficulties performers and listeners might encounter, that put the seal on his reputation.

In Sleep, in Thunder, commissioned by the London Sinfonietta and first played in London in October 1982, is a setting for tenor and fourteen players of six poems by Robert Lowell. Carter's score is headed "In memory of the poet and friend." In early years, Carter set Emily Dickinson, Hart Crane, and Mark van

Doren. There followed a long period of purely instrumental music, and then he returned to song with the Elizabeth Bishop cycle *A Mirror on Which to Dwell* (1975), for soprano and nine players, and the cantata *Syringa* (1978), a setting of a John Ashbery poem troped with a Greek anthology, for mezzo-soprano, bass, and eleven players. Both works last about twenty minutes, and so does the new cycle. The three form a kind of triptych inspired by contemporary American poets. In *Mirror,* poems of observation and description alternate with poems founded on the affections. *Syringa* is classical: the Greek text assembled by the composer—lines from Homer, Aeschylus, Euripides, Plato, Sappho, and lines that have been attributed to Orpheus himself—underpins Ashbery's temporal reflections. For the London commission, Carter first considered setting a group of poems from *The Dolphin,* written after Lowell's move to England. Then he thought of grouping some late poems in the context of Lowell's "In the Ward" (from the last collection, *Day by Day*), a memorial for the composer Israel Citkowitz, the second husband of Lowell's third wife. It contains the lines:

> . . . *the precision*
> *and daimonic lawlessness*
> *of Arnold Schönberg born*
> *when music was still imperfect science—*
> *Music,*
> *its ever retreating borderlines of being,*
> *as treacherous, perhaps, to systems,*
> *to fecundity,*
> *as to silence.*

Then, after sketching a dozen or so songs, Carter decided on a group of six of the fourteen-line poems—unrhymed sonnets—that make up the three collections Lowell published in 1973: *History, For Lizzie and Harriet,* and *The Dolphin.* (The first two volumes were quarried from the earlier *Notebook;* Carter uses the revised versions.) In a program note, the composer says that "what attracted me about these texts were their rapid, controlled changes from passion to tenderness, to humor, and to a sense of loss." He starts with the poem "Dolphin," which stands like a dedication at the close of Lowell's sequence (and again at the close of his *Selected Poems*); it begins beautifully and then moves to an octave that Adrienne Rich once described as—it is hard to disagree with her—empty eloquence, a poor excuse for a cruel book. He ends with "In Genesis," the fifth poem of *History.* In a *Tempo* essay on the new cycle, David Schiff, the author of *The Music of Elliott Carter,* says, "Clearly Carter wanted the poems themselves to suggest a form; and the pattern that eventually emerged was a portrait of the poet. . . . Carter removed the poems from their narrative contexts to heighten their reflections of Lowell's character and his obsessions; as he told me: 'There are three poems about women and three about God.'" The Lowell portrait of *In Sleep, in Thunder* is probably best viewed with some knowledge of those narrative contexts and of Lowell's life and his work. The poems can stand on their own but are also a part of what Lowell called his "verse autobiography" (which "sometimes fictionalizes plot and particular") and make fuller sense if one knows which "you" he is addressing in any of them; knows that in "Careless Night" his thought swings from the Christ Child to his own newborn son, and that "Dies Irae" arises from one of his spells of madness.

Ian Hamilton's biography of Lowell records several visits to the opera. In Brussels in 1952, Lowell saw five Mozart works in six days, and then, in London, *Der Rosenkavalier, Wozzeck,* and *Fidelio.* (I remember those performances; Erich Kleiber conducted the first two, and Clemens Krauss conducted *Fidelio.*) He declared himself "nuts about opera," read Tovey's analytical essays, and tried "to imagine, though tone deaf, modulating from the tonic to the dominant." In 1960, he was awarded a Ford Foundation grant to attach himself to the Met and the City Opera as a potential librettist. Melville's *Benito Cereno,* Richard Hughes's *A High Wind in Jamaica,* and Büchner's *Dantons Tod* were subjects he considered. He said he was feeling "wonderfully athletic, hackish, and ready for opera," and speculating "whether *Phèdre* or something like it could be given in a singing version." In September, he moved from Boston to New York and met Rudolf Bing, who recommended him to attend a Columbia beginners' course in opera. In November, the Washington *Star* reported that he had attended four Puccini operas in a week (presumably *Manon Lescaut, Bohème,* and *Butterfly* at the Met, and another *Bohème* or *Butterfly* at the City Opera). No Lowell opera resulted, although *Benito Cereno* was worked as a play. At some point, Lowell suggested to Carter that he should compose music for his *Phèdre* translation; Carter had already considered setting some Lowell poetry.

Music is quite often referred to in Lowell's pages: Beethoven, Mozart, Schubert songs, the "Archduke" Trio, Elisabeth Schwarzkopf appear. Yet before *In Sleep, in Thunder* there was doubt about how well his lines might lend themselves to music. I'd heard no previous settings (except Britten's *Phaedra* cantata, whose heroic couplets are a special case). In a *Paris Review* interview, Lowell said of Theodore Roethke—a poet who has been much set, notably by Ned Rorem and William Bolcom—"He wants a very musical poem and always would quarrel with my ear as I'd quarrel with his eye.... He rejoices in the rhetoric and the metrics." But there is a record of Lowell reading works of his at the 92nd Street Y in 1976 (Caedmon TC 1569) which is filled with "music"—with timbres (vowel colors more distinctly sounded than by many singers), carefully controlled pitches (the range employed generally narrow, the departures from it striking), and, above all, a wonderful play of rhythm, accent, and pace. This is the "voice" that sounds in the Carter cycle, although it wasn't heard at the British première. (I was not there, but, like most important European premières, it was broadcast, and soon circulated on tape.) The soloist was Martyn Hill, a sensitive, cultivated lyric tenor who has recorded much early music and attractive recitals of Reynaldo Hahn and Massenet songs. The New York soloist, Jon Garrison, was more robust, more forthright, and altogether admirable. And he had the advantage of speaking American, as Lowell did and Carter does. To British ears, Lowell's own speaking voice carries inflections and colors closer to forceful North Country speech than to standard southern British. One would not ask an English singer of the cycle to adopt a fake American accent, but if a Lancashire tenor were to essay it he might do well to use North

Country pronunciation. (I longed for those broad, singable vowels in my own Wagner translations: when "one" must be prolonged, better "wahn" than "wunn.")

Carter is a composer who as a point of honor does not repeat himself. The panels of the triptych are sharply distinguished. It was Lowell who directed him to Elizabeth Bishop when, intending to write a cycle for soprano, he sought poems by a woman, not a man, to inspire him, so that the singing would be emotionally direct. The vocal line of *Mirror* is but one strand in a chamber composition, prominent only because it articulates words. Each song has the Vermeer-like precision and balance of fine details found in its poem—a product of the "unerring Muse who makes the casual perfect" (Lowell's phrase for Bishop in a sonnet of *History*). *Syringa* is different. The bass, with guitar accompaniment replacing Orpheus' lyre as he enters the modern world, sings lyrically, in classical Greek; the mezzo patters the Ashbery poem. Two notions of time are superimposed, as so often in Carter's compositions—both measurably and on imaginative levels. The texture of *In Sleep, in Thunder* is different again. The singer is emphatically to the fore. The charge of the poems is carried in his line. (In practice, the instruments may overwhelm him at times, but that is an accident of a particular performance; the work is not easy to balance.) The vocal writing is more evidently vocal. The songs would make sense in a voice-and-piano reduction. They would be eloquent—as *Mirror* and *Syringa* would not—even if sung unaccompanied. This is not to say that the instrumental writing is any less intricate, fascinating, or picturesque but only to suggest Carter's differing approach to each poet. (Schiff recalls a remark of his, made "with an eager tone of creative delight," during the composition of *Syringa:* "I'm setting John Ashbery's poem because it will force me to do things I've never done before.") The three works have in common a quick, vivid response to the pictorial imagery of the poems. In the setting of Lowell's "Across the Yard: La Ignota," the trumpet carols the exuberant song the poet tells of, and the line "Brunhilde who could not rule her voice for God" is introduced with a subliminal touch of "Hojotoho!" In "Dies Irae," the trombone—Mozart's *tuba mirum spargens sonum*—is prominent. In the first song, "Dolphin," only strings are used; Schiff's observation that as Lowell invoked his muse Carter's thoughts turned to the string quartet is surely right. The bright details—a soaring, lyrical flute solo and a still, wide-flung string chord setting the scene for "Careless Night"; densely black, stark chords opening "In Genesis"—are picturesque but not merely incidental. They rise to the surface of structures taut yet flexible, and are part of them. This is music that etches itself on the mind and the emotions.

Speculum—versed in Carter's music, first interpreters (though the personnel has changed much over the years) of *Mirror* and *Syringa*—gave what seemed to me a marvellous performance. Robert Black conducted.

The Triple Duo, composed for the Fires of London and first played by them, at Symphony Space, last April, is a stretch of instrumental discourse marked by uncommon wit, attractiveness, and brilliance. The Fires treated it as chamber music; in the Speculum performance the six players had a conductor (Donald Palma). Their version was bolder and brighter than the Fires' but a shade less smiling. There was less sense of six individuals in conversation, but the definition of each phrase was sharper. The Fires' handling of the piece—as I noted after hearing two London performances of it this summer—has become more buoyant and confident than it was at the première. Speculum's handling will no doubt in time become more relaxed and joyous, without losing its virtuoso glitter.

Many modern composers have written substantial works for the guitar, and usually for a particular guitarist. Britten, Henze, Tippett, Peter Maxwell Davies, and Roberto Gerhard have written for Julian Bream. In this country, more than a hundred pieces have been dedicated to David Starobin. Carter's *Changes* is the latest of them. (Mr. Starobin played the important guitar part in the CRI recording of *Syringa,* and asked for more.) In a strange way, composers seem to become quintessentially themselves when writing for this instrument, unrivalled for intimacy and delicacy except by the clavichord yet able to summon tempests and pour out throbbing passions. The composer's own description of *Changes* can hardly be bettered: "music of mercurial contrasts of character and mood, unified by its harmonic and rhythmic structure." The piece lasts about eight minutes, and, in Mr. Starobin's performance, it proved captivating.

CHARACTERS

January 9, 1984

IAN HOBSON, the 1981 winner of the Leeds triennial international piano competition, gave a Sunday-afternoon recital in Tully Hall last month. He has recorded (for EMI) Mozart concertos, Chopin's studies, and Rachmaninoff transcriptions. This was his Manhattan début. He looks like a tall, modest schoolboy. By the fourth bar of Beethoven's Opus 10, No. 3, which opened the recital, he had caught mind and ear—by his bold placing of the sudden sforzando after an almost casually fluent start, and by his timing of the pause. The whole performance showed an attractive combination of ease and energy: the fierce dynamic contrasts were carefully observed, but with an absence of fuss; there was no self-conscious point-making. It was a fresh, free, thoughtful, athletic interpretation. Then came Schumann's F-minor Sonata, the "Concerto Without Orchestra," in the original version, which has two scherzos, two more variations in the slow movement than one usually hears, and other differences. When Horowitz took up the sonata (in its one-scherzo version), eight years ago, he described it as being "full of bold, wild ideas" and as having "astonishing symphonic unity." Mr. Hobson's performance was less choppy than Horowitz's (which was recorded), less sudden, more flowing. He played with evident enjoyment, with a command of long form and inner relationships, and with a pleasing romantic fancy.

The Leeds jury has regularly preferred grace to flashiness, poetry to pianistic fireworks. Radu Lupu was the 1969, Murray Perahia the 1972 winner. Sometimes

81

it has been charged with playing safe—with, as Dominic Gill put it in an account of the 1978 competition, when Michel Dalberto came first, rewarding "the evidently attractive and competent" at the expense of "the more subtle and controversial virtues ... real, dynamic and dangerous (but by its very nature fallible and vulnerable) talent." That year, two of the pianists whose individuality most excited Mr. Gill—Kristin Merscher and Gary Steigerwalt—did not reach the finals. Mr. Hobson did, and was placed fourth. As the Tully Hall recital progressed—the second book of Debussy studies, Bartók's Three Studies, and a group of Rachmaninoff preludes made up the second half—the impression formed of an admirable, exceptionally able pianist, one in whose playing love of the instrument, understanding of the music, and an ample technique unite. He was satisfying, but he was not stirring—except in the Debussy studies, where grace, beauty of timbre, and digital skills were most happily balanced. Mr. Hobson used a Hamburg Steinway, No. 425—an agreeable, protean instrument without much character of its own.

George Perle's Serenade III, for piano solo and chamber orchestra (ten players), had its first performance last month at one of Merkin Hall's Music Today concerts. (Perle's first Serenade, for viola solo and an ensemble of ten, appeared in 1962; the second, for an ensemble of eleven, in 1968.) The new piece has the lucidity and the quick, darting intelligence that mark all Perle's compositions and the lively charm that marks the best of them. There are five movements. The first and last are allegros, propelled by the same little germinal motif. The second and fourth are scherzos: a burlesco in which the pianist raps out, rather xylophonelike, a dry, bright, rhythmically teasing line, his hands an octave or two octaves apart; and a perpetuum mobile in which, with an unbroken flow of sixteenth notes, *ppp,* he traverses the upper half of the keyboard now at a straight-line tripple, now with limber, bounding figures. There is a slow movement at the heart of the work, an elegy "in memory of George Balanchine." It is a prelude, chorale, and variations, and is quietly, uneffusively moving. This movement contains lyrical piano writing of the kind, found also in Perle's Six Etudes and his Ballade, that has led to his being called a Chopin of the modern piano. Richard Goode was a soloist both poetic and witty. The Music Today ensemble, conducted by Gerard Schwarz, played deftly but did not convey that sense of mastery, of knowing intimately the work in hand, which marks Speculum and Parnassus performances.

The concert opened with Carlos Chávez's *Energia* (1925), a bold, vigorous composition with Varèse and Stravinsky connections. Luciano Berio's *Chemins II* had an expert viola soloist in Sol Greitzer, but the dream textures of the lovely, mysterious composition needed more careful balancing. After the Perle, there was another première, Neil Rolnick's *Real Time,* a concerto for Synclavier II Digital Synthesizer and an ensemble of thirteen. The synthetic sounds produced by the solo instrument, played by the composer, were revolting.

The Group for Contemporary Music's December concert, at the Manhattan School of Music, brought the première of Frederick Fox's *Nexus (Sonaspheres 2)*—old-fashioned, unattractive title for a firmly made, attractive composition whose ideas held one's attention. It is a stretch of colorful, often chunky music, with sharp profiles for flute, viola, cello, and piano. Fox works in Bloomington, Indiana; there were also pieces from San Diego and Champaign-Urbana, in New York premières. The former, Bernard Rands's *Obbligato* (1980), was an Arts Council of Great Britain commission for the Los Angeles trombonist Miles Anderson and the Sequoia Quartet. Rands's trombone solo *Memo 2*, an exuberant virtuoso monody, has been placed in a new context, provided by the string quartet, which glosses, colors, tropes, and develops the earlier ideas, transporting them into a new sound-realm that at the close confederates with the trombone's. (By a similar process, Berio converted his viola solo *Sequenza VI* into *Chemins II*.) A record is being made that will include both the solo and the quintet compositions. I look forward to hearing it. Mr. Anderson, a dazzling, mercurial player, was joined here by the Columbia String Quartet. John Melby's Concerto for Viola and Computer-Synthesized Tape (1982) was hard to listen to attentively, even though it seemed to have things to say. The tape was made on the IBM 4341 computer at the University of Illinois; the soloist, Benjamin Hudson, played a Barcus-Berry Violectra—a five-stringed fiddle, spanning viola and violin registers, with a microphone in its bridge and a timbre that emerged, lacerating in forte, from a small loudspeaker. This was music blasted out for the generation that has grown up deafened. (The car of the train I took last month to Washington was loud with various musics thudding from earphones pressed to young passengers' ears; I tried in vain to read a Handel score.) From the Violectra in full cry one could only flinch, consciously avoiding the noise, since focussing on it caused pain—as one did during Philip Glass's *The Photographer* at the Brooklyn Academy, as one does when an express passes through a local station. I hope Mr. Hudson wasn't harmed. He is a trenchant performer, and the violinist we probably hear most often in New York—first fiddle of Speculum Musicae, the Group, the Brooklyn Philharmonic, the Columbia Quartet, etc.

The program-note writer, having observed differences geographical and stylistic between the six composers on the wide-ranging bill, then turned to similarities: "All are male; all have received advanced academic training, and all are connected in some way with institutions of higher learning." Biographical notes further revealed that Roger Sessions, Luigi Dallapiccola, and Milton Babbitt each taught two of them. East Coast institutions (Columbia, Harvard, and Queens College) were represented by Arthur Kreiger's *Passacaglia on Spring and All* (1982), for chorus and electronic tape, which seemed to me an uninspired piece; by Donald Martino's *Quodlibets II* (1980), for solo flute, which is bracing and inventive, and was brilliantly played by Harvey Sollberger; and by Hugo Weisgall's *Translations* (1973), a song cycle that was commissioned by Shirley Verrett, was first sung by Elsa Charlston, was recorded by Judith Raskin (on CRI), and was sung on this occasion by Susan Belling. It is a modern *Frauenliebe und -leben* with some good poems in it—the best of them by, or translated from the Yiddish by, Adrienne Rich—and some well-written music. Weisgall, in a note on the cycle, points to three kinds of translation here: of texts; of women's feelings by a male composer; and of poetic form into musical structure. The recorded performance is dull: each word is clearly pronounced, but the poetry disappears and, with it, the expressiveness of Weisgall's music. Miss Belling's performance was electric—lieder singing on a high level, in which the lines flowed, the words were vivid, the eyes sparkled, and in each song a character stood before us. Her tones were flip, simple, sexy, tender, amused, wry, ardent, as each song required. The full sound was lustrous and unforced. Why do we hear so little of this remarkable soprano? The performance left one eager to discover her as Violetta, as Lulu, as any of Mozart's heroines. She has not been on the New York stage since creating the title role in Leon Kirchner's *Lily* at the City Opera, nearly seven years ago. Aleck Karis was the pianist—dexterous but unemotional.

Conductors of distinction are rare at the Metropolitan Opera. Bernard Haitink came two seasons ago, making his début there with *Fidelio*. He had a poor cast and a pedestrian production. It was a disappointing performance, and Mr. Haitink has not been back. Eight years ago, John Mauceri made his Met début with *Fidelio*. He had a good cast and a good production; Otto Schenk, who staged the opera in 1970, returned to rehearse the revival. It was a stirring and successful performance, but Mr. Mauceri has not been back. The recent triumphs of the young New York conductor have been with the English National Opera and the Royal Opera; in New York he does *On Your Toes*. [*Mr. Mauceri is now the music director of Scottish Opera*.] Last month, Klaus Tennstedt made his Met début with *Fidelio*. He had a cast that looked good on paper and a flabby production that seemed to be moves made "after the book" rather than in any endeavor to give theatre form to Beethoven's great score. It was an incoherent and disappointing performance. Mr. Tennstedt is an erratic conductor, inspiring at his best, splurgy and mannered at other times. This (I attended the second performance of the run) was one of the other times—a rough, untidy performance, with the emotion on the surface and little control of the long dramatic movement. Even on the simplest levels, things came to grief: the string turns in the prelude to Act II were smudges; the drums banged all else into inaudibility at the close of *Leonore* No. 3 (played to cover the scene change in Act II) and at the start of the finale; the strings under the trumpet signal boomed out oddly. The oboe, Elaine Douvas, was eloquent.

In the Met's century of history, most of the world's famous Leonores have sung the role there: from Marianne Brandt (1884) and Lilli Lehmann (1887) to Kirsten Flagstad (1936) and Hildegard Behrens (1978). The notable absentee from the annals is Lotte Lehmann; Flagstad had the role first, and Lehmann turned down an invitation to follow her. The Met's latest Leonore is Eva Marton, whose plain but very loud soprano is winning for her an easy international fame. She seems to me a potentially important but at the moment uncultivated singer. The timbre was unvaried and monotonous. The passages not plainly delivered sounded like applied effects: an exquisitely soft reprise of "Komm, o komm" was not worked into the long line of the aria; the second subject of the "Nur hurtig fort" duet with Rocco was delivered in a breathy stage whisper. One of the great passing moments of *Fidelio*—immortalized in a Lotte Lehmann record—is a fervently breathed "ja, ja" in the aria. Miss Marton did not sing the words but substituted "ich weiss."

For nearly a quarter-century, Jon Vickers has been a Met Florestan. Like all his operatic impersonations, this one is inspired by passionate identification with the character and his plights. Every ardent inflection, every long pause has been pondered, but it has become a disconcertingly elaborate interpretation: the form of the numbers is obscured; any simple momentum is lost. Mr. Vickers enacts an idea of the opera, powerfully imagined and powerful in execution, but on this occasion it related so little to the actual Leonore onstage and proceeded so nearly independently of the conductor as to seem almost self-regarding, self-centered. Mr. Vickers's latest "touch" is to play the Florestan of the finale as a shrinking, blinking White Rabbit unable, after years of dungeon darkness, to face Don Fernando, light, and life again. He all but hid beneath Leonore's coat. On a literal level, it makes sense; in the context of Beethoven's musical affirmation, it does not.

Two big Scandinavian basses, Matti Salminen as Rocco and Aage Haugland as Don Fernando, gave sonorous but somewhat lumbering performances—a Fasolt and Fafner pair. Roberta Peters's Marzelline was admirable; Michael Best's Jaquino was callow. In a smaller house, Franz Mazura's Don Pizarro would have been impressive, for it was trenchantly and stylishly delivered. But his voice is not large, and in the quartet confrontation he dwindled to a puny adversary, dwarfed vocally and physically by Miss Marton, Mr. Vickers, and Mr. Salminen. The spoken dialogue had been abridged to a point where the abruptness of some exchanges made the audience laugh.

The Powers of Music

February 20, 1984

The "new romanticism" and the "return to tonality" are trends surely not unrelated to Gustav Mahler's dominating position in contemporary concert life. Among the great composers of the late nineteenth and early twentieth century, Mahler was one who remained uncommonly independent of Wagner's harmonic influence. Ernst Krenek wrote in 1941—when Mahler's music was little played and largely scorned—of the composer's "unconscious reaction against Wagner," and claimed that his clinging to "a musical material which is not yet affected by the destructive principles let loose by Wagner against tonality" was "exactly what makes Mahler a propelling force in the evolution of music." In the late symphonies, Krenek continued, Mahler "succeeded in drawing the conclusions from this reaction and in laying down the foundations of the music to come." Some of that music to come, so far as concert-hall audiences are concerned, has been in a sense Mahler's own—symphonies known once to only a few enthusiasts but now everyday fare and extensively recorded. Conductors as diverse as Bernstein, Solti, Haitink, and Boulez have become Mahler champions. Composers as disparate as Weill, Shostakovich, Britten, Hans Werner Henze, Peter Maxwell Davies, and David Del Tredici have owned his influence.

This month, on consecutive days, Mahler's early cantata *Das klagende Lied* and his late symphony *Das Lied von der Erde* were played in New York. *Das klagende Lied,* his first large composition, is an astonishing piece. Completed in 1880, when he was twenty, it is less eclectic than prophetic—and less prophetic than already assured. Brahms and Wagner were still writing, but—as the composer Hugh Wood remarked in a program note for Boulez's London performance of *Das klagende Lied,* in 1975—"the influence of both these giant figures is subsidiary, almost bypassed, in fact, in favour of an extraordinarily fresh and independent empirical diatonicism." In this work, Mahler said, he "found himself as Mahler." On any page, its author is unmistakable. The sound of the orchestra is magical. The music has Schubertian freshness, boldness, beauty, and charm. The dew of early romanticism sparkles again here, yet the matter, both musical and textual, is disturbing. In 1880, Freud was still a medical student in Vienna; but poets and musicians often discover first what philosophers and scientists later formulate. *Das klagende Lied* is a tale of sibling rivalry, aggression, guilt, repression, and revelation. The roots of the narrative lie in folklore (many ballads tell a similar story) and go back to Cain and Abel. The score, amid all its picturesqueness, makes explicit—"analyzes"—dark currents of emotion and reasons for action. Mahler is easily enjoyed on the surface: the lyrical tunes—birdsong, folk melody—are so pretty, the passionate tunes so eloquent, the orchestration so delightful. Heady bursts of blatant popular music (already in *Das klagende Lied* they are present) exhilarate listeners independently of the ironic role the composer intends them to play. Sometimes it seems that is all that audiences—and several conductors, too—find in Mahler. He has been cheapened by many run-of-the-mill performances. There is more to him.

Mahler entered *Das klagende Lied* for the Beethoven Prize (Brahms was one of the judges), but without success; he remarked later that had it won he might have been spared "my whole cursed operatic career ... the hell of theatrical life." To "musicians of the future," the work was also unacceptable: Mahler sent the score to Liszt, the president of the Allgemeiner Deutscher Musikverein, and Liszt returned it with faint commendation of the music ("many praiseworthy details") and brisk condemnation, not altogether unjustified, of the text. The cantata was performed at last in Vienna in 1901, two decades after its composition. It was a public success but was vilely reviewed ("a flood of ugliness"). By that time, Mahler had removed the first of its three parts, "Waldmärchen." Mahler's nephew Alfred Rose owned a score, and he conducted a complete *Klagende Lied* over the Austrian radio in 1935. (His score of "Waldmärchen" is now at Yale, and the piece was published in 1973 by Belwin-Mills.) Mahlerians still disagree whether the composer's decapitation of his cantata was justified or not. Listeners can decide for themselves by playing, with and without the first part, the Boulez recording of *Das klagende Lied,* on Columbia. (Boulez recorded Parts II and III in 1969, and "Waldmärchen" the following year.) It is not quite an unloaded test, for Boulez's "Waldmärchen" has soprano and tenor soloists (Elisabeth Söderström and Ernst Haefliger) superior to those in the two other parts, and, in general, the performance of "Waldmärchen" is one of the most impassioned and colorful things he has put on disc. Nevertheless, the conclusion seems to me inescapable that *Das klagende Lied* as first conceived is a balanced and beautiful work, and one that should be performed complete. [*There is now a complete recording, conducted by Simon Rattle, on EMI.*]

There have been at least three three-part performances in New York, all brought to Carnegie Hall by visiting orchestras: the Minnesota Orchestra, under Stanislaw Skrowaczewski, twelve years ago (some cuts were made); the Buffalo Philharmonic, under Julius Rudel, three years ago; and, this month, the Boston Symphony, under Seiji Ozawa. Mr. Ozawa conducted a clear, straightforward account of the work, efficiently played and sung but rendered without poetic insight, without vision, without the delicate attention to Mahler's fine markings or the narrative urgency that distinguishes the Boulez reading. The *Times* critic was moved to describe the work as "fustian" and blamed Mahler, instead of his conductor, for a failure "to sustain epic length with dramatic specificity." The best of the four soloists was the Finnish baritone Jorma Hynninen; he had only a few phrases in the first part. The others—Esther Hinds, Janice Taylor, and David Rendall—were so-so. The piece was performed in German, and they pronounced words instead of bringing a narrative to life.

There seldom seems to be much point in attending Zubin Mehta's concerts with the Philharmonic, or in writing about them, except when a new or unusual work or a choice soloist is billed. Jon Vickers was billed as the tenor soloist in the Philharmonic's *Lied von der Erde,* and that promised something worth hearing. But Mr. Vickers was ill, and his place was taken by Jon Fredric West, who sang with rude, blunt enthusiasm. The alto part was done by Brigitte Fass-baender, a mezzo who specializes in breeches parts and had neither the warm, even tones nor the eloquence of phrase and utterance that the role requires. The Philharmonic's playing was undetailed and unbeautiful. The matinée audience applauded after each movement, as if at an operatic recital. It was an unworthy account of a composition that should leave listeners overwhelmed.

Handel's ode *Alexander's Feast, or The Power of Music,* is a masterpiece: his depiction of a very grand musical party—Alexander's victory feast in conquered Persepolis. Thais is at Alexander's side. The minstrel Timotheus sings, affecting his audience with a variety of passions. Part I ends with a lull: with wine and love at once oppress'd, the vanquish'd victor sinks upon Thais' breast and, as it were, snoozes through the intermission. Part II begins amusingly, recalling scenes common at concerts: at Timotheus' bidding, the band sounds "a louder yet, and yet a louder strain" until the hero jerks out of his slumber, stares about him a moment, and realizes where he is. Timotheus' stirring song of revenge then rouses Alexander to action. He seizes a flambeau, Thais seizes another, and they set fire to Darius' palace. Today, the banqueting hall of Persepolis is roofless, traces of the fire remain, polished reliefs of servitors bearing choice dishes still line the hall, and it is easy to imagine the scene. Easy, too, while listening to Handel's ode, for in the cut of its melodic gestures and in its instrumental colors it has the graphicness that makes him one of the most vivid of all composers. Soloists and chorus bring the conflagration to a climax. Then two recorders breathe gently over a viola bass, the tenor sings "Thus, long ago," Alexander's feast recedes, and St. Cecilia's more solemn music, which "enlarg'd the former narrow bounds," is hymned. As the chorus tells of "arts unknown before," its fugue touches within three bars on at least eleven of the twelve tones. Between sacred and secular, Handel refuses to judge:

> *Let old Timotheus yield the prize,*
> *Or both divide the crown:*
> *He rais'd a mortal to the skies;*
> *She drew an angel down.*

Newburgh Hamilton adjusted Dryden's 1697 St. Cecilia's Day ode for Handel's setting, in order, he said in his preface, that a great master "whose Compositions have long shewn, that they can ... inspire Life into the most senseless Words" might now have a worthy text. *Alexander's Feast,* which appeared in 1736 and was a public success, builds on *Athalia,* three years earlier, and adumbrates the great music-drama *Saul,* three years later. Handel's finest Italian operas had already been written. The ode pointed the way toward his still greater achievements. It reviews and at the same time demonstrates the powers of music ("the greatest blessing that's below") to instill awe, promote merriment, awaken compassion, incite amorous tenderness, and set the blood racing with wild, reckless excitement.

The ode was performed this month at the 92nd Street Y by the Y Chamber Symphony and the Y Chorale, conducted by Gerard Schwarz. The program bore the legend "Y Chamber Symphony Goes Baroque," but it hadn't gone quite baroque enough: the recorder parts were played by modern flutes; André Emelianoff's cello obbligato to "Softly sweet in Lydian measures" was Russianly ripe and throbbing; the band was top-heavy and often too strenuous and vibrant. But the chorus, trained by Amy Kaiser, was first-rate—light, lithe, steady, and clear. The four soloists had perhaps not given enough thought to the scene, the sense, and the poetry. They tended to sing at their scores and not to the audience. There were mispronunciations (of "Thais," "Bacchus," "deity"), and there were misaccentuations caused by banging down on the first beat of the bar instead of observing Handel's play of verbal against musical accents. The tenor, David Gordon, had very clear diction, but he chopped recitative lines into fragments. The second soprano, Kathryn Gamberoni (allotted "Softly sweet" and " 'War,' he sung"), marshmallowed her words. The principal soprano, Arleen Augér, was delightful—limpid, pure, gentle, witty and charming in her phrasing and her adornments. The bass, Ronald Hedlund, had some address, but his focus was unsure. Nowadays, one hopes to hear Handel conducted from the keyboard, with a nod, a glance, a toss of the head, an occasional wave of the hand. Mr. Schwarz stood on a podium, baton in hand, and beat time; and sometimes he seemed to be beating out every single beat of each bar in a way that kept the music earthbound. But not always: in particular, the choral finale of Part I soared aloft in free, sweeping arcs of glorious sound.

The Metropolitan Opera's revival of Verdi's *Macbeth* was a depressing affair. Peter Hall's controversial, arresting 1982 production, directed now by Paul Mills, has been reduced to routine. The broomstick rides are gone; the once apparently nude Hecate now sports brown briefs; Macbeth no longer plays an Albrecht attempting to grasp elusive Wilis; Lady Macbeth is less ready to roll about on the floor. The changes could be deemed improvements had anything but stock dreariness taken their place. John Bury's décor looks more coarsely executed than ever, and Gil Wechsler's follow-spot lighting more rudimentary. No one seems to have passed on to the Met chorus—surely one of the dullest and least dramatic opera choruses in the country—that injunction prominent at the start of the Verdi staging books:

> N.B. Make the choristers realize that they should not represent a meaningless mass of people but should each of them portray an individual character and, as such, act and move each on his or her own account, following his or her own sentiments, maintaining with the others only a certain unity of action devised to insure more accurate musical execution.

The choristers stood or sat about like dummies—features blank, postures inexpressive, eyes on the conductor—and produced much the same sort of timbre and attack whether they were playing warriors, courtiers, exiles, bards, or witches. The corps of cutthroats did sing their chorus at Verdi's *ppp,* and that was good, but they did so without whispered intensity; they might have been Mendelssohnian elves. (An equally stodgy *Don Carlos,* taped at the Met last season and put out this month by PBS, provided close-up views of lifeless pudding faces.) Sherrill Milnes, the Macbeth, was in good voice the night I went, but his interpretation was bland and blank. Renata Scotto's Lady Macbeth lacked the vocal resources for the role, and some of her histrionics were risible. James Levine's heavy conducting seemed less acceptable than ever after the alert, precise, colorful account of the score—Verdi's careful and copious dynamic indications accurately observed, choral and instrumental timbres matched to the situations—that Riccardo Muti and the Philadelphia Orchestra brought to Carnegie Hall last October.

St. Michael's, a good 1891 church by Robert Gibson on West Ninety-ninth Street, supports an ambitious and varied series of musical events. Some of them take place in the church, others in the octagonal parish hall, where last week the Columbia String Quartet, the church's quartet-in-residence, played a nourishing and beautiful program: Haydn's Opus 33, No. 3 (the "Bird"), Conlon Nancarrow's Quartet, and Schubert's C-major Quintet. The hall holds about a hundred and fifty. There was an audience of eighteen. It was an intimate occasion—chamber music played as if to a handful of friends—and would have been more intimate still had the room not been plunged into near-darkness when the music began. The Columbia is an ensemble of four sensitive and accomplished young artists (Benjamin Hudson, Carol Zeavin, Sarah Clarke, and Eric Bartlett), each also a soloist in her or his own right, and all versed in contemporary music. To the "classics" they bring a quick, keen appreciation of motivic variations and harmonic tensions which makes their interpretations more alert and more moving than those of some celebrated, lusher-toned, less finely sentient ensembles. The Haydn was bewitching. The Nancarrow—a score that looks almost amateurish on paper—is odd and adventurous in its modes and its rhythms. For the Schubert, Rosalyn Clarke joined the quartet, as second cello. The work, one of music's miracles, cast its unfailing spell. Uncommonly eloquent in this performance were the transitions in the slow movement from E-major bliss to F-minor fret, and back again: brief bars in which time stands still; moments that, when the sounds are as poignantly placed as they were here, fill listeners' hearts and minds with mysterious awe. Sometimes, in the small chamber, the playing could with advantage have been gentler still. In the finale of the Schubert, energy turned at the close to roughness. But the spirit—fiery, "symphonic," even heroic—was right. Strange that this could ever have been found an easygoing movement. The powers of music which Handel hymned and which Mahler deployed on an epic scale are all present in the four movements of this sublime, disturbing, beautiful quintet.

In Defense of Philidor

February 27, 1984

FRANÇOIS-ANDRÉ DANICAN PHILIDOR (1726–95), friend of Diderot and of Dr. Johnson, is remembered as a chess champion—the architect of Philidor's Defense, and probably the strongest player of his day. Music history knows him, too, as a key figure in French opera between Rameau and Gluck, praised by the latter, and admired by Burney. His pieces were in the Burgtheater repertory in Mozart's day; the young Beethoven played Philidor scores when he was a violist in the Bonn theatre orchestra. I first heard Philidor's music onstage when, in 1971, a group of Cambridge University undergraduates rediscovered his *Tom Jones* (1765), edited and translated it, and staged and sang it with persuasive zest and accomplishment. Their leader, Nicholas McGegan, the editor and conductor of the show, then undertook Philidor's defense in London and put on performances of his *Blaise le savetier, Le Jardinier et son seigneur, Tom Jones* again, and *Le Maréchal ferrant.* There were a few French productions in the late seventies: *Les Femmes vengées* at the Albi Festival, *Tom Jones* at the Opéra-Comique—where a descendant of the composer, his great-great- (or thereabouts) grandson, appeared on the first night. Mr. McGegan published his edition of *Tom Jones* in 1978 (Boosey & Hawkes), and there have been a handful of American productions. The latest of them was given this month by the Indiana University Opera Theatre, in Bloomington.

Tom Jones, an opéra comique, seems to me an excellent piece, and one apt for small-company or student performance. There are seven singing roles and one speaking role; a few male choristers provide a rollicking refrain to Squire Western's hunting song and, unaccompanied, sing a drunken catch in the Upton inn. The band is pairs of oboes and horns, a bassoon, and strings with harpsichord. It is tempting, and probably not inaccurate, to detect the hand of the master chess strategist in the careful planning, the neat ingenious constructions, and the adroit pacing of the score. The first number, a duet for Sophia and Mrs. Honour, employs a device less common then than it became: a verse in 4/4 for the heroine; another, in 12/8, to a different tune, for her maid; and then both together. The topers' catch lurches and staggers and recovers most cunningly. Michael Robinson, in his *Opera before Mozart,* cites the duet for Sophia and her father as an early example of dramatic conflict made manifest by both the cut of the vocal lines and the orchestration; the surprising septet that closes Act II extends the technique in an almost Mozartian way. The traditional vaudeville finale (musically identical verses, one from each member of the company, and a refrain in which all join) that ends Act III is saved from squareness and given piquancy by the fact that its phrases are five bars long. A brief coro built on its head-motif, in longer note values, rounds off the piece.

Fielding's novel appeared in 1749 (the year Philidor's *Analyze des Echecs* was published, also in London), and in French translation the following year. Coleridge deemed it one of "the three most perfect plots ever planned" (the others being *Oedipus Rex* and Ben Jonson's *The Alchemist*). Fielding began his career as a playwright. Molière adaptations were among his successes. For a time, he was manager of the Haymarket, producing good socialist plays there (which displeased Walpole's government and effectively ended Fielding's career as a dramatist) while Handel was bringing out opera seria at Covent Garden. *Tom Jones,* a great novel—and an extraordinarily modern novel, whose traces, as Austin Dobson observed in a Britannica essay, "are still discernible in most of our manlier modern fiction"—is also a drama with vividly visualized scenes and lively dialogue. (Coleridge links it with two plays.) Philidor's libretto, written by the despised Antoine Alexandre Henri Poinsinet but revised in 1766 by Jean-Michel Sedaine, that master of opéra comique (and a genitor of *Fidelio*), is expertly made. It simplifies the plot. (Stephen Oliver, in his *Tom Jones*— reviewed in *Music of Three Seasons,* p. 412—went to work more wittily and ambitiously.) Two-thirds of the novel is condensed into a single day: the marriage of Sophia and Blifil is arranged in the morning; Tom is expelled in the afternoon; and Act III plays that night in the inn at Upton, where all is resolved—as it would have been in Fielding, too, had he not contrived "many strange accidents" with a skill that chapters later he invites his readers to return to and admire. In the opera, Fielding's candid naturalism is bowdlerized. (Earthquakes that shook London in 1750 were by some declared to be God's wrath at the success of the book. "I scarcely know a more corrupt work," said Dr. Johnson.) Of Tom's carefree extra-Sophian amours, only a passing buss for Mrs. Honour remains; the Oedipal complication—apparent incest with an unrecognized, pretty mother—is omitted. Moreover, at the close Tom's parents are declared to have been properly, if clandestinely, wed. The Cambridge undergraduate translators—Andrew Nickolds; Adrian Salter, son of the musician Lionel Salter; and Nicholas Reynolds, son of the musician Gordon Reynolds, and director of the production—showed further skill in restoring much of Fielding's robustness and realism to the opera. Their spoken dialogue was in large part taken from Fielding's pages, in a controlled way that did not violate the musical characterizations or break with Philidor's style.

The Bloomington performance, sung and played by students but directed, designed, and conducted by their mentors, was rather disappointing. It lacked directness. *Tom Jones* was first done in the Hôtel de Bourgogne, the home of the Comédie-Italienne and the Opéra-Comique in the 1760s—an intimate little theatre whose stage projected well into the house. (There is a 1767 drawing of it in volume 14 of Grove.) The Cambridge revival was set in an even smaller theatre. In Bloomington, *Tom Jones* was done in the Musical Arts Center, an admirable building but a grand-opera house, larger than the grand-opera houses in several European cities. Max Röthlisberger, the designer, had diminished the stage opening with a false proscenium, incorporating three tiers of stage boxes on each side. Behind it, there were painted box sets. Costumed supers sat in the stage boxes and "acted" as they watched. The band wore eighteenth-century costumes (but played modern instruments). Since the auditorium could not be similarly diminished, the problem of scale remained. In any case, there is a big difference between a serious, thoroughgoing, committed attempt to revive an eighteenth-century opera in, so far as possible, eighteenth-century terms (Mr. McGegan's production of Handel's *Orlando* in St. Louis last year was a notable example) and the use of eighteenth-century trimmings to lend adventitious cuteness to a show. The décor sported coarsely limned, comic-strip putti. Ross Allen, the director, began things, needless to say, with flunkies touching tapers to a row of (electric) footlights, and he worked through many more such clichés before the evening was done. From Tony Richardson's *Tom Jones* movie he borrowed the famous seduction-through-munching sequence, and he used it to divert attention from the musical pleasures of the catch. There was much stock comic business unrelated either to the music or to character. What might be called a Cyril Ritchard approach to period comedy can be pretty tiresome even when it is executed with elegance; when students essay it the results are likely to be embarrassing. In opéra comique, the acting and the speaking are as important as the singing. There was some sweet, true singing to be heard—especially from Jane Giering, the Sophia—the night I went. But it seemed as if the performers had skimped classes in acting, in spoken dialogue, and in period deportment. (Nor had they noticed that in the English translation the heroine's name is rhymed with "desire" and "higher.") The orchestral playing, under Robert Porco, was not nearly light or active enough—the string phrasing airless, the woodwinds soggy. Although Philidor's orchestration is generally more functional than interesting, there is some delicate string writing; Mrs. Honour's first air has a bassoon obbligato; oboe and bassoon solos wind through Sophia's first air. None of this made much effect.

Tom Jones would have come across more strongly if its performers had cut the frills, hit the piece much harder, and performed it with musical-comedy high spirits and zest. The device of a costumed stage audience nearly always has a deadening effect on drama (more than one Handel opera has been killed in this way) and suggests a lack of belief in a piece's ability to hold its own before the real audience. Nevertheless, the evening, if but mildly entertaining, was instructive. Mid-century opéra comique was a fertile seedbed of ideas that later bore fruit in great operas. In Paris, Italian notions were refashioned by Frenchmen in subtle, inventive ways. (German ideas sometimes entered into opéra comique too: Philidor supervised the publication of Gluck's *Orfeo,* in

Paris, and calmly lifted Orpheus' "Chiamo il mio ben" into his opéra comique *Le Sorcier.* Berlioz called this "one of the most audacious plagiarisms in the history of music.") Charming, once widely performed and influential opéras comiques by Dauvergne, Monsigny, and Grétry are also revived from time to time. Philidor's scores stand up to scrutiny more securely than theirs. He avoids monotony—as even Gluck in his opéras comiques did not unfailingly do—by variety of form, of feeling, and of texture and scoring. Some of his airs are simple, others elaborate, with deft changes of rhythm. Tom's first air in Act II is a limpid, lyrical E-major song such as might fall from the lips of Gluck's Paris. Sophia's final number is a scena—dramatic recitative, brief adagio, fiery cabaletta—that recalls nothing so much as Beethoven's essays in opera seria. One number in this *Tom Jones* seemed out of place—Blifil's suave air in Act III. It *was* out of place; it comes from Philidor's tragédie *Ernelinde, princesse de Norvège.* Mr. McGegan added it (clearly identified as an insertion) to his edition so that Blifil would have more than one air to sing. The fact that it stuck out was convincing proof of Philidor's clever planning.

AIRS OF ENGLAND

March 5, 1984

POMERIUM MUSICES' Sunday-afternoon recital in Corpus Christi Church, in the Music Before 1800 series, was entitled "Madrigals and Motets for a King: Music from the Court of Henry VIII." Only one of Henry's own compositions, "O my hart and O my hart," was sung. There was music sacred and secular from the Newberry-Oscott Partbooks, that rich collection of Renaissance music assembled in Florence and sent to Henry. (Four partbooks are now in the Newberry Library, in Chicago, and the fifth is at Oscott College, Sutton Coldfield.) It included four Machiavelli settings by Philippe Verdelot; Claudin de Sermisy's powerful "Quousque non reverteris pax" (a prayer for the return to France of peace, "solace of the good, ever hateful to potentates"); and the dedicatory motet to Henry himself, "who cherishes in his bosom the shipwrecked alumni of the Muses." Sermisy, in Francis I's service, probably met Robert Fayrfax and William Cornysh, Henry's court composers, at the Field of the Cloth of Gold, in 1520, when the English and French royal chapels joined forces. Cornysh was represented at the Pomerium concert by his "Gaude virgo mater Christi," and Fayrfax by his glowing "Salve regina"—both in the Eton Choirbook. These pieces are pre-Reformation Tudor music at its richest and most splendid. Each was preceded by well-chosen groups of solo songs, duets, trios, full madrigals and motets, and lute pieces (played by Karen Meyers) reflecting both the cosmopolitan culture of Henry's court and the specific quirks of English music. The seven Pomerium singers, in varied combinations and as a body, were tuneful, supple, and well balanced. It was a good concert.

Nearly five centuries later, royal patronage of composers and performers has been replaced by public support. Queen Elizabeth II, we used to be told, spends more public money on her military bands than her government spends on all the many opera companies, symphony orchestras, chamber orchestras, and chamber-music ensembles in Britain. I don't know if the figures still hold. But I do know that when I visit London I find new music playing a more important role in everyday life than it does here. Probably as much gets performed in New York, but here people in general don't take the same interest in it. A composition of merit cannot count on receiving a dozen intelligent, eloquent reviews in the daily, weekly, and monthly press. Scores are not on sale in Carnegie Hall, Merkin Hall, Carnegie Recital Hall. (Lincoln Center does have a large subterranean bookshop, but seems to have no consistent policy of stocking—and displaying—scores and recordings of any new music due for performance in its halls.) Last summer, I suggested some concinnitory causes—among them enlightened public subsidy (as opposed to the American system of munificent public subsidy by way of tax deduction, determined by rich individuals' private whims); the BBC; careful music education from primary school onward—of England's being a land where new music seems to flourish. That was in an account of some composers born in the forties and fifties—Robin Holloway, Oliver Knussen, Robert Saxton, Giles Swayne, Colin Matthews, Philip Grange—who were being played in London's principal halls during August. The names of two young composers I'd read a good deal about were missing from the bills: George Benjamin and Jonathan Lloyd. But last month some Lloyd was played in, and some Benjamin within easy reach of, Manhattan.

George Benjamin, born in London in 1960, performed his Piano Sonata over the French Radio in 1978. It is now published, as is most of his music, by Faber (in exceptionally attractive scores), and it has been recorded on Nimbus. Benjamin came to wider attention in 1980, when his first orchestral piece, *Ringed by the Flat Horizon,* was played at Cambridge University, where he was an undergraduate. The work was acclaimed by the London critics, and later that year it was given at the Proms, by the BBC Symphony. Peter Heyworth wrote in the *Observer* of "a mastery that many labour half a life-time to acquire." Also in 1980, Benjamin's Octet (a 1978 piece) was played by the London Sinfonietta, under his baton, at the Aldeburgh Festival, and was played at IRCAM; in Carnegie Recital Hall a Duo for cello and piano had its first performance. Since then, Benjamin has composed *A Mind of Winter,* a Wallace Stevens setting for soprano and small orchestra, first done at the Aldeburgh Festival; a substantial piano piece, *Sortilèges,* first played at the Cheltenham Festival; *At First Light,* a chamber-orchestra tone poem inspired by Turner's "Norham Castle: Sunrise" (a Sinfonietta commission); a piano miniature, *Meditation on Haydn's Name* (a BBC commission); and the brief *Fanfare for Aquarius,* written for the opening concert of the new British ensemble Aquarius.

Two years ago, Christopher Keene conducted *Ringed by the Flat Horizon* with the German South-West Radio Orchestra, and admired it. He conducted it again last month, with his American orchestra, the Long Island Philharmonic. I attended the second performance, at the C. W. Post Concert Theater, a Beaubourg-like auditorium in Greenvale, architecturally adventurous and acoustically admirable. The title is from *The Waste Land*—from the passage that Eliot in his notes to the poem links with "the present decay of eastern Europe," Hermann Hesse's *Blick ins Chaos,* and multitudes marching in drunken ecstasy toward an abyss, singing songs that the blessed and the seers weep to hear. Benjamin's piece, however, is not political. The title, it seems, came after the composition. An inspiration for the music was a dramatic photograph by W. P. Winn (it is reproduced on the cover of the score) of a thunderstorm in New Mexico. In a program note, Benjamin says, "I wanted to portray an eerie tension as the landscape is overwhelmed by a vast storm. . . . Weird, soft bell chords, a sustained semitone clash, and deep tremors in the lower registers of the orchestra depict distant thunder." The storm gathers, comes to an unresolved climax. Then "for a moment the original semitone clash hovers motionless in the air, the thunder at last erupts in a violent explosion, and the work returns to a mood of unreal calm, ending as it began, with a soft bell chord." In *The Waste Land,* Benjamin found lines to verbalize his scene: "What is that sound high in the air," "Ringed by the flat horizon only," "Cracks and reforms and bursts in the violet air."

Last summer, I remarked the influence of Messiaen—once a mentor of Boulez, Stockhausen, Barraqué—on much new British music. Benjamin has been a pupil of Messiaen, to whom *Ringed by the Flat Horizon* is dedicated. The young composer has a complete control of timbre—of sounds that seem to suggest colors (violet, lemon, black, palest blue), Turneresque effects of light, and sensations of sultriness or, as in the Stevens setting, of icy cold. His palette is extraordinary. The imaginative sounds are inseparable from an equally complete control of harmony. If his music were merely picturesque, illustrative, sensory, it would already be well worth playing and hearing. But his command of form is impressive, too. His timing and placing are exact. Profuse in ideas, he is not profligate in his use of them; everything plays a necessary part. The time scale is not Messiaenic: Benjamin's longest work, *At First Light*, lasts twenty-two minutes; *Ringed by the Flat Horizon* eighteen. Both are large, beautiful, exciting compositions: music as a delight to the ear and a metaphor for adventures in life. The Long Island Philharmonic, a band of expert players, gave an admirable performance, colorful and strong. The twenty-two-hundred-seat hall was full.

Jonathan Lloyd, born in 1948, is rather like an Ives to Benjamin's Carter. He, too, was played at an early age—Andrew Davis and the English Chamber Orchestra did his *Cantique* in the Queen Elizabeth Hall in 1970—but he came to prominence only in 1981, when in quick succession Michael Gielen and the BBC Symphony did his *Toward the Whitening Dawn* (the *Sunday Times* review was headed "A New British Masterpiece"), Rattle and the Sinfonietta his Viola Concerto, Oliver Knussen and the Sinfonietta his *Won't it ever be morning*, and John Harle and John Lenehan his *John's Journal*. All were widely and favorably reviewed. Compositions and performances have been plentiful ever since. Michael Tilson Thomas and the Philharmonia gave the London première of Lloyd's *Everything Returns,* for large orchestra, in 1982. (At its New York concerts last week, the Philharmonia played no British music.) Boosey & Hawkes, Lloyd's publishers, list seven 1982 compositions in their pamphlet about him. His music had reached America back in 1973, when at Tanglewood his *Scattered Ruins* won the Koussevitzky Composition Prize. Last year, in New York, Musical Elements played his *Waiting for Gozo* (a 1981 Sinfonietta commission) at one of the adventurous and, I've always found, rewarding concerts it gives in the Great Hall of Cooper Union. Last month, Mr. Harle and Mr. Lenehan played *John's Journal* at their New York début recital, in Carnegie Recital Hall.

Thanks to tape, I've been able to hear several of Lloyd's compositions. They puzzle me if I start to think about them. While listening, I'm captivated by the easy, informal flow of invention, the casual command, the don't-care confidence. A preface to the Boosey pamphlet starts with a reference to Kipling's cat that walked by himself, talks of "a land where there are no monuments more ancient than Ives, and no evident boundaries of nationality or culture," and continues:

> The music itself—rejecting, in the name of free will, all but the simplest formal prototypes—obstinately refuses to disclose its route beforehand, or to describe its extra-musical surroundings thereafter. Its survival in transit depends on actions and reactions that seem purely instinctive: on multiple coordination in leaps and falls; on stealth and immobility in close cover; on double-jointed, arched, and swiftly recoiling movements in open combat. Strictly of its own making, and wholly deceptive, are its temporary pacts with domesticity. Catch it in a comfortable seat by the fireside and be sure of nothing except that it will leave again at nightfall, without warning, disdainfully. For only outside, on "the wild wet roofs," can it descry the path through the "wild wet woods"—and that to which everything returns.

Waiting for Gozo is a twelve-minute, twelve-player "piece about waiting," suggested by travel delays that beset the composer on his way to the Mediterranean island. A three-note cell runs hypnotically through the work. We hover, drift, start to move, have hopes roused only to have them dashed. Gozo looms up in a brass chorale, but then a soft, foggy drift of strings obscures it again. It's a light, attractive, fascinating, poetic composition. *John's Journal*, subtitled "a week in the life of a saxophonist," is a terse, dapper suite for saxophone (alto alternating with soprano) and piano, composed with what seems like nonchalant brilliance. On successive days, the soloist is "slow and lazy"; "fast, funky"; "nervous, hesitant" (and apt to rattle his keys); improvisatory; *"brutale ma brillante"*; "desolate, distant"; and, finally, *"disco non troppo"*—and off on a journey, no doubt, for the opening strains of Juventino Rosas's *Over the Waves* keep running through his mind. Mr. Harle, born in 1956, once a saxophonist with Her Majesty's Coldstream Guards, then a prize-winning graduate of the Royal College of Music, has become an eminent modern instrumentalist. For him, Berio recast *Sequenza IX,* for violin, as *Sequenza IXb,* for saxophone. Dominic Muldowney has written a concerto for him and the Sinfonietta. He has inspired important saxophone parts in most of Lloyd's orchestral works. He's a dazzling player, with an immense range of tones, and a magnetic musician; and Mr. Lenehan is a fine pianist. The published score of *John's Journal* includes their recording of the piece, tucked into a pocket at the back.

The Da Capo Chamber Players billed their concert in Carnegie Recital Hall last week as a salute to Great Britain. It began with Harrison Birtwistle's bright transcription (1969) of an Ockeghem motet—one of the tangy aperitifs he and

Peter Maxwell Davies devised for concerts of the Pierrot Players, who became the Fires of London—and ended with Davies's *Image, Reflection, Shadow* (1982), which the Fires brought to New York last year. At the Da Capo performance, the sextet played under a conductor, David Gilbert. The cimbalom player, Myron Romanul, could not match the mystery, the dusky-gold enchantment, the twangling frenzy that Gregory Knowles, of the Fires, brought to his star role. But there was much sensitive, adept playing. Once again, the long stretch of visionary music held its listeners spellbound.

Davies apart, the program hardly represented contemporary British music at its most inventive, stirring, or characteristic. (Time that New York heard some Muldowney, Nigel Osborne, and John Casken; more Knussen, more Holloway.) The five composers represented were born in the thirties. Bernard Rands's *Scherzi* (1974) is one of his less arresting compositions. John McCabe's *Movements* (1964), for clarinet, violin, and cello, is decently made but dry. Eleven years ago, I called Richard Rodney Bennett's *Commedia II,* at its première, "thin stuff that goes in one ear and out the other," and last week found no reason to change my mind.

The Nimbus record of Benjamin's Piano Sonata, played by the composer, also includes the Duo and Flight, *a captivating piece for solo flute. Another Nimbus record couples* Ringed by the Flat Horizon, At First Light, *and* A Mind of Winter. *Davies's* Image, Reflection, Shadow *is recorded on Unicorn-Kanchana.*

COMPLETEST CONCERTS

March 12, 1984

LAST week, Leonie Rysanek's twenty-five-year association with the Metropolitan Opera was celebrated by concert performances of Act II of *Parsifal* and Act I of *Die Walküre,* with Miss Rysanek as Kundry and as Sieglinde. Born in Vienna in 1926, she made her début in Innsbruck, in 1949. She sang at the first postwar Bayreuth festival, in 1951; at Covent Garden in 1953; and at the Met six years later. (Her American début was made in San Francisco in 1956, as Senta, Sieglinde, and Aida; the next season there she sang Turandot, Amelia in *Ballo,* Ariadne, Lady Macbeth, and Aida again.) For the first decade of her career, she was an uneven singer—very exciting when the voice poured out truly, with warm, ample radiance, but sometimes squally and wild. The terse comment of *The Record Year* on her Bayreuth début (Act III of *Die Walküre* was recorded) is "Rysanek as Sieglinde shows promise, but also a tendency to scream." When she reached New York, she had become a more disciplined and accurate vocalist, without losing the spontaneity, the womanly impetuousness, the dramatic directness that make people love her rather as Lotte Lehmann was loved.

97

The silver-jubilee concert was an occasion both moving and artistically rewarding. Miss Rysanek's Kundry—she first sang the role in Hamburg in 1976, did it at Bayreuth in 1982 and 1983, and brings it to the Met next season—is a serious, voluptuous, and stirring portrayal. When I heard the 1982 broadcast, I thought her voice could not do justice to her intentions. Last year, in the theatre, my reservations largely disappeared; her vivid presence made a difference, but she also seemed to have gained new force and freshness. The Met Act II was largely a Bayreuth reconstruction, with the same Parsifal (Peter Hofmann), Klingsor (Franz Mazura), and conductor (James Levine). The singers acted— with timbres, words, glances, gestures, and demeanor. And because Klingsor was not asked to cry his commands through a public-address system, because Kundry was not put through elaborate routines with maypole ribbons, the sense of Wagner's dramatic confrontations was actually clearer than it had been at Bayreuth.

The *Walküre* was also acted. Tensions between the three characters—Mr. Hofmann the Siegmund, John Macurdy the Hunding—ran across the platform. The "décor"—the Met stage walled and ceilinged in abstract, Appiesque manner, with constructions pleasing in form and color; the orchestra onstage—was hardly further from Wagner's scenic directions than that of many a contemporary *Ring* production. Sieglinde and Hunding wore the costumes—modern dress— that they often wear nowadays. The presentation was Wieland Wagneresque in its dependence on glance, posture, and a few clearly placed, potent gestures; details of realistic action were left to the spectators' imagination, not contradicted by some director's newly invented business. Since the orchestra plays so large a part in painting Wagner's scenes, there was no distraction in seeing it do so; it suggested, rather, a new, audacious "design concept" that invites the audience to interpret sound as colors, forms, and light. If the Met chose to stage its next *Ring* in this bold way, it could save a good deal of money on designer, sets, and stage crew. Mr. Levine had ranged his strings in almost the traditional fashion: second violins on his right, and therefore properly prominent in the opening pages; cellos facing out (and wonderfully eloquent throughout the evening); violas excellently audible. Only the double-basses, clumped to one side, let us down by not providing a balanced central foundation. There were some rough brass passages (had sectional rehearsals for the brass been skimped?), and the kettledrummer banged away with deplorable loudness. Otherwise, the orches- tral sound—rich and stirring, detailed in solos and glowing in tutti—made one eager for the Levine-conducted *Ring* long overdue at the Met.

Mr. Hofmann's Siegmund was less successful than his earnest, sharply focussed Parsifal. He lacked quick, generous reactions and charm of personality. During narratives, he fell into the pose of a handsome singing butler. But his line was clear and firmly molded. Mr. Macurdy's Hunding was dark, formidable, and incisive. Miss Rysanek's Sieglinde remains irresistible rather in the way that Hilde Konetzni's was—so warm, honest, and lovable. Sometimes she overdoes things. I wish she wouldn't scream with excitement when Siegmund draws the sword from the tree; if Wagner had wanted a scream he'd have asked for it. (And at each performance the scream gets louder and longer.) But one readily forgives her. In an age when some Sieglindes are Miss Mouse and others a

Brünnhilde manquée, she fearlessly projects feeling and character. There was much beautiful sound—phrases that shone and soared, luminous soft notes that floated through the house. She was a Sieglinde—as she had been a Kundry—intent on each turn of the score, whether she was singing or listening. Toward the end of the evening, her voice tired: small wonder, given her assignment. (Act II of *Parsifal* is a taxing warm-up for Sieglinde.) Besides, *Die Walküre* had been preceded by an affecting presentation, of a silver tray, with repeated plaudits from an adoring house as Frank Taplin, the president of the Metropolitan Opera Association, recalled her achievements, role by role, over the years. The performance was charged with high emotion. The act—and the evening—came to a thrilling climax.

Handel's *Rinaldo,* an opera about strife between Christian and Muslim in the Middle East, has been playing at the Met. It was the company's first Handel production—a good choice, for it is one of his most splendid and spectacular pieces. The program note, by Brian Trowell, referred, rightly, to "unusually serious subject matter" and to the applicability of the Renaissance epic on which *Rinaldo* is based—Tasso's *Jerusalem Liberated*—to the political situation in 1711, the year of its first performance. Today, the concerns seem even more urgent: this is a drama of ideologies in mortal conflict; of the distortions that personal partialities inflict on ideals; of captains distracted from and then recalled to their great enterprises, moving through trials and adventures to a last, decisive battle. The Met, however, did not produce the piece in this spirit. The show came to us from Canada, a centenary-season loan. It first appeared in Ottawa in 1982. Reviewing it then [*Musical Events: 1980–1983,* pp. 278–83], I remarked that there are two possible approaches to Handel opera. One was exemplified recently in the Cambridge and St. Louis productions of *Orlando* and is epitomized in Winton Dean's declarations that Handel "was not only a great composer; he was a dramatic genius of the first order" and that "the music of no other dramatic composer comes closer to Mozart in its detached but penetrating insight into human nature." The other approach is epitomized in Burney's defense of Italian opera against the taunts of Addison and Steele:

> Let it be remembered by the lovers of Music, that opera is the *completest concert* to which they can go; with this advantage over those in still life, that to the most perfect singing, and effects of a powerful and well-disciplined band, are frequently added excellent acting, splendid scenes and decorations, with such dancing as a playhouse, from its inferior prices, is seldom able to furnish.

It was as a "completest concert" that the Met *Rinaldo,* designed by Mark Negin and directed by Frank Corsaro, delighted its audiences. The settings and costumes were rich, gorgeous, and entertaining. A bright-eyed chariot-drawing dragon flew through the air, snorting smoke from his nostrils. Mermaids wagged their fishy tails. Stage magic held sway. The final battle was fought between golden boys (clad, here in New York, whereas in Ottawa they had been all but Greek-nude) and blue-armored paynims, with cartwheels and somersaults, while Rinaldo, aloft on a watchtower, sang his heroic "Or la tromba" against the pealing trumpet obbligatos.

This was not the opera Handel composed but a selection of numbers from it shuffled and reordered. Of the thirty-one arias in the 1711 score, only fifteen were done complete or nearly complete (one more than in Ottawa, for here Rinaldo regained his celebrated "Il Tricerbero humiliato," which had there been replaced by a piece from *Partenope*). Two great Handel sequences that are tonally coherent and dramatically overwhelming had been dismembered and were scattered through the evening. Two great arias, Rinaldo's "Cara sposa" and Armida's "Ah! crudel!," were sung out of context—the latter in two, divided installments. Act III, in particular, bore little relation to the act Handel composed: one of its arias was moved to Act I, three pieces from Act II were dropped into it, four arias were omitted, its duet was shortened, and a second duet, from *Admeto,* was added. I gave details of the damage in the Ottawa review and hoped—in vain—that it would be put right before the show came to New York. If the Met offered a *Tosca* in which Cavaradossi sang "E lucevan le stelle" (or perhaps "Che gelida manina") as his entrance air, "Vissi d'arte" brought down the second-act curtain, and the love duet from *Butterfly* enriched Act III—or if Susanna sang "Deh vieni" in Act I of *Figaro,* the Countess's "Porgi amor" became a finale, and Barbarina and the Count added "Là ci darem" to the last act—there might be some protest, however enjoyable the music was to hear.

Three of the Ottawa principals—Marilyn Horne (Rinaldo), Benita Valente (Almirena), and Samuel Ramey (Argante)—reappeared in the Met production. I heard some of the broadcast (Miss Horne was not in her best voice); when I attended the show there were new soloists. Ewa Podlés, a Polish mezzo, was a passable hero. Her voice was accurate and fluent, if a shade small for the house. Her acting was plain. (Addison called Nicolini, the first Rinaldo, "the greatest performer in dramatic music that is now living, or that perhaps ever appeared on a stage," and Steele declared that "every limb, and every finger, contributes to the part he acts.") There was a pleasing, poignant timbre in Gail Robinson's Almirena; a pity that, like her predecessor, she sang not a delicately varied da capo in the exquisite "Lascia ch'io pianga" but a dull descant. (Much of the vocal ornament seemed rote-learned.) Terry Cook's Argante was unimpressive. Carol Vaness, the Armida, was commanding and vivid enough (even though she sang "Ah! crudel!" lying down) to make the fragmentation of her grand scena doubly distressing; occasionally she sacrificed forwardness and precision to "richness" and volume. Dano Raffanti's Goffredo was a little raw but brought the pleasure of clear Italian sung as if it meant something. (Handel composed the role for a woman but twenty years later, in an unhappy rehash of *Rinaldo,* recast it for a tenor.) Most of the recitative was slowly and heavily delivered, against an almost nonstop harpsichord fantasia of arpeggios, figurations, and trills. Mario Bernardi's conducting was not unmusical but showed no special baroque skills. Could any true Handelian have agreed to conduct this edition?

Christ & St. Stephen's, an 1880 building on West Sixty-ninth Street, just north of Lincoln Center, is a happy country-church survival between Broadway and busy, bustling Columbus Avenue. It is one of New York's more agreeable concert places, and it has the civilized habit of providing not only a darkened listening area for those who want to snooze or dream during the music but also lit aisles for those who bring their pocket scores and for all those who take music seriously and find their attention heightened by being, European-fashion, in one room with the performers, not in a movie-house relationship. In Christ & St. Stephen's, the Guild of Composers gave a February concert. It was well attended. The program began with Schulamit Ran's clarinet monologue, *For an Actor*—a near-success, imaginative but slender. There was a première, Edward Cohen's Clarinet Quintet, but the evening was more notable for performances of three earlier works that have deservedly entered the modern repertory. Premières draw the critics, but deuxièmes, cinquièmes, dixièmes show that musicians continue to find the compositions in question worth performing.

I admired Robert Beaser's song cycle *The Seven Deadly Sins* (1979) when Paul Sperry sang it at a Musical Elements concert in 1982, and admired it again here—for its incisive word setting, its command of vocal gesture, its bold, sure piano writing, and its formal precision. The text is seven mordant, Blakean epigrams by Anthony Hecht. The singer was the baritone Richard Lalli. (The vocal line is "pointed" to make it compassable by either a tenor or a baritone.) His voice is not great, but he is a more cogent interpreter than many with better voices who put resonant vocalism before sense. He knew the music and did not read it off a score. He made much of the text. He was fearless. Where the composer wrote "freely," Mr. Lalli sang freely, adjusting note values to the length and stress of the words. There followed George Perle's Ballade, composed in 1981 for the pianist Richard Goode—a modern barcarolle, rhapsodic yet shapely, which Mr. Goode, who played it again here, plays ever more poetically. And then Yehudi Wyner's Concert Duo, for violin and piano, dating from 1957. There is a twenty-year-old recording, on CRI, played by Matthew Raimondi and the composer—a fine performance but an odd recording, with the violin down one channel and the piano down the other. (It sounds better when the mono switch on one's hi-fi is engaged.) The Duo is a terrific piece—rich, passionate, Brahmsian in its compound of lyrical ardor and constructive intelligence. Daniel Stepner and the composer gave a fiery performance.

Parnassus's February concert, in Merkin Hall, was also largely retrospective. Robert Hall Lewis's *Combinazioni I* (composed in 1974; recorded, on Orion, in 1978) had its New York première, and was followed by Lukas Foss's *Echoi* (1963; twice recorded). I felt that quartets of Parnassus players had worked hard at compositions that barely rewarded their industry. Then Frank Hoffmeister, with Edmund Niemann as pianist, sang Elliott Carter's early *Voyage* (1943), a broad and beautiful Hart Crane setting. But Mr. Hoffmeister had not mastered the song. On the simplest level, he had—unlike Mr. Lalli at the Guild concert—disobeyed that Golden Rule in Plunket Greene's *Interpretation in Song:* "The interpreter must memorise his work. . . . There will be no senses to spare for effect, or lilt, or magnetism, or illustration or anything else, if the eye is on the printed page."

In the second half, Stravinsky's *Ragtime* (1918) and *Reynard* (1917) were done, conducted by Anthony Korf. Parnassus players, as I have remarked before, are expert, earnest, dedicated musicians. That they came to what could have been a relaxed Sunday-afternoon concert dressed all in black, as if for a funeral, is unimportant. But that they played *Ragtime,* an unsolemn work, in stiff-collar-and-tie fashion mattered musically. *Reynard* was happier. It is a wonderful

101

composition—hardly worth staging, for the libretto is a bore, but well worth playing and singing, for the score is a cubist masterpiece. The Parnassus performance was beautifully bright, exact, and balanced. In the vocal quartet, Douglas Perry, the second tenor—bearer (most of the time) of the title role—was outstanding. The work was done in Russian. Afterward, I overheard a member of the audience say "I wish they had sung in English" and "I wish the singers hadn't kept their noses in their scores." I agreed.

PARADE

March 19, 1984

A REMARKABLE six-day run of orchestral concerts in Carnegie Hall began on a Monday with a program given by the Symphony Orchestra of the Curtis Institute, conducted by Sergiu Celibidache. Mr. Celibidache was making his American début. His engagement was a feather in Curtis's cap, for he has become a legend: a conductor who insists on between ten and eighteen rehearsals for each concert; who stipulates that players and soloists should have no other commitments during the rehearsal period; who now makes no records. Thirty and twenty years ago, when Mr. Celibidache was just one conductor among many, he was deemed vigorous (but not always: *The Record Year* in 1952 found his Mozart early G-minor Symphony "sleepy"), piquantly unpredictable, seldom dull, but an uneven stylist (his recording of Tchaikovsky's Fifth, for example, being "a very affected reading . . . full of exaggerated tempi and dynamics"). The Curtis concert revealed him to be a formidable orchestra trainer. The student playing was wonderfully exact and disciplined. There were pianissimi so soft that they fell below the ordinary fidget-and-rustle noise level of a filled hall. There was exquisite ensemble, meticulously tempered balance, phrasing polished to a phon and a microsecond. What one missed was any sense of musical impulse. Rossini's *Gazza ladra* overture was sedate—grotesquely so if one allowed a memory of Beecham or of Toscanini to cross one's mind. Debussy's *Iberia* was very carefully done—the colors applied with diacritical precision, the heady, precipitate gaiety of the score altogether absent. The *Tristan* Prelude and Liebestod emerged as an exercise in dynamics and sonorities which was perfectly executed. Prokofiev's rackety *Scythian Suite,* a coarse parergon to *The Rite of Spring,* had more vitality. How could it not, with all that banging and braying? Yet even here the players seemed more drilled, as if for a gym display, than personally exuberant. The evening was extraordinary for its demonstration of the instrumental excellence that seventeen rehearsals can achieve; its educational value, for listeners as well as players, was not in question.

Tuesday's concert, given by the Philadelphia Orchestra (forty-eight of whose members are Curtis graduates), conducted by Riccardo Muti, was full of grace. The main work was Bruckner's Fourth Symphony. The performance was fluent,

102

lyrical, admirably proportioned, and warmly played. It fell pleasingly on the ear. The symphony was preceded by Berlioz's cantata *The Death of Cleopatra*, the young composer's third unsuccessful shot at winning the Prix de Rome. *Cleopatra*, which has been recorded by Jennie Tourel, Janet Baker, Jessye Norman, and Yvonne Minton, is a stunning piece. In the accents of Berlioz's Dido but with more intricate emotions of grief, guilt, self-reproach, and wounded pride, the queen surveys her career and prepares to die nobly. At the Philadelphia concert, Miss Norman was the Cleopatra—regal, passionate, dignified, and poignant.

Simple superlatives can praise the concerts of the next three days, given by the Vienna Philharmonic, conducted by Leonard Bernstein. They offered the finest performances of Viennese symphonies I have heard in many, many years. They were concerts on the highest level one can hope to hear today. The programs were Haydn's Eighty-eighth and the Eroica; Mozart's late G-minor and Mahler's Fourth; the "Jupiter" and Brahms's Second. Although they came at the close of a seventeen-day, thirteen-concert American tour, there was no hint of fatigue or routine but, rather, a sense that orchestra and conductor were inspired to give the most profound and most beautiful performances of each work which they had ever given. In a dozen years here, I'd not heard orchestra playing at once so beautiful and so natural. The Berlin Philharmonic under Karajan has been sleeker and more patently amazing, and the Chicago Symphony under Solti has been louder and more brilliantly precise, but in their playing there was an element of display—apt to some scores, not to the Viennese classics—quite absent in the Vienna orchestra's performances. The Beethoven cycle that the Concertgebouw Orchestra under Bernard Haitink gave in Carnegie six years ago had much of this quality but not the extraordinary match of orchestral timbre and orchestral style to the works in question. Carnegie's February program book included an interview with Mr. Bernstein in which he expressed impatience with the notion of a particular conductor's or a particular orchestra's "sound": "I don't believe in *my* sound, or *Ormandy's* sound, or the *Chicago* sound, or the *Philadelphia* sound" and "I'm not interested in having an orchestra sound like *itself*. I want it to sound like the composer. That was my greatest pride with the New York Philharmonic—that they could switch on a dime, from Haydn, to Ravel, to Stravinsky, to Brahms, and it would always be stylistically right." But earlier in the interview he suggested reasons, technical and "not just mystical," that the orchestra of "the city of Beethoven, Brahms, Mozart, Haydn, and Mahler" should play their music more satisfyingly than any other orchestra does: "There's something about the tradition and the homogeneousness of that orchestra that makes a difference. The instruments in the string section are all matched, and the players all come from the same school—their grandparents played the same instruments in that orchestra."

Karajan to some extent internationalized the Berlin Philharmonic and turned it into the world's supreme virtuoso orchestra, adding suppleness to its solidity while maintaining the long, deep, firmly supported "breath"—of strings as well as winds—that has ever been its glory. The Vienna Philharmonic has been less colored by the introduction of foreign virtuosos with their different techniques and differently constructed instruments; its brass and its woodwinds sound different from those of other orchestras—especially the horns and the oboes. The blend, the cohesiveness, the absence of bite remain distinctively Viennese: the woodwinds are less keen and the brasses broader (and the tuba was rather too loose and plump of tone for my taste). The orchestra might not be able to switch on a dime from Brahms to Stravinsky, or perform, let's say, Elliott Carter's Symphony of Three Orchestras as well as the New York Philharmonic under Pierre Boulez did. (Maybe it could: in that interview, Bernstein claims that "with enough rehearsal, yes, one can make any great orchestra homogeneous in terms of whatever composer one is conducting.") I'm not sure that I'd want it as my only orchestra; after a week or so in Vienna I start to get itchy, find musical euphoria turning to restlessness, and feel that the place remains the complacent city that missed the point of Mozart, Schubert, Mahler, Schoenberg while they lived there. But its very conservatism, coupled with its wholehearted, if belated, devotion to past greatness, brings rewards; and these three days of concerts devoted to great music that lies at the center of Western civilization inspired nothing but gratitude and euphoria.

Mr. Bernstein has always been a conductor loving and giving. Sometimes in the past, he has been overenthusiastic and overemotional, wearing Mahler's, even Brahms's, heart on his sleeve, drawing out sentiment or whipping up excitement in his players in an almost unseemly way. But he has matured into a classical conductor probably unrivalled today—as warm, alert, and communicative as ever, but wiser and more disciplined. Great conductors—Weingartner, Furtwängler, Klemperer, Hamilton Harty, Albert Coates, Benjamin Britten—have often been composers. Mr. Bernstein has, as they had, a composer's instinctive grasp of why scores take the turns they do. The Haydn and the Mozart G-minor, done with reduced forces, were marvellously shapely; in the latter's Andante the sound of the Vienna strings and the loving way they laid entry upon entry brought tears of joy to listeners' eyes. The "Jupiter," done with a large orchestra, was grand but not heavy. The Eroica was noble; Tovey's phrase for the *poco andante* return of the theme in the finale, "like the opening of the gates of Paradise," was heard to be true. The performances were uneccentric. They were simply *right*. Just so should the horns sound the warm ray that lights the path into Brahms's D-major Symphony. Just so—with no more passionate intensity, for that would throw the movement off balance, but with no less—should the cellos play the *espressivo* melody at the start of the Adagio. Five of the six performances were confirmatory—fresh, joy-giving revelations of known glory, executed with energy, delight, beauty of sound and of phrasing, and an uncanny accord between conductor and players. Mahler's Fourth was more surprising. It has always been regarded as the sunniest, the least troubled, of his symphonies. Mr. Bernstein, largely by means of tempo transitions a shade less than easeful, of some stabbing accents and plangent timbres, made it a more disturbing work than usual. One recalled Mahler's observation. "Occasionally it darkens and becomes phantasmagorical and terrifying: not that the sky becomes overcast, for the sun continues to shine eternally, but that one suddenly takes fright; just as on the most beautiful day in a sunlit forest one can be seized with terror or panic." Mahler also said that when for reasons of musical logic he decided to alter a certain passage he found himself, to his amazement, transported from flowery

Elysian Fields to the icy gloom of Tartarus. Charm was not missing in Mr. Bernstein's performance. It seemed to compass—and to reconcile, memorably—both what Bruno Walter, smiling, and Klemperer, brooding, had discovered in the piece. A correspondent in the February issue of *Gramophone* asks "would it not be an interesting experiment to use a boy soprano" as soloist in the finale. Mr. Bernstein thought so, too, and in this performance he used a treble, young Alan Bergius, from the Tölz Boys Choir. (Master Bergius sings treble solos in the Telefunken series of Bach cantatas, and Amor in a recording of Gluck's *Orfeo* with Peter Hofmann as Orpheus.) As the last movement began, he rose up behind the orchestra, rather like Gottfried at the end of *Lohengrin*. He sang attractively, and Mr. Bernstein observed the Note to the Conductor set at the head of the finale: "It is of the highest importance that the singer should be accompanied with the *utmost* discretion." (Mahler uses the feminine form *Sängerin;* there is no evidence that he himself ever thought of a boy's voice here.) Mr. Bernstein said in that interview, "With a soprano, you don't get the low notes, and with a mezzo, you don't get the head tones. The only way you can get all of that is by using a boy." But this boy, at any rate from his station at the back of the platform, did not carry strongly enough. The delicate orchestral playing bore out the composer's declaration that the chief influence on his scoring in this symphony was that of Verdi. Mahler had conducted the Hamburg première of *Falstaff*, in 1894.

Karajan—in Helena Matheopoulos's fascinating book *Maestro*—says that a reason for the Berlin Philharmonic's and the Vienna Philharmonic's greatness is "that they give you what you want, but they also give you something more," and talks of rehearsing with an orchestra until "they carry *you* instead of you carrying them." Mr. Celibidache, for all his rehearsals, seemed not to have reached this point, and still to be, in Karajan's phrase, "conducting not music but notes and bar lines." In the three Vienna concerts, composers, conductor, and orchestra made one inseparable music.

The following Monday, WQXR broadcast a taped Boston Symphony concert including a performance of the Mahler Fourth, conducted by Seiji Ozawa, with Frederica von Stade, mezzo and soprano in one, as the soloist. It proved nothing, however, for Mr. Ozawa's account of the symphony was trivial, meaningless. Earlier that evening, the orchestra and Mr. Ozawa had appeared in Carnegie Hall. The concert began with Mozart's *Idomeneo* overture, in a performance that was firmly and pleasingly fashioned. Then Maurizio Pollini played Schoenberg's Piano Concerto—a problematic work, an early (1942) example, perhaps, of the "new romanticism." Neither Alfred Brendel (in the Deutsche Grammophon recording) nor Mr. Pollini seems to me to play it quite freely or lyrically enough. Schoenberg himself, in his essay "Heart and Brain in Music," cites the opening of the concerto as a melody in whose shaping "something like a human heart" was active. I've yet to hear it sound like the lilting waltz it is surely meant to be. The concert ended with Strauss's Symphonia Domestica, an orchestral showpiece that, despite some distinguished individual solo passages, showed the orchestra as a whole to be a rather strident, noisy, ill-blended band in climaxes. Although Mr. Ozawa is an efficient conductor, he often strikes me as a curiously empty one.

In the second circle of Hell, that abode of carnal sinners who subjected reason to lust, Dante encounters several operatic heroines and heroes: Semiramis, Dido, Cleopatra, Paris and Helen, Achilles, Tristan—and Francesca da Rimini and Paolo Malatesta, spirits who fly toward him, like a pair of doves, through the murky air. Francesca tells him her tale in lines so poignant and beautiful that the poet swoons—famous lines that a reader with any Italian at all still cannot read without emotion. (In 1300, the year of the *Comedy,* Francesca's husband and slayer, Giovanni Malatesta, was still alive; Caïna, in Hell's lowest circle, awaits him, she says. Dante spent his last years in Ravenna with Francesca's nephew.) D'Annunzio expanded the matter into a high-flown five-act tragedy for Eleonora Duse, which was first staged in Rome in 1901. Tito Ricordi acquired the operatic rights to the play for his protégé Riccardo Zandonai (D'Annunzio demanded, and received, twenty-five thousand lire, while the composer was paid three thousand for his score), and Zandonai's *Francesca da Rimini* first appeared in Turin in 1914. It reached Covent Garden later that year, and La Scala and the Met in 1916. In Italy, it has continued to be done from time to time. San Francisco presented it in 1956. Eve Queler conducted it in Carnegie Hall in 1973. The opera returned to the Met this month as the second of the centenary season's two new productions.

Francesca is one of the series of D'Annunzio operas which runs from Pizzetti's *Fedra* (1905), a noble work, through Franchetti's *La figlia di Jorio* (1906) and Mascagni's *Parisina* (1913), to Montemezzi's *La nave* (1918). They represent a postverismo, antiverismo movement toward a heroic, high-minded (and, all too often, highfalutin) new romanticism—a reaction against both Verdi's manly directness and Puccini's popular appeal. The symbolism of their librettos is chocolate-cream rich. The stage direction for the setting of Act III of *Francesca* (in which Wagner, Keats, Tennyson, Millais, and Oscar Wilde seem to combine) is characteristic. It reads, in part:

> There appears a room richly adorned, elegantly divided into panels bearing episodes of the romance of Tristan, amid birds, beasts, flowers, and fruits. Beneath the ceiling there runs, around the walls, a frieze in the form of festoons on which are inscribed some words from a love song:
>
> > *Melglio m'è dormire gaudendo*
> > *C'avere penzieri veghiando.*
>
> To the right, in the corner, is a bed, in an alcove concealed by rich curtains; to the left, an entrance covered by a heavy hanging; at the back, a tall window with many

panes, divided by little columns, that looks toward the Adriatic; there is a pot of basil on the window sill. Near the entrance, raised two feet above the ground, is a musicians' gallery whose compartments are adorned with delicate fretwork. Near the window is a lectern on which lies open the book of the History of Lancelot of the Lake, composed of large illuminated parchment pages constrained within the firm binding of two thin boards clad in vermilion velvet. Beside it there is a couch, a sort of chaise longue without back or arms, with many cushions of samite. . . .

The dialogue is similarly charged and clotted with allusive detail. Arthur Symons, who translated D'Annunzio's *Francesca,* observes in a preface to it that the poet "has learnt something from Wagner, not perhaps the best that Wagner has to teach, in his overamplification of detail, his insistence on so many things beside the essential things, his recapitulations into which he brought almost the actual Wagnerian 'motives.' " The composers of D'Annunzio operas had learned something from *Tristan* and something—whole-tone harmonies, indirectness, elusivity—from *Pelléas,* but none of them had Wagner's or Debussy's creative power. There is more music in Puccini's *Turandot* (1924), an aftermath of the crop, than in any of the D'Annunzio operas. *Fedra,* as I discovered at a 1959 Scala production, bears revival; it is large, dignified, colorful, and strongly made. The Franchetti, Mascagni, and Montemezzi operas seem, in vocal score, to be uninspired. Zandonai's *Francesca* has its admirers, but I am not among them. The mixture of Wardour Street medievalism (at the Met a stage musician in medieval costume plays a twentieth-century cello) and would-be passionate melody going through the motions of emotion has lost its savor. Ambitious construction, conscientious deployment of motifs, and careful scoring are no compensation for the absence of melodic phrases that bring characters to life. *Francesca* is an arty piece, historically interesting—but third-rate music.

The big dramatic sopranos, accomplished tragediennes, who used to sing Francesca—Rosa Raisa, Gina Cigna, Maria Caniglia—may have been able to persuade audiences otherwise. (The role combines traits of Isolde, Sieglinde, and Mélisande; lyrical and spinto sopranos—Louise Edvina at Covent Garden, Frances Alda at the Met, Raina Kabaivanska for Miss Queler—have also essayed it.) The new Met interpreter is Renata Scotto, in whose big dramatic assumptions there tends to be—for all her earnestness and endeavor—an element at best inappropriate and at worst somewhat absurd. What she did seemed calculated, mannered. She husbanded her voice and was less strident than usual, but she was unmoving. When Placido Domingo last sang Paolo here, for Miss Queler, he was monotonously loud; this time he was restrained, almost characterless. Cornell MacNeil's Giovanni was powerful but not always in tune. William Lewis turned the youngest brother, Malatestino, a vicious young firebrand, into a grotesque.

The director, Piero Faggioni, and the designer, Ezio Frigerio, observed some of but not all the stage directions. The topography of the Malatesta palace was hard to grasp, and the battle maneuvers of Act II were incomprehensible. It was an awkward staging, in giant, towering sets that dwarfed the principals. James Levine conducted as if he admired and loved the score; his advocacy was insistent, even in episodes where a light, charming touch might have been more

107

persuasive. The piece was done all but complete; Francesca's symbolic apostrophe to Greek fire, consuming and destroying whatever it touches, was, as usual, omitted.

Beaumarchais's third Figaro play, *La Mère coupable,* is a work often underrated. It appeared in 1792 (a few days after the first attack on the Tuileries)—seventeen years after *Le Barbier de Séville,* eight after *Le Mariage de Figaro,* and six after Mozart's *Le nozze di Figaro.* It is not a comedy but a daring essay in uniting the mechanics of comedy intrigue to *pathétique* action. The matter, Beaumarchais says in his preface, is "the inner griefs, dividing many a family, for which divorce, efficacious in other circumstances, provides no remedy . . . griefs that only paternal sentiment, goodness of heart, and forgiveness can cure." The scene is Paris in 1790, where the Count and Countess call themselves M. and Mme Almaviva, and their heir, Léon, is "a youth seized by the spirit of Liberty, like all ardent, new souls." Figaro is now "a man formed by experience of the world and by events," and Suzanne has "shed the illusions of youth." The play ends with forgiveness, reconciliation, and the betrothal of Léon, who has been revealed as the Countess's son by Chérubin (born while the Count was away governing Mexico), to Florestine, the Count's ward, who has been revealed as an illegitimate daughter of his and a Marquise Pizzarro. Beaumarchais suggests that in successive performances of *The Barber, Figaro's Marriage,* and *The Guilty Mother* the public can on the first day laugh at Count Almaviva's turbulent youth, on the second gaily observe the faults of his manhood, and on the third be persuaded that every man not irredeemably wicked becomes good when he grows old, "when the age of passions is past, and especially when he has tasted the sweet joy of being a father." William Mann, in *The Operas of Mozart,* says that this third play "was a total flop and deserved to be." But in 1792 the Paris public had other things to think about; when *La Mère coupable* was revived in Floréal of the Year 5 (otherwise May 1797) it was a great success, and Beaumarchais took the first curtain call of his life, delighted, he said, by applause not from aristocrats "the stupidest of whom thought himself superior" to a playwright but from "citizens who recognized no superiority but that accorded to merit or to talent, who wanted to see the author of a touching play."

La Mère coupable has its place in operatic history: Grétry considered an opera based on it, and so did Britten; Darius Milhaud composed one (which was performed in Geneva in 1965), and John Corigliano is composing, for the Met, *A Figaro for Antonia,* a "grand opera buffa" suggested by *La Mère coupable.* Daunting challenge, to complete a triptych whose other panels are by Rossini and by Mozart! In 1797, Beaumarchais declared that the two Spanish comedies had been written only as preparations for *La Mère coupable.* That's a view evidently determined by hindsight. What *La Mère coupable* seems to resolve is not so much *Le Mariage de Figaro* as *Le nozze di Figaro. Le Mariage* ends with a ten-strophe sung vaudeville. Suzanne observes that husbands' infidelities are condoned but wives' are punished; laws are made by men. The Countess remarks that whereas a proud woman might say she no longer loves her husband, and a less than truthful woman swear that she loves no one but him, a wise woman makes no avowal at all. Figaro reflects on Fate that causes one man to be born a king, another a shepherd, and sings Voltaire's praises. Chérubin once more apostrophizes the "beloved, volatile sex that torments us day and night." Suzanne draws a moral: that Nature in her wisdom achieves her ends by matching them to our desires. The stammering Brid'oison (Da Ponte's Don Curzio) tells the spectators that the comedy they have just seen reflects their own lives, and that all fi-fi-finishes in song. Ideas pass in rapid, brilliant review. There are strophes for Bazile and Marceline, and others (surviving in manuscript) for Bartholo and Franchette (Barbarina). Perhaps *La Mère coupable,* that mature, moving drama about guilt, remorse, and coming to terms with life, is already implicit here; but it springs more convincingly from *Le nozze di Figaro,* which has been well described as a transfiguration of *Le Mariage.* The Richardsonian truth in depiction of the human heart which Beaumarchais said was his aim in *La Mère coupable* already informs Mozart's setting of its predecessor. It is unlikely that Beaumarchais knew the opera before writing his third play; *Le nozze* was not done in Paris until 1793. Otherwise, one would be tempted to suggest that Mozart pointed the way to it.

Massenet's *Chérubin,* given its American première last month as the second presentation in Carnegie Hall's season of opéras comiques, is a quite different sequel to *Figaro.* The opera is based on a light, sentimental comedy by Francis de Croisset which Massenet saw at the Comédie-Française in 1901. Chérubin is preparing to celebrate his seventeenth birthday (so it is four years after *Le Mariage*). The Count and Countess and a Baron and Baroness have been invited. So has the dancer L'Ensoleillad, the king of Spain's favorite. All three women—and also Pepa, the mistress of a passing Captain, and Nina, a sweet country girl—set him aflutter. The heart of the opera is a touching love scene between him and the glamorous dancer, who is moved by the young man's ardor but is also realistic (rather like Zerbinetta in Strauss's *Ariadne*). All around, there is bright, busy comedy: rivalry between the women, jealousy on husbands' part. Act III finds Chérubin penning his will, in preparation for three duels. He leaves his fortune to L'Ensoleillad—"small reward for her kiss." The dancer returns to her royal protector. Chérubin's despair is lightened by a discovery that Nina, after all, is his true love. As the curtain falls, they embrace. Bystanders' comments add a dash of cynicism to the general sweetness: "There's Don Juan," "There's Elvira."

The opera was composed for Mary Garden, who created the title role in Monte Carlo in 1905 and, later that year, at the Opéra-Comique. In her memoirs, she is cool about the piece and cooler still about its composer. "But I enjoyed doing that little Chérubin of his, with his pranks and peccadilloes. . . . There was a certain dash and exuberance to the rôle." *Chérubin* had but fourteen Paris performances; productions in Antwerp, Brussels, Geneva, Magdeburg; no wide or long-lasting success. It is a soufflé calling for elaborate, expensive ingredients: a large cast of expert soloists, including three star sopranos (the title role is designated "soprano lyrique [petite Falcon]"; L'Ensoleillad, first played by the lovely Lina Cavalieri, simply "soprano"; and Nina "soprano de sentiment") and a notable "basse chantante ou baryton un peu grave" for the important role of the Philosopher, Chérubin's moral tutor. (Maurice Renaud sang it in Monte Carlo, Lucien Fugère in Paris.) Matthew Epstein, the artistic director of the Carnegie series, had obtained all these ingredients. To the title role Frederica von Stade brought the sparkle, the verve, the attractiveness that inform her account of Mozart's Cherubino. As in *La Périchole,* the first of the Carnegie opéras comiques, she was bewitching—in her timing, her phrasing, her sure sense of when to linger, where to invest a telling word with a new, telling color. Ashley Putnam was a L'Ensoleillad both glittering and romantic, even if at times she sang more loudly than needed. As Nina, Valerie Masterson made her New York opera début and perhaps for that reason was just a little too grand—more Countess than Barbarina—in her presentation. But she sang well. Samuel Ramey was a fine Philosopher. Judith Christin (the Baroness), Nico Castel (a Duke), and William Stone (the Count) were outstanding, and no one was weak. An anonymous orchestra played deftly. But Henry Lewis, conducting, laid a heavy hand on instrumental passages that should take wing.

Chérubin is a fluent and charming score, very skillfully composed—a pretty footnote to *Figaro.* It is not a neglected masterpiece; one would not urge its instatement in the repertory. But it was a pleasure to encounter it—especially in so polished a performance, with a troupe such as few regular companies could muster.

SHOWING A MYSTERY

April 2, 1984

BRITTEN's *Curlew River,* the first of his three "parables for church performance," is a small, powerful, and moving masterpiece. The fifteenth-century Noh play *Sumida River* underlies it. Britten saw the play in Tokyo in 1956, and for eight years, he said, the memory of it seldom left his mind. And he was moved to compose *Curlew River.* A woman driven mad by grief is ferried across the river, in search of her lost son; on the far bank she finds his tomb; the boy's spirit appears to her and comforts her. In Britten's version, which has a libretto by William Plomer, the river flows through the Fenland, and the actors are medieval monks presenting a mystery. They enter singing the compline hymn "Te lucis ante terminum." Their final amens dissolve the mode; a chamber organ sounds a long-sustained note cluster, and the Abbot, his phrases punctuated by the tapping of small drums, introduces the drama. The principal actors are ceremonially robed. The Ferryman's passengers assemble in his boat, singing the slow-flowing "river" motif. A Traveller joins them; his music, triadic melodies rising and falling over a trudging rhythm, sounds an echo of familiar Britten in a score that is mostly strange and new. Then, from afar, the cry of the curlew is heard, in the Madwoman's song—a rising tritone to the main note of the call, a glide off it to the fourth above. Mysterious low glissandos accompany the crossing of the river and the Ferryman's narrative about a boy who passed that way, slave to a brutal stranger who struck him and left him to die. Tension mounts, awaiting release in the woman's cry—the curlew call again—"He was

110

the child sought by this madwoman." An ensemble of prayer builds around the tomb, small tuned bells ringing through it; and suddenly the boy's voice is heard rising above it, sounding on when the other voices fall silent. It is a marvellous moment: somehow Britten has communicated to a twentieth-century audience the experience of being present at a miracle. The Abbot comes forward:

> Good souls, we have shown you here
> How in sad mischance
> A sign was given of God's grace....
> In hope, in peace, ends our mystery.

And "Te lucis ante terminum" returns as the recessional.

Curlew River is at once passionate and austere; freer, in point of harmony and of rhythmic patterns, than anything Britten composed before yet precisely controlled and formal; ritualistic yet emotional. The work appeared at a time when vanguard musicians were much concerned with "musical events"—not in the sense of the title this collection carries but as "notions" a few measures long, disparately set out, for performers to assemble at will in a composition that would be a different work each time it was played. (Sometimes composers would provide a few rules, such as "If you choose to start with B, then Y must follow.") In *Curlew River,* Britten broke music into its expressive elements, or "events": a motif, a cantilena, a drum rhythm, a chord. He gave greater play to individual executants' creative skills and fancies than he ever had before. (He also devised the "curlew" sign, ∞, to indicate a gathering point where individual rhapsodies must draw together; and it has passed into modern musical notation.) His wonderful musical mind, Mozart-like, perceived and seized on discoveries that were valuable, enriching, fruitful in the most vagrant experiments and explorations of his contemporaries, and he led them back into music's mainstream. (A study of Britten's use of twelve-note expressiveness needs writing.) *Curlew River,* which is unconducted, contains extraordinary passages of unmeasured ensemble—random polyphony. Other passages could be termed minimalist. Yet all its "events" are related to the hymn that opens and closes the opera. The whole is a rounded composition—new and strange, indeed, yet based firmly on plainchant, the foundation of Western music. "There is nothing specifically Japanese left in the Parable," Britten wrote in a short note on the piece. But surely there is: not only in the aspects of the sound world created by the instrumental ensemble (flute, viola, harp, horn, double-bass, percussion, and chamber organ) but also in the pacing of the drama—in the slow, tension-building spans, in the suddenness of revelation and release which is a feature of Noh. The tale follows its predestined course; there are no narrative surprises. Yet the shock of hearing the mother's cry "He was the child" does not diminish with repeated hearings (any more than does Oedipus' cry "All known! no more concealment!" after his dogged questioning of the Shepherd); nor does one's response to the boy's voice rising, radiant, from the tomb. In its formality, *Curlew River,* like *Sumida River,* communicates grief with an intensity that veristic drama can hardly achieve, and it brings the shine of the numinous into the presentation of a human plight.

The parable was first performed in 1964 in the church at Orford, beside the Alde, not far from Aldeburgh—a tall, spacious, airy building, large remainder of a once larger but unfinished fourteenth-century church. It is not one of Suffolk's spectacular glories—no Blythburgh, Lavenham, or Long Melford—but is gravely pleasing. When I visited it last, on a quiet, still evening, it seemed richly filled with remembered sounds: the ringing bugles and bright hand bells, the squeaks and shouts and happy singing of children in *Noye's Fludde,* precursor of the parables; the flute whirring, fluttering, looping around the song of the Mad-woman in *Curlew River;* the trombone's blaring of Babylonian splendor in *The Burning Fiery Furnace,* the second parable; the alto flute's telling of peaceful, diligent life in the fields and the trumpet's glittering lure to the heady delights of the city in *The Prodigal Son,* the third parable. The sense of place is always strong in Britten's music. Philip Brett's monograph on *Peter Grimes* begins well with E. M. Forster's evocations of Aldeburgh: "Crabbe without Aldeburgh, Peter Grimes without the estuary of the Alde, would lose their savour and tang." Suffolk seas and skies sound in the opera. More tangibly, more analyzably, Orford Church has left its mark on the scores of the parables: in its open, resonant acoustics, the echoes make sung melodies self-harmonizing, and Britten has reinforced the effect with his use of cluster-chord accompaniments built from the sung notes. The special sound of the parables in Orford—the space, the distances, the echoes, the way individual voices stand out in turn as processions pass the listener, the slow move of the action from right to left as the river is crossed—has been captured with astonishing success in three Decca recordings made there.

There are tall churches in New York with columned aisles, shadowy side chapels, and resonant acoustics which would house *Curlew River* well. Madison Avenue Presbyterian Church, where the Chamber Opera Theatre of New York played six performances of the piece, proves not quite the right place for it. Built in 1899 (but later altered), compact, galleried, unmysterious, it has neither the atmosphere nor the resonances of a medieval church. (St. Paul's Cathedral, in London, proved acoustically admirable for the parables, although visually unsuitable; here the Church of St. Paul the Apostle, on Columbus Avenue, might be a fine setting.) There were two excellent performers. Andrea Velis, who has been associated with the (tenor) role of the Madwoman for nearly twenty years, sang and acted it subtly and clearly, with a sure command of timbre, timing, and poignant formalized gesture. Randolph Messing, the Ferryman, has a bold stage presence and a bold, strong baritone. He did not force but molded his musical lines to the words and phrased cogently; he also listened intently. The others tended to sacrifice line, subtlety, steadiness of tone, and the sense of the words to mere loudness. The chanting was heavy, unflowing, unshaped. The flute, the viola, and the horn (Patricia Spencer, Martin Andersen, and Lucinda Lewis) were eloquent players.

As in every Chamber Opera Theatre production I have seen, talent and achievement were mingled with imprecision in the directing. I always hope to write with unclouded enthusiasm about the work of this company. Its aim is admirable, its repertory adventurous. There is nothing pinchpenny about the stagings. (*Ormindo,* two years ago, was a swagger show, even if queen and courtiers walked barefoot beneath their glamorous costumes.) And New York does need a first-rate chamber-opera troupe. But something seems to go slightly wrong, whether it's Cavalli-Leppard, Thea Musgrave, Menotti, or Britten that is essayed. The interpretations have been in varying ways off-key, obtuse, untrue to the creators' intentions. Points have been missed or misunderstood. In this *Curlew River,* it was a mistake, I think, to reintroduce Japanese references (in the costumes of Madwoman, Traveller, and Ferryman) that Britten and Plomer deliberately avoided; a mistake, I think, to invest the chorus of medieval monks with helmets, half masks, and chasubles of shiny white plastic. But they would not have been "mistakes" had the production as a whole been convincing. The director, Thaddeus Motyka, and the designer, Beni Montresor, had evidently thought out the drama afresh, and they were right to do so: Britten's operas have grown from local, particular sources to be enjoyed the world over, and they can be illumined by many different interpretations. The published score of *Curlew River* includes a detailed *disposizione scenica* by its first director, Colin Graham. Following it minutely, a director can hardly go wrong. Deliberately departing from it—as inspired Verdi directors have departed, with high success, from the authorized *disposizioni sceniche* published for Verdi's operas—an inspired director can add new insights. But in the Chamber Opera Theatre interpretation something essential to *Curlew River* was lost. The basic mistake, I think, was to let the performers play as if on a narrow, self-contained stage behind footlights: without full cognizance of the audience/congregation, without regarding the whole church as the setting, and without directing their voices so as to make every corner of the place—now here, now there—vibrant with sound. *Curlew River* is a play, but it is a miracle play, and even to an infidel it becomes more dramatic when it is performed as one. (Similarly, performances of the Matthew and John Passions prove overwhelming if, at least while they last, they contrive to fill renegades and infidels with Christian emotion.) Here the "parable for church performance" was treated as just another opera—theatrically—and as a result it was less operatic, less theatrical than usual. But Mr. Velis, Mr. Messing, and the instrumentalists seemed to be instinctively in tune with Britten's work, and in their contributions *Curlew River* was brought to life.

Pageant

April 9, 1984

Tamino, in *The Magic Flute,* enters a grove where stand three temples, bearing inscriptions to Wisdom, to Reason, and to Nature, and declares the place an abode of sagacity, industry, and the arts. These peaceable virtues and pursuits— and also the joys of wedded love—are hymned in *Solomon,* Handel's glowing triptych of a Golden Age. Act I pictures the dedication of Solomon's Temple—a scene of national industry and piety crowned by God's approval. It recalls the

113

celebrations that open *The Trojans at Carthage*. Then Solomon turns to his Queen and promises that his next building will be a splendid palace. She sings simply and radiantly of her love for him, with a candor that Victorian editors bowdlerized. They retire to the cedar grove, and the choir sings the Nightingale Chorus, "May no rash intruder," which is perhaps the loveliest chorus ever composed. The long, enchanted love scene may also bring *The Trojans* to mind, although Handel's delicate, rapturous idyll does not have the sultry, tragic overtones of Berlioz's garden scene. In Act II we see the wise laws of this happy state in operation, and justice is acclaimed. The plaint of the first woman, the true mother of the disputed child, is interrupted by a spiteful interjection from the second woman which cuts into the cadence and perverts the tonality. Solomon's calm "Justice holds the lifted scale" restores order. As the three pursue their own themes, the air becomes one of the earliest dramatic trios. Solomon sends for a falchion to divide the babe: the second woman sings a flashing, triumphant air, and the mother a deeply moving air in which she resigns her child so that his life may be spared. Solomon pronounces his judgment; the mother's final air, "Beneath the vine, or fig-tree's shade," is verbally irrelevant, but its lulling rhythms and drone basses seem at once to depict her cradling the child in her arms, gently rocking him while she pictures his growing up, and to afford a glimpse of the monarch's enlightened rule spreading from the magnificent capital to bring contentment through all the countryside. In Act III, the Queen of Sheba pays a state visit to Jerusalem, inspects the sights, and is entertained by a command performance, at which music's powers to lull, stir to action, tear at the emotions, and then calm are demonstrated. Rightly, the Queen admires the performance: "Thy harmony's divine, great king."

Georgian England may have been the starting point for this Triumph of Peace, but it is not occasional music. As Winton Dean has said, Handel in his last oratorios moves toward transcendence and "begins, perhaps unconsciously, to give a firmer expression to his personal beliefs." *Theodora* deals with pleasure, virtue, and a conflict of moral codes. *Jephtha* makes final, shattering statements on man and destiny. *Solomon*, their predecessor, is a vision of what a world well governed might be, and is warm with Handel's benevolence, his delight in nature, and his joy in generous, apparently effortless creation. (In fact, sketches survive that show the pains he took with the precise shaping of some melodies.) *Solomon* is one of the glories of English music. It covers an enormous range: the textures vary from massy splendor (several of the choruses are in eight parts) to the lightest tracery; the orchestration is rich. Musica Sacra, conducted by Richard Westenburg, performed it complete last month, in Avery Fisher Hall—the first complete performance, perhaps, since the three Handel gave in 1749. The oratorio seemed not at all long. Although Dean talks of "a certain amount of dead wood" and advises the pruning out of seven airs and one chorus, there was nothing one heard with impatience or would willingly have lost. Mr. Westenburg reversed the positions of the last two choruses. "Praise the Lord with harp and tongue!" is a grand, extended affair, and a more obviously effective finale, but Handel's earlier placing of it and his brisk signing off with "The name of the wicked shall quickly be past" is surely a deliberate artistic effect—unconventional, and worth trying.

The principal parts were written for two prima donnas Handel had trained. The mezzo Caterina Galli, who specialized in male roles, was the first Solomon. (Joseph, Othniel in *Joshua*, Alexander Balus, Joacim in *Susanna* were other parts she took.) The soprano Giulia Frasi had the wonderful triple role of the two queens and the mother. (Susanna, Theodora, Iphis in *Jephtha* were other parts Handel composed for her.) Kathleen Battle, the Musica Sacra soprano, yielded the central panel to another singer, and that was a pity: it lessened the emotional range Handel had devised, and, moreover, Miss Battle's singing of the two queens was so exquisitely beautiful and distinguished that one wanted to hear as much of her as possible. To put it simply: I thought her account of the Queen of Sheba's "Will the sun forget to streak Eastern skies with amber ray" the most ravishing performance of a Handel air I have ever heard. Throughout the evening, her timbre was clear, pure, and lovely. She felt the words, and she felt the phrases: her inflections were subtle and charming; there was wit in her delivery, piquancy in her well-chosen variations. She held one intent on each turn of each line. Miss Battle came to notice at a Brahms Requiem in Spoleto twelve years ago; at the Met five years later her Shepherd in *Tannhäuser* was delightful. But her more recent stage appearances, a shade pert and overbright—and her Despina in the Salzburg recording of *Così*—had hardly prepared one for this Handelian perfection. A Tully Hall lieder recital last month, given jointly with Florence Quivar, had: there, too, Miss Battle's tones were flowing, steady, and unforced, newly full and lyrical; her words were alive (in Purcell, arie antiche, Strauss's Brentano songs); and her presentation was at once candid, poised, and keen. She has matured into not just one of our better singers but one of the very best: a soprano whose sweet, sure voice—now smooth, now sparkling—and whose feeling for line, words, and musical character set one reaching back toward comparisons with Alma Gluck and Elisabeth Schumann.

To choose a countertenor for the mezzo title role was curious: one might as aptly—as inaptly—cast a countertenor as Cherubino or Octavian. Singing mezzo roles is one of the things that women—at any rate since gelding for art's sake was abandoned—do better than men, on the whole. James Bowman, the Musica Sacra Solomon, was steady, and he was precisely in tune; he has a good sense of rhythm and of stylish articulation. But the sounds he made fell unpleasingly on the ear: notes around treble C were sometimes shrieked and sometimes just faintly touched in. Janice Dixon, the mother, had a ripe timbre but one too vibrant for Handel. Susan von Reichenbach, the false claimant, was spiky, but that could be deemed not inappropriate. Carroll Freeman (Zadok, the High Priest) and John Cheek (a Levite) phrased squarely, dully, and showed no command of dramatic recitative. The Musica Sacra chorus, thirty-six strong, was in fine form—precise, clear, and deft. The band of thirty-eight instrumentalists was alert; Jerry Grossman was a supple continuo cellist. Mr. Westenburg directed from the harpsichord, sometimes with a nod and a wave, sometimes standing up to point the choral entries while the keyboard continuo passed to a chamber organ. His tempi were often brisk—convincingly so. There was no plodding, but

115

there were some unwanted gaps between movements. The recitatives were generally too slow, with delayed instrumental cadences that functioned as full stops, not as colons springboarding the sense into the following statement. The director's feeling for both the whole huge work and its marvellous details made the passing criticisms unimportant. This complete *Solomon* was a high point in New York's musical season. The lights in the hall were kept on, which not only allowed listeners to follow the libretto (printed in the program book) but added a sense of brightness and immediacy to the work and its performance.

In Carnegie Hall, the proud parade of visiting orchestras—this season, it seems, richer than ever—continues. After the Vienna Philharmonic, the Czech Philharmonic. I heard the first of its three concerts, which was devoted to Dvořák: the Carnival overture, the Cello Concerto, and the Seventh Symphony. It was slightly disappointing. Václav Neumann is a rather tight, dry conductor, and he seemed to have drained off some of the warmth of tone and the easy (though not undisciplined) charm of phrasing for which the Czech Philharmonic has long been famous. The strings sounded somewhat thin. To the concerto Mr. Neumann and Nathaniel Rosen, the American soloist, brought different approaches: the conductor was strict and the cellist wayward, even sloppily rhapsodic. The result was incoherent. In the D-minor Symphony, a stern, tragic composition, which Tovey had "no hesitation in setting ... along with the C major Symphony of Schubert and the four symphonies of Brahms, as among the greatest and purest examples in this art-form since Beethoven," Mr. Neumann stressed formal logic, at the expense of emotion. Eloquent woodwind soloists and a happily blended woodwind chorus provided the more striking moments of the evening. An encore, Dvořák's First Slavonic Dance, was played both subtly and joyfully.

Next came the Houston Symphony, conducted by Sergiu Comissiona, which brought with it a work new to New York, Paul Cooper's fifth symphony (1983), entitled Symphony in Two Movements. Like the other Cooper pieces I've heard—the Fourth Symphony, the Fifth and Sixth String Quartets, all recorded on CRI—it is an agreeable, thoroughly listenable composition, soundly constructed and attractively scored. There were passages whose timbres and texture brought the Ritual Dances in Tippett's *Midsummer Marriage* to mind. The concert closed with Tchaikovsky's First Symphony, "Winter Daydreams," which was given an elegantly understated reading, well matched to its mild melancholy. The Houston Symphony is a refined and accomplished orchestra.

I didn't hear the Orchestre National de France, conducted by Lorin Maazel, which played two concerts with a Rachmaninoff symphony in each, or the New Orleans Philharmonic, conducted by Philippe Entremont, which played Shostakovich's Ninth. The next visitors were the Rochester Philharmonic, conducted by David Zinman. They played Elgar's First Symphony. As someone who grew up with Elgar's Enigma Variations, *Dream of Gerontius*, and Introduction and Allegro in his ears, who shouted "Ecce Sacerdos Magnus" on high days at the local cathedral and piped "As Torrents in Summer" in prep-school singing class, who later got to learn and to love *Falstaff* and the Cello Concerto and even *Caractacus*—in short, as an enthusiast for about three-quarters of what Elgar composed, I'm bothered, and have been for years, by an inability to connect securely with the First Symphony. Musicians I admire acclaim it, and its appeal is not only to British ears: Solti, Daniel Barenboim, and Bernard Haitink have recorded it. I keep on trying—most recently, at the Rochester concert. Mr. Zinman has been championing Elgar in Rochester—with the Enigma, the Introduction and Allegro, the Serenade, *Falstaff*, and now the First Symphony. The Carnegie performance was trim and definite. The orchestral playing was clear-cut, not expansive; there was no rich string portamento of the kind the composer expected. This is the modern way with Elgar: I see that a British colleague approves Haitink's record highly because "several apotheoses are pushed towards their conclusion with something approaching impatience," the sound is "much leaner and harder-edged" than usual, and "the musical structure, the totally convincing symphonism, becomes paramount." I continue to find the themes beautiful and their assemblage, with much sequential linkage, less than cogent; "the passionate culmination of his long early struggle, the fullest of all his triumphs ... Elgar's supreme masterpiece" (phrases from another record review) still eludes me. The Rochester Philharmonic was impressive—a well-tuned and well-balanced orchestra, lively in tone, vigilant, never blatant. Only the harps sounded tinkly and tinny, unblended into the general ensemble.

Two earlier Carnegie concerts deserve a belated note. London's Philharmonia Orchestra gave an ample, well-shaped performance of Sibelius's Second Symphony, with Vladimir Ashkenazy as conductor. This was my first encounter with him in that role, and he was impressive. In the first half of the concert, he was both pianist and conductor, in Beethoven's Second Concerto, of which he gave a modest, gentle, and pleasing performance—but gentle almost to the point of being soft-edged.

The Cincinnati Symphony, conducted by Michael Gielen, brought Jonathan Kramer's *Moments in and out of Time* to Carnegie Hall four days after its Cincinnati première. It is one of seven large-scale pieces commissioned, from the seven faculty composers of the University of Cincinnati, by WGUC—a radio station that takes broadcasting seriously—to celebrate its twentieth anniversary. Kramer had the curious idea of using only six of Western music's twelve notes: a gapped hexatonic scale, C, D-sharp, E, F-sharp, G, B, C (comprising the triads of C major and B major—but that's not the way the music sounds). In a program note, he writes, "I chose to limit my material in this way to create a hypnotic stasis, a celebration of each moment as an unchanging eternity.... The piece moves and stands still *simultaneously*." The work was interesting for a while; there were ostinatos, chords with fragments of melody darting through them from one part of the orchestra to another, passages of very densely woven counterpoint. But it lasted a good half-hour, and that seemed too long. I missed the central work in the program, Berlioz's *Nuits d'Eté*, with Maria Ewing as the soloist, in order to slip into Carnegie Recital Hall and hear some new music there, but returned in time for the orchestral "suite" from Berlioz's *Romeo and Juliet*. Mr. Gielen is a sterling conductor, renowned for his command of large, difficult contemporary compositions—such works as Zimmermann's *Die Sol-daten* and Nono's *Al gran sole carico d'amore*. There is a Vox record of the

Eroica, made with the Cincinnati Symphony, which shows that he can also be a stirring conductor of classical music. The symphony receives a pure, strong, precise performance, held strictly to tempo. It is hard to define why a conductor like Mr. Neumann should seem "tight" and "dry," while another, no less strict, can ignite new, excited responses to a familiar work. Perhaps it is the intellectual energy in Mr. Gielen's approach that makes the difference—that and the energetic, precisely balanced, rhythmically taut playing he obtains. The *Romeo* excerpts weren't exactly memorable. Romance, sensuality, and abandon were absent. But in a lucid, rational way they were colorful and satisfying.

At all Carnegie concerts this season, even the Vienna Philharmonic's, I've regretted the newfangled orchestral seating plan, with the high strings grouped on the left and the lower strings grouped on the right. It probably sounds good to the conductor, who still has everyone facing him. But out in the hall the balance becomes lopsided and unblended. The audience that left the Vienna Philharmonic concerts was handed a brochure illustrating the orchestra in its home hall, the Musikvereinssaal, and in the traditional romantic formation: cellists playing out to the audience; double-bassists in a long row at the back, spanning the platform from side to side, providing a full central foundation and also playing out into the hall, not into the opposite wing. (An early photograph of the hall, in the "Vienna" entry of the New Grove, shows the double-basses similarly positioned.) I suppose there's a good reason for the modern disposition, else it would not have been so widely adopted. I've yet to hear it convincingly expounded. I'm old enough to remember the richer, warmer, fuller orchestral sound that came from the old, balanced seating plan.

For a March concert with the New York Philharmonic, in Avery Fisher Hall, Leonard Bernstein reseated the orchestra (which usually plays on a flat floor) on risers—as the Vienna Philharmonic sits in Vienna, though it didn't in Carnegie. I like risers: I have a feeling that if there is a direct sightline from the listener to, say, a solo oboe there may also be a direct acoustic line that makes the solo more vivid. It is possibly an acoustic illusion: at the Vienna Philharmonic concerts in Carnegie nothing was visible to listeners on the main floor but a solid bastion of strings, yet the woodwinds were clearly audible, and probably the effect differs from hall to hall. In Fisher Hall, the new eminence of the Philharmonic brass made them seem even more raucous than usual; and Mr. Bernstein did not observe the fourth and sixth of Richard Strauss's Ten Golden Rules for a conductor: "Never look encouragingly at the brass" and "If you think that the brass are not playing loud enough, damp them down two degrees." The program celebrated—rather earlier than Nature did—the arrival of spring, with Copland's *Appalachian Spring*, Schumann's "Spring" Symphony, and Stravinsky's *Rite of Spring*. After the *Rite*, one felt like echoing Stravinsky's terse comment on an earlier Bernstein performance of the piece: "Wow!" The Copland, insofar as it could be heard above the Philharmonic audience's foot-shuffling on Cyril Harris's resonant floor, danced along attractively. (The suggestion I once made that people should enter Fisher Hall as they would a Japanese temple or a Bavarian palace, having doffed shoes or donned felt overslippers, was not flippant; the audience noise both at *Solomon* and at this concert was such as to disturb the attention, again and again, of any serious listener.) The Philharmonic welcomed Mr. Bernstein with playing more exuberant and more ardent than usual, and he was in exuberant form. The Schumann was broadly laid out, but the sound of the orchestra was robust, not rounded, and the great new Bernstein who had conducted the Vienna Philharmonic became at times the old Bernstein whose enthusiasms overflowed.

THE TIDE OF POMP

April 16, 1984

IT is hard to assess *Dom Sébastien,* Donizetti's last and largest opera—first performed at the Opéra in 1843, and revived last month in Carnegie Hall by the Opera Orchestra of New York—without having seen it in the theatre. One calls it "Donizetti's" opera, but during its troubled genesis the musical structures he planned were mutilated both for the sake of the staging and at the behest of the singers. The baritone's barcarolle was cut by half, because the prima donna—Rosine Stoltz, *favorite* of the Opéra director, Léon Pillet—flatly refused to remain onstage, as the plot requires, and listen to all of it. An adagio from the Act III finale was shifted to Act IV, "reducing my finale to mere chatter," Donizetti said—"my third-act finale ruined because M. Scribe stubbornly insists that the scenic effect will gain." Donizetti himself initiated changes: among the Scribe papers in Paris I discovered an affidavit to the effect that the composer had rewritten the baritone's principal air, "O Lisbonne," between the dress rehearsal and the first night, and had required the poet to invent new lines to music already composed. (The next day, I found the original air—a beautiful piece—in the baritone's partbook, which survives in the Opéra library.) Donizetti went on making revisions during the Paris run, and made more for the Vienna première of the opera, in 1845. Arias come and go. Ensembles are rewritten. No two editions of the score coincide. In a preface to the libretto distributed at the Carnegie performance, Donizetti's biographer William Ashbrook tabled four differing versions of the opera (two French, one Viennese, one Italian), and could have added more: the work "as first composed," including the numbers that were dropped or replaced during the rehearsals and have never been performed or published but are recoverable from the Paris material; an Italian version put together by the Scala conductor Giacomo Panizza for the very successful Scala première of the piece, in 1847; Emanuele Muzio's attempt to straighten out—with the help of stray Donizetti pages from Vienna and elsewhere—the botch that he declared Panizza had committed. "It's a devil of a job," Muzio wrote in a letter; and preparing a critical score of *Dom Sébastien* would indeed make editing even such intricate pieces as Verdi's *Don Carlos* or Bernstein's *Candide* seem like child's play. There can be no "definitive" edition; in any case, the notion is inapplicable to operas of the period, which, like modern musicals, were altered during rehearsals, runs, and revivals to match most effectively the abilities of particular casts and the expectations of particular audiences. Some changes are forced on the composer against his will; others he himself effects or approves; still others represent his attempt to heal the wounds inflicted by cuts. (Some noble passages in the revised *Don Carlos* fall into that category.) What one needs is a critical score containing *all* the possibilities, with a clear account of what was done where, when, and—insofar as the evidence survives—why. Scores of this kind are now being prepared for Rossini's and Verdi's operas.

Is *Dom Sébastien* worth the labor? In these pages nine years ago, I called it "probably Donizetti's best *grand opéra*." Mr. Ashbrook said in his preface, "There is small room to doubt that *Dom Sébastien* is the most considerable achievement of Donizetti's busy career." But, after the Carnegie performance, I feel that we both somewhat overrated it. Julian Budden, in the New Grove, notes rightly that *Dom Sébastien* is the most patently Meyerbeerian of Donizetti's *grands opéras*. Of the three he completed, it was the only one planned as a *grand opéra* from the start. (*Les Martyrs* was an expansion of the shining, beautiful *Poliuto,* which had been banned by the Naples censors when it was already in rehearsal there, and *La Favorite* is an expansion of *L'Ange de Nisida,* which had been composed for the Théâtre de la Renaissance and shelved when that theatre went bankrupt.) Scribe's libretto—one learns, with some surprise, from Meyerbeer's diary—was originally meant for Mendelssohn. (Paris had hoped to be amused by seeing Mendelssohn and Meyerbeer locked in rivalry at the Opéra.) Meyerbeer got hold of it and said that at a first glance it seemed good but at a second glance too heavy by half. It went to Donizetti only when Meyerbeer, early in 1843, withheld once again the *Prophète* he had been working on since 1836, and Pillet commissioned Donizetti to provide the new work the Opéra needed. Meyerbeer eventually took thirteen years over *Le Prophète* and twenty-seven—ended only by his death—over *L'Africaine.* Donizetti was allowed a bare six months in which to produce *Dom Sébastien.*

The opera crowns those extraordinary years when, as if in a desperate attempt to numb his grief over the death of his beloved young wife, Virginia, he embarked on a round of creative activity which even for one who had ever been swift and industrious was prodigious. In 1837, the couple had moved into a new house, and life seemed smiling; but there Virginia gave birth to a stillborn son, and died herself six weeks later. Donizetti's letters are poignant: "This morning I gave away the new cradle. . . . Without father, without mother, without wife, without children, whom do I work for then? And why?" The following year, he left Naples for Paris. There, in 1839, he composed *Les Martyrs, L'Ange de Nisida, La Fille du régiment,* and a new version of *Lucia,* and began *Le Duc d'Albe.* He became Imperial Kapellmeister in Vienna. Without slackening pace as a composer, he found time to direct the Italian and Viennese premières of Rossini's Stabat Mater and to help introduce Verdi's *Nabucco* and *Ernani* to Vienna. The tally of his labors still grows: last week the young American scholar Will Crutchfield turned up in Covent Garden's basement Donizetti's previously unknown 1840 *rifacimento* of his 1827 *Otto mesi in due ore*—apt title! His last year of full activity, 1843, began with the première of *Don Pasquale,* at the Théâtre-Italien. Then he composed *Maria di Rohan* for Vienna, *Caterina*

Cornaro for Naples, and *Dom Sébastien* for the Opéra, and revised *Maria di Rohan* for the Théâtre-Italien. At *Dom Sébastien* rehearsals, a physical and mental deterioration—caused by the onset of tertiary syphilis—became apparent. (At the time, some thought suffering over what was being done to the piece had driven him mad.) He was not committed to an asylum until early in 1846, but after *Dom Sébastien* he composed little save revisions of that opera and a new finale for *Caterina Cornaro.* Swiftness of composition did not necessarily affect quality: *Don Pasquale, Maria di Rohan,* and *Caterina Cornaro* are excellent operas. *Dom Sébastien* is rather different. It is tempting, but probably unscientific, to view it along with other newly ambitious late masterpieces—final efflorescences, some but not all of them flawed, some left unfinished—that stricken composers, in prepenicillin days, produced at what was possibly literal as well as metaphorical fever heat: such works as Schubert's amazing Tenth Symphony, Schumann's underrated Mass and Requiem, Smetana's *The Devil's Wall* and Second String Quartet, Hugo Wolf's Michelangelo settings and scenes for *Manuel Venegas.* But it is simpler to conclude that a magnificent, visionary opera was compromised by Opéra exigences.

The libretto has plenty of Opéra spectacle. Act I shows the embarkation of a great armada. In Act II, a lush African oasis is followed by a desert battlefield, lone and level sands stretching far away. Act III contains—according to the version—either an immense funeral procession (in which, at the Opéra, six hundred performers took part) or a splendid coronation scene. Act IV is set in subterranean vaults where masked inquisitors gather and the flicker of torches and braziers reveals torturers and their instruments. In Act V, there is a final coup de théâtre; the tenor, with the soprano in his arms, attempts to escape from a high tower by means of a rope ladder, but a marksman's bullet severs the rope, and the pair tumble down into the sea. (In the Archives Nationales I found a sketch of the machinery needed.) Donizetti's music for the large chorus or solo-plus-chorus set pieces is grand but a little contrived; there is a certain stiffness of invention and shortness of musical breath. It is not for grandeur, however, that one loves Donizetti. His response to the personal scenes is more characteristic: Zaida, restored in honor to her native land, thinks of the Christian king who rescued her from the Inquisition's stake but has now come to make war on her people; Sebastian, defeated, alone on that desert battlefield, gazes bleakly at the future (to save his life, Zaida has promised her hand to a Moorish chieftain); in the great square of Lisbon, one tattered veteran begs alms of another—Sebastian and Camoëns, who had set out so bravely in Act I, meet again. *Dom Sébastien* is essentially a sad opera punctuated by scenes of extravagant spectacle. To what extent they are "effects without causes" only a stage production will show; Scribe does seem to have planned dramatic contrasts with some care. Yet it is perhaps significant that, while the huge Paris production was a success (despite such critical sneers as "a funeral ceremony in five acts"), the trimmer Vienna and Scala productions were triumphs.

Eve Queler, the conductor of the Opera Orchestra, who had already set us in her debt by revivals of *La Favorite* and *Le Duc d'Albe* (in Matteo Salvi's Italian completion), presented *Dom Sébastien* in an edition based on that of the Paris première. The displaced adagio, however, was duly returned to its original

121

position, and the third-act finale was further enriched by a bass solo that Donizetti added later. The ballet music was omitted. It was good to hear the opera (the previous New York performance seems to have been in 1864), even if the high expectations one had of it were—well, less than decisively fulfilled. The cast was hardly on Miss Queler's usual level. Klára Takács, the prima donna (Zaida), was often unsteady, out of tune, and strained of timbre. Lajos Miller, the baritone (Camoëns), and Sergej Koptchak, the bass (the Grand Inquisitor), were monotonously loud. Richard Leech, the tenor (Sebastian), brought more light and shade to his singing, but his high C's and D-flat from the chest—a specialty of Gilbert Duprez, who created the role—did not fall pleasantly on the ear. (Rossini likened Duprez's *ut de poitrine* to "the squawk of a capon having its throat cut.") Miss Queler, as if not quite confident in the piece, as if afraid of losing our attention, tended to push things along too insistently; to allow the music too little room to breathe and expand; to let her singers attempt conquest by force, not subtlety. A bigger, broader, more relaxed and various approach— such as she used in *Rienzi,* two years ago—would have made *Dom Sébastien* more exciting.

Dvořák's *Dimitrij,* the sixth of his ten operas, also sets textual problems for anyone who would perform it. The composer made minor changes and cuts after the première, in 1882; recomposed the last act in 1883, altering the dénouement; added a prelude and a beautiful tenor aria to Act III in 1885; and then subjected the work to a thoroughgoing—and commentators tell us, regrettable—revision in 1894. In 1906, the conductor Karel Kovařovic, the opera director at Prague's National Theatre from 1900 to 1920, and a committed "improver" (Janáček's *Jenůfa* has only recently been de-Kovařoviced), brought out a new version of *Dimitrij,* based on the 1882–85 scores but with passages of 1894 inserted, with vocal lines rewritten, and with many cuts. A 1941 vocal score edited by Otakar Šourek threads some of this maze, but the performing material that Dvořák's publishers supply is still the Kovařovic version. When the Nottingham University Opera Group, for the British première of *Dimitrij,* in 1979, sought to reinstate an 1882 or 1885 score, it could do so only in part, by the recovery (after burrowing in Czech theatre archives) of some of the passages Kovařovic cut. At the American première of *Dimitrij,* given in Carnegie Hall last month by the Collegiate Chorale, there were two large, clean cuts (the finale of Act II, which recalls a scene in *Ernani* as Shuisky and conspirators, in Ivan the Terrible's mausoleum, are surprised by Dimitri; and the 1885 Act III prelude and aria mentioned above) and several smaller snips. The opera was sung in the English translation John Tyrrell made for Nottingham. A libretto was distributed.

The Dvořák operas I have seen in the theatre—*The Cunning Peasant, Kate and the Devil, Rusalka* in several productions—hold the stage well. (*Kate,* I'm sure, could be a hit at the City Opera.) There is something so heartwarming about the flow of music and the way it is scored that the occasional dramaturgical clumsiness seems unimportant. I'd tend to mistrust anyone not moved by Dvořák's concord of sweet sounds. The Nottingham *Dimitrij* was greeted with enthusiasm, and so was the Collegiate Chorale performance. The opera is a sequel to Mussorgsky's *Boris Godunov.* Boris has died, and the false Dimitri claims the throne. Marfa, Ivan the Terrible's widow, professes—for complicated but honorable reasons—to recognize in him her son. Shuisky denounces him. By chance, Dimitri meets Xenia, Boris's daughter, and they fall in love. There has been trouble between him and Princess Marina: he criticized the dress she wore at their wedding, and he deplores her attempt to Polonize the Russians. There is a tense encounter between the two women. In the 1882 version, Xenia is killed; in 1883, she takes the veil. Marina denounces Dimitri as an impostor. Marfa is appealed to again—to swear, this time on the cross, that the Pretender is indeed her son. Dimitri, his life at stake, nobly tells her not to perjure herself; and Shuisky shoots him. It's a big opera, with many big chorus and double-chorus scenes—apt choice for presentation by a choral group—but its special glory is a series of lyrical duets filled with beautiful, shapely, unconventional melodies.

Dimitri is a long, taxing role. It was well taken by the young heroic tenor Cornelius Sullivan, who is very promising. He has a Slezak-like physique that supports a strong, firm, and well-focussed voice of fine quality. At the moment, both his demeanor and his musical manner rather suggest a sedate, solid, old-fashioned concert tenor—something very different from, say, René Kollo or Peter Hofmann. But if all goes well—if his imagination and responses quicken, if he learns to act with eyes, posture, and voice at once, and if he acquires the habit of joining good notes into a molded, expressive legato line, determined by the words—he should become a notable Lohengrin and Siegmund, and then Siegfried, Tristan, and Tannhäuser. The three women of the drama are well contrasted, and they were strongly cast. Martina Arroyo was a passionate, volatile Marina. Maralin Niska was a dramatic Marfa. Pamela Coburn, an American soprano who sings with the Munich Opera, was a clear, touching Xenia. In the cadet roles, Donald Osborne and Kevin Deas, as a pair of lively, lustful Polish soldiers, were outstanding. The orchestra, half of its players women (in contrast to the all-male Vienna Philharmonic and the all-but-one-harpist-male Czech Philharmonic that played in Carnegie recently), included some eminent names—Jerry Grossman leading the cellos, John Wion the flutes, Stephen Taylor the oboes—and sounded good. The Collegiate Chorale, a hundred and thirty strong, and very well prepared, sang with spirit and justified the "chorus as hero" claim in Milan Pospíšil's program note on the opera. Robert Bass, the Chorale's energetic conductor, often rendered downbeats as enthusiastic up-beats, and the burden of his direction seemed to be "More, more!" There were long sections in which the dynamic range was between loud and louder. But his enthusiasm proved infectious, and the performance was stirring.

In 1931, to celebrate its jubilee, the Boston Symphony commissioned several works: Stravinsky's Symphony of Psalms, Hindemith's Concert Music for Brass and Strings, Prokofiev's Fourth Symphony, and Roussel's Third were added to the modern repertory. Similar seventy-fifth anniversary commissions in 1956 produced Roger Sessions's Third Symphony and Leonard Bernstein's Third. To mark its centenary, the Symphony commissioned a dozen new pieces, for performance in the 1980–81 through 1985–86 seasons. Nine have so far been performed, notable among them Peter Maxwell Davies's Second Symphony and Sessions's Concerto for Orchestra, and—biggest of all the commissions—Michael Tippett's *The Mask of Time*, which had its first performance in Boston on April 5th.

The Mask of Time is an evening-long composition—the first part lasted forty-three minutes, the second fifty—for four soloists (soprano, mezzo, tenor, and bass-baritone), large chorus, and large orchestra. In a program note, the composer explains that "the word 'Mask' is used in the tradition of the Renaissance *Masque*, which was a theatrical display or pageant with a great diversity of ingredients, but embodying some lofty notions that come eventually into the foreground." The lofty notions of this modern masque for the concert hall are fearlessly stated:

> *The Mask of Time* is explicitly concerned with the transcendental. It deals with those fundamental matters that bear upon man, his relationship with Time, his place in the world as we know it and in the mysterious universe at large. But it subscribes to no particular liturgy or standard theory, Biblical or otherwise, about the creation of the world and the destiny of mankind.

In a work-in-progress essay on the piece which appeared in *Comparative Criticism* (1982), Tippett wrote of many creative artists' feeling impelled, toward the end of their lives (Tippett is a hale seventy-nine), "to give expression to the transcendental in some aspect or other." He cited Haydn's *Creation*, Beethoven's Missa Solemnis, and Mahler's Eighth Symphony—but as "negative" examples for him, since "our world has now acquired such vastly extended notions of space and time that any reliance upon past conceptions of the ontological and transcendental would for me be an error." It is hard—it has evidently been hard for the composer himself—to write about *The Mask of Time* without making it seem a pretentious work. It is not that; its author has not made inflated or unfulfilled claims. I think *The Mask* a masterpiece. Whether it is or not, time will decide. At the least, it is a major work of our day and a vast, stirring, challenging adventure for the ears and minds of those who hear it.

Tippett has retained, Wordsworth-like, a boy's undimmed wonder at the world; it informs and inspires the visions of a mature man who has observed, thought, and suffered much. He describes *The Mask* as "a multiple panorama of experience." A large inspiration for it has come from the most popular of modern media: television. This is probably the first considerable work of art that has captured for music the reflections awakened by new images television has brought us: of the natural world seen at depths, from heights, and in details where no man's eye looked before; of exotic, colorful places ("Chimborazo, Cotopaxi") and the whole varied life of animals and men; and of science that counts atomies and reaches out ever farther into space. In that essay, Tippett wrote that "the new cosmological discoveries alone are a constant stimulus to my sense of wonder and mystery." At the start of the libretto, "written and compiled by the composer," he owns a large debt to Jacob Bronowski's *The Ascent of Man*—both the television series and the resultant book—which "affected my conception of *The Mask of Time* in general terms and in its detailed contents." When Tippett writes and sets

> *O rose-red cinnabar, you sombre metal*
> *hell-heated*
> *hotter, hotter!*
> *radiant*
> *look, look!*
> *a silver and liquid pearl of mercury,*
> *For fire is alchemy,*

he is paraphrasing for and in music Bronowski's account of the medieval alchemists who "took the red pigment, cinnabar, which is a sulphide of mercury, and heated it. The heat drives off the sulphur and leaves behind an exquisite pearl of the mysterious silvery liquid metal mercury, to astonish and strike awe into the patron." Twenty pages on, in Bronowski, we encounter Joseph Priestley (to whom Thomas Jefferson said, "Yours is one of the few lives precious to mankind"), Antoine Lavoisier, their experiments with mercury, and a color plate of rose-red cinnabar in its crucible; and learn of the direct route, "the fire-walker's route," from Bronze Age metallurgy and medieval alchemy to "the most powerful idea in modern science: the idea of the atoms."

The Ascent of Man is not a popular history of science but, rather, an essay in natural philosophy; and *The Mask of Time* is, among other things, the composer's response to the scientist-philosopher's account of man's origins, his evolution, and his discoveries about the world and the universe he inhabits. But it grows, too, from thoughts Tippett has explored in his oratorios (*A Child of Our Time*, *The Vision of Saint Augustine*), his operas, and his symphonies: about time, with its ever-extending past and unknowable yet influenceable future playing upon our present; about human nature; about recurrence, metamorphosis, and fixed points in a changing context. Time, transformation, and recurrence are ideas meet for music. A partial analogue of *The Mask* is Hans Werner Henze's cantata *Novae de Infinito Laudes* (1963), his setting of musings on mutability by

125

Giordano Bruno, who went to the stake in 1600 for his noble insistence on viewing the world as it is, not as forced and distorted into an Aristotelian mold. In the *Laudes* we view the heavenly bodies moving on their appointed Copernican courses, each different yet obeying one law of motion; the four elements and the way in which, by a different arrangement of components, the variety of all known things can be achieved; slow metamorphoses; rapid movements between extremes; and the daily miracle of dawn, wrought by the operation of unchanging laws yet ever fresh and new. The first stirrings of day sound deep on the tubas; the mole burrows away from the approaching light; Tithonus' steeds paw the rosy east; donkeys bray, swine grunt; and a series of dawn choruses breaks from all creation, to praise "the infinite, simplest, uniquest, loftiest, and most absolute First Cause." I'm not suggesting that Henze's piece directly influenced Tippett. I don't know whether he's even heard it. In the "sunrise" movement of the *Laudes* the chorus produces an onomatopoeic patter of animal names (Bruno was fond of catalogues), and in a movement of *The Mask* the chorus produces an onomatopoeic patter of animal noises and names. Such things are a recurrent part of music. So is the depiction of dawn, of light breaking—memorable in Mozart's *Magic Flute*, Haydn's *Creation*, Weber's *Oberon*, Wagner's *Siegfried* and *Götterdämmerung*, Puccini's *Tosca*, and the Henze and Tippett works. It is one of the "extramusical" events that music, through its metaphors of timbres and harmonies, can most movingly portray. Music can provide, too, that sense of inner illumination for which the physical arrival of brightness is in itself a metaphor.

Light breaking is an important image in *The Mask of Time*—one among several. An aspect perhaps surprisingly unregarded in Tippett's "panorama of experience" is love and companionship—family, emotional, and sexual ties, and the large part they play in human existence. But he has treated of those in other works, and (*pace* Mahler) even a composition on this scale cannot hope to include *everything*. The recurrent scene in *The Mask* is of an individual trying to make sense of the immensity and variety around him. In the beginning, the chorus proclaims the composer's metaphor, crying the word "sound" to a long-sustained, slow-pulsing chord, swelling and diminishing on the open "ow" and the closed "oo" components of the diphthong. (It is a deep, complex chord, and yet its intervals—fourths, a fifth, a double octave—can be analyzed in pure, natural, Pythagorean 1:3:4 relationships.) The tenor soloist, the individual observer, protagonist of *The Mask*, breaks in with lines from Yeats's "High Talk." "All metaphor," he declares, and then—Yeats on his tower looks upward—a thin, high call from flutes and maracas (a recurrent theme) is heard, and the tenor continues the poem:

> *A barnacle goose*
> *far up in the stretches of night;*
> *night splits and the dawn breaks loose.*

In the next movement, the sounds consolidate. The world is being created in music. Shiva dances. Orpheus with his lute (a marvellously potent orchestral strumming) moves mountains into place. The laws of motion take shape. Tippett

126

recalls a childhood memory: being held up by his father in 1910, to see Halley's comet. (" 'Remember,' he whispered in my ear, 'it will come back.' ") The movement ends with a new chorus on Haydn's line "Achieved is the glorious work."

Wonders of the natural world inspire the next movement. The score contains some of Tippett's loveliest nature music, enchanted pages telling of bliss and awe in an unserpented paradise—until Nature red in tooth and claw with ravin intrudes, to cloud any uncomplicated rapture. Scenes of ecstasy, of cruelty (a giant water bug sucks the living essence from a frog), of puzzling waste (the lacewing, suddenly hungry, gobbles up some of the fertile eggs she has assiduously laid), and of transcendental, visionary moments are drawn from Annie Dillard's neo-transcendentalist book *Pilgrim at Tinker Creek*. Then we turn to man: his emergence from the Ice Age into a pastoral society; then violent civilizations where human sacrifice propitiates new, harsh gods. (A moment of Stravinsky's *Rite* resounds in the score.) Marvels—they are pictured in Bronowski—are touched on: incantatory cave paintings; the chance hybridization that turned wild grasses into wheat, plant that feeds man but needs man for its propagation.

There is humor in the work. The lacewing (as in Dillard) turns to God to echo the London taxi-driver's question reported in a story T. S. Eliot used to tell ("Only the other evening, I picked up Bertrand Russell, and I said to him, 'Well, Lord Russell, what's it all about,' and, do you know, he couldn't tell me"): " 'Well, Lord God,' asks the delicate, dying lacewing . . . 'what's it all about?' And do you know, he couldn't . . ."

There is both charm and humor. In the final scene of Part I, Adam, Eve, God, and a Dragon (the four soloists) enjoy cocktail hour in a Peaceable Kingdom, crooning "Evening shadows bring surcease across the meadows of our peace" in close harmony while the chorus paints the scene with lines from *Paradise Lost*. But things go wrong. A centaur leaps the protecting wall. ("In a sense, warfare was created by the horse," says Bronowski.) The Dragon dwindles to a serpent. God takes off for a "country . . . far beyond the stars" (the rhythm echoes Parry's famous Vaughan setting), declining to help but graciously permitting man to pray to Him. Adam and Eve lament the "loss of that sweet time," and the chorus, repeating the Milton lines, now mourns a vanished dream.

Part II opens with the "barnacle goose" call. This time, the watching poet is Shelley. His last, great, unfinished poem, *The Triumph of Life*, is texually abbreviated and musically expanded in wonderful depictions of his trance and his vision of the lurching, ill-guided chariot, bearing Life, and of the crowd that throngs its brutal progress. The music breaks off, as the poem does, before the watcher's question "Then what is Life?" can be answered; and we pass to scenes of Shelley's quest, his storm-tossed death, the pyre that could not consume his heart. The "fire-walker's route" is then traced: three canonic chorale preludes (limpid, increasingly complex) based on the plainchant "Veni creator spiritus" introduce evocations of Pythagoras and those who measured the world; of alchemists and chemists; of physicists who "unbind the structured atom to a whiteness that shall blind the sun." Lines from Anna Akhmatova's "Requiem" and

"Poem Without a Hero" underpin a threnody for all nameless sufferers; the soprano sings a transfigured, poignant blues, successor to those in the Third Symphony and *The Ice Break*.

For a while, Tippett felt uncertain how to end the work. "I cannot, after all, produce 'answers,'" he wrote—"answers to the ontological dilemma, answers to the apparently eternal eruptions of violence in the world as we have known it." He cannot seek to justify the ways of God to men. "What *can* we now praise, what can we affirm?" There follow three songs. The first is for the baritone: in lines from Rilke's *Sonnets to Orpheus*, the poet's severed but unsilenceable head continues to sing, and his lyre to play. The mezzo pictures a strange scene of endurance and hope: anti-Nazis in Japanese-occupied Peking gather to attend Helmut Wilhelm's lectures on the I-Ching, cast a hexagram, and read a message of Deliverance. (Orientally tinged music cites a figure from Tippett's Triple Concerto.) The tenor then recounts a scene from Mary Renault's novel *The Mask of Apollo*: the young actor Nikeratos, sightseeing in Olympia, stares open-mouthed at the great statue of Zeus, "till my eye, travelling upward, met the face of power which says, 'O man, make peace with your mortality, for this too is God.'" In the novel, it is a transient, unimportant scene, dismissed in the next sentence ("Going out, I had to shake off a low fellow who seemed to think a free supper would be my price"); Apollo, not Zeus, is Niko's tutelary deity. But Tippett has a fondness for arcane gnomes; Astron's pronouncement in *The Ice Break*, "Take care for the Earth. God will take care for himself"—sentences from a Jung letter—is another he lifted out of context and emphasized. The sentence that the god's face seems to say receives emphatic choral iteration. (The word "peace" is laid out on F's and F-sharps three octaves deep with a strange, calm effect of dissonances reconciled.) The choralelike dictum passes without break into a coda of wordless singing—wave upon wave of ecstatic utterance, apparently endless, but suddenly "cut off as though by the closing of a door."

The Mask of Time is Tippett's most lyrically abundant score since *The Midsummer Marriage*—filled with vigorous, leaping melodies, magically evocative and beautiful sounds, tenderness, episodes of hard, bright, deliberately brutal brilliance. Plainchant, chorale, Monteverdian monody and madrigal have contributed to the sonic pageant. Choral and solo-with-chorus perspectives devised by Handel, Haydn, and Mahler have played a part. The harmony is Tippett's own "disturbed diatonicism," which analysis of the notes and chords cannot explain, since its affecting powers—like those of Berlioz's harmony—depend so much upon timbre and register. The huge structure stands firm, for all its variety of sources and content. Recurrent themes, musical and verbal, underpin it. As one reads or rereads the literary sources of the libretto, congruences flood in, often from passages not specifically cited in *The Mask*. Halley's comet adorns the cover of the vocal score, and the words "turning, returning" provide an important motif. Bronowski writes that "in every age there is a turning-point, a new way of seeing and asserting the coherence of the world," and Rilke, in "Wolle die Wandlung," declares that "the moving spirit, master of the earthly, in the surge of shaping loves above all else the turning-point." Dillard's recurrent emblem of transcendence, in *Tinker Creek* (cited in the libretto in a way possibly mysterious to anyone who has not read

128

the book), is a cedar perceived as "the tree with the lights in it," and Rilke's first Orpheus sonnet begins "A tree sprang up. O pure transcendence!" It is not necessary for understanding to catch all Tippett's allusions; but if, say, the words "river noises" (which are sung in two separate movements of *The Mask*, to the same music) can bring to mind, on some level, the images of the Wallace Stevens poem from which they are drawn, then one's response to the music is likely to be fuller.

Colin Davis, long associated with Tippett's music, conducted an inspired performance. The Tanglewood Festival Chorus, a hundred and forty strong, prepared by John Oliver and Susan Almasi, sang exceedingly difficult lines with confidence; it had mastered the notes and moved beyond that point to expressing the music. The four soloists—Robert Tear as protagonist, Faye Robinson, Yvonne Minton, and John Cheek—were sure and eloquent. The Boston Symphony's playing was strong, subtle, and beautiful.

A recording of The Mask of Time, *with Miss Robinson, Sarah Walker, Mr. Tear, and Mr. Cheek as the soloists, the BBC Singers and BBC Symphony Chorus and Orchestra, and Andrew Davis as conductor, has been published by EMI.*

REËNCOUNTERS

April 30, 1984

PAISIELLO's *Il barbiere di Siviglia* (1782) was revived this month by the Opera Shop of the Vineyard Theatre, on East Twenty-sixth Street. I'd not heard the piece in some twenty-five years, and found it to be a better work than I remembered. Once, it was regarded as the opera that Rossini's richer, livelier, funnier *Barbiere* ousted from the international repertory. Today—after a quarter-century that has seen many revivals of operas by Mozart's and Paisiellos's contemporaries—it can be heard rather differently: as a precursor of *Le nozze di Figaro,* a first musical presentation of characters that Mozart knew and brought to fuller life. Mozart, in words of Grove, "after hearing *Il re Teodoro in Venezia* in Vienna in 1784 and perhaps also *Il barbiere di Siviglia,* first produced there in 1783, displayed discernible traces of Paisiello's style in *Le nozze di Figaro* and *Don Giovanni.*" That "perhaps" is perhaps overcautious: Paisiello's *Barbiere* was prominent in the Burgtheater repertory from 1783 to 1788; singers who were to sing in *Figaro* sang in it; it is hardly conceivable that Mozart did not hear it. When *Figaro* appeared at the Burgtheater in 1786, it had four performances in May and five scattered revivals later that year, starting in July. On four of those five occasions, Paisiello's and Mozart's operas were "paired." (A day intervened, because the Burgtheater alternated Italian operas with plays or Schauspiels. *Hamlet* was one of the intervening plays.) An intention of bringing the two Beaumarchais-based operas together seems evident. Perhaps it is also significant that Beaumarchais's

Le Barbier de Séville, a Burgtheater staple from 1776, reentered the repertory, after several months' absence, just eleven days before Paisiello's *Barbiere* first appeared. (Beaumarchais's *Le Mariage de Figaro,* to be presented by Schikaneder at the Kärntnertortheater, was announced in 1785, the year Mozart began *Figaro,* but was withdrawn at the last minute, when the Emperor expressed disapproval. The text was published, however.)

Edward Holmes, in his *Life of Mozart,* tells us that as Paisiello's "character possessed all the frankness and amiability of his own melody, Mozart became much attached to him. The two friends dined, walked, and drove out together." There seems to be no real evidence of this warm attachment, and I suspect Holmes of overamplifying a sentence in a 1784 letter of Mozart's to his father: he and his pupil Barbara von Ployer are playing a concert in Döbling, and "I am fetching Paisiello in my carriage, as I want him to hear both my pupil and my compositions." A 1789 remark of Mozart's about Paisiello's music comes from a source, Friedrich Rochlitz's "Authentic Anecdotes of Wolfgang Gottlieb Mozart's Life," whose authenticity has often been called into question. But its tempering of praise with implicit reservations (they escaped Holmes, who calls it a very favorable opinion) has a convincing ring: "Whoever seeks for light and pleasurable sensations in music cannot be recommended to anything better."

Paisiello's *Barbiere* leaves its listeners in small doubt that both Mozart and Rossini knew the work. The germ of the C-major section in the second-act finale of *Figaro,* "Conoscete signor Figaro," appears in Don Basilio's Calumny aria in Paisiello's *Barbiere;* Don Giovanni's servants, summoning the peasants to the party, do so to strains from the *Barbiere* quintet. Mozart's music is rich, developed, fully worked; Paisiello's is notable for melodic charm, shapeliness, and liveliness. In 1789, Mozart composed a number for Paisiello's opera: Rosina's Lesson Scene aria, "Già riede primavera"—or, rather, "Schon lacht der holde Frühling," since it was intended for a projected German-language performance of the opera in which his sister-in-law Josepha Hofer was to sing Rosina. Josepha Hofer was the first Queen of the Night. Mozart's aria has higher-flying and showier coloratura than the original piece, but also a tender lyrical middle section in G minor ("I sit alone in the meadow and weep, not for my lost lambkin but for the shepherd Lindoro"), which is at once exquisite in its own right and dramatically pointed. The music becomes more and more emotional, to reach a poignant cadence on Lindoro's name, and then very abruptly leaps back to the bright opening theme—as if Rosina realizes she is going too far, and Dr. Bartolo is suddenly aware that his ward has begun to address her music master in a surprisingly intimate manner. The Vineyard production of *Il barbiere* used Mozart's setting of the aria. It was good to hear it in context. (There is an excellent recording by Edita Gruberova, on London.) The difference between Paisiello's easy charm and Mozart's combination of charm with emotion, solid musical substance, and musico-dramatic subtlety was strikingly demonstrated. Although the scoring is unfinished, the vocal line and the bass are complete; the structure of the aria is all there.

The Vineyard is an intimate theatre: two rooms forming an L shape, with an acting space in the angle. Miriam Charney, who conducted, had reduced the score for an ensemble of flute, bassoon, two violins, cello, and harpsichord, which provided neat, ample support for Paisiello's melodies. There was a simple, effective set, by Sally Locke, that switched easily from the outside to the inside of Bartolo's house. Linda Melloy's costumes were handsome. Joseph LoSchiavo's staging was deft. The young singers, most of them familiar from previous Vineyard shows, had—all but the Bartolo—now got the measure of the house and did not sing too loudly. The Rosina, Anne McKenna, and the Almaviva, David Kellett, were winning, and a newcomer to the troupe, Karl Laird, was a lively, pleasing Figaro. The piece was sung in Italian (often bad Italian, in which a dear beloved became something like a "carro armato," or tank), and that was a mistake—especially in a theatre where every word can be heard. The details of Beaumarchais's cunningly wrought plot—letters figure in it as prominently as they do in *Figaro*—are by no means evident from the stage action alone, and the Vineyard might well address its dramatic productions to the full understanding of wider audiences than those who follow Italian. Most of the recitatives were taken too slowly—sung out in full voice, not "spoken on pitches" in speech rhythms. But, all in all, this *Barbiere* offered an evening filled with "light and pleasurable sensations."

Let me raise a small puzzle, in the hope that some reader has the answer. Michael Kelly (a tenor, Mozart's original Don Curzio) tells us in his memoirs that in the Burgtheater *Barbiere* "Signor Mandini and I played the part of Count Almaviva alternately." Stefano Mandini was later the Almaviva of Mozart's opera—a bass-baritone role. Grove tells us that he was both a bass-baritone *and* a celebrated Almaviva in Paisiello's opera (a tenor role). It has been suggested that Stefano's younger brother Paolo, described in Grove as a tenor, was in fact Paisiello's Almaviva. But (1) Kelly refers to only one Mandini, (2) Paolo was engaged for Haydn's troupe, at Esterháza, while *Il barbiere* continued its Burgtheater run, and (3) at Esterháza the part that Haydn composed for Paolo, Idreno in *Armida*, is a bass-baritone role. (Samuel Ramey sings it in the Philips recording.) When we examine other roles that Stefano played and that Paolo played—some of them tenor, most of them baritone—the mystery deepens. Was Stefano a baritone with tenor extension? (Both Almavivas sing up to F-sharp—but the tessitura of the two parts is quite different.) Or did he transpose Paisiello's music down? In that case, what happened during the ensembles? And is it likely that *Il barbiere* was played in Vienna with *four* bass-baritones or basses in the cast (Almaviva, Figaro, Bartolo, Basilio) and no tenor?

Another opera I'd not seen or heard in over twenty years and revalued on reëncounter is Kurt Weill's *Down in the Valley*, an Anglo-German production of which was shown on Channel 13 last week. Weill composed it for radio in 1945 (it found no takers), and revised and amplified it in 1948, for performance at Indiana University, Bloomington. It was a swift success: sixteen hundred productions—six thousand performances—were reported in the first nine years of its existence. BBC Television put out a rather feeble (and very British) account of the piece in 1961, which seemed to confirm the European consensus of the time that the Nazis had destroyed not only all Weill's scores they could lay their hands on but also, by driving him from Berlin to Broadway, his genius. (Virgil Thomson thought much the same.) In subsequent decades, the revaluation of his American scores began. I learned them from records and from the City Opera's revival of *Street Scene* in 1978 and 1979 (perhaps the company's highest achievement in the last decade). *Down in the Valley* has a deliberately naive libretto (by Arnold Sundgaard), an Alabama-set version of the tale of the fair, pure maiden and the lascivious squire who threatens to dispossess her poor old father unless ... The music is based on a handful of Anglo-Appalachian ballads, handled so subtly and sensitively that the sounds—I think it was T. W. Adorno who first said this of Weill's music—get under your skin. Or, as Virgil Thomson put it in a 1933 review of *The Seven Deadly Sins*, "If it really touches you, you go all to pieces inside." Weill's theatre music of every period now has this effect on me, and rational criticism becomes impossible. The Met is doing Gershwin's *Porgy and Bess* next season. It might do worse than follow it with Weill's *Lost in the Stars*.

The new production was very well conducted by Carl Davis. The impact of the opera was somewhat lessened by the decision of the director, Frank Cvitanovich, to interrupt and pad out the score (which lasts about half an hour) with long passages of silence, during which his cameras tracked over the English countryside (where the piece was filmed), through the jailhouse, and so on. There were oddities: Jenny, walking home from prayer meeting with Brack, whom she loves, sang of the night and its stars, but the sun cast its shadows on a brightly lit valley. Opera presented on film or television in "realistic" settings poses questions about the "conventions" harder than those the ordinary operagoer, in a theatre where paint and canvas set the scene and a proscenium defines the limits of illusion, has long since solved. "Where exactly *is* that orchestra that wells out over the landscape?" "Why do the voices sound so reverberant when the actors are apparently singing in the open air?" "Why do the voices remain in close-up when we see the singers in long shot?" And, in this opera, "Why do the lovers rashly burst into loud song, orchestra-accompanied, if they are trying to hide from a police posse?" Naive questions; but this production raised them, as the best film and television operas don't. The cast, led by Hutton Cobb as Brack and Linda Lou Allen as Jennie, was of modest but adequate vocal accomplishment. All the performers sang and acted with honesty and directness. Their unaffected sincerity made the piece moving. The designing was inspired, aptly, by the images in James Agee and Walker Evans's study of Southern sharecroppers, *Let Us Now Praise Famous Men*. Less happily, Weill's score was provided with a musical coda in the form of a gussied-up folk song sung by Judy Collins (elaborately accompanied, with none of Weill's genius) and then a snatch of the Second Brandenburg. The *Ring* broadcasts last year also had musical postludes. Are there no musicians at Channel 13?

BESIDE THE SEA

May 7, 1984

OLIVIER MESSIAEN's three most celebrated pupils—Pierre Boulez, Karlheinz Stock-hausen, and Jean Barraqué—pursued separate paths. Barraqué's was signposted by no manifestos; he blazed no trails for enthusiastic packs of followers, led no performing ensemble, was not prominent at the international festivals. G. W. Hopkins wrote in a 1966 *Musical Times* article:

> In his music, there are no flirtations with the exotic (his instrumentation has —exaggeratedly—been called "functional"), no aleatoric relaxations of control, no simplifications for the benefit of the tired or half-witted listener. Faceless music indeed, for those nurtured on the excitements and posturings of the Paris musical scene!
>
> In fact, his constant ideal has been to create a music in which technique and aesthetic are perfectly fused; his starting point has been scrupulous analysis of the scores of those few masters—Bach, Mozart, Beethoven, Debussy, and Webern—whom he considers to have most nearly approached this ideal fusion.

After producing his immense, thrilling Piano Sonata, his *Séquence* for soprano and ensemble, and an electronic Study, Barraqué encountered Hermann Broch's extraordinary book *The Death of Virgil*, in 1955, and thereafter devoted himself to composing a series of pieces based upon or related to it. He died in 1973, aged forty-five, having brought to performance ... *au delà du hasard* (Paris, 1960), *Chant après chant* (Strasbourg, 1966), *Le Temps restitué* (Royan, 1968), and an instrumental Concerto (London, 1968)—all but the last with texts partly from Broch and partly his own. Several other *Mort de Virgile* compositions are listed in Grove as "incomplete sections," for forces ranging from piano solo and string quartet to choruses and a *Discours* for eleven voices and a hundred and thirty instruments. Someday, I suppose, all the surviving music will be brought together in performance. I hope so, for what I have heard of it is inspired.

It is not difficult to understand how *The Death of Virgil* could provide a composer with inspiration for many years of creation. Hannah Arendt, in a 1949 *Kenyon Review* essay, called the book (begun in Vienna in 1935, completed in Princeton a decade later) "one of the truly great works in German literature." It grew from a twenty-page story to an eighty-page novella to a long, five-hundred-page book in just four chapters. whose sentences can span pages, written in a prose that requires surrender to its inexorable, hypnotic rhythms, repetitive as the arrival of wave after wave after wave on the beach, with phrases varied as waves are, rising, diminishing, overlapping, responsive to the slow

133

surgings and ebbings of the tides. It is not, in Jean Starr Untermeyer's English translation, a hard book to read—except in its demands on time, concentration, and submission. I own that I have not yet undertaken the single, unbroken, cover-to-cover traversal proposed by Hermann Weigand in his "program notes" to *The Death of Virgil* published in a 1947 *PMLA*—"at one sitting, as one sustained verbal symphony, punctuated by three brief pauses." A complete performance would take, he reckons, twenty-four hours—the period of "real time," as opposed to time remembered and visionary, transcendental time, spanned by the events of the book—"and when preceded by a proper regimen of training, it should prove no more difficult than Charles Lindbergh's solo flight from New York to Paris." I want to tackle it as soon as the world can be rather less with me for a while. In interrupted, piecemeal perusal, I've discovered the themes of what Weigand calls "a verbal symphony of overwhelming proportions," with its "differences of instrumentation, tempo and volume," its "solo parts and delicately blended voices of varying timbre," its "pulse of mounting tension," its "crashing climaxes of the full orchestra that leave [the listener] reeling as under the roar of the Day of Judgment."

In this four-movement "symphony," Virgil, in Augustus' train, enters the port of Brindisi; during a night of spiritual despair passes his career in review, pondering life and art, while a terrible imperative, "Burn the *Aeneid*!," forms itself and is succeeded by a vision of redemption; is persuaded (in dialogues plumbing what in life should be rendered unto Caesar, what unto God) that the greater sacrifice is for the artist to give up his work to the world; dies and, like a new Adam, passes into a Creation myth, but a reverse one, which leads from intricacy and richness to darkness and a world without form, and void—until in a final crescendo of light and sound he experiences Creation again, rejoices in a vision of a mother and child, and once more becomes specifically Virgil, an individual note even though it is lost in the sounding of a tone that is

> more than song, more than the striking of the lyre, more than any tone, more than any voice, since it was all of these together and at once, bursting out of the nothing as well as out of the universe, breaking forth as a communication beyond every understanding, breaking forth as a significance above every comprehension, breaking forth as the pure word which it was, exalted above all understanding and significance whatsoever, consummating and initiating, mighty and commanding, fear-inspiring and protecting, gracious and thundering, the word of discrimination, the word of the pledge, the pure word . . . a floating sea, a floating fire, sea-heavy, sea-light . . . incomprehensible and unutterable for him: it was the word beyond speech.

But *The Death of Virgil* can't be potted, summarized, any more than can *The Divine Comedy* or *Faust*: sounds in time and the slow building of the movements are part of its sense. The four movements are titled with elementary prefixes: "Water—The Arrival," "Fire—The Descent," "Earth—The Expectation," and "Air—The Homecoming." In musical terms, their basic tempi might be designated Andante, Adagio, Scherzo (bringing the relief of dialogue exchanges after the long-sustained paragraphs), and Maestoso.

Barraqué's aim was not to compose a concert-hall analogue of the verbal symphony (I suppose that symphonies of twenty-four hours' duration have been written; the notion is daunting) but, rather, in separate works to illumine, interpret, make more vivid, give sonic form to some episodes, ideas, beliefs, visions woven into the rich fabric of the book. His *Chant après chant* explores ideas and images in Broch's second chapter. Key phrases are "seas of silence," "strange unity," "hearkening to the inaudible," "the melodic invisibility in which all artistic creation is rooted." Composed for soprano, piano, and six percussionists commanding a very large sonorous battery, it is made of resonances, silences, grand statements that die into the empty air, pregnant statements that burgeon and are later recalled. It is an adventure—lasting about twenty-three minutes—in sounds now delicate and enchanting, now awesome, and a discourse both poetic and lucid. A score was published in 1967. A recording (now on the Astrée label) was made in 1969. *Chant après chant* had its New York première in March, in Symphony Space, at the inaugural concert of Prism, a chamber orchestra founded and conducted by Robert Black (who gave the American première of Barraqué's Piano Sonata in Merkin Hall two years ago). A big-city Barraqué première—even one so long delayed—is an important event. The critic of the *Times* admired the performance but briskly dismissed the music as "warmed-over Boulez—a hybrid of bright, brittle violence and spurious academic theories." It didn't seem that way to me. Barraqué is generally deemed the romantic among the postwar serialists. Before Stockhausen moved into mysticism, before Peter Maxwell Davies went to live on an Orkney island, Barraqué declared himself a Breton by adoption, "fascinated by the sea, the rocks, the tides, the rhythm of life," dreaming as a child of "refashioning something as the tide does," dreaming later of his *Death of Virgil*. Academic theories—"spurious" or not—seem to have played no part in his utterances or, more important, in his compositions. He suggests, rather, the old-style composer—seized, visionary, inspired, building on the work of his predecessors, seeking to refine and extend his technique only so that his music may be more precisely eloquent. It is very difficult music. I find that I must listen to the works again and again. (The Piano Sonata, *Séquence*, and . . . *au delà du hasard* are also on record.) As Mr. Hopkins says, "whatever links with the past there are in Barraqué's music are, in fact, deeply embedded in a personal style of such complexity as to offer the listener very few immediately recognizable points of reference in the traditional sense." And he "largely avoids parading the rational processes of composition on the surface of his works, expecting the listener's response to be primarily an irrational one."

The text—most of Barraqué's compositions have sung texts—often provides the easiest point of entry into the music. The soprano in *Chant après chant* is not dominant. In the words of André Hodeir's program note, "she slips, sometimes stealthily, into the clear spaces of a polyphony of variable density." Sometimes she murmurs, sometimes cries, through the last shudder or shimmer of a dying resonance. Whatever she says has a defining effect. Margaret Ahrens, the soloist of the Prism performance, is not exactly the "dramatic soprano" specified in the score, but she was beautifully clear, beautifully exact, and pure in tone—an impressive artist. The piano part (it was ably played by Elizabeth DiFelice) seems to suggest at each entry the "real" world—or, at any rate, something on a different plane from the metaphorical dream discourse of the six percussionists. They carry the burden of the piece. Their music—now beguiling, now blustery; sometimes delicate, sometimes anguished or brutal—flickers, suddenly surges, darts from player to player around the platform, solidifies, crests, dies into silence, resumes. The listener is caught in an enchanted web of sonorities, densities, durations. The Jersey City State College Percussion Ensemble (Michael Hinton, Edward Brunicardi, Mark Christofaro, Chris Deczynski, Matthew Patuto, and Robert Romeo) gave a virtuoso performance. Mr. Black conducted with the warming combination of advocacy, emotional commitment, and accuracy which distinguishes all he does. A pity that Prism was not invited to repeat *Chant après chant* at the Horizons '84 Festival next month. The wide public hears too little Barraqué.

On to slighter things. Ambroise Thomas's *Mignon*, the third of Carnegie Hall's opéra-comique series starring Frederica von Stade, was somewhat disappointing. Miss von Stade, who earlier this season was a bewitching Périchole and a captivating Chérubin, gave us a Mignon who from the start to almost the end of the opera was lackluster, depressed, undervitalized. As in the 1982 Santa Fe production, she was, quite simply, dull, despite the beauty of her tone and her careful, delicate attention to the phrases. When she plays unhappy, put-upon heroines—Massenet's Cendrillon and Rossini's Desdemona are others—it is almost as if she turned some mental switch to a "sadness" setting, producing rhythmic inertia, monotony of timbre, and a curious blankness. It's disconcerting. One can't recognize the artist whose Cherubino, Chérubin, and Rosina have held one spellbound. She seems to miss the point of the opéra-comique Mignon created by Thomas and his librettists, Michel Carré and Jules Barbier (a team adept at simplifying for the operatic stage such intricate literary works as *Hamlet*, *Faust*, and *Wilhelm Meisters Lehrjahre*), and to adopt, as it were, a Philine's-eye view of the character. (Philine is the glittering actress who dazzles Wilhelm Meister and thinks Mignon a quaint, dreary little waif.) Goethe's Mignon was given her musical setting by Hugo Wolf; in his Mignon songs we recognize the mysterious child who (as Carlyle put it in a preface to his translation of *Wilhelm Meister*) "at length overpowers [the reader] with an emotion more deep and thrilling than any poet since the days of Shakespeare has succeeded in producing." Thomas's Mignon doesn't quite succeed in doing that to the listener, but she blends pathos, piquancy, charm, and ardor in a winning, touching way. She can be heard in Conchita Supervia's records of "Connais-tu le pays" and the Swallow Duet.

The opera went through several changes of plot and design before it reached the stage of the Opéra-Comique, in 1866 (the year before *Don Carlos* at the Opéra), with Célestine Galli-Marié, later the first Carmen, as Mignon. Other large changes—for Germany, for London, for revivals in Paris—were made thereafter. (I sketched some of the tangled history when reviewing the 1974 Dallas production of *Mignon*: *Music of Three Seasons*, pp. 50–54.) The Carnegie presentation confined itself to familiar printed music, without recourse to alternative numbers recoverable from the Paris material, or even to the early editions; in fact, it simply followed the ordinary Schirmer score. This was

136

defensible except, perhaps, in one respect: it was odd in the context of a "French Opéra-Comique Festival" to choose the grand-opera sung recitatives instead of spoken dialogue; they are undistinguished and, like those added to *Carmen*, clog the flow of a drama originally planned for enactment in speech that breaks into song.

The Philine and the Wilhelm, Gianna Rolandi and Barry McCauley, were also those of the Santa Fe production. She was nimble and animated but lacked the bright, exact purity that Philine's coloratura must have; some high notes struck too hard went out of focus. He was rather a dull stick in music that calls for elegance. As the Harper, Robert Lloyd, Covent Garden's King Philip and Boris Godunov, made his New York début and sang agreeably but unmemorably. (He was the only artist to use a score.) As Friedrich, Colette Alliot-Lugaz, a star of the Lyons Opera, made her American début and was nimble but not quite sparky enough. In the subaltern roles, Barry Stilwell (Laertes), Kurt Link (Jarno), and James Busterud (Antonio) were good, and the Orpheon Chorale was a dapper chorus. Kenneth Montgomery conducted, as he had at Santa Fe. Everything was neatly turned and carefully shaped, but there was a lack of aristocratic lightness and grace. It was not Beecham-like. (Beecham conducted *Mignon* at the Met in 1943, with Risë Stevens.) The orchestra seemed rather too large and rich. There was some exquisite playing from the anonymous first clarinet.

If this seems a shade unappreciative, it is only because Carnegie's operas-in-concert series devised by Matthew Epstein (three Rossinis with Marilyn Horne last season; the three opéras comiques this season; three Handels, two with Miss Horne, announced for next season) lead us to expect the highest and have so far seldom failed to approach it. The "trimmings"—platform deployment to mirror the dramatic shape of the scenes, sensitive platform lighting, the provision of bilingual librettos and of light enough by which to read them—are not neglected. Not everything has been perfect (the stage directions of the *Mignon* libretto were skimpy), but in general both the casting and the presentation have set musical standards such as the Met and the City Opera, churning out up to seven or eight performances a week in full stagings, can hardly maintain.

Ivo Pogorelich gave a piano recital in Carnegie Hall last month, and the place was packed. He has the reputation of being a flamboyant artist. At the 1980 Chopin Competition in Warsaw—a biographical note in the program book told us—his appearances "aroused the sort of frenzied mass demonstrations usually reserved for rock stars." But the recital was outwardly a sober, gentlemanly affair. There were just three sonatas on the program: Mozart's in A, K. 331; Chopin's Third; and Prokofiev's Sixth. The Mozart was largely unstylish—a romantic pianist's Mozart, with unpleasing rhythmic distortions, in the first two movements. The *alla turca* finale, however, had an admirably steady beat and delightfully bold yet unexaggerated sonorities. Both the Chopin and the Prokofiev were odd performances—rhythmically and dynamically wayward in fashions that seemed sometimes inspired but sometimes pointlessly capricious. Prokofiev once analyzed four strains in his creative personality—neoclassical, ostinato, lyrical, and "the modern trend . . . the search for a language in which to express powerful emotions"—with a possible fifth that he preferred to regard as an intensification of the others to a "scherzo-ish" degree. All five can be discerned in almost any of his compositions. All five appear in the Sixth Piano Sonata, a large, ambitious, and wide-ranging composition. The first two seem to me—but evidently not to Mr. Pogorelich—to call for strongly defined and steady rhythms. If the first movement is not held to a crisp 4/4, how can the off-beat accents make their intended effect? Mr. Pogorelich, Yugoslav-born and now London-based, is Russian-trained, but his is hardly an "authentically Russian" way of playing Prokofiev. (I don't know Prokofiev's own recording of the sonata but have heard other celebrated Russian pianists play the piece.) The slow, free lilt that he brought to the third movement (marked "like a very slow waltz") was more convincing.

He played across a very wide dynamic range without ever becoming clangorous. His technique was effortless and unshowy. Whenever the dynamic indications dropped below *mf*, he tended to depress the soft pedal; I don't think I've ever heard a recital with so much *una corda*. He played a Hamburg Steinway that was dusky and unassertive of tone—too sober an instrument to set the vast spaces of Carnegie Hall ablaze. He is a real pianist, with personality, temperament, and alertness. But he seemed to have left the original scores too far behind—to revel in detail at the expense of form. Chopin's sonata was a no less beautiful and a more coherent work in Robert Taub's balanced performance earlier this season. Mr. Pogorelich's encores—a Scriabin study, a Chopin prelude, and a Scarlatti sonata—were delectable.

RIDING THE WAVES

May 14, 1984

THE demise, five years ago, of the Juilliard's Twentieth-Century Music concerts, conducted by Richard Dufallo, left a hole in New York's musical life. In a city that lacks any counterpart of the London Sinfonietta and any counterpart of the BBC's Radio 3, the Juilliard concerts brought us performances of works by Boulez, Berio, Stockhausen, Ligeti, Xenakis, Gilbert Amy, Messiaen, Peter Maxwell Davies, Oliver Knussen, Barry Conyngham and by the Americans Charles Wuorinen, Ralph Shapey, Jacob Druckman, Earle Brown, Richard Wernick, Joel Hoffmann which kept listeners riding the waves of contemporary music or tumbling, exhilarated, into the tangy sea. And it was all happening at Lincoln Center. I've no objection to travelling uptown to Symphony Space, downtown to the Kitchen and to Cooper Union, or under the East River to the Brooklyn Academy to hear new music. But it's important that there should be a heartbeat at Lincoln Center invigorating the staider, safer offerings of the Metropolitan Opera House, the New York State Theater, and Avery Fisher Hall. I hope that whoever becomes the Juilliard School's next president sees it as the place by which the enterprise of the other Lincoln Center houses is judged. Those Juilliard concerts were very well played: looking over my reviews of them, I find name after name of performers who have gone on to fame. In the "outside world," economic pressure often prescribes skimpy rehearsal schedules, and therefore programs—particularly of orchestral concerts—in which compositions difficult to prepare make way for more easily achievable but less important pieces. Something of the sort seems to have affected the program of the Brooklyn Philharmonic's Meet the Moderns concert last month, given in the Lepercq Space of the Brooklyn Academy and the next night in the Great Hall of Cooper Union. (I attended the former.) It was entitled "Berio, Boulez, and New Europeans." It delivered them, but not at strength.

The concert began with three small, choice chamber blooms from *A Garland for Dr. K*—a garland woven by eleven composers and presented to Alfred Kalmus in London in 1969 as an eightieth-birthday tribute. Dr. Kalmus (who died in 1972) was a remarkable man. When he was twenty, he joined the Viennese music-publishing house Universal Edition, where he was associated with Schoenberg, Berg, Webern, Bartók, Kurt Weill. Driven from Austria in 1936, he went to London and there ensured the continuance in print of Universal composers denied musical existence in the Third Reich. During the war, his Universal Edition (London) worked under the aegis of Boosey & Hawkes; for a time Mahler study scores bore the Boosey imprint. After the war, Boulez, Berio, Harrison Birtwistle, Brown, Richard Rodney Bennett, David Bedford, Sylvano Bussotti, and Stockhausen were among the composers Dr. Kalmus published. His New Grove entry—written by a fellow-publisher, Alan Frank of the Oxford University Press—ends, "No publisher in the twentieth century could have pursued more assiduously the task of gaining recognition and financial reward for composers of new music." The history of music is made primarily by its composers but also by those who recognize genius and, in a wider sense than by simply getting the notes into print, "publish" it. The three *Garland* pieces on the Brooklyn program—Birtwistle's "Some Petals from the Garland," Boulez's "Pour le Dr. Kalmus," and Berio's "The Modification and Instrumentation of a Famous Hornpipe as a Merry and Altogether Sincere Homage to Uncle Alfred"—are more than conventional pièces d'occasion. Each of them represents a major composer working, although on a small scale, at the top of his bent, in "altogether sincere homage." Dr. Kalmus was a familiar, courteous, very correct, slightly austere bearded figure at London concerts, somewhat awesome to shy young critics. (We nicknamed him Dr. Marianus, from Mahler's Eighth Symphony.) In Brooklyn, the *Garland* morceaux had their New York premières—belated but welcome, for Dr. K left his mark on a half-century of musical history.

Four of the five other pieces on the bill used electrical amplification, and used it crudely. Louis Andriessen's *Disco* (1982), a duo for amplified violin and piano (played by Benjamin Hudson and Kenneth Bowen), sounded shrill and empty. Louis Andriessen, born in 1939 (a brother of Jurriaan Andriessen, whose *Berkshire Symphonies,* used for the ballet *Jones Beach,* I remember with pleasure; a son of Hendrik Andriessen, whose opera *Philomela* I remember with mixed feelings), is a striking, inventive composer, who, like all composers, works within a context—in his case, Dutch vanguard music. Most composers are local or, at best, national prophets, prominent members of and important to the societies that they live in and serve. Great compositions serve the world (and need Dr. Kalmuses to see to it that they do). Since my transposition from Europe to America, I have become increasingly aware that there are also pieces important, even revelatory, to audiences who have followed their composers' careers step by step which are probably not worth exporting. And in this huge country there are works that matter in New York even though their California performances may add little to the lives of those who hear them there. And vice versa. (Haydn's famous letter regretting that admirable operas he has composed specifically for Esterháza can have little appeal to metropolitan audiences makes the point strongly.) Against that, of course, must be set musicians' curiosity to discover what is being done elsewhere; and also the danger that if a "context" has not been established, important, world-serving compositions may fall upon minds and ears unprepared for their full comprehension. (This seems to have happened with Haydn's operas in Vienna, with Davies's First Symphony at the Philharmonic in 1978, with Barraqué's *Chant après chant* at Symphony Space in March.) Perhaps I'm saying no more than that international and transnational programs should be assembled with great care. Boulez's metaphor of a waterline—works that rise above it matter, while those below it, whether just below or fathoms deep, can well be ignored except by swimmers in local waters—seems relevant. There is too much music being made in the world for a listener to be able to keep up with more than, on the one hand, the best of it and, on the other, the works of the composers who live in his particular part of the world. Andriessen has written better pieces than his duo *Disco*. And Arne Nordheim (born in 1931) has written better works than his trio *Signals* (1967), for amplified accordion, electric guitar, and percussion, which was the next work on the Brooklyn program. It was played by Guy Klucevsek, David Starobin, and Joseph Passaro.

Knussen's *Coursing,* a chamber-orchestra piece commissioned by the London Sinfonietta, was originally announced for the concert but was replaced by his *Hums and Songs of Winnie-the-Pooh,* for soprano and instrumental quintet. It was composed in 1970, when it had an informal hearing at Tanglewood, and was revised last year for performance at the Aldeburgh Festival. Like all Knussen's music, *Hums and Songs* is written with a marvellously exact and imaginative ear. It avoids coy whimsy. It is poised, charming, and amusing: a happy blend of miniature tone poem and tiny song cycle, with deliberately blurred narrative—a young man's memories of childhood Pooh-musings, after bedtime reading, between lights out and falling asleep. *Hums and Songs* deserved a place on the program; it provided an introduction to *Where the Wild Things Are,* the opera Knussen wrote with Maurice Sendak, which receives its American première next month. Karen Beardsley, who will play Max in *Wild Things,* was a limpid, accurate, and winning soloist. Her appearance is fresh and boyish, but it was odd of her to wear a bare-shouldered red dress that seemed very far from the world of Pooh and Christopher Robin.

After the intermission, there were first performances of two works for larger forces. *Trajet* introduced, both as composer and as pianist, the Belgian Luc Brewaeys (born in 1958). The piece was written at the invitation of Lukas Foss, the music director of the Brooklyn Philharmonic; it is dedicated to him, and he conducted it. *Trajet* is based, the program note told us, on a five-note chord representing a musical encipherment of the letters L-U-K-A-S and on the rhythms of the dedicatee's name tapped out in Morse code. Well, a composer has to start somewhere. The piece is composed for "slightly ring-modulated" (i.e., electronically distorted) piano and eleven instruments. Mr. Brewaeys showed himself to be a swift, able player and an evidently efficient composer with a quick, sure ear, definite about what he wants. It's a kind of music that, like Xenakis's, I respect but can't engage with. Then there was *Offrande* (1982), by Sharon Kanach, an American who lives in Paris—a long gallimaufry for soprano, orchestra, and tape, which struck me as pretentious, self-indulgent, undisciplined, and tedious to listen to. The starting point here was casts of the I-Ching. Voices on the tape recited poetry in various languages. (Dante, Rilke, the start of "Ash-Wednesday" appeared; I thought the T. S. Eliot estate was more discriminate about releasing his lines for use in musical compositions.) The orchestra played. The soprano Diamánda Galás sang both high and low in lines sometimes heavily vibrant and sometimes steady. I admired her legato. But she was grossly overamplified. Since the composer's fingers were on the electronic controls, this was either what she intended or a miscalculation, at her station among the players, of what would reach the audience in the Lepercq Space's awkward acoustics.

The Tremont String Quartet's concert in Merkin Hall last month was a rewarding event: confirmation of the string quartet's survival into our times as an ideal medium for the communication of intimate thought; and revelation of a young American quartet (formed in 1977) dedicated to contemporary music and able to play it with technical proficiency and emotional commitment. Paul Griffiths, on the first page of his survey *The String Quartet*, a book of brilliant aperçus and cunning formal design, observes that "more than any other sort of music in the western tradition, the string quartet has enjoyed the stability yet also the capacity for a constant renewal of a living species." And on the last page he has a pleasant fancy: the eighteenth-century quartet party reported by Michael Kelly in his memoirs—Haydn the first violin, Dittersdorf the second, Mozart the viola, and Vanhal the cello ("There was a little science among them")—sits down to tackle a composition by Carter or Xenakis and, although somewhat disconcerted by the difficulty of the parts, "which leaves little room for an individual moulding of statement or response," discovers the essential continuity of the genre and its modes of expression. The Tremont Quartet—Richard Balkin, Laura Mahan Balkin, Linda Walton Kirkwood, James Kirkwood—played four quartets. Three of them were new to New York, and the fourth had its world première. They represented four very different approaches to the medium. Three of them were works I look forward to hearing again.

R. Murray Schafer's String Quartet No. 2, "Waves" (1976), is a product of his World Soundscape Project—which (to put it simply) explored natural "musics" of the world and related them to man and the music he makes. (The results are recounted in Schafer's book *The Tuning of the World*.) Recording and analyzing the patterns of waves breaking on the Atlantic and Pacific shores of Canada revealed that "the duration from crest to crest usually falls between six and eleven seconds"; and "it is this wave motion that gives the quartet its rhythm and

141

structure." The sea has long been a potent source of musical inspiration—to Debussy, Vaughan Williams, Britten, Barraqué, Davies. (Do people who were born far from the sea and grew up without having its rhythms, its sonic and visual metaphors of recurrence and variety, tempest and calm, violence and cradling, etched in their psyches respond differently to sea music and sea poetry?) Schafer's quartet is no academic "transcription" but an imaginative composer's response to observation, shaped by art into a beautiful stretch of music.

James Willey's String Quartet No. 3 (1981), composed for the Tremont, is in manner a more traditional quartet discourse. It is a fresh, worthwhile piece, in one movement—lasting about fifteen minutes—with six clear sections. And it is very well written. A program note remarked that "the sounds and textures of hymns and fiddle-tunes are never very distant." That may suggest some neo-Ivesian pastiche, but in fact the popular elements are sublimated, turned into true quartet material, as surely as are the Russian tunes of the Razumovskys. Willey's command of modern harmonies, his metrical astuteness, shaping of form, and handling of textures delight ear and mind. There are several solo or solo-with-accompaniment passages. In the Schafer piece, the players murmured, lapped wave upon wave, surged, subsided in beautifully disciplined poetic ensemble. The Willey gave each of them chances to come forward as an individual and display color and character. The instructions in the score are vivid—"scruffy, full of bow noise," "mysterious, a bit playful," "*pp*, but clearly audible as a ghostly backdrop"—and so was the Tremont's playing. Willey, who teaches at the State University of New York at Geneseo, where the Tremont is quartet-in-residence, was a composer new to me. I've made a note to obtain the Spectrum record on which the Esterhazy plays his First and Second Quartets.

The score of Ben Johnston's String Quartet No. 5 bears a 1980 date and the inscription "For the Kronos Quartet"; according to a New World Records note accompanying Johnston's Sonata for Microtonal Piano, the quartet was composed in 1975 for the Concord Quartet; the Tremont Quartet gave the work its first performance, in Chicago last year. I find it easy to get lost in Johnston's microtonal compositions, based on "extended just intonation" and set out in notation of formidable complexity whose signs may provide for up to twenty-two different degrees of sharpness, twenty-six of flatness. But in the Fifth Quartet there is something not difficult to follow—the Appalachian tune "Lonesome Valley," a guiding thread through the labyrinthine adventure of unfamiliar concords and discords where the composer's concern, as he once put it, is "to reopen doors closed by the acceptance of the twelve-tone equal-tempered scale as the norm of pitch usage."

Marc-Antonio Consoli's String Quartet (1983), commissioned by the Tremont and receiving its first performance, ended the concert. It seemed to me insistent, rebarbative, long-winded, and graceless in its writing.

VOICES OF ROME

May 21, 1984

Two seventeenth-century Roman sopranos have been in the news lately: Marc'-Antonio Pasqualini and Loreto Vittori. Both began their careers as choirboys and went on to fame in Urban VIII's papal choir and also on the operatic stage—notably in the splendid productions of Cardinal Antonio Barberini, Urban's nephew. They seem to have been the Faustina and Cuzzoni or Callas and Tebaldi of their day, their names linked in several memoirs. John Evelyn, in his diary, placed Pasqualini first in his list of Rome's "chiefe Masters of Music," and Vittori second. But when Luigi Rossi's seven-hour Ariosto opera *Il palazzo incantato* was presented at the Barberini theatre, in 1642, Vittori (the Angelica), not Pasqualini (the Bradamante), was adjudged the star of the show.

Pasqualini, born in Rome in 1614, was the younger of the two singers, and a favorite of Antonio Barberini. One day when Vittori complained it was so cold in St. Peter's that he had no spirit to sing, Pasqualini had simply skipped the service and was elsewhere with his "Signor Cardinal Protettore"; Margaret Murata, in a 1980 *Analecta Musicologica* article, records this and other occasions (noted in the Sistine Chapel *Diario*) when Pasqualini showed up late or not at all and often gave as an excuse that he was otherwise engaged with the Cardinal. (They seem to have been a lively bunch, these papal choristers; the soprano Angelo Ferrotti—he played the allegorical figure of Magic in *Il palazzo incantato*—once "with his wonted merriment" provoked a shocking outburst of giggles during the recessional.) Iconography as well as documents and the music written by and for these seventeenth-century musicians helps to bring them to life. The Metropolitan Museum has recently acquired the celebrated and splendid life-size portrait of Pasqualini painted by Andrea Sacchi. Pasqualini (who was short, and once referred to "my genius contained within a small frame") stands on the left of the picture, looking out at the spectator with calm, confident intelligence in his clear features. A leopard skin is draped over his white surplice; his right hand rests on the keyboard of a clavicytherium, or upright harpsichord. A tall, blond nude Apollo, derived from the Belvedere figure, stands center, a lyre in his left hand, in his right a laurel wreath, which he holds above Pasqualini's head. On the right, an open-mouthed, discomfited Marsyas is bound to a tree. The prospect behind may be of the Alban hills. In the February *Early Music*, Terence Ford assembles some facts about the picture and follows Sacchi's biographer Ann Harris in suggesting that Giulio Rospigliosi (the librettist of *Il palazzo incantato*, and later Pope Clement IX) was probably its original owner. It seems to me a thoroughly Barberini picture in scale, spirit,

143

and detailed content. A black-and-white reproduction in *Early Music* gives but small idea of its strange, arresting power.

Pasqualini left nearly fifty solo cantatas, "in which more grace and facility appear than force and learning" (Burney's *History*), "which excel in grace and charm" (Gloria Rose in the New Grove). Those I have seen are indeed graceful and charming. Vittori (who was born in Spoleto in 1600 and as a boy sang in the cathedral there when the future Urban VIII was bishop) composed on a larger scale, but the music of all save one of his dramatic works has been lost. The survivor is the opera *La Galatea,* published in Rome in 1639, with a dedication to Antonio Barberini. No evidence of a Roman performance survives, but it was produced in Naples in 1644, and it was produced in New York last month and this by the Mannes Camerata, in Christ Church United Methodist, a picturesque building on Park Avenue. *La Galatea* has had a good press through the centuries. In 1711, Andrea Adami, a papal soprano and a music historian, told of its success, and Burney's *History* has kept the report before the eyes of opera lovers. In 1921, the French musicologist Romain Rolland called it "the finest lyric drama of the first half of the seventeenth century"—a remark given prominence in Donald Grout's *Short History of Opera,* where it has astonished generations of Monteverdi admirers. In 1939, the Italian musicologist Francesco Vatielli called it "one of the best examples of Roman seventeenth-century opera, for its magnificent scenario, the deftness of the scenic action, the happy distribution of solo arias and ensembles, the effective use of choral sections," and continued, "The last act is a true masterpiece for its nobility of expression and grandeur of design." His observations were given prominence in Loewenberg's *Annals of Opera.* And the New Grove tells us that on occasion Vittori surpassed Monteverdi: "Vittori's recitative style is, on the whole, blander than those of Peri and Monteverdi, but moments such as Galatea's [in fact Acis'] lament 'Pur mi lasci, crudele' (in Act 3 scene i) are more intense." All this made one eager to hear the piece. The Mannes performance was no disappointment.

Vittori, his own librettist, seems to have made a conscious attempt at a "reform" opera: a return to tight, moving music drama such as Peri's *Euridice* (1600; produced by the Mannes Camerata last year), Monteverdi's *Orfeo* and Gagliano's *Dafne* (1608; produced by the Camerata in 1982) had been—in contrast to spectacular extravaganzas such as *Il palazzo incantato.* The plot is the familiar one told by Ovid and treated by Handel—the Galatea-Acis-Polyphemus triangle—with the addition of Venus and Cupid and of Cloris (an elderly nymph) and Lucindo (a young shepherd) as participants in the action. Neptune, Jove, and Proteus also put in appearances. The chorus plays sylvans, tritons, and satyrs. The plot spans a day by the Sicilian shore, below Mount Etna. Verbal and musical imagery are vivid; the immortals seem to arrive as embodiments both of smiling, bounteous Nature and of forces within human nature which move men and women to enjoyment or, beneath lust's lash, to perfidy and unkindness. At the start, Acis and Galatea meet eagerly in the sparkling dawn; but Galatea reveals the vein of swift jealousy that (in Vittori's version of the tale) precipitates the tragedy. At the close—after misunderstandings, murder, metamorphosis, and reconciliation—Acis and Galatea join with Proteus in a serene sunset trio. The music is varied in tone—tender, sensuous, merry, poignant, angry—and in its vocal textures. The alternation of dramatic declamation with aria, strophic set piece, or chorus is sure. The emotional climax is "Pur mi lasci." (It was sung with feeling by William Mitchell.) Galatea, too easily persuaded that Acis is untrue, has spurned him cruelly; the faithful, bewildered youth pours out his grief and swoons beneath the weight of it. There follows a monologue for Polyphemus—a little absurd (the Cyclops has combed and adorned his shaggy locks, and trimmed his beard, for Galatea's sake), a little touching, and more than a little alarming in its portrayal of impatient brute violence. Polyphemus comes upon Acis' senseless form and crushes him beneath a rock. The opera moves to its close with a great exequy—choruses and solos as character after character joins the company—enshrining an impassioned lament from Galatea. The flow of music passes, at Jove's decree, into Acis' fluvial transformation and to rejoicing. The physical aspect of the tale—Galatea, a water nymph, can now bathe in her lover, and he envelop her—receives more sensual expression than in any other handling I know. All in all, *La Galatea* is the work of a highly intelligent dramatist and composer, alert both to theatrical technique and to psychological nuance. Martin Morrell, in a program note for the Mannes production, suggests that Cupid would have been Vittori's role had he taken part in a performance. It is more tempting to cast him as Galatea—his singing of a plaint of Mary Magdalen was famous—and the saucy little Pasqualini as Cupid, the breaker of hearts.

The performance was staged and conducted by Paul Echols, the director of the Mannes Camerata, and his presentation was imaginative. Ralph Adam Cram's Christ Church (1932), romantic-Romanesque in manner, is aptly described by the AIA Guide as "an archeological and eclectic stage set." Before the opera began, conches sounded on all sides from the shadows, heralding the arrival of Neptune, who prefaces the opera with a plot summary in five strophes. The band was a consort of strings (both violin and viol families) and organ on one side; on the other, a continuo group of lutes, harp, and harpsichord, with recorders, flutes, shawms, dulcians, a cornet, a sackbut, and percussion to color the various episodes appropriately. The singing, acting, playing, and dancing were, by and large, modestly accomplished—stylish in manner and good enough in execution to let the work come through. The piece was sung in Italian; a bilingual libretto was provided.

The concerts of the Chamber Music Society of Lincoln Center (sometimes dubbed the Sight-Reading Society of Lincoln Center), in Alice Tully Hall, have seldom in my experience maintained a consistently high level, although individual works on a program have on occasion been well performed, with character and conviction. On the whole, the fare has been agreeable and unexacting, offered to an unexigent audience by expert players functioning at reduced voltage. I simply stopped going, preferring to pick out any works or performers of special interest from the WNYC broadcasts of the concerts (at noon on Sundays) and to listen to the masterpieces of the chamber repertory in a chamber more intimate than Tully Hall, performed by artists playing as if their lives, and not simply a livelihood, depended on the result. But the Society looms large on the New York scene: fourteen programs (thirty-five concerts) a season;

145

occasional repeats in Washington; occasional previews elsewhere; nationwide broadcasts. Three premières—commissions from John McCabe, John Harbison, and Ellen Taaffe Zwilich—appear on the 1984–1985 bill. The Society can't just be ignored. I attended the final program, last month, of the 1983–1984 season, which was played by the Emerson String Quartet. (In 1982, the Society decided to engage a quartet-in-residence, instead of entrusting a major part of the chamber repertory to ad-hoc foursomes drawn from the team of Society players, and chose the Emerson.) The concert began with Mozart's late C-major Quartet, the "Dissonanzen," K. 465. I like the Emerson's thin, refined tone, its careful balance, and its elegant sense of rhythm. I admired those qualities when it played the "Dissonanzen" in Tully Hall five years ago, the year after it won the Naumburg, but complained then that the reading lacked force, that even in violent episodes it remained gentle to the point of blandness. Nothing much had changed: once again the dynamic contrasts were reduced; once again we glided over the grit that should make the work ever-startling.

There followed the première of George Tsontakis's String Quartet, commissioned by the Society. It is a four-movement piece, subtitled "Emerson"—not with any transcendentalist intent, it seems, but simply for its first performers. In a program note, the composer described his work as "severely introspective, consistent with a clear reaction to our times; unleashed, relentless, with no editing or tempering of fears and frustrations save careful thought to balance and form." I couldn't engage with it at all—it seemed to me a construction, not an eloquent work of art. The second movement made interesting sounds: Beethoven's "Muss es sein?" question, posed here by viola and cello, was answered by faint, glinting strains from the violins, damped by metal practice mutes ("like stars" is the instruction in the score), while viola and cello, sometimes in octaves, sometimes diverging, continued a dramatic recitative.

OUT OF THE MAZE

May 28, 1984

I BEGAN an evening's listening on Monday last week in Carnegie Hall, where the Danish National Orchestra, conducted by Sixten Ehrling, introduced Hans Abrahamsen's *Nacht und Trompeten* to New York. Abrahamsen, born in Copenhagen in 1952, came to attention when he was eighteen as a highly talented exemplar of Denmark's "new simplicity." Europe's musical "minimalism" was not like America's: it began as something closer to Stravinskian neoclassicism; "concretism" was another name for this reassembling of the stuff of traditional music in modern patterns unrestricted by the traditional canons of relationship and consequence. As the Danish critic Jan Jacoby put it: "History cannot go backwards, and the 'new simplicity' was, in fact, a new way of looking at old material. The well-worn tonal phrases no longer impart their full emotional value. They have become neutralized and can be utilized by the composer like toy bricks, free for him to manipulate. The old gestural coherence has lost its impact, and a new meaning must be sought." But, of course, tonal phrases haven't lost their emotional value; and in their different ways newly simple composers (Kurt Schwertsik in Austria, Jonathan Lloyd in England, Abrahamsen in Denmark, Conrad Cummings in this country) find their way back to what Abrahamsen has called "real music"—new music cognizant of both the adventurous past and the adventurous present. *Nacht und Trompeten*, composed in 1981, was given its first performance in 1982, by the Berlin Philharmonic. It is a short piece (lasting about nine minutes) for classical orchestra—strings, double woodwinds, two trumpets and two horns, kettledrums, no trombones—plus high trumpet, piano, and four more percussionists, called on to play four differently pitched and "beautifully resonant" matched gongs. A program note left the title unexplained. The music suggested that "night" was the confusion of wonderful ideas that the past has left with us, and that "trumpets" heralded an attempt to make sense of it all. Both Abrahamsen's ear for scoring and his inventions were cogent. I look forward to hearing more of his music.

The Danish concert began with Dvořák's overture *Carnival*, of which Mr. Ehrling conducted a gruff, insensitive performance, and continued with Mendelssohn's Violin Concerto—Peter Zazofsky as soloist—and Carl Nielsen's Sinfonia Espansiva. I was tempted to stay; but in a critic's calendar new music takes precedence of old, and at Alice Tully Hall the American Composers Orchestra was offering two world premières and a New York première. To hear the Abrahamsen, I had missed the start of the ACO concert, an account of Randall Thompson's Second Symphony, composed in 1930–31, and revived in honor of his eighty-fifth birthday; there are two recordings of it. The new works that followed were all three easy to listen to, but all three seemed slightly stale. They were by composers older than Abrahamsen—Otto Luening, born in 1900, and Les Thimmig and Joseph Schwantner, born in 1943—and were in comfortable middle-brow manners covered by the fashionable umbrella of the "new romanticism." A composer's age, of course, has no direct bearing on the freshness of his music—next year we celebrate the quatercentenary of Heinrich Schütz, who broke new ground in his eighties—and pieces worth hearing can be written in almost any idiom. (Every musician discovers styles that attract him, others that repel him. Critics try to keep themselves open to as many as possible; I draw a line at music mechanically amplified to a point where it inflicts physical pain and aural damage). There was no harm in these works. It just seemed a pity that performers and listeners were devoting time and attention to commonplaces.

Thimmig's Concerto for Bass Clarinet, commissioned by the ACO, alternated smoochy mood music for the soloist with jazz-inspired episodes for the orchestra. The composer was a polished soloist; Paul Dunkel conducted. Luening's Symphonic Fantasia No. 4, conducted by Leonard Slatkin, was a civilized, unexacting five minutes of musical small talk by a man who has touched and influenced the music of our century at many points—small talk proceeding from a well-stocked and witty mind.

For a while, Schwantner seemed to be an interesting and promising composer. His *Aftertones of Infinity*, commissioned by the ACO (and recorded on Mercury), won a Pulitzer Prize in 1979. The later works of his I've heard have struck me as pretty empty—conventional responses to poetic texts, carried out, admittedly, with confidence, technical skill, and an able command of color. *Magabunda* (*Witchnomad*), first performed in St. Louis last year, ended the ACO concert. It is a setting for soprano and orchestra of four poems—two in English, two in Spanish—from Agueda Pizarro's collection *Sombraventadora/ Shadowinnower*. The English pair first appeared in 1980 for soprano and piano, and were commissioned by Lucy Shelton, who has been the muse of several Schwantner pieces. (Her recording of his *Sparrows*, a cycle for soprano and eight players, in the Smithsonian album N 022, provides a good example of his deft, superficially attractive music.) In the orchestral version and in the new songs Schwantner uses an orchestra as large as Strauss's in the Four Last Songs; and Miss Shelton used a microphone when singing them. Even so, she didn't quite come through. She is a good artist, but her voice is small and often a shade edgy. Although *Magabunda* was written for her, it seemed to be written as if for a fuller and more dramatic soprano.

The conductor was again Mr. Slatkin. In the June *Keynote*, he writes:

> It seems as if the experimentalists of the Fifties and Sixties, although having not completely faded, have been pushed into the background by a school of composers who wish their music to be understood immediately by audiences hearing their works for the first time. This is a great help to the performer as well. Too often I have found it difficult to communicate a work successfully to an audience when I myself have great difficulty understanding all of the musical elements in a given piece.

I can well imagine Mr. Slatkin's having difficulty with, say, such a masterpiece as Elliott Carter's Symphony of Three Orchestras. Composers he commends are David Del Tredici, Schwantner, Christopher Rouse, John Adams, Steve Reich, Robert Beaser, and Jacob Druckman. Well, I've enjoyed works by those able composers, too, but haven't coupled my commendation with sneers at more challenging music appreciated by what Mr. Slatkin calls "just a handful of so-called 'musical élite.'" The "new romanticism" draws close to old commercialism and old laziness. Roger Sessions's chapter "The Listener" in his *The Musical Experience of Composer, Performer, Listener* (a Princeton paperback) provides a thoughtful rebuttal of "the slogan, sometimes couched in more refined and even quasi-intellectual terms . . . 'Give the public what it wants' "; and his chapter "Hearing, Knowing, and Understanding Music" in *Questions About Music* (a Norton paperback) offers encouraging and helpful counsel to the listener with "a willing ear" who is baffled by a difficult new work yet feels that there is "something there." Some good works can be "understood immediately" by audiences hearing them for the first time. Many great works waited long before being understood and enjoyed.

With this concert, the ACO completed its eighth season. It is plainly a valuable, important element in our musical life, this full-sized symphony orchestra devoted largely to contemporary American music. It has championed no special trends. Its programming has had a middle-of-the-road, fair-shares-for-all, something-for-everyone quality. Two paths—one creative, one commemorative—have been pursued. The bills look as if they were drawn up by a middle-aged, fair-minded committee, not by fiery, committed individuals. It is not an organization like the London Sinfonietta, which Nicholas Kenyon, in an article in the June *Keynote* comparing New York's and London's musical life, describes as

an orchestral-sized group that for sheer commitment and excellence outshines anything I encountered in New York. It achieves more than the American Composers Orchestra, because its artistic policy is more characterful, its personnel is more regular, its administration full-time, and its concerts more frequent. It achieves more than Speculum Musicae, because it operates on an altogether larger scale. And in one important sense it achieves more than the New York Philharmonic (and more than London's main orchestras) because the new music it commissions and the contemporary classics it constantly keeps alive are performed with an absolute belief in their worth.

Beside Britons young and old, Gilbert Amy, Berio, Boulez, Earle Brown, Carter, Crumb, Henze, Ligeti, Lutoslawski, Messiaen, Sinopoli, Stockhausen are among the composers played by the Sinfonietta. It has probably given more Carter performances than any other orchestra. (It commissioned *In Sleep, in Thunder*, and took it on tour earlier this year.) Its *intégrales* of Varèse, Webern, Stravinsky, and Roberto Gerhard enriched recent London seasons. It ventures into opera: played for Covent Garden's production of Henze's *We Come to the River* and La Scala's of *The Rake's Progress*; performed and recorded Harrison Birtwistle's *Punch and Judy* (with Phyllis Bryn-Julson and Jan DeGaetani) and Tippett's *King Priam*; next month does Tippett's *Knot Garden* in a run with *La Calisto* at the Royal Court Theatre. (I go into this detail because my remark two weeks ago that New York "lacks any counterpart of the London Sinfonietta" was challenged.) The American Composers Orchestra has its eponymous brief and within it ranges permissively and promiscuously. The lack of partisanship, the refusal to play favorites, is plainly a good thing in some ways but makes it hard for one to get excited about the orchestra. Representation for all is worthy; ardent championship—such as Speculum's, Parnassus's—blazes more brightly. Scanning the ACO's 1984–85 bill, one sees without enthusiasm what are likely to be conscientious, professional performances of several decent compositions from fifty to twenty-five years old, all of them available on record. But sees, too, enough new music, from American composers of every stripe, and even some young ones, to ensure that audiences will be eager to hear at least a part of every program.

Peter Lieberson's Piano Concerto—one of twelve compositions commissioned by the Boston Symphony to mark its centenary—was played in Boston in April last year, and later at Tanglewood. It was revived in Boston this year, and was brought by the orchestra to Avery Fisher Hall last month. It is a substantial three-movement piece, and a fine one—a major addition to the modern concerto repertory. I have admired and liked Lieberson's music since first I heard it—the Concerto for Four Groups of Instruments, played by Speculum in 1973, the

Cello Concerto in 1974. Those works were not easy; I couldn't grasp them at first hearing. But the Concerto for Four Groups was recorded (on CRI), and the Cello Concerto had three performances in successive years; by the third of them I began to hear how its quicksilver ideas fitted together. Then Lieberson stopped composing for a while. He spoke of "musical claustrophobia"; he'd possibly written himself into a postserialism impasse. The Piano Concerto, on which he worked for three years, represents an extraordinary release. It's his first orchestral composition. It's larger, richer, and more confident than anything he's done before. It's music attractive and impressive at a first encounter which becomes more so at each subsequent hearing. [A *recording is now available on New World Records.*]

There are several ways of entering the concerto. The first movement begins with low F-sharps and resolves at length on a bright F-sharp and A-sharp (spelled B-flat) chord. The central movement opens with the same chord but ends with a solo A from the oboe, prepared by a long leading-note trill. At the start of the finale, A's glint through many octaves (rather like the G's at the start of the Nile Scene in *Aida*), but the concerto ends with soft-pulsing F-sharps, to which a crotale at last adds the major third (though it sounds more like a soft, shimmering overtone brought forward than a positive A-sharp or B-flat added). So there is a tonal structure to hang on to. There is also a "program"; for, the program note told us, "each movement reflects in a musical way the composer's 'poetic vision' as based on the Buddhist principles of heaven, earth, and man." The first movement, "earth," is often solid, massy, in low registers. In the second movement, a scherzo enclosing an adagio, "man" is unstable, unpredictable, driven, and—in the adagio—yearning. In the finale, the composer says, "the music is inspired by 'heaven,' not in the theological sense, but in the Buddhist sense of spaciousness, and room for things to take place." Its huge spread of A's at the start seems to lay out a calm universe embracing all. The programmatic summary makes things sound too simple, however; it provides just a starting point for the large, energetic, purely musical adventures. There are also melodies. Lieberson tells us ("It sounds so corny to say this, but it's actually true") that while "sitting around, waiting for something to happen in terms of the piece," he heard a bird sing, and the song suggested a tune, and the tune suggested a twelve-note set, "so I had some material to work with, and that's where it started." The twelve-note melody is a beautiful one—easy to memorize, easy to sing, even easy to harmonize over a ripe Elgarian chord sequence. There is another beautiful melody in the adagio, played by a solo cello accompanied by four violas. The work freely makes use of the gestures, the textures, and the harmonies of romantic piano concertos from Brahms to Rachmaninoff. The piano writing has Chopinesque, Bartókian, Schoenbergian elements; it is fluid, decorative, purposeful. The *Times* critic said, "Mr. Lieberson's intent seems to have been to compose a virtuoso piece that would synthesize many of the influences on twentieth-century music," and found that "the work went along in a disjointed way, one densely packed section following another without discernible logic or sense of inevitability." I didn't find that, and would therefore put it somewhat differently: in giving shape to his clearly formed vision of the concerto, the composer boldly availed himself of still eloquent procedures, timbres, rhetorical modes from the past, as all concerto composers have done. The result never sounds stale or secondhand. It is a thoroughly composed, beautifully worked, excellently balanced, and spacious concerto. At first hearing, I was mildly puzzled by episodes in the finale where the impulse seemed to falter or where joins seemed to show. At later hearings, these became necessary transitions or points of repose.

The piece is dedicated to its first soloist and its first conductor, Peter Serkin and Seiji Ozawa. The piano part is immensely taxing; I thought Mr. Serkin played it superlatively well—with intellectual and physical vigor, lyricism, clarity, and brilliance. Mr. Ozawa's players sounded assured, colorful, committed, and individually eloquent in their solo lines.

CHATTER, PATTER, AND RANT

June 4, 1984

APRIL 5TH was Louis Spohr's two-hundredth birthday. In London, his opera *Faust* (1813) has been revived. In Carnegie Hall last month, his Third Symphony (1828), in C minor, was given what was billed as its American première, by the Youth Symphony of New York, conducted by David Alan Miller. It was hard to credit the first-performance claim: Spohr's name is prominent in nineteenth-century American orchestral history. The New York Philharmonic in its initial brochure, in 1842, announced that it would be performing "the Grand Symphonies and Overtures of Beethoven, Mozart, Haydn, Spohr, Mendelssohn, and other great Masters, with a strength and precision hitherto unknown in this country." In 1844, it pressed Spohr to come over and conduct it. (He wanted to, but said his employer, the Elector of Hesse-Cassel, would not grant him leave of absence.) And, in fact, a glance at Krehbiel's published early annals of the Philharmonic (or a call to Avery Fisher Hall) could have saved the Youth Symphony from pretension: the Philharmonic played Spohr's Third Symphony on February 20, 1875. Well, that's unimportant—unless it was the glamour of a "première" that induced the orchestra to choose for revival the Third Symphony rather than the Fourth. One feels genuinely curious about the Fourth Symphony (1832), entitled "Die Weihe der Töne." It was the first of Spohr's four "program" symphonies. The Philharmonic played it in 1846, 1847, 1850, 1852, 1854, 1857, 1860 (two movements), 1870, 1875. It must have had something, to keep this hold on the repertory while Spohr's other compositions came and went. His first two symphonies (1811 and 1820; played by the Philharmonic in 1848 and 1844) are said to have left their traces on Beethoven. His Third, composed after Beethoven's death, bears traces—in the form of a recurrent *ta-ta-ta-tum* refrain muttered under the melodies—of a rather more famous symphony in C minor. Hearing the piece hardly modified what the textbooks have taught us to think about Spohr's music: "euphonious and amiable but lacking in energy and

151

profile." The phrase, from Gerald Abraham's *Concise Oxford History of Music*, can be paralleled in almost any history of music. Abraham also talks of, and illustrates in a page of music type, Spohr's "imaginative orchestration." That, too, was evident in this performance of the Third Symphony. Euphonious, amiable music; imaginative orchestration; aural confirmation of what the textbooks say—I mustn't sound ungrateful. There are worse ways of spending time. One might be—a critic often is—listening to discordant, disagreeable music ineptly scored. If I sound less than ardently appreciative, it is only because when there is so much music in the world waiting to be played one wants to feel sure that a work by a minor master has been chosen for revival as being an example of the best he has to offer. *Vita brevis* . . .

Admission to the Youth Symphony's concerts is free. The programs are adventurous. (Last season, Schubert's marvellous Seventh Symphony in Brian Newbould's performing edition was a true première, and an important one.) The players, who range in age from twelve to twenty-two, play with an eagerness and spirit seldom heard at the Philharmonic, and they are accomplished. Mr. Miller, a gifted young conductor, led a supple, graceful performance of the symphony—one that made it seem closer to Mendelssohn than to Beethoven. There followed the first movement of Mozart's Sinfonia Concertante for violin and viola, with Nicholas and Victoria Eanet, aged twelve and seventeen, as the soloists. Master Eanet, who has already played with the Philharmonic, is an astonishing young fiddler; his tone is clear and true, and his phrasing had shape and character. His sister was able. The movement was conducted by Alan Kay, the orchestra's assistant conductor.

William Moersch, a marimba virtuoso well known for his work in ensembles, gave his first New York solo recital last week, in Merkin Hall. He played six pieces, the oldest of them written in 1975, drawn from four continents. The marimba has come far both in esteem and in repertory since in the fifth Grove (1954) it was defined as "a curious instrument in use in the southern parts of Mexico." Well before then, Clair Omar Musser's hundred-piece marimba band had played in Carnegie and Milhaud had composed his Concerto for Marimba and Vibraphone. The New Grove traces the instrument's progress from light music to the regular modern orchestra. It was probably Messiaen, in works from *Chronochromie* (1960) on, who made the marimba a familiar sight on the concert platform. Peter Maxwell Davies's *Ave Maris Stella* is at times almost a marimba concerto. The marimba plays a colorful role in Elliott Carter's Triple Duo. It sounds in his Symphony of Three Orchestras, in Tippett's Fourth Symphony and *Mask of Time*, in Davies's two symphonies, in Roger Sessions's later symphonies, *Montezuma*, and *When Lilacs Last*. It's established. But a whole evening of solo marimba? During Mr. Moersch's first piece, Irwin Bazelon's deftly made Suite for Marimba (1980), one began to wonder whether one might get bored with the sound of it. It is not exactly a versatile instrument. It has its specialties, and very striking and effective they are: the pattering tremolo of rapid repeated strokes which is its way, kin to the mandolin's, of sustaining long notes; four-part chords (two beaters in each of the player's hands); sudden flurries; melodies darting through the range of the instrument;

a "mellow" timbre warmer than the incisive "wooden laughter" of the xylophone, less piercingly sweet than the vibraphone's. But once it's been put through its paces?

Well, the marimba was put through its paces again and again in this recital, and there was no boredom in the result. For one thing, each composer used its specialties for his own musical ends (and it was fascinating to hear him doing so). For another, Mr. Moersch is a performer who makes one listen—listen, above all, to a range of pianissimi within pianissimi that hold an audience rapt and silent. Much of the evening was as intimate as a clavichord recital. Both Hans Werner Henze in his *Five Scenes from the Snow Country* (1978) and David MacBride in his *As Before* (1978) employed the device of conjuring a note from silence to just the threshold of audibility—a sonic metaphor of rare charm. Mr. Moersch played a Rolls-Royce of marimbas—a four-and-a-half-octave Yamaha instrument, reaching up from low F. When it was whacked *very* hard, the tone was unpleasing: the chock of the beater on the bar overwhelmed the singing response of the resonator below it. Bazelon used the sound—deliberately, arrestingly, in "dead strokes," where the beaters, having hit, remain in contact with the bars—as a shock device, but elsewhere there were moments when it seemed that either the composer or the performer strove for bigger sounds than the marimba can lyrically provide. Most of the evening, however, was spent in enchanted landscapes created by fine distinctions of timbre and timing. The richest pieces were Henze's *Scenes*, first played by Michiko Takahashi in Tokyo two years ago, and here given its American première, and Richard Rodney Bennett's *After Syrinx II* (1984), composed for Mr. Moersch, and here given its world première. Like Bennett's *After Syrinx I*, which is for oboe and piano, *After Syrinx II* is a flight of musical thoughts inspired by Debussy's *Syrinx*. It is a poetic and beautiful composition. On Yoshihisa Taira's *Convergence I* (1975) Debussy's music, a program note told us, was also an influence. In *For Marimba and Tape* (1982), by the Australian composer Martin Wesley-Smith, the tape sounds, created on Sydney's Fairlight CMI (Computer Musical Instrument), evoke a strange marimba world where instruments can skitter from side to side of the platform, glissade in chords, and sustain resonances without repeated beating. They provided a new, challenging "environment" for the live player in their midst.

The Opera Orchestra of New York's concert performance of *Nabucco* in Carnegie Hall last month brought the local début of the Bulgarian soprano Ghena Dimitrova, who has sung with success in Dallas, London, Milan, Vienna and has been acclaimed as one of the few singers around today with voices big enough for Verdi's dramatic roles and for Santuzza, la Gioconda, Turandot. In an *Opera News* interview last month, Miss Dimitrova told of her realization about two years ago that "there was no one singing my roles with the vocal weight to cover, technically and with volume, this dramatic repertory." She later conceded that there are perhaps two other singers with the necessary physical equipment: "As a dramatic soprano, with the exception of Eva Marton and Angeles Gulin, I believe I am vocally without rivals in this repertory." She made it clear that she was talking about calibre of voice: "I'm not talking about artistry—that's quite another thing." And she has a point. Roles that in Verdi's day Teresa Stolz and in our century Rosa Ponselle, Elisabeth Rethberg, Eva Turner, Maria Caniglia, Zinka Milanov, Maria Callas, Renata Tebaldi sang (the list is easily prolonged) are often now sung by lyric sopranos pushed to—and beyond—the limits of their natural resources. Naturally huge voices have become rare. Miss Dimitrova has one. Her Abigaille in *Nabucco* was loud—excitingly loud. One must not underrate—or overrate—the dramatic force of sheer volume. In answer to Joseph Kerman's celebrated strictures on *Tosca* a prima donna can say "I refute him *thus!*" and cry the final "O Scarpia, avanti a Dio!" with a B-flat riding the orchestra's *fff tutta forza con grande slancio* outburst in a way to turn the "shabby little shocker" into Euripidean tragedy. When Callas sang Tosca at Covent Garden in 1964, the historian Wilfrid Mellers, as stringent a critic of Puccini as Professor Kerman, was sitting behind me, and like everyone else in the house he was overwhelmed by the drama enacted there. I then read with admiration his endeavor in the *New Statesman*, where he reviewed the performance, to reconcile accurate scrutinies of Puccini's skillful, meretricious opera and of Callas's tragic performance. Since opera began, both composers and critics have been at the mercy of singers, who can by genius magnify and by mediocrity obscure the merits of operas, distorting cool, sane judgment.

Commanding the right volume is important, but the sound should be beautiful as well as big—or when not beautiful, at any rate expressive. And the role of Abigaille, like that of Lady Macbeth, calls for much soft, dramatically intense singing. I was impressed by Miss Dimitrova but not "carried away." Mme Milanov, cheered by the public as she entered the Carnegie lobby, attended this *Nabucco*. I felt that those who rose later to cheer Miss Dimitrova to the skies either had short memories or were young and phonographless. Some of her notes were hard and ugly—notes that one flinched from. The sound was more forceful than full, shining, or generous. Her style was plain and energetic; Abigaille may be a two-dimensional character, but Verdi wrote phrases for her, especially in recitatives, that need subtle, imaginative handling. Miss Dimitrova, a tall handsome woman, is due at the Met in 1987–88, as Turandot. The Milan correspondent of *Opera*, reviewing her Turandot at La Scala last year, told of her success, regretted that "delicate singing does not excite the public as much as powerful, loud notes," and wrote of the soprano's "huge voice, her steely tone" and "a certain lack of refinement in her singing." But much can happen in three years. Miss Dimitrova is potentially an important performer.

The hero of the evening was Paul Plishka, the Zaccaria—a prophet apparently compounded of Jeremiah, who did not go Babylon, and Ezekiel, who did. (The Biblical Zechariah was a post-Exile prophet.) On the Met stage, Mr. Plishka sometimes seems to lack character and authority, well though he sings. But here he was imposing: in the stirring cavatina; in the strange, beautiful prayer accompanied by the dusky glow of six cellos; in the fierce prophecy (with its violent dynamic contrasts) of a Babylon laid low, home of hyenas, serpents, and screech owls. By paying careful attention to Verdi's markings, by using the words, by singing in firmly focussed tones what other basses often boom out fuzzily, he made of Zaccaria as noble and dominant a figure as Moses is in Rossini's revised *Mosè*. Allan Monk, a late addition to the cast (he stood in for

Matteo Manuguerra), sang the title role cleanly but with no great dramatic force. The Spanish tenor Jesus Pinto made his American début in the small role of Ismaele, producing much sound from a slight frame, so fervently as to be at once winning and a little absurd. Fenena is also a small role: Patricia Schuman replaced the brief *preghiera* in the score with the somewhat grander setting of the same text which Verdi supplied for the Venetian première of *Nabucco*, in 1842, when the soprano Almerinda Granchi (the Anaide of the Scala's 1840 *Mosè*) was the Fenena. It is less touching, less dramatically apt than the original, but interesting to hear in context. Eve Queler's conducting was spirited and natural.

AIMING HIGH

June 18, 1984

ON the day of the eclipse, Paul Earls's *Icarus*—a "sky opera" that opens with an apostrophe by Pasiphaë to Helios, her father, and ends with a threnody for Icarus, who flew too close to the sun—had its American première, in the Kresge Auditorium of the Massachusetts Institute of Technology. (The Cambridge sky, alas, was sodden that day, the sun invisible.) Earls is a fellow of MIT's Center for Advanced Visual Studies, which collaborated with the Boston Musica Viva to present his opera; eight years ago I admired his one-act *The Death of King Phillip*, performed in a Brookline church with astonishing electronic and CAVS light effects—laser-projected imagery, strobe snapshots of action lingering in silhouette on the scenery after the actors had moved on. *Icarus*, which lasts about fifty minutes, was scenically an even more elaborate affair, to which Otto Piene, the director of CAVS (and scenarist and artistic director of *Icarus*), had contributed inflatable sculpture; Günther Schneider-Siemssen scenery (painted on glass slides and projected from four Pani lanterns) and films; and Earls himself a music-activated computer drawing, laser-projected, of Icarus' flight and fall. The opera has been a long while in the making. Episodes—drafts and sketches—appeared in Washington, in Vienna, in Guadalajara, and at MIT from 1978 to 1981. Ian Strasfogel, as librettist and director, and the Boston Musica Viva, conducted by Richard Pittman, joined in the creation of the full première, at the Ars Electronica festival in Linz in 1982. Last year, the team put on a different production, in a lakeside open-air stadium in Munich. The Cambridge production (with Mr. Schneider-Siemssen as a new collaborator) was different again. Although Eero Saarinen's Kresge Auditorium, housed in a vast, light concrete shell that touches the ground at only three points, is a dramatic place, it is more of a concert or meeting hall than a fully equipped theatre, and it has a platform rather than a stage. Projections must come from the front; Mr. Schneider-Siemssen when painting his slides had to allow for actors' shadows cast on the backcloth. He did so effectively and fulfilled his expressed hope of making the spectators "feel as if they are sitting in a cosmic room, with none of the usual boundaries they are accustomed to experience in the theatre." The human actors of Daedalus and Icarus could not fly aloft on pinions but remained earthbound, waving their arms and shifting their weight, and this was somewhat less than magical. But the evening as a whole was filled with visual marvels close-matched to Earls's imaginative and capable score.

The incidents treated are Pasiphaë's lust for the strong, beautiful bull; the birth of the Minotaur; the building of the Labyrinth; the flight. The work is composed for just three singers (treble, mezzo, and baritone, as Icarus, Pasiphaë, and Daedalus), an unseen amplified speaker (Minos), boys' choir, six instrumentalists (clarinet/saxophone, trumpet, horn, trombone, percussion, piano/synthesizer), and tape—chamber forces, and yet the sound was full, the effect grand. One felt that *Icarus* could as easily fill the State Theater or the Met with music as it did the twelve-hundred-seat Kresge. I should like to see and hear it in a setting where its spectacular elements could be more cogently integrated. In this production, there was a sense that practical limitations had perhaps determined a seriatim display—albeit a fascinating and showy one—of high scenic possibilities rather than a coherent dramatic adventure: item, one inflatable sculpture; item, a live-video sequence of an ambulant singer with simultaneous giant close-ups of his face; item, a montage of the foregoing device and a prerecorded video sequence (Daedalus sings a duet with himself); item, a line drawing laser-projected in glittering sapphire, modulating to emerald, changing its size and jittering into strange distortions at the music's behest.

Each episode was striking in itself and was strongly enacted. Nelda Nelson, the Pasiphaë, a passionate, fearless performer, gazed out with wild surmise as the fruit of lust stirred in her womb and grew before our eyes into a towering, obscene, red Minotaur. Timothy Noble, a singer with a powerful vocal and physical presence, played a Daedalus puffed with pride, glorying in his powerful inventions, careless of the uses to which others might put them. The Treble Chorus of New England, in which boys' distinctive timbre is mixed with girls', voiced Icarus' chromatic—and enigmatic—plaint "What is the use of being a little boy if you are going to grow up to be a man?" with assurance, and Icarus himself, Joseph Olefirowicz, sang his song of soaring aspiration with zest and confidence.

Since American opera houses are evidently unable to offer conductors like Claudio Abbado, Carlos Kleiber, Riccardo Muti, and Georg Solti, all active in European theatres, the working conditions they ask for, they would go unheard here in opera were it not for concert performances. Mr. Muti's *Macbeth* this season, with the Philadelphia Orchestra, was rehearsed to a finer point of musical execution than the Met's. In Chicago, with the Chicago Symphony, Sir Georg conducted two concert performances of *Moses and Aaron*—an opera whose scenic requirements are formidable—and Mr. Abbado three performances of *Wozzeck*. His *Wozzeck* was the most accomplished and accurate account of the score I have heard, with matchless instrumental playing exquisitely balanced. The international cast, led by Benjamin Luxon in the title role and Hildegard Behrens as Marie, both first-rate, was strong. Yet somehow

I found the presentation curiously unmoving, even though it was on a musical level that one should be greeting with rapture. And I'm puzzled to know why. One reason may be that the tone of the Chicago Symphony—strings, winds, and brasses—is less warm, less emotional, less tender than that of, say, the Vienna Philharmonic. Everything is well-nigh perfect, but with an almost inhuman perfection. Another reason may be that the mode of presentation fell awkwardly between a concert and a theatrical performance. This *Wozzeck* was fully enacted, in costumes, on a stage—a broad wooden platform above the instrumentalists, ringing the apse of Orchestra Hall. There were "locations," each lit up in turn, but there was no scenery: the Captain's room imagined right; Marie's room at the center, represented by a chair; the pub left, represented by the out-of-tune piano. The actors made entrances and exits or moved from one "scene" to another. A large circle on the central bank of organ pipes glowed red to serve as the setting sun in the second and as the blood-red moon in the penultimate scene.

Concert presentations of opera, if they are to be more than "stand up and sing when your turn comes," need tactful handling. Entrances and exits can be useful. In Ottocento works, the great moment of a prima donna's entrance aria is effectively enhanced if she sallies on for the first time during the ritornello. Singers' moves between side seats and center seats can help an audience to know who's meant to be onstage at any moment—addressed, or perhaps eavesdropping—and who's not. Carefully chosen modern costume can suggest character: a Julius Caesar or a Tamerlane sung by a bejewelled mezzo in a low-cut, billowing evening dress would inhibit the idealized "staging" that takes shape in listeners' minds when, libretto in hand, they attend to a concert performance. Much depends on the nature of the work. Newell Jenkins's Clarion Concerts, Eve Queler and her Opera Orchestra of New York, the Sacred Music Society, Carnegie's recent Rossini and opéra-comique presentations have addressed the problem in different ways and have shown what works, what doesn't. (Clarion's *La pietra del paragone*, the Sacred Music Society's *Il crociato in Egitto*, and Miss Queler's *Rienzi* were particularly successful.) The Chicago *Wozzeck*, which was directed by Roberto Goldschlager, attempted too much theatrically, I think, and adulterated the fine musical rendering with a half-baked staging. (Not Mr. Goldschlager's fault; he did what could be done in absence of a theatre.) In a concert hall, one can't have the best of both worlds, music and drama. "Drama through music" must be the aim, aided by some discreet theatrical touches that enhance but do not distract from the special merits of concert performance: concentration on the music itself; musical excellence difficult to achieve when not just the music and its meaning but also moves, costumes, scenery, the practical difficulties of keeping together must all be considered. Concert opera is not a substitute for the real thing but a close-up of some elements—the most important—of the rich amalgam from which operas are made. I'd like to hear the Chicago *Wozzeck* again as a broadcast, following it with libretto or score in hand. (In Orchestra Hall, we sat in the dark.) But in one respect, at least, a broadcast would be unable to do justice to it. Berg asked for the chamber orchestra of Act II, Scene 3, to be "distinct if possible from the main orchestra," and in Mr. Abbado's performance this separation and the balance between the chamber orchestra, the main orchestra, and the voices were more beautifully achieved than in any theatre production I have heard.

Gerhard Unger—for decades a sweet-voiced, youthful David and Pedrillo—was a trenchant, testy Captain. Robert Cole's Simpleton was striking. The other tenors, Philip Langridge as Andres and Jacque Trussel as the Drum Major, were both able but rather dry of tone. Alexander Malta was an excellent Doctor. Fiona Kimm, always a vivid performer, was the Margret. Richard Cohn and Paul Kreider, the two Apprentices, were good. Thinking back over the performance, I recall passage after passage of finely wrought instrumental playing and of careful, intelligent singing but not a complete, overwhelming dramatic event.

Chicago Opera Theatre, which began its performances in 1974, has in most of its seasons presented a Mozart opera, a contemporary opera, and (since 1979) a third opera often not standard fare: *The Pearl Fishers*, *Martha*, *La rondine*. It plays in the Athenaeum Theatre, a nine-hundred-seat house in the former German neighborhood of Chicago, built early this century as a home for Singspiel and operetta. I had heard good things about the company, which rehearses its productions for five weeks, and found them to be justified when I visited its *Mother of Us All* last month. *Mother*, an irresistibly attractive and moving masterwork, can triumph in small-scale redactions with a handful of instrumentalists and a handful of singers doubling up in the numerous roles, but in a performance with the full orchestration and the full cast Virgil Thomson's extraordinary achievement glows even more brightly. His ear for exact rhythmic inflections and for melodies that turn American speech into memorable song is matched by a command of clear, bold, suddenly thrilling instrumental color. When listening to *Mother*, I'm tempted to consider it the best of all American operas; and on calm reflection I'd hardly modify that beyond "one of the three or four best." Though I think I've got to know the piece well, each performance brings new discoveries. There's a mystery here. Thomson describes his score as "an evocation of nineteenth-century America, its gospel hymns and cocky marches, its sentimental ballads, waltzes, darn-fool ditties, and intoned sermons . . . a memory book, a souvenir of all those sounds and kinds of tunes that were once the music of rural America and that are still the basic idiom of our country." The ingredients used are simple—limpid tunes, diatonic harmonies—but the detail is so subtle, dexterous, and elegant that Gertrude Stein's text and Thomson's music unite in an opera at once charming, serious, and important, even heroic.

Carmen Pelton—also the heroine of the small New York production last year—was a serene, sensitive, resolute, vulnerable, shining Susan B. Anthony, steady and clear and unforced of voice. Twenty-four others made up a cast of delightfully varied character and almost uniform accomplishment. Mary Griswold designed the sets and Kate Bergh the costumes. Geoffrey Bushor's lighting was adept and was executed with split-second precision. Frank Galati was the stage director. Steven Larsen conducted a poised, well-paced, well-played performance. Verdi once said that a single directing intelligence should take responsibility for every detail of an operatic performance; and here, the program told us, "the entire production [was] under the artistic supervision" of Alan Stone, the founder and the artistic director of the company.

Paean

SAN ANTONIO, with its riverside walks through the heart of the city, its flowers and trees and birds, its ethnic diversity, its comfortable hotels, and its warm climate, makes a good festival place, and the San Antonio Festival, now in its second year, is generously and exuberantly planned. Amid plays, ballets, shows, concerts of all kinds, there were five operas to be heard during its three weeks: *Carmen* (a Berlin Opera production reworked for an open-air riverside theatre), three Brittens (the English National's *Gloriana* and *Turn of the Screw*, and *Noye's Fludde*), and Rossini's *Guillaume Tell. Tell*, it seems, had been unstaged in this country for over half a century, although it is not a rarity in Europe. In London, I saw four different productions in fifteen years. (Last month, for a change, Grétry's *Guillaume Tell* was done there.) But all four were much abridged and all were in translation, Italian or English. Uncut performances—perhaps the first since the opening night, at the Paris Opéra in 1829—were provided by Riccardo Muti, at Florence's 1972 Maggio Musicale, and by the 1973 Angel recording, with Montserrat Caballé, Nicolai Gedda, and Gabriel Bacquier. (The recorded account is "more than complete" in that it includes, as an appendix, an unpublished air for Jemmy, Tell's son, which Rossini decided not to use.) The San Antonio production was sung in an Italian translation (why not in English or in Spanish, if an original-language version presented difficulties?) and was very heavily abridged. It offered only two and a half hours of music—against the four hours of the Angel recording. *Tell* is customarily shortened, but these cuts were crippling—especially those at the start and the close of Act II (an act Donizetti declared to have been composed not by Rossini but by God) and in the finale. An admirer of Rossini's last opera was torn between pleasure that the piece had been revived at last, tolerance of the shortcomings ascribable to practical necessity, and indignation at the further, wanton injury that had been inflicted on the work.

Tell is an elevated, austere composition: a four-act grand opera conducted in ensembles, choruses, and recitatives, with only four solo numbers—the soprano romance "Sombre forêt," an air apiece for the soprano and the tenor, and the baritone's twenty-eight-bar "Sois immobile," as Tell warns his son to keep very still while balancing the apple on his head. And only the last of them was regularly sung: the tenor air disappeared after the first night and was not reinstated at the Opéra until 1837; the soprano's air was customarily omitted, and her romance sometimes went, too. The drama is that of a people's rebellion slowly gathering force—incident upon incident conspiring to strengthen resolve either generally or in individuals until in Act IV the storm breaks at last, both as

159

a scenic metaphor and in the patriots' hearts. Austrian tyranny is overthrown. And then, as Desmond Shawe-Taylor has put it:

> The last pages of *William Tell* are among the great inspirations of operatic music. The storm has cleared away, and an immense view opens up: in the distance, snowy peaks glisten in the sunshine. A single motive (suggesting the *ranz des vaches*) is passed upward from horn to woodwind, moving through numerous keys both major and minor, while the characters contemplate the scene, their hearts filled with joy, and at last unite their voices in a great paean to liberty. After this apotheosis, it is almost understandable that Rossini should never have written another line for the theatre.

In liberal Tuscany, *Tell* could be performed (in 1831) in straight Italian translation, but in Hapsburg-ruled Milan the tale of Hapsburg oppression was safely distanced to Scotland, as *Guglielmo Vallace*, and in papal Rome *Tell* became *Rodolfo di Sterlinga* and *Giuda Maccabeo*. This opera, composed during the closing stages of the Greek War of Independence, while in Italy the Risorgimento was stirring, can still chime with what we read in newspapers each day. I'm not suggesting that Frank Corsaro, the director of the San Antonio production, should have relocated the action in San Salvador, Manila, Warsaw, or Johannesburg—only that he should have perceived more clearly what the opera is about and how its drama is paced. Act II ends with a secret assembly—the men of Unterwalden, the men of Schwyz preceded by a cautious horn call, the men of Uri accompanied in their passage across the lake by a soft-lapping cello melody—and a conjuration of the cantons, resolving to rise when a signal fire flares out. Mr. Corsaro ended it with a Swiss-Austrian skirmish. Act III ends with the populace crying imprecations on Gessler, the Austrian governor, but restrained from armed defiance by his threat to kill Tell on the spot. Mr. Corsaro ended it with a Swiss-Austrian skirmish. And thus he leached out tension that should mount until in Act IV, at the height of the tempest, Jemmy gives the signal for rebellion by setting Tell's house ablaze. Had Mr. Corsaro cast more than a perfunctory glance at the libretto? In Act I, Tell saves a patriot's life by rowing him across the lake while his pursuers stand baffled on the shore; in Mr. Corsaro's version the pursuers themselves arrived by boat, and the episode lost its point. In Act III, there is an entrance for Princess Mathilde, come to put a stop to Gessler's atrocious behavior; Mr. Corsaro brought her on at the start of the scene, and she sat there enthroned, mute, making ineffectual moues of distaste, until the moment for her intervention arrived. Earlier, there's a striking tableau: Gessler has ordered the Swiss to bow down to his hat, set up on a pike, and at the end of the dancing they do so—all except two who remain standing, Tell and Jemmy. And that's what brings about the appleshooting episode. There was no such tableau in Mr. Corsaro's staging. On the simplest level of theatrecraft, the shooting of the apple off Jemmy's head was muffed; it's a stage trick I've seen brought off in a town-hall production in a way that made the audience gasp.

The evening began well, for the opera was presented in the Majestic Theatre, a late-twenties extravaganza by John Eberson (known in New York for his Loews Paradise, on the Grand Concourse—a house now unhappily "quadded," and ruined). The Majestic went dark in the mid-seventies and was rescued in the early eighties by the Pace Management Corporation, of Houston—to join the lengthening list of show palaces happily saved for the arts. The audience sits in a Hispano-Moresque courtyard surrounded by towers, turrets, and balconies. The ceiling simulates a deep-blue night sky with twinkling stars. Doves perch on the balustrades. Cypresses rise against the dusk. The Majestic originally held some thirty-seven hundred. Now (the "colored balcony," with its separate entrance, once a regular feature of Southern theatres, has been closed off) it holds about a thousand less. It is a place made for a Sarah Caldwell production of *La Favorite* or *Il trovatore*. Alhambran enchantments play no part in *Tell*, however; the stars were switched out when the opera began. The orchestra pit is long but narrow; five double-basses were stationed outside it on the house floor, to the left, and the harp and the percussion battery to the right. The conductor, Carlo Franci, presided from the house side of the pit rail. But the sound was full-bodied and the balance was fine where I sat, toward the front of the main balcony. The overture was well played. Later, Mr. Franci tended to hold his singers to the beat in places where expressive phrasing was called for. He was efficient but unyielding. Franco Colavecchia's décor was skillful—the boat service on Lake Lucerne was frequent—but not picturesque. The 1829 designers visited Switzerland to seek authentic inspiration.

Tell is hard to cast. Of the three principals, only Giorgio Zancanaro, in the title role, reached an acceptable festival standard. Margaret Pent, the Mathilde, and Giuliano Ciannella, the Arnold, were taxed beyond their resources. (Miss Pent included Mathilde's air—at any rate, its first movement—which I had never heard onstage before; it had been shifted from Act III to Act IV.) Harolyn Blackwell was a bright, clear Jemmy. The chorus—most of it from Bloomington, Indiana—was small (thirty-eight voices) but sang strongly. I'd be prepared to commend the show blandly as a brave stab at a difficult opera had I not seen *Tell* productions by even more modest forces which realized the innate grandeur of the work—and had not San Antonio itself, in a *Rienzi* seven years ago, shown that it can do grand opera in a grand way. *Guillaume Tell* has merits that were unrevealed here.

GOLDS AND BLUES

July 2, 1984

LAST June, the New York Philharmonic, once its regular season was done, presented a seven-concert contemporary-music festival called Horizons '83, subtitled "Since 1968, a New Romanticism?" With the question mark, Jacob Druckman, the Philharmonic's composer-in-residence and the artistic director of the festival, proposed that in music there had been a swing from what he called (in a program-book essay) "the Apollonian, the Classical—logical, rational, chaste, and explainable" toward "the Dionysian, the Romantic—sensual, mysterious, ecstatic, transcending the explainable." Among the works played at the festival were David Del Tredici's *All in the Golden Afternoon,* Aaron Jay Kernis's *Dream of the Morning Sky,* Frederic Rzewski's *Le Silence des espaces infinis.* Composers not played were Pierre Boulez, Milton Babbitt, Iannis Xenakis, and Elliott Carter—grouped in Mr. Druckman's essay as presenting "the quintessential statement of those Apollonian ideals ... an elevation of rationalism to unprecedented heights." That there has been "a return to romanticism" was not really in question—a return to tonality, to the sound of the full symphony orchestra, to the symphony itself, to opera. Mahler's music fills our concert halls. Close academic study of once-scorned composers such as Donizetti, Bellini, and early Verdi flourishes and is found respectable. Modern composers are carried on the tide and help to swell it. Karlheinz Stockhausen is engaged on an opera more ambitious than *The Ring*; Peter Maxwell Davies proclaims the influence of Schumann and Sibelius on his symphonies; Charles Wuorinen proves Schoenberg's dictum that there is still plenty of good music to be written in—or at least on—C. Mr. Druckman was criticized by some both for his categorizations and for his choices. In fact, Horizons '83 presented seven concerts of uncommon interest, which stirred debate, inevitably inconclusive, on reasons for the new romanticism and on its dangers as well as its delights. (Boulez, in an interview reported in the current *New York Review of Books,* discerns a "protective phenomenon ... a kind of anxiety in trying to find a refuge in old values that are no longer relevant.") And it demonstrated the very wide diversities of matter and manner, of intent and technique, to be found in scores that could all fairly be placed within the pale.

This year, the Philharmonic gave us Horizons '84, subtitled "The New Romanticism—A Broader View." It was a ten-concert event (in nine days), and one of even greater interest. Several essays in a good program book, edited by Linda Sanders, pondered the broader issues. Three concerts devoted to music in whose creation computers had played a part formed a small festival within the festival, and two concerts presented "The New Virtuosity"—in works by composer-performers who have mastered extended instrumental and vocal techniques. I'll leave consideration of those to later reviews, even though it means delaying any account of the most exciting première, Wuorinen's *Bamboula Squared,* for orchestra and quadraphonic tape. I've not attended another contemporary-music festival on this scale with so few duffed or dull pieces. Admittedly, the programs were largely retrospective, reaching from Babbitt's *Correspondences,* of 1966–67, toward only three large premières: works by Roger Reynolds and George Crumb, and the Wuorinen. "Where have we got to?" rather than "Where are we going to?" was the question. If there was not the excitement of a pathbreaking new piece by a Stockhausen, a Boulez, a Ligeti, there were few pigs in pokes. Only one of the composers—Diamánda Galás—was under thirty.

Plainly not by chance, those four composers named for exclusion in 1983 were this year all represented: Boulez by *Domaines,* Babbitt by *Correspondences,* Xenakis by *Khal Perr,* and Carter by his Brass Quintet. "Today's exceptions," Mr. Druckman wrote in the program book, "are often as

162

worthy of attention as that music which moves with the tide," and "this year we can take a broader view and include some of those other musics which are in no way romantic but which are also strong and vital." Stronger, more vital, worthier of attention, many listeners may have felt; three, at least, of the four pieces dominated the programs in which they were played, and *Correspondences* might have done so, too, had it been interpreted and executed with the verve and brilliance that Babbitt's music always calls for. The Carter was played by the American Brass Quintet, for whom it was written, ten years ago. Three of the players have changed since then, but the ensemble's performance becomes ever more lyrical, confident, and nuanced. And it is hard to think of a definition of "romantic" that must exclude this character-filled, vivid dialogue. In Avery Fisher Hall (where all the concerts were held), the big solo calls and the full, solemn, swelling chordal passages rang out bravely, while the fleet, scurrying, whispered episodes were excellently audible. In fact, Fisher Hall, so often found unsatisfactory as a home for nineteenth-century romantic music, lent itself admirably to bright modern music for small forces and to works meant to be heard partly or wholly through loudspeakers.

The program including the Carter Quintet was completed by four orchestral pieces, played by the Philharmonic, conducted by Leonard Slatkin. Christopher Rouse's *The Infernal Machine* (1981) is a five-minute trifle for large orchestra which is going the rounds as a piece of modern music making few demands on listeners' intelligence or patience. The title is from Cocteau, but there is nothing Oedipal about the program. The work is, in its composer's accurate description, "a brief orchestral showpiece inspired by the vision of a great self-sufficient machine eternally in motion to no particular purpose." It's cleverly scored. The St. Louis Symphony, conducted by Mr. Slatkin, gave the New York première in March, in Carnegie Hall. I thought it ingenious but empty both then and at this second hearing, yet would defend its inclusion on the Horizons bill, if only as an example of what our more conservative conductors are choosing to play. There followed Robert Beaser's *The Seven Deadly Sins*, a song cycle composed in 1979 for baritone and piano, here receiving its première in a recension where the baritone (Jan Opalach) was drowned by an accompaniment for full orchestra. I've admired *The Seven Deadly Sins* in its piano-accompanied version; the orchestra obscures its trenchant, witty setting of Anthony Hecht epigrams. Next, there was Thea Musgrave's *Peripeteia* (1981), a capable, modestly adventurous composition, which needs more carefully balanced and more colorful execution than it received. The concert ended with Donald Erb's *Prismatic Variations* (1983), a harmless, agreeable work, made entertaining by the presence of about a hundred extra players (here the Bergen Youth Orchestra) scattered through the audience and blowing harmonicas, delicately tinging on telephone bells, ringing glasses, or blowing across the tops of soda-pop bottles. Mr. Slatkin prefaced the performance with a demonstration of these effects; the last of them gave forth an ethereal, dovelike sound, reminiscent of the twelve ocarinas in Penderecki's *And Jacob Awaked*.

The Babbitt and Xenakis works appeared in computer-music programs. The Boulez ended an evening of mainly French music, conducted by Gilbert Amy,

163

which began with Betsy Jolas's elegantly terse *Quatre Plages* (1968), for string orchestra—not a beach piece, but with *plage* signifying "a portion of time occupied by a specific type of sound-structure." Amy's own *Shin'anim Sha'-ananim*, or *Angels of the Throne* (1979), which was played by Speculum Musicae, is a glowing, ecstatic composition. For years, Boulez has spoken of reworking *Domaines* (1968)—limpid stichomythia between a peripatetic clarinettist and small groups of players seated on points of a circle around him—in a more elaborate way. "I shall integrate the soloist with the group in front of which he is playing. . . . The structure is too simple. . . . What is needed is a more complex structure, and above all more ensemble work." The result should be enthralling. But there is something very satisfying in the lucidity of the familiar *Domaines*, with its "geographical representation of what happens in the score." Stanley Drucker was the accomplished protagonist.

The festival opened, aptly, with Henze's *Tristan* (1973), in its American première. Henze has ever been a romantic. As Paul Griffiths puts it in the program book:

> When, in the middle 1950s, Stockhausen was working on *Gruppen* and Boulez on *Le Marteau sans maître*, Henze was writing opera, ballets, and symphonic pieces. For him, the only change brought about by the new climate of the 1970s was a change in status. Instead of being regarded as an outsider, he became a rallying point for young composers, particularly in Germany, and this coincided with the change in his political outlook, his resolve to march with his younger colleagues on the road to socialism.

Tristan, commissioned by the London Symphony Orchestra, is a long (nearly forty-five-minute) six-movement composition for piano, electronic tapes, and large orchestra. It grew from Henze's dreams, his nightmares, his mourning political (for Salvador Allende, for Chile) and personal (for his librettists W. H. Auden and Ingeborg Bachmann, who both died while he was engaged on the fifth movement); from adventures with strange new sounds discovered and collected in Peter Zinovieff's electronic studio; from memories; from citations direct or oblique, newly scored or electronically transformed, of Wagner's *Tristan*, the old Florentine "Lamento di Tristano," Brahms's First Symphony, Chopin's Funeral March. The first movement opens with the exposition of a twelve-note row, "tenderly," on the piano—a slow melody lapped in chromatic harmonies—and ends on a long, soft chord of A minor. Into the chord there steals a quaint, sweet twangling—the "Lamento" played on Renaissance instruments, tape-transformed. The fifth movement is a set of three alarming dances, "tormenting, reeling hallucinations and grotesques" (the quotations are from a vivid essay Henze wrote about the piece), silenced at last by "a scream of death—no longer simply that of Isolde or Tristan, but of the whole suffering world—which seems to burst the bounds of concert music." In the finale, a boy's voice (an echo of Stockhausen's *Gesang der Jünglinge*?) reads two moving sentences telling of the death of Yseult, from the *Tristan* of the twelfth-century poet Thomas, in A. T. Hatto's English translation, while a heartbeat thuds on the tape and the strings play the start of Wagner's third act. Then bells ring out, as if from Venice's many towers, and from the tape there sounds, like a chaconne, swelling and waning, electronic transformations of this ancient music, glittering like the sea on an autumn evening when the golds and blues so often evoked by Trakl are shining and red maple leaves float on the canals. In this light, in these sounds, in the lamenting and the silences, all that has accompanied the composition comes together: places and people, the Klagenfurt cemetery, the Santiago football stadium, the deaths and the manners of death which have impoverished mankind. . . .

A black gondola appears, comes from the portal of the Vendramin Palace, bearing a veiled woman and the coffin that accompanies her; Tadzio disappears over the horizon. . . . Buffets of wind greet me. Dust and yellow maple leaves blow across the Campo, and a flock of grey pigeons flutters toward me as if bringing further fearful news.

In its richness of allusion, in its multiplicity of techniques, in its tonal episodes, in its use of orchestra, of tape music, and of soloist, and in its programmatic content, *Tristan* brought together much of what was separately explored during the succeeding days. It was well played, with the Philharmonic under the composer's baton and Emanuel Ax as the pianist—if not quite as securely as it is on the Deutsche Grammophon recording. A second performance would have formed a fitting, culminating close to the festival.

Henze has from the start—when, after the war, he emerged as a prodigiously accomplished young composer with Schoenbergian and Stravinskian techniques at his fingertips and something of his own to say—been an absorber: heedless of fashionable fame (like Romain Rolland's Jean-Christophe, he fled the "music marketplace" to pursue his own visions) but quick to discern what might be valuable, eloquent, and pertinent to his own purposes on the waves thrown up by the busy fifties, sixties, and seventies. Boulez, in that interview, talks with not unjustified scorn of fashion—"the 'stereophonic' year, the 'chance' year, the 'formless' year, the 'novel tone colors' year." He might have added the "total serialization" year, the "peripatetic players" year. But during those years Boulez himself made waves, testing notions of, especially, total serialization and determinate choice to what might have proved their breaking point had the compositions in which he embodied them not been so strong, so logical, and so musically rewarding. And in most of those years discoveries were made that composers have continued to profit by, as Henze does. Where Boulez can say, "The phenomenon of our heritage is no longer important to me," Henze brings the past and an ever-expanding present together. Penderecki, whose First Symphony (1973) completed the first Horizons concert, has been a man of mode, applying vanguard manners to big themes (the Passion and the Resurrection of Christ, Auschwitz, *Paradise Lost*) in a way that has impressed the public. The symphony was commissioned by Perkins Engines, a British diesel manufacturer, and was played for its workers, in Peterborough Cathedral, by the LSO. They may have been diverted by hearing factory noises so skillfully imitated and organized. At a talk before the concert, Penderecki said he no longer composed music in this manner, because orchestras hated playing it. Yet the Philharmonic's performance, under the composer's baton, seemed efficient enough.

At the penultimate concert, Oliver Knussen's one-act fantasy opera *Where the Wild Things Are* (1979–83) had its American première. It was the only Horizons event conducted by Zubin Mehta (who the day before had been conducting Covent Garden's new production of *Aida*). The opera is based on Maurice Sendak's story-and-picture book of the same title (1963), whose hero, Max, seems to be as familiar to children today as Alice, Winnie-the-Pooh, Peter Rabbit, and Mrs. Tittlemouse were in my nursery. Sendak wrote the libretto. The opera, incomplete at its Brussels première in 1980 and at a London concert performance in 1982, was staged with considerable success at London's National Theatre earlier this year, in a Glyndebourne production directed by Frank Corsaro, designed by Sendak, and played by the London Sinfonietta, under the composer's baton. The book's lack of morality bothers me somewhat. Max behaves very badly—in a way to recall an Auden-Britten petition in the closing litany of their *Paul Bunyan,* for deliverance from "children brought up to believe in self-expression"—and is sent to bed without his supper. But instead of being punished he is rewarded with an exciting adventure, and supper waits for him at the end of it. The opera, however, adds a touch missing in the book (and Mr. Corsaro's production underlined it): during a wild rumpus, one of the Wild Things "literally loses its head in the chaos," and Max realizes that bad behavior may be not merely uncouth but also destructive and unkind. And so, like the Child in the Colette-Ravel opera *L'Enfant et les sortilèges,* which underlies *The Wild Things,* he "earns" his reward. Nevertheless, I remain uneasy about the implicit allegory of a white boy's being innately superior to lesser breeds without the Law and about his ability, Mowgli-like, to subdue wild creatures by looking them straight in the eye.

The Philharmonic performance was high-spirited but coarse-grained. The voices were rudely overamplified, and the orchestral playing had none of the delicacy and shimmer and fine, sensitive phrasing that the Sinfonietta brought to the piece. In fact, if I'd not heard (on tape) and seen (on videotape) the Glyndebourne production—with the same delightful Max, Karen Beardsley—I'd be wondering why *The Wild Things* has been so much praised.

Another British music-theatre piece, Harrison Birtwistle's *Down by the Greenwood Side* (1969), had its New York première at the final concert. This is a grimmer drama, its central figure being the Cruel Mother of the old ballad (played by Susan Belling) who plunges a penknife both long and sharp into the hearts of her two unwanted babes. Like *The Wild Things,* it suffered from the lack of dramatic presentation, from unnatural amplification of the voices, and from being played in a hall far too large for it.

The Knussen was preceded by Crumb's *A Haunted Landscape,* conducted by Arthur Weisberg—a Philharmonic commission. This is eighteen minutes of exquisite mood music; perhaps one should say "moods music," for the composer in his program note talks of the "tiny, subtle nuances of emotion and sensibility" induced by contemplation of landscapes that history has made numinous; he instances Jerusalem, Delphi, and West Virginia woods where "one senses the ghosts of the vanished Indians." It's a mysterious, transcendental emotion (Boulez might grow impatient with it) that lends itself to music; passages of *The Ring,* Holst's *Egdon Heath,* Tippett's *The Midsummer Marriage* come to mind. Crumb's score, laid out over an unchanging *ppp* low B-flat pedal on two double-basses, is a thing of rustlings, tappings, tickings, fine-spun hazy chords, pulsings, sudden chirrups, exclamations or solemn proclamations from brasses or winds. In one passage, three clarinets seem to wheel overhead like birds of augury.

SOUND-HOUSES

July 9, 1984

IN 1624, Francis Bacon, in *The New Atlantis*, predicted with some accuracy what would be happening at IRCAM and in the computer-music studios of San Diego, Stanford, Murray Hill, and elsewhere three and a half centuries later:

> We have also sound-houses, where we practice and demonstrate all sounds, and their generation. We have harmonies which you have not, of quarter-sounds, and lesser slides of sounds. Divers instruments of music likewise to you unknown, some sweeter than any you have; together with bells and rings that are dainty and sweet. We represent small sounds as great and deep; likewise great sounds extenuate and sharp; we make divers tremblings and warblings of sounds, which in their original are entire. We represent and imitate all articulate sounds and letters, and the voices and notes of beasts and birds. We have certain helps which set to the ear do further the hearing greatly. We have also divers strange and artificial echoes, reflecting the voice many times, and as it were tossing it: and some that give back the voice louder than it came; some shriller, and some deeper; yea, some rendering the voice differing in the letters or articulate sound from that they receive. We have also means to convey sounds in trunks and pipes, in strange lines and distances.

In 1906, Thaddeus Cahill demonstrated his two-hundred-ton Telharmonium, which generated sound by electricity, and which led Busoni, in his "Sketch for a New Aesthetic of Music," to ask, "In what direction does the next step lead?" and answer, "To abstract sound, to unhampered technique, to unlimited tonal material." The development of the valve oscillator, a decade later, and the inventions of the Theremin, the Ondes Martenot, and the Trautonium made new sounds less cumbrously achievable. But only the advent of the tape recorder (which composers began to compose with in the fifties—Cage's *Imaginary Landscape No. 5*, Varèse's *Déserts*), then the electronic sound synthesizer (which Stockhausen used, together with tape-manipulated natural song, to create *Gesang der Jünglinge*), and now the computer has made possible that complete control of sound which Bacon described: analysis, dissection, whole or partial metamorphosis, and reassembly, as required, of all existing sounds; the invention of sounds unheard before, precisely formulated, in precisely determined structures; the ability to make sounds walk or dart or whirl through space along plotted paths.

167

The medieval theorists related music to mathematics: 4:5:6 represents a perfect major triad. Today, any sound or combination of sounds, however intricate, can be represented by numbers—digital recording depends on this. Time, expense, and the composers' technological skills are the only impediments to composition. When IRCAM was conceived, in 1970—readers of the June *Ambassador*, TWA's flight magazine, discover—"even the most powerful musical computers, or 'signal processors,' could take a week to produce a sound after receiving a direction, months for an entire short composition." And in the program book of Horizons '84—the Philharmonic's contemporary-music festival, at which three concerts were devoted to music in whose making computers played a part—Richard Moore, the director of the San Diego Center for Music Experiment and of its Computer Audio Research Laboratory, writes:

> A ten-minute musical composition done in stereophonic sound . . . might require about one hundred twenty million eight-bit bytes of computer memory just to hold the sound itself, exclusive of the computer program. Simple musical sounds might require about a hundred computer operations to calculate each number. Assuming that a good-sized modern computer can execute a million operations per second, it would take about seventeen hours to compute that ten-minute piece of music. More complex sounds might require ten or a hundred times more computation.

It's a far cry from a composer who, pen or pencil in hand, sets down on staff paper notes that indicate pitch and relative durations but cannot with precision define timbre, changes of timbre, changes of speed. And a farther cry from the composers who would turn out a long opera in weeks, in days, and count upon its executants to add the necessary "finishing touches"—different at every performance—to the music.

The Horizons concerts were prefaced by a two-session symposium on computers and art in which famous figures in the field, their names familiar from the textbooks—Richard Moore, Max Mathews, Benoit Mandelbrot, Harold Cohen—took part, along with the two composers, Charles Wuorinen and Roger Reynolds, who had planned the concerts. The participants stressed that full-scale computer composing was an expensive business and that only the well-equipped and generously supported studios can provide an ambitious composer with complete control of all sound. (IRCAM is subsidized to the tune of about four million dollars a year; I don't know what the San Diego, Stanford, Bell Labs budgets are.) They also stressed that the instruments of electronic music are still developing very fast, and that computers are one of the few things in the world that become cheaper. (Xenakis, in a program note for his *Khal Perr*, given its American première at a Horizons concert, looked forward to a time when all would be able to compose freely on their home computers, linked into immense sonic and system resources held at "university centers, conservatories, and all cultural centers.") Many musicians have had mixed feelings about electronic music. Boulez, after composing his electronic Etudes, in 1952, wrote, "Everything that was limited becomes unlimited; everything that was 'imponderable' can now be subjected to precise measurement." But in 1969 he told the *Times*: "This same frenzy for technology began in Europe about 1953. By 1958

168

it had all died down. The idea of electronics as the big future of music is just an American trick of fashion. Next year they'll discover the viola da gamba." Boulez now heads IRCAM, and his *Répons* (1981)—unheard so far in America but being considered for a Philharmonic performance—is, to judge from what a tape recording can capture of it, a dazzling sonic adventure that makes full use of IRCAM's technological wizardry. [Répons *reached New York in 1986; see p. 465.*]

Répons is a "real time" composition: it uses live players, and none of the sound is prerecorded. A CRI album, SD 268, celebrating ten years of composition at the Columbia-Princeton Electronic Music Center, 1960–1970, presents a rich survey of the different ways natural or traditional sounds, those sounds transformed, synthesized sounds, and living performers have been used, separately or in combinations. It includes Varèse's *Déserts*, for orchestra and tape (in its 1961 recension); Milton Babbitt's *Vision and Prayer* (1961), for soprano and synthesized accompaniment; Mario Davidovsky's *Synchronisms No. 5* (1969), for percussionists and tape; and two purely electronic pieces by Vladimir Ussachevsky (1968 and 1971) in which, the composer says, "it is likely that all known methods of generating sounds with the digital computer are illustrated." Paul Griffiths's *A Guide to Electronic Music* is a handy and readable survey of the subject, with a useful discography. But, written five years ago, it stops short of the latest computer developments. The Beatles', Frank Zappa's, the Grateful Dead's recourse to electronics is considered. Since then, Michael Jackson's *Thriller*, product in part of a Baconian sound-house, has become the best-selling record of all time.

The Horizons concerts illustrated many of the different ways in which computers can be used. The first piece heard was Michael McNabb's very attractive *Dreamsong* (1978), which has become something like a classic of the genre. McNabb used digital processing to achieve transitions from unaltered natural sounds to synthesized sounds—"more poetically, from the real world to the realm of the imagination," as he put it in a program note. A movement of Laurie Spiegel's *Music for Dance* (1975), composed on Mathews and Moore's GROOVE system, seemed musically unimaginative. Charles Dodge's *The Waves* (1984) is an eloquent, shapely composition—a setting, for the soprano Joan La Barbara, of the opening sentences of the Woolf novel, accompanied by a tape in which Miss La Barbara's reading of the passage and examples of her remarkable vocal techniques served, the composer said in his note, "as a sound-source for computer extension and enhancement, and also as a model for the frequency and amplitude of computer-synthesized sounds."

The second concert was played by the Group for Contemporary Music, conducted by Harvey Sollberger. It opened with Xenakis's *Khal Perr* (1983), for brass quintet and percussion—live players of a score in part freely composed, in part computer-calculated. It is a bright, exciting stretch of music. Jean-Claude Risset's *Profils* (1982), for seven players and computer-synthesized tape, proved fascinating in its sound effects—in the interplay, especially, of bell timbres and gong timbres both natural and synthesized (Bacon's bells and rings that are dainty and sweet)—but it seemed more a demonstration of possibilities than a satisfying piece of music. So did York Höller's *Arcus* (1978), for seventeen players and tape—a pioneering work in IRCAM history. On the other hand, Paul

Lansky's *As If* (1982), for string trio and computer-synthesized tape, was an elegant and arresting composition.

The third concert, played by the American Composers Orchestra, conducted by Mr. Wuorinen, began with Babbitt's *Correspondences* (1967), for string orchestra and synthesized tape (not a computer piece). The tape sets standards of accuracy in pitch, rhythms, and dynamics which players find hard to keep up with. Like most of Babbitt's music, the piece is fiendishly difficult to perform, and this seemed to be a skin-of-the-teeth performance, with little dynamic nuance. Babbitt's music, so cogent and convincing in masterly, confident, high-spirited, colorful performances, easily disintegrates if the players seem to be still wrestling with the notes instead of enjoying them; then the lines don't hold. Earlier this season, there were at least four very enjoyable Babbitt performances: *My Ends Are My Beginnings* (1978), a long clarinet monologue, poetically played by Charles Neidich at a Parnassus concert in Merkin Hall; *Images* (1979), for saxophone and tape, played with brio by John Sampen at a New Music Consort program in Carnegie Recital Hall devoted to music with tape; *Sextets* (1966), for piano and violin, in a spirited, dazzling performance by Alan Feinberg and Rolf Schulte at a League-ISCM concert in Carnegie Recital Hall; and *Groupwise*, given its première at a Group concert at the Y honoring Harvey Sollberger—flutist, composer, and, with Wuorinen, co-founder of the Group. In *Groupwise*, a flute is the protagonist, and violin, viola, cello, and piano are his companions in adventures sometimes lyrical, more often tense.

At the Horizons computer symposium, Mandelbrot showed pictures of beautiful landscapes, seascapes, and cloudscapes which his computer, instructed by him in the characteristics and the characteristic irregularities of the natural world, had invented, composed, and set down. Idealized, almost Platonic scenes they seemed to be. Wuorinen, whose *Bamboula Squared*, for orchestra and quadraphonic tape, had its première at the third concert, was influenced by Mandelbrot's work to use computers, he said in a program note, in a way that "creates situations in which—most emphatically according to *my* rules, taste, and judgment—a 'music of nature' emerges from the mingling of traditional compositional values and approaches with numerical models of certain processes in the natural world." I grope to understand the procedure, which seems to be a subtle extension of the basic mathematical harmonic relationships mentioned earlier, but I had no difficulty at all in responding to the composition that resulted: sixteen minutes of energetic exhilarating music, starting and ending on a fundamental C, ranging through timbres and rhythms and harmonies—from the orchestra and from the loudspeakers—of uncommon eventfulness. There's something sunlike about Wuorinen's best works: he cometh forth as a bridegroom out of his chamber, and rejoiceth as a giant to run his course.

There followed the première of Reynolds's *Transfigured Wind II*, for solo flute (Mr. Sollberger), computer-processed sound, and orchestra. If Wuorinen had used the computer as a form of artificial intelligence, Reynolds had used it first as an instrument of analysis and dissection—rather as one uses field glasses to scan and marvel at details of drawing and paint in the Sistine ceiling—and then as a projector. Computers, he wrote in his program note, "allow us to recast musical materials, to transform them in ways that are intriguing and let one retain that delicious and mysterious *sense* with which a fine performer imbues a musical line." *Transfigured Wind II* began with flute solos played by a live performer and recorded; that way, composer and performer together provided material that "once inside the computer ... could undergo a host of transformations before reëmerging on the tape." With computers, one can view musical gestures as if in slow motion. One can dissect and examine them both "horizontally," in time, separating attack—of breath upon mouthpiece, string upon bow—from the note that follows, and "vertically," in their timbre structures. One can then prolong, emphasize, transform, or remove any of the elements. The sounds that music is made of, we have learned, are far more complicated than once was thought. There were sounds in Reynolds's piece— the soft sizzle of the player's breath seemed to be one—that have long been a part of music although not before prominently heard. New sounds can in themselves be eloquent, and the discovery of new instruments and of new sounds is important. But what matters more is the use that composers then make of them. The eighteenth-century clarinet with downward extension would be forgotten today had Mozart not composed a quintet for it. Reynolds is at once an explorer and a visionary composer, whose works can lead listeners to follow him into new regions of emotion and imagination.

I've not had much experience of computers under my own fingers. (I'm writing this piece with a fountain pen, not on a word processor.) As Boulez prophesied, I've discovered the viola da gamba—as being the only instrument on which music written for the viola da gamba can be executed with the kind of accuracy that Boulez himself (if he has any use for such music) would admire. It seems to me oddly arrogant to view the present as all-important or as more than a speck on the long stream of time. Yet even someone who lives his imaginative life in a continuum where Bach and Babbitt, Monteverdi, Mozart, and Messiaen are living musical presences can appreciate the artistic importance of the computer and of what it renders possible. These Horizons concerts made it clear that—like the viola da gamba, the fortepiano, the pianoforte, the tape recorder, Wagnerian harmony, Schoenberg's twelve-note method, Elliott Carter's metric modulations, and so much else—it has enormously increased the range of musical adventures on which a composer, and then his listeners, can embark.

HIGH ENCOUNTERS

SIEGFRIED, the third installment of the San Francisco Opera's new *Ring*, staged during the company's summer season, is a very successful production—close to the opera that Wagner composed, uncontroversial, unquirky, but not unimaginative in its presentation of what Wagner called "deeds of music made visible." The conductor was Edo de Waart, the director Nikolaus Lehnhoff, and the designer John Conklin. Last summer's *Rheingold* and *Walküre* by this team were striking and beautiful but carried some clutter from modish *Ring* stagings of our day—by Patrice Chéreau, Götz Friedrich, Joachim Herz, Luca Ronconi—set in worlds far removed from Wagner's mythical epoch. By such stagings, the great allegory is limited, reduced to specific (albeit ingenious and entertaining) similes, even representations. (Turning Loge, the god of fire, into a sharp modern lawyer, nattily suited and reading *The Wall Street Journal*, is the sort of thing I mean.) In the San Francisco *Siegfried*, Mr. Lehnhoff has shown himself readier to think for himself, along Wagnerian lines. He is a bold, intelligent director with a feeling for precise, revealing details of behavior and an eye for strong, eloquent stage imagery—a worthy disciple of Wieland Wagner, on whose 1965 Bayreuth *Ring* he worked. He is not afraid of color and knows that picturesqueness is a necessary weapon in Wagner's expressive armory.

In Act I, Mime has made of his cave a kind of mini-Nibelheim, equipped with a traditional forge (no nonsense about a modern hydraulic press) and other cunning devices—such as a door swinging up on counterweights—that give testimony to his skill and ingenuity. When he recalls the toys he made to beguile Siegfried's young years, he pulls from a dusty recess a cuddly black beastie on wheels. The strong sense of a sun-filled forest outside is not lost. Act II is an open evocation of a Caspar David Friedrich landscape—specifically, "Graves of the Fallen Freedom Fighters," in the Hamburg Kunsthalle. The dragon is a shade disappointing: we see only its head—huge (sixteen feet long), pterodactylic, with snapping bony jaws, but no fiery breath or glowing eyes. Act III opens on the classical terrace (recalling the Friedrich painting of Agrigento now in Dortmund) where in *Das Rheingold* the gods assembled. Then it was already a noble ruin (Mr. Lehnhoff began his cycle in a degenerate society, not at the dawn of civilization) but a neat one; now brambles and further decay have romanticized it. And the Valkyrie Rock of the final scene, once a way station on the flight path to Valhalla, has similarly lost much of its high, godlike aspect and become an abandoned, lonely place. The tree sheltering Brünnhilde's long sleep has grown taller; there are drifts of fallen leaves. The collaborators on this *Ring* intended to suggest a four-seasons progress, and their *Siegfried* has a warmly autumnal tone.

René Kollo seems to me, on balance (by which I mean a balance of voice, acting ability, interpretative insight, and appearance), the most satisfactory Siegfried around. When he sang the role—but not the *Götterdämmerung* Siegfried—in the first years of the Chéreau *Ring* at Bayreuth, he was variously deemed "completely miscast vocally" (*Opera* in 1976) and "youthful and agreeably fresh" (*Opera* in 1977). In San Francisco, he didn't have loud, beefy trombone tones. (I doubt whether Jean de Reszke had them, either.) The sound was bright, lyrical, easily produced, excellently focussed, unforced, and always energetic and audible. I'd have enjoyed a little more volume in the forging song—but not if it meant the thick, dry, prosaic timbre that most loud Siegfrieds suffer from. In voice, Mr. Kollo recalled Wolfgang Windgassen (another tenor usually declared insufficiently a Heldentenor), and he's a better, a more poetic actor. But he overclowned—as Mr. Windgassen used to—the youth's attempts to converse on his reed with the Woodbird.

Francis Egerton was a trim, incisive, precise Mime. Thomas Stewart, as Wotan the Wanderer, was warm, noble, and wise. Once—to a generation brought up on Hans Hotter's god—he seemed to be a new-style Wotan. (Did Hotter seem that way to the generation brought up on Friedrich Schorr's god?) The years go by—Mr. Stewart first sang at Bayreuth twenty-four years ago—and now in San Francisco he brought into the performance an air of old, high Wagnerian breeding: calm, authoritative, and all but lost today. (Wieland Wagner's *Ring* productions, found iconoclastic when they appeared, are now remembered as "classic.") It was apt to the encounter between the god and his impetuous, uncouth modern grandson. (Mr. Kollo began his career as a pop singer.) Wotan's acknowledgment that things are changing was poignantly enacted.

Stanley Wexler (who sings Sweeney Todd at the City Opera later this season) was a vivid, alert Alberich, until his voice tired during the argument with Mime. James Patterson gave Fafner a big, steady, impressive bass. (Fafner when dying here reverts from dragon to giant form—one of Mr. Lehnhoff's few endorsements of modishness.) Cheryl Parrish's Woodbird was bright and clear. Helga Dernesch sang her first Erda. She has been a soprano (the Marschallin in Glasgow; Brünnhilde and Isolde in Salzburg, for Karajan) and is a mezzo (Goneril, Herodias, Fricka in San Francisco) whose performances leave an indelible impression. In this *Siegfried*, Erda totters forth like a dying lady, lean and pale, wrapped in a gauzy veil, at Wotan's stern summons. Miss Dernesch made every word clear. The sense of an old order's coming to an end and the once all-wise woman's distress at a confused, unpredictable future were potently conveyed. The encounter between god and sibyl carried its full symbolic charge and was also—this is a general virtue of Mr. Lehnhoff's staging—a clash of characters. On one level, it might have been Siegfried Wagner informing Cosima that he intends to introduce new ideas into Bayreuth, or even a mature Pip confronting Miss Havisham: primeval matriarchy's days are done. On another, it was a man's last farewell to his mistress of many years before, aged now but still beautiful. Those notions are too definite. Enough, perhaps, to say that the great scene seemed to be a necessary interview—a psychic liberation that Wotan must achieve before he himself can freely resign the conduct of the world and entrust it to younger hands. When the scene that Wagner wrote, and not one possible interpretation of it, is played as intensely and beautifully as it was here, its manifold resonances—half-defined but fully felt—sound more stirringly.

Eva Marton sang her first Brünnhilde, and it was promising. Her voice is perhaps unremarkable except for its power, but vocal power is a good foundation for a Brünnhilde to build on. She played the role with simple, straightforward dignity. Sometimes she pushed too hard, and notes that should have a steady shine acquired a shudder. "Ewig war ich" was smoothly and tenderly sung.

The complete *Ring* is due in San Francisco next summer, and one looks forward to it. So far, it seems to me the best-looking—and aptest-looking—of contemporary *Ring* stagings, and so far it has been, on the whole, as well cast as any I know, with experienced Wagnerians and accomplished newcomers carefully blended. Mr. Lehnhoff will no doubt rethink some aspects of last year's *Rheingold* and *Walküre*—where sometimes he seemed too much concerned to make a striking "personal statement"—in the light of this confident, masterly *Siegfried*. My chief reservation concerns the conducting. Mr. de Waart is scrupulous and careful. The orchestral playing is well rehearsed, well balanced. What one misses is what is loosely called "inspiration": a sense that the music—singers and instrumentalists together—has taken on a life of its own, that it is moving in huge, inevitable spans. With Mr. de Waart, one is often aware of a man in the pit beating four, three, whatever to the bar. Nevertheless, it's decent, respectable conducting. Furtwängler is dead, and Reginald Goodall conducts only in Britain.

Thomas Munn's sensitive lighting was, at the performance I attended, the last of the series, spoiled by the flashing on and off of "supertitles"—tags of the text in English translation—above the scenes. If singers would learn English or—better—if audiences would learn German, supertitles wouldn't be necessary. On a television screen, subtitles can be taken in almost subliminally. In the theatre, supertitles divide the attention of those who follow them between the actors and the summary script, disturbing the direct communication that is one of the joys of living theatre; and for those who try to ignore them they are a flickering distraction. But words need to be understood. It's a tricky subject. Wagnerians tend to be more serious and better prepared than other operagoers, readier to listen, less in need of visual aids. Only two of San Francisco's five *Siegfried* performances were supertitled.

CLIPPED WINGS

July 23, 1984

My fondness for *Madama Butterfly,* one of the first operas I saw, has never faltered. I'm prepared to defend the piece against all detractors, to praise its formal structure, scoring, subtlety, emotional honesty, relevance to modern life. But what I defend and praise is not always what gets performed. Most accounts of the opera declare simply that a first-night failure was followed a few months later by a revised version, which triumphed. In fact, there are four main versions of *Butterfly.* I'll refer to them as "Milan," "Brescia," "Washington," and "Paris."

The fiasco of the first performance, at La Scala in February 1904, is a mystery of music history more puzzling than the failures of *Il barbiere di Siviglia, La traviata,* the Paris *Tannhäuser,* and Britten's *Gloriana* at their opening nights. Plausible reasons—if not justifications—for the initially bad reception of those operas can be found, but no reasons sufficient to explain why *Butterfly* should have been received with such derision that Puccini immediately withdrew it. Critics by no means deaf to the merits of the opera seemed equally surprised. Giovanni Pozza, in the *Corriere della Sera,* reported that "the public that had assembled in the theatre in the assurance of witnessing a new triumph for its favorite composer passed without transitions from excessive optimism to harsh criticism, condemning without consideration."

There was a strong cast: Rosina Storchio in the title role, Giovanni Zenatello as Pinkerton, Giuseppe De Luca as Sharpless—singers whose accomplishment can still be admired on records. The second act (which in modern librettos and most modern performances is divided into Acts II and III) was long, it is true. Puccini himself while scoring it had called it "eternal." Giuseppe Giacosa, who collaborated on the libretto with Luigi Illica, had called it "interminable" and "against common sense." Giulio Gatti-Casazza, the manager of La Scala, tells in his memoirs of animated discussion, after the pre-dress rehearsal, about whether the act should be divided. Puccini was against it. Back in 1902, he had insisted to Illica that there should be only two acts—"reaching the end having held the public nailed to their seats for an hour and a half! Monstrous, but the life of the opera depends on it." Act I was based on John Luther Long's story "Madame Butterfly" (1898), Act II on the one-act play David Belasco made from it (1900). And Belasco thought Butterfly's night-long vigil (where in the opera the second intermission would come) the supreme achievement of his theatrical career. In *The Theater Through Its Stage Door,* he wrote: "To portray this episode, Blanche Bates was compelled to hold the stage for fourteen minutes without uttering a word. . . . There was not a dissenting voice in the criticism of that scene. My experiment was hazardous, but it succeeded, and its success was

175

due entirely to its imaginative appeal." Puccini saw Belasco's production in London in 1900. He clad the famous scene in his humming chorus and the orchestral interlude depicting daybreak, the stirring of activity in the port below, and the thoughts passing through Butterfly's mind as she stands there in her wedding dress, awaiting her errant husband's return. The composer, like the playwright, set great store by the scene. His experiment was hazardous, and it did not succeed: to the dawn birdsong, the Milanese audience added its own chorus of avian and animal noises.

Three months later, *Butterfly* appeared at Brescia, with a new heroine, Salomea Krusceniski, but the same Pinkerton and Sharpless and the same conductor, Cleofonte Campanini. Then, in July, Toscanini conducted *Butterfly* in Buenos Aires, with Storchio, Edoardo Garbin (the first Fenton), and Pasquale Amato. These very successful performances made *Butterfly* the repertory opera it has been, nationally and internationally, ever since. The controversial Act II was now divided by an intermission. Puccini rewrote the principal motif of Butterfly's entrance song, whose earlier kinship to a phrase of Mimì's the Milanese audience had been quick to spot and mock, and rewrote key phrases in the final scene. A few cuts were made (the only substantial ones being Goro's presentation to Pinkerton of the bride's friends and relations en masse and Uncle Yakusidé's drunken song). The tenor arietta "Addio fiorito asil" was added. The show must have lasted longer than the Milan première, for several numbers were encored, among them "Un bel dì," the letter duet, the flower duet, and the humming chorus. (In Milan, added reasons for the spectators' displeasure had been the composer's refusal to come onstage for a call after the flower duet—one piece that did please them—and the absence of an encore.) A revised score ("Brescia") was published.

In 1906, *Butterfly* had its first English-language performances, in America. The Savage Opera Company took it on a six-month coast-to-coast tour, opening in Washington in October and playing in New York in November. Tito Ricordi, who had directed the Scala première, came over to supervise it. A third, bilingual score ("Washington") was published. Five further cuts had been made: two more scraps of the wedding scene, a stretch of the flower duet, Butterfly's little song to the baby before the vigil, and the episode in which with quiet dignity she refuses the payoff money that Pinkerton has left with Sharpless.

So far, the characterization of Butterfly has not changed, though she loses some telling passages. "Addio fiorito asil" gives the tenor more to sing but, with its repeated "Son vil!," makes a callous, cowardly fellow maudlin as well. The drastic alteration of *Butterfly* was done for the Opéra-Comique production of December 1906. Numerous cuts were proposed by its director, Albert Carré, and his wife, Marguerite, who sang Cio-Cio-San. Puccini accepted them, despite his initial doubts; he had nicknamed Marguerite Carré "Mme Pomme de Terre." Two more large cuts were made in the wedding scene. Pinkerton was further "prettified": he no longer decides to call the servants Mugs 1, 2, and 3; no longer orders them to serve candied spiders and flies and other disgusting dainties of *Nipponeria* to the bridal party. Kate Pinkerton was all but written out of the final scene. (Sharpless and Butterfly take over most of her lines.) Eighteen orchestral bars were inserted into the flower duet, to allow more time for floral

176

arrangement. Mme Pomme de Terre's role was lightened, and she was simplified into a straightforwardly pathetic heroine. All this had a sentimental-izing effect: passages that are sharp, ironical, critical, or dramatically intricate have gone. The French Cio-Cio-San no longer says that since she has cost Pinkerton a hundred yen, she will make it up to him by living frugally. In the love duet, she skips thirty-seven bars—the shy confession that when the marriage-broker first approached her she was reluctant to be sold to a foreign barbarian. From the suicide scene she drops her murmuring of an old song (accompanied by bare parallel fifths):

> *He entered the closed gates,*
> *took the place of everything—he left—*
> *and left nothing behind,*
> *nothing but death.*

The Paris *Butterfly* was a success. Puccini now had a surefire, performer-proof version, less adventurous and less interesting than the work he first composed but unproblematical and easier to stage. A fourth score ("Paris") was published, and became the definitive version. Julian Smith, who has edited a new edition of the opera for Ricordi, summed it up thus, in a paper read to the Royal Musical Association in 1980:

The original *Butterfly* was a daring opera, unconventional in its structure, and unsparing in its delivery of what for its time was an unusually pointed moral and social message. The Milan audience of 1904 rejected the former, and Albert Carré, on behalf of the bourgeois Parisians, successfully diluted the latter. And so Puccini's original *Butterfly* underwent a tragic metamorphosis, from which it emerged perilously close to sentimental melodrama.

Since the sentimental melodrama has been delighting audiences for seventy-seven years, the work's vicissitudes in the three years before that might seem to be old history that can be left to academe. Not so, however: opera companies the world over have begun to abandon unquestioned adherence to the standard version—the Berlin Comic Opera, the Welsh National, the Opera Company of Boston, the English National, the Paris Opera. In eleven days of 1982, La Fenice, in Venice, played four performances of "Milan" and four of "Paris" in alternation. Recently, the Opera Theatre of St. Louis produced "Washington" (closer to "Brescia" than it is to "Paris"), while City Opera's revival of "Paris" afforded a comparison.

But not a straight comparison. If the St. Louis production proved far more enjoyable, interesting, and moving, this was not solely because "Washington" is a richer score. The show started with three other advantages (and one disadvantage). It was sung in English; it had principals with fresh young voices; and the director, Bliss Hebert, had directed the opera Puccini wrote. (On the other hand, since the pit is too small to hold Puccini's orchestra, Ettore Panizza's reduced score was used. It is skillfully made, but the climaxes lack emotional punch.) The City Opera had the full orchestra, but the piece was sung in Italian; the soprano and the tenor sounded frayed; and Frank Corsaro had directed a variation on Puccini's drama which was at many points at odds with the music and in most points less effective than the original. Neither décor was pleasing, but Allen Charles Klein's, in St. Louis, was at least practicable. In New York, Lloyd Evans awkwardly divides Butterfly's dwelling into two buildings.

In St. Louis, Maria Spacagna was a touching, detailed, and delicate heroine. Sopranos of every kind have undertaken the role with success—from (at Covent Garden) Emmy Destinn, an Aida, to Maggie Teyte, a Mélisande; from (at the Met) Destinn and Elisabeth Rethberg to Renata Scotto and Teresa Stratas. Storchio, Puccini's first Butterfly, made her Scala début in 1895, aged eighteen, as Sophie in *Werther*. She was a Susanna, a Manon, Toscanini's Gretel. Krusceniski, the second Butterfly, was Toscanini's Salome and Isolde at La Scala, and a Brünnhilde. The heavy Butterflies excel in emotional force and tragic power, the light ones at portraying the fifteen-year-old "plaything" (as Mrs. Pinkerton, in the story and the play, calls Butterfly) whose trust, dignity, maternal tenderness, and depth of feeling shame the insensitive, patronizing Westerners. Miss Spacagna is a young lyric soprano whose tones are still sweet, true, and unforced. In her phrasing, her acting, and her use of the words she covered, as if by instinct, a wide emotional range. The lullaby was particularly beautiful. Tonio DiPaolo, the Pinkerton, had some brave, ringing notes, but the voice did not flow effortlessly, and his mind seemed to be more on his singing than on the character. Joseph Rescigno conducted a performance admirably responsive to the singers' phrasing.

The City Opera staging—Mr. Corsaro's production has been revived by Christian Smith—is a bag of tricks. At the start, Pinkerton has brought three tippling shipmates along with him—three stooges who pour whisky down the servants' throats, who clown mutely except for an enthusiastic shout of "Whisky!" when Pinkerton offers the consul milk punch or whisky. In Act II, Butterfly has adopted American dress, a tall American demeanor, a Louise Brooks bob, a pump-handle way of shaking hands. She decides *not* to wear her wedding dress during the vigil. There are several bits of "cameo" scene-stealing to take the attention off the principals and what they are singing: by a natty Western photographer, who lights a cigarette and is chided for doing so by Suzuki; by Kate Pinkerton, who runs a finger over some steps to see if they are clean enough to sit on (while the trio, an emotional peak of the drama, is being sung). The raid on the garden, to fill every corner of the house with flowers, yields just one posy in a vase and a single chrysanthemum, whose petals are scattered over the king-size futon Cio-Cio-San has spread in readiness. The production—first staged in 1967, with Francesca Roberto and Placido Domingo—was no doubt once coherent. I hadn't seen it before. It is now an unappealing parade of undergraduate touches sticking out from a background of routine chorus work—in marked contrast to the vivid, musically and dramatically focussed playing of the St. Louis comprimari and choristers. Some of Mr. Corsaro's ideas can be traced back to Long and Belasco; they would be better served by an earlier version of the score. Catherine Lamy's tone broke up and became impure under pressure, and her pitch was often unsure. Riccardo Calleo's timbre was bleak and prosaic. (In 1907, the Savage company recorded the principal numbers, for Columbia; through the heavy surface there rise shining, unforced streams of free, steady sound—and also very clear words. The singers—Renée Vivienne as Butterfly, Vernon Stiles as Pinkerton—were not famous; they achieve a purity and beauty of tone rarely heard, or even sought, today.) Christopher Keene's conducting was alert to the instrumental marvels but emotionally somewhat thin-blooded.

After St. Louis, the "Paris" version seemed impoverished. But straight "Washington" is perhaps not the ideal version for audiences readier than those of 1904–06 to appreciate what Puccini called "the most modern of my operas." As with all works surviving in multiple but not mutually exclusive versions, one must distinguish critically between evident improvements (the "Brescia" rewriting of Butterfly's entrance and of "O a me, sceso dal trono," in the final scene) and compromises of the initial vision made to satisfy a particular singer, director, or audience. Some things are perhaps not in doubt: *Butterfly* is better without a second intermission and without "Addio fiorito asil." (The preceding trio does all that is dramatically needed there.) How much of the wedding scene is retained must depend, in part, on the rehearsal time available. How much of Butterfly's role—and what exactly she sings—must depend, in part, on the individual artist. (Destinn, in her 1909 recording of the final scene, keeps the phrase "fior di giglio e di rosa" in the lower octave; for Carré, and the definitive edition, it was raised an octave.) At the Fenice, straight "Milan" was generally deemed inferior to "Paris," but that was a confrontation of extremes. Joachim Herz's blending of "Milan" and "Brescia" (in Berlin and Cardiff) and the English National's similar "best of both" approach seem wiser.

In telling the tale of the four main versions, I have left out much detail. Other scores, old records, and old librettos reveal various transitional stages. What St. Louis performed should perhaps be called "Washington 2"—the third version slipped with two pages containing the "Paris" addition to the flower duet. This score remains in print (Kalmus) and, in fact, has never quite disappeared from English-language stages. (It's the *Butterfly* I got to know at Sadler's Wells and at Covent Garden.) The State Theater had two different librettos on sale: in the lobby, Souvenir Book Publishers' reprint of the current Ricordi libretto ("Paris," with Ruth and Thomas Martin's English translation), and at the box office something more interesting—a reprint, by the Program Publishing Company, of a 1906 Ricordi libretto, basically "Washington" but including some "Milan" lines and even some lines Puccini never set. The libretto to have, however, is that in the English National Opera/Royal Opera *Opera Guide*, No. 26, edited by Nicholas John; it provides the full "Milan" text, with the subsequent cuts and revisions recorded in footnotes, and also includes Long's story.

TRIUMPH OF ORIANA

July 30, 1984

THE English National Opera visited America in May and June, three hundred and thirty strong, appearing in Houston, Austin, San Antonio, New Orleans, and New York. It presented a kind of opera that does not exist here: the work of a large, year-round ensemble company playing music dramas in the language that the singers and their audience have in common. The City Opera's *Street Scene*, last done in 1979, was rather like an ENO performance; that company's new recourse to "supertitles"—tags or loose paraphrases in English projected on a screen above a foreign-language enactment—underlines its preference for presenting what Dr. Johnson called "an exotic and irrational entertainment." (He was defining not "opera" but Italian opera in London.) In New York, the ENO appeared at the Met, the world's largest opera house, and one too large to allow the company to come across at full strength. Although its home theatre, the Coliseum, is London's largest, holding something over twenty-three hundred people, it was built, in opulent Edwardian days, on music-hall, not gilded-horseshoe, lines, which cluster the audience as close as possible to the stage. Sarah Bernhardt and Ellen Terry appeared there; *Annie Get Your Gun*, *Guys and Dolls*, *Kiss Me Kate* were done there in days before musicals were electrically amplified. Both sight lines and acoustics work for an intimacy that was lacking at the Met.

Benjamin Britten's seventh opera, *Gloriana*, written for Elizabeth II's coronation, in 1953, had a concert performance in Cincinnati in 1956 (with an arresting cast: Inge Borkh, Suzanne Danco, John Alexander, Theodor Uppman, Donald Gramm). The American stage première was given last month: the ENO played *Gloriana* in San Antonio, New Orleans, and New York. There have been only three stage productions of the piece: Covent Garden's, at the time of the coronation; the ENO's, new in 1966; and Münster's in 1968, with Martha Mödl as its heroine. This is surprising, for *Gloriana* is an opera both attractive and impressive—unconventional, it is true, but not in ways that deter public enthusiasm. At every performance—since the unhappy first one—I've attended, there have been cheers at the end. In New York, there were standing ovations. That notorious first night is a matter of history. As the Earl of Harewood (the Queen's cousin, largely responsible for the commission, suggester of the subject, now head of the ENO, and a force for good in England's artistic life) puts it in Kobbé, "that it was misunderstood and intensely disliked by a 1953 assemblage of grandees and courtiers provides a rather acid comment on the different standards prevailing in the mid-twentieth and the late sixteenth centuries, when a luminary of the aristocracy could be the author of the words

180

'Happy were he.' " (William Plomer's libretto incorporates that lyric by the Earl of Essex.) The columnists ("an insult to our beautiful young Queen"), the gossips, and the writers of letters to the press ("Surely our wonderful Queen has had enough ordeal during the past few weeks without having to sit through an evening of Benjamin Britten") had a field day. The music critics were not imperceptive, even if legend has it otherwise. They questioned the aptness of celebrating a new Elizabethan age with the representation of a bald, aging, unhappy, infatuated queen but praised Britten's resource and invention, technical brilliance, choral writing, orchestration, masterly, original formal structures, and dramatic eloquence. In *Music and Letters*, I hazarded a guess that "of all Britten's operas *Gloriana* is the one that contains most elements likely to win popular favour" but prudently added a "Time alone will show." Time, still at work, has already shown that, although *Peter Grimes* remains the international favorite, followed by *The Turn of the Screw* (unwritten in 1953), *Gloriana* increasingly delights musical listeners. The title role has attracted a series of successful interpreters: Joan Cross, Constance Shacklock, Sylvia Fisher, Miss Borkh, Miss Mödl, Ava June. Leontyne Price has recorded one of the scenes. The latest in the line is Sarah Walker, a tall, regal mezzo, an imposing and skillful actress, a strong singer, but one taxed by the upper reaches of the role. (Miss Cross, the first Gloriana, once remarked that "Ben never seemed to make up his mind whether I was a contralto or a soprano.")

The libretto is based on Lytton Strachey's *Elizabeth and Essex*, a psychological history (Freud sent Strachey a congratulatory letter on it) that has been likened to a five-act tragedy—Strachey's *Anthony and Cleopatra*. (Michael Holroyd, in the ENO/Royal Opera *Opera Guide* to *Grimes* and *Gloriana*, suggests that it also contains autobiographical elements.) Plomer, I think, may have looked through Rossini and Donizetti librettos about Elizabeth; the riverside love duet of Act II which becomes a quartet and the soloists-and-chorus second-act finale are in forms those composers would recognize. Much else is adventurously untraditional: the first dance sequence is accompanied by surely the longest stretch of a-cappella music in opera, and the second by an onstage consort of just five players, plus drum; one scene is chiefly a gittern-accompanied ballad; the end is a monologue for the Queen, largely spoken, between bursts of music during which her life passes through her mind in review.

Gloriana is the most objective of Britten's operas: lapped portraits of a great monarch in relation to her people; of her intricate policy; and of a woman vowed to virginity but erotically not untroubled. In Strachey's words, "Though, at the centre of her being, desire had turned to repulsion, it had not vanished altogether. . . . Though the precious citadel itself was never to be violated, there were surrounding territories, there were outworks and bastions over which exciting battles might be fought." He traces her trouble back to an imagined childhood trauma: by Essex's death, "manhood—the fascinating, detestable entity, which had first come upon her concealed in yellow magnificence in her father's lap—manhood was overthrown at last, and in the person of that traitor it should be rooted out. Literally, perhaps . . ." (Castration was part of a traitor's punishment.) It's complicated stuff. The politics are complicated, too. We need to know that Cecil represents the new men whom Elizabeth brought to power, and Essex's rebellion (in Strachey's view) the last uprising of England's ancient chivalry. ("The flame was glorious—radiant with the colours of antique knighthood and with the flashing gallantries of the past; but no substance fed it.") Perhaps we don't need to know, in the quartet, that Essex is the stepson of Leicester, Elizabeth's former favorite; that Lady Essex is the widow of Sir Philip Sidney; that Penelope Rich, Essex's proud sister, was Sidney's Stella (and bore five children to her lover, Lord Mountjoy); or that Anne Boleyn's sister was Essex and Penelope's great-grandmother. If we do know, the emotional and conspiratorial network draws tighter. History, Strachey's artful patterning of it, and Plomer's and Britten's repatternings for the operatic stage are curiously mingled. On the surface, *Gloriana* is self-explanatory, as Rossini's *Elisabetta* and Donizetti's *Roberto Devereux* are. All three works become more interesting, more profoundly enjoyable the more one studies them, but only *Gloriana* is many-layered. It ties fascinatingly into real history, into musical history, into Freud (Strachey's brother James was Freud's translator), and even into Bloomsbury (most of *Elizabeth and Essex* was written at Ham Spray, in Carrington days). On a musical level, too, the opera glows under close scrutiny, although its trove of melodies—phrase after phrase sings on in the mind—and exciting timbres is sufficient to afford delight at a first encounter, even before one has begun to trace the musical connections running through the pageantry of public and private scenes.

Colin Graham's production for the ENO is excellently clear and bold but subtle in its details. He is one of the best opera directors of our day—musical, imaginative, adept at laying out a composer's work effectively, sensibly, eloquently, and accurately, without fuss but not without finesse. Alix Stone's décor looked good in the Met. Miss Walker had a triumph. Arthur Davies caught both the high gallantry and the romance of Essex—at once dashing popular hero and Strachey's "pale boy who would lie for hours, obscurely melancholy, with a Virgil in his hand." He sang the lute song "Happy were he" exquisitely. Elizabeth Vaughan was a flashing Penelope (an early Joan Sutherland role), and Jean Rigby a moving Lady Essex. Mountjoy (Neil Howlett), Cecil (Alan Opie), Raleigh (Richard Van Allan) were surely played. The chorus was wonderful. Mark Elder and, at the last of the three New York performances, Noel Davies were expert conductors. It is rare in New York to see a large, difficult opera so consistently well executed, with every part intelligently in place. The Met's own *Grimes* and *Billy Budd* revivals, earlier this season, contained several individually splendid performances, but the operas as a whole were less surely in focus.

Prokofiev's *War and Peace* is another opera that makes sense on its own but fuller sense to listeners who know its source. Prokofiev, assuming such knowledge, set not a connected narrative but scenes from Tolstoy's novel—scenes heightened by lyrical, stirring, and brilliantly theatrical music. His opera achieves coherence through musical means—repetition, juxtaposition, carefully graded contrasts—and also through the perspective that places Natasha's, Pierre's, Andrei's personal destinies against the great theme of national, general resistance to the foreign invader. When the fortieth anniversary of D day was celebrated recently, military historians reminded us that it was also, and perhaps principally, on the Eastern front, at terrible cost, that the evil might of Nazism was destroyed. The ENO production chimed with this. But reaction to heroic music is often personal. The *Times* critic spoke of "cheap pageantry," "hollow rhetoric," "claptrap," "agitprop set to music," and called Field Marshal Kutuzov, who led the resistance to Napoleon while counting the cost with a heavy heart, "a cartoon figure . . . an early model of Josef Stalin." I found the patriotic scenes and the figure of Kutuzov (fervently sung and played by Norman Bailey) profoundly stirring, and surrendered to emotion as readily as Verdi's audiences did when "Va, pensiero," "O Signore, dal tetto natio," "Si ridesti il Leon di Castiglia," and "Patria oppressa" first burst upon them. Prokofiev, like Verdi, found music for popular feeling which continues to make even listeners who have led comfortable, untroubled lives "vibrate in unison with it" (Luigi Dallapiccola's phrase for the effect of Verdi's Risorgimento strains). Napoleon's invasion of Russia is a metaphor for the Nazis'—and, beyond that, for all aggression against peoples.

The ENO production, first put on in 1972, is by Mr. Graham and has the virtues of his *Gloriana*. It is the fullest version of *War and Peace* on the contemporary stage, and the most exciting. Erwin Piscator's famous theatrical distillation of the novel may have influenced the staging, which moves swiftly, economically, yet spaciously, in sets with projected backgrounds (designed by Mr. Graham and Margaret Harris)—in contrast to the Bolshoi's heavier, realistic presentation. There are seventy individual roles. Naming a few principals—Eilene Hannan (Natasha), Ann Howard (Hélène), Kenneth Woollam (Pierre), Arthur Davies (Anatol), Neil Howlett (Andrei)—and blanket admiration of all must suffice. The choral singing was noble, and the orchestral playing, under James Lockhart, was bright and accurate.

The other two operas played in New York (to San Antonio only the company took *The Turn of the Screw*) were entertainment. One was Gilbert and Sullivan's *Patience*—an elegant and stylish show (directed by John Cox, designed by John Stoddart), if a little lost in the vast space of the Met. It's good to be entertained, and Sullivan was a graceful and masterly composer. His score blossomed under the musical care that Derek Hammond-Stroud (Bunthorne), Alan Opie (Grosvenor), Anne Collins (Lady Jane), and the others bestowed on it. And again the chorus shone.

The second was *Rigoletto*. Verdi, to be sure, intended his opera seriously. Although Italian censorship of the day proscribed a historical king (Francis I, in the Victor Hugo play on which the opera is based)—or, indeed, any king—in the cast list, in an anonymous Duke of Mantua Verdi still had a figure to illustrate preoccupations that run through his work: responsibility, the conflict of public duty and private inclination. Jonathan Miller, the director of the ENO *Rigoletto,* sought to make the familiar drama newly vivid by transferring it to a modern setting: "Little Italy, that part of New York under the control of the Mafia, in the 1950s." (Thus the London program; in New York it was just "New York in the 1950s.") The Duke becomes Dook, capo (while still young enough to pass himself off as a student) of a crime family, and Rigoletto a bartender. Mr. Miller's attempt misfired. In place of sixteenth-century Mantua—a theatrical metaphor that has gripped audiences since 1851—we are confronted with a musical-comedy never-never land: a Little Italy where a free-lance, nonunion assassin can offer his services nightly with impunity; where someone in a bar, when it comes on to rain, says not "Call me a cab" but, to the proprietor, "Why don't you sleep in the outhouse? Go to blazes. I'll have to stay here." The response is "How thoughtful. ... I'm delighted to offer you my bedroom if you would like it. Come, I will show you up there." (I quote from the published translation, by James Fenton, but changes were made in the performance; I even heard lines of my own *Rigoletto* translation—which, being devised for the Mantuan setting, sounded even more unnatural than Mr. Fenton's in the new locale.) The building where Gilda lived had incompatible façades: one warehouse, the other tenement. In London, the production seemed unrealistic, un-Verdian, and faintly absurd; in New York, even more so. Verdi, often compelled to change the century and the setting of his operas, was always insistent that whatever was chosen had to match the tone of the drama and the tone of his music. (The score of *Ballo*, he said, predicated a court of some elegance, not Mediterranean, and postmedieval; the baritone had to be able to say to the protagonist "To your life ... the destiny of thousands and thousands of other lives is linked.") The ENO has other out-of-period productions—of Monteverdi's *Orfeo*, Dvořák's *Rusalka*, Debussy's *Pelléas*—that seem to me not frivolous but revelatory. This *Rigoletto* was often ingenious and amusing, but the big, straightforward, powerful emotion on which it depends—the tragedy, if you like—was diminished. It was fairly well sung. Arthur Davies was a debonair and attractive Dook. Mr. Elder's conducting was crisp but unidiomatic.

SACRIFICE

August 6, 1984

GLUCK is a great composer honored more often by dutiful praise than by impassioned performance. All that gets done with any frequency is *Orfeo*—and that usually in a text where music that he composed for a tenor is transposed for an alto and mixed in with the original alto music in a way to produce tessituras, textures, and even melodies that Gluck never wrote. But perhaps things are beginning to change. St. Louis this summer staged a 1762 *Orfeo* adulterated only by the flute-solo dance of 1774; both Riccardo Muti (Angel) and Sigiswald Kuijken (Accent) have recorded the original version; Concert Royal stages it, with period band, later this month; and Mr. Muti gives a concert performance with the Philadelphia Orchestra in October.

Gluck is not easy to get right. In an 1854 communication to the *Neue Zeitschrift für Musik*, Wagner—making an earnest point with Shavian exuberance—proposed a moratorium on his music, since it was as a rule so unintelligently performed that the reverence for the composer instilled from youth up and the impression left by his works in actual performance proved incompatible and utterly confusing. In Dresden, Wagner himself had conducted

Armide in 1843 (with Wilhelmine Schröder-Devrient) and *Iphigénie en Aulide* in 1847. For the latter production, whose staging and designing he also supervised in detail, he made his own edition of the score. It has been preserved; in fact an RCA recording of *Iphigénie en Aulide* was Gluck-Wagner, in German, with Anna Moffo, Dietrich Fischer-Dieskau, Thomas Stewart, and Bernd Weikl in the cast. Wagner's edition is a fascinating document—music criticism written in music—of what he admired in Gluck and what he thought could be bettered. (But also, of course, of what he thought needed adjustment to the taste of a particular audience and to the capabilities of a particular cast; that factor makes the document less than straightforward to assess. If the Dresden tenor had been able to compass with ease Achilles' air as Gluck wrote it, Wagner would presumably not have "repointed" it, removing high notes to the detriment of the melodic contours.) This Gluck-Wagner *Iphigénie en Aulide* had what seems to have been its American première at the Waterloo Festival last month.

The vocal score Wagner began with was a bilingual one by F. Brissler, published in Berlin in 1839. (There's a copy in the New York Public Library.) His orchestral material came from Berlin and had been worked over by Spontini. Dissatisfied with Brissler's German translation, Wagner revised it thoroughly. Dissatisfied with Spontini's orchestration, he sent for Gluck's original, published in Paris in 1774. Wagner's own copy of the French score survives. (It was formerly in the Burrell Collection in Philadelphia's Curtis Institute and is now in Bayreuth.) It is larded with inserted pages and papillons (those pinned-on or pasted-on scraps of paper that easily flutter off when scholars pry for readings concealed beneath them), and on almost every page it bears Wagner's revisions and performance instructions. In his autobiography, Wagner described his aims:

> I sought to bring the libretto as far as possible into agreement with Euripides' play.... For the sake of dramatic vitality, I tried to join the arias and choruses ... by connecting links, postludes, and preludes, doing my best to use Gluck's own motifs so as to make the interventions of a strange composer as unnoticeable as possible.... I revised all the instrumentation more or less completely, but only with the object of making what was already there tell effectively.

Euripides' *Iphigenia in Aulis*, even in the imperfect form that has come down to us, is one of the most powerful of antiwar—and, in modern jargon, antimacho—plays. It throws into question all received Homeric values. Agamemnon, Menelaus, Clytemnestra, Achilles have been corrupted by power games. The four have decent qualities. Perhaps even Calchas—offstage in Euripides but brought on by his successors—has decent qualities, although he seems to embody superstition and state religion as inhumanely as any Verdian priest. By allowing the decent qualities to show, Euripides emphasized the extent of the corruption. Against it are set the chorus—women who know what war means to those who don't glory in it—and Iphigenia herself, a naive young victim in her acceptance of the man's values but a shining heroine and redeemer in her readiness to sacrifice her own happiness for the general good.

When Racine rewrote the play, in 1674, he turned the villains into heroes driven by inexorable decrees. He added a "love interest," between Iphigenia and Achilles. And by a Gilbertian dénouement he saved Iphigenia from

185

immolation: one Eriphile, a daughter of Helen and Theseus, and herself in love with Achilles, commits suicide at the altar; her real name, it transpires, is Iphigenia, and so the letter of the oracle—calling for the sacrifice of an Iphigenia—is fulfilled and (except for Eriphile) all can end happily. There was classical precedent for this version of the tale. Apostolo Zeno adopted it for his Iphigenia libretto, much set in the first half of the eighteenth century. Then a back-to-Euripides movement began. Francesco Algarotti ended his influential *Essay on the Opera* (1755) with an *Iphigenia in Aulis* libretto, offered as a model, in the last scene of which Diana (as narrated in Euripides) descends to whisk Iphigenia away into her service, leaving a hind on the altar. A flood of Iphigenia operas followed. The libretto for a 1768 Berlin revival of Carl Heinrich Graun's *Ifigenia*, in whose writing Frederick the Great probably played a part, specifies in its preface that while the action is imitated from Racine, the ending follows Euripides. Gluck and his librettist, the Bailli du Roullet, also followed Racine but provided a different ending, neither Racine's nor Euripides'. Two endings, in fact. In 1774, Calchas suddenly announces that the sacrifice need not take place after all. In 1775, Diana herself descends to announce that the gods, moved by the daughter's virtue and the mother's tears, have abated their wrath: the Greek armada, no longer becalmed, can sail for Troy, and the young lovers can be happy. Of four *Iphigénie* productions I've seen, two used the 1774 close and two the 1775. The former is more effective. It can even be realistically played: as if the wily Calchas, perceiving that Achilles and his Myrmidons have invaded his temple and will prevent the sacrifice or, at least, make it an occasion of general carnage and rebellion—and at the same time, perhaps, perceiving that the wind is about to change anyway—bows to the inevitable and expediently declares it to be the goddess's decree. Rummaging through libraries and archives to discover a composer's alternative treatments of difficult scenes is not just a pastime; it has practical consequences for performance, whether the work concerned is from the eighteenth, the nineteenth, or the twentieth century. How to end *Iphigénie* is a problem.

Wagner found it one. He didn't know the 1775 dénouement (a critical score was published only in 1873), and he didn't like the 1774. Therefore, he devised his own and composed an intervention by Diana, unaware that Gluck had already done so. His goddess prepares the way, as Racine's does not, for *Iphigenia in Tauris*, declaring that she thirsts not for Iphigenia's blood but for her exalted spirit. She will take her into her service, and one day Iphigenia will redeem the curse on the house of Atreus. Gluck's quartet follows (here amplified by chorus), and the opera ends abruptly with a cry of "Nach Troia!," recalling the cry of "Nach Rom!" that ends the second act of *Tannhäuser*. Gluck's 1775 close was equally abrupt: Calchas interrupts the final chaconne with a cry of "Volez, volez à la victoire!" But in 1774 this was followed by an exciting unison chorus, Berlioz-bold, of "Partons, volons." Brissler omitted it; strange that Wagner didn't restore it, once the 1774 score was in his hands.

Wagner's other changes can be briefly summarized. He omitted Gluck's three dance-and-song divertissements, one in each act. The only dance remaining in his score is a little D-major minuet. He cut a good deal else and—this is surprising—abridged petits airs in *aabb* form to a plain *ab*, thereby making them sadly short-breathed. He elided many full closes into what follows, both within and at the end of numbers. He lowered the Iphigenia-Achilles duet by a tone, and by the repointing of Achilles' air removed eighteen A's and eight B's above the staff. (In Paris, the whole air was on occasion simply lowered from D to C—whether to spare the tenor or to give him the chance of showing off a high C or two is unclear.)

Wagner's principal additions are two. Iphigenia's air of farewell to Achilles is reconstructed. Gluck wrote an andante *aabb*, "I must submit to destiny," followed by a long lento, "Remember that Iphigenia loved you." Wagner, in his expressed desire to eliminate the Racinian love interest, reduced the andante to *ab*, removed the tender lento, and composed a new passage in which Iphigenia, in the tones of Elisabeth and accompanied by *Tannhäuser* harmonies, declares that Hellas' fate depends on her. Then the abridged andante is repeated—creating the da capo form that Gluck in his reform operas sought to avoid. Artemis' arioso-recitative speech, on the other hand, clearly anticipates Lohengrin's "In fernem Land." These additions are accompanied—like Elisabeth's prayer, in *Tannhäuser*—by winds only. So are Iphigenia's air of farewell to her mother and—another episode Wagner himself composed—her slow departure for the altar. The passages are assigned to a backstage wind consort—an ethereal effect. Once, at a Karajan production of *Tannhäuser* in Vienna, I heard Elisabeth's prayer similarly accompanied.

Wagner made much of his discovery that the 1774 score (unlike Brissler's) bears no indication for tempo change after the slow introduction: "How incredibly Gluck's overture has been disfigured by playing it twice too fast!" Wagner's deliberate pace is certainly impressive, but if he'd pursued his researches further he'd have found in the Paris performance material (preserved at the Opéra) a "Grave" at the unison "motif of power" and then an "Animé" where the main movement begins.

Iphigénie en Tauride—"Gluck's last French opera," I nearly wrote, forgetting, as people often do, the final *Echo et Narcisse*, which is filled with greatness and beauty, and is most unjustly neglected—is by general consent his masterpiece. *Iphigénie en Aulide,* his first work for Paris, is also a great opera. So are *Orfeo, Alceste, Paride ed Elena,* and *Armide.* But none of them are performer-proof. In inspired productions, they touch the very heart of one's being; reveal music's power to sound every string of a listener's psyche; make the theatre what it should be, a place of, at once, ecstasy, entertainment, and moral and political enlightenment; join the spectators with all those who through twenty-four centuries have discovered in contemporary stage enactments of the ancient myths new ways of understanding the world they live in. But in unworthy performances the operas can seem to show Gluck as an aspirant, earnest calculator—an intelligent plodder with sensible ideas but not heaven-sent felicity, melodic fertility, and grace. A contemporary reproved Gluck for giving the army in *Iphigénie en Aulide* always the same tune to sing as they call for Iphigenia's death. He retorted that crowds that assemble with one object in view always chant the same slogan, over and over again ("Dump Reagan," as it were); as a musician, he could well have written differing melodies, but as a dramatist he'd done what he'd done quite deliberately. The performance will determine whether the effect is chillingly realistic or simply monotonous. Wagner decided to recompose one of the choral interjections.

The success of *Orfeo, Alceste, Armide,* and *Iphigénie en Tauride* depends very much on the dramatic and vocal abilities of the protagonist. *Iphigénie en Aulide* has the practical advantage of spreading that burden pretty well equally across the soprano, the mezzo, the tenor, and the baritone. It is perhaps Gluck's most varied and tautly exciting opera, with great scenes for Agamemnon and Clytemnestra, and eventful, surprising action. Wagner produced it with his *Tannhäuser* cast: Johanna Wagner (Elisabeth, Iphigenia), Schröder-Devrient (Venus, Clytemnestra), Joseph Tichatschek (Tannhäuser, Achilles), and Anton Mitterwurzer (Wolfram, Agamemnon, later the first Kurwenal). He interrupted the composition of *Lohengrin* to undertake the revision. If Gluck-Wagner rather than Gluck is to be revived, it must be done, wholeheartedly, in a way that enables listeners to visit a staging post on the journey that leads from *Tannhäuser,* through *Lohengrin,* to *The Ring,* in which Attic drama, ancestral myth—and just about everything that men have thought, done, written, composed—play a part. The RCA recording is pointlessly "de-Wagnerized"; transitions that Wagner added have been deleted. The Waterloo performance was in concert form, and Wagner might not have approved; he once wrote, "I can imagine no more hideous travesty of a dramatic and, especially, a tragic piece of music than to have, say, Orestes and Iphigenia—in tailcoat and ball dress, complete with posy, holding their scores in kid-gloved hands— proclaiming their death agonies in front of a concert orchestra." No half-loaves for him: "Where an artistic illusion is not fully at work on me, I cannot be even half content." But without concert performances the modern operatic repertory would be meager. The Waterloo performers had no posies or kid gloves. Nor, it seemed, had they thought themselves deeply into the drama or pondered the ways that by glance, by demeanor, and, above all, by declamation, accent, and phrasing concert performers can create an illusion. They seemed to be singing off their scores, not from their hearts. Except for the Iphigenia, Alessandra Marc. She has a large, shining, steady soprano. It is not quite technically finished but is blessedly unforced and already impressive. She sang the music with simple, unaffected dignity and phrased with tender feeling. Katherine Ciesinski, the Clytemnestra, pushed her voice into harshness and impurity. Gary Lakes, the Achilles, is a promising young heldentenor, solid and sure. Norman Bailey, who has sung Wotan's and Hans Sachs's words so eloquently, was a disappointing Agamemnon: "zart," "teuer," "grausen" all sounded much the same. His reading lacked passion. Justino Diaz, the Calchas, produced some big, strong notes. Communicativeness was impeded by the use of a translation intended for a Dresden, not a New Jersey, public. All appoggiaturas—as vital in Wagner as they are in Gluck—were ignored and were turned into ugly "blunt endings" (repeated notes at the end of phrases).

The performance, conducted by Gerard Schwarz, seemed underrehearsed. The Waterloo Festival Orchestra, a mixed professional and student body, accompanied recitatives as if it didn't know the singers' lines—bumping in on the conductor's beat, not moving with the actors' minds. Much of the playing was undercharacterized, undramatic, and mezzo-forte; many of Wagner's careful

188

dynamic inflections went for little. It was not a carefully studied, stylishly convincing re-creation of the 1847 drama. But I'm glad to have heard it, for I'm a half-loafer myself: rather this moderately competent, uninspired (except when Miss Marc sang) *Iphigénie* than no *Iphigénie* at all. Waterloo is a pleasant place—an eighteenth- and nineteenth-century village carefully and unobtrusively restored, set in broad parklands beside lakes and the Morris Canal. Woodland or waterside strolls—and serious catering—induce a tolerant frame of mind. The performance was warmly received. But Wagner and Gluck deserved better.

GIVE HER BLACK EYES

August 13, 1984

THE City Opera's 1984 season began, last month, with a senseless and deplorable new production of Rossini's *Barbiere di Siviglia,* directed by Toby Robertson, who seemed not to have noticed that the plot turns on gaining entrance to and escaping from a close-guarded house. Ladders led up to its second-floor balcony. Even before Rosina's appearance there, Almaviva and Fiorello had been charging through the house; Figaro began "Largo al factotum" inside it and made his entrance down a ladder. This was not a high-spirited, neatly fashioned comedy of intrigue and character but an any-old-joke affair. Bartolo had a laboratory in a corner of his salon; at the climax of the calumny aria, retorts exploded and a skeleton began to waggle. Twelve supers (one of them dressed as Rossini) mimed the overture and remained onstage to share the action with the singers. Judith Forst gave Rosina some well-turned phrases; for the rest, the singing tended to reflect the stage horseplay and was without grace, charm, or supple, individual inflections. Lloyd Evans's décor was hideous. Christopher Keene's conducting was careful but chilly, unsmiling.

The company put on five shows—three of them Puccini operas—during the first three days of the season. A matinée *Magic Flute* (done in my English translation) was intelligently staged by Jay Lesenger and brought the company début of Walter MacNeil (Cornell MacNeil's son), as Tamino. The sound was good, the interpretation dull; he tended to give equal emphasis to each word and each note of a phrase—singing, as it were, "Can, These Be Pangs Of Love I Feel?" Let him study Plunket Greene's *Interpretation in Song*. William Parker, on the other hand, was a Papageno whose clear diction and feeling for musical and verbal stress delighted a translator's heart. *La Bohème* that evening brought another tenor débutant, Richard Leech, whose light, pure, blessedly unforced Rodolfo did much to redeem a mainly ill-sung performance. He has an easy, natural stage presence. The next day's matinée *Butterfly* I've already written about, and I missed the *Turandot* that followed.

A week later, there was a new production of *La traviata,* directed by Frank Corsaro, in Zack Brown's dowdy 1981 scenery "remounted" by Mr. Evans. Its spaces are poorly defined. The sets, with rostra left and right, look like store displays of crude period furniture, not rooms that anyone really lives in. In the new staging, Violetta and Flora have swapped salons, to mutual advantage. Marianna Christos's first New York Violetta was promising. She is a vivid and passionate artist, with a gleaming presence, a voice both flexible and lustrous, and strong musical and dramatic instincts. But she seemed ill at ease, and she had reason to be so: in the pit, Klaus Weise, the music director of the Kiel Opera, showed no idiomatic feeling for the flow of Verdi's music and no consideration for the artists he should have been accompanying. Miss Christos's "Sempre libera" was moving—the first verse sung with reckless determination, the second (after Alfredo's declaration of love drifted in to her) as if with a breaking heart. Her Alfredo was a fairly good young tenor, Robert Grayson, with a light, free-flowing, and well-focussed voice and an honest manner. He wasn't quite aristocratic in style; his rhythms were a shade metronomic, but hardly more so than in most modern performances. Although Mr. Corsaro's production had its oddities—Alfredo reappeared in person at the end of the first act (a modern cliché, and a bad one); Annina, forgetting her station, settled down unbidden for a cozy chat with the master; Violetta spent the Act III prelude wandering about on the terrace in her ball dress but with bare feet—on the whole the characters' emotions and behavior were nicely observed.

Candide as performed at the City Opera is a coarse cheap travesty of Bernstein's opera. The shape and spirit of the original are destroyed, and number after number is deprived of meaning. This season's revival was made tolerable, just, by David Eisler's light, true, frank singing of the title role. Leigh Munro was a brittle, edgy Cunegonde. It has been a season, so far, marked mainly by acceptable tenors. Its summer segment (the first ten of the twenty weeks) is also a Corsaro-Evans season: six of the thirteen operas are directed by Mr. Corsaro, and six of them are designed by Mr. Evans.

The revival of their *Cavalleria rusticana* and *Pagliacci* was not happy. The sets are ill-painted; the *Cav* church is an architectural muddle. The direction is one of Mr. Corsaro's most perverse, not because of any freakish change of period or place—the basic style is stock traditional: realism from the principals, and a chorus of stooge peasants who line up like a choral society—but because he seems to have gone out of his way to destroy every theatrical effect devised by the composers. An entry of red surplices, lace, and blue-and-silver banners takes the attention from Santuzza and Mamma Lucia during the tense pause while they await the outcome of the offstage duel. Nedda shares most of her aria with a dwarf, and the latter part of it with Tonio. Her pretty little pantomime as Columbine is appropriated by two acrobats. During Canio's "Vesti la giubba," an onstage Nedda provides an alternative focus of attention; Silvio does so during "No! Pagliaccio non son"; and "La commedia è finita!" is capped by a chorister's scream and prominent exit. These are not little things; they're big theatrical moments of the dramas diminished. I have never known a *Cav* and *Pag*—or, for that matter, a *Butterfly*—so untheatrical, so feeble in emotional impact. It's puzzling. Mr. Corsaro evidently gives thought to motivation and character. But sometimes he directs as if he were tone deaf, missing the point of the music, muffing dramatic point after point that has been made with notes as well as with

190

words. Sometimes he seems merely contrary: the composer, using a rich operatic language compounded of words, notes, and stage actions, asks for one thing, and Mr. Corsaro does something else; words and music can't be changed, but he changes the actions. (This is equivalent to saying, "I'm a better dramatist than Mozart, Verdi, Puccini." But Mr. Corsaro isn't. He usually provides inferior—albeit novel and interesting—variations on successful dramas.) Sometimes he reminds me of a conductor who, faced with a familiar work, decides to refresh it by "bringing out inner voices" even if the main theme is thereby obscured. And sometimes he is like a conductor who adds inner voices of his own composition: most Corsaro casts include characters uncalled for by the dramatist. I like elaborate, detailed stagings of *Cav* and *Pag* (though a plain, starkly beautiful Brechtian production I once saw in Parma was also impressive). Franco Zeffirelli's are far more elaborate and realistic than Mr. Corsaro's: the chorus looks and moves like a crowd of individuals; the priest behaves like a real priest; real water trickles from a public fountain; the Francofonte wine is of authentic color. (I'm recalling the Covent Garden productions; I have not seen Mr. Zeffirelli's versions for the Met.) But the musical and dramatic focus is sure. At the big moments, all attention is directed on the principals. Composer, director, and singers work together, help one another.

Operas are often staged nowadays as if to help audiences in every way from having to do anything so exacting as to use their ears and listen in detail to what is being sung, said, and played. Overtures and instrumental interludes are made accompaniments to pantomime. (An excellent episode in the *Candide* overture was drowned by the gabble and cries of an assembling chorus; the *Cav* and *Pag* intermezzi were mimed.) Audiences do their bit by blotting out passages with their applause for the scenery, for visual gags, or when a slow curtain starts to fall on a quiet coda. It's true that the City Opera's *Cav* and *Pag* casts were hardly worth listening to (with the exception of Frederick Burchinal's firmly sung Tonio); that the intermezzi were dryly played, without ripe portamento, as if they were twentieth-century compositions; that Mr. Weise's conducting was leaden, without emotional surge. But the production was surely not planned with those as données; if one doesn't intend to *use* the music, spoken drama would be preferable.

The employment of supertitles further encourages people to pay but small attention to the singers—to what they are saying and with what tones, inflections, and expression they say it. Audience reaction at the State Theater this season has been determined by and timed to the words on the screen above the stage; jokes projected there are laughed at before the actors have made them. These supertitles are evidently planned for intent, not occasional, following: whenever, having missed a sung line and forgotten what it should be, I've glanced up for guidance, it has been to a screen already blank. Stray lines that have caught my eye at other times have been as often as not somewhat misleading. In the bohemians' mock-informal farewell to their landlord, "vostra signoria" ("your lordship") became "your wife." Santuzza's "A te la mala Pasqua, spergiuro!" was "May you be punished this Easter." Canio-Pagliaccio, returning home earlier than expected "ma in tempo!"—in good time to witness his wife's infidelity —was made to say "not early enough." In the *Traviata* second-act finale,

Germont, who had the dominant line, seemed to be declaring that "Baron Douphol's sword shall defend her honor." Alfredo's exclamation "Mille serpi divoranmi il petto" ("A thousand serpents devour my bosom") was glossed over; if it's thought to be too strong an expression for modern ears, why not change the Italian, too? There's been nothing quite as jolly as the supertitle reported from Houston which accompanied Tosca's sly, tender, cajoling remark to Cavaradossi as she looks at his painting of the Marchesa Attavanti. To the displeasure of the prima donna, Eva Marton, a rehearsal audience roared with laughter when she sang the line. It read "Give her black eyes!" (in itself, a not inaccurate translation of "Ma . . . falle gli occhi neri!").

Mistakes and miscalculations can be righted. It's the device that—for all its evident usefulness—bothers me. The main fault of most American singing is already insufficient care about the text. "Make the words live, let them determine the timbre and the timing, and the music will be brought to life" has been the counsel of singers through the centuries. Supertitles are likely to encourage audiences, and then singers, to care less and less about the way the words are sung. Beverly Sills is on record as saying, "This will revolutionize opera. You don't have to sit there for hours anymore, wondering, 'What the hell is going on?' " Is that all she thought people did when, with careful attention to word color, she sang Manon, Elizabeth, Mary Stuart?

ANOTHER TIME, ANOTHER PLACE

August 20, 1984

THE days are done when *Così fan tutte* was deemed a frivolous divertimento, its plot an unworthy vessel for some of Mozart's loveliest music. If anything, the opera is perhaps now treated with—well, not exactly undue seriousness but, let's say, insufficient appreciation of its comedy. The best performers get it right, of course. Elisabeth Söderström's Fiordiligi made me cry when the martial music returned during the wedding feast and she looked up stricken with the realization of how far and how swiftly emotion had carried her from her intended path. And she made me smile as well, for it is, after all, a comedy situation. The *Don Giovanni* trio—Juan's burlesque serenade to Elvira—is a locus classicus of mingled heartbreak and clowning. *Così* is a yet more complicated compound. Just how complicated I discovered when I tried to make an English translation that would be straight Da Ponte, without the added larkiness and witticisms of English versions that invite frivolous performances.

In recent years, there have been at least three productions of the opera at once serious, moving, and entertaining: Peter Hall's for Glyndebourne, Jonathan Miller's for St. Louis, and now Peter Sellars's, staged this month at the Castle Hill Festival, in Massachusetts. Mr. Sellars uses Da Ponte's poetry but an American setting. Da Ponte's action opens in a *bottega di caffè;* here a neon sign proclaims

"Coffee Shop." In the words of the director's synopsis, "Don Alfonso, a Vietnam Vet who is having trouble hanging on, has been seeing Despina, the proprietress of the shop, for a few years now. At breakfast one summer morning, two loud guys start talking about their girlfriends in big terms, offering to hurt anyone who contradicts them." And so on. "Reagan has decided to invade Nicaragua—Ferrando and Guglielmo have been mobilized in the Naval Reserve." That's a gloss on "To the field of battle by royal command they are summoned," but much of the synopsis is straight Da Ponte. For example, a chorus extols "beautiful military life! Every day you change locations, and the firing of guns and bombs increases the force of your arm and of a spirit which dreams only of triumph."

Alfonso "introduces two wild and crazy friends of his who claim to be from Albania, where they were very big in the entertainment industry." Soon we are in deep waters. The disguises don't really hold for long, but this is not like that old adaptation of *Così* as *Tit for Tat; or, The Tables Turned,* in which Despina gives the plot away to her mistresses; it is something subtler and far more disturbing, for no one is prepared to admit—not even one sister to the other—that the real identities are recognized. It throws "real" identity into question. The sisters offer the men a chance to come clean, with their direct question "Cos'è tal mascherata?" near the start of Act II. The men, taken aback, make confused replies; the women take the lead and continue the masquerade. Their earlier discussion about doing so has already caused a little shiver of excitement. All four are playing with fire. Soon Dorabella has slept with her sister's boyfriend—her own boyfriend's best friend—and has enjoyed doing so, while Fiordiligi and Ferrando are wrestling with deep emotions. At the end, there is no simple reconciliation in either possible pairing; to the women's protestation of eternal devotion the men return Da Ponte's lines "I believe you, fair jewel, but I don't want to prove it." Maybe something can be worked out later, when all the bewildering experience has been digested.

The Despina, Sue Ellen Kuzma, was the wittiest I have seen, and the most surprising; her two arias—outbursts at male behavior, analysis of how women learn to deal with it—ended in angry tears. I can't believe it is what Mozart consciously intended, but it made excellent sense. In the words of the synopsis, "She tells what it is like when you have to go with hundreds of men—and give to them all whether they're beauts or brutes—without blushing, without confusion, how to live a lie. And finally how to make them pay for it by enforcing obedience. Viva Despina who knows how to serve!" It's exactly what Mozart's Despina sings, and Miss Kuzma's performance made excellent musical sense, too: while none of the cajolery or sparkle was lost, the tempo changes, the hesitations, and the repetitions seemed to be motivated.

Everything that happened made excellent musical sense. Mr. Sellars, quick to each shift of tempo and harmony, each instrumental entry, whether he's engaged with Handel's *Orlando*, *The Mikado*, Peter Maxwell Davies's *The Lighthouse*, or *Così*, evidently works from the full score. In a world where so many famous directors seem to be tone deaf or, at least, unmusical, he invites us to hear with our eyes and see with our ears. He trusts great composers, doesn't try to vary or improve or "criticize" their work but stages their scores as vividly as possible. His means are bold. This *Così*—like the *Orlando* in Cambridge a few years ago—employed Oriental theatre techniques, eighteenth-century formal conventions, and contemporary references. It distressed conservatives who want the opera to be elegantly and prettily artificial, and distressed those who want it to be Puccini-veristic in its depiction of emotional plights. It upset the literal-minded who heard the dark-haired Ferrando referred to as "il biondino" and Despina in notary disguise (here as Ms. Beccavivi, a smooth, cool lawyer) called "un uom nascosto." It delighted everyone who can watch and hear theatre moving as metaphors—even mixed metaphors—on many levels at once, with quicksilver responsiveness to the mirth, the profundity, and the unresolved ambiguities of the music. Much was surprising, startling, and delightful. It was a *Così* that kept listeners on the edge of their seats and left them emotionally in a whirl, as the characters are left.

Much has been written about parallels between *Così* and its creator, who in life loved one sister and then married another. It has also been suggested that the original performers of Alfonso and Despina, the veteran intriguer Francesco Bussani and his flighty young wife, Dorotea, may have been models for their roles. (Dorotea, Da Ponte says in his memoirs, "built up a great following among cooks, grooms, waiters, lackeys, hairdressers, etc., and was consequently considered a gem.") Despina's remark to Alfonso "An old man like you is no use to a girl like me" seems near the knuckle. I'm still pondering Mr. Sellars's demoticized and very physical treatment of their relationship: in the text I find only a hint of passing tease, not a physical entanglement, and in the music hear minds, not bodies, moving together. And I was disturbed by the couple's failure to address the line "Aftereffects of the poison" (when the Albanians become amorous) to Fiordiligi and Dorabella, for musically and verbally it is part of a dialogue.

In this production, meant for nimble minds, there was room for funny, fleeting allusions to television commercials; for exotic, ecstatic mime in "Un'aura amorosa," where Ferrando seemed to be caressing the lovely melody with hands and voice at once; for a refinement of Mr. Miller's broad jukebox joke in *Rigoletto* (a swift, entertaining reference at "una bella serenata," not the awkwardness of a jukebox apparently playing accompaniment to a tenor's song). A distinction should be made between veristic, literal out-of-period presentations, such as that *Rigoletto*, in which the setting and the tone of the original are mismatched, and this *Così* (or the English National's production of Dvořák's *Rusalka*), in which initial realism breaks into a theatrical adventure where anything may happen next, at the composer's bidding, and for which Wagner's phrase "deeds of music made visible" seems apt.

The singers had the light, unforced quality too seldom heard in New York. Susan Larson (Fiordiligi), Miss Kuzma, James Maddalena (Guglielmo), and Sanford Sylvan (Alfonso) are prized Boston musicians. Freda Herseth (Dorabella) is a Stuttgart Cherubino. Carroll Freeman (Ferrando) was a bright tenorino transfigured. Mr. Sellars seems unfailingly to draw wonderful performances from his casts—as musicians, as actors, as movers. Michael Nishball's set—the green plastic banquettes and Formica tables of Despina's diner—and Dunya Ramicova's costumes made a work of art. Craig Smith, Mr. Sellars's regular collaborator, conducted a band of expert young Boston players with his rare insight into the meanings of a score. Sometimes his reluctance to let go of enchantments verged on the indulgent—a tendency easy to understand and forgive.

Castle Hill is a large William-and-Maryish house built in the 1920s, about thirty miles northeast of Boston, and set in a park with a *grande allée* sweeping down to the sea. In its casino, sunken Italian garden, and a concert barn, summer music and theatre are played. Picnics on the lawn suggest Glyndebourne (without the formal dress). But there's no opera house. *Così* was done in the Italian garden, and some of the orchestral impact was lost to the night air. There is talk of reviving it in a theatre. There it should run and run (as *Orlando* did, for forty performances). It is something one would like to hear and see many times.

The City Opera's new production of *Carmen*, with Victoria Vergara as its heroine, directed by Frank Corsaro, designed by Franco Colavecchia, and conducted by Christopher Keene, is a success. There is plenty to be said against it, but then there is always plenty to be said against any production of *Carmen*. Bizet's bold challenging of opéra comique produced an unconventional masterpiece that no single performance seems able to compass. A vision of the work as it might ideally be is built up from the best elements of many performances: in my case, the Carmens of Anna Pollak, Winifred Heidt, Martha Mödl, Regina Resnik (and, on record, Emma Calvé, Maria Callas, and, above all, Conchita Supervia); Melba's pure, shining Micaëla (imagined by the mind's ear, for although Melba sang the role she did not record it); the impassioned José of Jon Vickers; a production by Tyrone Guthrie; the conducting of Claudio Abbado (and on record Beecham). Add Maria Gay, Victoria de los Angeles, Teresa Berganza. Let each listener add elements of any *Carmen* that has stirred him: perhaps the high spectacle of Karajan's Salzburg production and—incompatibly—the sheer effectiveness of the piece, even in a stock revival, on the small stage of the Opéra-Comique itself. How can one production contain them all? Nevertheless, there are performances that in their own right hold off comparisons and keep the spectator intent on the drama enacted before him. Much of the time, the City Opera's was one of them.

Miss Vergara, a Chilean mezzo-soprano who made her début as Micaëla, in Santiago fifteen years ago, has sung Carmen widely in leading opera houses of Europe and America. To New York she gave a performance untouched by any hint of routine, quick in reaction to each turn of the action around her. She is wonderful-looking—tall, strong, beautiful, with lustrous Latin features. Her eyes, her mouth, her abundant black hair, her body are eloquent. She moved magnificently, combining animal grace with intelligence and dignity. She spoke and sang French fluently, commanding the text, able to bend it to her bidding. Her voice is rich and colorful. Had there not been moments when under pressure it lost focus, became smutched with ambient sound around the pure pitch, there would be few reservations in my praise of her.

The production was first seen in Philadelphia last year, also with Miss Vergara. Mr. Colavecchia's décor—basically a well-shaped gray box, differently decked for each scene—and Michaele Hite's largely black costumes look good. Mr. Corsaro has moved the action forward from 1820 to 1936, and Carmen and her crew are not smugglers but heroes in the fight against Franco. It doesn't make much sense if one stops to think about it: Bizet's drama is about a decent, albeit quick-tempered, fellow drawn down by passion into criminal activity, whereas in this version the criminals are the good guys. Bizet's Carmen, who represents an abandonment of conventional morality, and champions personal freedom whatever the cost to others, is hardly a convincing political heroine. The "liberté" she and the gang invoke at the end of Act II is not freedom for the people but escape from social responsibility. All the same, the notion doesn't get in the way too badly, for the basic drama—the José-Carmen relationship—is clearly perceived and clearly presented, and the freedom-fighter glosses can be overlooked, or even enjoyed as lively trimming. Most of the time, not always: Bizet's precise music for the smugglers has a furtive, avaricious quality ill-matched to the expression of civil-rights sentiments; "La fortune est là-bas" does not—despite the declaration of the City Opera supertitles—mean "The enemy is waiting for us down below," and "Notre métier est bon" does not mean "This is the good fight." (It's disconcerting to hear one thing and read another; the supertitles either become irrelevant or constitute an invitation to pay no close attention to the performance. "L'auberge devrait être fermée depuis dix minutes" does not mean the inn "will be closed in ten minutes." "La chose, certes, nous étonne" does not mean "We're not too surprised." "Si tu m'aimes" does not mean "Do you love me?") Things go seriously wrong only in the last act, where the climactic duet, in itself well staged, is made to compete for our attention with preparations by the partisans for an assassination—snipers scaling towers, etc. José's last cry is trumped by the offstage salvos and screams of the coup. Mr. Corsaro's sense of effective theatre strays here; he muffs the close, and the decision to adulterate Bizet's taut finale with music that the composer himself rejected makes things worse. But until then this *Carmen* is gripping.

When Jacque Trussel sang José for the Welsh National Opera last year, he was required, by the Rumanian director Lucian Pintilie, to portray him as a bearded baldpate. (That *Carmen* was staged as a street-carnival extravaganza after a revolutionary coup; a blind Micaëla entered on point.) Mr. Corsaro allowed him to be young and romantic, a plausible magnet for Carmen's affections, neurotic, tormented—in short, Bizet's José. Mr. Trussel acted the role admirably, with strength, subtlety, and passion, but his singing was effortful, and the voice rang freely only in the last act. Escamillo was described in a preliminary interview with Mr. Corsaro as "an aging bullfighter well past his prime . . . a local hero playing the Fascist side . . . easily seduced by Carmen for her own purposes." That belies both the plot and the torero's athletic music, but Robert Hale went along with it, staggering and puffing between the verses of his song, and relying on two henchmen to save him from José's knife. In Act III, he essayed an otiose offstage cadenza that Bizet deleted. The Micaëla, Maryanne Telese, pushed her high notes into unsteadiness and impurity. Mr. Keene conducted a briskly insensitive musical reading that allowed his singers and woodwind soloists small chance to breathe or to shape their phrases expressively, and ensemble between the stage and the pit was sometimes ragged. Nevertheless, this was, all in all, a production fresher, more serious in intention, more like a real opera performance than anything else at the State Theater this season. The chorus was alert and animated. If Mr. Corsaro continues to work at the show, refining and rethinking some of his ideas, if Miss Vergara can bring the peaks of her voice into clear focus, and if a conductor responsive at once to the score and to his singers takes over, this could become a notable *Carmen* indeed. Already it is one that prompts new, alert responses to the opera from performers and audience alike.

LOVE IN A GARDEN

August 27, 1984

LEONARD BERNSTEIN's latest opera, *A Quiet Place,* commissioned jointly by the Houston Grand Opera, the Kennedy Center, and La Scala, had its première in Houston last year. This June, it was given six performances at La Scala, and then, in July, it came to the Opera House of the Kennedy Center. Milan and Washington saw a rather different work from Houston. *A Quiet Place* was originally a two-hour, one-act opera, played on a double bill with Bernstein's *Trouble in Tahiti*. *Tahiti* (1952) is a wry, tuneful tragedy of American suburbia, at once serious and entertaining, composed for a mezzo-soprano and a bass-baritone (Dinah and Sam), a chorus of three who offer commentary in the sweet, insidious manner of a radio commercial, and a chamber orchestra. *A Quiet Place,* for a large cast and a full orchestra, is set thirty years later. In brief (I wrote at length after the première: *Musical Events: 1980–1983,* pp. 474–78), Dinah has been killed in a car smash. At her funeral, Sam is reunited with his neurotic forty-year-old son, still called Junior, and his daughter, Dede; and meets his son-in-law, François, who was Junior's lover before he married Dede. Through a jangle of painful memories, recriminations, and gropings toward understanding and reconciliation, the family finds its way at last to a "quiet place" such as Dinah—relating a dream to her analyst—sang of in *Tahiti*:

> *There is a garden:*
> *Come with me . . .*
> *There love will teach us*
> *Harmony and grace,*
> *Then love will lead us*
> *To a quiet place.*

It's a bold, ambitious, and very interesting opera, containing some of Bernstein's most richly wrought music. I thought so in Houston and thought so again in Washington. Bernstein and his librettist, Stephen Wadsworth, have worked with a candor that is almost shocking; they have "bared their souls." *A Quiet Place* is no opera for people who want art to keep its distance and behave with decorum. Bernstein, as concert-hall audiences know, does his best to put Beethoven's injunction "Seid umschlungen, Millionen" into practice, spiritually and literally. *A Quiet Place* received some thin, prim reviews in this country, from those unwilling to accept the composer's embrace. (The Milan critics were more welcoming.) But his warmth and generosity of spirit, his emotionalism, his love of music and love of humanity are inseparable from his music-making; and he is a wonderful musician.

A Quiet Place is unlike any other opera I know (some Janáček scenes afford the closest parallel) in its attempt to fashion a coherent work of art from the disorderly speech and disorderly thought of uneducated contemporary people who can't express their thoughts clearly and don't even finish their sentences. The music makes clear what they are trying to say and gives form to their messy lives. In Houston, the opera had something of the shape of a four-movement symphony, with a complicated, many-themed exposition, a slow movement of linked nocturnal duets, games in the garden as a scherzo, and an apotheosis of tempests followed by a rainbow. In Washington, it was divided into three acts, the second of which (the former slow movement) incorporated *Trouble in Tahiti* as two segments of flashback. Several little cuts had been made, and some large ones. Here and there, the orchestration of *A Quiet Place* had been thinned and that of *Tahiti* amplified. In one important respect, the dramaturgy had been much strengthened: Dinah no longer leaves an arcane suicide note that— somehow, mysteriously—points the way to the quiet place, and François no longer preaches a sermon with this letter as his text. The finale is more naturally and more smoothly achieved. For the rest, I am unsure whether all is gain. In the first scene, the funeral, Dinah's brother Bill, her friend Susie, and, especially, another friend, Mrs. Doc (who later realizes she was in love with Dinah), are vividly presented—strongly drawn in brief but telling strokes. In the Houston version these characters return to resolve their own problems in the general harmony; in the Washington version, they don't. The result is simpler, the denseness of the emotional thicket has been pruned, but there seems now to be an imbalance between the well-stocked first scene and the no-more-than-quartet scenes that follow. Besides, we lose some beautiful music.

The *Tahiti* flashbacks are skillfully introduced, but they break the flow of the nocturne and make for an oddly proportioned opera: the three acts last about forty-five, sixty-five, and twenty-two minutes. After Houston, I described *Trouble in Tahiti* as "the necessary exposition to the grand opera that follows." I am no longer sure whether that is true. There are musical links between the two operas, but *A Quiet Place*, I now think, can stand alone (as *Figaro's Wedding* can, without needing *The Barber of Seville*—either as preface or in flashbacks—to explain how the present situations have been reached). Perhaps the two operas should be performed on consecutive nights (as in Vienna Paisiello's *Barber* and Mozart's *Figaro* once were): *Tahiti* with a suitable companion piece, *A Quiet Place* restored to its full length but with the dramatic improvements of the Washington finale retained.

The revised version had been newly directed, with a sensitive and subtle hand, by Mr. Wadsworth. The Houston scenery was reused, adapted to the requirements of the new ordering. It looked rather dowdy, and added nothing to the drama, but served to house a production whose strengths lay in the accuracy and acuteness of the individual performances. Chester Ludgin (Sam), Peter Kazaras (François), and several others repeated their Houston roles, and were even better than before. There was a new Dede and a new Junior, Beverly Morgan and Robert Galbraith, and both were excellent. Miss Morgan gave the performance of her life, vocally secure, and alive in every glance, move, and inflection. Mr. Galbraith is a splendidly vivid young character baritone—someone to watch for. In *Tahiti*, Diane Kesling repeated her shining Dinah, and a new Young Sam, Julien Robbins, was vigorous, if backward of tone. John Mauceri, who had helped in the refashioning of the operas, conducted with the mixture of passion and control, of freedom and discipline, that makes him one of our best opera interpreters. It was an exciting evening for American opera.

The Vienna State Opera has announced *A Quiet Place* for its 1985–86 season. [*And a live recording of the Vienna production has now been published by Deutsche Grammophon.*]

PepsiCo Summerfare is a season of opera, theatre, music, and dance performed on the Purchase campus of the State University of New York. The campus has four theatres, designed by Edward Larrabee Barnes. Robert Venturi, Paul Rudolph, and Philip Johnson have also built there. PepsiCo's headquarters (the buildings by Edward Durrell Stone) and famous sculpture gardens (landscapes and planting by Russell Page) are across the road. The place is not far away—about forty-five minutes' drive, closer than Glyndebourne is to London. One of the four theatres is a "black box" that allows for varied seating plans; the others hold five hundred, seven hundred, and fourteen hundred people. The houses are intimate; the fare is international. The main theatre event this year was Giorgio Strehler's celebrated production of *The Tempest,* brought by the Piccolo Teatro di Milano. The main "creation" was of Conrad Susa's one-act opera *The Love of Don Perlimplín.*

Lorca's *Amor de Don Perlimplín con Belisa en su jardín* is a play that approaches the condition of music. It is shot through with songs; the first stage direction includes the instruction "A sonata is heard." Lorca was a composer himself. Francisco García Lorca, his brother, remarks that the four characters "interweave their voices in a kind of concerto grosso for four instruments," and that "none of Lorca's plays shows with more poetic evidence the musical influence in his theatre." One can almost imagine the play's being "performed" on the harpsichord. Lorca said Domenico Scarlatti would have been the man to set it. Small wonder, then, that it has attracted several musicians. There have been operas by Vittorio Rieti, Claire Kessler, and Wolfgang Fortner (I remember Rieti's as a delicate, poignant piece); a radio opera by Bruno Maderna; a powerful and poetic ballet, *Il mantello rosso*, by Luigi Nono.

And on the strength of Susa's previous operas, *Transformations* and *Black River*, I suspect that there may be a rewarding small opera lurking within what one saw and heard at Purchase. But it was hard to perceive it. The staging, by David Alden (in the seven-hundred-seat theatre), was grotesquely elaborated, overblown, and unfocussed. The set, by Douglas W. Schmidt, was a huge, high room containing the various scenes—study, bedchamber, garden, etc.—within it. It was decked with expressionist props (books the size of a steamer trunk) and was traversed by a Brechtian *gardine*, or half-curtain. Belisa's mother was presented as a cross between Miss Havisham and Mother Ginger in *The Nutcracker*. The singers—junior members of the San Francisco Opera—knew their notes but not, it seemed, their roles in a drama that needs poised and precise playing. Lorca's *Don Perlimplín*, a tragic verso to *Don Pasquale*, is written with epigrammatic, sometimes enigmatic terseness, which Susa has respected. The libretto, by the composer and Richard Street, based on the English translation by James Graham-Lujan and Richard O'Connell, is economical, as the staging was not, and does not try to explain things, although it swells Lorca's two sprites into a chorus of six, and swells their wedding-night interlude by Lorca's "Ballad of the Unfaithful Wife," sung and danced. Mr. Alden kept the singers and dancers onstage and gave them prominent parts in some private scenes. Susa's music is aptly lean and bright, elegant and animated, passionate without being lush. It seemed to be cunningly scored, but it was hard to tell, for Andrew Meltzer conducted a pretty consistently mezzo-forte performance. The show left the impression of having had too large a production budget and too little rehearsal.

ROUNDUP

September 3, 1984

MINIMALISM, though unrepresented this year at the Philharmonic's Horizons festival, is not yet, it seems, a spent force. The Brooklyn Academy has announced Steve Reich's *The Desert Music* and a revival of Philip Glass's *Einstein on the Beach* for next season. The City Opera does Glass's *Akhnaten* in November, and in London the English National Opera does it in June. This season in New York we had a performance, at the City Center in May, of Act V, composed by Glass, of *the CIVIL warS: a tree is best measured when it is down. the CIVIL warS* is a long, long theatre piece, devised, designed, and directed by Robert Wilson, working with various composers, which has been in piecemeal creation all over the world and would have been assembled at the Olympic Arts Festival in Los Angeles had funds not run short. Act V, commissioned by the Rome Opera, was produced there in March. The City Center performance, in concert form, was given by the New York Opera Repertory Theater, conducted by Leigh Gibbs Gore. Without the "visuals," it seemed a slight, sometimes agreeably quaint, sometimes boringly repetitious piece. The mezzo and soprano of the cast (one doubled as Earth Mother and Mrs. Lincoln, the other as Snow Owl and Alcmene, Hercules' mother) were so unsteady and approximate that the common chords of which most of the music is made, instead of shining, became murky and unpleasant.

The St. Louis Symphony and Symphony Chorus, conducted by Leonard Slatkin, brought John Adams's *Harmonium* to Carnegie Hall for its New York première in March. This expansive diatonic choral setting of poems by John Donne ("Negative Love") and Emily Dickinson ("Because I Could Not Stop for Death," "Wild Nights") is an impressive piece, with slow-motion Victorian harmonies, a shimmering, colorful surface, and some wonderful deep sonorities. "Wild Nights" begins as if in Wagnerian darkness. But for some reason the work didn't swell, surge, and glitter as it had in San Francisco, where it was first performed, in 1981.

Edmund Niemann, an able pianist, devoted the first half of a Merkin Hall recital in May to minimalism, with Adams's *Phrygian Gates*, another attractive and impressive piece, as its climax. But then he devoted his second half to music by Stefan Wolpe and ended with the tremendous Passacaglia—music whose power and substance made the minimalism of the first half seem mere flicker, ripple, and foolery.

Some other works—and performances and sounds—of the season deserve at least brief mention before 1984–85 brings its new crop. Peter Lieberson's *Lalita*, subtitled "Chamber Variations," had its première at a Speculum Musicae concert at Symphony Space in May. The title, a Sanskrit word meaning "passionate sport" or "play," occurred to the composer immediately, he said in a program note, when he began thinking about a work for Speculum. *Lalita* consists of a theme, eight variations, and a coda; it lasts about twenty minutes and is written for ten players (violin, viola, cello, double-bass, flute, oboe, clarinet, horn, piano, and percussion). The transformations of the theme prove hard to follow at a first hearing, but the articulation of the work is clear, especially in the variations where individual players assumed star roles. It is a shapely, graceful, engaging composition.

Three days later, again at Symphony Space, the Kronos Quartet gave the première of Tod Machover's First String Quartet, followed by the New York première of his *Chansons d'Amour* Part II, "Zwischen Himmel und Erde," played with magnificent bravura and passion by Alan Feinberg. Machover is director of musical research at IRCAM. I've not made much of the earlier music of his I've heard, most of it involving computers, but these two works for live performers were gripping. Each evinced what the composer in a program note described as a "search for unity and harmony amidst seemingly insurmountable complexity." Each began with a unison; broke into torrents of notes, floods of harmony; soared, wrestled; achieved moments of strange, transfigured calm; ended surely—the quartet with a reiterated, affirmative unison, the piano piece with a soft, wide-flung chord enclosing a gentle, questioning dissonance.

Sounds from Horizons concerts which I go on thinking about are the noble tones of Stuart Dempster's trombone, recorded in Clement VI's abbey at Avignon, with its fourteen-second resonance, and reproduced in Fisher Hall with Mr. Dempster's live "overlay," in his *Standing Waves—1976*; the irides-cence of Dean Drummond's zoomoozophone (a kind of super-marimba with thirty-one notes to the octave, tuned in just intervals) in works of his own and by Joan La Barbara; Miss La Barbara's astonishing bird imitations (squawks, chirrups and twitters) in her *After "Obervogelsang"*; and Robert Dick's virtuosity on flutes in his $T \approx C^{10}$, for solo bass flute, and in Martin Bresnick's *Conspiracies*, for solo flute and four other flutes, whose parts in this performance had been prerecorded by Mr. Dick.

At a Merkin Hall concert in June presenting music by eight young composers who had won ASCAP grants, Mr. Dick played Todd Brief's *Canto*, which, like the Horizons pieces, draws polyphony from the single instrument. The outstanding work here was Rand Steiger's *Quintessence*, a mercurial construction for clarinet, cello, percussion, and piano duet, which was elegantly played by the New York New Music Ensemble.

In the Juilliard Theater, Joel Krosnick embarked on a big, six-concert survey of twentieth-century American cello music. His fourth program, in May, contained a vivid performance of Mario Davidovsky's *Synchronism No. 3*, for cello and tape, and a polished performance, with Elizabeth Wright as pianist, of Ben Weber's excellent Five Pieces.

At the 92nd Street Y in March, Gerard Schwarz—that busy conductor who has sometimes seemed to be tackling more repertory than he is able to enter profoundly—and the Y Chamber Symphony gave an elevated account of Shostakovich's Fourteenth Symphony. I remember it as one of the most moving events of the season. It was poignantly phrased and extremely well played, and had two eloquent soloists—Alessandra Marc and John Cheek.

At a League-ISCM recital in Carnegie Recital Hall in May, given by the Pro Arte Quartet, Bethany Beardslee, without fanfare or fuss, made what was said to be her last New York concert appearance. For three and a half decades (she made her New York début in 1949), she has been a muse for contemporary musicians. Milton Babbitt, Robert Helps, Fred Lerdahl, George Perle, Roger Sessions, Ralph Shapey, and Ben Weber are among the composers she has championed—composers whose music she has recorded memorably. At this concert, she sang Mel Powell's *Little Companion Pieces* (charming, poetic companions for Schoenberg's Second Quartet), for string quartet and soprano, so truly, sweetly, and sensitively as to make any thought of retirement seem premature. Her place in musical history and in musicians' hearts is assured. [*A happy postscript: Miss Beardslee changed her mind, and has continued—on rare, precious occasions—to sing; see pp. 288–89.*]

This season, the Northeast Orchestral Consortium—composed of the Albany Symphony, the Hartford Symphony, the Hudson Valley Philharmonic, the New Haven Symphony, and the Springfield Symphony—organized the commissioning of six substantial orchestral works. Two commissions came from Albany, one from each of the other places; and the five orchestras concerned agreed that all would play all six works at least twice, over a three-season period, thus ensuring a minimum of ten performances for each commission. The works are John Harbison's *Ulysses' Raft* (New Haven), Earl Kim's *Cornet* (Hartford), Tobias Picker's *The Encantadas* and Charles Wuorinen's Third Piano Concerto (Albany), Ned Rorem's Violin Concerto (Springfield), and Robert Starer's *Hudson Valley Suite* (for the Hudson Valley Philharmonic, which is Poughkeepsie-based).

Starer's *Hudson Valley Suite* is a twenty-minute tone travelogue in five movements: "Sources," "The View from Olana," "Dances on a Terrace," "A Glimpse of West Point," and "Past Gotham and On to the Sea." It is a conventional and undistinguished example of its genre; "Sources" is rather pretty, and then it's downhill all the way. That's how rivers run, it is true, but the Hudson swells to grandeur and romance that find small reflection here. And the scoring strikes me as workaday.

Picker's *The Encantadas* is also a picturesque work, but a rich one that I have now heard several times with pleasure. It lasts about half an hour and is for speaker and orchestra—a combination that is seldom successful but is here brought off. At the second performance, in Springfield, Picker himself recited the text, with inflections and timing that made it seem part of the composition, not a distraction. The words are descriptive passages from Melville's Piazza Tale, telling of the mysterious island's desolation, of the ponderous tortoises, of Rock Rodondo, rising towerlike from the sea, with its tiered population of birds. The six movements are entitled "Dream," "Desolation," "Delusion," "Diversity," "Din," and "Dawn." Melville's charged prose spins exotic metaphors of the human condition; Prospero, Caliban, and Ariel seem not far away. Picker responds with romantic, colorful music. His materials are conventional, often Mahlerian in cut; his use of them is fresh and imaginative. One passage seems out of place—a penguins' waltz so Ravel-like that it whisks one from the enchanted Galápagos Islands to a European ballroom.

Wuorinen's concerto was the most exciting of the four new pieces I have heard: the only one to challenge an audience, the only one recognizable as music of our day—not something that might have been written at any time during the last half-century. Albany audiences are accustomed to new music. The eight programs in the orchestra's major 1983–84 series and the eight announced in its 1984–85 series (each of them played both in Albany and in Troy) contain contemporary or near-contemporary American music on every bill (except the last, in which Griffes's *Pleasure-Dome of Kubla Khan* commemorates his centenary and Penderecki's Viola Concerto has its American première). These concerts constitute the Merrill Lynch American Music Series. I heard the Wuorinen in Troy—in that famous 1,250 seat concert hall, over the Troy Savings Bank, that opened in 1875. The hall was full, and the applause for the new piece was warm.

The concerto lasts half an hour. The soloist is playing just about all the time: the work is like a huge piano piece in which the orchestra supplies an extension of the instrument's timbres and dynamics. It is energetic, packed with ideas, exhilarating. There is a vigorous first movement; a highly developed slow movement with beautiful sonorities (the orchestra has a more nearly independent role), eloquent lines, and powerful harmonies; and a trenchant finale. In lieu of a program note, there was the transcription of a fascinating conversation between Wuorinen and Scott Cantrell, the Albany *Times-Union* critic. Wuorinen deals briskly with critics (especially those of the New York *Times*) and their "combination of pusillanimity and arrogance"; with the charge that much music is being written not for audiences but for the composer and his colleagues

("This means ... simply that the critic doesn't like it"); and with "neo-romanticism." He tries to distinguish between "nostalgia ... which tends merely to regurgitate the gestures of music which belongs to another time and another place" and "the restoration of a continuity, a link with the music of the past." In Wuorinen's recent music I sense that restoration, that link. (No doubt this means simply that I do like it.) In this piano concerto, as in Peter Lieberson's (but less patently), there is also a link with romantic piano concertos, insofar as the soloist can put his mastery of big, bravura techniques at the service of a contemporary work. The piano writing implies a player for whom Brahms and Rachmaninoff hold no terrors.

The soloist here was Garrick Ohlsson, who filled that bill. He gave what seemed to me a masterly performance—big, brilliant, unflagging, lyrical in the slow movement. The orchestra, conducted by Julius Hegyi, sounded good; but at later hearings, which I followed score in hand (Albany concerts are broadcast on WMHT, the Schenectady public-radio station), I began to imagine an orchestral performance with sharper, more shapely details and more careful observance of dynamic distinctions.

Ulysses' Raft and *Ulysses' Bow* are ballet scores that Harbison embarked on after seeing and being stirred by a production of Monteverdi's *Il ritorno d'Ulisse* in the summer of 1982. "I decided to make my own Ulysses opera without singers," he says in a program note. Each ballet—or, rather, each part of the two-part ballet, for that is how the work seems to have been conceived—contains five scenes, introduced by a prelude and divided by interludes. *Ulysses' Raft*, the longer of the two, has for concert performance been divided into two suites. The first suite, played at New Haven, conducted by Murry Sidlin, begins with the prelude (Ulysses starting his journey home, and, in another image, the waiting Penelope) and the first scene (in Polyphemus' cave), and then jumps to the fourth interlude (Ulysses on his raft, after leaving Calypso's island, and his struggle with Neptune) and the fifth scene (Nausicaa). This leaves, for a second suite, the scenes of Circe, of the Underworld, and of Calypso, and the interludes "Aeolus' Winds Released," "Penelope at Her Weaving," and "Sea Perils and Shipwreck." *Ulysses' Bow* is set on Ithaca. The five scenes are "Ulysses' Return," "The Suitors," "Penelope," "The Trial of the Bow," and "Reunion," divided by the interludes "Ulysses and Argos," "While the Suitors Sleep," "Penelope's Dream," and "The Ritual of Purification." This part, composed for the Pittsburgh Symphony, was played in Pittsburgh in May and brought to Avery Fisher Hall twelve days later.

I find it a puzzling work (or pair of works). On the one hand, it is a large, carefully planned score by an able and distinguished composer inspired by a great subject. Ulysses and Penelope provide the main themes. Music provides a means of tying Ulysses to his adversaries—Polyphemus, Neptune, the suitors—in ways that define differences between them, and of presenting Penelope and her rivals Circe, Calypso, and Nausicaa as aspects of the anima, related yet very different. The composer points this out in his program note; in the score one can discern the relationships and the differences; and even at a first hearing one can perhaps catch something of the process. There is also a good deal of picturesque incident—the roars of the blinded Polyphemus, Ulysses' struggle with the waves, the murder of the suitors—that lends itself to graphic musical treatment. Harbison is good at this, and he scores very well.

On the other hand ... But I find it hard to define my uneasiness about the piece. (Perhaps it will disappear after a whole performance.) I can't escape a feeling that Harbison has settled a little too readily for familiar musical imagery. There seems to be precious little here that, say, Albert Roussel could not have composed. Difficult questions arise. If this Ulysses ballet were in fact a work of the 1930s, not the 1980s, would we hear it differently today? And should we? Such questions underlie one's feeling about "neo-romanticism" in general. So much of it—George Rochberg, David Del Tredici—sounds like comfortable, unchallenging acceptance of the traditional. In *Ulysses' Raft* and *Ulysses' Bow* I hear inspired passages, and others in which Harbison seems to be not at full stretch but merely filling—diligently, conventionally—his grand design.

Harbison's First Symphony is a similarly disconcerting work. One of the Boston Symphony's centennial commissions, it was first played in Boston in March, conducted by Seiji Ozawa, and then at Tanglewood in July, conducted by the composer. The first, rather Shostakovich-like movement is fine, with a stern, metallic first subject (the music came to Harbison in a dream, he revealed in his program note) and a quirky second subject. It promises much. But there follows a gauche, wispy scherzo, gone almost before it has registered; a slow movement that seems like movie music, with Max Steiner-ish moments; and a final toccata in scrubbing-brush neoclassical style.

Harbison's Ulysses' Bow *is recorded by the Pittsburgh Symphony, conducted by André Previn, on Nonesuch, and his First Symphony by the Boston Symphony, conducted by Mr. Ozawa, on New World Records.*

THE PATH OF DUTY

September 10, 1984

IN some forty Italian operas and twenty English music dramas, Handel gave expression to just about the full range of human experience. Myth, history, and romance—the Bible, Sophocles and Euripides, Herodotus and Xenophon, Tasso and Ariosto, Corneille and Racine, Milton, Dryden, and Pope—supplied his subject matter, and he composed so abundantly that there are likely to be new adventures in store all life long for even the most assiduous Handelian. There are ten Handel operas I've never seen on the stage; one of them, *Teseo*—a heroic, spectacular drama, with a tremendous role for Medea—is due in Boston next May. Handel's three-hundredth birthday falls in February, and many commemorative performances are planned. Carnegie next season does *Orlando, Ariodante, Semele,* and *Alessandro,* with starry casts. A full performance of *Israel in Egypt*—the triptych, not just its customary second and third panels—is announced by the Sine Nomine Singers. As a tercentenary prelude, Handel's penultimate opera, *Imeneo,* was given its New York première last month, performed by the LaGuardia Music Theatre, a troupe of young professionals, at LaGuardia Community College, in Long Island City.

Imeneo has been a rediscovery of our day. Handel left the autograph in a mess. Burney's *History* provides a number-by-number account of most Handel operas, but when the author reaches *Imeneo* he says, "It is not in my power to give the reader a regular review of this little opera, for Handel's original foul score is very incomplete." (Nevertheless, Burney's comments on "the principal airs that I have been able to decipher in the hasty sketch" are apt.) Friedrich Chrysander's 1885 score, in his great Handel edition, is still confused. *Imeneo* was brought into focus only in 1961, when Anthony Lewis—drawing on materials unavailable to Chrysander—prepared a performing edition and conducted it at the Barber Institute of Birmingham University. He conducted it again, in London, in 1972 (at the Royal Academy of Music) and in 1980 (for the BBC), and at each performance his edition was refined. It was published in 1980, by the Oxford University Press. (The score represents a careful choice between alternatives, not a complete or definitive text, as Sir Anthony made clear in his preface.) *Imeneo,* neglected and slighted for over two centuries, is now one of the few Handel operas for which respectable performing material is readily available. It was done in Princeton in 1965 and in Boston in 1975. Winton Dean, in his book on Handel's opera (1970), said of it that "its individual flavor almost entitles it to rank as a minor masterpiece." That "almost" seems needlessly cautious.

One's heart sank when one saw that LaGuardia had billed it as a "comic opera." It's true that *Imeneo* was announced by the London *Post* in 1740 as "a New *Operetta,*" but that meant only that it was brief, unheroic, modestly scored (a pair of oboes, strings, and continuo), unspectacular (a single set), and dramatically straightforward, with a small cast. The plot can be represented as:

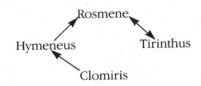

The arrows indicate affection. The action turns on Rosmene's perfectly serious plight: her heart and her hand have been promised to Tirinthus but are sought by Hymeneus as reward for his having rescued her—and, with her, many other Athenian maidens—from pirates. Both men urge their claims, and Rosmene is torn between love and civic obligation. The latter carries the day, and the opera ends sadly: Handel sets the final coro—"If a noble spirit or a noble heart considers duty, it never yields to its desires but follows reason"—in a cold, bleak E minor. There is nothing comic here. It would have been easy with a twist of the plot to pair off Clomiris and Hymeneus, and Rosmene and Tirinthus. Instead, we are left with only one satisfied lover, Hymeneus. As Mr. Dean puts it, "instead of a conventional happy end we have a profoundly moving statement about human nature." Handel emphasized the unhappiness when he performed *Imeneo* in Dublin, by adding—for Rosmene and Tirinthus, the true, loving pair who must part—the wonderful *Sosarme* duet "Through the gates of torment."

Imeneo, composed at the same time as *Saul*, has some musical parallels with that Aeschylean drama and some preëchoes of *Messiah*. Handel worked on a small scale but on his highest level. The music is rich and varied. The work is also excellent theatre. When I first saw *Imeneo* (the 1972 production), I had gone without having read the libretto, or even a synopsis, and until the end was kept wondering how Rosmene would decide. Act II reaches its climax in a marvellous trio—an unresolved conflict dramatized, as Mr. Dean remarks, much as Mozart or Verdi would have dramatized it. The rivals implore Rosmene to choose between them, and she is rent between inclination and duty. In Act III, her decision has been taken, but she cannot bring herself to accept it fully or declare it openly. Hamlet-like, she feigns madness; the others—and the audience—are still kept in suspense while, to extraordinary music, she conjures a vision of Rhadamanthus, judge of the underworld, come with sword and balance to direct her. At last, swooning, she summons the resolution to force herself into Hymeneus' arms. It is a psychologically complex episode: Rosmene's madness (like Hamlet's in some productions of Shakespeare's play), though initially assumed, threatens to become real—the welcomed escape from responsibility of an overcharged mind. The audience asks itself, "Is she still pretending or has she really gone mad?" And that is what the dramatist seems to intend. It is also a musically complex episode: the traditional devices of an operatic mad scene are donned as a mask beneath which to make statements too painful for conventional utterance.

I'd love to see *Imeneo* staged by Peter Sellars. Even in this LaGuardia presentation, which had just about nothing but Handel's music to commend it, the force of the opera was apparent. "Contractual problems," we were informed, had led to the disappearance of the string sextet billed in the program; the opera was accompanied by harpsichord and a woodwind quartet of two oboes, flute, and bassoon. The players were deft, but the effect was as of watching a colorful television program on a black-and-white set. (A good deal still comes through.) The singers couldn't act for toffee. Absurdly, the drama was presented in Italian—in largely lame, bad Italian. (I wonder how many members of the audience realized that one air tells the story of Androcles and the lion.) There is a perfectly good English translation in the Lewis edition. Recitatives were slowly declaimed, not at speech pace or with speech inflections. Some of the aria tempi, set by David Pasquale at the harpsichord, were plodding. The singers— even though the hall held only a little over two hundred, and addressing the audience was easy—often pushed their voices. The Rosmene, with a tone of inherently beautiful quality, was sometimes out of tune and unsteady. The Argenius (Clomiris' father, spokesman of the Athenian senate, a bass) wobbled. Lynnen Yakes, the Tirinthus (a castrato role, sung four years ago by Janet Baker, in English), gave the most pleasure, with a brave, ringing, but unforced account of "Sorge nell'alma mia" (a clarion air that Burney characterized as being "of great spirit, in a style that was then new") and an inspired, moving delivery of "Pieno il core" (which Burney rightly called "grand and original"). Talmage

Fauntleroy's production included two anxious-looking, toga-clad secretaries, who made mirror images of Argenius' gestures or else, wielding a long, waggly quill on a parchment scroll, pretended to take down lines as they were sung; and four soldiers who, though armed from head to ankle, from helmet to greaves, pranced about, rattling wooden swords against cardboard shields, on bare feet.

LaGuardia Community College is a good modern building, designed by Stephen Lepp & Associates. (It is just across the Queensboro Bridge, and is easily reached by subway.) A long, tall corridor, with bright-red central columns, leads to the auditorium. The sight lines are good. A thrust stage places actors and audience in one room. There is no pit, and so the instrumentalists can be in direct touch with the stage. But it is not quite an ideal home for intimate opera; for speech it would be fine, but it does not have the warm resonance that singing voices need.

PART
II

1984–1985

Un Viaggio a Pesaro

October 1, 1984

THE recovery of a lost opera by a great composer is a rare and exciting event. Monteverdi's *Il ritorno d'Ulisse,* composed in 1641, was found in Vienna in the 1860s; several of his operas are still missing. Unknown scenes from known operas turn up more often, and the boom in nineteenth-century studies has accelerated the pace. Bizet's *Carmen* gained new episodes in 1949 and 1965, and Verdi's *Don Carlos* new numbers in 1970. Rossini's *Tancredi* acquired an alternative, tragic finale in 1976. This year, the Donizetti *rifacimento Elisabetta* was discovered in Covent Garden's cellar (and there is plenty more unperformed, unpublished Donizetti around). Two works of Rossini's high maturity, the thirty-fifth and thirty-sixth of his forty operas, have long been missing. One is *Ugo, re d'Italia,* promised to London in 1824, unperformed (the impresario of the King's Theatre went bankrupt) and therefore probably unfinished, and last glimpsed in the hands of one Jas. Kemp, the messenger who in 1831 signed for the receipt from a London bank, of "two Packets of Music purporting to be the Opera of Ugo, Rè d'Italia." The other is *Il viaggio a Reims,* Rossini's last Italian opera and his first for Paris. *Il viaggio,* one of a slew of works composed to celebrate the coronation of Charles X, was staged at the Théâtre-Italien in 1825. It was, one learns from reviews of the time, a much-admired one-act opera, lasting some three hours, that contained a fourteen-voice ensemble and a medley-finale of national airs. About half the music was later reused in Rossini's bewitching comedy *Le Comte Ory* (1828). The libretto of *Il viaggio* survived, but the score was scattered. Now the young American scholar Janet Johnson has reconstructed it; and *Il viaggio a Reims* received its first modern performances in August, at the Rossini Festival in Pesaro, the Adriatic town where Rossini was born. People gathered there from all over the world to hear it.

Miss Johnson retrieved and reassembled the score from several sources. The autograph of four numbers not used in *Ory,* presented by Rossini's widow to the family physician, had found its way to the Santa Cecilia library, in Rome. In Paris, some of the 1825 performing material—instrumental and vocal parts—remained. Similar material for two pasticcios employing *Viaggio* music—*Andremo a Parigi?,* concocted in Paris to celebrate the 1848 revolution, and *Il viaggio a Vienna,* concocted in Vienna to celebrate the wedding of Franz Joseph I and Elizabeth of Bavaria, in 1854—and the published score of *Le Comte Ory* filled gaps. All that is missing now of *Il viaggio* is a few phrases of secco recitative (for Pesaro they were composed anew) and a chorus to launch the finale, which will no doubt turn up sooner or later. In Pesaro, a fascinating and delightful opera, different in character from any other that Rossini wrote, was revealed.

A *pièce de circonstance*, it was devised to show off the Théâtre-Italien troupe at strength. The cast—ten famous principals and eight cadet singers—was led by the great Giuditta Pasta, later Bellini's first Amina and first Norma. She played Corinna, the Roman *improvisatrice*—a heroine borrowed from Mme de Staël's once-famous novel *Corinne*—and was dressed after François Gérard's painting "Corinne au Cap Misène" (for which Mme de Staël herself sat). Laure Cinti, later the heroine of Rossini's four works for the Opéra, played the Comtesse de Folleville, a lively young widow. Ester Mombelli, who had been the heroine of Rossini's very first opera, *Demetrio e Polibio,* thirteen years earlier, was Mme Cortese, the *patronne* of the Golden Lily, the thermal hostelry where the opera is set. Domenico Donzelli, later the first Pollio (in *Norma*), played the Chevalier Belfiore, a dashing young French officer, also based on a *Corinne* character. And so on: the original cast list is a glittering roll call of prima donnas soprano or contralto, first tenors, and first basses buffo or *cantanti*. The opera is hardly dramatic—except in its musical events. An international group of travellers (Italian, French, British, German, Spanish, Russian, Polish, Greek), bound for Rheims and the coronation, finds itself stranded at the Golden Lily; there are no fresh horses to be had. Amorous crosscurrents—flirtations, wooings, jealous quarrels, reconciliations—provide such action as there is, and the travellers' decision to hold their own celebration, since they can't get to Rheims, provides the climax, a sequence of national airs echoed by ensemble and chorus. Baron Trombonok, the master of ceremonies, leads off with Haydn's Hymn to the Emperor. Melibea, a Polish marchioness, sings a polonaise. Count Libenskof sings a Russian song, and Don Alvaro a Spanish one. Lord Sidney (based on Lord Nelvil, the hero of *Corinne*) offers "the only tune I know"—which is, of course, "God Save the King." Comtesse and Chevalier join in a lilting French song, and Mme Cortese, supported by Don Profondo (another character with a counterpart in *Corinne*), yodels a tyrolienne. Corinna crowns things by "improvising," to harp accompaniment, five noble stanzas in praise of the new monarch. The libretto, by Luigi Balocchi, the Théâtre-Italien house poet, is deft and light-hearted. The emotions of opera seria are prettily parodied: the loss of the Comtesse's new finery in an overturned coach inspires an aria of high tragedy ("Più fieri amari spasimi/Non ho provato ancor"), and the recovery of one dear little hat inspires a glittering cabaletta ("Grazie vi rendo, o Dei!"). Balocchi's stanza for a thirteen-voice unaccompanied ensemble of consternation when the news about the absence of horses is brought is a witty assemblage of tags from earlier Rossini operas:

> *A tal colpo inaspettato,*
> *Palpitando va il mio core . . .*
> *Cruda sorte! Il tuo rigore*
> *Troppo, oh Dio! penar mi fa.*

The score is cast in the form of nine extended numbers, each of several movements: an introduzione, arias, duets, a quintet enclosing an offstage aria for Corinna, the thirteen-voice ensemble capped by a fourteen-voice stretta. In 1825, the single act was broken by two intermissions, and in Pesaro by one. There was about two and a quarter hours of music—delectable music, for the score is an exuberant, captivating display of science, charm, melodic invention, grace, skill, and formal precision. *Le Comte Ory* has been aptly characterized as a bridge, musically, between *Così fan tutte* and Berlioz's *Béatrice et Bénédict*. *Il viaggio a Reims* is a companion piece of similar calibre—a theatrical divertimento, a scenic cantata spun on a thread of plot offering situations that Rossini knew well how to dissolve into music. It is at once refined, beautiful, and entertaining.

Pesaro sought to assemble a worthily all-star cast. Claudio Abbado conducted, Luca Ronconi directed, and the ten principals were Cecilia Gasdia (Corinna), Lucia Valentini Terrani (Melibea), Lella Cuberli (the Comtesse), Katia Ricciarelli (Mme Cortese), Edoardo Gimenez (the Chevalier), Dalmacio Gonzales (Count Libenskof), Samuel Ramey (Lord Sidney), Ruggero Raimondi (Don Profondo), Enzo Dara (Baron Trombonok), and Leo Nucci (Don Alvaro). But things didn't work out as well as that lineup promised. In different ways, the conductor and the director had missed the point of the piece. Mr. Abbado's reading, neatly executed by the Chamber Orchestra of Europe (a band of players, largely British, aged between eighteen and twenty-four), was tight, tense, airless, and hard-driven. It lacked playfulness, humor, and any touch of the easy, relaxed, aristocratic grace that conductors such as Beecham and Vittorio Gui brought to Rossini. It was often too fast and sometimes crassly, noisily energetic. The soloists—both vocal and instrumental—were not encouraged, or even allowed, to breathe their phrases with individual delicacy and charm. The recitative was accompanied not by an 1820s piano but by two busy harpsichords. Many necessary appoggiaturas were missing. Pesaro's Rossini Foundation houses expert Rossinians, whose advice the conductor can hardly have taken. It seemed wrong to incorporate in this first modern revival of *Il viaggio* some second thoughts (however delightful) that Rossini had had only when recasting his music for *Ory*, and to add an anachronistic—in the context, even treasonable—"Marseillaise" counterpoint to a finale lauding Charles X.

The opera was staged—though "staged" is hardly the word—not in Pesaro's charming small Teatro Rossini but in the even smaller concert hall of the Rossini Conservatory. Simultaneously, the show was televised and shown on a giant screen to a popular audience in the town piazza. It was, in effect, a concert or studio performance in costume, larded with slapstick. The setting, by Gae Aulenti, a fashionable Milanese designer, was not Rossini's but a row of eight modern bathtubs, as in a school changing room, on a bare stage flanked by two towers of scaffolding. The concert-hall organ formed the background. Singers emerged from the tubs draped in their national flags; Lord Sidney later sported a Union Jack cummerbund. Miss Cuberli sang her grand aria dressed in underclothes. Miss Gasdia, wearing a little lyre as a comic headdress, sang Corinna's exalted improvisation ambling about in affected Greek poses, as if guying its sentiments; during the last verse she and her harpist went up on an elevator in one of the towers. Television crews, onstage and in the house, formed part of the show and dominated the final tableau. Pitched electrical hums disturbed the music. It was a staging that treated the opera with contempt, as matter for an undergraduate romp, and the approach got into the music. Mr. Ramey, for example, sang Lord Sidney's confession of love with no trace of

213

tender, confiding intimacy, and while he sang his Corinna (who shouldn't be present) attitudinized upstage. Miss Ricciarelli was in poor voice. (At the second of the two performances I saw, she broke down in the introduzione and withdrew.) Miss Valentini Terrani's once-reliable tones sounded worn at both the upper and the lower edges. Pasta's music seemed to lie awkwardly for Miss Gasdia, usually so attractive a soprano. (Pasta at the time of *Il viaggio* was termed a prima donna contralto.) The grossness of the direction and the strictness of the conducting must temper any harsh criticism of the singers; they weren't given a chance to shine, to be anything but blunt. Only Mr. Gimenez showed any Rossinian sparkle and lightness.

The other festival opera was *Le Comte Ory,* performed in the Teatro Rossini. It was no better conducted and no better directed. Donato Renzetti drove his cast and the London Sinfonietta through another trim but graceless, unbreathed, unshaped reading. His handling of the enchanted, Berlioz-like trio "A la faveur de cette nuit obscure" was especially painful. Pier Luigi Pizzi, both director and designer, inflicted a heavy, humorless staging on the elegant comedy. The overture was mimed. The décor was not prettily medieval but a solid pitch-pine affair suggesting a modern hotel lobby. The chorus, uniformly dressed in navy blue, primped and postured and pranced by rote; in Act II the men pretending to be nuns broke into a hearty cancan. "A la faveur" was sung by three singers rolling around on a big bed, until the Countess fell out of it. Such larks! In spite of all this, two artists managed to give delight. As the Countess, Miss Gasdia, suited now by a true soprano role, sang with uncommon charm. There is something pleasingly definite about everything she does, and her voice flowers as it rises. And as Isolier, the page, Zehava Gal produced fluent mezzo tones of attractive, individual quality and phrased with spirit. Rockwell Blake's singing of the title role was nimble, but his timbre was raw, not sweet; at my performance it was announced that he was unwell and the audience's indulgence was asked. As Raimbaud, Alessandro Corbelli sang with his wonted forwardness and clarity, but his aria was delivered without wit. Gregory Reinhart, as the Tutor, was loud and plain, and seemed to relish the clowning that Mr. Pizzi had devised.

Hearing *Ory* soon after *Il viaggio* prompted admiration for Scribe's skill at composing new, apt words to existing music. One would never guess that Raimbaud's account of his sortie upon the castle cellar had started life as Don Profondo's catalogue of the travellers' belongings. Hearing and seeing both shows prompted despair at the way Rossini is commonly treated today: by conductors insensitive to the poised wit of the music, by directors who pile on the broad, coarse clichés of low comedy, by singers who docilely don vocal straitjackets, dim their prowess (and dim Rossini's music), and, apparently unprotesting, allow themselves to be put through vulgar, unstylish stage paces. Booing in the theatre is an ugly sound, but it was reassuring, almost a relief, to hear at least a few voices objecting vociferously to what Mr. Pizzi had done to *Le Comte Ory*. The Rossini Foundation, which along with the Comune of Pesaro organizes the annual festival, takes care to provide the performers with accurate musical editions. I wish it would now start insisting that those editions should be stylishly and accurately performed.

A recording of Il viaggio, *drawn from the Pesaro performances, has been published by Deutsche Grammophon. Anyone hearing it is likely to think my comments far too harsh; I thought so myself, listening again to the sparkly music while undistracted by the stage antics. But I decided to let them stand after listening again, on records, to Beecham's and Gui's way with Rossini.*

TRANSMUTATION

October 15, 1984

KARLHEINZ STOCKHAUSEN'S *Harlequin* (1975) had its New York première last week at the League-ISCM concert in Symphony Space. A forty-five-minute solo for a clarinettist-dancer-actor, it was executed with high accomplishment by Jean Kopperud. It cannot be easy to warble while pirouetting, play a steady glissando while doing a split, keep a cantabile smooth while stumbling or tottering about the stage, pipe roulades en arabesque. Miss Kopperud made it all seem easy as without a puff or a pant she continued to phrase with aplomb and command a full palette of colors and dynamics. At the end, someone should have given her a gold medal; when Mary Lou Retton, at the 1984 Olympics, won hers, she didn't have to play the clarinet while going through her paces. In Stockhausen's piece, Harlequin is reborn as a musician, and his traditional spiels are transmuted into melody. It is an entertaining, engaging, and sometimes poetic work, even if it does go on, rather. The choreography of this performance was by Jesse Duranceau, and some of his ideas were glib and repetitive—responsive to the chirpy moments but neglectful of the romance. The composer's demands are not light, and his aims are high. Of one episode he writes (in a program note), "Those who listen very quietly at this moment will be able to sing this melody eternally in their dreams and will be able to transform everything that is ugly into something of beauty." I did listen very quietly but have failed to acquire that useful transmutatory skill. The idea could be developed. One might add Columbine and compose a flute-and-clarinet pas de deux; add Pierrot, Brighella, and Pantaloon and set a full woodwind quintet capering. Peter Maxwell Davies's *Le Jongleur de Notre Dame*, a drama whose actors converse by way of their instruments, already does something of the kind.

The concert began with the American première of Davies's *Sea Eagle* (1982), a brief tone poem for solo horn. William Purvis played it with technical brilliance, but his "presentation" of the soaring, swooping music was plain. (The whole concert, not just *Harlequin*, was given under theatrical rather than concert-hall lighting, of a kind that called for performers unreticent in manner.) Two other brilliant instrumentalists, the violinist Rolf Schulte and the pianist Alan Feinberg, joined Mr. Purvis for the New York première of György Ligeti's Trio (1982)—an event eagerly awaited, for this was his first substantial composition after the opera *Le Grand Macabre* (1978). The inner movements, with

215

their metrical intricacies, reflect the composer's excited discovery of Conlon Nancarrow's music; the elegiac finale, like the last scene of the opera, evokes a world in which old, familiar musical gestures have survived but have lost their formerly accepted relationships and meanings. Subtitled "Homage to Brahms," the Trio is a disquieting and beautiful piece—at once an individual's commentary on "process music" and on "neo-romanticism" and a new, exploratory composition. The players gave a poised, rapt performance. [*They have now recorded it, on Bridge.*]

The fourth work on the program was a classic: Boulez's Two Improvisations on Mallarmé, composed in 1957. A quarter-century ago, these pieces broke on astonished and delighted ears, and gave rise to many other compositions using soprano filigree amid a delicate flicker and tintinnabulation of percussion. They grew into two movements of the mighty *Pli selon pli.* In the original, chamber version, the combination of *Lakmé*-like charm and formal precision remains unfaded. They were very deftly performed by Margaret Ahrens and an instrumental ensemble conducted by Robert Black. It was a good concert for the start of the season. The hall was nearly full, and Ligeti's Trio was greeted with cheers.

Delibes's *Lakmé*, a pretty opera, was a Met staple of the thirties and forties, with Lily Pons as its heroine. It has come to the City Opera in a performance laid out on acceptable, traditional lines but not, so far, quite graceful enough in execution. Gianna Rolandi, the Lakmé, sounds the notes accurately, and on the first night there was sweet pathos in her phrasing of the final scene. But her words were uncolored, not forward, and her features were inexpressive; they came to life only at the curtain calls. Barry McCauley's Gerald, also accurate, was dry, not sweet and winning, in timbre. Harry Dworchak's Nilakantha was strongly voiced. Imre Pallo conducted. It was all a little too full, musically overweight, Italianate, too far from opéra comique. (The version with sung recitatives—Delibes's own—was used, which is right for a large theatre, but the recitatives needed to be livelier.) Pasquale Grossi's scenery, originally designed for Trieste, looked more attractive—like Gérômes brought to life—when I saw it in Dallas four years ago. As displayed in the State Theater, it suggested warehouse stock, crudely painted, with strings of paper flowers hanging down. Fabrizio Melano's stage direction was modest to the point of verging at times on a parody of old-style opera. He made, however, two unhappy departures from tradition: in Act I the British party settled down, incongruously, to a picnic tea in the temple garden it was profaning; and "La Forêt," the entr'acte before Act III, was demoted to serve as an accompaniment to a pantomime.

The City Opera waited long to produce Stravinsky's *The Rake's Progress*— some three decades—while elsewhere the opera became pretty well standard fare. Having done it at last, the company has done it well, with an exceptionally strong and spirited cast. Last week, I caught the last of the four performances, and it played to a full and enthusiastic house. May *The Rake* henceforth be a house staple: it is written in American, it suits American singers, and besides being a masterpiece it is the freshest, most melodious, attractive, and exhilarating of modern operas. There have been dark productions, garish productions,

216

steamy productions, productions foolishly or frivolously overelaborated. The City Opera production is bright and clear with a clarity that lets the power of the parable shine through. The staging is based on Glyndebourne's second production, of 1975, which had three American principals and was directed by John Cox and designed by David Hockney. Mr. Hockney's elegant, sensitive scenery, hatched or crosshatched sometimes in clear colors, sometimes in black and white, looks as delightful as ever in its big-house version. (It has also been seen at La Scala and in San Francisco and Dallas.) The production, staged for New York by Robin Thompson (Mr. Cox's assistant in San Francisco), was no tired, dutiful copybook replica but a crisp, lively reworking that took account of the temperaments of the current cast.

Jerry Hadley was the boldest and most cleanly sung Tom Rakewell I have heard—every word clear, every note firmly and truly struck—and he was an eloquent actor with his own approach to the role. This Tom was self-aware but not self-pitying. Frederick Burchinal's Nick Shadow was also cleanly and strongly sung but was a shade heavy, not witty enough. His words, while excellently clear, were clearly *pronounced* rather than, like Mr. Hadley's, supply and energetically used to determine the shape and the inflection of the musical phrases. (There's a difference between singing intelligibly in English and singing good English.) Baba the Turk's music, which lies awkwardly for many mezzos, rang out zestfully from Joy Davidson. She carried her chest tones uncommonly—I hope not harmfully—high. Her characterization was generous and flamboyant without being overdone. Jonathan Green's Sellem was nimble and precise. Erie Mills's Anne Trulove was the weak member. There was a moment of poignant emotion in the street scene, when Anne learned of Tom's marriage, but most of the time the voice sounded thin, lacking in body and in lyrical tenderness. The dense wig and overpainted eyes were unsuited to Anne. The small roles were cast at strength: Joyce Castle (Mother Goose), Mr. Dworchak (Trulove), and Ralph Bassett (Keeper of the Madhouse). The chorus was alert. Christopher Keene was an acceptable, if not a distinguished, conductor. If possible, a way must be found, before the revivals, to effect the scene changes more swiftly and less noisily; Stravinsky's score was broken by unwanted pauses.

Davies's opera *The Martyrdom of St. Magnus* had its first performance seven years ago in the twelfth-century Orkney cathedral, in Kirkwall, where Magnus lies buried, and its New York première last month from a new troupe, Operaworks, in Larry Richardson's Dance Gallery, on East Fourteenth Street. *St. Magnus* recounts a historical tale, found in the Orkneyinga Saga, about the good, God-fearing Earl Magnus, who was treacherously murdered by his cousin, Earl Hakon, in 1117; and it is a timely parable about moral integrity in conflict with brute political expedience. The libretto, the composer's own, is a brilliant reduction for music of George Mackay Brown's poetic novel *Magnus*. The one-act opera lasts about ninety minutes. Five singers play all the parts, and the orchestra is an ensemble of ten (the Fires of London sextet plus guitar, two trumpets, and horn). The music has its foundation in plainchant such as Magnus himself knew, but the chant, as Davies says in a program note, has been adapted

217

and extended "to encompass as wide an expressive musical and operatic vocabulary as possible." It is a ruthlessly contemporary score with its roots in the fundamentals of musical expressiveness.

A few days before the *St. Magnus* performance in New York, I was wandering through Roman London, which now lies nearer to the surface of the commercial City than it has for centuries, and musing on cloud-capped towers, solemn temples (Wren churches are thick-clustered here; Mithras has yielded to Christ), and the fading of insubstantial pageants. In the clean Orcadian air, away from city din and city distractions, Davies has been able to clarify and formulate in music the vague thoughts about the past beating upon the present which can fill a musician's mind, and to reconcile opposed yet simultaneous views of the present as urgent and important and as no more than a speck drifting on the long stream of time. Nature, the seasons, the elements, ocean and sky, Orkney's awesome prehistoric monuments, its turbulent ancient history (racked by Norsemen and by Scots), and its modern history of attacks by invaders greedy for uranium and for oil play a large part in Davies's later scores, as they do in Mackay Brown's writings. Ligeti's Trio and *The Rake's Progress*—although that opera is by now itself a part of history—deliberately put imagery of the past into a modern context and test its applicability to contemporary life. Both the dramatic matter and the music of *St. Magnus* (not that the two are separate) do so, economically, directly, and potently, in ways that might perhaps affect—confirm, challenge—a listener's decision about how to vote in the forthcoming election. "All a poet can do is to warn": Britten used Wilfred Owen's line as epigraph to his *War Requiem*. And that's probably all a composer can do. Warnings are not always unheeded.

The Operaworks performance was good and would have been better had the director, Joel Casey, tried harder to stage the opera Davies composed. Instead, Mr. Casey had tinkered with it. The cast was swelled to seven, and the carefully planned doublings were shuffled. Instead of ritual simplicity, there was elaboration of the action, the costumes, the setting. There was a sandbox at the center of the acting area. The instrumentalists were concealed behind a black screen, over the top of which the conductor, David Leighton, peeped. (Better if the players can see the singers; this is chamber music.) The nightmare sequence of dances, shouts, and commentary during which singers and players should move into the hall and mingle with the audience was prerecorded and was played through a loudspeaker into a dark hall. This scene whirls through the centuries. The subsequent scene, "The Sacrifice," should take place in the present and "in the place where the opera is performed." Mr. Casey gave it a Nazi setting. Much about the presentation was misconceived, jejune, and weakening to the work. Yet the performance was ambitious, serious, committed, and so in sum not unworthy. David Eisler gave a beautiful, quietly radiant account of the title role; his tenor is pure and unforced, and he uses words well. Hilda Harris was a vivid Blind Mary.

The Finnish baritone Jorma Hynninen made his Carnegie Hall recital début last week, in a concert that confirmed neither his reputation nor the excellent impression left by his Frick recital last year. In the first half, he sang four Yrjö

Kilpinen and five Sibelius songs, one after another, rather as if polishing them off; a true lieder singer makes of each song something exquisite and distinct. His voice was not in focus. One presumed that he was nervous and had not got the measure of the hall. The second half, devoted to *Die schöne Müllerin*, was even more disconcerting, for he gave what seemed to be a thoroughly rattled and uncontrolled performance of the cycle. The fast songs were generally too fast; the slow ones tended to get slower and slower as they went on. Sometimes Mr. Hynninen crooned; sometimes he shouted. Many of the little notes were inaudible. All that could be praised was the rude vigor of the singer's response to the verses. The pianist, Ralf Gothóni, was a polished player but one given, in interludes and postludes, to grotesquely extravagant rubato. I'd pass over the whole disappointing event in silence had not Mr. Hynninen been acclaimed at the end as if he were a new Gerhard Hüsch and Dietrich Fischer-Dieskau in one.

Serious, Beautiful Operas

November 5, 1984

Gluck's *Armide*, with Olive Fremstad its heroine, Caruso as Renaud, and Toscanini as the conductor, opened the Metropolitan Opera's 1910–11 season. W. J. Henderson, in the *Sun*, admired the work and its execution but said, "It is hardly likely that the majesty and justice of the composer's declamation will be wholly recognized, for the work requires a higher degree of musical knowledge than the general public could be expected to have." After three performances that season and four the next, *Armide* left the bills. *Orfeo* apart, Gluck's noble operas have won no secure place in the modern repertory. Maria Callas's Alcestis and Iphigenia, Janet Baker's Alcestis stir excitement for a while, but it quickly subsides. The composer's champions continue to proclaim his high virtues, but even they after actual performances are usually compelled to admit that the operas are uncommonly difficult to bring off in modern theatres, with modern artists. Already in 1854, Wagner proposed a moratorium on Gluck presentations, so hard was it to square the composer's reputation with anything one saw and heard. In our day—a recent clutch of Gluck recordings widely varied in character, and none wholly satisfactory, affords evidence—Gluck's greatness can seem more elusive than ever. In big houses, modern concern for authenticity often undermines the assured old-fashioned approaches; and some of the thoroughgoing historical re-creations have verged on the precious.

On records and in concert performances, one of the difficulties for regular companies—the large part that dance must play in the dramas—is avoided. The concert performance of *Orfeo* that Riccardo Muti and the Philadelphia Orchestra brought to Carnegie Hall last month illustrated many of the others. The original, 1762 Vienna score was used. Inevitably, the particular colors of Gluck's instrumentation were lost; only a band with cornets, chalumeaux, and, in general, preclassical woodwinds, brasses, strings, and harp can render them faithfully—and that only in a hall smaller than Carnegie. (When Gluck revised the opera for Paris, in 1774, with a tenor protagonist, he modernized and simplified his orchestration.) This large-scale presentation with contemporary forces fell between several stools. It did not have the heavy, confident grandeur that Furtwängler, Knappertsbusch, and Karajan brought to the score, in readings that were stylistically questionable but dramatically overwhelming. Mr. Muti used a reduced orchestra, based on six cellos and four double-basses. (In Paris, Gluck seems to have had twelve and five.) There was a harpsichord centerstage, but, being pretty well inaudible, it served little more than a cosmetic function. The instrumental playing, on the other hand, was still old-style romantic— vibrant, plush-toned, not lightly articulated. There was an enormous chorus— the Westminster Choir, nearly two hundred strong—but its tone was soft-grained and a shade genteel: not keen in mourning or fierce in infernal challenge. Insufficient attention to the words smoothed syncopations implicit in the Furies' music. The scholarly edition of the Vienna score, by Anna Amalie Abert and Ludwig Finscher, was used, but in no scholarly way. Necessary appoggiaturas, which are spelled out above the staff in that edition, were often ignored. (Rendering notes *come scritto* is rather like seeing "Mr." in a printed text and pronouncing it "Mrr," not "Mister.") Necessary, corona-signalled cadenzas, such as should close the three strophes of Orpheus' first plaint, were omitted, and reprises were unvaried. (The elaborate decorations introduced by Gaetano Guadagni, Gluck's own Orpheus, perhaps strain bounds suggested by the composer's professed aim of "a beautiful simplicity," but this literally graceless rendering was simpleminded and inexpressive.) Mr. Muti's tempi were mainly on the "traditional" slow side, and Gluck's two-in-a-bar movements—the mourning chorus, Orpheus' first two songs to the Furies and "Che farò," the Orpheus-Eurydice duet—always difficult to pace convincingly, seldom flowed easily.

Agnes Baltsa, the Greek mezzo-soprano, took the title role, as she does on Mr. Muti's Angel recording. She has a beautiful voice—strong, forward, cleanly focussed, individual in its candid, dusky timbre—but she performed only to her score, not to the audience, and as a result was not especially eloquent. Her heart didn't seem to be in the drama. Margaret Marshall, a Scottish soprano, was the Eurydice, as on that recording. She has a clear, true, steady voice; her performance had no passion in it and little character. Arleen Augér, the Cupid, seemed to wish to present the bright, saucy boy portrayed in Gluck's music but to be inhibited from doing so by the seriousness all around her. This was not a careless, thoughtless, or unfeeling account of the work, and in its chosen way the execution was highly polished. But it made the sublime opera seem rather a dull one.

[*It has lately been questioned whether the decorations published by Domenico Corri in 1779 are in fact Guadagni's; Corri's phrase "Sung by Sigr. Guadagni" may apply simply to the arias.*]

The Met has staged Mozart's *La clemenza di Tito* as a companion piece to its 1982 *Idomeneo,* in the same basic set, with some of the same backcloths, and with costumes that draw parallels between Idomeneus and Titus, Idamantes and Sextus, Electra and Vitellia, Ilia and Servilia, Arbaces and Publius. The two rulers share the same desk and chair, the same posse of guards. The designer and director of both shows is Jean-Pierre Ponnelle, whose productions of *Tito* and *Idomeneo* have been going the rounds of the world's houses for some fifteen years and growing more classical in each edition. At the Met, they ingeniously and handsomely come together. The space is a columned courtyard or square, rising at the sides and the back. The centerpiece at the back is in *Idomeneo* an immense stone mask of Neptune, in *Tito* a version of the Arch of Titus (erected to celebrate the emperor's less than clement conquest of Jerusalem and destruction of the Temple). Dropcloths alter the background and provide varying depths of scene. The execution is in grisaille, which makes a slightly arty effect; but the stage pictures, achieved in a romanticized neoclassical manner, are large, serious, and beautiful. The costumes are eighteenth-century. The worst to be said against the staging is that it approximates two operas of sharply distinct character—each of them a powerful and personal transformation of opera seria—to a generalized idea of opera seria as something conventional, stately, and decorative. The same scenery and costumes could equally well clothe a hundred other operas. That would be no bad thing in these days of financial stringency if the Met also has thoughts of doing Handel's *Admeto*, Gluck's *Alceste*, Mozart's *Lucio Silla*, Traetta's *Antigone*, Vivaldi's *Tito Manlio*.

Mr. Ponnelle's penchant for perking up a composer's action with vulgar little details of his own devising is not unchecked. The opera opens *Rosenkavalier*-fashion with Vitellia in a double bed from which Sextus has evidently just risen. Annius and Servilia at the close of their duet sink into an amorous clinch on the paving stones of the piazza. A pantomime of a mute Berenice's departure from Rome, in a galleon that must have added quite a lot to the budget, is both unnecessary and puzzling to any members of the audience ("Who she?") not well up on their Roman history. It is also quite unmatched to the music of triumphal assembly to which it is enacted. At the end, Mr. Ponnelle pairs off Vitellia and Sextus. Metastasio did so, too, in the libretto from which Mozart's was adapted, but Mozart did not. The omission is surely deliberate: that particular marriage hardly bears thinking about. Mr. Ponnelle's penchant for adding eavesdroppers is less in evidence than in his *Idomeneo*, but the whole gang did drop in around the edges during Titus's interview with Servilia. If some crucial lines of recitative had not been cut, what they overheard there would have put paid to any further action. These are things that can easily be righted during the run. Cast changes may right the main dramatic fault of the performance: that Vitellia and Titus are played as comic-cut caricatures. In *Idomeneo*, Hildegard Behrens's Electra moved the audience to mirth by the silent-movie frenzy of her final scene. In *Tito*, Renata Scotto's Vitellia drew laughter as, with loping, cameline gait, dressed in an immense blue crinoline, suggesting nothing so much as the Duchess in *Alice*, she advanced upon Servilia; as she crouched beside the prompt box in voodoo attitudes to listen to Sextus' "Parto"; as, in the second act, she paced swiftly in small circles to register agitation. And Kenneth Riegel invested Titus with popping eyes, sudden, jerky gestures, and choppy utterance that made him an emperor more grotesque than gracious.

The greatness of Mozart's opera was revealed by Covent Garden's 1974 production, a landmark in Mozart history, a presentation that caused widespread revaluation of the work and gave practical demonstration of what some modern Mozart scholars, turning up new facts about the genesis of *Tito*, had started to claim: that the opera, long regarded as a cynical potboiler dashed off by a sick man, is in fact a carefully considered piece of work; that (as I put it after the City Opera's 1979 production: *Music of Three More Seasons,* pp. 455–63) Mozart's thought had for years been turning toward the composition of an opera seria that would also be—in his own phrase—"a real opera," one that in richness of music and depth of true emotion would transcend the facile opere serie of his contemporaries as completely as his human comedies had transcended their lightweight opere buffe. Mr. Ponnelle's production, first seen in Cologne in 1969, had prepared the way for the revaluation. It used all Mozart's numbers, in Mozart's order. (A 1949 Salzburg production had embellished the score with gems from *Idomeneo*; the City Opera text was shortened and shuffled.) But it was, and is, a less nearly complete representation of Mozart's drama than Covent Garden's version, which treated the opera as a masterpiece needing no apologies and no tricking out for a modern audience. Some of Mr. Ponnelle's embellishments have been mentioned; in addition he obscures the clear shaping of Mozart's score by introducing many more scene changes than the composer called for. And to some extent he slights the drama by his very heavy abridgment of the recitative. Covent Garden cut some of it. Here great chunks are missing—even, at the very start, Sextus' account of Titus' character and citation of his famous utterance ("Amici, diem perdidi," at the close of a day on which he had not done his good deed), and, later, the imperial contribution to the Vesuvius Relief Fund. The recitatives were not composed by Mozart, and they are musically undistinguished, and so it is tempting to cut them to the bone. But they are part of Mozart's scheme, they delineate the characters, and they create the situations then explored in the musical numbers. Moreover, they are written in noble dramatic verse that lends itself to noble dramatic declamation. Voltaire, in the preface to his *Sémiramis*, described Titus' interview with Sextus and his subsequent soliloquy as "two scenes worthy of the finest that Greece ever produced, if not superior . . . worthy of Corneille when he is not ranting, and of Racine when he is not flimsy." Caterino Mazzolà, who adapted Metastasio's libretto for Mozart, kept the former scene intact (at the Met it is much shortened) and abridged the second but lightly. Miss Scotto—the only Italian in the Met cast—showed how powerful and interesting the recitatives can be when they are freely and tellingly delivered. For the rest: well, I suppose most people pay small attention to the words of a musical drama when it is sung in a foreign language. The Met has published an admirable new bilingual libretto of *Tito* that sets out the complete text; passages that audiences might like to know about even though they will not hear them sung are indicated as such. The stylish English translation is by David Stivender.

The instrumental performance, under James Levine, was on a high level: clear, lively, and well balanced. His tempi were convincingly chosen. Each number was given its distinct musical character. Roger Hiller was an expressive clarinet soloist in "Parto," and Vincent Abato an expressive basset-horn soloist in "Non più di fiori." The singing was patchier. Titus, a tenor, is a steady font of clemency. The drama depends on the prima donna, Vitellia, an emperor's daughter, proud, passionate, and unscrupulous (has anyone written a study of the fiery, vengeful women recurrent in Mozart's operas?), finally repentant; and on the primo uomo, Sextus, Vitellia's lover and Titus' friend, torn between sexual enslavement and moral imperatives. (The first Sextus, in 1791, was the castrato Domenico Bedini, described by a contemporary as a mountain of flesh unpleasing to eye and ear; three years later in both Vienna and Prague a woman took over the role.) Vitellia and Sextus open the opera with dialogue and a duet (her line proud and scornful, his drooping from resolution into spaniel curves), and toward the end each has a great rondo—Sextus' "Deh, per questo istante" and Vitellia's "Non più di fiori." Miss Scotto's Vitellia, as I said, was exaggerated in her acting and vivid in her recitatives. Her singing was uneven, and of "Non più di fiori" she gave a cautious, pianissimo account, the notes barely sounded. Tatiana Troyanos was due to sing Sextus, but on the first night she was ill; this was disappointing, for her Sextus in Mr. Ponnelle's television version of the opera was magnificent—one of the best things she has done. Ann Murray, billed as Annius, took over (she was the Sextus of the City Opera staging) and gave an accomplished but, in the context of this large production, somewhat small-scale performance. All Tituses I've heard have been defeated by the coloratura of the emperor's final aria, "Se all'impero." Mr. Riegel was no exception; in fact he made heavier weather of it than most. In the smaller roles, Gail Robinson (Servilia), Ariel Bybee (the substitute Annius), and John Cheek (Publius) were fairly able but unremarkable.

Mixed feelings, then; but preponderantly gladness that the great opera has joined the Met repertory at last, in a handsome staging and on Mr. Levine's secure musical foundation. An early critic of *La clemenza di Tito*, Heinrich von Kleist's uncle Franz Alexander, who attended both the Prague première and its 1794 revival, wrote about it well: "The singing line is constant, most excellent in the andantes, heavenly sweet, filled with emotion and expression. The choruses have pomp and are noble. In short, Gluck's nobility is united to Mozart's original art, his outpouring of emotion, and his irresistible harmonies." Perhaps only his conclusion goes too far: "Connoisseurs are uncertain whether *Titus* does not even surpass *Don Giovanni*."

LINE AND COLOR

November 12, 1984

MILTON BABBITT'S *The Head of the Bed* (1981), composed for the Chamber Music Society of Baltimore and the soprano Phyllis Bryn-Julson, had its New York première last week at the first Parnassus concert of the season, in Merkin Hall. It is a setting for soprano and four instruments (flute, clarinet, violin, and cello) of John Hollander's long, dense, difficult poem with the same title—225 decasyllables, fifteen stanzas of fifteen lines each. The soprano sings throughout, across a range firmly defined by frequent B-flats below the staff and A's above it, and with many wide leaps; there are no instrumental interludes, and the work lasted about twenty-five minutes. Judith Bettina's performance at the Parnassus concert was a tour de force. She sounded unstrained, confident, clear of tone, and fresh to the end. One's only complaint might be that she narrowed the dynamic range and the extreme dynamic contrasts called for in the score— called for, however, with such profusion that literal adherence to the jostling *fff* and *ppp* markings would probably break the line. And line—a flexible, fascinating vocal line quick to the rhythms, the imagery, and the sounds of Hollander's words—is at the heart of the composition. Each of the stanzas has a different instrumental accompaniment—the fifteen possibilities offered by four instruments playing solo, *a due, a tre,* or all together. The textures are flickering, alert. The Parnassus players—Keith Underwood, Charles Neidich, Carol Zeavin, Chris Finckel, unobtrusively conducted by Anthony Korf, the ensemble's director—seemed at once assured and delighted by their parts. This "dream-journey" (Hollander's description of his poem) is one of Babbitt's most lyrical compositions. [*It has been recorded on New World.*]

The concert began with the late Charles Whittenberg's arresting, rhetorical Three Pieces for Clarinet Alone (1963), which were given a dazzling performace by Mr. Neidich. Then several generations of Princeton composers with master-pupil links were represented: Paul Lansky (born in 1944), David Rakowski (born in 1958), Roger Sessions (born in 1896), and Babbitt (born in 1916). Lansky's Serenade (1978), for violin, viola, and piano, was composed (the composer said in a program note) after "a long and difficult bout with a computer." It is unstringent—especially in the third and fourth of its five brief movements—to the point of self-indulgence, but the writing has Lansky's wonted elegance. Rakowski's *Slange,* written for Parnassus, had its first performance. The composer calls it a "miniconcertino in five sections." It is a short stretch (about six minutes) of finely worked, agreeable, but unmemorable music, for eight players, with the sound of clarinet and bass clarinet together, as the composer heard them in Parnassus's recent performance of the Schoenberg Serenade, one of its sonic inspirations. Sessions's Six Pieces for Violoncello (1966) were eloquently played by Mr. Finckel, who showed himself to be an artist able to cast a spell, to make an audience hang on each turn of the music's progress. A good concert.

Sessions's twenty-minute-or-so Piano Concerto does not have the place in the repertory one would expect a work so exhilarating and, in the slow movement, so beautiful to have won for itself. The program note for a New York performance last month suggested that since the première, in 1956, it had been revived only three or four times. The concerto was commissioned by the Juilliard Musical Foundation and was first played by Beveridge Webster and the Juilliard Orchestra, conducted by Jean Morel. *Musical America* hailed it as "a major addition to the repertory." There were BBC studio performances in 1966 and 1971–72. Last year, Monique Duphil and the Cleveland Orchestra, conducted by Yoel Levi, did it in an all-Sessions concert, later broadcast in New York, by WQXR. It was a performance slightly too strenuous at times, poetic at others, and distinguished by limpid playing of the many woodwind solos. I had not heard the work live before last month's performance, which was given by Rebecca La Brecque and the American Composers Orchestra, conducted by Larry Newland, in Alice Tully Hall. Coming at the end of a program that otherwise consisted of three murky world premières (two other piano concertos and an orchestra piece), it made a powerful impression: after muddle, mastery; after confusion, clarity. Wilfrid Mellers, in an essay at the time of the BBC's 1966 performance, wrote of Sessions's liaison of "New England Puritanism with the nature mysticism of Debussy and the elegiac sensuality of Mahler," and of his fusion of "Berg-like European sensuousness with a religious austerity more typical of his New England heritage." The concerto is dedicated to the memory of Artur Schnabel; the soloist's part includes passages of the rapt, softly ecstatic figuration and also the "speaking" melodic lines for which Schnabel's playing was famous. Composed for a large orchestra (triple woodwinds), the work is brilliantly and lucidly scored—some tambourine strokes are peculiarly telling—and the soloist is never overpowered. Sessions's reputation for seriousness is well established; perhaps it is time for commentators—and performers—to make more of his music's sensual charm. There is one busy episode in the finale of the concerto which seems a shade dry, less than inspired; but no doubt when one gets to know the work better it falls into place.

Miss La Brecque is a dedicated and energetic champion of contemporary American piano music in general and Sessions's in particular. She has recorded an album of his three piano sonatas (Opus One records). This concert was an ambitious affair. But it hardly seemed to have had the long, careful rehearsals that such a program needs. In the two other piano concertos—the more interesting, by Daniel Brewbaker, completed a month before the concert; the other, entitled *Metanoia*, by Joseph Gabriel Maneri, written in 1962—there were torrents of notes but little balanced or coherent discourse to be heard. The playing of the Composers Orchestra seemed to be more efficient than loving.

The English National Opera opened the 1984–85 season with a revival of *The Flying Dutchman*, and the Metropolitan Opera with one of *Lohengrin*. Covent Garden's second new production of the season was of *Tannhäuser*. All three shows missed the straightforward theatricality that makes old-fashioned faithful stagings of these early Wagner operas surefire, allowing picturesque scenery and dramatic confrontations to be at once enjoyable in their own right and potent metaphors for Wagner's inner themes. The ENO *Dutchman* was a black-and-gray affair directed by David Pountney. It was not especially outré, just drab, and simple, exciting effects Wagner prescribed, such as Senta's "starting up from her seat, carried away by sudden inspiration," to sing the *allegro con fuoco* episode that ends her ballad, were ignored. (Senta was already standing.) The opera was played without intermissions, on a turntable, and ended with comedy as Senta, struggling to reach the Dutchman, ran anticlockwise while the turntable moved clockwise at the same speed. Josephine Barstow, the Senta, seemed ill at ease. Neil Howlett, the Dutchman, sang soundly but acted stolidly. Walter Weller, once concertmaster of the Vienna Philharmonic and now principal conductor of the Royal Philharmonic, gave a plain, coarse reading of the score.

Tannhäuser was a disaster. Its director, Elijah Moshinsky, in a naïve preliminary essay in *Opera*, dismissed the Met's noble, sensitive, inspiring production of the work as "a mere historical pageant ... a performance of the stage directions, not the inner spirit of the opera." He must have attended an unspirited performance. His own decision to alter the composer's stage directions can be likened to that of a conductor who after hearing a dull musical account of the work—"a performance of the notes"—thinks that the notes should therefore be altered. Mr. Moshinsky's effort was a callow, sub-Wieland affair, ineptly executed. It was set on a circle, bare in the outer acts, ringed with benches in Act II. Spectators in the upper parts of the house, I was told, enjoyed a colored floorcloth, but from the orchestra the set looked bleakly monochrome. The bacchanale, with choreography by Kenneth MacMillan, was reduced to a clinically copulative demonstration by two couples in body tights. The Act II assembly for the song festival became a religious procession—in motley costumes, said to be based on Giotto, that looked as if they had been pulled from various "period" hampers. (Wagner wrote that if his own ideas for the scene were not fulfilled "then I merely beg the band to play some march from *Norma* or *Belisario*, but not my music," whereas "if one prefers to retain my music, the entry of the guests must be so ordered as to thoroughly imitate real life in its noblest, freest forms.") There was an entertaining moment when at Tannhäuser's mention of the Mount of Venus a posse of little nuns went skittering across the stage in high agitation. Eva Randová, dressed as a nightclub hostess, was a squally Venus. Klaus König, a Dresden tenor, was a plain Tannhäuser who sang at the ground. Gwyneth Jones's Elisabeth was warm and emotional, and some of her notes shone beautifully. The vocal honors of the evening went to Thomas Allen, who with a shade more smoothness will be a fine Wolfram, and to Master Nicholas Sillitoe, a free-voiced shepherd boy. Colin Davis's conducting was solid, heavy. The 1860, or so-called Dresden, score was used—a mistake— and a monstrous cut was made from the Venusberg music of the overture into the Venusberg scene itself.

The Met *Lohengrin* is maimed by Ming Cho Lee's ill-devised and ugly scenery. Elsa must sing her Song to the Breezes popping, like a cuckoo from a cuckoo clock, through a little window set in a blank wall spanning the stage. The wall is an inadequate representation of "the Antwerp citadel, with the knights' dwelling center back, the women's dwelling left front, the minster portal right front." Later in the scene, it lifts, to reveal an awkward set, neither quite indoors nor quite outdoors, in which Ortrud's interruption of Elsa's procession to the minster, usually a big moment, goes for little. August Everding's staging included actions that did not improve on Wagner's. Lohengrin won his duel not by valor but by a magic trick. (Wagner is clear that Lohengrin should strike the first blow.) At "Atmest du nicht mit mir die süssen Düfte," where the pulsing strings provide a foretaste of *Tristan* enchantments, he drew his bride's attention not to the fragrant night outside but to some awful little posies clipped to their fourposter bed. Anna Tomowa-Sintow's Elsa was purely and sensitively sung. Eva Marton's Ortrud was loud and crude. Placido Domingo sang his first Lohengrin since the two performances he gave sixteen years ago in Hamburg (the city that also heard his first Radamès, Duke in *Rigoletto*, Don Alvaro, and Otello). His account of the part, carefully studied, carefully (but not smoothly enough) phrased, and carefully voiced, lacked freedom and romance. He wore—at any rate, on the second night—the worried expression of a charming Labrador uncertain of his master's approval, and it seemed to get into the singing. Fernando De Lucia, bright and forward in timbre, provides the touchstone for Latin Lohengrins; Mr. Domingo did not savor and color the German words as De Lucia does the Italian translation. James Levine's reading was broad, purposeful, and very well played.

I am prevented from drawing any simple moral—such as that Wagner's stage directions, indissoluble from his music, should always be observed—by the fact that the most exciting productions of the three operas I have seen were Wieland Wagner's, at Bayreuth, close followed by Götz Friedrich's Bayreuth staging of *Tannhäuser*. And those were certainly untraditional. It is hard to define the reasons—easier just to state—that they were strong while these later productions are weak. But perhaps some points can be made. First, the Bayreuth productions all showed an awareness that there are high dramatic moments in these early operas which it is foolish to forgo—*azione scenica* that, like Verdi's *parola scenica,* makes apparent the inner situation. The Dutchman's sudden appearance in Act II—muffed in the ENO production—is one such. Second, if Wagner's basic stage plans are not adhered to, the musical execution is jeopardized, balances go awry, and the musical structures may seem unmotivated. Bernard Shaw, reviewing the first Bayreuth *Lohengrin*, in 1894, instances an episode of choral traffic devised by Cosima for a modulation in the first-act finale as "a piece of stage management of the true Wagnerian kind, combining into one stroke a dramatic effect, a scenic effect, and a musical effect, the total result being a popular effect the value of which was proved by the roar of excitement which burst forth as the curtains closed in." In the Met *Lohengrin*, both the Herald and King Henry sing their first utterances from high above the stage on the edge of a wharf, an acoustic perch that diminished their voices. Third, these operas that Wagner himself—writing to Liszt, after he had embarked on the *Ring*—described as "things that I have outlived" owe their continuing popularity not just to their inner seriousness, dealing in elevated fashion with matters that affect all our lives, but also to the composer's practical stagecraft and his extraordinary mastery of ordinary operatic pleasures. The *Dutchman, Tannhäuser, and Lohengrin* all have the categorization "Romantic Opera." They are spectacular, colorful, popular. Shaw enjoyed that Bayreuth *Lohengrin* because "its stage framework is immensely more entertaining, convincing, and natural than it has ever seemed before." In both Covent Garden's *Tannhäuser* and the Met *Lohengrin*, twentieth-century haircuts above medieval garments looked unnatural, unconvincing.

DESERT SONG

November 19, 1984

PHILIP GLASS's latest opera, *Akhnaten,* appeared at the State Theater last week, in a production that was first seen in Houston in October and goes to the English National Opera next year. It is the third in a series of "portrait" operas—successor to *Einstein on the Beach* (1976) and to *Satyagraha* (1980), which dealt with Gandhi's career in South Africa. Glass has described the themes of the three as science, politics, and religion. Akhnaten (Akhenaton, Ikhnaton, etc.) was the name adopted by Amenhotep (Amenophis) IV, the fourteenth-century-B.C. pharaoh who declared that there was only one God, symbolized by the sun, the giver of life, and that he, Akhnaten, was His son. He destroyed images of the old gods, built a fair new city, and lived there pacifically with Queen Nefertiti (whose portrait bust is in Berlin) while the far-flung empire his forebears had won crumbled. After his death, the old gods were reinstated, and his capital was abandoned. Some thirty-two centuries later, there were found among its ruins state documents and communiqués, tomb scenes depicting the life of the city, and hymns to the Sun God whose imagery anticipates that of the Old Testament:

> *Thou hast filled every land with thy beauty . . .*
> *All the beasts are satisfied with their pasture,*
> *Trees and plants are verdant,*
> *Birds fly from their nests, wings spread,*
> *Flocks skip with their feet,*
> *All that fly and alight live when thou hast arisen.*
> *How manifold is that which thou hast made!*
> *Thou sole God, there is no other like thee.*

James Breasted, whose *History of Egypt* (1909) is cited as a source of Glass's libretto, called Akhnaten "the world's first idealist." Karl Abraham, in the first issue of *Imago* (1912), discerned in him a forerunner of Mosaic monotheism, and even of Christ. And Freud, in his last work, *Moses and Monotheism* (1939), wrote of "the first and perhaps the purest case of monotheistic religion in the history of humanity."

Glass was drawn to the pharaoh by a reading of Immanuel Velikovsky's

Oedipus and Akhnaton (1960), a popular work in which speculation about parallels between the history and the myth moves to confident statement: "Freud did not realize that his two heroes—Oedipus, of his first book, and Akhnaton, of his last book—were one person." Glass at first considered a double-stage drama but then concentrated on Akhnaten only and plunged into eighteenth-dynasty history and texts. The libretto, credited to the composer and four collaborators, is drawn from these texts (sung or spoken in Egyptian, Akkadian, or English translation), together with verses from Psalm 104 (sung in Hebrew) and, at the end, sentences from Fodor's and Frommer's guides to Egypt, accompanying modern tourists as they potter through the remains of Akhnaten's city. There are ten scenes, between a prelude and an epilogue, arranged in a narrative sequence: from the funeral of Amenhotep III, through the new king's coronation, his proclamation of the new religion, his building of the new city, and his peaceable life there, to a rebellion against him and the restoration of the old order. It is an interesting story and makes good matter for an epic opera: processions, dances, hymns, love duets and ensembles, conspiracies, attacks, triumphs provide an almost Meyerbeerian framework for music. Glass's setting of the hymns aspires to a mystical, ecstatic quality, but the spiritual aspirations of the opera are to some extent undermined, I think, in the City Opera production by the presentation of Akhnaten as a flighty, ineffectual hermaphrodite and not much else. The printed libretto bears a composer's note saying that the text "represents the conception of the opera as originally intended by its creators," although "it is possible that different productions will depart in some detail from the descriptions contained herein." This production does. (So, by all accounts, did the Stuttgart première, in which the opera was designed, directed, and "adapted" by Achim and Ilona Freyer.) According to the libretto, Act I ends with Akhnaten alone, "gazing at the distant funeral cortege floating on barques across a mythical river to the Land of the Dead." But at the State Theater the young king, his mother, and his bride went capering about like giddy flower children—to the dismay of their subjects—for what seemed like five minutes.

The settings, by Robert Israel and Richard Riddell—two of the collaborators on the libretto—evoke images of sky, sands, and the Nile. (Strips of real water traverse the forestage.) They are beautifully conceived, but their technical execution is not deft: the backcloths hang rumpled, and a doorway into the sky, toward which Akhnaten ascends at the close of Act II (another departure from the libretto, but a symbolically apt one), is clumsily built. In David Freeman's staging, the ritual elements of the work are understressed: two further visions of Amenhotep III's funeral cortege on its journey to the heavenly land of Ra—in Act II and at the very end—are also omitted. Mr. Freeman (whose production of Monteverdi's *Orfeo* for the English National I described in *Musical Events: 1980–1983,* pp. 125–28) is the founder and director of small, carefully rehearsed operatic ensembles, called Opera Factory, in Sydney, Zurich, and London. He cites Martha Graham, Peter Brook, and Jerzy Grotowski as influences on his work, and he expects his actors to be able to move as freely and expressively as they sing. I have not seen his small-scale presentations, but in the big-house shows—*Orfeo* and now *Akhnaten*—excitingly complete individual performances have mingled with episodes that look dangerously close to amateurish group improvisation. (There is a caucus-race in Act II of *Akhnaten* that might have come straight from *Alice*.) He is not afraid of cliché: at one side of the *Akhnaten* stage, throughout the evening, there is a man winnowing, and, at the other side, a man fashioning mud bricks; pharaohs come and go, but ordinary life continues. Akhnaten's new city is built onstage as a sand castle and then stamped and kicked to bits by the insurgents' feet.

There are differences between *Einstein,* created jointly by Robert Wilson and Glass, and its successors. *Einstein* was a four-act opera, without intermissions, that lasted nearly five hours. It was scored for the Philip Glass Ensemble (five instrumentalists, amplified), a violinist, a singer, speakers, and a company that danced, acted, and sang, its text being numbers to count the rhythmic patterns of the score or sol-fa syllables naming the notes sung. There were no "characters," although the violinist could be seen, in Glass's words, "perhaps as Einstein himself." The imagery was abstract, nonrealistic. *Satyagraha* and *Akhnaten,* on the other hand, are sequential narratives composed for regular opera-house forces (opera singers, chorus, and orchestra) and at not immoderate length. (The three acts of *Akhnaten* lasted about forty-five, forty, and thirty-five minutes.) They are less demanding works than *Einstein,* simple, straightforward, and more general in their appeal.

Glass's music for *Akhnaten* uses Victorian harmonies, moving at a slower pace than almost anything in nineteenth-century music except the first thirty pages of *Das Rheingold.* Woodwinds, much of the time, limn the harmonies in arpeggio figures. (One began to feel sorry for the relays of wind players called on to sound endless pages of toccata-like keyboard figuration.) The only section of the score I have seen, the Akhnaten-Nefertiti love duet, is 275 bars stuck in an arpeggiated E minor, colored by passing notes and added notes. There are pedals and some slow, occasionally dissonant counterpoints in the form of climbing chromatic scales. The lovers' voices shine out above this in a slow, chorale-like melody, crossing, overlapping (Akhnaten is a countertenor, Nefertiti a mezzo), and ending each phrase on a unison, octave, or fifth. The meters and the phrase lengths vary. It is a carefully composed, carefully proportioned stretch of music.

The principals—all of them City Opera débutants—sang surely and purely. Christopher Robson took the title role, Marta Senn was Nefertiti, and Marie Angel was Queen Tye, Akhnaten's mother. Kurt Link was Aye, Nefertiti's father; Peter Lightfoot was Horemhab, a general; and Michael Austin—vivid of presence and strong of voice—was the High Priest of the old order. Christopher Keene conducted with unflagging enthusiasm. There should perhaps be a word for the six living Segals who stood near-motionless in complicated group-wrestling poses throughout the evening.

Steve Reich's *The Desert Music,* commissioned jointly by the Brooklyn Academy of Music and West German Radio, was played in the Academy's Opera House last month, as part of its Next Wave Festival. (*Einstein on the Beach* has a revival there next month.) It is a cantata, lasting about fifty minutes, for chorus (twenty-four voices in eight-part writing) and large orchestra (fourfold woodwinds, full brasses and strings, eight percussionists, two four-hand piano duos). The voices are amplified, each group of three clustered round a separate microphone, and are doubled throughout by woodwinds or by muted brass. The woodwinds are also amplified. The general timbre seemed to be dense and dark, very different from the bright shine of Reich's *Tehillim,* though people seated on other levels of the house reported otherwise, and a critic of the Cologne première told of "extraordinarily colorful sound" and of "rich, many-hued, shimmering orchestration." The soprano voices, emerging from loudspeakers, sounded canned, and there was an almost Andrews Sisters effect in the swells and diminuendos created by closing in on, then withdrawing from, the mikes, in close harmony. *Tehillim*—four Psalm settings—had a dancing, joyful quality and a glittering surface. *The Desert Music* uses a darker, plainer text—lines drawn from poems by William Carlos Williams, a poet that Reich also set in his early days—to which darker, denser music is appropriate. The five movements are built on long, slow-moving harmonic cycles of squidgy added-note chords, unresolved or irrationally resolved, rolling inexorably on and on. At the center of the work there is a six-part double canon for women's voices, setting and illustrating (at length) the lines

> *It is a principle of music*
> *to repeat the theme. Repeat*
> *and repeat again.*

The work does not have the melodic buoyancy of *Tehillim,* but it brings together, in a long, elaborately planned score, many of the ideas with which Reich has latterly been working (constantly changing meters within a steady tempo being one) and adds a new element in the form of big, slow, resonant choral writing such as might fill a great cathedral. There is also plenty of the familiar pulsing. The Brooklyn performance was given by twenty-seven singers (there were three extra first sopranos) and an orchestra of eighty-nine (seventeen members of the Reich ensemble and the Brooklyn Philharmonic, with the Colorado Quartet leading the string sections). Michael Tilson Thomas conducted.

Both Glass and Reich apply busy, animated surface activity to slow, repetitive underpatterns. A difference between them might be described, baldly, as that between arpeggiation and pattering: where Glass goes *diddle-diddle-diddle* or *diddledy-diddledy-diddledy,* rocking up and down, Reich goes—to quote the text of the first fourteen pages of *The Desert Music*—"*De De De De De De De De De*" on repeated chords. (The chorus sings that syllable hundreds of times there, and perhaps thousands of times before the work is done.) A likeness between them in recent years is that each, who used to work mainly with his own specialized, dedicated ensemble, has now been composing for regular, established forces—opera companies and symphony orchestras. Linked reflections arise that may help to explain why some people who were once captivated or, at the least, fascinated by Glass's and Reich's music are now beginning to feel some dissatisfaction, disillusion, and perhaps even the hostility of Pauls become Sauls. It may be—it seems even likely—that the minimalist idiom is one better suited to chamber than to large forces. And it is certain that in the work of the Philip Glass Ensemble and of Steve Reich and Musicians there is a virtuoso performance element, adding to the allure, that executants with more traditional skills find hard to capture. (Both points were illustrated when *Tehillim,* which had been so sparkling when Steve Reich and Musicians did it at the Metropolitan Museum, sounded stodgier, even bloated, in the full-scale version given by the Philharmonic at the start of the 1982–83 season.) Moreover, when this music is no longer a refreshing occasional alternative but seeks to enter the mainstream it tends to be judged—however unfairly—against a different background. Episodes of pounding, irregularly accented "stamping," of ever-unresolved "altered" chords, or of single harmonies endlessly sustained through changing orchestration can seem childish, simplistic, poster-crude to the listener through whose mind there moves a memory of *The Rite of Spring, Tristan,* or *Das Rheingold.* Despite the variety—the little changes of notes or stress, the sudden drastic shifts, the iridescence of timbres—that Glass and Reich employ, there is still an immense amount of straight repetition in their music, of a kind hard to bear patiently unless one is spellbound, numbed, or soggily inattentive.

Critics may breathe out threatenings and essay verbal slaughter of minimalist music, but it continues to draw the public. (The Sold Out sign goes up at the State Theater when *Akhnaten* is on; in Brooklyn *The Desert Music* played to three full houses.) Performances proliferate here and in Europe. In this world that's so full of a number of things, minimalism is not one of those that mean most to me—I'd rather listen to Carter, Maxwell Davies, Wuorinen, Babbitt and have my powers of understanding, not my patience, challenged—but I don't feel any call either to rave and thunder or to "rave" in the opposite sense. *Akhnaten* offers an unusual, interesting, and at times moving theatrical adventure. I enjoyed and was impressed by *Satyagraha* when it was spaciously laid out at Artpark, and was then bored stiff by the repetitiveness of the music when a Stuttgart production of the work was compressed onto a television screen. But the appeal of minimalism as a socio-musical phenomenon needs consideration. Wim Mertens, a young Belgian musician associated with the movement, considers it in his *American Minimal Music.* After short studies of La Monte Young, Terry Riley, Reich, Glass, and their methods, there is an Adorno-influenced section on "the historical development of basic concepts"; Schoenberg, Webern, Stockhausen, and Cage pass in brief review. Then there is a section—not clearly formulated or argued, but worth wrestling with—on "ideology." Mertens contrasts Adorno's critical theory and defense of dialectical art with the "libidinal philosophy" of Gilles Deleuze and Jean-François Lyotard—nondialectical, anti-intellectual—and reaches disturbing conclusions: that minimalist music may provide at best Freud's "return to the infantile experience of hallucinatory satisfaction," and that one of the main reasons for its popularity is "the drug-like experience and the imaginary satisfaction it brings about . . . even more obvious in disco music and space-rock, the popular derivatives of repetitive music." Finally, he suggests that what began as a liberating movement—a possible escape from an impasse toward which modern art unwelcomed by large audiences seemed to be heading—may have become something more sinister. Invoking Marcuse (who "says that late-capitalist society has an extraordinary capacity to turn emancipatory movements into movements that accommodate the ruling monopolistic powers"), he ends, "The breakdown of dialectics . . . the desertion from history

232

in favour of a utopian world ... can bring only pseudo-satisfaction and will probably serve to strengthen the historical impasse." Mertens wrote his book a few years ago. (It first appeared, in Flemish, in 1980.) Since then, Glass and Reich have been taken up by big—well, fairly big—business in the form of major opera houses, record companies, and music publishers as well as by big audiences. In an increasingly uncritical and irresponsible society, it is perhaps harder than ever for a musician to surrender to their beguiling, mesmeric *diddledy-diddledy* or *de-de-de-de* with anything approaching an easy conscience—even when the subject matter and the texts are elevated.

The minimalist discography is large. Of the works mentioned here, the 1979 recording of *Einstein on the Beach* has been recut and reissued by CBS, and *Tehillim* is on the ECM label. The Brooklyn performance of *The Desert Music* is on Nonesuch. A City Opera recording of *Satyagraha* and a Stuttgart recording of *Akhnaten* are on CBS.

Ascendant

November 26, 1984

The music of Karlheinz Stockhausen is not much played in New York—the Philharmonic has done nothing since *Jubilee,* three years ago, and several large works remain unheard here—but his influence is strong. He has been and remains at once a pioneer in many fields—musics serial in more elements than pitch, electronic, aleatory, spatial, "intuitive," mystical—and the great synthesizer of our age, giving order and coherence to his discoveries, inventions, and dreams. On American campuses, he and his music have been inspiring. And his works, unlike those of the minimalists, grow with the passing years, lose none of their freshness and fascination. Each new encounter with *Momente* (which Martina Arroyo and Gloria Davy used to sing), *Hymnen, Stimmung* (of which a new recording has just appeared, on Hyperion), even the early *Gesang der Jünglinge* proves exciting. Most of one's listening has to be done on records— several of Deutsche Grammophon's Stockhausen recordings are in the domestic catalogue, and more are available as Polygram Special Imports—but there are occasional performances. Last month in Alice Tully Hall, Cameron Grant and James Winn gave what was billed as the New York première of *Mantra*—a two-piano piece composed in 1970 and published in 1975.

Mantra is a masterwork of our age. I thought so in a woolly, first-impression way when I heard Alfons and Aloys Kontarsky play it in London thirteen years ago, and now feel sure of it. The composition appeared to Stockhausen in a vision as he was being driven one day from Madison, Connecticut, to Boston, in 1969: "I was humming to myself ... I heard this melody ... I had the idea of one single musical figure or formula that would be expanded over a very long period of time." And he jotted the melody down on the back of an envelope. The following year, he was in Osaka, at Expo '70, where his music was performed daily for six months in the German Pavilion. For some time he had been composing mainly "intuitive" music, of the kind represented at an extreme by *Gold Dust,* the penultimate work in the collection *From the Seven Days* (1968). The complete "score" of *Gold Dust,* for small ensemble, is:

> *Live completely alone for four days without food*
> *In complete silence without much movement*
> *Sleep as little as necessary*
> *Think as little as possible*
> *After four days late at night without conversation beforehand play*
> *single sounds*
>
> *WITHOUT THINKING which you are playing*
>
> > *Close your eyes*
> > *Just listen*

Busy New York professionals can't find *Gold Dust* an easy work to prepare and perform. (Even Stockhausen's own group waited four years before adding it to the recording of the rest of the *Seven Days* on a seven-disc Deutsche Grammophon album.) In Japan, the composer gave form to *Mantra,* his first fully notated score for a decade. He has said, "Perhaps the influence of the daily performances in Osaka of our intuitive music—working with a few instructions and then playing completely freely—brought me to *Mantra.* . . . I felt that I wanted to develop further a kind of music that only I was responsible for and not only make music with our group or with other musicians where I proposed rather than 'ordered.'" And *Mantra* is a reassuring piece for musicians to whom such "compositional procedures" as

> *Play a vibration in the rhythm of dreaming*
> *and slowly transform it*
> *into the rhythm of the universe*

(an excerpt from the *Seven Days* nocturne) seem altogether too muzzy, too mystical, and too much dependent on the chances of individual execution. *Mantra* is thoroughly composed in all its aspects: the pitches, the durations, and the dynamics are defined. The mantra itself is a slow twelve-tone melody thirteen notes long, beginning and ending on A, and ever repeated—but not mindlessly or identically. During the hour-long composition, it is expanded across gapped scales and expanded or compressed in diverse time modes. Various elements of the original melody—tremolos, mordents, grace notes, stuttering attacks, chordal accompaniments—come to the fore and dominate long paragraphs. Some of Stockhausen's earlier inventions—the "Morse code" muttering of Piano Piece X, the Noh percussionist's cries in *Telemusik*—find their way into the fabric. Each pianist has a set of tuned antique cymbals mounted above the keyboard, and a woodblock; their timbres enrich the texture and sometimes provide clear, bright articulation of the structure. Electronic ring-modulation colors the piano tone, adding consonances to the tonic and

234

dominant of any section and dissonances to distant intervals, and in general functioning not unlike those eighteenth-century tempered tunings that favor the home key and emphasize the extent of departures from it. And there is much more. There are jokes: one player uses his woodblock to imitate the snap of a switch, cutting short the other player's mimicry of a studio tape loop. The piece is high-spirited (Stockhausen called his work on it "the happiest composition time I have ever spent in my life"), abundant (there are passages that seem to join hands with Cage, with Schoenberg, with Bartók, with Balinese music), and lucid.

The Kontarskys have made a splendid recording, on Deutsche Grammophon, but it is also good to hear the work live, to share in the performers' adventures as they traverse it. Mr. Grant and Mr. Winn gave an assured, unflagging, engrossing account of the piece—a little too broadly joky at times, perhaps, as if encouraging the audience to titter, but excellently energetic, and poetic, too.

Musik im Bauch (1975), a fable for six percussionists and music boxes, shows Stockhausen in lighter vein. It had its genesis one day when the stomach of the composer's two-year-old daughter began to rumble gently, and her father said to her, "Why, Julika, you have music in your tummy." With delight, Julika began to laugh and to cry out "Musik im Bauch! Musik im Bauch!" The fable took shape later: from the belly of a giant figure hung with jingles three brothers extract music boxes and then imitate their tinkling tunes on a little glockenspiel. (The tunes are chosen from a set of twelve, which went on to achieve independent existence in *Tierkreis*. Four of them also figure in the central section of *Sirius*.) Meanwhile, on a battery of bell plates on one side of the stage and a marimba, played four-hand, on the other, the same music is sounded in immensely slow motion. The carillonneur, with a good deal of variety of dynamics and attack, peals out the tunes in succession, a note at a time, while the marimba duo, imitating mechanical dolls, spreads one tune through the length of the performance. The work ends when the music boxes run down. *Musik im Bauch* was given what was billed as the United States première by the New Music Consort in Carnegie Recital Hall this month.

Robin Maconie, in his Stockhausen monograph, calls the piece "an odd moral tale on the conflicting values of mechanical versus intuitive timing, of true versus false precision, of independence versus cooperation, of a questioning versus an unquestioning attitude to musical performance and the composer's instructions." And adds, "To a child, however, it is simply an enchanting fable about a giant with the secret of music hidden inside him." But in a performance less than finely tuned it can seem trivial fare. The New Music Consort's presentation had an unexpectedly grim flavor. All six players were dressed in black, with faces painted and hair lacquered to look like metal. The three brothers, not only the marimbists, moved like robots. Percussion players are usually the lithest and most theatrical of instrumentalists, the easiest movers, the readiest to be eye-catching (there was a moment in Peter Brook's *Tragédie de Carmen* when Daniel Druckman, tuning his timpani, took the limelight off the singers), but these didn't seem altogether unembarrassed. The bell plates were replaced by tuned gongs, whose sound is less bright and gleaming—*bong* rather than *ding*.

The concert began with Lukas Foss's Quartet for percussion, which looks more fun to play than it is to listen to, and was rendered with a physical grace lacking in the Stockhausen. Jalalu-Kalvert Nelson's *Albatross* (1981)—which expresses "what I imagine to be a day in the life of an albatross," the composer said in a note—had its American première. Two Orpheus songs by Anne LeBaron, "Lamentation" and "Invocation," for baritone, clarinet, harp, and cello, had their world première and left a stronger impression, for they are thoughtful, imaginative pieces, precisely and delicately "heard"; each utterance tells. Charles Wuorinen's sextet *Speculum Speculi* (1974), a closely argued and sensuously exciting composition, had a welcome revival.

I use the cautious formulations "billed as the New York première" and "billed as the United States première" because a few weeks ago I too readily accepted a program book's claim that Stockhausen's *Harlequin* and Ligeti's Trio were receiving their United States premières at the October concert in Symphony Space. Readers quickly let me know that *Harlequin* was played in Ann Arbor last March, and that Ligeti's Trio was played in Portland, Oregon, last July.

What does seem—surprisingly—to have been the New York première of Schoenberg's *Die Jakobsleiter* was given in Carnegie Hall last month, brought here by the Cleveland Orchestra, conducted by its new music director, Christoph von Dohnányi. Schoenberg completed, in short score, only the first part of what would have been a long oratorio. After his death, in 1951, the orchestration was undertaken by Winfried Zillig, and *Die Jakobsleiter* was first heard in 1961. The American première was in Santa Fe, staged, in 1968; and Santa Fe revived the work in 1980. A CBS recording with BBC forces conducted by Boulez has just been released in this country. A critic of the album remarked that the oratorio "seems to embrace the worlds of Mahler's Eighth Symphony and Stockhausen's *Sirius* in its visionary grasp." It is an immense conception: a vision of mankind—represented both by numerous, disparate choruses and by solo spokesmen—mounting, some groups eagerly, some reluctantly, "the mystical ladder of the seven spiritual worlds hung one above another in space, and seen by the floods of light that fall in cascades down the steps of the heavenly floor." The quotation is from Balzac's *Seraphita,* which inspired Schoenberg's text. For the end, set in a Swedenborgian Heaven where offstage voices and offstage orchestras join the soloists, chorus, and main orchestra until, as Schoenberg said in a 1921 note, "music is streaming into the great hall from all sides," we have only the composer's libretto. There has been much speculation about why Schoenberg, having composed some six hundred bars of *Die Jakobsleiter* at white heat, in three months of 1917, could not find his way back into the score after the interruption caused by a very brief spell of military service. It was not for want of trying: between 1918 and 1922 he made fifteen attempts on passages of Part II, and in 1944 he took up the work again for a while. Two not exclusive explanations seem to me likely. One is suggested by Hans Keller's challenging remarks in a 1968 essay introducing BBC broadcasts of *Die Jakobsleiter* and the Matthew Passion. "Bach was a religious finder where Schoenberg was a searcher," Mr. Keller says. "Which is about all the difference one can make between the Matthew Passion and *Jacob's Ladder;* for the rest, the two are virtually identical, in all that matters in music." That *Die Jakobsleiter* is a chapter of spiritual autobiography no one has doubted. And that Schoenberg, ever-questing, could find music to make vivid the conflict, the dilemma, the aspiration, but not the victory, the resolution, the arrival seems at least likely; the history of the unfinished *Moses and Aaron* points the same way. Second, as has often been noted, both the words and the music of *Die Jakobsleiter* adumbrate ideas that led to the "method of composing with twelve notes." And once that path—that highway, that "discovery thanks to which the supremacy of German music is ensured for the next hundred years" (Schoenberg to his pupil Josef Rufer)—had come clearly into view there could be no easy backtracking.

Die Jakobsleiter is not overwhelming as *Moses and Aaron* is. Or the Matthew Passion. Or an inspired performance of Mahler's Eighth. (If I don't add *The Dream of Gerontius,* one of the works that first moved me to live a life in music, it is only because I've not heard it for many years.) But Schoenberg's great vision is there to catch. There are marvellous, inspired pages, although there are others where—dare one say it—the notes seem a bit dull. And although Gabriel, the principal character—hustler-on of the throng and respondent to the other soloists—is rather hard to take: he scolds in tones of priggish righteousness. To the Chosen One, who has aimed "to shape a model certainly new, possibly higher" but is ever misunderstood and derided—and who is generally considered to be a self-portrait of the composer—Gabriel is fairly indulgent. But the other soloists, it seems to me, are also aspects of the questing Schoenberg. To a Called One who "sought after beauty . . . perceived only the rhythm of beauty" and found joy in doing so, Gabriel sternly says, "You are self-satisfied. . . . Self-sufficiency (too simple a formula, for all progress is torment) keeps you warm." And to a Monk who gave up the joys and delights of the world he says, disagreeably, "You were richer before you became more perfect; you have sacrificed all brightness for one gloomy insight—into your own inadequacy!" The oratorio tends to reinforce the emotions of anyone who, while an unreserved admirer of Schoenberg's genius (how can anyone not be?), finds it hard to love the man. Yet in the end the genius triumphs. Gabriel doesn't only hector in Sprechgesang; he also has passages of broad, lyrical song. His last words—the last words Schoenberg set—are "When you complain no more, you are near. Then your Ego is dissolved": a condition implying uncritical acceptance. There follows high solo-violin song and rapt, wordless vocalises of a Soul who has ascended the ladder toward bliss—both haloed in distant ethereal music. The glimpse of ecstasy is beautiful and moving as it fades into the silence where Schoenberg left his piece.

The choral writing is very difficult, calling not only for song but for precise speaking on pitch. The Cleveland Orchestra Chorus, prepared by Robert Page, was in splendid form. The orchestra played surely and warmly. Julian Patrick was a Pizarro-like Gabriel. Celina Lindsley was an exquisitely pure, radiant Soul. (At the close, where—space and time dissolved—the Soul breaks into metaphysical duet, she sang both lines, on a prerecorded tape.) Helga Pilarczyk, once the vivid heroine of so many contemporary operas, spoke the pitched words of the Dying One with fervor. William Johns, Jaroslav Kachel, Andrew Foldi, Oskar Hillebrandt, Richard Brunner, and the solo violins of Daniel Majeske and Lev Polyakin all contributed to a remarkable performance. The new music director has begun bravely.

December 10, 1984

ANDRZEJ PANUFNIK's latest work, *Arbor Cosmica,* a substantial and stirring composition, had its first performance last month, in Merkin Hall's Music Today series. No work of his has made a stronger first impression on me. Like his best-known piece, *Lullaby* (1947), it is scored for a body of solo strings: twenty-nine of them (together with either one or two harps) in *Lullaby,* twelve in *Arbor Cosmica.* (The Violin Concerto, written for Menuhin in 1971, also uses only string orchestra.) *Lullaby,* which came to prominence at the 1948 ISCM Festival, is historically important: in its sounds and its procedures it anticipated music that Lutoslawski, Penderecki, Xenakis, Ligeti wrote much later. The composer Nigel Osborne, in a recent *Tempo* essay, recalled his first encounter with *Lullaby* while in 1970, in Warsaw, he was studying and analyzing the latest Polish music: "There it was, rather like looking at one of Leonardo's aeroplanes, a forgotten prototype of Polish School texture, created some twenty years ahead of its time: silvery wisps of tremolo quarter-tones, unfolding across each other, settling like mist around a simple diatonic line—or, as the composer has described it, like clouds passing the moon."

Panufnik, celebrated and honored in his native land as a composer and a conductor—holder of the Standard of Labor, First Class, and twice State Laureate—left Poland in 1954, in protest at political interference with creative artists, and settled in England. Five years earlier, his *Sinfonia Rustica* had both won the Chopin Prize and been officially condemned as "alien to the great Socialist era." But in England—or so *Arbor Cosmica* now leads me to think—not quite enough was made of him. True, he was performed, published (by Boosey & Hawkes), and recorded. (Six of his eight symphonies and much else have appeared on disc.) The world acknowledged him: there were premières in New York (the *Katyń Epitaph* in Carnegie Hall in 1968, the Alexander Pope setting *Universal Prayer* in St. John the Divine in 1970, both conducted by Stokowski), Houston, Paris, as well as in several British cities. The Boston Symphony commissioned his *Sinfonia Votiva* for its centenary and recorded it on Hyperion. He had some ardent champions; in general, there was temperate admiration for a series of works—*Sinfonia Sacra, Sinfonia di Sfere, Sinfonia Mistica*—in which veins of deep patriotism, Catholic mysticism, and aristocratic niceness flow quietly through carefully planned structures. Ten years ago, Panufnik described the three stages by which he makes a composition. First, there is "the purpose or reason for which the work is composed." ("Some spiritual or poetic content is ... for me essential.") Then "the architectural structure" is devised and designed. (Several of his works are published with preliminary diagrams, blueprints, of the musical framework.) Then "the material of which it is to be built" is determined. (Often this is three-note or four-note motivic and harmonic "cells.") It is a sensible and not at all uncommon way of working; but some of Panufnik's pieces sound as if they were produced by following a formula rather than by whatever mysterious processes produce music that is moving and exciting to hear. His intentions have ever been high: "to compose a large-scale work to express my deep sorrow for *all* the war victims of *all* nationalities, religions, and races: a work which, at the same time, would be an anti-war protest against violence and the aggressive element in mankind" (the *Sinfonia Elegiaca*); "to compose a prayer ... in which the spiritual content might help to unite the feelings of all people, now so tragically divided in this disturbed world" (*Universal Prayer*). It may be that a disparity between the lofty aims and music of more modest, worthy achievement clouded due appreciation of its merits.

Panufnik was seventy in September. Mr. Osborne suggests that his music "has now come into its own," after being "rejected by the Stalinists, cast aside in the fever of modernism itself, and ignored in the flabby reaction that followed," and that it can now be appreciated by "a generation of 'post'-post-modernists" which "sees the need to pull the strands tightly together." *Arbor Cosmica* certainly fell as refreshment on ears wearied by the harmonic triteness of insistent minimalism or by the cloying reminiscences of neoromanticism. It sounded new, and yet it is built on the traditional foundations of Western music: the twelve movements (or "Evocations") span the great circle of fifths, from C to F, that provide us with our twelve notes, and each movement ends with a tonic chord major and minor at once, with both thirds present. The piece was commissioned by the Koussevitzky Music Foundation. In a preface to the score, the composer says:

> This work has grown out of my lifelong admiration, almost worship, for trees. ... Beauty, harmony, strength and order, the tree conveys to me; but it communicates to me something much more than its sheer physical presence. Beyond the aesthetic pleasure and sensual delights of appearance, touch or smell, the tree seems to me to emanate some mysterious power through its moods, and through its soul.

The "cell" here is simply the notes C, D, E-flat. Repeated in ascending sequence, it climbs a nine-note scale from which melodies are made; the first, the central, and the last notes of this scale yield a triad (C, F-sharp, B) that, in constant transpositions, provides the "vertical" element of the work. There is a diagram, tree-shaped, that shows a trunk built from the cell and its transpositions, crowned by twelve branches that lead to the twelve tonic triads. The Cosmic Tree, Panufnik tells us, sometimes appears in art and literature with its roots in Heaven and its foliage running down to earth; his movements alternate patterns of ascending triads with descending melodies, and vice versa.

The plan does sound—it is—schematic, but the music itself is inspired; that imprecise word must serve. The form—twelve short movements, lasting in all about forty minutes—saves the composer from any formulaic filling-out of ambitious long-movement designs. Nothing outstays its welcome. The scoring is skillful. In that preface, Panufnik talks of "the dance-like rocking of branches in the wind," of "the song-like groaning and sighing, the leaves rustling and whispering, full of mysterious secrets." I happen to share his arboreal love: spend part of each summer lulled at night by the susurrus of a wide-branched poplar; can recall individual trees in the parks of Thames-side Twickenham, where Panufnik lives; and after twelve years in New York still feel a pang when passing the sickly planes that fight bravely for life in the poisoned earth and air. But one need not be a tree-lover to enjoy *Arbor Cosmica*. Even without the "program," without the titular clue, a listener would respond to the sounds and the way they move. The separate Evocations are well contrasted but form a coherent sequence. The composer allows that, although the work was composed as an entity, segments of it may be performed separately, provided that the movements chosen are consecutive. He says nothing about increasing the string forces, but I imagine that large orchestras as well as small will find the score rewarding; a Berlin Philharmonic performance might be breathtaking. The twelve Music Today players, conducted by Gerard Schwarz, were eloquent, and filled Merkin Hall with beautiful sound.

George Perle will be seventy next May. In a *Tempo* essay three years ago, the composer Oliver Knussen told of his delighted discovery of Perle's later music, from the Seventh String Quartet (of 1973) on; and over the years I have chronicled the appearance of small-orchestra works Haydnesque in their wit and technical mastery, and of piano works—the Etudes, the Ballade—Chopinesque in their lyricism. Knussen wrote of "a profound 'late flowering,' in the sense of Janáček or Gerhard"—without forgetting the early force and fire of Perle's Three Movements for Orchestra or the grace and clarity of his Fifth String Quartet, both composed back in 1960. Two of Perle's later pieces for piano and small orchestra had welcome revivals last month. Serenade III, for piano and ten players (first heard at a Music Today concert last year), was done by the Chamber Music Society of Lincoln Center, in Alice Tully Hall; and the Concertino for piano, fourteen winds, and timpani (first heard here at a Group/Parnassus concert in Symphony Space four years ago) opened the Music Today program that ended with the Panufnik. Richard Goode was the pianist of both. An advocate of Perle's music, he was poetic, playful, and deft. Both performances—the Serenade conducted by Fred Sherry, the Concertino by Mr. Schwarz—confirmed, as later hearings don't always do, favorable first impressions. Haydnesque, Chopinesque, and, one might add, Stravinskyesque are simple critical labels that indicate not imitation but ways in which a listener may respond to music where the notes seem to fall in the right place, where (as in Handel) texture may thin to essentially two parts and still sound rich, and where a single theme can provide lively matter for cogent discourse. Harmonically, Perle has become another healer of wounds the twelve-note system inflicted on consonances and their traditional connotations. But he is a pioneer moving onward, not a nostalgic lost in dreams of the past. Moreover, the themes seem to generate the forms, and the context to determine the procedures. Perle is fairly well represented on disc. Of the works mentioned above, the Fifth Quartet is on Nonesuch, the Seventh Quartet and the Three Movements on CRI, and the Etudes on New World.

*   *   *

Andrew Imbrie, born in 1921, has—to judge by two pieces performed here this season—flowered into a new lyricism. Once, he seemed to be the type of an academic, "Princeton" composer. His vivid *Roethke Songs,* heard three years ago, while still spiky, pointed toward a freer, fuller way of writing. *Campion Songs,* a Naumburg commission that was given its first performance, by the New York Vocal Arts Ensemble, in Alice Tully Hall in October, attains it. The songs are difficult; we were warned that the Ensemble—a vocal quartet—might not essay them after all, but in the event it gave an account of them good enough at least to show that Imbrie's attempt "to capture [Campion's] spirit of courtliness combined with passion" (as he said in a program note) was successful. It was bold of him to reset lyrics that the poet-composer, a famous matcher of tone to word, had written for his own music, but Alfonso Ferrabosco the younger, in the early seventeenth century, and Hubert Parry, in the early twentieth, gave precedent. The poems are "O never to be moved," "Fire, fire, fire," and "Come, o come my lifes delight."

Imbrie's *Pilgrimage,* commissioned by the New York New Music Ensemble and given its New York première, by the Ensemble, in Carnegie Recital Hall last month, was even more surprising and more enjoyable. The other day, a London colleague, after a concert by the Fires of London (*olim* Pierrot Players) which included Elliott Carter's Triple Duo and Peter Maxwell Davies's *Image, Reflection, Shadow*—both written for what he called the "starkly unblended timbres of flute, clarinet, violin, cello, piano, and percussion"—asked, "Why should the accidental fact that Schoenberg chose these instruments (without percussion) for *Pierrot Lunaire* still condition the sort of music composers are writing seventy-two years later?" I think the question is easily answered—simply by pointing to the quantity and the variety of admirable music composed for and performed by the Fires and for and by the New Music Ensemble, which has the same constitution. The sextet seems to inspire, not to limit, composers' invention. Imbrie's *Pilgrimage* sounds quite different from works for the same forces by Davies, Carter, Harrison Birtwistle, Richard Meale, Charles Wuorinen, Bernard Rands (whose *Déjà* was also on the Carnegie Recital Hall bill). *Pilgrimage,* which lasted about twenty-three minutes, is an astonishingly lush, colorful, and picturesque composition; there were even moments when the Act III dawn of *Tosca* seemed not far away. The program note vouchsafed no program; in fact, it specifically described the work as "non-programmatic: absolute music, dissonant but adhering to no fixed system of tonality, descriptive of moods and architectural structures." I'll describe it as euphonious, descriptive of moods, uninhibitedly emotional as I've never known Imbrie to be before, and masterly. The Ensemble, conducted by Robert Black, gave a shining performance.

241

CRYING FOR PEACE AND LOVE

December 17, 1984

SIMON BOCCANEGRA is a somber, beautiful opera, which most Verdians hold especially dear. True, it lacks contrast: there is no trace of the laughter and brilliant high spirits to be found in every act of *Ballo* and in all but the first of *Forza. Don Carlos* is larger, grander, more colorful, more ambitious, and *Aida* more surely fashioned, although its subject matter is conventional. The first version of *Boccanegra* (1857) marked Verdi's return to Italy after more than three years spent mainly in Paris, and his return to dramatic matter like that of the early *I due Foscari,* treated now in a richer and subtler manner. The revised *Boccanegra* (1881) broke his seven-year silence after the Requiem, and work on it proceeded while *Otello* was already being planned. In both cases, *Boccanegra* holds a special position in Verdi's career. In 1880, as he contemplated the revision, he wrote of the first version, "The score is impossible as it stands. It is too sad, too depressing.... I'll need to redo all the second act [by which he meant what we know as Act I, for the context shows that he was thinking of the Prologue as the first act] and give it contrast and variety and more life." In fact, what he did was to remove the lively festive music of the first version—the Genoese people's anniversary celebration of Boccanegra's election, complete with stage band and ballet—and make the opera darker and more serious still. He directed the attention of his new collaborator, Arrigo Boito, to "two stupendous letters of Petrarch's, one written to Doge Boccanegra, the other to the Doge of Venice, telling them that they were about to embark on fratricidal strife, since both were sons of the same mother, Italy, etc. Sublime, this feeling for an Italian fatherland in those days! All that is politics, not drama, but a man of resource could well dramatize it." Boito responded by citing another Petrarch letter: "It is fine to overcome a foe by the test of the sword, but finest to conquer him by magnanimity of heart." He was a man of resource. The Council scene he devised for Verdi, embodying the Petrarchian pleas for peace, is moving and magnificent. He sent it to the composer along with a bold alternative scheme in which the old Acts I and II are conflated and an entirely new act, set in the besieged church of San Siro, follows. But then he added his opinion that the opera was not worth resuscitating. The characters were weakly delineated. Profound virtues were trivially treated. The drama, after the Prologue, lacked tragic power and theatricality: it was like a rickety table that continued to wobble whichever leg one propped. (Boito later refused to let his name be associated with the revision, although the critics of the day made no secret of his share in it.) In reply, Verdi praised the novelty and theatricality of the San Siro act but said it was too much for him to tackle. He welcomed the Council scene. "Your criticisms are just, but you, immersed in loftier tasks, and with *Otello* in mind, contemplate a perfection unattainable here. My aim is lower, and, more optimistic than you, I don't give up hope. I agree that the table is rickety, but, after some adjustment of a leg here and there, I think it will stand firm." He suggested that there certainly was something to be made of the characters of Simone and Fiesco.

Verdi's revision was thorough, and it eventually affected every scene. The piece was well received, and Verdi hoped it would make the rounds as most of his earlier operas had done, "even though the subject is very sad." ("It's sad because it has to be sad," he told a friend, "but it's gripping.") *Boccanegra* did not catch on, however, and even today it is less often played than *Ballo, Forza,* and *Don Carlos.* The Met is probably the only company that for over forty years (from 1932 to 1974) has given it with some regularity. The early Met casts were grand: Lawrence Tibbett, then Leonard Warren, in the title role; Maria Müller, then Elisabeth Rethberg, as Amelia; Giovanni Martinelli as Gabriele; Ezio Pinza as Fiesco. On pirate discs, 1935 and 1939 performances can still be heard; in *Opera on Record* Lord Harewood remarks that "few of us since the war have heard more than a handful of Verdi performances to compare at any point." Now, after a ten-year absence, *Boccanegra* has returned to the Met. We were originally promised a new production by Peter Hall, and then one by John Dexter, but in the event the opera has been newly staged by Tito Capobianco in old scenery borrowed from Chicago.

The first-night performance was not altogether satisfying; in fact, by high standards it should be called an unworthy one. The sets are large and handsome, but they look as though they had been pulled from stock, and they jar with the scenes that Verdi envisaged and regarded as essential to the proper enactment of his music. Mr. Capobianco's production included a good deal of amateurish-looking jostling by the chorus and eyes-on-the-conductor action by the principals. In its routine way, it was preferable to a perverse fancy staging, however well drilled, but not to a serious, stylish, imaginative presentation inspired by an accurate response to character, situation, and the music. There were compensations. James Levine's handling of the score, although hardly idiomatic, was carefully considered and was well played. (Perhaps it was an inflexibility of beat that led the *Times* critic to describe the famously delicate and original instrumental writing of Amelia's aria as "organ-grinder accompaniment.") And in the title role Sherrill Milnes gave a performance of deep feeling and some grandeur.

Chicago's 1974 production of *Boccanegra* has a certain historical importance. The Lyric Opera was host at the time to an international congress planned by the Parma-based Institute of Verdi Studies and devoted to *Boccanegra.* The disparity between the work the Lyric presented and the work Verdi composed was so great that dismayed American Verdians set about the creation of an American Institute for Verdi Studies, and today that institute, housed at New York University, has a rich archive of prime materials for serious conductors and directors to consult before embarking on a Verdi production. (Mr. Levine and Mr. Capobianco are members of the advisory board.) There they can discover, for example, that in *Boccanegra* the cries of rebellion at the close of Act II should be not simply sung in by a stationary offstage chorus but treated dynamically. A page of the 1881 production book describes the needed effects, with detailed stage plans showing how they were attained at the Scala première; directors are told to test these and, if necessary, modify them to match the acoustics of a particular theatre. Verdi composed the opera with both ear and eye. "Take great care over the staging," he wrote in a letter. "It is essential that everyone should see Simone when [in the Prologue] he enters the house and when he comes out onto the balcony and takes down the lantern; here, I believe, I have achieved a musical effect that I do not want ruined by the staging." For the next scene he suggested practical ways in which, by gauzes and lights, the scene painter could second the ripple and sparkle of moonlight on the sea so delicately portrayed in his music. At the end of the opera, the lights of Genoa en fête should be clear and brilliant on a distant backcloth and then go out one by one until at Simone's death all is dark—"a powerfully effective moment, I believe, and it would be a disaster if the staging were not good." In Chicago, none of these things happened. Nor did they at the Met; the scenery—originally designed by Pier Luigi Pizzi, but at the Met modified and uncredited—does not allow them to. Act II (the Doge's room in the palace) and Act III (a large hall in the palace, open at the back to a wide prospect of the city) are now played in the same setting, without an intermission between them. This saves time, but the compromise set—a vast loggia with the Doge's study curiously laid out in one corner of it—destroys the intended contrast between a closed, intimate scene, without chorus (except offstage), and a public one. (At the back, a gilt equestrian statue of St. George and the dragon is three centuries out of period.) Another of Verdi's requirements—that the scene change in Act I should be made without dropping the front curtain and in the course of a single measure—was also unmet. The sudden transformation from the garden by the sea to the thronged council chamber would produce a powerful effect. The staging book sets out one way of accomplishing it, and the music is paced so as to give Simone time enough to don the ducal regalia, and Paolo and Pietro, who end the first scene, time enough to reach their appointed places in the second.

The opera can be approached in different ways. Detailed adherence to nineteenth-century stage techniques is not essential. (Musical authenticity is perhaps more important. Julian Budden, in his splendid three-volume study *The Operas of Verdi,* has pointed out that the trombone writing in the Council scene requires the valved instruments of Verdi's day, not our modern slide instruments.) La Scala's 1971 production—directed by Giorgio Strehler, designed by Ezio Frigerio, conducted by Claudio Abbado, and musically preserved on a fine Deutsche Grammophon album—is famous. (In 1976, it visited London and Washington.) There was only one intermission. The scenery was simplified. The stage directions were not literally observed. But Strehler proceeded from a profoundly Verdian perception of the drama, as remarks of his gathered in a booklet accompanying the DG album make clear. Simone's story, he rightly says, is coherent, although "the libretto complicates and obscures the events" by its recourse to the old devices of melodrama—disguises, false names, discovery of the long-lost child, assassins' daggers and poison. "Everything may seem confused and jumbled, but it has sense in Simone's soul." In the Prologue,

244

personal tragedy and public triumph follow one on the other (as they did at the start of Verdi's own career), and the theatrical scene—shadows, the sudden flare of torches, cloaked figures, mysterious encounters—is a potent metaphor. The sea—cradling, eternal, sometimes fierce, sometimes a gentle mother—is an ever-present symbol, both musically and scenically, as it is in *Peter Grimes*. It murmurs in the opening pages, sparkles brightly in Amelia's love song, and at the close calls to the dying Doge. The plebeian seaman rises to the highest office. Lonely, misunderstood, unappreciated, attacked, he goes through life holding to his ideals of courage, honesty, duty, and generosity of spirit. The vanity of hoping in this world for happiness and peace, the real, if fleeting, consolations of tender love, and the duty to endure without weakness or compromise were Verdi's recurrent concerns; in Francesco Foscari they found an early, in King Philip a late, and in Simon Boccanegra perhaps their most affecting and beautiful embodiment. Mr. Milnes understands this. In a *Times* interview before the performance, he said:

I think Simon Boccanegra is the most profound character ever created by a French or Italian composer. [The national qualifications suggest that, as others have done, he holds Hans Sachs and Wotan to be comparable characters.] Otello also comes to mind, but he was concerned only about his own personal problems. Boccanegra has these, too, but his heart is immense—he goes much farther. I know of no other character who speaks with such love of mankind and who tries harder to do what we are trying to do now—getting people in conflict to live in peace. If he has a fatal weakness, it's his idealism.

The Council scene—Simone's plea for peace and love—was well described by Budden as "a hymn to the ideal of universal brotherhood as uplifting as Beethoven's 'Ode to Joy'" and as "perhaps the highest expression of social idealism in opera ever penned." Things seem to be coming right for Simone at last, but only when—unknown to himself—he is dying, poisoned by a traitor he trusted. Strehler replaced the final, symbolic extinguishing of the lights by a different image: a great sail fell as the corsair-doge died.

Another approach than Strehler's would be one attentive—but in no pedestrian or mere "blocking" way—to the prescriptions of the staging book: respectful of moves and stations that at once reflect the relationships, indicate changing patterns of dominance, clarify the musical structure, and help to ensure an accurate musical balance. Such a production need be no more inhibiting to a sensitive director than the attempt at a faithful execution of the notes is to a conductor. A celebrated Fiesco remarked to me, during an interval of the Met performance, that across the years he'd been offered just two ways of singing "Il lacerato spirito": stage left or stage right. The production book sets the aria within a fairly elaborate stage crossing keyed to particular bars and carefully motivated. About the Amelia-Boccanegra duet, however, it says:

His questions, her replies, the eagerness and ever growing interest of the Doge are too clearly defined by the music to make any minute description of the moves necessary: this is one of those music-drama scenes that draw their effect from the talent and intuition of the artists; and no cold scenic description would achieve the desired result when the actors did not have natural understanding and could not give form to the powerful emotions that stir them.

And so only a few key moves are specified, to provide a framework within which the artists can work.

Amelia was sung by Anna Tomowa-Sintow. On the first night, her aria was disappointing, the timbre a shade dirty; but then the voice cleared, and her lines flowed fully and truly. She is a correct and well-trained artist, if not an exciting or individual one. Vasile Moldoveanu was the Gabriele Adorno. I like the bright, virile ring and sharp focus of his tenor. There is something of Martinelli about it. It is a sound more incisive than, say, Placido Domingo's. The performance was unsubtle—eyes front, and give it to the audience—but not mere provincial belting. Paolo, a role usually assigned to budding Boccanegras (it was Leonard Warren's début role at the Met, and Mr. Milnes has sung it there), was on this occasion taken by a veteran Boccanegra: Peter Glossop, burly-voiced and bulldog-firm as ever. Fiesco is a part for a primo basso profondo, and Paul Plishka didn't quite fit the bill; he was unsteady in the aria and did not have the dominant personality of the proud old patrician. Simone's political and social adversary wasn't formidable enough.

So, in effect, Mr. Milnes had to carry the show, and this he did by honesty and force of feeling, physical presence, and strength of voice. He has matured into an uncommonly interesting and impressive Boccanegra, less concerned than before with brilliant top notes and generalized magnificence, readier to seek the specific eloquence of each episode and of each incident within it. Reaction to Milnes's performances is seldom straightforward. His voice is unconventional and is produced now in ways that seem more willed than natural. The vocal naturalness and ease that Piero Cappuccilli and Renato Bruson—the other international Boccanegras of our day—display at their best are absent. Sometimes Mr. Milnes hits notes that, while still powerful, are plain and bleak in timbre—patches where the nap seems to have gone and only the strong, tough backing shows through. On the other hand, Mr. Cappuccilli and Mr. Bruson when unprodded by firm direction are apt to amble through the opera in an uncommitted and monotonous fashion, whereas Mr. Milnes is always engaged with the sense of what he does. About his stage portrayal one has similarly mixed feelings. The emotional projection is vivid, but, however subtly conceived and intricate the emotions may be, his theatrical devices tend to be old-fashioned and unsubtle. In the Council scene, he made such play with the ducal robe that it began to distract attention from the man within it. At the end, he crashed to the ground in a melodramatic stage fall that was very striking but surely less moving than the death described in the production book: "Suddenly the Doge rises, extends his arms toward his daughter, and with a supreme effort cries 'Maria!' He would say more, but he cannot; he falls back on the seat [which has been described as broad, low, and backless] and looks for the last time at the sea. His head falls back; he is dead." At the Met, the applause broke out before the curtain had fallen or the music had ended (whereas when the Strehler *Boccanegra* played at Covent Garden the editor of *Opera* reported a fifteen- or twenty-second silence, into which the first clapping broke as an unwelcome intrusion).

Mr. Milnes's histrionics were partly to blame, but in fairness it should be noted that even the greatest artists seem unable to quell the ill-timed enthusiasms of Met audiences. There are always (I'd add "except on Wagner nights" could one be sure of hearing the last chord of *Tristan*) some unmannerly and ignorant persons there who do not want to listen to the music or let others do so. The magical close of the Amelia-Boccanegra duet—the Doge's poignant, loving exclamation "Figlia!" on a soft high F, as his eyes follow his departing daughter—was ruined. It tells of the new ray of happiness that has entered his life. But it went unheard: some of the audience had begun applauding loudly long before Mr. Milnes breathed the tender cry.

The scenery will presumably go back to Chicago. The production is presumably a stopgap affair assembled when the Met's plans for its own *Boccanegra* fell through. The way is still open for a serious, studied new production of the great opera.

Riches in Little Room

December 24, 1984

Two short pieces by Elliott Carter were introduced to New York last week by the Chamber Music Society of Lincoln Center. *Riconoscenza* (a title that combines senses of recognition and gratitude), for solo violin, celebrated the eightieth birthday of the composer Goffredo Petrassi. It was first played at the Pontino Festival, in Italy, in June. *Canon for 4* (which is subtitled "Homage to William"), for flute, bass clarinet, violin, and cello, honored the achievement of William Glock. It was first played at the Bath Festival (where, in 1980, Carter's *Night Fantasies* had its first performance), in June, on the occasion of Sir William's retirement as the festival director. Neither is a miniature or mere albumblatt; each lasts about four minutes and is plainly destined to outlive its occasional origin. Carter—in a conversation with the cellist Fred Sherry printed in the Lincoln Center program book—says that neither work is a study for a larger composition: "These pieces were individual pieces that worked for themselves. I was just interested in trying to solve the problem of writing short pieces." The conversation ranges beyond the two new works: "The composer who has always meant the most to me, all my life, has been Mozart. He's interesting because he was very concerned with the change in human feeling, constantly seeing things in different and varied lights." And: "Much of the music of the twentieth century has disturbed me because it's trying to avoid just this flexibility, developing a primitive, almost hypnotic effect which I find very dangerous, having lived through the time of Hitler." Mr. Sherry remarks on the "rapid and incredible changes" that characterize much of Carter's music, and instances the Symphony of Three Orchestras. The composer in reply talks of "one of the most interesting things music can present—the way human feeling can change and vary—the way we look back on what we've just experienced."

Riconoscenza, a large adventure in small space, is concerned with seeing things in different and varied lights and looking back on what we've just experienced. It's a flight for the solo violin, but every so often he and, with him, his listeners pause—hovering, *tranquillo*, on long-sustained consonances (thirds, fourths, fifths, sixths), as if to consider and reconsider before moving off again. Ground level is represented by G, the violin's lowest note. At first, the pause points seem to be harmonies resting for the most part on the open strings—G, D, A, E—but soon it becomes plain that things are not as simple as that; the implied progressions defy any easy analysis. And so *Riconoscenza* becomes a challenging piece, limpid yet elusive.

The three-page score of *Riconoscenza*, which is published by Boosey & Hawkes, is satisfying and beautiful to contemplate. But—as Frederik Prausnitz observes in the introduction to his *Score and Podium*—"central to the musical experience itself is the fact that, although a qualified beholder may find beauty in a page of music, his listeners will not see that page [but] will hear it performed." (*Score and Podium*, published last year by Norton, is subtitled "A Complete Guide to Conducting"; embedded in the clear technical advice is a consistent philosophy of the way creators' musical visions are made manifest to the listening public.) Mr. Prausnitz quotes Roger Sessions's remark, "I am convinced that the performer is an essential element in the whole musical picture." Similarly, Carter, in that program-book conversation, says, "I consider the music I write as concerned with performers; the music is concerned with dramatizing the performer's activity." The performer of *Riconoscenza* was Eugene Drucker, a violinist of the Emerson Quartet. To suggest that he didn't discover all that the piece has to offer is perhaps no harsh criticism; it merely suggests a listener's eagerness to hear what other performers will make of the work. [*In August, Rolf Schulte had introduced* Riconoscenza *to America at the Monadnock Festival.*] All the same—the three printed pages are laid out before me as I write—it was hard not to feel that Mr. Drucker was simply getting through the notes and coping with the tricky metrics rather than being in full command of the composition and interpreting it.

Canon for 4 is at once musically denser and more readily charming. The charm derives in part from the play of instrumental timbres (the work lends itself to performance by a *Pierrot* ensemble) and in part from the pleasures, as in Bach's Art of Fugue, of audible contrapuntal play. In the score, the cello line is indicated as "basic form," the violin line as a retrograde inversion, the bass-clarinet line as a retrograde, and the flute line as an inversion. One can't consciously hear all that happening, through a composition 132 bars long, but—particularly in the central episode, *tranquillo*, where the rate of incident decreases and one melody at a time spins on its way through sustained harmonies—one can observe and enjoy some of the structural detail. The turning point on the bar line between measures 66 and 67 is plain: the flute runs for a few paces beside the violin and then, as it were, takes over the baton. The tempo signature, 6/8, is constant throughout—rare occurrence in a Carter score—and the pulse, dotted-quarter about 69, stays constant, too, but within the regularly marked-out course the music moves at many paces. A call to attention—a sharp short chord, a gesture from the flute—opens the work.

(Reversed—as a gesture of farewell from the violin, a final chord—ends it.) Then the four players burst forth at once, with melodies so devised that, although each has its own rhythmic shape, their lapping causes every sixteenth of each measure to be sounded, toccata-like. Initially, the players set out as two couples: flute and clarinet are in step, violin and cello play a two-part invention. Then they become individuals. Quite soon, the texture thins, the pace becomes less emphatic, and group activity turns to conversation. Dotted sixteenths appear, producing a two-against-three metrical interplay. Long notes appear, and it is beautiful to hear one instrument's quick response to another's sudden fancy. The notation avoids the mathematical intricacies of, say, the Second and Third String Quartets: there is just one septimole (each player, of course, has it in turn), in the flow of the running theme through the center point. Perusing the score is a delight in itself: I keep finding new subtleties of construction and feel I have barely touched the surface of its ingenious secrets. But more important is the way the music sounds: the product of calculation, certainly, but of joyful, lyrical calculation such as Mozart's must have been when he worked out the canons and combinations of the "Jupiter" finale. The performers were Paula Robison (flute), Virgil Blackwell (clarinet), Philip Setzer (violin), and David Finckel (cello), and I thought they played brilliantly.

Carter's picturesque Symphony of Three Orchestras, a Bicentennial commission, was given its first performance, in 1977, by the New York Philharmonic, conducted by Boulez. The work is dedicated to them. Last month and this, the Philharmonic, conducted by Zubin Mehta, revived the piece. I heard the last of the four performances. It began impressively. Although Gerard Schwarz's playing of the great trumpet flight—soaring, arching, suddenly dipping—that rises out of the shrill dawn tumult of the start is legendary, Philip Smith's solo was also impressive. Boulez and the Philharmonic (with Mr. Schwarz on first trumpet) have recorded the symphony, in a very fine performance (CBS), but the music needs space—large physical space. The three orchestras are arranged on the platform according to a careful plan. Perspectives shift. Sound answers sound. So the live Philharmonic performance offered something that a record can't. But, after the good start, it did not have the lucidity of the Boulez interpretation. The colors were bright, but the details were not sharply focussed. What should be keen and clear seemed incoherent, not precisely balanced. Returning to the record, one can hear "the tunes" again, and find that it all makes sense.

Carter performance on the highest level was heard in Cincinnati earlier this season, when Ursula Oppens and the Cincinnati Symphony, conducted by Michael Gielen, played the Piano Concerto, of 1965. It's a heroic work, violent and dramatic: a battle without quarter between ideas represented by the soloist, with her small band of supporters and sympathizers—seven other solo players— around her, and ideas represented by the rude might of the main orchestra. It's a work that engages listeners in the fight, recruits them on the soloist's side, rouses feelings of something close to hatred for what the orchestra represents. The conflict is not a simple matter of the orchestra's trying to batter the soloist into submission—though sheer brute force of sound is at times one of the weapons employed—but a subtle matter of ways of thinking and ways of behaving represented by harmonies, timbres, dynamic levels, and the shape of melodies. I had heard Miss Oppens play the concerto before (in New York in 1978, with the Philharmonic and Mr. Mehta). I had read high praise of performances in Britain given by Charles Rosen and by her. I had not before heard so stirring and cogent an account of the work as a whole, one where everything seemed to fall tellingly into place. Mr. Gielen has the ability to make hard music not easy—the Carter Piano Concerto can never be *easy* listening— but gripping, emotionally intelligible, intellectually exciting. The orchestra's stretches of sullen inertia—soft dense chords that gather like stifling fog banks—and its jabs and jeers and volleys were vividly realized. The seven soloists of the concertino were eloquent. (Phillip Ruder's violin and Thomas LeGrand's bass clarinet deserve special mention.) And Miss Oppens, in a virtuoso role calling for technical and emotional resources of the highest order, was astounding—glittering in bravura, graceful in cantilena, passionate in protest, lyrical in the long, humane recitative of the second movement, poignant in the soft, wounded bars of the close.

[*The Cincinnati performance of Carter's Piano Concerto, coupled with the Variations for Orchestra, has appeared on a New World Records disc.*]

MUSICA DA CAMERA

December 31, 1984

MERKIN HALL was pretty well full for Charles Neidich's Sunday-afternoon clarinet recital last week. He is an artist of uncommon merit—a master of his instrument and, beyond that, an interpreter who keeps listeners hanging on each phrase he utters. The recital began with the Morceau de Salon, Opus 229 (1862), of Johann Wenzel Kalliwoda, once a violinist under Weber and for many years the distinguished director of Donaueschingen's musical life. Of Kalliwoda's compositions, about several of which Schumann wrote appreciatively, the fifth Grove (1954) said, "Their day is now over," but wind players keep Opus 229 alive—there are at least three modern recordings, on clarinet or on oboe—and in the New Grove the Kalliwoda entry is twice as long as before. The Morceau de Salon—a recitative, aria, and cabaletta for a woodwind virtuoso—is a charming piece when played as Mr. Neidich played it, with the grace, the phrasing, the heady bravura, and the teasing wit that singers like Sembrich and Tetrazzini once brought to comparable vocal morceaux. There followed Schumann's Three Fantasy Pieces, which Mr. Neidich played with poetic insight and in a text that he had freed from Clara Schumann's editorial interventions. Then Carl Reinecke's program sonata *Undine*, Opus 167 (c. 1885). Reinecke is another romantic composer who has returned to favor; the list of recordings in the Schwann catalogue is surprisingly long, and contains five versions of the *Undine* sonata in its original, flute form. [*1989: Reinecke continues to flourish*

250

in Schwann's CD catalogue.] In a program note, Mr. Neidich suggested that no mere arranger but the composer himself may well have prepared the clarinet version, since it departs from the original and is beautifully written for the instrument; and by his performance he argued the case even more eloquently. The clarinet has a more varied and more moving voice than the flute's, one better suited to this tale of mystery, enchantment, love, tragedy, and final transfiguration. By comparison with, say, James Galway's swift, perfunctory performance of *Undine,* on RCA, Mr. Neidich's *Undine* was a marvel of romantic storytelling—in its ripples, its rocking, its whispers, its cries, its passages of passionate song. The soft-breathed notes at the very end were magical.

All three pieces are for clarinet and piano. The pianist was Elena Ivanina, who is Mrs. Neidich—Crimean-born and Moscow-trained. Mr. Neidich, the first Fulbright scholar to have studied in Russia, is a graduate both of Yale and, like his wife, of the Moscow Conservatory. In the Reinecke, she was rather too reticent, too much an accompanist. (The New Grove rightly praises the "Brahmsian majesty and warmth" of Reinecke's later chamber music, which calls for big, uninhibited playing.) But it was not altogether her fault. Merkin Hall's piano is a full-size, full-strength concert Steinway, and not for the first time I wished that the hall had also a smaller, beautiful instrument that could accompany singers and play in chamber music without needing to be held at half throttle. Berg's Four Pieces, Opus 5, which opened the second part of the recital, presented a more even duo—a meeting of two keen minds in one of our century's small masterpieces. Mr. Neidich played the quick, nervous phrases and touched the soft pulse tones with miraculous art. The second part was all twentieth-century. Meyer Kupferman's *Sound Spells No. 6* (1982), written for Mr. Neidich, is a duo for live clarinet and "larger-than-life" tape-recorded clarinet— an arresting dialogue, sometimes suggestive of schizophrenic musings with a doppelgänger. Edison Denisov's finely wrought Sonata for unaccompanied clarinet (1972) has two movements—the first ruminative and sad, with micro-tonal inflections, the second pipping and playful. Finally, there was Daniel Paget's *Romania!* (1979), a work that in various instrumentations, its composer told us in a program note, "has delighted audiences around the country." It's not much more than ethnic café music, exuberantly and skillfully written, but it gave the protean Mr. Neidich a chance to display yet two more of his tone colors: a low, husky murmur and high, gypsy keening.

Merkin Hall, in the Hebrew Arts School, on West Sixty-seventh Street, is not officially part of Lincoln Center, but in effect it is the intimate hall for chamber music which the Center itself lacks. Since its opening, six years ago, it has gone from strength to strength: seventy-five concerts in the first full season, 1979–80; two hundred and sixty this season. Attending concerts there has proved an unfading pleasure. Although ideally I'd like just slightly warmer acoustics—not simply true but positively flattering—I'm not complaining. Accuracy and clarity of sound, agreeable architecture, comfortable seats, excellent sight lines, sensitive lighting of the platform and the audience, and the courteous welcome from those who work there conspire to heighten enjoyment of the perfor-mances. The hall has four resident ensembles—Music Today, Musica Camerit, the Mendelssohn String Quartet, and the Hebrew Arts Concert Choir—and is the

New York home of the Boston Camerata. A few days before Mr. Neidich's recital, the Mendelssohn Quartet completed a three-concert cycle in which Schoenberg's four quartets and three of Mendelssohn's were played. The final program was Schoenberg's Third and Second, divided by Mendelssohn's Opus 44, No. 2, in E minor.

The young quartet—it made its début, in Merkin Hall, in 1981—has grown into an alert, finely tempered ensemble whose playing holds one intent on the progress of the music. The cellist, Marcy Rosen, is perhaps the strongest personality, but not in any way that unbalances the team: the sense of four well-matched but distinct characters pursuing one musical end gave the performances more interest and liveliness than those of homogenized ensembles. The players are supple. No blanket epithets for their timbre will serve, since it varies responsively to the music, from delicately dry to warmly emotional; it is never routinely sleek. Their intonation is pure, and their rhythms are athletic. Schoenberg's Third began just a shade tentatively but quickly gathered strength. Mendelssohn's E-minor—less adventurous than the A-minor, which was played in the first program, but exquisitely fashioned—was lyrical, elegant, and warm. Schoenberg's Second received the most gripping performance of all—its discourse impassioned, its tempo fluctuations beautifully judged—until the soprano soloist, Phyllis Bryn-Julson, entered. Usually so sure an artist, here she uttered "Tief ist die trauer" so loudly as to break the spell, and she seemed unable to weave her lines into the string players'. Her share of "Ich fühle luft von anderem planeten" lacked legato and remained earthbound, unecstatic.

Lincoln Center was further enriched, last month, by something that for twenty-five years was missing: a well-stocked record store open after concert time and final curtains. It's Tower Records, on the block between Alice Tully Hall and Merkin Hall, and in its bins recorded riches imported from all over the world are displayed. What the area still lacks is a comparable music and book shop. [*In 1989, I add, sadly, that Tower Records is no longer what was: the stock of rare LPs has shrunk.*]

I had not been in Wilmington, Delaware, in eight years. In 1976, I went there to hear the première of Alva Henderson's *The Last of the Mohicans,* a Bicentennial commission, given in the town's newly restored Grand Opera House. The restoration was not yet finished, but nearly enough so to show that the theatre, an eleven-hundred-seater that opened in 1871, is a highly attractive place. And it is one apt for voices overtaxed by the immense "arts centers" that make opera in many cities something different from sung drama in which almost every word is audible and every expression legible. The restoration is now complete: the foyers are handsomely frescoed; a bookshop and a restaurant lead off the lobby. By German standards, the public spaces are, admittedly, meager. (So they are in most Anglo-Saxon theatres; at Covent Garden the room that on the Continent would be the spacious grand salon is all too aptly designated the "crush bar.") But some intermission discomfort—mitigated on warm nights by the theatre's position on tree-lined, traffic-free Market Street—is a small price to pay for the intimacy and warmth of sound in the auditorium.

I returned to Wilmington this month for OperaDelaware's production of *Aida*. It is not an opera that lends itself to small-company performance. It is hard to stage in a theatre that has no flying space above the stage. But it was conducted by David Lawton, and he is a Verdian whose high merits as scholar and performer would warrant a longer expedition than that from New York to Wilmington. (In fact, it's an easy excursion, provided one doesn't mind the late hour of arrival home by Amtrak's Night Owl. The opera house is a short walk from Wilmington's railroad station.) Mr. Lawton had newly edited the score from Verdi's autograph, as he had for the *Traviata* he conducted last year in Wilmington and the *Macbeth* he conducted at Stony Brook in 1981. In a program note for *Aida* he wrote: "The changes I had to make with respect to dynamics, phrasing, and articulation alone number in the thousands. These alterations, though perhaps not immediately obvious to the listener, should result in greater clarity of texture and variety of expression, as they did in *La Traviata*." They did so in *Aida*. But more obvious to the listener were the changes of tune between Verdi's first ideas, set down in the autograph, and the revised versions found in the early printed scores. That curiously dapper little melody to which Ramfis in the second-act finale sings "Son nemici e prodi sono" once continued less squarely. Amneris once gave a dramatic scream on high A (the autograph specifies "un grido") when hearing the sentence—to be entombed alive—pronounced on Radamès by the priests. Aida's question to Radamès at the end of the Nile scene—"By what route can we avoid the army squadrons?"—once followed the contour of the first-violin line, and only later did it double the second violins and then the cellos. The familiar printed scores are not "wrong" on these points. The composer himself directed several productions of *Aida,* and it is inconceivable that he would have allowed material to circulate, through several editions, that in melodic matters did not represent his final intentions. An autograph is not always a better guide to a creator's considered text than the first edition—let alone later, corrected editions that pass under his eye. (In the coda of "Caro nome," the new critical edition of *Rigoletto* follows the autograph rather than the printed texts in a way that seems to me a shade less than convincing.) On the other hand, in the hurly-burly of the performing arts little is definitive, and—as I can attest in a modest way from my own experience as a translator—changes made to suit the caprices or capabilities of a particular interpreter sometimes get into print and stay there even though a later artist may reveal an initial idea to be more effective. At all events, it was interesting and valuable to hear these episodes of *Aida* as Verdi first wrote them. Whether to bring any of them into general use can be left to individual taste and discernment, and must depend, in part, on the singers concerned.

That the orchestral materials in common use for Verdi's operas are corrupt is not, however, in dispute. Instrumental parts were prepared in the first place by copyists who in matters of phrasing and dynamics tended to make regular what the composer may have intended as fine distinctions. Later editing produced further regularization, and conductors' added markings also found their way into some printed texts. The work was not all bad: someone has to edit what Verdi wrote and to make decisions before the parts can conveniently be set out on the stands and rehearsed. (There is plenty of "editing" in the new *Rigoletto* score, but whereas in the old scores one can't tell what's Verdi and what's not, the new editor of *Rigoletto,* Martin Chusid, has clearly distinguished his markings from the composer's.) In general, today there is a greater readiness to prize composers' discrepancies and find significance in their quiddities. One couldn't draw any instrumental conclusions from the Wilmington performance, however. The score did sound more transparent than usual; but since a much-reduced orchestration was used, that wasn't surprising: nice points of dynamic distribution in a tutti passage can hardly be judged when the lines for second oboe, second bassoon, third and fourth horns, and three of the four trombones—or, in the Amneris-Radamès interview, second oboe, English horn, bass clarinet, and two of the horns—are missing.

The singing was marked more by feeling for the music than by technical accomplishment. Although Daisy Newman, the Aida, spun some exquisite high notes, she was much of the time afflicted by tremolo. The Amneris, Janis Eckhart, had a ripe wobble. The Radamès, Lawrence Bakst, had a well-formed and unforced tenor. But he sang his phrases. As if they were punctuated. Like this. He came to full stops instead of carrying the sense through the frequent rests of the hero's line. Leland Kimball's direction drew intelligently on the published production book, in ways that clarified musical and dramatic balances. He then spoiled the effect with idiotic added inventions of his own. The opera begins with Ramfis and Radamès in mid-conversation: that the first word is "Yes" makes this plain, and the production book spells it out. In Wilmington, Ramfis advanced to address a Radamès seated at a café table, and interrupted his gaming with two vivandières and a veteran—who remained onstage to eavesdrop on the intimate exchanges that follow. The "serto trionfale" with which Amneris later invested the hero was a long daisy chain of bright paper flowers; the poor fellow had to wear it, an unheroic stole, during his triumphal scene. Aida wore a short tennis dress and, when flung to the ground in the Nile scene, strove valiantly to avoid immodest exposure. The production book says, "At the announcement of 'Radamès!' as supreme commander, some of the chorus turn to their neighbors to communicate the news; others point him out with a little gesture. . . . Well executed, the scene takes on a splendid aspect of truth." As executed with high enthusiasm by an amateur chorus, the scene was less than veristic. All in all, this *Aida* was an odd mixture of village-hall grand opera and accurate Verdian endeavor. Mr. Lawton's conducting made it worthwhile. He has a natural feeling for tempo, a grasp of the way Verdi's music moves, a command of balance between outer and inner voices which are altogether remarkable. To these virtues he adds the daring of a true dramatic conductor—the readiness to seize chances, to breathe and feel with the singers as some important moment approaches. (I can't think why the Met and the City Opera aren't competing to engage him. Have their talent scouts not attended his Verdi performances?) The Wilmington audience was enthusiastic but musically barbarous. Amneris had to launch her cry of "Ritorna vincitor!" through a storm of applause after the hanging dominant-seventh chord that closes the "Guerra!" chorus; and the coda of Aida's romanza "Ritorna vincitor!" was similarly obliterated. Will one ever hear the scene change of Act I performed as Verdi conceived it: the last note of Aida's romanza dying away as she walks into the wings; a swift open-scene transformation to the temple while the music continues unbroken; the prima donna's voice floating back, over the harps, as she herself voices the offstage priestess's invocation to mighty Fthà?

CHIVALRY

January 14, 1985

THE career of John Christian Bach—the London Bach, born in 1735, Johann Sebastian's youngest son and the eighteenth of his twenty children—links into the lives of greater composers in attractive and interesting ways. He made his name in Italy, where his first opera, *Artaserse* (Turin, 1760), starred Gaetano Guadagni—pupil of Garrick and of Handel—who two years later was Gluck's first Orpheus, in Vienna, and in 1770 introduced Gluck's opera to London in a version expanded by John Bach. Bach came to London in 1762 (three years after Handel's death), at the invitation of Colomba Maffei, the woman who ran the King's Theatre, and he died there twenty years later. The prima donna of his first London operas was Anna de Amicis, who was later Mozart's prima donna in *Lucio Silla* (Milan, 1772). Bach reset the *Silla* libretto in 1774, for Mannheim, with three of the singers who later created Mozart's *Idomeneo*. (Anton Raaff, Bach's Silla and Mozart's Idomeneus, had a decade earlier sung in Bach's Neapolitan operas.) Bach's last London opera, *La clemenza di Scipione,* had in the title role the tenor Valentin Adamberger, who later created Belmonte in Mozart's *Die Entführung*. (Both operas contain an extended soprano aria with flute, oboe, violin, and cello obbligatos.) Bach befriended the eight-year-old Mozart in London in 1764. They gave a long recital together for George III and Queen Charlotte, Mozart sitting on Bach's lap; and in the playful dedication to Mozart's Opus 3 to the Queen "Your Majesty's very humble and very obedient little servant" boasts presciently that one day "I shall become immortal like Handel . . . and my name will be as celebrated as that of Bach." Fourteen years later, Mozart was delighted to meet Bach again, in Paris. Bach had come to hear the Opéra singers—Gluck's tenor Orpheus, his Alcestis, Armida, Agamemnon— since he had been commissioned to write a work for them.

Mozart and Bach were in Paris at a time when musical fashion was divided between Gluckistes and Piccinnistes. Bach's French opera, *Amadis de Gaule,* appeared between Gluck's *Iphigénie en Tauride* (1779) and Piccinni's *Iphigénie en Tauride* (1781) and seems to have pleased nobody. According to Baron von Grimm, "the Gluckistes find that it has neither Gluck's originality nor his sublime *élan,* the Piccinnistes that the vocal lines lack Piccinni's charm and melodic variety." Yet *Amadis* is certainly a charming opera and an almost bewilderingly various one, as was revealed at its American première, given by Bel Canto Opera in the theatre of the Joan of Arc School, on West Ninety-third Street, earlier this season. Some of it is like the *galant* Bach whose "natural,

255

flowing and easy style" Leopold Mozart commended to his son in 1778, urging him to compose something that would sell instead of "all those harmonic progressions, which the majority of people cannot fathom." Some of it is like the Italianate Bach of the opera *Temistocle* (usually heard in a modern pasticcio edition that includes numbers from six of Bach's operas). Some of it sounds like Gluck imitation, some like Rameau imitation. There are also episodes to set beside the taut, startling inventions of Bach's G-minor Symphony. The mingling of manners suits the subject: the marvellous adventures of Amadis, Prince of Wales, flower of chivalry, in quest of his beloved Oriana, Princess of Great Britain. The epic, in its various incarnations, captivated readers as different as Francis I, Charles V, Ariosto, and Montaigne. It was the first of the books the Priest and the Barber spared in the holocaust of Don Quixote's library. And it provided matter for many operas. Handel's *Amadigi* is another of them.

Bach, like Gluck in *Armide* and Piccinni in *Roland,* chose to set a century-old Lully libretto. (Lully's *Amadis* was in the Opéra repertory from 1684 to 1759, and it reappeared as late as 1771, worked over by P.-M. Berton and J.-B. La Borde.) Odd procedure: rather as if, to demonstrate the increased expressiveness of modern music and to satisfy contemporary taste, Elliott Carter were to reset Verdi's *Aida* libretto, or Pierre Boulez Wagner's for *Tristan und Isolde.* (Just so, in 1868, young Constantino Dall'Argine reset Rossini's *Il barbiere* libretto, for an up-to-date Bologna public.) Lully's book was simplified and condensed for Bach's use by Alphonse de Vismes, an artillery officer, the Opéra director's brother. The first act was omitted (we plunge into the midst of things in a way confusing to listeners unfamiliar with the Amadis story), and the fourth and fifth acts were made into one: rather as if, Grimm remarked, one tried to strengthen a building by digging up the foundations and knocking off the roof. The tale as it unfolded in the Joan of Arc School was jerky and elliptical in a rather pleasantly modern way. I know not whether to credit Bach or some modern editor, for I have not seen the original score. (It was published in about 1780, and a reprint was announced in 1972, but the copy the New York Public Library ordered has not yet arrived.) *Amadis* was revived in Hamburg in 1983 (with Helen Donath as the heroine and J. Patrick Raftery as the villain, Arcalaus), and since that show lasted nearly four hours and the New York show closer to three, there was presumably some cutting. The Hamburg staging, "conceived" by Michael Beretti and executed by Marco Arturo Marelli, was, to judge by reviews, idiotic. So was the New York staging, which was directed by Mr. Beretti himself. His notion was that, as the Hamburg correspondent of *Opera* put it, "Bach and de Vismes were trying to reform tragédie lyrique and French society—decadently symbolized by the Marquis de Sade (Arcalaus) replete with whips, leathery costumes, torture, bloody sacrifices, and deviation—by proposing a people's monarch (Amadis) who would ward off the coming Revolution." The New York staging had little to do with anything perceivable in Bach's opera, and even on its own distasteful, silly terms it was ineptly executed. But the music remained, and a bilingual libretto—albeit one innocent of stage directions—was on sale. The music was fascinating to hear: a panorama of late-eighteenth-century operatic manners, a Grand Tour conducted in melodic accents now French, now Italian, now German. And everything has the deftness and grace that Mozart admired. The orchestration is inventive and captivating. Bach's long-lasting influence on Mozart has often been observed, but generally in terms of the instrumental works. His operas are worth reviving. London did *La clemenza di Scipione* in 1972 and *Adriano in Siria* in 1982. *Lucio Silla* and the *Temistocle* pasticcio have appeared as Voce albums. And Garland Publishing has a Complete Works in progress.

James Richman, the conductor of Bel Canto's *Amadis,* set apt tempi. There was a small but able orchestra. Ann Monoyios was an Oriana pure of voice and pure in style. Cynthia Miller brought passion to the heroic role of Arcabonne, her rival. Trudy Ellen Craney gave a glittering account of a coryphée's display air. The men were less satisfactory: the Amadis made little of his words, and the Arcalaus tended to bluster. The important dances were sensitively choreographed by Ann Jacoby in period style, and were danced by members of the New York Baroque Dance Company, led by Miss Jacoby and Catherine Turocy.

Last month, I heard three song recitals. Jan DeGaetani's, in Carnegie Hall, began with Duparc's "Phidylé" and included groups of songs by Tchaikovsky and Charles Ives. Beverly Morgan's, in Merkin Hall, included groups of songs by Tchaikovsky and Ives. Kurt Ollmann's, in Merkin Hall, ended with "Phidylé." The first was given by a celebrated and well-loved mezzo-soprano who made her New York début a quarter-century ago but was giving her first Carnegie Hall recital; the second by a soprano whose vivid musicianship I've admired since first I heard her, eight years ago (in Boston, in Paul Earls's *The Death of King Phillip*), and who came to new prominence last year as the heroine of Leonard Bernstein's *A Quiet Place*; and the third by a new young baritone of exceptional promise. Long years as a critic have taught me the dangers of overpraising newcomers, in eager response to fresh talent, and of underrating those whose merits have become so familiar as to be taken for granted. Nevertheless, after allowing for that I must still report that Miss DeGaetani's and Miss Morgan's recitals were somewhat disappointing, while Mr. Ollmann held his listeners intent on every song. His voice was more beautiful than theirs, but that was not the only or the main reason. It was that he gave life to the words.

All three artists subscribed to what that great American singer David Bispham called the "foreign-language fad." In *A Quaker Singer's Recollections,* Bispham wrote:

> To all American singers I say, sing your songs in well-chosen English if singing to an English-speaking audience, and sing them so that everyone understands your words; enunciate so clearly that the audience can tell even how every word is spelled. Get away from this foreign-language fad and you will find yourself nearer the heart of your public. I often quote from the fourteenth chapter of St. Paul's First Epistle to the Corinthians, where he says: "Now brethren, if I come unto you speaking with tongues, what shall I profit you? . . . Except ye utter by the tongue words easy to be understood, how shall it be known what is spoken?" And the Apostle goes on to say, "I will sing with the spirit, and I will sing with the understanding also. . . . I had rather speak five words with my understanding, that by my voice I might teach others also, than ten thousand words in an unknown tongue."

I own that, as a listener, I'm also a subscriber to the foreign-language fad—when it is a language that both I and the singer understand, and even when it is one of which I have just a few phrases, provided that the singer commands it fully. I wouldn't have wanted Oda Slobodskaya to sing her Russian songs in anything but Russian. She gloried in the language. Miss DeGaetani and Miss Morgan didn't: they pronounced it. When they got to Ives, I found Miss DeGaetani's words to be incomprehensible without the aid of the printed texts, and Miss Morgan's words, while clear, to be so oddly stressed as to recall that quaint air-hostess lingo in which auxiliary verbs carry the emphases ("until the captain *has* switched off the seat-belt sign and the plane *has* come to a complete standstill"). "Stronger comes the breeze from *the* ridge," Miss Morgan sang, and "ma-ri-gold," in Ives's "Two Little Flowers," giving equal weight and length to each syllable.

Miss DeGaetani, with Gilbert Kalish as her pianist, sang in French (a Duparc group), Russian (the Tchaikovsky group), German (a Schumann group), and English, and introduced songs written for her by Mario Davidovsky, Richard Wernick, and George Crumb. She has been an inspiration for many contemporary composers, as a singer able to compass any interval, across a very wide range, with instrumental accuracy, steadiness, and purity of tone. Wernick's "I, too..." (a setting of a poem by Charles Lee) ended with a beautiful soft-shining high note to the word "stars." She also presented an attractive Copland song, "Alone," newly rediscovered, which dates from 1922 and his time of study with Nadia Boulanger. But there was much cooing and crooning through the long evening, and few of the songs were given a sharp, individual character.

Miss Morgan's recital was marked, more disconcertingly, by a bleakness and monotony deliberately cultivated—by a stricken, tragic demeanor, both of voice and of physical presence, suggesting that all colors and all strong contrasts had faded from the world. The first half contained groups of mostly melancholy songs by Tchaikovsky, Prokofiev (his Akhmatova settings), and Rachmaninoff. Even those not intrinsically sad—such as Rachmaninoff's "How fair this spot" (once memorably recorded by Slobodskaya)—became tragic. The deadpan manner was suited to the wry comedy of the scena "Northeast Reservation Lines," which was given its first performance. It is a setting by Hayes Biggs of verses by Jane Shore that begin "Northeast Reservation Lines are busy. As soon as an agent becomes available we will connect you" and move into increasingly surrealistic variations as that message returns, returns, returns. Mark Pakman was the alert and accomplished pianist.

Mr. Ollmann's program was all-French: Rameau's cantata *Thétis,* groups of songs by Gounod and Poulenc, single songs by Albert Roussel, Louis Aubert, Jacques Leguerney, and André Caplet, Duparc's "Elégie" and "Phidylé," and, at the heart of it, a magical performance of the second book of Debussy's *Fêtes galantes.* Mr. Ollmann showed a true lieder or mélodie singer's ability to give each song its particular setting, atmosphere, character, characters—to conjure up a scene, a mood, a drama in small space. The readiest comparison is with Gérard Souzay, with whom he has studied: Mr. Ollmann has a comparable delicacy, variety and subtlety of inflection, gentleness, and beauty of timbre. His French was flawless; words and music lived together. For some of the songs, I thought, he chose needlessly low keys: his baritone flowered freely in the upper reaches. It was not surprising to learn that La Scala has invited him to sing Pelléas. A program calling for precise, poetic understatement gave no idea what he might make of a forceful, overtly dramatic ballad such as, say, Walter Damrosch's "Danny Deever." (It comes to mind because David Bispham, in 1906, recorded it so vividly; the disc has been reissued by New World Records.) Michael Pisani was a supple, responsive pianist and partner.

MELODIOUS WINDS HAVE BIRTH

February 18, 1985

THE Winds of Parnassus blew featly, neatly, fleetly, sweetly through Alice Tully Hall at their inaugural concert this month. Parnassus has ever been an ensemble renowned for the strength and virtue of its wind sections. For New World it has recorded Charles Wuorinen's *The Winds* (eight winds and piano). Its CRI record of works by Milton Babbitt, Donald Martino, and Anthony Korf is entitled "Music for Winds." It has given noble performances of Stravinsky's Symphonies of Wind Instruments and of Varèse's *Octandre* and *Intégrales*. Twelve Parnassus players and seven assisting artists came together to form the new Winds of Parnassus. They played Mozart, Dvořák, Stravinsky, and Wuorinen.

The Mozart was the B-flat Serenade, K. 361, a long work but a bewitching one when done as deftly and lovingly as it was here. Often it sounds chunky, even lumpy; the Parnassus players moved through its varied patterns with the grace, the poise, the courtesy of Balanchine dancers. Special praise to the first oboe (Stephen Taylor), the first clarinet (Charles Neidich), the basset horns (Dennis Smylie and Marjorie O'Brien), and the first bassoon (Steven Dibner); praise to all for balance and elegant ensemble interplay as now one soloist or couple, now another came forward to lead the lovely dance.

The Dvořák was a nonet arrangement—pairs of oboes, clarinets, bassoons, and horns over a string bass—of three of his Slavonic Dances. They acquired a Janáček-like tang in this garb (Janáček's *Mládí* is a work for the Winds of Parnassus to take up) and were done with lilting, happy enthusiasm. The Stravinsky was the neoclassical Octet, of 1923. Trumpets and trombones made their only appearance of the evening—joined by flute, clarinet, and a pair of bassoons. The sounds were exquisite. Sonority, Stravinsky said, was not his first concern here, but this account of the Octet demonstrated his inability to set down a note in the wrong place. The performance was intelligent and winning; it had both grandeur and charm. The Wuorinen was a première, a Concertino newly composed for the Winds of Parnassus. It is for fifteen players (the thirteen of Mozart's Serenade plus two flutes) and lasts about fifteen minutes. The first half or so proved arresting in a neo-Stravinskian manner; as the music moved to a slower gait, became chordal, then blurting, its hold on a listener slackened.

Inspiration seemed to have flagged. But it ended with a memorable, Berliozian sound—a B blown out across seven octaves.

All these pieces—every beat of them, sometimes needlessly—were conducted by Mr. Korf, the founder and music director of Parnassus and now of its Winds. By Parnassus performances and Parnassus commissions he has put New York and the musical world in his debt. He has gathered some of the most brilliant players in the country and forged them into an ensemble. He has championed composers—Babbitt, Wuorinen, Varèse, Stefan Wolpe—whose works need virtuoso performance and has interpreted them with passion and precision.

Prism, a chamber orchestra founded and conducted by Robert Black, gave its first concert in March last year and introduced Jean Barraqué's *Chant après chant* to New York [see pp. 133–36]. At its second concert, in December in Symphony Space, Prism introduced to America Barraqué's Concerto. After *Chant après chant* and after Mr. Black's performance in 1982 of Barraqué's towering Piano Sonata (*Musical Events: 1980–1983,* pp. 246–48), I wrote of my conviction that Barraqué (who died in 1973, aged forty-five) is a giant of that exciting period—the postwar fifties and sixties—when waves of discovery and invention flooded Europe's concert halls. He was not particularly prominent then; unlike Pierre Boulez and Karlheinz Stockhausen—former Messiaen students, as Barraqué was—he headed no fashionable movements, signed no dashing manifestos. Discovery of his stature came—is still coming—slowly. Performances are few. For the last eighteen years of his life, he worked at a series of pieces related to Hermann Broch's extraordinary book *The Death of Virgil. Chant après chant* is one of them. But the Concerto, his last completed composition, which had its first performance in London in 1968, has no evident links with *The Death of Virgil* except in being—as the composer put it—"a work that casts its gaze upon another work." It is a long (thirty-five-minute), taxing, spellbinding composition—difficult to describe, difficult to analyze, absorbing to listen to. The critic and composer André Hodeir, an ardent champion of Barraqué, has declared that "in the works of Barraqué, music may well have attained the world of utter strangeness which was partly glimpsed by Beethoven in his last quartets, by Debussy in *La Mer,* and by Berg in *Wozzeck*—a world in which musical form as such remains entirely submerged in the music, defying any attempt at analysis."

The Concerto has two principal soloists, clarinet and vibraphone, who are surrounded by an ensemble of eighteen players grouped into six trios: violin, bassoon, and trumpet; viola, English horn, and trombone; cello, alto flute, and tenor saxophone; harp, bass clarinet, and baritone saxophone; harpsichord, oboe, and horn; guitar, flute, and alto saxophone. Each trio thus has a stringed, a woodwind, and (reckoning the saxophones as brass) a brass instrument. Violin and English horn also have important solo episodes. Each mixed trio has its special character, and other trios are drawn from the company. The Concerto begins with a brief, trenchant violin solo, continues as a string trio (violin, viola, and cello), and then as a harp, harpsichord, and guitar trio. The clarinet makes just four brief—and commanding, very dramatic—appearances in the first third of the work, before coming forward as the principal soloist. The vibraphone enters only two-thirds of the way through. I don't understand the logic of this unconventional structure, and simply report that I found the journey through it to be a stirring and beautiful adventure filled with marvellous events—the clarinet's unaccompanied flights, a long clarinet and vibraphone passage, a passionate English-horn solo.

Jean Kopperud was a bold and brilliant clarinet soloist. Daniel Druckman's vibraphone playing was poetic. Ronald Oakland (violin), Jennifer Graham (English horn), and Chris Finckel (cello) made eloquent contributions. Mr. Black had assembled a sensitive, expert band, and he conducted an inspired, dedicated performance.

Milton Babbitt's latest work to appear, Composition for Guitar, had its world première—followed by its world deuxième—last month at a Speculum Musicae concert in Columbia University's McMillin Theatre. It is an eight-minute stretch of animated, attractive music, composed for and dedicated to David Starobin, who has done so much to enrich the modern guitar repertory. His performances of the piece were at once incisive and poetic; I would happily have listened to it yet again. [*I've now done so. Composition for Guitar was recorded, by Mr. Starobin, on Bridge.*] The program, all Babbitt, began with *Phonemena,* done first in its version for soprano and piano (1969) and then in the version for soprano and synthesized tape (1975). This is a captivating scena, the text an assemblage of English phonemes, or small sound units of speech. (Twenty-four consonant and twelve vowel sounds are employed.) They were chosen, the composer says in a program note, "for such acoustical properties as formant frequencies, envelopes, and durations," but they sound like poetry in a lively, expressive language that one happens not to understand. Judith Bettina was a brilliant soloist—alluring, witty cabaret artist and virtuoso soprano in one. It was interesting to hear the two versions in succession. In the first, Miss Bettina was a star supported by a deft accompanist, Aleck Karis; in the second, she had to fit the tape, to be an element in a strictly plotted ensemble—a creature that moves in determinate grooves, in fact not a bus but a tram.

The interplay of live soloist and prerecorded tape has fascinated many composers. Babbitt's *Images,* for saxophone and synthesized tape, first played in 1979 by Harvey Pittel, reappeared at this concert, with John Sampen as soloist. The medium did not inhibit him. The composer in a program note spoke of "multiple musical mutualities between what issues from the loudspeakers and what emanates from the performer's instrument, particularly the complementary parallelisms of transformation between temporally proximate events produced by the different media"; in less precise language, one might liken the soloist to a poet advancing through dreamscapes spun from the loudspeakers—pausing, pondering, and then, like another Orpheus, singing commentary so eloquent that at his strains the trees, mountaintops, billows move into new patterns. The program included the Second String Quartet (1952) and ended with the Composition for Twelve Instruments (composed in 1948 and revised in 1954), which is Babbitt in the pointillistic vein—pips, plinks, and pops, with never a lyrical line, never a tune—that eludes my ear.

*   *   *

The New Music Consort's January program, given in the Borden Auditorium of the Manhattan School of Music, where the Consort is in residence, included two local premières—one by a young Mexican musician, the other by a young Cuban musician, both of whom now live here. Juan Carlos Arean's *Musica para un tercer otono* is a brief trio (flute, clarinet, and guitar) that started attractively enough but outstayed its welcome during the wind-down of its closing pages. Tania Leon's *Momentum,* a piano solo—it was played by Martin Goldray— revealed a pleasantly determined and accomplished personality. The concert began with a glittering account of Luciano Berio's *Sequenza V,* for solo trombone. Leonard Krech was the player, and he demonstrated—as Miss Bettina had in Babbitt's *Phonemena*—how much more vividly a work comes across when the performer has it by heart. Oliver Knussen's *Hums and Songs of Winnie-the-Pooh* were prettily sung by Daniela Sikora, with Robert Black conducting the small ensemble (unaccountably, he left a long gap after the colon of "And as he climbed he sang a little song to himself, and it went like this:"). The concert ended with Elliott Carter's Double Concerto, Ursula Oppens the harpsichordist, Mr. Goldray the pianist, and Claire Heldrich the conductor. The performance was trim and spirited, but it was hard to enjoy it very much: the Borden stage is too small to allow separation of the two orchestras, and the harpsichord tone—electrically amplified to a point where it drowned everything else—was revolting.

Larry Bell's Second String Quartet was given its first performance, this month, by the Columbia String Quartet (Benjamin Hudson, Carol Zeavin, Sarah Clarke, Eric Bartlett), in the hall of St. Michael's Church, on West Ninety-ninth Street. It is a fourteen-minute work in three movements: a scherzo that becomes an adagio, a central lament that encloses a rather bitter serenade, and an adagio that becomes a scherzo. It is elegantly and thoroughly composed, and dramatic in its progress. Some of the gestures of passionate grief it makes struck me as being a shade conventional. The program ended with Brahms's C-minor Quartet, which was ardently played—albeit in the modern manner, without the touches of expressive portamento which players of Brahms's day employed. St. Michael's Hall is a good chamber for chamber music—intimate but not squashy, warm in sound.

A Long Pull to Get There

February 25, 1985

GERSHWIN's *Porgy and Bess* opened at the Metropolitan Opera this month, half a century after its first performances, in Boston and then on Broadway. If Otto Kahn had not died in 1934, the Met might have created the work. Kahn had approached Jerome Kern, Irving Berlin, and Gershwin about composing for the

Met; his fellow-directors there had less enthusiasm for a "jazz" opera. (The first *Porgy and Bess* records, however, were made by Met singers, Lawrence Tibbett and Helen Jepson, in 1935, and are reissued on a Victrola disc along with *Porgy* excerpts by Eleanor Steber, Risë Stevens, and Robert Merrill.) There are other ifs in *Porgy* history: if plans for a Jerome Kern and Oscar Hammerstein musical with Al Jolson as Porgy had not fallen through, Gershwin's opera might not have been written. On Broadway, the opera had only 124 performances, and so it was counted a failure; the backers lost their investment. The success came after Gershwin's death. *Porgy and Bess* arrives at the Met not as a novelty but as a classic that many opera houses have mounted. Glyndebourne stages it next year.

The Met production, which ran for nearly four hours on the first night, was not altogether an unmixed delight. It raised old questions about the work which I thought had been laid to rest for me in a buoyant, stylish, and totally enjoyable performance by the Indiana University Opera Theatre five years ago [*Music of Three More Seasons*, pp. 534–35]—questions about the merit of both the score and the subject. Gershwin aimed high. Talking to the *Herald Tribune* about *Porgy and Bess* in 1934, he said, "If I am successful, it will resemble a combination of the drama and romance of *Carmen* and the beauty of *Meistersinger*, if you can imagine that. I believe it will be something never done before." The *Carmen* analogies are obvious. *Die Meistersinger* doubtless suggested community hymn singing (here spirituals, not Lutheran chorales), the choral fugue for the quarrel, and perhaps the street cries. There is also something of *Louise* in the work, some influence from Berg's *Wozzeck*, an opera Gershwin much admired, and some influence—as the Gershwin scholar Wayne Shirley has pointed out—from *Der Rosenkavalier*. Good models. Received wisdom about *Porgy and Bess* declares that it contains excellent songs and duets connected by stretches of recitative and instrumental interludes of markedly lower quality. Between 1935 and 1976—in which year a complete London recording appeared, with Willard White and Leona Mitchell in the title roles, and the Houston Grand Opera staged a full production that later came to Broadway for fifteen weeks and was recorded by RCA, with Donnie Ray Albert and Clamma Dale—*Porgy and Bess* was revived in abridged versions from which much of the connecting matter had been removed. Back in 1935, Virgil Thomson wrote that "Gershwin has not and never did have the power of sustained musical development." In 1976, David Hamilton, reviewing the complete London recording, wrote:

> In much of the scene music, there isn't any consistent idea of how to get from one place to another, except to write lots of music, and ambitious-sounding music, at that. But the musical development is consistently short-breathed, undercutting both the ambition and the need to fill large spaces of time. Much of it isn't really very good: The Hindemithy fugue to which Porgy kills Crown [a reprise of the choral fugue to which Crown kills Robbins] is quite dreadful, scholastic and meaningless. The problem of what kind of musical fabric would best surround, connect, and set off these wonderful songs has not really been faced.

But Gershwin did, I think, face the problem, although he failed to solve it. If his "in-between" passages are feeble, it is not for lack of care and effort on his part. I spent a fascinating day last week poring over the *Porgy and Bess* sketches now in the Library of Congress. In them one can discover not only the famous tunes moving through draft versions to their definitive forms but also many studies for the music that links the numbers: development passages, contrapuntal essays, thematic transformations and conjunctions, harmonic experiments. Melodies are written out in inversion, in retrograde, in retrograde inversion. Motifs are tabled. Such preliminary toil, of course, affords no guarantee that good music will result. Received wisdom is not wrong. But it is at least plain that Gershwin did not simply write inspired songs and then join them up with musical Scotch tape. His goal was a through-composed and thoroughly composed grand opera, a *Wozzeck* in an American idiom. That he did not achieve it—and that *Porgy and Bess* has succeeded most often when reduced to a ballad opera—is due partly to his lack of technical command; partly to the nature of his musical material, its frequent unaptness to the kinds of procedure through which he puts it; and partly to the "book."

Linking the first and second points, Mr. Thomson wrote that Gershwin's "lack of understanding of all the major problems of form, of continuity, and of straightforward musical expression, is not surprising in view of the impurity of his musical sources and his frank acceptance of them." (Those impure sources are devastatingly described as "at best . . . a piquant but highly unsavory stirring-up-together of Israel, Africa, and the Gaelic Isles.") About the libretto, separate points—sociological and dramaturgical—need making. It derives from the play *Porgy*, by Dorothy Heyward and DuBose Heyward, which the Theatre Guild staged with success in 1927. And the play derives from DuBose Heyward's novel *Porgy* (1925), an evocation of Charleston black scenes that he knew well—"my own white man's conception of a summer of aspiration, devotion, and heartbreak across the colour wall," as he put it in a preface to the play. The novel begins: "Porgy lived in the Golden Age. Not the Golden Age of a remote and legendary past; nor yet the chimerical era treasured by every man past middle life, that never existed except in the heart of youth; but an age when men, not yet old, were boys in an ancient, beautiful city that time had forgotten before it destroyed." Heyward envies the Negroes, he says; and he seems to envy them simplicity, naturalness, the ability to sing away their cares. Credulity, fecklessness, gullibility are found charming. *Porgy* is affectionate, and not patronizing by intention, but some things about it give one pause. From the start, Gershwin's opera has inevitably aroused a certain uneasiness in both blacks and whites—and in both performers and spectators. Duke Ellington scorned Gershwin's "lampblack Negroisms." Douglas Watt, reviewing the London album in these columns, noted that it is "hard to find trained black singers willing to immerse themselves, with what must amount to almost atavistic abandon, in a white man's version of black folkways and characterizations from which their race has so painfully fought to escape." It's a tricky matter. Maybe it is enough to conclude that when a black cast today is prepared to throw itself heart and soul into the work, white spectators should simply forget their scruples and enjoy the show. The Met has expunged the word "nigger" from the libretto.

The dramaturgical side is easier to discuss. *Porgy* the play already included a deal of music; when, for the opera, Heyward added songs (the lyrics for some of them written by Ira Gershwin) and devised ensembles, he broke the dramatic narrative into what can seem like a succession of loosely connected genre scenes. There are stretches of *Porgy and Bess* that bump from episode to episode, from number to number. It is a perfectly good dramatic technique when deliberately employed, but it seems like clumsiness in a work evidently intended for straight-line, veristic presentation.

Any simple, unquestioning surrender to *Porgy and Bess* was made difficult at the Met by the less than convincing presentation of the two principal roles. On Simon Estes, the Porgy, judgment must be reserved. At the dress rehearsal, he had dislocated his right knee, and on the first night he sang the part resting on his left knee with his right leg stretched out straight before him. It is an uncomfortable and soon becomes a painful posture, and so one can hardly blame Mr. Estes for not enacting the role or giving it much expression. Heyward envisaged Bess as "a gaunt, tragic figure," and in the play she is described as "slender, but sinewy; very black, wide nostrils, and large, but well-formed, mouth. She flaunts a typical, but debased, Negro beauty." However, the first Bess of the opera, Anne Brown, was (to judge from photographs) slender, attractive, and of distinguished appearance. She was only twenty, and so she had to don years for the role. ("Dat girl's thirty if she's a day!") So did my first Bess, Leontyne Price, who was twenty-five when I saw her. (Miss Price made beautiful *Porgy* recordings, now reissued on RCA; John W. Bubbles, as in 1935, is the Sportin' Life.) Grace Bumbry, the Met interpreter, looked rather mature for the part, and short, tight-fitting dresses did not flatter her. Still, we have seen affecting Butterflys who plainly carried more than fifteen years, and matronly Mimìs who were nevertheless moving. The trouble was more that Miss Bumbry played not so much Bess as a world-famous diva attacking the role with undisciplined, even vulgar, relish. She didn't suggest the sort of person who would naturally say, "Porgy, I's yo' woman now, I is!" She did, however, sing the notes securely.

Otherwise, the cast was pretty strong. Gregg Baker, the Crown, was Heyward's "huge Negro of magnificent physique," and he sang vigorously. Bruce Hubbard, the Jake, sang even better, resisting the temptation (to which many others succumbed) of oversinging—pushing—in an endeavor to fill the enormous auditorium. Myra Merritt, the Clara, began a shade thinly but then improved, and she has the "sweet, wistful face" Heyward asked for. Florence Quivar's Serena was admirable. Charles Williams's Sportin' Life was spry. There were many new faces and voices on the stage, and there was a large new chorus, which made a fresh, full, and lively sound. (The Gershwin estate insists on an all-black cast in American performances of the opera.) Nathaniel Merrill's production was a routine affair, neither punchy nor poignant. Robert O'Hearn's design for Catfish Row was traditional but carried little suggestion that the tenement court had grown up in what was "in Colonial days one of the finest buildings of the aristocracy." His set for Serena's room was very awkward—the people huddled together as if packed on a narrow shelf. The style veered between stock verismo and—in the dances, done by a gleaming, long-limbed ensemble from Dance Theatre of Harlem, and in Sportin' Life's songs—show numbers. James Levine's conducting was at once energetic, heavy, and bland. By comparison with the youthful Indiana presentation, everything seemed rather heavy and overblown. Perhaps in the Met that's inevitable.

After Indiana, I wrote that "the genre scenes built into a coherent whole; the threads of personal tragedy ran through them unbroken; the sense of a linked community and of the individual sufferings and solaces of those within it was vividly conveyed." And also that "the more of the score that is done the better." I can't say as much after the Met production. It seemed badly in need of cutting—though perhaps all it needs is a lighter, keener, more imaginative touch in the execution. If, on the other hand, the Met feels like *adding*, there's a scene for Bess and Serena, in Act III, that has never been staged. It needs orchestration. Mr. Shirley found it in Gershwin's pencil short score of the opera, which is also in the Library of Congress (as is the autograph full score, some of whose readings should be used to correct what is generally performed). He described it in the summer 1981 issue of the Library's *Quarterly Journal,* which includes a recording of the scene, given with piano accompaniment. It provides Bess with a solo ("Oh let me be, Serena, can't you see I's changed? ... I's done with yesterday an' I got a new tomorrow"), which otherwise the heroine lacks, and it closes with a duet, "Lonesome boy," which the two women sing tenderly over Clara's orphan baby.

THE SILVER ANSWER RANG

March 4, 1985

ONE of the warmest receptions for a new work I've heard in a long while greeted the New York première of Dominick Argento's song cycle *Casa Guidi,* in Carnegie Hall last month, sung by Frederica von Stade and played by the Minnesota Orchestra, conducted by Neville Marriner. *Casa Guidi* is an attractive piece, and it was beautifully performed. Argento has a gift for finding unusual and thoroughly musicable texts—as in his cycles *Letters from Composers* (1968), for tenor and guitar, and *From the Diary of Virginia Woolf* (1975), for medium voice (Janet Baker's in the first performance) and piano. The text of *Casa Guidi* is drawn from letters that Elizabeth Barrett Browning, in Florence, sent to her sister Henrietta. Mrs. Browning wrote good letters. They were—as another of her correspondents, Mrs. David Ogilvy, noted in a memoir—"written in minute scratches no thicker than the hairs on a daisy stalk, on tiny note sheets, folded sometimes into tiny envelopes, the whole forming apparently a doll's epistle. But if the writing was thin, the thoughts and feelings were stout and strong." Argento has in five songs made music for stout and strong thoughts and feelings: about the Brownings' Casa Guidi apartment (which literary visitors to Florence still enter with emotion); about friendly argument between Wilson, the North Country maid Mrs. Browning brought to Italy with her, and the cook Alessandro (whom Mrs. Ogilvy described as "a fantastic old fellow"); about Robert, movingly ("It is strange that anyone so brilliant should love *me,* but true and strange it is. ... Here am I, in the seventh year of marriage, happier than on the seventh day!"); about Mr. Barrett's death:

Occupation is the only thing to keep one on one's feet a little while, that I know well. Only it is hard sometimes to force oneself into occupation . . . there's—the hardness. I take up books—but my heart goes walking up and down constantly through that house of Wimpole Street, till it is tired, tired, tired. The truth is, I am made of paper, and it tears me.

And, finally, about quiet-glowing domestic happiness and the gently conflicting, soon reconciled loving claims of husband and child. Argento has deftly, unobtrusively shaped the prose into lines and stanzas. The vocal part is a supple flow of full, thematic melody shading into and out of arioso and recitative. The harmonic language recalls Britten's extended diatonicism. The start of the fourth song, "The Death of Mr. Barrett," is even a paraphrase of the dawn scene in *Peter Grimes*—the same repeated high E's with the F-natural grace note, a vocal entry of similar melodic contour, the same A-major harmony welling beneath the A-minor high above. The orchestration is warm, tender, sensitive: at times the bells of Florence are heard sounding outside. *Casa Guidi* draws listeners surely into the Anglo-Florentine idyll—a felicity not mindless but active, intelligent, and creative. The music rings true with the woman whom one loves from her letters and her poetry. The cycle compasses her capacity for delight, her quick observations, her sense of humor. Argento's music both paints the scenes and paints the woman Mrs. Ogilvy described:

> The full silky curls falling round her face like a spaniel's ears, the same pathetic wistfulness of expression. Her mouth was too large for beauty, but full of eloquent curves and movements. Her voice was very expressive, her manner gentle but full of energy. At times she became intense in tone and gesture [Argento's cycle shows it], but it was so spontaneous, that nobody could ever have thought it assumed.

Casa Guidi, first performed, in Minneapolis, in 1983, was written for Miss von Stade, and it matches her direct, sincere art as exactly as the Virginia Woolf cycle matched Dame Janet's. The best song composers compose not just with notes but with scenes, literary resonances, and particular interpreters in mind.

Two days later, the Chamber Orchestra of Europe, conducted by Claudio Abbado, visited Carnegie Hall. The orchestra, nearly fifty strong, was founded four years ago by veterans of the European Community Youth Orchestra who had reached retirement age—twenty-three—and wished to keep together. Its history has been a swift success story of international tours, festival appearances (in Pesaro, Rossini's *Donna del lago* and *Viaggio a Reims*), and recordings. The personnel is international—more than half the players are British—and the average age is now about twenty-five. The Carnegie concert displayed the young orchestra's prowess in music of three centuries. It began with Brahms's first orchestra piece, the D-major Serenade, which was freshly and buoyantly played and gracefully shaped. Then came György Ligeti's *Ramifications* (1969), for strings divided into two groups, one group tuned slightly over a quarter-tone sharp, at A = 453. The composer has likened the work to lianas twining through clockwork in motion and has also called it "an example of decadent art," with harmonies that "smell high." It is a brief essay in sonorities—in blurred, unsettling sounds. *Ramifications* had a vogue for a while; there have been at least four recordings. Today, it seems more a careful experiment of the past, carried out by a subtle and scrupulous creator, than a lasting work of art. Among Ligeti's compositions of the time, *Lontano* and the Chamber Concerto have a stronger claim on the modern repertory. But maybe *Ramifications* is a better piece than I thought it: the Carnegie audience, both restless and bronchial, added unwanted noises to the score which hampered nine minutes of intent, close listening.

A vocal soloist, Hildegard Behrens, then joined the orchestra to sing Beethoven's "Ah, perfido!" and three of Mahler's *Des Knaben Wunderhorn* songs—the three Mahler conducted in Vienna in 1900, with Selma Kurz as soloist. The Beethoven was presented in the fearless, candidly passionate manner that brings life to everything Miss Behrens does. It was even a little too bright, a shade too fierce for an eighteenth-century scena; it was delivered in accents and tones that suggested Leonore rather than Metastasio's Deidamia. It was an exciting performance, if not a classically poised one. In the first Mahler song, "Wer hat dies Liedlein erdacht," Miss Behrens's voice did not flow easily through the lilting, innocent roulades. But the other songs, "Das irdische Leben" and "Wo die schönen Trompeten blasen," were magical. Singer, conductor, and players conspired to cast the spell that makes the *Wunderhorn* songs one of music's marvels—scenes that stir in a listener the responses to history, to literature, to nature which were Mahler's; scenes executed not at length or with bombast but in keen, small strokes that cut deep. "Das irdische Leben" chimed with what we read of hunger and starvation in the world today. "Wo die schönen Trompeten blasen" must have filled even the most materialist listener with a sense of tender awe. There were no texts in the program book, and Miss Behrens sang the songs in German; they can have made their full effect only on those who knew that language. But her timbres and timing and those of the players were in themselves enough to hush the hall into rapt attentiveness. In an age when just about every conductor is ready to turn his hand to Mahler's music, and workaday performances rub off its bloom, Mr. Abbado is a conductor who reveals afresh its strangeness, its poetry, its beauty.

There followed a performance of Mozart's "Posthorn" Symphony—three movements drawn from the "Posthorn" Serenade—which was exquisitely formed and was filled with delightful detail. This ended the announced program. The audience showed no wish to get up and go, and was accorded two encores: the Scherzo of Mendelssohn's *Midsummer Night's Dream* music and Rossini's *Scala di seta* Overture, both of them in fine-grained performances. It would happily have listened to more, but Mr. Abbado at last signalled to his players to follow him off.

The *Times,* in an account of a Philharmonic December concert, reported that "fully a third of the audience stampeded from Avery Fisher Hall before the program's final piece"—the Three Fragments from *Wozzeck* which Alban Berg extracted from his opera for concert use. The Philharmonic is honoring Berg's centenary this season, and in February, two days before his hundredth birthday, it gave his Seven Early Songs (composed in 1905–08, with piano accompaniment, and orchestrated in 1928) and his Five Orchestral Songs to Picture-Postcard

Texts by Peter Altenberg (1912). The soloist was Jessye Norman. There was no stampede. There was even excessive applause, I thought, after the earlier cycle, for although Miss Norman sang it with richly sounded notes, she seemed reluctant to join those notes into eloquent phrases. She is a disconcertingly unpredictable performer: majestic of presence, majestic of voice, sometimes thrilling, sometimes sluggish and stately as if she were "editing" each individual note before preparing to form the next one. I remember when I first heard her, at the Spoleto Festival fifteen years ago, and reported on a young singer (she was twenty-four) who—in Wagner's Wesendonk songs and in Mahler—poured out warm, generous, full-toned sound with an ease to prompt memories of Kirsten Flagstad. She has gained in grandeur since then but has lost spontaneity, swiftness of response, urgency. Or so it seems much of the time. Not always: her heroic Dido at the Met, in Berlioz's *Les Troyens,* moved from regal dignity to quick, raw passion in the death scene, and at the Philharmonic concert, after merely voicing the early Berg songs (in splendid tones), she gave a sensitive, beautifully shaped account of the Altenberg cycle, creating the atmospheres and rendering the images accurately and vividly.

The Berg songs were framed between Mozart's first and last symphonies, which share a four-note figure (do-re-fa-mi—schoolboy mnemonic for the keys of Brahms's four symphonies) that runs through much of Mozart's music. The humdrum account that Zubin Mehta, who was conducting, gave of K. 16 offered little inducement to hear what he might make of the "Jupiter," K. 551, and I joined in a small stampede that took place after the Altenberg songs.

LIGHT

March 11, 1985

ANDREW LLOYD WEBBER's Requiem—already available on an Angel record—had its public première last month in St. Thomas, that large, fashionable Episcopalian church on Fifth Avenue known for its music. (It is apparently the only church outside Europe to maintain a resident choir school.) The performance was given for the benefit of the Holy Apostles Soup Kitchen. It was a grand affair. The boys and men of the St. Thomas Choir were joined by those of Winchester Cathedral, brought over for the occasion. The soloists were Paul Miles-Kingston, a Winchester treble; Sarah Brightman, ex-*Cats;* and Placido Domingo. Lorin Maazel conducted the Orchestra of St. Luke's—an orchestra that has come to the forefront of New York's musical life. (The day before, it had been playing Handel's *Semele* in Carnegie Hall.) Television was there: at the start of the show, Humphrey Burton instructed the audience in how to comport itself before cameras and not disturb the taping; on Good Friday, PBS brings the Requiem to the nation in its Great Performances series.

The composer of *Joseph and the Amazing Technicolor Dreamcoat, Jesus Christ Superstar, Evita, Cats,* and other successful shows describes the Requiem (in a note accompanying the record) as "the most personal of all my compositions." The BBC, he says, invited him in 1978 to write a Requiem for Northern Ireland, but he was too busy then to undertake it. Some years later, three events moved him to the composition. His father died, and the Requiem is dedicated to him. (William Lloyd Webber was an honorable minor composer and a man respected and liked by all who knew him. When he was secretary of the Royal College of Organists and I edited *The Musical Times,* which publishes RCO news, he told me that his boys showed musical promise. Andrew's brother Julian is now a well-known cellist.) A journalist who had recently interviewed Andrew Lloyd Webber was killed by the bomb that the IRA set outside Harrods. And a *Times* account of a young Cambodian boy who had to decide whether or not to kill his sister, who had been horribly mutilated, seared the composer. His Requiem is not exactly a distinguished piece of music, but it is a "felt" work and an honest one. The effects are obvious, but they are effective. Lloyd Webber—as the success of his theatre pieces attests—has a flair for lyric invention, for tunes that catch. The Requiem begins with a motif—a falling E-B-E motto—that moves into a well-devised theme. He is not a composer on a grand scale; he thinks of a tune and then plugs it. The Recordare is built in this way. So is the Hosanna, whose tricky rhythms and brash orchestration come closest to the manner of the shows. So is the Pie Jesu, a melody of sentiment sung by the soprano, by the soprano and the treble, by the chorus, then by the soprano and the treble again. This is unchallenging music—unless the challenge is to a listener to set aside any ideas of development, difficulty, and such subtlety as informs the varied repetitions of the Agnus Dei in Verdi's Requiem. The "Mors stupebit" tercet of the Dies Irae is declaimed by the boy, unaccompanied. "Confutatis maledictis" is a brutal march. At the end of the piece, a series of fierce organ chords smashes into the boy's singing of "et lux perpetua luceat eis." As they die away, he, alone illuminated in the darkling church, is still heard singing "perpetua, perpetua . . ." to the initial motif. The orchestra, with precedent from movements of the Brahms and Fauré Requiems, is violinless, and the scoring is functional rather than striking.

The performance was excellent. Master Miles-Kingston has a sweet, slightly breathy treble and is of exquisite appearance. Miss Brightman has a natural, steady production and a fine way of placing words on an unforced stream of tone. She sounded better in the church's warm acoustics than she does on the record. Mr. Domingo poured out big, brave, opulent sound in his familiar manner. The Requiem lasted forty-seven minutes. Before it, the Winchester Choir, conducted by Martin Neary, gave a polished—an almost overpolished—virtuoso account of Purcell's "Jehovah, quam multi sunt" and "Hear my prayer," and the St. Thomas Choir, conducted by Gerre Hancock, a buoyant, if slightly soft-focus, account of Bach's "Singet dem Herrn."

Earlier in the day, Pomerium Musices had made music on a very different scale, in the Music Before 1800 series in Corpus Christi Church. There were five singers: Marcella Calabi and Kathy Theil, sopranos; Patrick Romano, tenor; and Alexander Blachly and Peter Stewart, basses. The music was fourteenth-century

Italian. Each part of the program began with a plainchant transcribed from the glowing pages at a Florentine gradual on display at the Morgan Library last month. What followed was sometimes sacred, more often secular. (It was almost unseemly to hear two young men, standing before the altar, sing gleefully of a day on which, hidden among the bushes, they watched naked girls—some redheads and some blondes—bathing.) One or two pieces, I thought, were taken rather too slowly, but all were sung with a distinctness and purity of pitch and a rhythmic alertness that gave delight in the play of voice against voice, in both the vertical and the horizontal aspects. "Fresh, luminous polyphony" was Gustave Reese's phrase for Italy's fourteenth-century music. The concert rose to grandeur with Marchetto of Padua's motet written, probably, for the Scrovegni Chapel, with its Giotto frescoes.

Dominick Argento's *Postcard from Morocco* (1971) was revived last month at the Juilliard American Opera Center. It's a long one-acter—ninety minutes—for seven singers, two mimes, and eight players. The characters are gathered in "the railway station of Morocco or some place, hot and strange, like the interior of a glass-covered pavilion or spa." The band, in costume, plays behind a screen of cardboard ferns. It might be the start of an Agatha Christie story. Instead, the action proceeds as a surreal drift of dreams, encounters, confrontations, confidences. Each of the characters clings protectively to a suitcase or box, holding some cherished or feared part of his personality. Most of them play more than one role: a little hatmaker has a passage of transfiguration as a sultry cabaret star; a nervous spinster and a shabby old man become the juvenile leads of a romantic operetta. There is boasting and prying; there are episodes of cruelty, others of companionship and comfort. At last, one of the boxes—belonging to Mr. Owen, who emerges as the protagonist—is forced open, and it proves to be empty. But Mr. Owen summons the ship of his dreams, and on it he sails out for adventure. John Donahue's libretto is a moving and skillful piece of work. Argento's score is eclectic in manner—Stravinsky, Schoenberg, and Britten are brought to mind—and masterly in its flow, its command of textures, its formal poise, and its sensitive word setting. *Postcard from Morocco* is at once a pleasing, a poetic, and a practicable opera.

The Juilliard production—the third in New York—did not reveal all the merits. Thirteen singers, not seven, took part, without doubling of roles, and there were twelve mimes. This had the advantage of involving more students in the show, but it diffused the economy that is one of the pleasures of the piece. Calvin Morgan's set was an open desert oasis, not a waiting room. The director, David Ostwald, had the notion of identifying characters with Mr. Owen's mother, father, and young self—but these gratuitous identifications remained on the page of the program and did not noticeably affect the action. It was a production that must have left many spectators with little idea of what was happening—an imprecise realization of something delicately and deftly planned. But the execution was trim, and, on its own terms, the production worked well. The show looked good, it was enacted in a lively fashion, and it sounded good. Ronald Braunstein conducted.

The Metropolitan Opera's revival, last month, of *Die Meistersinger,* a work missing from the house for eight seasons, had its points, but perhaps the return should have been delayed until a Hans Sachs more distinguished than Franz Ferdinand Nentwig could be found. Mr. Nentwig was acceptable—not more— about half the time. He understands the role. He plays and pronounces it clearly. But he has neither the physical nor the vocal presence to fill it. The great moments went for nothing. There were stretches—at any rate on the first night—when he was simply insignificant. The cobbling song was a puny affair. The Elder monologue had no broad, tender climax at "Lenzes Gebot." At the close of it, during the coda and the start of the duet with Eva, this Sachs hammered noisily. (It's true that the stage direction says "Sachs resumes his work with cheerful composure"—but surely not *hammering*, through that music!) The Eva was the Swedish soprano Mari Anne Häggander, making her Met début. She has sung the part at Bayreuth for the last four years, and she is perfectly efficient, but she brings to it no special charm of personality or interpretation and no great radiance of timbre. Peter Hofmann was the Walther. He played the part keenly, giving life to what he said, listening to what others said, but he portrayed the knight as a sullen, truculent, dislikable young man. It's a possible view of the character—it's Beckmesser's view—but constitutes a "criticism" of Wagner's plot rather than a happy presentation of it. Walther is supposed to win us over, despite his evident character failings. Mr. Hofmann's singing was bold and clear but seldom winningly lyrical. His costume was peculiar: a little sword dangled from his tunic with no sword belt to support it.

Dieter Weller, so admirable a Beckmesser eight years ago—a tall, personable young town clerk, a plausible suitor for Eva's hand—was now quite different. He played a pallid clown and no longer sang his serenade or prize song with beautiful tone. The Pogner was Gwynne Howell, who does have a beautiful voice but used it with a lack of legato surprising in a singer who has worked with Sir Reginald Goodall. David Rendall, the David, had both charm and clarity of utterance. He savored the words and he shaped the phrases. I've never heard him better. But—there's a "but" to be butted against each of the principals—he was an uncomfortably bulky apprentice. For no good reason, Richard J. Clark played Kothner as an antique dodderer, while shouting the difficult coloratura music and forcing it out of tune. The minor masters were a sorry bunch who bawled their various adsums straight out into the house. Matthias Hölle, a fine bass and Bayreuth's regular Nightwatchman, made his Met début in that role—all twenty bars of it. (Later in the season, he does Pogner.) The ten-o'clock call rolled out beautifully. So did the eleven-o'clock—but not in the "gently tremulous voice" that Wagner specified. The choral singing was rich and full.

Christof Perick, Generalmusikdirektor of the Karlsruhe Opera and soon to be conductor at the Berlin Opera, made his Met début. Good reports of him have been coming from Europe. He obtained warm, richly colored playing, marked by vitality of individual instrumental lines and careful balance. Within each long paragraph, the music moved well, but one missed a large, broad approach that joins the paragraphs into hour-long or two-hour spans. The production, directed by Nathaniel Merrill and designed by Robert O'Hearn, dates from 1962. (Bruce

Donnell was named as director of the revival.) It's a plain, routine staging within which stronger principals could enact a moving drama. The ensemble scenes needed abler management. Acts I and II both ended with a choral-society lineup, the second fronted by a frieze of supers waving their arms about and throwing pillows. The set for Act I is traditional and pleasing. Act II (which was very badly lit) is a vulgarized parody of the traditional set, pointlessly flopped left to right—as is the first scene of Act III. The final scene is a glitzy horror out of key with Wagner's opera.

The American Composers Orchestra gave two concerts in Alice Tully Hall last month, four days apart. The first was conducted by Gunther Schuller, the second by Dennis Russell Davies. The programs included a world première—Vivian Fine's *Poetic Fires*, for piano and orchestra—five New York premières, and two revivals. They were, on the whole, pretty dismal concerts. Sad that those responsible for ACO artistic policy (Francis Thorne, Charles Wuorinen, Mr. Davies, Jacob Druckman, John Duffy, and Peter R. Kermani) don't come up with more exciting programs. Sad that the orchestra players—in whose ranks are many of New York's ablest instrumentalists—must spend time on music that they surely can't admire. They do a decent professional job; in other ensembles, one hears them playing with joyful enthusiasm. I'll pass over in glum silence the concertos by Fine, William Thomas McKinley (first heard in Boulder in 1980), Alexei Haieff (recorded in Vienna in 1952), Ramon Zupko (first heard in Kalamazoo in 1980), and Gerry Mulligan (first heard in Treviso last year). The three other pieces bore listening to. Thomas Oboe Lee's *Phantasia for Elvira Shatayev* (1981), for soprano and orchestra, which opened the first concert, was his Harvard doctoral exercise. The work is a setting of a poem by Adrienne Rich so powerful in its matter and its imagery that no composer with a modicum of technique could go far wrong with it. Lee—who was born in China in 1945 and was trained at the New England Conservatory, where he now teaches—has plenty of technique. His piece—a solo cantata, shaped as introduction, exposition, recitative, aria, and coda—was striking. Christine Schadeberg was a secure and imposing soloist, although her timbre at climaxes was not pleasant.

Robert Hall Lewis's *Osservazioni II* (1978), for twenty-four winds, harp, piano, and five percussionists, which opened the second concert, is an "academic" construction—handy epithet for music that seems to be the product of will, not of inspiration or expressive need. Some of it proved horribly noisy in Tully Hall. But some of the ideas were arresting. The concert ended with Walter Piston's Seventh Symphony, first played by the Philadelphia Orchestra, under Ormandy, in 1961. Its pure, powerful inventions, its cogent and never merely conventional discourse, its formal and instrumental precision made all else that had been heard at the concerts seem low-grade music.

Airs of Earth and Heaven

March 18, 1985

Robert Beaser and Daniel Asia, the musical directors of the ensemble Musical Elements, regularly devise coherent, attractive, and satisfying programs. An Elements concert in the Great Hall at Cooper Union last month consisted of music by Hans Werner Henze and Peter Maxwell Davies, along with music by two younger Europeans, Hans Abrahamsen and Robert Saxton, who have come to prominence in recent years. It began with Henze's *Carillon, Récitatif, Masque* (1974), for mandolin, guitar, and harp—a small neoclassical suite of uncommon refinement and beauty. The performers were Peter Press, David Starobin, and Susan Jolles, who have recorded the work on the Bridge label. Abrahamsen, a Dane, born in 1952, was introduced to New York last year with *Night and Trumpets,* played by the Danish National Orchestra. (It was first played by the Berlin Philharmonic, conducted by Henze.) Elements gave the American première of his *Winter Night* (1978), a four-movement suite for seven instruments (flute and clarinet, cornet and horn, piano, violin and cello). Abrahamsen has been called a European minimalist—a misleading term except insofar as it can describe uncomplicated thematic material and limpid facture. His music is composed with subtlety and grace. It is unschematic and always lyrical. *Winter Night* proves captivating at a first hearing and loses none of its charm on repetition; rather, admiration grows for the deft, unconventional textures, metrical ingenuities, and unself-conscious contrapuntal play. The Elements instrumentalists, conducted by Mr. Beaser, played it with exquisite skill.

Paul Sperry then joined the ensemble to sing seven numbers from Henze's *Voices* (1973)—an album of twenty-two songs, lasting nearly two hours, for mezzo-soprano, tenor, and fifteen players who among them command some eighty instruments (and to one song add choral accompaniment). Rose Taylor, Mr. Sperry, and the London Sinfonietta, conducted by the composer, gave the first performance, in 1974. *Voices* stands high on the list of Henze's achievements. The text is an anthology of poems—Italian, German, Greek, Cuban, Chinese, American—that caught the composer's attention. The first of them, Heberto Padilla's "Los poetas cubanos ya no sueñan," tells of lyricism invaded by horror as "the world flows over [the poets'] mouths and the eye must look and look and look." In the last of them, Hans Magnus Enzensberger's "Das Blumenfest," the poet overwhelms his foe by drowning him, smothering him—like Boito's Mephistopheles—in flowers. The uniting themes are artists' responses to all the oppressions that are done under the sun and the tears of those who are oppressed and have no comforter, while the power is on the side of the oppressors. The poems range from chiselled strophes by Heine,

Ungaretti, and Brecht to the rawest of anti–Vietnam War verses. Not all is angry, bitter, or denunciatory; there are episodes of consolation, hope, and humor. The music is an anthology of manners ranging from Kurt Weill and Paul Dessau, through electronic collage, Cuban rhythms, Dixieland, pop protest song, aleatory music, and parody, to Henze's personal vein of tenderest lyricism. Each song is differently accompanied. The album is like a rich sketchbook, tracing in epitome procedures and notions that had been or would be more fully explored in other Henze pieces. But these are "finished sketches," each fully worked, complete in itself. *Voices* presumes an educated listener able to respond to verses in Italian, Spanish, German, and English. (Lines by Ho Chi Minh are translated into English, and by Michalis Katsaros into German.) A sense of fellow-feeling spanning countries and centuries, of musics of many kinds turned to moral ends, and of artists as unacknowledged but influential legislators of the world is strong. In 1974, *Voices* was topical. Today, unfaded, it remains what Shaw in 1898 called *Das Rheingold*—"frightfully real, frightfully present, frightfully modern." Elements offered only a sampler, but one that included some of the best songs and was enough to show the force of the work and the genius of its composer.

Davies's *Seven In Nomine* (1965), which followed, is also a moral piece—though less evidently so, in that its message is not spelled out in words. It was one of the works (others are the two orchestral Fantasias on John Taverner's In Nomine, of 1962 and 1964) that he created on the way to the completion of his opera *Taverner* (1962–68). The concern of the opera is the role that creative artists—and, by extension, all those who live by, in, or on art: performers, managers, publicizers, musicologists, critics—can in conscience play when they consider all the oppressions that are done under the sun. *Seven In Nomine,* less exigent than the opera it led to, explores music's expressive possibilities. It begins with Taverner's own In Nomine, from the Benedictus of his "Gloria tibi Trinitas" Mass, scored by Davies for string quartet. The fourth and sixth movements are Davies's scorings of In Nomine by John Bull and John Blitheman—two of the hundred-and-fifty-odd developments from Taverner's idea which English composers of the sixteenth and seventeenth centuries essayed. The four other In Nomine are Davies's own new workings of the chant in the light of music's progress through the four and a half centuries since Taverner's Mass. The sequence as a whole brings the past into the present, makes us one with the ages, and proclaims the steps and leaps of plainchant as basic metaphors relating music to life. On the local level, the scoring (for flute or piccolo, oboe, clarinet, bassoon, horn, harp, and string quartet) delights the ear; a listener smiles happily as the instruments mimic the timbre of the little eighteenth-century chamber organ (the harp providing the "chiff") on which the composer played the pieces to himself.

Saxton, born in 1953, has taught with Davies at the Dartington Summer School of Music, in Devon. His latest work, *Sentinel of the Rainbow,* was written for the Fires of London, the ensemble that Davies directs. At the Elements concert, Vicki Bodner and Elizabeth DiFelice gave the American première of his *Arias* (1977), for oboe and piano—a chain of lyrical, shapely miniatures. The program ended with Davies's *Runes from a Holy Island* (1977), composed for the Fires sextet, playing alto flute, clarinet, celesta, percussion, viola, and cello. The *Runes* are mysterious, cabalistic utterances. They sound like beautiful spells. A thread of plainchant running through them surfaces from time to time. In a program note, the composer invites listeners to find in them also "miniature sea and island soundscapes." The performance, conducted by Mr. Asia, was delicate and intent.

The audience was not large. Cooper Union, in whose Great Hall Abraham Lincoln and Susan B. Anthony once spoke, now lies off center of New York's musical life. Vauxhall Gardens and the Astor Place Opera House disappeared long ago (but the Public Theater is a new neighbor). The 1974 reconstruction of the Union cased the hall's slender iron columns in cement, and from many seats the sight lines have become tricky. There's no bar, no buffet, only a water fountain. In winter, an excursion to a Cooper Union concert offers few incidental pleasures. (It's different on long summer evenings, for the neighborhood contains many buildings worth looking at, and a preconcert hour or two can be enjoyably spent.) After a decade in New York, I've learned to stop regretting the extramusical amenities that European audiences can take for granted; but this program of European music reminded one that over there concertgoing is a sociable activity.

In 1983, I wrote about Saxton's orchestral piece *The Ring of Eternity,* a work springing from contemplation of Henry Vaughan's "I saw Eternity the other night Like a great *Ring* of pure and endless light, All calm, as it was bright." [see p. 29]. Ideas of music as a metaphor for light, and of both as emblems for transcendental adventure, have run through Saxton's work. He first set the Vaughan poem at the age of eleven—the year before his first opera was staged in London. *The Ring of Eternity* opposes images of shining calm and shadowy turmoil ("And round beneath it, Time . . . Like a vast shadow mov'd"). At last year's Proms, Saxton's Concerto for Orchestra had its first performance, given by the BBC Symphony, conducted by John Pritchard. The idea behind the work, the composer revealed in a program note, depends from "the Hekhaloth tracts, Jewish writings which describe the mystical experience of journeying through the seven heavens and the seven palaces in the highest heaven until the Divine Presence is reached; after the brightness and sometimes fearful qualities of the celestial palaces the eventual goal is total simplicity, calm and infinite light." It is music that juxtaposes shimmering, active chords from the upper strings (the violins in twelve parts, each oscillating in thirty-second notes); slow brass chords that well up, note added to note; bursts of splendor from the woodwinds as they take over the string music with a brighter shine; silvery glints from piano, celesta, and harps; occasional trumpet fanfares. There is a clear sense of stages along a journey. There is a large-scale harmonic ground plan. The goal is reached when the shimmering turns to a steady radiance, and a serene English-horn melody—some of its contours intensified by clarinets, alto flute, or trumpet—sings out. The vision does not last long: a sudden flicker passes across it, and it is gone. The mystical progress is apparently one that souls can make repeatedly.

There is perhaps something of Messiaen here, and something of Ligeti in the writing for the large orchestra. But it's new music, of the kind that Constant Lambert called for half a century ago in *Music Ho!*—music that cannot be labelled "the new This" or "the new That," music that, while consolidating "the reckless and fascinating experiments" of pioneers, neither truckles to topicality nor loses itself "in a dream world of forgotten loves and vanished days." One aspect of the Concerto for Orchestra bothers me a little: the solo-violin passages. Saxton has illustrious precedents: Beethoven, Mahler, Schoenberg in *Die Jakobsleiter* used the solo violin in episodes of mystical rapture. But the sound of it brings one down to earth, draws attention to an individual, human player. Of the solo violin in the Benedictus of the Missa Solemnis, Martin Cooper (in *Beethoven: The Last Decade*) remarked, "It would hardly be more unsuitable to introduce a ballerina into the sanctuary."

Acts and episodes from Karlheinz Stockhausen's opera-in-progress *Light*, a seven-day work, have been performed in many European cities, and the complete *Thursday* and *Saturday* from *Light* have been staged by La Scala. An album of *Thursday*, assembled from episodes recorded in Cologne, Paris, Hilversum, and Hamburg, has been published by Deutsche Grammophon. [*Monday has now been done, too, and a recording of* Saturday *has been published.*] At the 92nd Street Y last month, the trumpeter Stephen Burns played and danced the final section of *Thursday*, called *Michael's Farewell*. The protagonist of the opera, the plot of which is largely autobiographical, is Michael, the archangel, incarnate as a mortal musician. He, like the other main characters, Eve and Lucifer, is played by a singer, an instrumentalist, and a dancer. Michael's instrument is the trumpet, Eve's the basset horn, and Lucifer's the trombone. At La Scala, Matthias Hölle, the Met's Nightwatchman in *Die Meistersinger,* sang Lucifer. Mr. Sperry was the tenor Michael of Act III; the composer's son Markus was the trumpeter Michael. But the *Farewell* was sounded by five trumpeters in Michael costumes, illuminated like tower statues, who stood—two on the outer balcony of the opera house, three on the palaces that front the other sides of the vast Piazza della Scala—and exchanged Michael calls across the piazza for about half an hour. On the recording, Markus Stockhausen, doing all five parts, plays a condensed version, lasting about eleven minutes, recorded in a Hamburg studio. At the Y, Mr. Burns had prerecorded four of the parts and played the fifth, dancing the while. Aged twenty-five, he's fresh-featured, slim, and graceful (the *Farewell* in this form is not a work that more burly trumpeters—Maurice André, for example—could easily tackle); the simple, well-judged steps, turns, gestures, and attitudes mirrored the phrases and made pleasing images. Heard out of context, *Michael's Farewell* is perhaps hardly more than an impressive series of lapped trumpet calls, but the general effect was one of awesome, joyous majesty. [*An account of* Thursday *appears on pp. 366–71.*]

The concert began with a sonata by Pietro Baldassare, composed for cornet and strings, and Alessandro Scarlatti's cantata *Su le sponde del Tebro,* composed for soprano, baroque trumpet, and strings. Mr. Burns played both on a rotary-valved piccolo trumpet with warm, bright, rounded tone. Beverly Hoch, the soprano, showed disappointingly little feeling for the words. In the Stockhausen, in a workaday sonata by Kent Kennan, and in a bold transcription of Schumann's Fantasy Piece Opus 73, No. 3, Mr. Burns played the regular instrument. Encores produced trumpets in other sizes and a flugelhorn. His tone was unfailingly delightful—now brilliant, now gentle, never blaring or aggressive. His manner was buoyant and winning. He's a virtuoso (as can be heard on his first record [Musicmasters], a concert of seventeenth- and eighteenth-century music). But his sense of baroque style was less than sure.

There Is a River

March 25, 1985

For her sixth opera, *Harriet the Woman Called Moses,* which had its première this month in Norfolk, Virginia, Thea Musgrave chose an American subject. Harriet Tubman "deserves to be placed first on the list of American heroines," said the prominent abolitionist Samuel May. In 1863, when Harriet Tubman still had fifty years to live, the Boston *Commonwealth* wrote:

> It was said long ago that the true romance of America was not in the fortunes of the Indian, where Cooper sought it, nor in New England character, where Judd [the author of *Margaret*] found it, nor in the social contrasts of Virginia planters, as Thackeray imagined, but in the story of the fugitive slaves. The observation is as true now as it was before War, with swift, gigantic hand, sketched the vast shadows, and dashed in the high lights in which romance loves to lurk and flash forth.... The desperation or the magnanimity of a poor black woman has power to shake the nation that so long was deaf to her cries.

That year, Harriet Tubman was in South Carolina with a Union raiding party that rescued eight hundred slaves. She was likened to Joan of Arc by her memorialists. John Brown, who sought her advice, called her "the most of a man naturally that I ever met with." The opera, however, deals not with Harriet Tubman's Civil War exploits but with the earlier years when, an escaped slave, she returned again and again to Maryland to guide other slaves along the Underground Railroad to freedom. For those deeds she was (as a memorial tablet in Auburn, New York, where she settled, records) "called the Moses of her people." She had escaped to Philadelphia herself, but after the passing of the Fugitive Slave Law she had to take her charges to Canada before they were safe.

The biographies of this remarkable woman are contradictory about details and tantalizingly incomplete. She left no autobiographical narrative—such as Frederick Douglass or Sojourner Truth did—but in old age delighted to recount her adventures. The passages in purported oratio recta which others set down bear out the claim of one of her biographers that "she had a highly developed sense of the dramatic, a sense of the comic, and ... the surge and sway of the majestic rhythm of the King James version of the Bible was an integral part of her speech." Of Robert Gould Shaw's attack, with his black regiment, on Fort

Wagner, she said: "And then we saw the lightning, and that was the guns; and then we heard the rain falling, and that was the drops of blood falling; and when we came to get in the crops, it was dead men that we reaped." And of the day she crossed the state line into Pennsylvania:

> I looked at my hands to see if I was the same person now I was free. There was such a glory over everything, the sun came like gold through the trees, and over the fields, and I felt like I was in Heaven.... I was free; but there was no one to welcome me to the land of freedom. I was a stranger in a strange land, and my home after all was down in the old cabin quarter, with the old folks, and my brothers and sisters. But to this solemn resolution I came: I was free, and they should be free also; I would make a home for them in the North, and, the Lord helping me, I would bring them all here.

In youth, she suffered a head injury—an incensed overseer flung a heavy weight at her—and throughout her life she was the subject to sudden bouts of trancelike sleep. She told Thomas Garrett, the Wilmington Quaker, that she talked daily with God, and He with her. She had mysterious premonitions of impending danger and to them ascribed her ability to avoid it. Gerrit Smith, the millionaire abolitionist, wrote that he listened often to Harriet Tubman with delight, "and I am convinced that she is not only truthful but that she has a rare discernment, and a deep and sublime philanthropy." References to her in letters and memoirs are numerous but brief. The chronicles are scrappy, and the personality of the woman, I find, remains elusive.

In a program note Musgrave set out "some of the reasons why I, a white woman of Scottish descent, felt moved to write about Harriet Tubman": the subject embodies Lincoln's "eternal struggle between two principles"; Harriet Tubman inspires an answer to the question "But what can one person do?" And:

> There is another overriding reason why composers are drawn to subjects that cross political and temporal boundaries and venture into different, often exotic settings for their works.... Most composers want to underline and emphasize the eternal nature of human conflicts and emotions which transcend time and place.... Harriet is every woman who dared to defy injustice and tyranny; she is Joan of Arc, she is Susan B. Anthony, she is Anne Frank, she is Mother Teresa.

Operas with which *Harriet* can fairly be compared and contrasted are Hans Werner Henze's *We Come to the River* (1976) and David Blake's *Toussaint* (1977). Henze's librettist, the playwright Edward Bond, has declared it his aim "to create public images, literal or figurative, in sight, sound, and movement, of the human condition." Their opera, like Musgrave's, ends beside a river, with a chorus of oppressed preparing to cross:

> *We stand by the river.*
> *If the water is deep we will swim....*
> *We will stand on the other side.*
> *We have learned to march so well*
> *that we cannot drown.*

There was an incident in Harriet Tubman's life when, warned by an inner prompting, she saved her party from capture by leading it through a swift, deep, apparently impassable stream. In the metaphors of art, as in life, rivers play a double role. Their flow, an everlasting stream, is an emblem of time, of immanence against eternity. But they are also boundaries marking stages in life's journey—for Caesar, for Alice, for Pilgrim. Harriet Tubman used to dream of flying over fields and towns, rivers and mountains, until she reached a last river over which she would try to fly: "But it appeared I wouldn't have the strength, and just as I was sinking down, there would be ladies all dressed in white over there, and they would put out their arms and pull me across." The river at the close of Musgrave's opera is at once a potent metaphor and the actual Niagara, with Canada, freedom, and the welcoming ladies in white on the other side. The opera's final chorus runs:

> We will fight
> So no one is a slave,
> So all can live together
> In peace,
> In harmony
> And in freedom.

Blake's *Toussaint,* on the other hand, ends with no optimistic affirmation but a questioning chorus, as—Toussaint dead in his Jura prison, Dessalines enthroned—Haiti embarks on its modern history of insurrection, assassinations, and tyranny:

> Hide in the fields,
> Hide in the forests,
> Live in the blackness of the blood.
>
> What will be the end of the fire?

The goodies-and-baddies characterizations of Henze's and Musgrave's operas are eschewed. Blake's aim is to present a clear picture of confusions, not a simplified didactic parable and not a mere entertainment with a historical subject. All three operas are operas of "ideas"—what Verdi, referring to his *Forza* and *Don Carlos,* called "opere a intenzioni." In an introduction to *Toussaint* Blake wrote, "The beauty and truth of an *idea* is often more profoundly moving than the all-too-easily-won emotionalism which music, and operatic music in particular, is notoriously good at evoking." All three are by intention operas of a higher order than, say, Puccini's *Tosca* (of which the Met has just mounted a lavish new production). That is not to say they are more successful operas. One must distinguish between aim and execution. Puccini aimed low and hit his mark surely. Of composers who face a higher challenge more is asked.

Musgrave, I think, has to some extent compromised her opera of ideas and ideals by an excess of caution. She has perhaps not demanded enough of herself, her performers, or her audience. She plays safe, as neither Henze nor Blake did. She has ever been a thoroughly commonsensical composer, with her feet on the ground even while her glance was on—but her head not in—the clouds. Her works have not lacked vision. *The Voice of Ariadne* (1974) is a poetic and beautiful creation. *Mary, Queen of Scots* (1977) is an exciting combination of history, politics, pageantry, and character study. As I observed after *Mary,* because everything Musgrave does is so lucid and intelligent, listeners struck mainly by her patent abilities may miss the veins of romance, ambition, and poetry. At second and later hearings they become apparent, once first-encounter admiration of her competence, her matching of means to ends and of demands to executants' skills, has been remarked and can be taken for granted. Competence and careful planning for effectiveness are virtues, but they can be limiting ones, and in some recent works I have wished Musgrave remained more a Jill-o'-dreams. A *Christmas Carol* (1979) seemed to me—and still seems, after rehearings—an efficient but earthbound composition. Her D. H. Lawrence theatre piece *The Last Twilight* (1980), less meticulously worked, even sketchy, is more stirring to the imagination.

The composer was her own librettist. *Harriet* begins with the well-worn device of flashback. The heroine, escaped, lies in the house of Thomas Garrett, and in a dream she hears her people calling "Moses! Moses! Lead us out of bondage!" Then we are back in the slave quarters. Harriet breaks into the slaves' singing and dancing with "Go down, Moses . . . Let my people go!" and is whipped for introducing a forbidden song. There is a love scene between Harriet and Josiah, a fellow-slave. There is a long scene in the Big House between the Old Master, a slaveowner of benevolent disposition, and his wicked son Preston, who has incurred gambling debts and asks his father to meet them by selling some slaves into the harsher slavery of the Deep South. Then Preston tries to seduce Harriet. The Master decides to sell the best of his slaves; Josiah escapes. The Master has a heart attack, and Harriet, rather than become Preston's slave, chooses to escape. The act (which lasts about eighty minutes) ends with her back in Garrett's house, resolving to return as a deliverer of her people.

The opera bears the subtitle "A Story of the American Underground Railroad." Act II (which lasts about an hour) starts with a pantomime:

> Harriet rescues another group of slaves. She leads them in a variety of ways through the assembling groups of the patrol. When they reach safety in the North they are greeted by Mr. Garrett and other Abolitionists.

Harriet meets Josiah again; they sing a duet and quarrel. ("At last we's together, I won't let you go!" "I must make just this one more journey South . . ." "Then go alone! And stay alone!") Josiah is recaptured. Harriet rescues her parents, Rit and Ben. In the North, Quakers and blacks free Josiah from a slave pen. (The incident is adapted from a celebrated rescue at Troy, New York, in which Harriet Tubman took part.) The vindictive Preston pursues the couple to the Canadian border and fires at Harriet as she crosses the bridge. Josiah receives the shot and sings a duet of reconciliation and farewell with Harriet before he dies.

In life, Harriet Tubman had an unsatisfactory husband. Musgrave omitted him and invented Josiah, and with him she introduced both a conventional love interest and—but halfheartedly, not convincingly—a conventional operatic conflict between love and duty. (Verdi in *Giovanna d'Arco* did the same thing more boldly.) It blurs Harriet's character. Musgrave invented a good deal else, including Preston, his attempted seduction of Harriet, and his pursuit of the fugitives. There are stretches where the story of Harriet is lost in operatic cliché. Something had to be done to fill out the narrative and give it dramatic shape (Harriet Tubman's history is not like that of Toussaint, so rich in documented incident that there it was a matter of what to leave out), but this libretto seems to me commonplace at times—weakened by concessions to a notion of what the public expects all operas to contain.

The music is thoroughly planned. There is a recurrent "freedom" motif—seventh and ninth chords sung to the words "Freedom! Freedom!," clearing to B major (with a long high B from Harriet) at the end of the first act and to A major (with a long high A from her) at the close. There are stretches of whole-tone harmony such as Puccini used in *La fanciulla del West*. There are old spirituals—"Go Down, Moses," snatches of "Swing Low, Sweet Chariot"—and there are new ones, composed by Musgrave. There are arias and duets, but only one set number—Rit's "How can I live without my Ben?"—invites (and received) applause. Dramatically, this number functions like Serena's "My man's gone now," in *Porgy and Bess*. In its long melodic spans it recalls Hannah's aria "Stranger and darker" in Tippett's opera *The Ice Break*—but that comparison turns Musgrave's melody to fustian (as does any comparison of Musgrave's spirituals with Tippett's in *A Child of Our Time*). On the whole, the music of *Harriet* strikes me as workaday—functional but undistinguished. It doesn't soar. In the love episodes, it drops into the short-breathed idiom of minor verismo. (I except one happy, memorable invention—Josiah's song in the slave pen, "Wonder where my brother gone.") Moreover, Musgrave's strange reluctance for pages on end to take the orchestra below middle C gives much of the score an insubstantial quality.

The heroine was played by Cynthia Haymon, a rising and promising young soprano, who gave a fervent and subtle portrayal. She is more beautiful than the historical Harriet Tubman was, and is so direct and convincing an actress that I almost forgot to mention that, having broken her leg in rehearsal, she played the role in a cast and on crutches. Alteouise DeVaughn, a tall young mezzo, subdued her glowing looks and transformed her personality to give a strong, mature performance as Rit. Ben Holt, an alert artist, was a vigorous and sensitive Josiah. Raymond Bazemore was good as Ben. Damon Evans, as Benjie, Harriet's brother, was entertainer-bright, working rather too hard at being animated. The whites, including Jay Willoughby as the Old Master and Barry Craft as Preston, did what they could in near-parody roles. Jeffrey Beecroft's settings shifted within a basic frame suggesting the hold of a slave ship. Gordon Davidson's stage direction was fluent and conventional. Accents were all over the place, varying from stage black and stage Southern to standard singing-teacher American. There's a problem here, as there is with *Porgy and Bess*. (In quoting utterances ascribed to the real-life Harriet Tubman, I have removed the various attempts to represent her pronunciation.)

Harriet, commissioned jointly by the Virginia Opera Association and the Royal Opera House, Covent Garden, is the third Musgrave opera the Virginia company has staged. *Mary* had its American première and *A Christmas Carol* its première in Norfolk, where Musgrave is a local heroine and her husband, Peter Mark, is general director of the company. He conducted *Harriet* ably. The work had ten sold-out performances (two of them in Richmond; four of them school matinées). It was carried across the country, directly or in a delayed broadcast, by ninety radio stations and across the Atlantic, live, to BBC listeners. At the two performances I attended, the public enthusiasm was immense. The Virginia Opera, ten years old, has from the start worked for and won wide community support. In connection with *Harriet,* three intelligent and imaginative "curriculum guides," related to music, "language arts," and social studies, and tapes of excerpts had been prepared for use in schools; children guided by them would certainly approach the opera—and opera in general—with intellectual curiosity and understanding whetted. Any personal disappointment in the piece was tempered by the pleasure of seeing a new opera so warmly welcomed.

To Stir, to Rouse, to Shake the Soul He Comes

April 1, 1985

THE Handel tercentenary season brings a rich feast: in New York alone, Carnegie Hall's *Orlando, Ariodante, Semele,* and *Alessandro; Serse* at the Juilliard; concert performances of *Deidamia* and *Agrippina*; the oratorios *Theodora, Belshazzar,* and *Israel in Egypt*; and much else. In other cities, stagings of *Agrippina, Rodelinda, Giulio Cesare, Teseo, Tamerlano*; *Jephtha,* the Occasional Oratorio, the newly reconstituted Vespers of 1707.

Aci, Galatea, e Polifemo, a cantata that Handel wrote in Naples in 1708, when he was twenty-three, was brought to the Metropolitan Museum last month by Washington forces. It is a less dramatic score than *Acis and Galatea* (1718): for the English masque, Galatea's tale as recounted in the *Metamorphoses* was elegantly dramatized; in the Italian cantata, it is a thread on which a duet, fourteen arias, two trios, and a short finale, linked by recitatives, are strung. Acis in this earlier version is a soprano, Galatea an alto, and Polyphemus a bass who enters not in amorous vein ("O ruddier than the cherry") but with the angry trumpet aria "Sibilar l'angui d'Aletto," better known from its reuse in *Rinaldo.* Both trios are remarkable. In the first, a threat from Polyphemus, a reproach from Galatea, and reassuring words from Acis are laid out in turn and then cunningly interwoven. The second is a melting love duet broken into by blustering recitatives from Polyphemus, who is watching the pair, and whose jealous fury grows until it explodes in a two-octave drop, from the D above the bass staff to the D below. Unaware of his presence, undisturbed, the lovers continue to spin their dulcet strains. It is a vivid piece, precursor of high dramatic strokes in the operas. There are several graphic simile arias. When Polyphemus observes that a river confined flows more swiftly, the instrumental bass compresses the violins' ample figure into a rushing torrent. The aria recurs in *Deborah,* when Abinoam sings:

> Swift inundation
> Of desolation
> Pour on the nation
> Of Judah's foes.

When Galatea sings of a small vessel tossed by the waves but guided by the stars, the recorders rock to and fro while plucked strings wink and twinkle. The most striking aria of all is perhaps Polyphemus' "Fra l'ombre e gl'orrori," as he likens himself to a butterfly blundering and plunging in the sudden dark after a lamp has been extinguished. It has, in Winton Dean's phrase, "a sublime spaciousness worthy of Sarastro." The vocal line plummets, flutters to rise, only to fall again, until there's a straight drop of two octaves and a fifth, from the A above the bass staff to the D below it. The Naples bass must have been an exceptional singer. When Handel rewrote the "river" aria for Antonio Montagnana, the first Abinoam, he took out the low E. When he used the "butterfly" aria again, in *Sosarme,* and reworked the music, again for Montagnana—a bass renowned for his extension and (according to Burney, writing of "Fra l'ombre") "peculiar accuracy of intonation in hitting distant intervals"—he took out the low E-flats and D and the high G's and A. Another striking piece is Acis' death aria, sung over a quiet, steady, chromatic F-minor throb of strings which falters at last as he expires.

Handel's early Italian cantatas are a treasure house of music too little explored. They have the exuberance—and on occasion the exaggerations—of buoyant youth. He himself roamed among them freely throughout his career, borrowing, refining, and transforming ideas from them (as he freely borrowed, refined, and transformed ideas of his fellow-composers). Even when there are no straight note borrowings, notions recur. In the *Acis* trio, the lovers also sing a duet ("The flocks shall leave the mountains") that continues on its way undisturbed by Polyphemus' rumblings; and again Acis expires over slow-throbbing chromatic string chords in F minor. I hope the Handel year will bring us more cantata performances. On disc, there has appeared the captivating *Aminta e Fillide* (Hyperion), instrumentally less ambitious than *Aci*—it is accompanied by strings only—but wonderfully fresh and inventive. In the Metropolitan Museum's *Aci,* Richard Crist was a bass taxed by the range (who would not be?) but able to sound the notes. Hilda Harris was a pleasing Galatea. Linda Mabbs was an Acis not quite forward or bright enough of voice for Handel until she reached the final aria, which she sang exquisitely. Stephen Simon, conducting an adept little band, revealed the expressive beauties of the work.

After his three years and more in Italy, Handel came to England as a thoroughly trained German composer fired with the melodic vivacity and theatrical brilliance that Italy had taught him. His mind was so well stocked with melodies and procedures that when composing he was never at a loss what to do next. His genius ensured that whatever he did sounded new, and specific to its situation. On the one hand, he was a rapid, fluent composer. On the other, he was—to an extent that modern scholarship increasingly reveals—a perfectionist, swift to reject and replace anything that displeased him. (To take just one example: he composed the opening scene of *Tamerlano* again and again and again before arriving at the stark, powerful version that he brought to performance.) He settled in England and there enlarged his art with ready responses to Purcell, reflected in many compositions, and to English literature as he set Dryden, Milton, Pope, and, above all, the cadences of the James Bible. His music became greater and greater, until, in some forty Italian operas, some twenty English music dramas, and many anthems and odes, it had embraced the full range of human experience.

Last year [see p. 87], I wrote of the glories of *Alexander's Feast* (1736), a Dryden setting that at once details and demonstrates the manifold powers of music upon the human spirit. It's a work that, like *Semele*, needs to be heard at least once a year: a Handelian deprived of it suffers some musical analogue to vitamin deficiency. The National Chorale Soloists sang *Alexander's Feast* in Merkin Hall last month, but, alas, their performance gave insufficient nourishment. It was below any acceptable level.

A theme central to the work is the rise and fall of mighty empires—the long stream of history with a world dominated in turn by Persia, Macedon, Rome, Spain, Britain . . . and whom next, as would-be conquerors vie? The setting is Persepolis, with Alexander enthroned in triumph and "Darius great and good . . . fall'n from his high estate." Handel returned to the theme in *Belshazzar* (1745), one of the grandest of all music dramas, a work to place beside *The Ring*. Nitocris, the Empress-Mother of Babylon, sets the stage with a tremendous monologue:

> Vain, fluctuating state of human empire!
> First, small and weak . . .
> > Anon, it strives
> For pow'r and wealth, and spurns at opposition.
> Arriv'd at full maturity, it grasps
> At all within its reach, o'erleaps all bounds,
> Robs, ravages, and wastes the frighted world.
> At length, grown old and swell'd to bulk enormous,
> The monster in its proper bowels feeds
> Pride, luxury, corruption, perfidy,
> Contention . . .

And then the scene—in that idealized theatre of the mind (its settings painted by music and the phrases of the word book) wherein Handel laid the action of his dramatic oratorios—moves from the imperial palace to "The Camp of Cyrus before Babylon. A view of the City, with the River Euphrates running through it. Cyrus, Gobrias; Medes and Persians. Chorus of Babylonians on the Walls, deriding Cyrus, as engaged in an impracticable undertaking." Nitocris, Cyrus, Belshazzar, Daniel, and Gobrias (a Babylonian, victim of Belshazzar's tyranny, who has joined with Cyrus) are strongly characterized. So are the choruses of Babylonians, of Jews, of Medes and Persians. The Babylonians revel within their vaunted defenses, even while Cyrus undermines them. Daniel, in music of sweet, solemn beauty, reads to his people the prophecies of Jeremiah and Isaiah.

285

Nitocris tries in vain to check her son's descent into drunken, blasphemous megalomania. At his feast, Belshazzar, swilling wine from sacred vessels looted from the Jewish Temple, calls wildly for "Another bowl! . . . Another bowl!" The mysterious hand appears (a wonderfully eerie scrape of staccato violins, an amazing invention), and the king "turns pale with fear, drops the bowl of wine, falls back in his seat, trembling from head to foot, and his knees knocking against each other." In Act III, with Macbeth-like defiance—but newly drunk—he reels into battle with Cyrus, and is vanquished. The magnanimous victor promises the Jews their freedom and a rebuilt Jerusalem, and the work ends with a full-throated magnificat.

To recount the marvels of *Belshazzar*—melodic, harmonic, instrumental, formal—to tell of its grandeur, variety, vividness, and profundity, would take many pages. The Pro Arte Chorale and Orchestra, conducted by Roger Nierenberg, presented a fine performance of it last month in Alice Tully Hall. It was done in a dramatic way. The orchestra was lowered to house-floor level. The soloists, uncostumed but acting, made entrances and exits: Babylon was stage left, and Cyrus was encamped stage right. The chorus was ranged behind them, and the organ closed the prospect. Scenery was two thrones. Props were the sacred scroll and a wine cup. The mysterious writing on the wall was a projection. Nicholas Deutsch, the stage director, had devised a powerful, well-judged "production" effected by simple, telling strokes. (In the chorus "Recall, oh king! thy rash command," each chorister fixed his eyes on Belshazzar, standing stage left, and the massed accusatory effect was chilling.) There was skillful, unfussy lighting, by Jackie Manassee. I've seen Handel's dramatic oratorios, including *Belshazzar,* presented in manners ranging from straight concert performances—the soloists on a row of chairs, book in hand—to full-fledged operatic shows. The Pro Arte production, so potent and so practicable, was a new landmark.

The role of Daniel was composed for Susanna Cibber, Garrick's leading lady for two decades, and that of Cyrus for Miss Robinson. (Her Christian name is unknown, but she was evidently a fine artist, since she was also the Dejanira of *Hercules*.) In the Pro Arte performance, two men, Drew Minter as Daniel and Jeffrey Gall as Cyrus, usurped the roles—as countertenors often do in these days when true female altos are rare and mezzo-sopranos' aspirations are usually upward. (This season, Mr. Gall had already undertaken Francesca Bertolli's part in *Orlando,* Mr. Minter Francesca Boschi's in *Agrippina,* and James Bowman Maria Negri's in *Ariodante*.) Both of them gave beautifully firm, precise performances, with clear, shapely words and stylishly expressive phrasing. Mr. Gall used chest voice and head voice in striking, sometimes startling contrast. Mr. Minter's voice is more even, more sweetly melodious. David Gordon was a bold, splendid Belshazzar. The role of Nitocris needs a more mature, commanding personality than Linda Wall brought to it, but her singing was fluent and assured. The chorus and the orchestra were spirited. Mr. Nierenberg's conducting was alert, confident, and convincing.

The performance had been announced as complete. In the event, Cyrus lost "Dry those unavailing tears" and the second verse of "Great God! who, yet but darkly known," Daniel lost "Can the black Aethiop change his skin?," and the da capo numbers were reduced to first section only (all but one, and of that the reprise was shortened). Nevertheless, it was a much fuller *Belshazzar* than one usually hears. And a noble one.

From Handel to Puccini, from *Belshazzar* to *Tosca,* represents a drastic, a positively Polyphemic descent. The Metropolitan Opera's new *Tosca,* designed and directed by Franco Zeffirelli, is a big, expensive-looking show, with more elaborate scenery and more supers than Puccini's opera usually has. It is handsome, in a rather overdone way, but not more effective than the 1968 production (designed by Rudolf Heinrich and staged by Otto Schenk) that it replaces, and cannot hold a candle to the less grandiloquent, more sharply focussed *Tosca* that Zeffirelli designed and directed at Covent Garden twenty-one years ago. Act I ingeniously mingles built scenery and cloth painted in perspective. In Act II, Scarpia's room is a library, dominated by tall bookstacks. Both scenes pose architectural puzzles: the Attavanti chapel seems to run back into the nave of Sant'Andrea della Valle; the Palazzo Farnese fireplace is set in the window wall looking onto the courtyard. The painter's scaffolding and Scarpia's table and sofa are not in their usual places; the pointless departures from tradition prescribe actions and aria positions less telling than usual. Into Act III Zeffirelli has introduced scene changes. The prelude is set on the platform at the top of the Castel Sant'Angelo, but the statue of the angel, not the prospect of St. Peter's which Puccini specified, dominates the background. For "E lucevan le stelle" and the duet with Tosca, the platform is then slowly jacked up out of sight, to reveal Cavaradossi's dungeon below it. (The Met audience breaks into applause, seeing scenery shift before its eyes, and blots out the music.) For Cavaradossi's execution we return to the platform—hastily, for there are only eight bars of music between Tosca's "Così" and her "Come è lunga l'attesa!" (The latter remark—"How long the waiting!"—now seems absurd.) The dungeon is a romantic scene, heavy with classical architecture (the castle was built by Hadrian as his mausoleum), but it's not wanted. It disturbs the shape and flow of a short, carefully planned act— shorter than the intermission that preceded it. In later performances, the intrusive scene changes can easily be omitted. The opera will gain.

Zeffirelli's London *Tosca,* which initially had Maria Callas in the title role and Tito Gobbi as Scarpia, was so tellingly planned that it served, and continues to serve, as an enhancing frame for more ordinary interpreters. His Met *Tosca*— bloated, as his Met *Bohème* was in relation to his Scala *Bohème*—is a spectacle that must steal the show from all but very strong performers. In a smaller, German house, Hildegard Behrens would probably be a striking and interesting Tosca. In this show, she was dwarfed by the stage pictures, and nothing much came across. Placido Domingo, the Cavaradossi, sang bravely and fully; Zeffirelli had not inspired him to go beyond his usual "generalized excellence" to give an individual and imaginative performance. Cornell MacNeil was a blunt Scarpia, taxed beyond his vocal resources by "Già. Mi dicon venal." Italo Tajo's Sacristan was horribly overplayed. Giuseppe Sinopoli, making his Met début, standing and waving so high that he was often more noticeable than the singers, conducted a performance that included much colorful orchestral playing but did not flow easily or naturally.

SUCH AS FOUND OUT MUSICAL TUNES

April 8, 1985

ROGER SESSIONS died last month, in Princeton, aged eighty-eight. For music, he embodied what is finest in American thought, character, and genius. In nine symphonies, in concertos, two operas, and many other works, he gave it utterance. He was one of the country's—and the world's—great men. In his life, he was not honored here by frequent performances: New York has still to hear his requiem *When Lilacs Last in the Dooryard Bloom'd*; the Metropolitan Opera has not produced *Montezuma*. But he was and is honored and loved by those—listeners, generations of pupils, friends—who met the music or the man and felt the inspiring touch of his integrity, his questing intelligence, his gentleness, his toughness, his refusal to compromise with anything seamy or second-rate. One day, the people will tell of his wisdom, and audiences will show forth his praise.

In memoriam, Bethany Beardslee and Alan Feinberg began a Guild of Composers concert in Merkin Hall last month with Sessions's James Joyce setting "On the Beach at Fontana," a 1929 song epitomizing what Aaron Copland later said about the First Piano Sonata, of 1931: "Sessions has presented us with a cornerstone on which to base an American music." Mr. Feinberg then played Susan Blaustein's Fantasy (1980), and later in the program he gave the first performance of George Edwards's *Suave Mari Magno*. Mr. Feinberg sets problems for critics: he's a Callas of contemporary-music pianists. He makes whatever he plays sound arresting, exciting, and important. Cool perusal of the scores, after the concert, confirmed that the pieces merited his championship. The Fantasy is a rich, imaginative composition, at once carefully planned and warm in feeling. *Suave Mari Magno* takes its title from the second book of Lucretius ("'Tis pleasant, safely to behold from shore, The rowling Ship, and hear the Tempest roar," in Dryden's translation), but acquired it, the composer revealed in a program note, after the completed music had suggested the marine imagery, not vice versa. It is not as turbulent a piece as that might suggest, but sets the activity within a long, controlled framework. Not having read the program note in advance, and vaguely associating the title with an antiphon incipit, I seemed to hear chant soar through a great building, break into subsidiary echo flurries, move deep spaces to sympathetic resonance. In any event, it is a remarkable study in sonorities, and surely fashioned. Eric Chasalow's *The Furies*, a setting, for soprano and tape, of four poems from Anne Sexton's collection of the same title, also had its première. It seemed an effective enough cycle—nothing special—and was effectively sung by Christine Schadeberg.

The second half was *Pierrot Lunaire*, with Miss Beardslee as the singer-speaker, Jacques-Louis Monod the conductor. I'd never heard a *Pierrot* with, on the one hand, so much life and force in each individual phrase—sung, spoken, or played—and, on the other hand, so just and delicate a balance and ensemble. It was enthralling. The players were Robert Stallman (flute), Anand Devendra (clarinet), Shem Guibbory (violin/viola), Timothy Eddy (cello), and Christopher Oldfather (piano).

Aleck Karis at a League-ISCM piano recital in Merkin Hall last month played five modern classics—Stravinsky's Serenade, Schoenberg's two Piano Pieces, Opus 33, Webern's Variations, and Boulez's First Sonata—as a frame around two contemporary works. The Stravinsky and the Schoenberg were given dutiful, undercharacterized performances. The Webern was better, warmed by the lyricism that Peter Stadlen brought to the surface in his 1979 edition of the Variations. (He gave the first performance in 1937, and his edition shows in red the expressive marks that Webern pencilled into the printed copy that he and Stadlen worked from, and in green the composer's verbal instructions and recommendations. From the cool, black-and-white score one might not guess that, in Stadlen's words, "a fervently lyrical mind bent on expressiveness has been at work." Webern's intentions—as surely as Handel's, Mozart's, Verdi's—are misrepresented by blinkered performances rigorously intent on exactly what appears in the score and nothing more, no "interpretation.") At the close of the evening, Mr. Karis came fully to life: the Boulez sonata was given a buoyant, committed, excited and exciting performance. Boulez's Second Sonata is a monument of our time. This First Sonata—a twenty-year-old genius's new edifice on a Schoenberg foundation—has a freshness and a boldness that are irresistible, and they stirred Mr. Karis to produce colors, inflections, contrasts, drama such as one missed earlier in the evening. The contemporary works were *Pieces of Piano* (1982), by Scott Lindroth, born in 1958, and Four Impromptus (a première) by Daniel Grey, born in 1954. The Impromptus seemed to me mere note-spinning. *Pieces of Piano* is a strong, craggy, percussive composition—cogent, if initially unappealing, even brutal at times. It's a work that (to apply a critic's simplest test) I'd be glad to hear again—but perhaps in a performance more dramatic and forceful.

Robert Starer's *The Last Lover,* first produced at the 1975 Caramoor Festival, was revived last month by the American Chamber Opera Company, in the hall of St. Michael's Church, on West Ninety-ninth Street. It is a one-act chamber opera, lasting less than an hour, for three singers and a wind quintet, and recounts the Thaïs-like life of St. Pelagia the sinner—she who (in the words of Father Hippolyte Delehaye, in the eleventh Britannica) "was a celebrated dancer and courtesan, who, in the full flower of her beauty and guilty sovereignty over the youth of Antioch, was suddenly converted by the influence of the holy bishop Nonnus, whom she had heard preaching in front of a church which she was passing with her gay train of attendants and admirers." The libretto is by Gail Godwin. Starer is spare, almost parsimonious, with his music, but the lean, slim inventions have distinction. It is an intelligent, cultivated, entertaining yet serious little opera—more laconic, even, than Stravinsky's *The Soldier's Tale.* Like that work, it deals with big themes in terse, telling fashion.

Margaret Astrup, the Pelagia, caught the tone precisely. Her aria—parallel to the Meditation in Massenet's *Thaïs* entrusted to the solo violin—was movingly sung, and beneath her monk's cowl (Nonnus, overcoming his canonical scruples, allowed Pelagia, like Leonora in Verdi's *Forza,* to pass as a male penitent), her features shone with spiritual beauty. The other singers—one doubling as Pelagia's maidservant and a nun, one as her good and evil geniuses—had their moments but spoiled their performances by striving for volume. The St. Michael's hall is a place where a whisper carries, where singers can concentrate on gentleness, easiness, refinement and charm of timbre, and delicately shaped words. No need there to push, force, and coarsen the tone; no need to yell. Douglas Anderson conducted.

Young Handel, in Rome in 1707, was made welcome by the Arcadian Academy, among whose shepherds were Arcimelo and Terpando, better known to us as Arcangelo Corelli and Alessandro Scarlatti. The Academy had been founded in Queen Christina's honor in 1690, the year after her death, and it was modelled on her Accademia Reale. A composer once in the Queen's service and later active at the Teatro Tordinona, which she supported, was Alessandro Stradella. He died three years before Handel was born, and he was one of the seventeenth-century composers from whom Handel borrowed. He was an innovator: Burney praises his "ingenious imitations, elegant passages, and new expressions of words and modulation, at the time they were composed." He wrote an oratorio about St. Pelagia. And, like Handel, he wrote one about Esther, which was given what was announced as a New York première last month in Corpus Christi Church, in the Sunday-afternoon Music Before 1800 series. Stradella's *Ester, liberatrice del populo ebreo,* is a simpler work than Handel's *Esther* (which is based on a Racine play), but it is not undramatic. The heroine is characterized with clear, gracious music. Ahasuerus (Xerxes) comes to life in a chivalrous, flowing aria; after learning of Haman's treason, he declares that he must calm himself by walking amid trees and flowers (and one is reminded of Handel's Xerxes, whose first utterance is a love song to a plane tree). But their roles, and that of Mordecai, are small. Somewhat surprisingly, the dominant figure of the oratorio is the ambitious Haman, the villain of the piece. He has the first big solo. Part I closes with a long, powerful, rhetorical dialogue between him and Celestial Hope; at its climax the two break into each other's sentences, and it ends abruptly as Hope, determined to have the last word, flings back at Haman—after the cadence, unaccompanied—a phrase he used earlier. This is a lively account of a dignified argument turning into a spat. In Part II, Haman, on learning of his condemnation, has a wonderful recitative-arioso sequence, punctuated by a recurrent line. (This is a frequent device in the work.) He turns to the Queen and asks her to plead for him, but Xerxes intervenes before she can reply. The final scene—after Celestial Hope has returned to Haman, to point out that she has won the argument broken off at the end of Part I, and to draw a melodious moral—is an extended, Macbeth-like monologue for Haman, with astonishing harmonic leaps: "Son fabbro de' miei danni, Ed ingannato son da' propri inganni. . . . O superbia, o miseria, o fato, o sorte!" Some phrases of narrative, sung by artists not engaged in the action, bridge the scenes and keep the story moving. The few choruses (sung by the soloists in concert) are dramatic, not gnomic: at the start, lamentations by the Jews; in Part II a general cry of "Fall, perish, die, villain," which reinforces Xerxes' sentence and recurs suddenly at the very end. (The effect is like that of the brief cries that succeed Macbeth's dying monologue in Verdi's 1847 opera.) There may once have been string parts. If so, they are lost. What survives is a vocal score.

Robert Kuehn was a striking Haman. The others in a pleasing cast were Cheryl Bensman (Esther), Lisa Nappi (Celestial Hope), Kurt-Owen Richards (Xerxes), and Michael Brown (Mordecai). Louise Basbas, at the harpsichord, directed a performance that moved well. Judith Davidoff, viola da gamba, was the string bass.

Later that day—the Fourth Sunday in Lent—the New Amsterdam Singers, in Merkin Hall, sang three well-contrasted masterpieces of Handel's church music, from three decades: the Chandos anthem "O sing unto the Lord" (1717), the coronation anthem "Let thy hand be strengthened" (1727), and the funeral anthem for Queen Caroline, "The ways of Zion do mourn" (1737). The first was written for James Brydges, soon to become Duke of Chandos, and his musical establishment at Cannons: an altoless choir of about eight singers, each a soloist in his own right, and a little band. "O sing unto the Lord" is an expansive, elaborate piece for small forces; the tenor solo "The waves of the sea rage horribly" is vivid. For George II's coronation, in Westminster Abbey, Handel commanded (according to a report in the Norwich *Gazette*) a chorus of forty and a band of a hundred and sixty. "Let thy hand" is grand and simple, apt for a very resonant space, and not merely ceremonial. It takes a somber E-minor turn when justice and judgment, mercy and truth are enjoined on the new sovereign. The funeral anthem was sung in the Henry VII chapel of the Abbey, and now Handel commanded (according to a report in the *Grub-Street Journal*) "near eighty vocal performers and a hundred instrumental." (But what the papers say must always be treated with caution.) This was Handel's first large composition after his physical and mental breakdown, earlier in the year, and it reveals his powers fully, gloriously recovered. Handel had known the Queen as a young princess; he was music master to her daughters; she had long been his loyal champion. Deep personal feeling seems to mingle with the national mourning for one of England's most cultivated and estimable queens. "Her judgment was a robe and a diadem."

On his copy of the Order of Service book for the 1727 coronation the Archbishop of Canterbury jotted down, "The anthems in confusion; all irregular in the music." And after Queen Caroline's funeral the Duke of Chandos wrote to his nephew, "The composition was exceeding fine . . . but I can't say so much of the performance." There is something to be said for concert-hall conditions, which allow for neater execution. Merkin Hall is less resonant than and very different in atmosphere from the Abbey or St. Lawrence's, the church near Cannons where the Chandos anthems were probably first sung. But the performances by the New Amsterdam Singers—sixty-one strong and accompanied by a small, adept band—were neither confused nor irregular. Bart Folse conducted an enthusiastic account of "Let thy hand," and Clara Longstreth, the

Singers' musical director, conducted the Chandos and funeral anthems with a beat that looked tight and constricted but in fact allowed the long periods to flow. Since the choir abounds in altos, it was understandable that the Chandos anthem was done in a modern edition that (not unskillfully) rearranges the soprano-tenor-bass disposition for soprano-alto-tenor-bass. In the funeral anthem, some passages were assigned to a quartet of soloists, which may be unauthentic but could hardly be deplored in this intimate performance—especially when it brought us the radiant soprano of Dawn Upshaw and the exquisite singing and diction of the countertenor Drew Minter.

Christopher Hogwood's *Handel,* just published by Thames & Hudson, is a clear, well-proportioned, readable biography, made vivid by copious contemporary comments and—since great men's works do follow them—brought to the present day. It uses the new information about Handel that has turned up since Otto Erich Deutsch published his big documentary biography, thirty years ago—material that has been available, for the most part, only scattered through many articles, reviews, prefaces, etc. The illustrations are numerous and well chosen. There is no list of works, but there is a valuable, trustworthy chronological table, in parallel columns of biographical incident and performances, by Anthony Hicks.

TRUE COLORS

April 15, 1985

THE Metropolitan Opera's production of the three-act *Lulu,* in 1980, was serious and beautiful. This season's revival is even finer—one of the best things the company has done in years. Anyone tempted after *Francesca da Rimini, Ernani, Porgy and Bess, Tosca* to dismiss the house as a place of serious artistic endeavor must think again. One reason for the higher excellence may be that in 1980 three of the principals—Teresa Stratas as Lulu, Franz Mazura as Dr. Schön and Jack the Ripper, and Kenneth Riegel as Alwa—came to the production from the première of the three-act *Lulu,* in Paris the previous year, and had not quite freed themselves from its influence. That Paris production, directed by Patrice Chéreau and designed by Richard Peduzzi, was imposing, but in a perverse fashion—musically and dramatically at odds with what Berg wrote. It was conducted by Pierre Boulez in a cold, analytical manner. At the Met, on the other hand, the conductor, the director, and the designer—James Levine, John Dexter, and Jocelyn Herbert—addressed themselves to Berg's score as champions and allies of the composer-dramatist, and their decision to present rather than to contradict, subvert, and alter his work bore rich fruit. In the revival, Mr. Mazura, Mr. Riegel, and in the title role Julia Migenes-Johnson (who sang some of the 1980 performances) seem more confident and more Bergian than before.

Miss Herbert's settings and costumes are at once exquisite and theatrical; moreover, they are cunningly planned to overcome so far as possible the disadvantages of the enormous house and to give immediacy to the drama. Mr. Dexter's direction is filled with careful, vivid detail—none of it obtrusive or gratuitous, all of it springing from character. (The nearest thing to a conventional "director's stroke" is a tableau of Jack the Ripper standing vampirelike in the moonlight, after "Wir brauchen kein Licht, der Mond scheint.") Mr. Levine's conducting is likewise marvellously detailed yet wholly unaffected. His command of motif, instrumental color, and formal structure is complete, and at the service of expressiveness. The orchestral playing is superlatively good. One could attend this *Lulu* with eyes shut, ignoring the drama, and be thrilled by what happens in the music. When the music conspires at almost every point with so lively and precise a visualization and enactment of the score, the result is overwhelming. Mr. Levine and Mr. Dexter are embarrassed by neither the comic-strip incidents that are a part of the work nor the passages of lyrical effusiveness. This is an art in which farce and tragedy can be present at once, as they are in the Elvira-Leporello-Giovanni scenes of Mozart's opera.

The critic must add just a few buts. Miss Migenes-Johnson—a slender, graceful young woman, a remarkable actress, an exceptional musician, and a highly accomplished singer—comes as close to being the ideal Lulu as one is likely to see and hear in a single interpreter. She has the vocal and the emotional range for the role. She holds eye and ear intent, and delights the listener with her delicate timing and inflections. She is a "star," yet there is nothing stagy in her portrayal: she has Lulu's naturalness and spontaneity. But one wishes that her timbre were a shade fuller in the large soaring phrases. Evelyn Lear, the Countess Geschwitz (and once a notable Lulu herself), plays the tragic role with dignity and presence and is very moving, but her tone is not pure. Mr. Riegel has become an entirely convincing Alwa, as singer and as actor, in every way but one: he still flecks his performance by beat-watching; in the love duet his attention seemed divided between Lulu and the conductor or the prompter. No reservations, no buts, about Mr. Mazura; I cannot imagine the complicated role of Dr. Schön more clearly or more powerfully done. There are good performances by Edward Sooter (the Painter, the Negro), Lenus Carlson (the Animal Tamer, the Acrobat), Hilda Harris (the Wardrobe Mistress, the Schoolboy, the Page—but odd of her to keep the schoolboy cap on in Lulu's salon), Robert Nagy (the Prince, the Manservant, the Marquis), and Ara Berberian (the Theatre Manager, the Banker). Above all, there is the sense of a company rapt in the work and building on the foundation of its earlier performances. Andrew Foldi has been the Schigolch since first the Met did the opera, in two-act form, eight years ago, and he has been the Schigolch of many other productions. His portrayal of the old man's relationship with Lulu was even subtler than before. The execution of the elaborate gambling scene was still not quite expert—the busy realism that Mr. Dexter has rightly striven for yields to a few frozen groupings when the trickiest ensemble moments arrive—but it is far more nearly right than before, and one feels that this cast will not rest until it does the scene better still.

Small things: Lulu shouldn't point the revolver at Dr. Schön at the start of her Lied ("Wenn sich die Menschen"), where Berg instructs her to lower it. The murder of Alwa would be more convincingly effected by means of a blackjack, a life preserver (called in German a *Totschläger,* a "death dealer"), as the composer requires, than by knocking his head against a post; the music allows for just one fatal whack, not repeated knocking. Jack shouldn't wipe his hands on Lulu's portrait; there's no portrait motif in the music here. The large point is that this is in sum a wonderful performance. *Lulu* remains a bewildering opera but a rich and engrossing one—more so than ever in this production not simplified to embody a single directorial "concept." It is sung and spoken in German—clearly pronounced and, by nearly all the cast, tellingly used.

Handelian adventures and revelations continue. *Saul,* the grandest of Handel's music dramas, begins with an epinicion and closes with an exequy. *Israel in Egypt,* the oratorio that followed, reverses the order. Part I is the "Lamentations of the Israelites for the Death of Joseph," and Part III, "Moses' Song," is a setting of Exodus 15:1–21: "I will sing unto the Lord, for he hath triumphed gloriously: the horse and his rider hath he thrown into the sea." Between them is "Exodus," an epic narrative of the plagues and the crossing of the Red Sea. Handel began with Part III (three days after finishing *Saul*). Perhaps he embarked on it as an anthem and later realized that it might well crown an oratorio. The autograph of "Exodus," begun a fortnight later, is headed "Act ye 2," which suggests that he had already decided that Part I should be his Funeral Anthem for Queen Caroline—music too noble not to survive its occasion—preceded by an overture and adjusted by a few changes of text (mainly "he" for "she," and so on). *Israel in Egypt* had its first performance, at the King's Theatre, in April 1739. It was not a success. The pious debated the propriety of singing biblical words in a public playhouse. (*Messiah,* which had its London première in Covent Garden, four years later, was still more strongly censured.) Opera fanciers were unentranced by an elevated score containing very few arias and no solo characters except, briefly, Miriam the prophetess—a soprano who in twelve solo bars proposes the theme of the final chorus. At the second performance, *Israel* was announced as "shortned and Intermix'd with Songs," and in time it lost Part I altogether. Without Part I, it became a Victorian favorite. The first recording of classical music ever made was, it seems, of an *Israel in Egypt* chorus sung by four thousand voices at the 1888 Crystal Palace Handel Festival. The *Illustrated London News* of the day declared that it "reported with perfect accuracy the sublime strains, vocal and instrumental." The cylinder is now at the Edison National Historic Site, in West Orange, New Jersey.

Since 1739, the oratorio has rarely been heard complete, and the published scores contain only Parts II and III. But it was done in full in Carnegie Hall twenty years ago. Last year, reports came from Boston of a full, three-part performance by the Cantata Singers and of its success. And last month in Merkin Hall the Sine Nomine Singers and Baroque Orchestra, conducted by Harry Saltzman, presented a full performance that triumphantly vindicated Handel's original scheme. Without the elegy, we plunge too soon into the comedy numbers of Part II: the hippity-hoppity figures of "Their land brought forth frogs, yea, even in the King's chambers"; the buzzing and itchy violin runs of "And there came all manner of flies and lice in all their quarters"; the "plop . . . plop-plop" with which the hailstorm begins. Without the elegy, the oratorio seems unbalanced, both musically (for the final choruses are weighty) and emotionally (for the uninhibited jubilation needs to be justified by the earlier tribulation). *Israel* need never again be done in truncated form. The Sine Nomine performance lasted only three hours. The 1739 performance must have lasted longer; it included, according to the *Daily Post*, "several Concerto's on the Organ."

"Sublime" and "sublimity" are recurrent words in commentary on the oratorio. Sedley Taylor, for example (in his book on Handel's borrowings), calls the chorus "He led them through the deep," in Part II, "that superb oceanic commingling of sublimity and loveliness," and the chorus "The people shall hear," in Part III, "probably the greatest of all Handel's polyphonic compositions, and certainly one which both as respects construction and sublimity has been surpassed by the choral masterpieces of J. S. Bach alone." The passage telling of "thick darkness over all the land, even darkness, which might be felt" is harmonically as dense and mysterious today as it must have seemed to Handel's contemporaries; the chorus in its first five bars sounds all twelve tones. But *Israel in Egypt* presents the problems of Handel's borrowings from other composers in acute form. Part III is largely recomposition of a Magnificat by Dionigi Erba; Part II is largely recomposition of a serenata by Alessandro Stradella (one dealing with two gentlemen wooing a fair lady) and includes a choral transcription of a keyboard piece by J. K. Kerll—a composer who also contributed to *Messiah*, and who supplied Bach with the start of a Sanctus. The sublime choruses mentioned above seem to be Handel's own inspirations, and that's reassuring. It is disconcerting to find that other high moments—the plop of the hailstones, the serene pastoral lilt of "He led them forth like sheep"— were composed by Stradella.

But in performance there is one glorious sweep of music, with its climaxes and its points of repose carefully placed. Handel repaid his debts with interest. Mr. Saltzman's account of the work was surely fashioned. He, his singers, and his players had a true Handelian response to imagery. The words were clear; the phrases were sharply defined; the colors of the baroque strings, woodwinds, brasses (*Israel*, like *Saul*, uses trombones as well as trumpets), and drums were bright.

A test of a music school's liveliness is its students' eagerness—and ability—to play contemporary music. Indiana University's Music School, at Bloomington, passes with high marks on the strength of the two concerts that its New Music Ensemble brought to Symphony Space last month. The ensemble's director is Harvey Sollberger, well known in New York as a conductor, flutist, and composer. The first concert began and the second ended with a piece from the past: Edgard Varèse's *Octandre* and Aaron Copland's *Appalachian Spring* suite, in the small-orchestra version. Otherwise, the oldest work was Charles Wuorinen's *Hyperion*, for twelve players, of 1975. I underrated it at its première; perhaps it was less well played then. Speculum Musicae later took it up and brought it to life. The Bloomington performance was bright, assured, very well balanced, wholly enjoyable.

Four works by Indiana University composers had New York premières. None of them call for either enthusiasm or disdain. Juan Orrego-Salas's *Cinco*

Canciones a seis (1983–84), a cycle for mezzo-soprano and five players, foundered on a mezzo-soprano who had an agreeable voice but delivered the poems as if she had learned only how to pronounce Spanish, not how to speak the language and bring it to life. Frederick Fox's *Sonaspheres 5,* for ten players, matched expectations roused by the title and by a program note announcing "a sixteen-minute work in five major sections delineated by tempo and extreme character change," in which "all pitch material is drawn from a chromatic pitch-set and is developed by a variation process." That's unfair criticism—there are masterpieces to which similar sentences apply—but it suggests the kind of work that, a listener feels, has been conscientiously and thoroughly constructed but not written because the composer felt a burning need to share a vision. Sollberger's own *The Humble Heart/cat Scan* (1982), a woodwind quintet, is hardly more than adept doodling over and around two Shaker tunes. One of them is "Simple Gifts," the song that is also the making of Copland's *Appalachian Spring.* The other, "The Humble Heart," is set going at five different speeds simultaneously; the passage is phase music that builds up a blurred seven-note chord of modal E minor. The end, a musical disintegration "symbolic of the dispersal of the Shakers" (the composer says in his program note), is striking; but, like the tune-superimposition episode, it seems more a promising notion mechanically worked out than inspired composition. Donald Erb's *The Devil's Quickstep* (1982), for seven players, made attractive and ingenious sounds, as does all the music by him that I have heard.

Milton Babbitt's *Four Play* (1984) is more challenging both to its four players and to its listeners. Listeners whose discernment I trust told me that the four young players—Michael Chesher (clarinet), Chris Chappell (violin), Karl Parens (cello), and Efrain Amaya (piano)—met the challenge magnificently. But this is one of the Babbitt works—here a sound, there a sound—that I can't begin to enter into or make sense of. Some of his pieces seem so lyrical, so exciting, so lovable; others prove impenetrable. "Inspired composition" is what I heard in John Eaton's *The Cry of Clytaemnestra,* represented at these concerts by the protagonist's central aria and final scene. The opera was performed first in Bloomington in 1980, and later that year at the Brooklyn Academy. Since I have lately been collaborating with Eaton (as librettist) on a forthcoming opera, I'll confine comment to what I wrote about *Clytaemnestra* back in 1980, before I knew him: that he has a born opera composer's mastery of vocal gesture, a full armory of expressive devices, a fine ear, and a soaring musical imagination. In Symphony Space, Nelda Nelson, the original Clytaemnestra, gave a tremendous performance—dramatic, noble, and impassioned. The electronic music was missing—someone forgot to throw a switch—and yet, while this lessened the impact of the whole, it emphasized the power of the purely vocal and instrumental writing.

April 22, 1985

THE Metropolitan Opera's Easter revival of *Parsifal* was very well conducted and very well played. There are occasions when a listener seems to know from the opening bars that an evening is going to be good—or no good. The opening of this *Parsifal*—the five and a half bars of unison line ascending through an octave, then falling back—gave assurance of a lovingly rehearsed, pondered, serious performance. Wagner's marking for the passage is "very slow" and "very expressive," and it was both. The timbre is complicated: clarinet, bassoon, and one player at each desk of the violins and the cellos, muted; English horn joining in at the crest of the phrase and then falling out again. James Levine, conducting, and his players made it marvellously eloquent—a unison of blended, living, subtly shifting colors. There are two sixteenth-notes in the phrase. Felix Mottl, who helped to prepare the première of *Parsifal,* in 1882 (and also prepared the Met stage première, in 1903), edited a score of the opera to which he added numerous extra indications, musical and scenic, based on his observation of the Master at work. Under the opening bars he has the footnote "The sixteenths always tranquil and drawn out." ("Don't hurry the little notes; sound them; enjoy them; give them their full value—and then some" is a maxim apt to the execution of many slow melodies.) Mr. Levine didn't skimp them. And by his broad, tenderly weighted delivery of the bars he laid surely the foundation for the great span of music that ended, in the same key, nearly five and a half hours later. *Parsifal* is a work that moves slowly in some ways, but few operas are more richly packed with incident calling for bar-by-bar concentrated attention. Lucy Beckett, the author of the Cambridge Opera Handbook for *Parsifal,* after devoting more than four pages of her synopsis chapter to just four minutes of the work (the first dialogue between Parsifal and Gurnemanz in Act III), says, rightly, "Nothing happens—two characters stand still on the stage and sing in turn, while a third listens—and yet a great deal takes place." Bayreuth is the house for *Parsifal,* but there is something to be said for hearing it in a conventional theatre with an open orchestra pit; as Richard Strauss once remarked, "Many of the inexhaustible riches of the scores are lost at Bayreuth." At the Met, one is in closer contact with the eventfulness in the orchestra. This may not be what Wagner intended, but it provides a complementary revelation of the opera. Mr. Levine (who is now also Bayreuth's regular conductor of *Parsifal*) obtained a broad, smooth sound, not a fierce one, and a balance that allowed the voices to come through almost as freely as they do at Bayreuth. And in New York he has a finer orchestra. The only passage that disturbed one was his hearty handling of the communion hymn. He invested it with a "Pomp and

297

Circumstance" swagger. But Wagner marked each phrase of the hymn to begin piano and to swell only in its final bars to full-throated affirmation: that way, it could seem devotional.

Kurt Moll sang his first Met Gurnemanz. He gave a wise, noble performance, especially notable for clear, telling pronunciation of the words—for utterance in which consonants, vowels, sense, and sound made one memorable shape. His voice is powerful, steady, and firmly focussed, without woofiness; he drew precise and beautiful lines. In the rapturous outbursts, his tone did not flower as generously as Ludwig Weber's once did, but since Weber there has perhaps not been a Gurnemanz more poetic or more moving. (Hans Hotter was as poetic and moving but less firm of voice.) Leonie Rysanek sang her first Met Kundry. She left it late. In the big scene of Act II, she sometimes felt her way into each sustained note (while little notes fell by the way) and then opened into it; this made the slow phrases sluggish. When, on the other hand, she sang impetuously, she lost control of the line. Act II calls for a lustrous vocalist at the height of her powers; otherwise Kundry is not exactly a "singing" role. Her part in Act I is largely exclamatory ("Hier! . . . Nimm du! . . . Balsam"), while in Act III she is onstage for the full eight minutes but sings only four notes. (Timings of this act vary from sixty-five minutes, in Pierre Boulez's Bayreuth performance, to ninety, in Toscanini's.) Miss Rysanek is very good at exclamations, as she is famous for her screams. "Kundry emits a horrifying yell" and "Kundry gives vent to a howl of despair, dropping from the greatest force to a frightened whimper" are directions in Act II which she fulfilled memorably. But it was as an actress that she triumphed, revealing in each move, gesture, or episode of stillness the woman that Miss Beckett calls "certainly the strangest and perhaps the most profound of all Wagner's characters."

Jon Vickers returned to the title role—which he has been singing for over twenty-five years—with undiminished vocal vigor and with force of character perhaps even greater. In Act I, as an impulsive boy he was visually unconvincing, and his timbre was too mature, too heroic; but there seemed to be limitless grandeur and gravity in the Parsifal of Act II (after Kundry's kiss has changed him from heedless youth to holy redeemer) and of Act III. Spiritual radiance appeared to flood him. Sympathetic pain rent him. The combination of earnestness with compassion, of sternness with sweetness was overwhelming. It was not a comfortable performance. The confusion of Parsifal with Christ is Kundry's—the heated Kundry of Act II—not Wagner's. Parsifal (I quote Miss Beckett again) "must not be seen as Christ, the Redeemer, but only as a man redeemed, who nevertheless carries the responsibility of revealing Christ's continuing redemptive power to the world." Yet Mr. Vickers's and Miss Rysanek's reënactment of Christ and the Magdalen and his mystic celebration of the Last Supper were so vivid as to make their presentation in a common playhouse almost unseemly. Still, the Met program translates Wagner's term for *Parsifal,* "Bühnenweihfestspiel," as "stage-consecrating festival play," and in a performance like this the Met stage does become a consecrated place. Mr. Vickers is a tenor who avowedly "carries the responsibility of revealing Christ's continuing redemptive power to the world," and he does so here in a performance that transcends mere aesthetic appraisal. On that lower level, however, let it be noted that, although a brutal snarl entered his timbre at times, usually on an *e* vowel ("*e*wig"), the *ai* and *a* ("*eine* Waffe"), *o*("*O*!"), and *i* ("schl*i*esst") sounds rang out with force and freedom. And noted, too, that today there are no other tenors, and few singers, who interpret with such intensity.

The rest of the cast was Met routine. The performance was dedicated to the memory of George London; he and Hotter were the great Amfortases of their day. The part was sung by Simon Estes—an unsatisfactory performer, for although there are striking sounds in his voice, he tends to bugle them out at the audience in a way that says "Admire me" and undermines belief in the character he portrays. Klingsor was Morley Meredith. Titurel was Julien Robbins, admirably dark and steady. The knights, squires, and flower maidens were cast with the regular Met comprimari. Some of them were good. But it is hard to believe that if Mr. Levine carefully combed through his company, choristers included, he could not assemble posses of steadier, smoother, well-matched voices to fill these important roles. If there are no poetic, radiant contraltos left in the modern world (and I can't think of one), perhaps the utterance stealing from on high at the close of Act I should be entrusted to a countertenor—Drew Minter, Jeffrey Gall—who could invest it with the beauty and significance it requires.

The production, designed in 1970 by Robert O'Hearn and directed by Nathaniel Merrill, is undistinguished. It's Wieland Wagner softened around the edges. It adds nothing but is not offensive. (The only absurdity now is the entry of the knights in Act III, staggering in lockstep like drunken sailors.) There is a sad lack of color, however. Wagner's Hall of the Grail glittered with bright mosaics, and his flower garden was gaudy. Here the Good Friday meadow remained drab even while the orchestra painted the bright burgeoning scene. (The audience had to carry into the theatre the sight of the city outside, bursting with the annual miracle of spring.) The lighting, uncredited, was careful, except when it belied Gurnemanz's remarks in Act I that "the sun is high now" and in Act III that it is noon.

The first-night Met audience gave its own virtuoso performance, by sustaining a steady obbligato of open, unstifled coughing for over five hours. (Each passing hour was signalled by electronic beeping from unmuted wristwatches.) Seldom did two consecutive bars go by undisturbed by coughers, answering one another from side to side of the theatre, now high, now low, like farm dogs in the hills on a moonlit night.

The opening notes of the *Parsifal* prelude, with the same note lengths, occur in the long melody at the start of Beethoven's A-flat Sonata, Opus 110, and Wagner's theme closes into its cadence and into a stirring of A-flat arpeggios much as Beethoven's does. Wagner's thoughts moved to Beethoven's late sonatas while he was composing this music. On September 25, 1877, Cosima noted in her diary, "R. says that, if he were to try to visualize Beethoven 'in his starry glory' he would have to think of the second movement of Opus 111 (the Adagio with Variations); he knows nothing so ecstatic, yet at the same time it is not at all sentimental." On the twenty-sixth—which Cosima recorded as "a strange, wonderful day"—he played the *Parsifal* prelude to her, from the orchestral sketch: "Wonderful mingling in the prelude, of mysticism and chivalry. The D-major modulation is for him like the spreading of the tender revelation throughout all the world." Their conversation turned to Christ: "The Gospel account of the day before His death mankind's most sublime achievement, incomparable, divine!" Musical settings of that Gospel account—by Schütz, by Handel, above all by Bach—have been among musical mankind's sublime achievements.

On Good Friday, in Alice Tully Hall, the Florilegium Chamber Choir and Baroque Orchestra, conducted by JoAnn Rice, sang and played Bach's Passion According to St. John. There were twenty-eight choral voices, a band of seventeen, and continuo shared between a harpsichord, played by Miss Rice, and the Tully Hall organ, played by Walter Hilse in semitone-downward transposition to match the baroque pitch of the others. (The use of the harpsichord, as Arthur Mendel says in the introduction to his edition of the Passion, "has little historical justification" but is "in no way artistically disturbing.") It was a well-paced and well-balanced performance, cleanly and vigorously sung, with variety—but not exaggeration—of expression. Florilegium has become a much stronger chorus than it was three years ago. A new English translation, by Miss Rice, was used. I was brought up on the Ivor Atkins edition of the St. John Passion and the Elgar-Atkins edition of the St. Matthew, both published by Novello. ("The treatment of Bach's recitative in relation to the English Bible marked an important stage in the appreciation of Bach's Passion settings in England," says Grove.) In America, Henry S. Drinker's translations (given new currency by the New Bach Edition vocal scores, published by Bärenreiter) and, for the St. John, Mendel's revision of Drinker, published by G. Schirmer, are familiar. An announcement of the Rice version said, "Unfortunately, most published translations of the St. John Passion reflect the language used in the King James Bible." Fortunately, Miss Rice did not stray disturbingly far from that language. And the Evangelist—Frank Hoffmeister, who was clear, direct, and admirable—sometimes returned to the Mendel text. In the arias and chorales, Miss Rice sought to avoid "Victorian-style poetry." The soprano aria "Ich folge dir gleichfalls mit freudigen Schritten" was translated by Atkins "I follow, I follow, in gladness to meet Thee," which fits the music well. Mendel has "I follow Thee also with joy-lightened footsteps." Miss Rice's "I'll follow Thee gladly and cheerfully serve Thee," although adding a new idea, improves on Mendel, if not on Atkins. A few things in her version jarred: "verlacht, verhöhnt and verspeit," in the chorale that opens the second part, became "taunted, flaunted, and defiled," and, in the penultimate chorale, "O hilf, Christe, Gottes Sohn,/durch dein bittres Leiden" was most oddly rendered as "When the world with devils filled/threatens to undo us."

Two days earlier, in Carnegie Hall, there was a St. John Passion—or, rather, a Johannes-Passion, since it was sung in German—which opened Carnegie's "Choral Celebration of Bach." The St. Matthew Passion—the Matthäus-Passion—followed on Holy Saturday, and the B-minor Mass on Easter Day. All three were conducted by John Nelson, played by the Orchestra of St. Luke's, and sung by the American Boychoir and the Male Choir of St. Luke's. Elly Ameling was the soprano soloist of the St. John and the Mass, Sylvia McNair of the St. Matthew. Jorma Hynninen sang Christ in both Passions. Chris Merritt was the Evangelist of the St. John and the tenor soloist of the St. Matthew. The countertenor Paul Esswood, the tenor John Aler (Evangelist of the St. Matthew), and the bass John Cheek sang in all three works. It should have amounted to something marvellous. It didn't, for reasons hard to understand. The choir sounded thin and weak; in the St. John it was not until the final chorus that it produced any real *tone*. (There were twenty-two trebles, and six men to a part in the St. John and the Mass, four to a part in the double-choir St. Matthew.) Carnegie Hall is smaller than St. Thomas's, in Leipzig, but also a good deal drier; it doesn't "fill out" voices as church acoustics can. Odd things happened to the balance. In the "Qui tollis," two (modern) flutes drowned the full chorus. But often the orchestral playing seemed indistinct. The throbbing bass notes of the "Crucifixus" ran together. The lack of a crisp, solid organ, such as underpinned the Florilegium choruses, was felt; there was just a whiffling little positive organ (two of them in the St. Matthew), adequate for accompanying recitative and aria, not for the full ensemble.

To undertake three immense, engrossing choral masterpieces in the space of five days was no doubt presumptuous—too much to ask of any singers and players. Yet the works had been carefully prepared, and Mr. Nelson had clearly given thought to their architecture and to the style of execution. The performances foundered, probably, on his fondness for excessively, eccentrically brisk tempi. Singers and players seldom had much chance of listening to themselves and to each other, of tuning and shaping their phrases in balanced counterpoints or full, sonorous harmony. "Ich folge dir" was pushed through at such a lick that Miss Ameling and the flutes could not breathe and define their lines or answer one another in happy dialogue. Likewise the "Laudamus te," with Kathryn Bouleyn, the second soprano of the Mass, and the solo violin. "Cum sancto spiritu" aspired to the condition of Mendelssohn's *Midsummer Night's Dream* scherzo. When Mr. Nelson did give the music time to register, there were some wonderful moments. One was the choral cry "Wahrlich, dieser ist Gottes Sohn gewesen," in the St. Matthew. The Benedictus was not taken too fast, and Mr. Aler and the solo flute could both be eloquent. Nor was the Agnus Dei, of which Mr. Esswood—who until then had sounded frayed of voice—gave an exquisitely molded and moving account.

EXPRESSIVE, LUCID, ROMANTIC

April 29, 1985

THE Juilliard String Quartet, forty years old next year, has introduced new quartets by the dozen. Some of them go on to enter the repertory (Elliott Carter's Second and Third Quartets come to mind), some are soon forgotten, and some are revived from time to time. Prophecy is rash, but Donald Martino's String Quartet, of which the Juilliard this month gave the New York première, at a recital in the Juilliard Theater, seems to me to be a work that should enter the repertory. It proved enthralling at a first hearing, and repeated hearings (by way of a tape recording) each time left me eager to listen to it yet again. It is a rich piece. The quartet was commissioned by the Elizabeth Sprague Coolidge Foundation, to celebrate the Juilliard's twenty years as quartet-in-residence at the Library of Congress, and was first played in the Library last October. It has also been played in Cambridge. It lasts just over half an hour. There are four movements—distinct, but linked by adagio cadenzalike passages. The opening is a twelve-note melody, *ansioso* (a recurrent expressive indication). The first six notes limn a wedge shape, in even quarters: B-flat, A, B, A-flat, C, G. There's a brief hold, and then, in eighths, the next six notes close down again, onto E. The first strain is unisono or in octaves, begun by the cello, with viola, second violin, and then first violin stealing into the melody (with octave displacements that give to each player's line a different shape and subtly shift the color balances on each note). The second strain has holds that add harmonies to the melody. Then, differently transformed on each instrument, the shape is speeded up, slowed down, and speeded up again to lead into the energetic first subject, on the first violin, which springs recognizably from the same shape but leaps exultantly across octaves and has a sharp rhythmic profile.

The score is published by Dantalian. I've made small analytical sorties into it, always with satisfying results. But analysis—discovering the constructional details of a span of music—tells nothing about merit. I must use more emotive language—as Elaine Barkin, the author of the New Grove entry on Martino, does when, after speaking of "the projection of 'simultaneously-progressing total-set forms' . . . delineated by registral stratification and differentiated dynamics and articulation," she concludes: "Martino's music has been characterized as expressive, dense, lucid, dramatic, romantic, all of which are applicable. But it is his ability—as he engages himself in a world of virtuoso music-making—to conjure up for the listener a world of palpable presences and conceptions . . . that seems most remarkable." The vigorous melodies of the quartet are elating, the slow melodies affecting. Beneath much of the first movement there seems to run a vein of seductive, lilting waltz tune. The second movement is a mercurial scherzo-rondo, the third a set of variations, each tautly characterized. The finale contemplates what has gone before; in the words of the composer's program note, "at first it seems to be trying to find a resolution to the problem of summarizing previous arguments," until after alternate propositions "the ultimate solution is found in music reminiscent of the Andantino cantabile of Movement III."

The music is precisely imagined and is set down with meticulous instructions to the performers about articulation, tempo, and rhythm. However, they are then urged, after "having observed the mathematics," to let "expressive character" and "rubato character" be their guides. The music is alive in every line. As one gets to know it better, delight in the progress is enhanced by appreciation of the fine contributory details. I'm no string player, but it seems to me this quartet must be good to play. It's certainly good to listen to. The Juilliard Quartet's performance was eloquent—amazingly brilliant and sure, always expressive.

The concert began with two of the earlier works composed for the ensemble:

Irving Fine's String Quartet (1952), a dramatic piece (there is a recording by the Juilliard, with its original personnel, on CRI); and Fred Lerdahl's First String Quartet (1978), an interesting and skillful composition, which I described after its New York première (*Music of Three More Seasons*, pp. 360–62) and was glad to hear again.

André Emelianoff and Anne-Marie McDermott began their recital in Merkin Hall this month with Samuel Barber's early Cello Sonata, Opus 6, and ended it with Brahms's F-major Cello Sonata, Opus 99. The Barber is a lyrical, beautiful work, and Mr. Emelianoff's performance was poetic. He gave a fervid, large-scale account of the Brahms, pausing to mop his brow after the first movement and giving the listener a chance to metaphorically mop his. This was cello playing in the large grand manner, in the line of Piatigorsky and Rostropovich, but it wasn't too much—not even for listeners attuned to the more classical Brahms of, say, Pierre Fournier. The passion that informed big melodies and exquisite pianissimi alike was communicative. What was odd was the player's avoidance of rich portamento, which cellists of Brahms's day would certainly have used and which would have matched and intensified the other aspects of Mr. Emelianoff's approach.

George Perle's Sonata for Cello and Piano, composed for Mr. Emelianoff, had its first performance. It's an eighteen-minute work in three movements preceded by a long, striking cadenza—almost a movement in itself—for the cello, unaccompanied except at two points. The piece has the elegance, the grace, the deftness so regularly discerned in Perle's recent scores that he may be wondering whether he, the critics, or both are starting to repeat themselves. The new Cello Sonata inhabits the world of Serenade III and the Concertino. The forms are clear, the textures limpid. There is also a vein of elegiac poetry, apt to the cello's emotional tones. Some of the espressivo melodies, moving by semitone over rich harmonies, even brought César Franck to mind.

Two happy finds completed an enjoyable and varied program: Nicolai Roslavets's Cello Sonata, billed as a New York première, and the epilogue of Charles Wakefield Cadman's *A Mad Empress Remembers*. Roslavets is known for having arrived at a twelve-note system independently of Schoenberg; this short one-movement sonata, however, dating from 1921, is closer to Scriabin in its dense, rapturous harmonies. *A Mad Empress Remembers* is a late work of Cadman, for cello and orchestra, dating from 1944 and composed for (but not played by) Piatigorsky. When I heard a studio performance of Cadman's opera *Shanewis*—first done by the Met, in 1918—I thought he deserved to be known by more than the songs "At Dawning" (recorded by Mary Garden, John McCormack, Richard Tauber, and many others) and "From the Land of the Sky-Blue Water" (recorded by Lillian Nordica, Alma Gluck, Jeanette MacDonald, and many others). The epilogue of *A Mad Empress Remembers* (the Empress is Carlota of Mexico), a poignant and striking piece, roused curiosity to hear the complete work, in its orchestral dress.

Miss McDermott, an accomplished and sensitive pianist, played boldly. The balance was not that of a soloist-with-accompanist recital—not in terms of sound. But in terms of temperament it was. I often wonder why at violin or cello recitals the string player turns his back on the pianist—why the platform layout is not so arranged that mutual glances, such as string-quartet players exchange, can pass between the partners before important entries. As it was, Miss McDermott had to read her cues from Mr. Emelianoff's back. She did so ably—the ensemble between the pair was, in fact, excellent—but, particularly in the Brahms sonata, she scarcely took the lead decisively, even in passages that require it.

Stephen Paulus's *Reflections: Four Movements on a Theme of Wallace Stevens*, composed for the St. Paul Chamber Orchestra, had its première last month at a concert conducted by Pinchas Zukerman in St. Paul, and was brought to New York last week, over WNYC, by an American Public Radio presentation of the concert. The movements are entitled "The Holy Hush," "Unsubdued Elations," "Isle Melodious (Remembrance of Awakened Birds)," and "Where Triumph Rang Its Brassy Phrase"—tags from the Stevens poem "Sunday Morning." The music, however, didn't seem to me to have much to do with the poem. The lines are rich in phrases from which almost any pieces of music might be titled. (How about a suite with the titles "Ambiguous Undulations," "The Strings of Our Insipid Lutes," "Love Whispered," and "Chant in Orgy"? Or maybe "Spontaneous Cries," "Echoing Hills," "Grievings in Loneliness," and "A Chant of Paradise"?) It's an agreeable twenty-minute stretch of music that slips down easily. Paulus is a bright, fluent inventor with a ready lyric gift. Yet it is disconcerting to hear music by a fairly young composer (he was born in 1949) that could have been written seventy years ago—and some of it earlier than that. A hint of Wagner here, of Rimsky-Korsakov there, of early Stravinsky everywhere. I suppose there's no reason that the ascent in the *Tristan* Act III prelude shouldn't climb from a soft bell-tree shimmer to depict holy hush. The surging violin unisons that open *Die Walküre* can well serve to depict unsubdued elations. (Are Paulus's unisons also played across two strings at once? It sounded as if they were.) In an intermission talk, the composer said he'd become more conservative than he used to be. And I, who so much enjoyed and admired his first opera, *The Village Singer,* six years ago, could only agree.

Reflections is dedicated to the memory of William Harwood, who conducted *The Village Singer* and also Paulus's second opera, *The Postman Always Rings Twice.* Mr. Harwood died last year, suddenly, and America lost one of its most inspiring young conductors. I first heard his work ten years ago, at a Yale student performance of *Idomeneo,* and on the strength of it called him one of the finest Mozartians of our day. A *Magic Flute* in St. Louis in 1980 confirmed that estimate. He would have made his City Opera début last season.

The broadcast was in good sound but was presented in a way to provoke any musical person to switch off before the concert itself began: first a signature tune, then background music played behind some drivel about music's magic powers, the announcement of the program, and preliminary conversation with the composer. Musicians boycott restaurants, stores, hotels that pipe in music as a "background," flinch when to reach the offices of W. W. Norton, the publishers of "Books That Live in Music," they must ride in a music-loud elevator. They don't expect to hear background music from a serious radio station.

IMMORTAL?

May 6, 1985

THOMAS CARLYLE'S *Life of John Sterling* is the exception: a masterwork of biography written by a great man about a lesser. Most famous biographies shine with reflected glory, and the author becomes altogether invisible in the modern genre of "documentary biographies," such as those Otto Erich Deutsch assembled for Handel, Mozart, and Schubert: compilations of all known facts and contemporary commentary, untouched by what Deutsch called "personal elaborations." Such comprehensiveness becomes impossible when the subjects enter our zealously preservative, overdocumented age; then even the most objective of documentary biographers must begin to show something of himself as he decides what to include, what not.

When Edward Elgar was nine, his mother began to keep press-cutting books about her son's public appearances. His wife continued them, and, later, his daughter. His wife kept a daily diary through the thirty years of their marriage; his daughter kept a diary. Over ten thousand letters written to the Elgars survive; so do many of the replies. Jerrold Northrop Moore, Elgar's latest biographer, mentions this in a preface to his *Edward Elgar: A Creative Life*. It is a long book—850 pages—and a good one, and I think it represents something new in musical biography. The *Times Literary Supplement* reviewer, Donald Mitchell, called it "a work that assiduously collects the facts and attempts rather little in the way of interpreting them." It is true that Mr. Moore says rather little about Elgar's music, essaying neither formal analysis nor descriptive rhapsody. Nor does he intrude presumptuous speculation of his own about Elgar's psyche, personality, or soul. What he has done, with modesty, industry, precision, and discernment, is to master the immense amount of biographical material, both printed and surviving in the memories of those who knew Elgar, and then—this is his high achievement—to recount the details of Elgar's life while trying "to understand what it is to look at the world through creative eyes, to listen through creative ears." Particular attention, therefore, is paid to the circumstances in which arose a new musical idea or a new musical work, and those in which an old idea reoccurred. Interpretation is left to the reader—and to the listener. Mr. Moore does have a thesis, adumbrated in his first sentence—"Music and biography share the expression of time remembered"—and recapitulated in his last sentences: "Those years [1857–1934, Elgar's life span] had seen change accelerate as never before in human history. His response had been to seek the illumination of time remembered. For all of his generation and the future who would feel the insight of retrospection, he had made of that evanescence his music." The thesis is not pressed, nor need it be. The composer Roger Reynolds,

305

lecturing last month at the City University, distinguished between "makers," who order and explain past experience, and "searchers," who through sounds and structures unknown before strive to enlarge the range of that experience. In those terms, Elgar was a maker. Neville Cardus wrote, "He pointed no new direction. If he had never composed a note, there would today be no link missing from the main evolution of the vocabulary and syntax of music." But the world would be poorer. Mr. Moore does not assess Elgar in relation to his contemporaries: Janáček (born in 1854), Mahler and Wolf (1860), Debussy and Delius (1862), Richard Strauss (1864), Sibelius (1865). When he writes about the music, it is usually to show the persistence, reëmergence, and development of shapes, ideas, and images.

It is easy to go on about Elgar "enigmas" and contradictions. The tradesman's son, without university education, suffered slights that were not imaginary. The Roman Catholic composer, in a dominantly Protestant Britain, died, it seems, an unbeliever. The poet who found inspiration in the English countryside and the patriot who wrote "Land of Hope and Glory" composed music whose worth Germans—Hans Richter, Richard Strauss, A. J. Jaeger (Nimrod)—were often swifter than his compatriots to recognize. (Mr. Moore relates Beecham's nasty quip when at a sparsely attended Elgar concert in 1916 someone asked where the composer's friends were: "They've all been interned.") In 1913, when Elgar was famous and honored, *Falstaff* had its London première to rows of empty seats. In 1931, the composer C. W. Orr wrote, "He has been given the Order of Merit by the King and the cold shoulder by the public. . . . He is politely disregarded by the older and patronized by the younger generation of musicians." Confidence, high spirits, even swagger sound in some of his music; Arnold Bax recalled that in 1901 "his appearance was rather that of a retired army officer turned gentleman farmer than an eminent and almost morbidly highly strung artist." But the eyes of a wounded, lonely poet look from his photographs. Mr. Moore does not set out to find neat, easy answers to enigmas. In his pages, which are lit by letters, diaries, reviews, we traverse the events private and public, the triumphs and troubles, of a long, complicated, and interesting life: interesting for its incidents but more so for the way those incidents gave rise to music. Recurrent shadows are cast by the shabby meanness of publishers eager to profit by musicians' work. Recurrent rays are the perceptiveness and support of two critics, Bernard Shaw and Ernest Newman.

The first issue of *Music and Letters,* in 1920, contained a Shaw essay on Elgar. The estimate is high: "To the north countryman who, on hearing of Words-worth's death, said, 'I suppose his son will carry on the business' it would be plain that Elgar is carrying on Beethoven's business." Whether it is justified, Shaw says, only time can show: "Contemporary judgements are sound enough on Second Bests; but when it comes to Bests, they acclaim ephemerals as immortals, and simultaneously denounce immortals as pestilent charlatans." Mr. Moore cites the essay. On the next page he has a passing reference to "a younger composer whose genius seemed clear to almost everyone in England then, Rutland Boughton." Boughton has proved an ephemeral. I was surprised to come across his opera *The Immortal Hour* in New York last month, put on by

Bel Canto. In London, I'd heard enthusiasts' revivals of *The Immortal Hour, Bethlehem, Alkestis* (first done at Covent Garden, in 1924), and *The Queen of Cornwall* (a Tristan opera, its text the Hardy play) with bored, unappreciative ears. Last year, a recording of *The Immortal Hour* appeared, on Hyperion. What on earth did people hear in this music? How could Elgar (according to Kobbé) declare *The Immortal Hour* to be a work of genius? Boughton's biographer Michael Hurd says, "Of the many English composers whose careers overlapped those of Elgar and Vaughan Williams . . . none enjoyed greater success during his lifetime, nor a more total subsequent eclipse, than Rutland Boughton." My parents were among the hundreds of thousands who fell under the spell of *The Immortal Hour* when, in London from 1922 to 1924, it ran and ran and ran. The piano bench at home—like most piano benches of the day, I guess—held a tattered copy of "How beautiful they are, the lordly ones," the Faery Song from the opera.

In 1911, Boughton, aged thirty-three, had published his manifesto *Music Drama of the Future*. Inspired by William Morris, Carlyle, Tolstoy, and Wagner, he proposed to build a theatre in which "dramas of the spirit" would be played: "There have been many communes and they have failed—for lack of a religious center. Our theatre supplies that. It shall grow out of the municipal life of some civically conscious place if we can get such a place to cooperate with us. Failing that, a new city shall grow around the theatre." Letchworth Garden City was considered. Glastonbury was chosen: hallowed Glastonbury, to which Joseph of Arimathæa brought the Grail; which is the Isle of Avalon, where Arthur lies buried; which was once a famous place of pilgrimage. The first Glastonbury Festival would have been held in 1913—a production of *The Birth of Arthur,* the first of Boughton's five Arthurian operas, was planned—had not local supporters been dismayed by the discovery that Boughton and his companion, the artist and designer Christina Walshe, were unwed. The festival was moved to more tolerant Bournemouth. But the following year it was back in Glastonbury, and there for twelve years it continued. The Clarks, a Quaker family, the well-known shoemakers, lent moral and financial support. Glastonbury became a place of pilgrimage again. Seven of Boughton's operas, Purcell's *Dido,* Matthew Locke's *Cupid and Death,* John Blow's *Venus and Adonis,* Gluck's *Iphigenia in Tauris,* plays by Sophocles, Laurence Housman, Lady Gregory were done. By 1924, more than three hundred and fifty operatic performances had been given. The end came when, in 1926, Boughton presented his *Bethlehem* in London in support of the miners' and general strike: Herod a top-hatted capitalist (Shaw's account of Alberich and the Tarnhelm pointed the way), and Christ born in a miner's cottage. Glastonbury collapsed, and Boughton joined the Communist party. He left it in 1929, rejoined it from 1945 to 1956, and died in 1960.

I wish I'd sought him out in his last years. But so total was the eclipse that I didn't even know he was still alive. In any case—beguiled then by Fritz Busch's and Carl Ebert's Glyndebourne, by a Covent Garden where (whatever the attendant shortcomings) Kirsten Flagstad, Ljuba Welitsch, Hans Hotter, and Ludwig Weber were singing, by Benjamin Britten's Aldeburgh, and by Wieland Wagner's Bayreuth—I hardly believed that Glastonbury could have been more than a worthy British endeavor: homemade opera, piano-accompanied, in a village hall. I realize now that I should have been more attentive to a postscript in Shaw's *The Perfect Wagnerite*:

> Mr. Rutland Boughton began in ordinary village halls in Somerset, with a piano and his own fingers for orchestra, his wife as scenepainter and costumier, and a fit-up for a stage. The singing and acting was done by the villagers and by anyone else who would come; and a surprising number of quite distinguished talents did come. On these terms performances were achieved which in point of atmosphere and intimacy of interest were actually better than the performances at the enormously more pretentious Festival Playhouse at Bayreuth.... His festival is now a yearly event.... But it still has no theatre, no electric light, no convenience for Wagnerian drama that every village does not possess. Yet it is here that the Wagnerist dream has been best realized in England.

It is plain now that Boughton's Glastonbury prepared ground for the flowering of music—of all the arts—through postwar Socialist Britain. Bliss was it in that dawn to be alive, and to be young was very heaven! Bright dawns yield often to louring day. In 1899, the year of the Enigma Variations, Elgar stormed from the offices of his publisher, Novello, shocked at the "sheer brutality" of its chairman. To Jaeger he wrote, "I confess the prospect of a rich man seriously considering the fleecing of those poor underpaid, overworked devils in the orchestra *quite* prevented me from feeling Xtian. If that is 'business'—well *damn* your business—I loathe it." At the City University, Roger Reynolds was bitter about the effects of commerce on musical life. And the critic who for a review of a composition may be paid more than its composer earned by weeks, months, years of toil examines his conscience and—until the next deadline calls—indulges in William Morris dreams of a simpler, juster, more beautiful society.

None of which must stop me from saying that I think *The Immortal Hour*—first heard at Glastonbury in 1914—a feeble piece, unworthy of revival while many works of greater merit remain unperformed. The libretto is a play by Fiona Macleod, the alter ego of the Scottish poet and editor William Sharp (who, according to his wife, underwent frequent Tiresian transformations, especially during thunderstorms). Both authors turn up in the pages of Yeats, who knew Sharp and corresponded with Macleod. The plot is tushery from the Celtic Twilight: Eochaidh, High King of Ireland, meets and marries Etain, a fairy princess, "daughter of Kings and Star among the dreams that are lives and souls." A year later, a minstrel comes to the palace, sings the Faery Song, reveals himself as Midir, a prince of the Shee, and draws Etain back to fairyland. Through the action there stalks the mysterious Dalua, the Son of Shadow—rather like the Dark Fiddler in Delius's *Village Romeo and Juliet*. The Bel Canto program note spoke enthusiastically of a drama that "furnishes substance for endless hours of thought and discussion as one peels away layer after layer of meaning in an attempt to find the mysterious core." But Fiona Macleod was no Yeats, and *The Immortal Hour* is no *Countess Cathleen*. The language is fustian. The music has a faint, wispy, not irresistible charm. The second scene—the meeting of Etain and Eochaidh—is threaded with a melody that Ravel's *Bolero* has made familiar. (Ravel was often in London during the vogue of *The Immortal Hour*.) The Faery Song is pentatonic and catchy.

Bel Canto presented the opera with accomplishment and conviction. Unlike Boughton's Glastonbury, the theatre of the Joan of Arc Junior High School, on West Ninety-third Street, where the company plays, does have electric light. (The 1940 building has a noble, aspirant portal; the street culminates in a mounted statue of the Maid, high above the Hudson, whose base incorporates stones from Rouen and Rheims.) There was an orchestra of twenty-one, conducted by Victoria Bond, and a chorus of fifteen. Frank Corsaro, the director, his set designer, Paul Robinson, his costume designer, Dain Marcus, and his lighting designer, Julia Rubin, used simple means to striking effect. In 1897, Yeats wrote to Fiona Macleod about his plans for an Irish theatre: "My own theory of poetical or legendary drama is that it should have no realistic, or elaborate, but only a symbolical and decorative setting. A forest, for instance, should be represented by a forest pattern and not by a forest painting. . . . This method would have the further advantage of being fairly cheap and altogether novel." It's a novel method no longer, but it still works well. When Shaw saw the Glastonbury *Iphigenia* in 1916, piano-accompanied, he rejoiced that there was "no scenery and no opera house: in short, no nonsense"—just "sufficient decoration by Miss Walshe's screens and curtains to create much more illusion in the big schoolroom than I have ever been able to feel in Covent Garden."

In one important respect, however, the Bel Canto troupe let us down. Instead of bel canto the singers produced something close to bawling. Instead of scaling their voices to the small, very resonant hall, they pushed them hard, sacrificing beauty and sweetness of tone and subtlety of inflection to noise. When all else was delicately and sensitively imagined, and enacted with a feeling for mystery and marvel, the vocalizing was indelicate. London's famous Etain, Gwen Ffrangçon Davies, was a light, silvery soprano (a light, silvery actress, with beautifully clear words, when I came across her, much later in her career). Shaw admired the Glastonbury Iphigenia, Gladys Fisher, because she "sang very agreeably, with adequate power and presence"; he reflected gloomily that "when she becomes a thoroughly sophisticated *prima donna,* and learns to shriek every note above the treble staff as if it were her last gasp, the audience will wonder at her prowess; but she will no longer be Iphigenia." The Bel Canto principals—Elizabeth Szczygielska (Etain), Stan Blair (Eochaidh), Gordon Vorhees (Dalua), and Rick Christman (Midir)—had voices; perhaps it had simply not occurred to them to sing gently, with refinement. A partial exception must be made for Mr. Christman, who spun some of Midir's music beguilingly. Hollie Stein and Frank Barr, in the smaller roles of Maive and Manus, were less violent.

309

GERMANIA, first produced in 1902 at La Scala, is an opera by a Jewish composer, Alberto Franchetti, that celebrates Germany's War of Liberation against Napoleon. The librettist was Luigi Illica, who six years earlier had brought the French Revolution to the stage of La Scala in Giordano's *Andrea Chénier*. The *Germania* cast enrolls many early-nineteenth-century celebrities—among them Humboldt, Fichte, Lützow, Blücher, Schlegel, Körner, Chamisso, Kleist, Hölty, Jacobi, Queen Louise, the future Frederick William IV, and Napoleon. They don't all have singing roles; only an attentive reader of Illica's libretto can know who all of them are. (Weber, "his eyes brilliant with a double fever, that of genius and that of phthisis," is one of those introduced onstage by name; the company welcomes him by breaking enthusiastically into his patriotic partsong "Lützow's wilde Jagd.") It is a high-flown libretto, with empurpled stage directions that sometimes fill a page. On a simpler level, the plot is propelled by the fact that the tenor and the baritone, the students Friedrich and Karl (Caruso and Sammarco at the first performance), while comrades in the struggle, are rivals for the love of the soprano, Ricke. The first scene is a vast mill on the banks of the Pegnitz, outside Nuremberg, housing an underground press where, in 1806, students print inflammatory literature pouring in from Germany's great writers. The last scene is the battlefield after the Battle of Leipzig (1813): Napoleon and his defeated grenadiers pass across the back; Karl lies dead; Friedrich dies with a cry of "O libera Germania!" on his lips; and, in a blood-red sunset, Ricke, beside him, enters upon "her first and eternal wedding night."

Franchetti, once spoken of in a breath with Mascagni and Puccini, had a sound German training. He excelled in the handling of large-scale scenes; he was called "the Meyerbeer of modern Italy." Toscanini conducted *Germania* at the Met in 1910 and 1911 (with Destinn, Caruso, and Amato), and it was well received. Today, little more than the arias recorded at the time of the première by Caruso, Sammarco, and Amelia Pinto (the first Ricke) and some later records by Caruso and Amato is remembered. But last month and this Bel Canto Opera revived *Germania,* on a modest scale, in the theatre of the Joan of Arc Junior High School, on West Ninety-third Street. It proved to be a melodious and skillfully fashioned piece, a little square in the cut of its melodies, surprisingly diatonic, and very different from the coarseness of lesser verismo. The temperate conclusion of the 1954 Grove entry on Franchetti is just: "His music is not profoundly emotional, not very often distinguished, but his workmanship is sound and scholarly, and the fact that he owes little or nothing to Wagner and stood entirely apart from the hysterical school of young Italy, in the ascendant during Franchetti's youth, should not be reckoned against him."

Bel Canto, within its limitations, did well by the opera. April Evans-Montefiore (Ricke), Henry Lackowski (Karl), and Joseph Wolverton (Friedrich) were principals of some merit. Maroun Azouri, the director and designer, set the piece in a white box on which the décors of the Met 1910 production were projected. (The projections were continued onto the walls of the theatre; the idea of thus enlarging the effect of the tiny stage was good, but the whirr of projectors in the auditorium, further muddying the already murky acoustics, was too high a price to pay.) One was left with mixed feelings. Pleasure in the piece and admiration for the company's enterprise and ingenuity were tempered by regret that so much of the opera remained unrealized. The role of Jane, Ricke's young sister (created by Jane Bathori in 1902 and sung by Alma Gluck in 1911), was omitted altogether. A chorus of twelve could do little justice to scenes for which two hundred choristers and supers would not be too many. The big symphonic intermezzo evoking the Battle of Leipzig, its content prescribed by Illica ("What supreme vision lights your dying eyes, ye new heroes? Heaven and Myth mingle there in a supreme embrace of poetry, bloodshed, and glory with Earth and History. . . . All the ancient heroes on their white steeds descend from mystic Valhallas to witness Arminius' renewed glory"), was missing. An orchestra of nine fiddles, two horns, timpani, and one each of viola, cello, double-bass, flute, oboe, clarinet, bassoon, trumpet, and harp produced a sound far from anything Franchetti could have had in mind. It was stationed off to one side: blend, balance, and ensemble were insecure. Victoria Bond conducted; her beat was trim, but her approach was unidiomatic.

If Bel Canto confined its efforts to works in which there is less disparity between its resources and those required, New York would in recent years not have heard and seen—albeit imperfectly—such pieces as *Les Huguenots, Prince Igor*, Saint-Saëns's *Henry VIII*, Filippo Marchetti's *Ruy Blas*, and Catalani's *La Wally*. Some of the big works revived by Bel Canto have then found their way, it is true, to the Metropolitan (*La Favorite, Thaïs, Esclarmonde, The Carmelites*), to the City Opera (*Lakmé*, Cherubini's *Médée*, Ambroise Thomas's *Hamlet*, Montemezzi's *L'amore dei tre re*), or to Carnegie Hall (Thomas's *Mignon*, Glinka's *A Life for the Tsar, Semiramide*). A full staging of *Germania* at Lincoln Center seems unlikely—even though odder and less meritorious things, such as Zandonai's *Francesca da Rimini*, do get done there. A full concert performance of *Germania*—complementary to the Bel Canto staging as Eve Queler's concert *Nerone* was to the Amato Opera's doll-house (but exciting) production of Boito's opera—would not be unwelcome.

The latest presentation of Miss Queler and her Opera Orchestra of New York, in Carnegie Hall last month, was Edouard Lalo's *Le Roi d'Ys*, last done at the Met in 1922. At the Opéra-Comique, where *Le Roi d'Ys* had its première, in 1888, it won for Lalo what Paul Dukas, in his slightly catty obituary of the composer, called "more than just success: glory." There, he said, "to the profound stupefaction of the director, the conductor, the singers, the dancers, the choristers, the stage hands, and the lighting staff of the Opéra-Comique, *Le Roi d'Ys* was welcomed as a triumph." It was given nearly five hundred times before, in 1941, it was transferred to the larger spaces of the Opéra. There was no triumph at Covent Garden, where, in 1901, it failed after two performances. Or at the Met, where it failed after five, despite a cast including Ponselle, Frances Alda, and Gigli. I remember rather enjoying the records of *Le Roi d'Ys,* with Rita Gorr as Margared, which came out years ago. (The set is still around.) I can't think now why I did, unless I was bowled over by the performances. Mylio's famous aubade, "Vainement, ma bien-aimée," is a pretty piece; Rozenn's reply, based on a Breton folk tune, is charming; and their love duet is tender. But those numbers are exceptions—the light relief in an otherwise strenuous score. For the rest, one must endure an awful lot of fanfarade and chordal chant, often organ-accompanied—State and Church at their dreariest. *Le Roi d'Ys* was once influential. Dukas can be forgiven his malice in the light of his conclusions: that although sickliness is often found more interesting than health, and unlike health, proves contagious, "Gounod is not a greater composer than Berlioz by reason of being more widely imitated, nor Massenet than Bizet." Dukas's own *Ariane et Barbe-Bleue* (1907) is a more considerable opera than *Le Roi d'Ys.*

Miss Queler is a conductor of wide sympathies and enthusiasms who responds to greatness (I recall her 1978 *Tristan* with gratitude), who can quicken uneven scores by great composers in ways that make their merits outshine their weaknesses, but who does not have Beecham-like alchemic power over dross. Weber's *Oberon,* Berlioz's *Lélio,* Wagner's *Rienzi,* Donizetti's *Gemma di Vergy,* Verdi's *I lombardi* and *I masnadieri,* Smetana's *Dalibor,* and Puccini's *Edgar* have been among her successes. (I like her work least when she allows singers to bawl their heads off to an audience that then bawls back its approval.) In points both of repertory and of roster she has provided New York with high adventure. Smetana's *Libuše* is promised. Gluck's *Armide,* Spontini's *La Vestale,* Fauré's *Pénélope,* Szymanowski's *King Roger,* Janáček's *Osud,* and Franz Schreker's *Der ferne Klang* are works she might consider. Pizzetti's *Fedra* deserves a hearing, if a new Phaedra—once one of Régine Crespin's great roles—can be found.

As Margared we heard the Rumanian mezzo Cleopatra Ciurca, and heard some of the loudest noise above the treble staff since—well, since Eva Marton's Ortrud at the Met this season. In fairness, it should be added that the yells were cleanly focussed and accurately pitched notes; but they were not pleasant to hear. The title role was taken by Marc Vento, a reliable Paris bass-baritone of the old school, with focussed, unforced tone and clear, forward words. The baritone Mark Pedrotti, a New Zealander active in Canada, had the same qualities and a bright young voice; one regretted that his role, Jahel, was small. The baritone Alan Titus, as Karnac, the heavy villain, sang boldly, not quite stylishly. The casting seemed undecided between Opéra and Opéra-Comique scales: on the one hand, Miss Ciurca in full cry, with a boisterous orchestra; on the other, Barbara Hendricks, a very light, pretty (but not quite steady) Rozenn. Mylio is one of those French tenor roles calling for both elegance and heroics. The first Mylio, Jean-Alexandre Talazac, was the first Hoffmann and Des Grieux and also the first Paris Samson; in London he sang Faust and Nadir in *The Pearl Fishers.* (Shaw remarked that his figure offered a terrible temptation to the hungry shark.) Miss Queler had the young Corsican tenor Tibère Raffalli, who plies a similar repertory. He did some agreeable things but seemed unformed: a composite of tenorial mannerisms rather than a polished artist.

Jewish Opera at the Y, a series produced by Hadassah Markson, the director of the Y School of Music, has been a creatively fruitful enterprise. Bruce Adolphe's *Mikhoels the Wise* (1982) and his *The False Messiah* (1983), two intelligent and unusual music dramas, have been among its successes. David Schiff's *Gimpel the Fool,* based on the story by Isaac Bashevis Singer, was done at the Y six years ago and again in 1980, and it was revived last month, in a new production. The opera was composed and first sung in Yiddish. The revival was given in the composer's English translation; he wrote in a program note, "I have discovered that there are very few singers, especially outside of New York, who can sing Yiddish authentically with the proper pronunciation and inflection." Schiff's music is eclectic, with touches that recall Mahler, Stravinsky, Kurt Weill, and Jewish cabaret song; the eclecticism, he says, "reflects the basic eclecticism of the Jewish musical inheritance." The orchestra of fourteen has a klezmer tang, with trumpet and clarinet solos, busy fiddle, tuba bass, accordion, mandolin, and an electric harpsichord to stand in for the cimbalom. The score is catchy, varied, entertaining, and often moving. It is written in traditional Jewish modes and employs figures from cantorial chant. Some of the numbers, with exotic melodic inflections and piquant instrumental timbres, reminded me of the Iranian cabaret—folk and animal tales retold to satirize both shah and mullah—that in pre-Ayatollah days used to flourish at the Shiraz Festival. It's not a pastiche score but a modern one with roots in the past. Schiff's inventions are distinguished, and his technique is precise. He tells of entering, by way of Singer's story, into "the world of my ancestors . . . an irrational world full of ghosts and demons but also a world saturated with the moral and spiritual values of traditional Judaism." It's a world close enough to basic human nature and universal myths to be recognizable, yet particular enough to be picturesque. The opera is at once sharp-eyed, sharp-eared, and kindly: a modern successor to *The Soldier's Tale* and *Reynard,* but more warmly emotional than those masterpieces. Gimpel, a baker's apprentice in a Polish shtetl, is partly the butt of Polish jokes, played on him by the townspeople, and partly a Holy Fool. One night, the Evil One tempts him to take revenge on the people of Frompol by fouling their challah dough; the ghost of his wife, who betrayed him lustily while she was alive but is now atoning for her misdeeds, dissuades him. There's a cast of twelve; some of the roles can be doubled. It's a good opera for campuses and colleges, and it might be a hit at the City Opera.

The Y performance, conducted by Amy Kaiser, directed by Dan Held, and designed by Tony Castrigno (sets) and Karen Hummel (costumes), was keen, bright, and sensitive. William Parker, as Gimpel, and Barbara Martin, as his errant wife, led an adept professional cast. The band, which included some well-known New York players, was first-rate. Amid the city's operatic ventures, which range from Zeffirelli spectaculars at the Met to amateur grand opera with a troupe of ten, piano-accompanied, in church halls, the Y has put on chamber opera—and new opera—with full resources, imagination, and technical accomplishment.

*   *   *

313

A series of five Carnegie Hall concerts given last week by the Chicago Symphony Orchestra began on Monday with a hard-driven, even brutal account of Verdi's *Falstaff*, conducted by Sir Georg Solti. One is tempted to call it a *Falstaff* starring the high-powered Chicago brasses and cymbals, accompanied by strings, woodwinds, and a cast that contained some good singers. The conductor stood high on a ziggurat of podium upon podium. The singers, corralled behind a barrier of music stands, were in mid-orchestra, upstage of the strings, and not able to come forward to sing to the audience. One or two of them remained masked from any listener whose seat was on the floor of the hall: all I could see of Christa Ludwig, the Mistress Quickly, was—except when she moved right to join Guillermo Sarabia, the Falstaff, in their second-act interview—a section of midriff visible through Sir Georg's legs. And since Miss Ludwig was giving a dramatic performance, not simply singing the notes, this was frustrating. Her Quickly—what I saw of it—was something to set beside her Amneris: an assumption in which glances, gestures, changing timbres, and savoring of the text conspired to create a character. Mr. Sarabia also gave a performance. His Dutchman at the City Opera nine years ago was blunt; now he has become an artist. His voice had the needed fatness and fullness, but he could use it lightly, conversationally, to etch remarks with fine, telling line. Mr. Sarabia and Miss Ludwig took part in the *Falstaff* production Sir Georg conducted in Vienna five years ago; so did Heinz Zednik and Yordi Ramiro, the Dr. Caius and the Fenton of the Carnegie performance. Mr. Zednik was incisive, witty, charming in a role often caricatured. Mr. Ramiro sang tastefully but plainly, in tones not displeasing but of no special quality. No one seemed to have determined in advance whether the style of presentation was to be vivid, heightened by glances, expressions, reactions, and—within concert-platform convention—gestures, or whether it was to be an "oratorio" performance. Each singer went his or her own way. Katia Ricciarelli, the Alice, elected just to sing; her singing lacked merriment and rhythmic verve. Kathleen Battle, the Nannetta, sang exquisitely, tracing the phrases of her duettinos, recitative, and aria with full, gentle, sweet tone. Wolfgang Brendel, the Ford, was inclined to bluster. Ann Murray was a lively Meg, Francis Egerton a nimble Bardolph, and Aage Haugland a thunderous Pistol.

A cast that could have brought Verdi's lyric comedy to life was given little chance to. The limelight was on the conductor and his orchestra. Sir Georg is not—it was a common complaint during his Covent Garden years—an opera conductor responsive to a drama being enacted onstage, either in general or as it takes shape on a particular night. And even at a concert performance the conductor should be both an inspirer and an accompanist quick to adjust balances and phrasing to what the singers actually do. I recall four outstanding Solti performances in which protagonist and conductor worked together as one, in which mutual fire blazed generously: a Frankfurt *Zauberflöte* with Fritz Wunderlich, and at Covent Garden an *Otello* with James McCracken and an *Elektra* and a *Tristan* with Birgit Nilsson. Those were wonderful—and exceptional. Sir Georg is as energetic as ever. Age has not mellowed him. He conducted *Falstaff* at Covent Garden twenty-two seasons ago and recorded it in 1964, and essentially his approach to the piece is unaltered. His enthusiasm for

Verdi's score is not in doubt; nor, in Carnegie Hall, was the virtuoso quality of the instrumental playing he secured. What one missed was grace, elegance, relaxed, easy wit, laughter, enchantment, warm yet delicate feeling, and anything but the more obvious responses to the quicksilver emotions and profound wisdom of the score. The frenetic bang-crash closes to every scene but the fifth were vulgar.

Gentleness and Chivalries

May 20, 1985

Witold Lutoslawski began his Third Symphony in 1972 and completed it early in 1983. That September, the Chicago Symphony, which had commissioned the piece, gave the first performance, conducted by Sir Georg Solti. (It was broadcast across the country and to Britain, Canada, Sweden, and Germany.) Since then, the symphony has been widely played, in a dozen countries, and has been widely admired and enjoyed. It has been done in Milwaukee, Aspen, Los Angeles, St. Louis. The first live performance in New York was given in Carnegie Hall this month by the Chicago Symphony, conducted by Solti. In November, the Philharmonic plays it.

Each of Lutoslawski's symphonies (the First appeared in 1947, the Second in 1967) has summed up a period both in his own career and in the history of contemporary music: each is at once a firm, surely fashioned statement based on the new ideas and inventions and, as it were, a completed, fully civilized staging post to linger in and explore before setting out on new adventures. He has been in both senses of the word an admirably reflective composer: open, as anyone of sense must be, to the exciting thoughts, techniques, and discoveries of others; and critical, personal in his observance, testing, acceptance, and development of them. Between the inception and the completion of the Third Symphony he composed *Les Espaces du sommeil, Mi-parti, Novelette,* the Double Concerto. Each is a finished, elegantly turned, progressive score. Each evidently played a part in determining the form of the Third Symphony.

In a program note, the composer owns that, much as he loves Brahms's big works, he finds them exhausting. (One recalls the anecdote of the young man who at the first London performance of a Brahms symphony turned to his companion and said, "What a beautiful melody! Do let's leave before he starts *developing* it.") Lutoslawski's "model of a perfectly balanced large-scale form" is provided, he says, by Haydn. The Third Symphony lasts about half an hour. (The composer's performance with the BBC Symphony, last year, lasted a minute more, Solti's in Carnegie about five minutes less.) The music is continuous, but within it can be discerned an introduction (a variety of ideas proposed by winds over a soft, octaves-deep pedal E on the strings); a first movement of three episodes, each followed by a rondo refrain of long, twined melodies on

315

woodwinds; a main movement, which carries the burden of the symphonic argument; an epilogue, or perhaps third movement, of high emotional content, in which the strings are prominent; and a brief, muscular coda. A mottolike figure of repeated E's articulates the structure. The scoring, in concerto-for-orchestra fashion, keeps the instrumental families distinct; each has its own kind of material, and all is lucid except when a deliberately dense climax is built. Any overt programmatic intent is disavowed, but the symphony is potently moving, and the remark of a London colleague, reviewing the broadcast of the Chicago première—"music for a possible unwritten tragedy"—seems apt.

The Chicago Symphony's performance was strong and sure. The BBC Symphony's performance conducted by the composer, which I know on tape, seems to me more poetic, thoughtful, and colorful. The Chicago orchestra played the work at the third of the five concerts it gave in Carnegie in six days. These were not all happy events. The crowd conditioned to respond to musicians' reputations rather than to what they achieve on a particular occasion rose to its feet as usual at the end of each concert and cheered; but the orchestral sound at the three concerts Solti conducted was hard and unlovely. Last week, I wrote about the first concert, a performance of Verdi's *Falstaff*. The second consisted of two ninth symphonies, Shostakovich's and Bruckner's. The Shosta-kovich is a strange, unsettling piece when beneath the brittle gaiety, the fluent rhetorical lamentation, and the banalities a conductor finds pain, bitterness, and poignant lyrical feeling (as Bernard Haitink does on a London recording of the work). Solti stayed on the surface; his reading was undercharacterized, unmov-ing. In the Bruckner one missed warmth, breadth, fullness, and what might be called a sense of spiritual elation. On the technical side, one heard string tone with too unyielding a surface and strident, aggressive brass. The Lutoslawski symphony was preceded by Brahms's Variations on a Theme of Haydn and followed by Beethoven's Fifth. Both of them were joyless, driven performances, without grace, without charm. Max Kalbeck, Brahms's biographer, once de-scribed the Variations as a mystical depiction of St. Anthony's wrestling with terrible temptations of the flesh: "It was to no avail that he flagellated himself bloody in order to mortify the desire of his senses, because the blood dripping from his whip was transformed into fragrant roses." It's a bizarre interpretation of a work so freshly and healthily abundant, but even as an illustration of some such dæmonic program Solti's tense performance wouldn't do, for it lacked sensual allure. There are many ways of molding the *dolce* second subject of the Beethoven symphony; here it was unshaped. Tovey's famous sentence about the second movement—"Shakespeare's women have the same courage, the same beauty of goodness, and the same humour"—was irrelevant to this performance.

The fourth and fifth concerts were conducted by Claudio Abbado. The fourth was devoted to Mahler's Seventh Symphony, which Abbado has also recorded with the orchestra. The Chicago players regained color and character—that sense of making individual contributions to a musical discourse, not pushing forward like highly disciplined, all-conquering attack troops. There were mysterious, radiant, transfigured moments in the inner movements. The finale— Mahler's "riotously robust revelling," Neville Cardus called it—was unconvinc-ing, as it nearly always is, but at any rate it was rendered in well-balanced sound, brave without being brazen. String portamento was avoided: not simply the regular portamento that Mahler would have taken for granted but the emphatic portamento specially asked for in, for example, the main theme of the fourth movement. The last concert began with a lustrous account of Berg's Three Orchestra Pieces, followed by a very beautiful account of his Violin Concerto. Salvatore Accardo was the soloist. This was exquisite almost—not quite—to the point of being sentimental. It was emotional, as the concerto should be. The fine string lines for the orchestra were played with a refinement to match the soloist's. Then Tchaikovsky's Fifth Symphony, in a warm, graceful performance, with a slightly heftier finale than that of Abbado's 1972 recording. Again there was no portamento, such as Tchaikovsky would have expected and such as can be heard in Willem Mengelberg's 1928 recording of the symphony (now reissued, in surprisingly good sound, on the In Sync cassette 4138, along with the Fourth Symphony). How would a modern audience respond to a performance as turbulent and personal as Mengelberg's?

Lutoslawski's next work after the Third Symphony, *Chain I,* had its New York première in March at a Music Today concert in Merkin Hall, conducted by Gerard Schwarz. A nine-minute divertimento for fourteen players, it was written as a surprise present for the London Sinfonietta and its artistic director, Michael Vyner—"as a souvenir of our common music-making"—and had its première in London five days after the Third Symphony was first played in Chicago. "Chain" refers to a structure of lapped "links" of music, each link traced, in a different instrumental color, until toward the end a tutti of cantabile melodies is sounded. The close is a shower of pizzicato sparks that explode, twinkle, and fade. It's a delightful piece, and Mr. Schwarz's ensemble evidently enjoyed playing it.

It was altogether a good and interesting concert. Nicholas Thorne's Double Quintet (woodwind quintet and string quintet), in its New York première, proved to be a buoyant, polished, unlabored composition. Gerald Levinson's *Light Dances, Stones Sing* (1978), a tone-poem for eighteen players, is Monet-inspired and makes attractive neo-Debussyan sounds. Miriam Gideon's *Songs of Youth and Madness* (1977), Hölderlin settings for high voice and thirteen players, is sensitively and carefully worked. (There is a CRI recording.) Finally, *Michael's Greeting*—Stockhausen's bright, elaborate, extended fanfares for brass octet, piano, and three percussionists which salute the audience gathering for a performance of his opera *Thursday*—had its American première.

Tadeusz Kaczyński's *Conversations with Witold Lutoslawski,* published in Polish in 1972, has appeared now in English translation. Lutoslawski's compositions up to *Mi-parti* are discussed; so are many other topics that make the volume an excellent introduction to the thoughts and personality of the cultivated, finely tuned creator. Lutoslawski even has a good word to say for music criticism: "It is eagerly read, it allows a listener to compare his impressions and opinions with those of a professional, and as such it becomes a noble intermediary between a work and its hearers."

Last week, in Carnegie Hall, the Philadelphia Orchestra, conducted by Riccardo Muti, played Bruckner's First Symphony with a warmth of string tone, a breadth of full, unviolent brass tone, and a wonderful deep blend of strings, woodwinds, and brasses such as the Chicago Symphony had not found in its account of Bruckner's Ninth. The concert began unpromisingly with a hoked-up "flute concerto" by Handel (four arias from his opera *Flavio* arranged for flute and strings), played by a small band, with harpsichord continuo, in a style appropriate to the arrangement but not at all to Handel. There was the New York première of Raymond Premru's Music for Three Trombones, Tuba, and Orchestra—a drab composition. Then the Bruckner. There was both tenderness and grandeur in the performance. The orchestra seemed to be finding joy in the music, and it played with unaffected, unforced beauty of sound.

Courtesy, Humanity, Hardiness

May 27, 1985

The Baltimore Symphony, conducted by David Zinman, gave a pleasing concert in Carnegie Hall on Sunday last week. It began with Charles Wuorinen's *Crossfire,* commissioned by the orchestra, which had had its première, in Baltimore, three days earlier. This is a brilliant, energetic score, dominated (at any rate in this performance) by the utterances of the brasses, and it becomes increasingly interesting when, toward the close, there are surprises of texture, of gait, and of harmony. It lasts eleven minutes. The composer (in a program note) calls it "extroverted, direct *allegro*." He also writes of "two distinct layers of music . . . juxtaposed and indirect," but these were not easily discerned by the ear.

Dvořák's Violin Concerto followed. It's not a work that has meant much to me in the past, so this extraordinarily poetic performance had a revelatory quality. Joseph Silverstein, the soloist, showed his mastery of romantic style from the start, shaping the triplets of the main theme not evenly but eloquently. Soloist, conductor, and orchestra were as one in their presentation of a score unconventionally fashioned and warmly felt. Their manner was not effusive, not splurgy; the emotion rang true and ran deep. They were more moving because there was a touch of reticence in the interpretation. There are people for whom "romantic" is almost a dirty word, who tend to sympathize with the heroine of Strauss's *Intermezzo* exclaiming against "the conductor who, to amuse a well-fed audience, lays bare his burning passions in 4/4 time! Disgusting!" There are interpreters who seem, as it were, to tenderly part leaves so that we can admire the blossoms beneath; others, of the same works, who seem to thrust full-blown flowers into our faces. (One might push the metaphor to cover "analytical" performers who seem to offer desiccated and dissected flowers, tidily mounted.) But one can't generalize: some scores positively ask for uninhibited, gaudy treatment; others respond in different, complementary ways to different manners of approach. I miss Edwin Fischer, and miss Bruno Walter, but last week approved of Willem Mengelberg's turbulence in Tchaikovsky's

Fifth Symphony (on record), and three seasons ago—to take an extreme example—was bowled over by Leonard Bernstein's heart-on-sleeve account of the Enigma Variations. At any rate, previous performances of the Dvořák concerto—I've not heard many—now seem to me to have been either underinterpreted or overplushed. Previously, I'd admired Mr. Zinman mainly as a polished conductor of *galant* and early-classical music. This Dvořák showed why enthusiastic accounts of his Mahler have reached us from Baltimore. The combination of emotion and distinction, of enthusiasm and discipline was uncommonly impressive. Mr. Silverstein's savoring of the difference between the quarter-note and the two eighth-notes which alternately top the second strain of the concerto was one memorable detail among many. The dynamic levels of the performance were "European" rather than those customary in America's giant auditoriums: there was no pumping up of the tone; one had to *listen*—but in Carnegie's fine acoustics listeners hear well. One cavil: the woodwinds weren't bright enough. The first oboe in his duetting with the soloist and the first bassoon in his were shy. The flute's Mozartian tune in E major and the oboe's A-major answer were not forward; the delightful episode (which doesn't return, though one hopes it will) made less than its due effect. The orchestra's home, Meyerhoff Hall, has closer, brighter acoustics than Carnegie; perhaps the players hadn't allowed sufficiently for the "mellowing" effect of the larger space.

The concert closed with Bartók's Concerto for Orchestra. In my pocket score of the piece I've pencilled a record of the more notable performances heard over the years, among them Furtwängler's with the Philharmonia, which was deep-toned, personal, and vibrant, and Szell's with the Cleveland, which was magnificently exact and no less impressive. I met Furtwängler after that performance of the Concerto for Orchestra, and he gave me what was left of the baton he'd broken while conducting it; I used it thereafter whenever I conducted. Another associative glow played on me during the Baltimore performance: misled by misinformation in the printed score ("First performance on December 1st, 1944, by the Boston Symphony Orchestra under the direction of Dr. Serge Koussevitzky, at Carnegie Hall, New York"), I imagined that I was hearing the Concerto for Orchestra in the place where it had first been played. (The première, in fact, was given in Boston, the first Carnegie performance a month later.) Associative glows may quicken a listener's attention, but they don't affect critical assessment. By the most objective standards, Mr. Zinman's performance was remarkable: for its colors, its control, and its contrapuntal force. Performances of the Concerto for Orchestra often stress orchestral virtuosity. It is an extraordinary masterpiece—a work as detailed and intimate as a string quartet, yet one that glances at Stravinsky, Shostakovich, Strauss in episodes that constitute a critique of twentieth-century orchestral manners. Not only in the raspberries blown at the "Leningrad" Symphony but also in subtle and appreciative ways does it comment on big-orchestra repertory (in the years before the enthronement of Mahler), big-orchestra prowess, and concert-hall taste. But, above all, the Concerto for Orchestra is rich, individual music. The Baltimore performance made much of the play of theme against theme, timbre against timbre, rhythm against rhythm. It was not obviously but

319

inwardly high-powered. It left one thinking not so much "What a stunning orchestra!" as "What a marvellous work!" That's meant as high praise. The orchestra looks young. It sounds fresh and lively. There's no conceit, no ostentation in its playing, but rapt, keen attention to the work in hand.

On Monday, the Toronto Symphony, conducted by Andrew Davis, came to Carnegie, to give two concerts on consecutive days. The second of them began with Bartók's Divertimento, played by the full string body; the composer sanctioned such forces, although he wrote the work for the Basle Chamber Orchestra. There was no heaviness in the Toronto playing, plenty of energy, and brilliance in the finale. But for this sinewy music I prefer the leaner sound of a small band. Mr. Davis had ranged his eight double-basses evenly across the back of the platform, in their traditional place, to provide a solid Brahmsian foundation for the score. They moved back to the modern position, far right, for the next work, R. Murray Schafer's *The Garden of the Heart,* which received its American première. Schafer is always a surprising composer. The surprise here was encountering kitsch. *The Garden of the Heart* (1980) is a setting for contralto and large orchestra, twenty-two minutes long, of a text the composer derived from *The Thousand and One Nights.* "The nightingale makes her sweet complaint. . . . The flowers are fairer than the lips of the beloved. . . . Streams move through the grass like silver snakes. . . . The south wind murmurs like a flute, and the west wind blows languishing." The lines are lapped in the lush clichés of early-twentieth-century exoticism: Ravel with rosewater; Delius's *Hassan* music laced with honey; melodic arabesques, whole-tone and pentatonic scales, gongs, chimes, tinkles. The performance was appropriately colorful. Maureen Forrester, although taxed now by some of the higher phrases, sang warmly and ripely.

Brahms's Fourth Symphony followed. Feeling rather as if I'd eaten a box of Turkish delight, I couldn't face it.

The Aspen Wind Quintet, winner of the 1984 Naumburg Chamber Music Award, gave its victory concert in Alice Tully Hall this month. The program included the New York première of Hans Abrahamsen's *Walden* (1978), which, like everything else I've heard by this young Danish composer (he was born in 1952), proved to be an attractive and poetic composition. Thoreau provided inspiration for music straightforward and honest in its statements, stripped of superfluities, simple in its communicativeness, yet subtle in its thought. Nature seems to be present, in the form of stirrings, cycles, and marked rhythms—like those of sleepy birds, crickets, tree frogs on a hot, still night—not measured by the regular tick of man's clock. The world of men is not forgotten: horn calls steal from afar. The audience is invited to be still, and to listen intently. I mustn't make it sound *too* simple. Abrahamsen was part of a movement called "the new simplicity," but his music has nothing in common with the mechanical repetitiveness and busy insistence of urban minimalism. He works here in silver-point, not acrylics. Every detail tells.

Each year, there is a Naumburg commission for the winning ensemble (and some excellent works have resulted, among them John Harbison's Wind Quintet, for the Aulos). The Aspen commission was Frank Zappa's *Time's Beach.*

Zappa doesn't make it into John Rockwell's *All American Music* or into the New Grove (Francesco Zappa, an eighteenth-century cellist-composer, is there), but he does get one long sentence in Charles Hamm's *Music in the New World*, which tells us that Varèse is one of Zappa's favorite composers, that his band the Mothers of Invention "included several players with extensive classical training and experience," and that the album *Freak Out* (1966) and its successors contained "music of greater rhythmic and structural complexity than had yet been accepted into popular music." Now that Boulez has championed Zappa, by conducting and recording his music with the Ensemble InterContemporain, I suppose we'll be hearing more of him at Lincoln Center. I couldn't make anything of *Time's Beach*. It seemed to be quite unidiomatic in its writing for the instruments—undifferentiated in a way that turned long stretches into horn with scurrying woodwind accompaniments—and metrically intricate in ways more readily compassable by Zappa's own electronic synthesizer, the Barking Pumpkin Digital Gratification Consort of the Utility Muffin Research Kitchen, than by mere live instrumentalists. The Aspen Quintet essayed only four of the five movements and seemed to be wrestling with them bravely. The Abrahamsen, which is composed with a sure, delicate ear for individual sonorities and characters, Paul Taffanel's Quintet (1880), which is more pleasing for polished, instrumental manners than for any great strength of invention (Taffanel was the father of modern French flute playing), and Villa-Lobos's bright Quintette en Forme de Chôros (1928, revised in 1953) gave the players more chance to show their merits. They are a good group, even though the flute, while admirably steady, her tone unpolluted by the ceaseless wobble that so many players affect, is not quite strong enough to top the ensemble.

New music must take precedence of old; but, baffled and bored by the Zappa, I felt sorry that I hadn't slipped up the road after the Abrahamsen to Merkin Hall, where Pomerium Musices was celebrating the quatercentenary of Heinrich Schütz's birth. Schütz is never boring. He inspires unfailing awe, wonder, and delight. During a long life, he poured out a stream of masterpieces—some large, some small—inexhaustible, always refreshing. Like many of the great composers—Isaac, Handel, Bach, Mozart, Schubert, Wagner—he reconciled the best of Italy and of Germany. He turned words into music that makes texts glow with new intensity. He never staled, and in old age wrote works as youthfully zestful as Verdi's *Falstaff*. Though with a pang I passed up the Pomerium concert, three days later there was more Schütz in Merkin: the Sine Nomine Singers, conducted by Harry Saltzman, sang two of his best-known works, the St. John Passion (1665), in English, and the *Musikalische Exequien* (1636), in German.

Brahms conducted Schütz's dramatic "Saul, Saul" in Vienna in 1864. Hans Joachim Moser's big Schütz biography appeared in 1936. (In it he described "Saul, Saul" with tumbling phrases of enthusiasm: "A pinnacle of old music; a piece of spectral dramatic art; a distant whispering and rustling, the approaching threat, the roaring, the nightmare of a colossal cloud shadow finally dissipating itself specterlike into the mist, as it had begun like the inescapable voice of conscience.") But the wider rediscovery of Schütz began only in the fifties, aided by long-playing records and by the Schütz festivals sponsored by the publisher Bärenreiter, which in 1955 embarked on a new edition of the Complete Works. I first heard the Exequies "live" in the great church of St. Bartholomew's, Smithfield, at the inaugural concert of Roger Norrington's Heinrich Schütz Choir, in 1962, and likened it to a seventeenth-century *Dream of Gerontius*. It was composed for a princely funeral. A "composition in the form of a German funeral Mass" is built on the texts the prince had had inscribed on his sarcophagus—an unbroken sequence of moving ensembles, solos, and cho-ruses. There is a double-choir motet. Then the "voices on earth" sing the Nunc Dimittis while in the distance—as it were, from Heaven—the voice of the departed prince, baritone, joins with two soprano seraphim to sing "Blessed are the dead which die in the Lord."

There are churches in New York better suited to the work, acoustically and spiritually, than Merkin Hall is. The Exequies lost something in emotive power. There could be only small separation between the two choirs. The Heavenly trio stole in not from on high but from the wings. Nevertheless, it was a gravely beautiful performance. Schütz disliked gabbled performances—what he called "eine *Battaglia di Mosche*, oder Fliegenkrieg" (a battle of flies). Mr. Saltzman set easy, flowing tempi that allowed the words and the movement of the harmonies to tell. The voices were well balanced and true. Sometimes one wanted a little more emotional force in the declamation. The little organ didn't always sound quite in tune: perhaps the hot night had ruffled some of its ranks; perhaps the choir was instinctively adopting juster intonation than a machine can manage. The unaccompanied Passion was very well done, in a manner that combined drama with formality. The soloists in both works were drawn from the choral ranks. The contralto Harriet Kapner delivered one of the funeral sentences with outstanding fervor. Gregory Purnhagen was an exceptional Evangelist—his tenor clear, free, and beautiful in timbre, his words distinct, his phrasing sensitive.

O GLAD, EXULTING SONG

June 10, 1985

LAWRENCE KRAMER's *Music and Poetry: The Nineteenth Century and After* is an intelligent, perceptive, and elegantly disciplined investigation into ways that poetry and music affect readers and listeners. The study grew from the author's conviction that "the way I read certain poems was intimately bound up with the way I heard certain pieces of music." Kramer is well-read, "well-heard," and persuasive. His book runs from Wordsworth and Beethoven to John Ashbery and Elliott Carter, and their *Syringa*. Using, and adapting, some approaches more familiar in literary than in music criticism, he pursues analogies and also the direct confrontation of the two arts when they are brought together in song. Recurrent names are Walt Whitman and Wallace Stevens, two poets who were

322

much concerned with the effects of music and with "musical effects" achievable by verse. Kramer is both a critic and a composer: his song cycle *That Music Always Round Me,* for tenor and piano, was performed at Bard College in April and in Merkin Hall in May. It is a setting of three Whitman poems: "I Hear America Singing," "Dirge for Two Veterans," and "That Music Always Round Me." The first song begins with wide, open sonorities, defining a space that is gradually filled, texturally and rhythmically, as the poet catalogues the "varied carols" rising from carpenter, mason, boatman, woodcutter, plowboy, mother, young wife at work, girl sewing or washing. The "Dirge" is one of the *Drum-Taps* poems, its scene a double funeral, of father and son, beneath a moon like "some mother's large transparent face." Kramer's setting makes mimetic use of "the great drums pounding, and the small drums steady whirring," and the "coming full-key'd bugles," but does so in no obvious way: the beats and calls are transmuted into musical imagery. In the last song the singer threads a free, rhapsodic line, almost as if improvising his commentary, through long, surging, ebbing and flowing but unbroken music—music that sounds big, brave, and sonorous independently of the vocal line.

There are dozens—probably hundreds—of Whitman settings: inspired ones by Delius, Vaughan Williams, Roger Sessions, Carter, and Hans Werner Henze. Rutland Boughton and Arthur Bliss, Carl Ruggles and Ned Rorem, Castelnuovo-Tedesco and Coleridge-Taylor, Holst and Hindemith, Charles Villiers Stanford, Franz Schreker, and Othmar Schoeck have set Whitman. He's a poet that (like Vaughan, Herrick, Milton, Pope) I first met in music, piping his verses well before I read them unclad in harmonies other than their own. Whitman, along with James Fenimore Cooper (whom Schubert read avidly, whose *The Bravo* Wagner borrowed from his stepdaughter when in need of light reading) and Mark Twain, provided the European's romantic vision of America. It's a vision still recapturable, even in days when "Dallas" and "Dynasty" are the images of America propagated abroad. Whitman's range is wide. He didn't only sing in exuberant celebration or exhortation. What he wrote in 1865, on seeing Union soldiers returned from Southern prison camps, sounded echoes in 1945, and again this year when 1945 was recalled: "Can those be *men*—those little livid brown, ash-streak'd, monkey-looking dwarfs?—are they really not mummied, dwindled corpses? . . . Probably no more appalling sight was ever seen on this earth. (There are deeds, crimes, that may be forgiven, but this is not among them. It steeps its perpetrators in blackest, escapeless, endless damnation.)" Rorem in the powerful, chilling, tender cycle *War Scenes*—dedicated "to those who died in Vietnam, both sides," during the ten days of 1969 in which he composed it—found song for this side of Whitman. (There is a recording on Desto.) Sessions in the great requiem *When Lilacs Last in the Dooryard Bloom'd*—dedicated to the memory of Martin Luther King, Jr., and Robert F. Kennedy—sang Whitman's deep, beautiful song of healing. (There is a recording on New World.) In the very multiplicity of the musics Whitman has called forth there is an image of his abundance. One could embark on an invocatory catalogue in his own exuberant manner. Kramer adds a new voice to the chorus: lucid, lyrical, unemphatic, quietly fervent, exact.

The songs were written for and were sung by Darrell Lauer, who has a small, ripe tenor and uses it with art and with charm. He gave a pleasing recital: an old-style program of carefully chosen groups in which familiar and rarer songs were mingled—each of them carefully studied, lovingly presented, and sung by heart. The first half was three songs by Beethoven, five by Brahms, and Ottavio's airs from *Don Giovanni*; the second, three of Liszt's Victor Hugo settings, the new Whitman cycle, and a clutch of ballads, including "I hear you calling me" and "Mother Machree." John McCormack seems to be Mr. Lauer's exemplar, and he's a good model. There was care for communication, feeling for line, and detailed shaping of the phrases. But by comparison with McCormack Mr. Lauer was a shade lazy-lipped; the sounds of the words (whether German, Italian, French, or English) were not always savored. Michael May was a fluent accompanist; on a smaller piano he could have played out more bravely.

Two works performed by the Cleveland Orchestra in Cleveland this season would have been welcome in New York when the orchestra came here last month to give three concerts: Charles Wuorinen's *Movers and Shakers* and Henze's Seventh Symphony. The programs the orchestra did bring, under its new conductor, Christoph von Dohnányi, were not exactly conventional, but they contained nothing newer than Bartók's Divertimento, composed nearly half a century ago. They closed with Brahms's First Piano Concerto, with Tchaikovsky's Fifth Symphony, and with the "Eroica."

The Bartók was played with slightly—not much—leaner sound than it had been the day before by the Toronto Symphony, and it was not particularly exciting. Janáček's heroic tone poem, or "rhapsody for orchestra," *Taras Bulba* followed. It's a strange work, as is the epic tale by Gogol on which it is based. In the book there is a touch of Fenimore Cooper (whom Gogol admired) and the oddest mixture of rough humor, tender romance, adventure, and tragedy. Janáček's response was vivid. He composed the piece, in 1915–18, because, he said, "in the whole world there are neither fires nor tortures strong enough to destroy the strength of the Russian nation." There are three movements: the indomitable Cossack hetman Taras kills his second son, Andrei, who has fallen in love with a Polish maiden and joined forces with the Poles against his people; he witnesses the death by torture, in Warsaw, of his elder son, Ostap; and, captured by the Poles, being burned alive, he cries the words that Janáček paraphrased as his reason for composing *Taras Bulba*. In Gogol—but not in Janáček—Taras continues by prophesying that one day "a czar will arise on the Russian land, and there'll be no power on earth that won't submit to him." The prophecy was quoted in the Cleveland program note, and presumably it incited the comments from the *Times* critic that *Taras Bulba* is a "noisy and tawdry essay in pre-Soviet Realism" and that Janáček "was not the first nor the last Slav to yearn for domination by Mother Russia." I don't see—or hear—how anyone familiar with the mind and thought and nobly generous personality of the composer, detester of tyranny in any form, can bring that charge. *Taras Bulba* played in Poland today could be a musical symbol of solidarity and hope. Jaroslav Vogel, Janáček's biographer, is nearer the mark when he likens the final pages to "the arch of a rainbow of peace spanning the earth" and records that "even in countries where the background . . . could not be expected to commend it to the listener," the tone-poem was highly successful—"proof enough of its musical wealth and elemental expressive strength." *Taras Bulba* is no simple hymn to heroic resistance and national freedom but, like Gogol's, a complicated and not uncritical one. Andrei is beguiled into treachery not merely by love but by his glimpse of all the allurements of a life gentler and more chivalrous than the rude, hard-drinking barbarity he was raised in. And some of the most beautiful, tender music is devoted to them. The scoring is as personal and colorful as anything in Janáček. For an episode in Gogol where Andrei, on his way to his beloved, passes through a Catholic service, in all its mystic splendor, and is deeply moved by the sound of the organ, Janáček makes use of that instrument; and he brings it back to underpin the final pages. Carnegie Hall has no large pipe organ but only an electronic substitute, and the sound was not pleasant. Otherwise, the performance was stirring.

In the Brahms concerto that followed, Alfred Brendel was the soloist. His playing was active and energetic, but it was not really an enjoyable performance. The piano tone was shallow, clanking. It was not a big, warm, noble interpretation. Let me, after disagreeing with my *Times* colleague about *Taras Bulba*, agree with him about Brendel: "In agitated passages he sometimes sounded like a professor angry over the loss of an umbrella rather than a heaven-storming Brahmsian."

Two questions for some chronicler of concert-hall practice to answer: When did it become the rule for the conductor of a piano concerto to tuck himself away on the far side of the piano, unable to see the soloist or the first violins except by craning over his left shoulder? And when did the current introductory rituals become standard practice? I mean expectant hush, entry of the concert-master, applause for him, bow, public tuning session—first winds, then strings—directed by the concertmaster, entry of the conductor, more applause, acknowledgment of it, orchestra brought to its feet, more applause, resettling, and, at last, the concert. (A simplified variant of this is for the players to rise in tribute at the conductor's entrance, instead of waiting for his signal to rise and be applauded along with him.) Nothing so elaborate happened in my young days. Henry Wood, it's said, made the players file past him, each sounding his A, on their way to the platform; concertmasters didn't make formal solo entrances and take preconcert solo calls; tuning sessions were swifter and softer. And in Sir Henry's little handbook on conducting he instructs the conductor of a piano concerto to be sure he is stationed where he can see the keyboard clearly.

The Cleveland's first concert was in Carnegie Hall. The second was in Avery Fisher Hall. It began with Ruggles's *Men and Mountains,* a good, strong piece. Then Stravinsky's *Reynard,* sung in French translation. (When it's not done in the language of the singers and the audience, it might as well be done in the composer's original Russian; *Reynard,* he said, "is phoneme music, and phonemes are untranslatable.") It was mimed and danced by members of the Cleveland ballet and was neatly played by an ensemble from the orchestra. But it needs a smaller hall. The third concert, back in Carnegie, began with Haydn's Symphony No. 64, subtitled on an early manuscript copy "Tempora mutantur, etc." It's certainly an extraordinary and adventurous piece, evidence of changing times; Dohnányi's performance was a little ordinary, a Kapellmeister performance—nothing exactly wrong and nothing memorably right. Then Schoenberg's Six Songs, Opus 8, with Anja Silja the soloist. I'm always glad to encounter Miss Silja, who made her début at fifteen, who has tackled roles from the Queen of the Night (I first heard her in that part twenty-six years ago, when she was nineteen) to Isolde and Brünnhilde, and who has been arresting in everything she does—a magnetic performer even when her singing has been shrill or strident. In Carnegie, she was on her best vocal behavior—perhaps even too much so. The songs were sung more carefully than in her recording of them (with Dohnányi and the Vienna Philharmonic, on London) and a shade less impulsively. Her voice still shines.

In London, with its five full-time symphony orchestras, there's usually a kind of "ranking table," its order determined largely by who "has"—who is the chief conductor of—each orchestra. (At the moment, Klaus Tennstedt has the London Philharmonic, Claudio Abbado the London Symphony, Giuseppe Sinopoli the Philharmonia—posts held before by Bernard Haitink and then Georg Solti, by André Previn, and by Riccardo Muti. The BBC Symphony gives adventurous programs; one hears less about the Royal Philharmonic.) Management also plays its part in making reputations: orchestras in robust financial health can attract the best players and engage eminent guest conductors. In New York, with only one full-time symphony but a splendid parade of other orchestras passing through Carnegie Hall, the league table is on a national basis, and although the positioning is usually less clear, there have been times when the Chicago under Fritz Reiner or the Cleveland under George Szell or the Chicago under Solti has seemed by consensus to head it. On the basis of what I've heard this season, I'd be inclined to put the Philadelphia under Muti current top—while readily admitting that scattered concerts afford but a flimsy basis for any such opinion. The Cleveland under Dohnányi has still to regain the distinction and character that the Cleveland under Szell once had. I don't have a clear idea of Dohnányi; I've not heard enough of him in basic classical repertory, and what I have heard hasn't tempted me (amid the orchestral riches offered in this city—the Beethoven, Brahms, Bruckner from the world's greatest) to hear more. I first heard him conducting Schreker's *Der ferne Klang,* in Cassel, and the première of Henze's *Der junge Lord,* in Berlin, twenty years ago, and was impressed; also at the première of Henze's *The Bassarids,* at Salzburg in 1966. He's probably best known for his recordings of *Wozzeck* and *Lulu,* with Miss Silja their heroine. Perhaps his forte is as a champion of the new and the neglected. *Taras Bulba* was the high point of the Cleveland concerts.

A 1989 postscript: I can't let that 1985 "ranking" stand without adding that my admiration for Dohnányi and the Cleveland grew and grew, while Muti, in the years that followed, refashioned the Philadelphia tone into something harder, more "Chicago-like." And I can't think why I made no mention of Michael Gielen and the Cincinnati Symphony, whose prowess, in the December 24, 1984, review of the Carter Piano Concerto, I had so much admired. But, as I said, any orchestral "league table" is a fluctuating affair and rests on a flimsy basis. The only constant, in my decades as New York critic, has been the unfailing beauty of the Vienna Philharmonic's playing at each of its New York visits.

ST. LOUIS, that handsome, tree-rich city beside the Mississippi, is an agreeable place. As in Edinburgh or Salzburg, a visitor, whatever his special interests may be—buildings, plants, pictures—finds that there is more to do and explore than there seems to be time for. After a dozen visits there, I still have a list of "things to do next time." (And each year has also brought something new. Sullivan's Wainwright Building and C. Howard Crane's fabulous Fox Theatre have been restored to life; now it's the turn of the grandly romantic Union Station.) Meanwhile, the Opera Theatre of St. Louis, which plays in a small, pleasing 1966 theatre, the Loretto-Hilton, set on lawns aflicker with fireflies, continues to offer some of the most satisfying opera performances in the country. In its tenth season, just ended, it maintained the successful pattern of recent years—a Mozart, two (or more) uncommon operas, and one standard piece—with unusually adventurous and varied fare. There were twenty-five performances in the course of a month. The Mozart was *Idomeneo,* the standard piece was *The Barber of Seville,* and two full-length operas composed for the company—Minoru Miki's *Jōruri* and Stephen Paulus's *The Woodlanders*—had their world premières. Both were conceived by, have librettos by, and were directed by Colin Graham, the artistic director of Opera Theatre. In the progress of twentieth-century opera, Graham is an important figure: a stage director who has played an increasingly creative role as ideator, collaborator, mentor, and animator. In London, at the English National Opera, his powerful productions of Janáček's *House of the Dead,* Britten's *Gloriana,* and Prokofiev's *War and Peace* were particularly influential. He collaborated with Britten on the formation and presentation of *Noye's Fludde,* the three church parables, *Owen Wingrave,* and *Death in Venice.* As a director of the English Music Theatre Company, he commissioned new pieces. His work in America builds now on those foundations and has its own continuity.

Miki's earlier opera *An Actor's Revenge* was commissioned by Graham for the English Music Theatre Company and was first performed in London in 1979. It was done in St. Louis two years later, and by then Miki and Graham were already working on a successor. *An Actor's Revenge* is a Kabuki opera: the protagonist is a Kabuki actor, and the "real-life" drama in which he is involved is played out within Kabuki conventions. The librettist was the poet James Kirkup. *Jōruri* (the name of a medieval princess, adopted as a general term for the narrative ballad style in which her tale was told, while the Japanese characters can also mean "paradise") was inspired by Chikamatsu Monzaemon (1653–1725), who brought new refinement, realism, and poetry to the Japanese puppet play and was celebrated for his love-suicide tragedies. The characters are Shōjō, the old, blind master of a puppet troupe; his young wife, Otane; and young Yosuke, who both carves the puppets and animates them in performances while Shōjō chants the narrative. They are another Mark, Iseult, and Tristram. In a preface to the libretto, Graham notes that a conflict between *giri,* obligation or loyalty, and *ninjō,* human feelings, underlies Chikamatsu tragedy, and so it does this drama, which is not an adaptation from Chikamatsu but an original play, embodying some of his themes, conceived for music and for the modern theatre—and specifically for the all-in-one-room intimacy of the Loretto-Hilton. The action is as simple as that of Wagner's *Tristan,* and the working is rich, subtle, and skillful. The basic style is the (comparative) naturalism of *sewamono,* or domestic drama. In each of the three acts there is also a Kabuki episode, as three supernatural visitors—embodiments of memory or thought—come to Shōjō. The first is the tyrannical magistrate who blinded him as punishment when he intervened to save the child Otane from the magistrate's lust; the second, Otane's jeering, mercenary mother; the third, Shōjō's doppelgänger, come to debate with him once he has realized that his wife and his disciple love one another. There is an episode of *kyōgen,* comedy intermezzo, as three theatre assistants comment on and parody their master's plight. And there are excerpts from three puppet plays. The first, "straight," introduces the troupe. The second, the rehearsal of a new play, is broken off when parallels to the real-life situation prove too painful. (The heroine is loved by a blind lord; Yosuke has carved the puppet as a likeness of Otane; later, Shōjō's fingers trace its features and sense the passion that went into the carving.) The third, the climax of a love-suicide tragedy—and at the same time the resolution of the opera—is enacted not by puppets but by Otane and Yosuke themselves. Like the characters they play, the lovers disappear into a waterfall, and Shōjō is left alone with us in the darkling theatre. The simple, ever-effective play-within-a-play device—as of *Pagliacci*— has become something subtler, more intricate, opaline. The contrasted dramatic styles are different kinds of metaphor which mysteriously act upon one another, light the central situation from different angles, and explore the shifting relationships between actors and their audience.

The influence of Japanese theatre upon Western theatre has taken many forms—in the work of Yeats, Brecht, Britten, Peter Brook, Peter Sellars. *Jōruri* embodies new, fine-grained Western responses to the formality, to the contrasts of obliquity and directness, to the startling changes of pace (near-static musing, sudden violence), to picturesqueness that serves poetic ends. Miki's score matches—animates, enacts—the drama at every point. He uses an orchestra of moderate size and three Japanese instruments. The movements of a *koto* (Japanese long zither) concerto provide the overture, the prelude to Act II, and, in Act III, a poignant interlude functioning like "The Walk to the Paradise Garden" in Delius's love-suicide drama *A Village Romeo and Juliet.* A *shaku-hachi* (bamboo flute) breathes the tenor of Shōjō's sad reflections. A twangling or thrumming *shamisen* (Japanese lute) accompanies the puppet plays. Of all the cross-culture composers, Miki has perhaps most successfully united Japanese and Western elements in a personal and highly expressive language. His musical training, in Tokyo, was Westernized; the assimilation of Japanese timbres and inflections came later. The score of *Jōruri* is notable for delicate, unconventional, affecting color combinations, for supple rhythms and pacing, and for eloquent melodic lines. In a program note, the composer writes of a melodic style growing from "the tone of speech inherent in Mr. Graham's libretto, fused with my kind of arioso singing." The music changes idiom to match the changing dramatic styles. The mother-in-law's scolding is pretty well a cabaret song.

Miki writes, too, of a presentation in which "the performers make use of their whole body and spirit in their burning desire to communicate with the audience." The St. Louis production—directed, as I said, by Graham, conducted by Joseph Rescigno, designed by Setsu Asakura, lit by Peter Kaczorowski, and choreographed by Onoe Kikushiro—was a marvellously communicative ensemble of song, instrumental sound, acting, and movement. Faith Esham, the Otane, looked exquisite and moved exquisitely, and her voice has become a flexible, beautiful instrument. John Brandstetter, the Yosuke, acted intently, sang well, and manipulated puppets with skill. Andrew Wentzel was a moving Shōjō. Mallory Walker was brilliant in the three Kabuki roles. The three assistants—John M. Sullivan, Gordon Holleman, and Stephen Kirchgraber—deftly played "invisible" assistants in the puppet episodes, similar roles (in a different dimension) within the actions of the opera proper, a sprightly *kyōgen* trio, and three lively individuals. At the performance I attended, the audience seemed spellbound, and at the close the silence that is the deepest mark of appreciation yielded gradually to cheers and a long standing ovation.

The Woodlanders is not quite as successful a work. Britten might have brought it off. Paulus's music, while sensitively and attractively made, is rather too conventional to give artistic verisimilitude to Hardy's otherwise bald and unconvincing narrative, and rather too modest to develop any strong life of its own. In rude summary, the plot reads much like that of an old opera seria: Grace Melbury, a country maiden gentrified by attendance at Cheltenham Ladies' College and a Continental finishing school, returns to deepest Dorset; she abandons her childhood sweetheart, Giles Winterbourne, for the fascinating Dr. Fitzpiers, whom she marries; when Fitzpiers deserts her and goes off with Mrs. Charmond, the lady of the manor, she takes up again with Giles; when Giles dies, she returns to her husband. It could all happen in real life, but Hardy, a peremptory puppetmaster, put the characters through their paces so abruptly that it is difficult to believe in them. E. M. Forster, in *Aspects of the Novel,* says of the Wessex tales in general:

> Sometimes a plot triumphs too completely. The characters have to suspend their natures at every turn, or else are so swept away by the course of Fate that our sense of their reality is weakened. . . . Hardy arranges events with emphasis on causality, the ground plan is a plot, and the characters are ordered to acquiesce in its requirements. . . . His characters [Tess alone is excepted] are involved in various snares, they are finally bound hand and foot, there is ceaseless emphasis on fate, and yet, for all the sacrifice made to it, we never see the action as a living thing as we see it in *Antigone* or *Berenice* or *The Cherry Orchard.* The fate above us, not the fate working through us—that is what is eminent and memorable in the Wessex novels. Egdon Heath before Eustacia Vye has set foot upon it. The woods without the Woodlanders.

Holst found stark, memorable music for Egdon Heath. Paulus's music for the woods is no more than mildly, gently descriptive, in a vein that recalls Delius with Delius's force of feeling. In any case, as an opera composer he must concern himself chiefly with the woodlanders. "Trees, trees, undergrowth, English trees! How that book rustles with them" was Forster's exclamation. Indeed it does. The scenes are vivid. But Hardy's endeavors to link the scenes with his characters' emotional progress can seem labored, even inviting of parody:

> The time was that dull interval in a woodlander's life which coincides with great activity in the life of the woodland itself—a period following the close of the winter tree-cutting and preceding the barking season, when the saps are just beginning to heave with the force of hydraulic lifts inside all the trunks of the forest.... It was dusk: there were no leaves as yet; the nightingales would not begin to sing for a fortnight; and the Mother of Months was in her most attenuated phase—starved and bent to a mere bowed skeleton, which glided along behind the bare twigs in Fitzpiers's company.

Graham's libretto and his staging begin promisingly. A semichorus materializes in a tree-filled scene—woodlanders who might be the trees themselves commenting on human actions that passed beneath their boughs. But the image is not sustained or pursued; the singers soon become stage gaffers. At other times, one glimpses again an opera Graham probably wished to create—for example, when Giles on his deathbed breaks into a simplified version of Hardy's poem "The Tree and the Lady":

> *I have done all I could*
> *For the lady I knew!*
> *Through the heat shaded her*
> *When summer jaded her . . .*

And the notion of Giles-as-tree chimes with Grace's vision of him: "He rose upon her memory as the fruit-god and the wood-god in alternation: sometimes leafy and smeared with green lichen, as she had seen him amongst the sappy boughs of the plantations; sometimes cider-stained and starred with apple-pips, as she had met him on his return from cider-making." (By this time, late in the novel, Hardy seems to be sharing Grace's view of Giles as "Autumn's very brother," sticky and fragrant with apple juice. When we first meet him, he is less romantically described: "A man not particularly young for a lover, nor particularly mature for a person of affairs—each of which functions he in some degree discharged.") But in the end librettist, composer and performers alike seemed hampered by the sheer amount of plot that requires getting through. Changes of temper barely motivated even in the novel become a switchback scramble in the reduction for the stage. (The same is true in Peter Tranchell's Hardy opera *The Mayor of Casterbridge*. I don't know Frédéric d'Erlanger's *Tess*, which has a libretto by Luigi Illica; Edward Harper's brief, effective *Fanny Robin* uses only episodes of *Far from the Madding Crowd*.) Graham has ingeniously worked in a good deal—probably too much—of *Woodlanders* incident. The dialogue is largely in end-stopped blank verse, as in this first exchange between Mrs. Charmond and Grace:

> *And so, you're back from Dorchester, my dear.*
> *Some weeks ago—how strange we've never met. . . .*
> *You must let me call on you some afternoon.*
> *I wish you would—this place depresses me,*
> *and soon I'll have to go abroad again.*

For the "numbers," Graham adapts poems—by Chatterton, Shelley, Edmund Gosse—and folk songs that Hardy cites in the book, and also introduces Hardy poems freely rewritten (with results disconcerting to the extent that one knows the originals) either to fit the new situations or to eliminate Hardy's distinctive quirks of diction and meter. (Britten, in his cycle *Winter Words*, found the apt music for Hardy's poetry.)

The Woodlanders is not an uninteresting or unrewarding opera, but I doubt whether the subject has brought out the best in Paulus. His three operas have all been written for St. Louis. The one-act *The Village Singer* (1979), after the story by Mary Wilkins Freeman, was fresh and masterly—an American opera with a universal theme and with a particularity of setting and local color reflected in the score. *The Postman Always Rings Twice* (1982), which Graham devised for Paulus, after James M. Cain, was classical tragedy reënacted in a low, steamy verismo setting, and it called for a composer who combines the raw passion of Mascagni with the compassionate vision of Alban Berg. Paulus's response was thoughtful and careful but not inspired. Something like James Fenimore Cooper's *The Spy*—a strong novel successfully dramatized the year after its publication—might be the right subject for him. Hardy's *The Woodlanders*, Wessex-rooted, has a particularity both of local color and of speech patterns which seemed to elude him. One was left admiring not the work as a whole so much as many fluent, lyrical inventions and a generalized savoir-faire. Giles's aria that opens Act III (a setting of Gosse's "Two Points of View") left the strongest impression, and Giles's deathbed aria (its text compounded of Hardy's "The Voice" and "The Tree and the Lady") was also effective. Although Grace is at the center of the novel, Giles is the operatic character most consistently and fully rendered, and in James McGuire he had an interpreter admirably direct and credible. Mr. McGuire sang on the words and sang with candid feeling in a fresh, pleasing baritone that one might describe as still unspoiled by a voice teacher—natural, unforced, unmannered.

Carol Gale's Grace and Mark Thomsen's Fitzpiers were good but more conventional. Dan Sullivan's Mr. Melbury, Grace's father, was excellently clear. Lisbeth Lloyd's Mrs. Charmond was alert and lively. All did what they could to bring the roles to life. Cory Miller's Marty South—the working girl who never speaks her love for Giles—was movingly enacted and was sung richly, but in "rounded" tones in which all vowels were tinged toward "waw." Mrs. Melbury, the most congenial character in the book (she makes few appearances, but every one of them tells), is omitted in the opera. The gaffers—young men sporting white whiskers, painted wrinkles, and stage-old-man shuffles—let down Graham's reputation for shows in which all the movement carries conviction. There was perhaps too much open sky, not an oppression of clustering trees, behind Richard Isackes's basic set. Richard Buckley's conducting was confident.

Idomeneo was done in my English translation, but that must not stop me from praising Robert Carsen's arresting and finely detailed production, which held many memorable images. His device of "framing" the opera as a ritual enacted in a modern Cretan village was unnecessary and added an extra level of unrealistic convention—remarkable that these fishermen knew their Mozart so well—but it was not disturbing, and it suited this theatre where the audience, seated on three sides of the stage, can seem an extension of the chorus. There was a strong cast—Michael Myers (Idomeneus), Patricia Schuman (Idamantes), Sylvia McNair (Ilia), Ashley Putnam (Electra), John LaPierre (Arbaces, arialess but allowed his poignant recitative), and Hans Gregory Ashbaker (the High Priest)— and an excellent chorus, trained by Donald Palumbo. John Nelson's conducting was deft, but the orchestral playing, by members of the St. Louis Symphony, was disappointing. The Loretto-Hilton pit is unhappily deep: the instrumentalists cannot see and, I imagine, can hardly hear the singers with whom they are making music.

WAGNER GOES WEST

July 8, 1985

THE San Francisco *Ring*, designed by John Conklin, is probably the best-looking production of the cycle to be seen today. *Das Rheingold* and *Die Walküre* appeared in 1983; *Siegfried* was done last year; and this summer a completed cycle had three performances. (Tickets sold so well that the first of them was carried by television to a giant screen in Davies Symphony Hall, across the street from the Opera House, as a "video *Ring*" for the overflow audience.) The new *Götterdämmerung* is as handsome as its predecessors. Caspar David Friedrich and Karl Friedrich Schinkel, who provided Conklin's main inspiration, were good choices—the romantic painter whose landscapes are imbued with moral fervor and the neoclassical architect who began his career in the theatre. At the start of *Götterdämmerung,* the Norns have taken up their station on the former "terrace of the gods"—a noble classical ruin when we first saw it, in the second scene of *Das Rheingold,* and now picturesquely cracked, crumbling, and brambled. Day dawns on the Valkyrie Rock (a scene derived from Arnold Böcklin's "Isle of the Dead"), where during Brünnhilde's long sleep—between *Die Walküre* and *Siegfried*—the spreading fir tree that sheltered her has withered and died. The Gibichungs live in ostentatious luxury and grandeur, in a neoclassical palace decorated with giant busts of the Nordic gods; the scene suggests one from Visconti's film *Götterdämmerung* (*The Damned*), peopled with arrogant, decadent offspring of some armaments baron. The terrace outside, the setting of Act II, has many steps (too many to allow an easy assembly of armed guards, vassals, and women). The first scene of Act III, "a wild and wooded rocky valley on the Rhine," is a three-dimensional free stage transcription of Friedrich's "Winter," in Hamburg, with the Gothic arches of the Eldena abbey ruins—Friedrich's recurrent image of a splendor no longer mighty—made Romanesque. (A cycle of the seasons runs through the colors and general feeling of the designs for the four operas.) The final scene is a version of Friedrich's "Arctic Shipwreck" with, superimposed on it, a silhouetted observer like that of his "Traveller Gazing at a Sea of Fog." (Those pictures are also in Hamburg.) All these scenes—and those of the earlier operas, inspired by Friedrich, Schinkel, and, for Valhalla, the architects Etienne-Louis Boullée and Gottfried Semper—are striking, and many of them make appropriate settings for Wagner's drama. The sense of the natural world and of man in relation to it is strong. There is plenty of color and plenty of light. The costumes are colorful, too, and eclectic: Botticelli goddesses, gods garbed as if for *Orphée aux enfers;* Sieglinde the heroine of a German rural romance, Siegmund in pop-star leather, with naked torso, the *Walküre* Fricka suggesting variously a Byzantine or a Prussian empress; *Star Wars* guards for the Gibichungs, Gunther and Gutrune in glamorous negligee (they dress in more seemly fashion when their visitor is announced), Hagen buttoned in a long, tight black trenchcoat. The characterizations by means of costume are a shade obvious; the results are attractive, but sometimes a shade frivolous in effect.

Loge, the god of fire, is the one who sticks out painfully, and that was evidently the intention of the director, Nikolaus Lehnhoff. Loge is dressed in a natty nineteenth-century suit, has dove-gray spats and gloves, and carries the *Wall Street Journal* under his arm. In 1983, he looked like a sharp lawyer; this year, with abundant sideburns and a vest of burgundy brocade, he suggested a fashionable artist, and perhaps he was even intended to represent Wagner. Lehnhoff's *Rheingold* ends—to the accompaniment of Wagner's magnificent Valhalla music—with Loge dominant. From a throne, he retrieves his newspaper (somewhat crumpled by now, for Fricka has been sitting on it); centerstage, he peels off his elegant gloves and tosses them over his shoulder. (On the first night, one of them landed on Donner's cloak and was carried into Valhalla.) Lehnhoff's *Götterdämmerung* ends with Loge dominant—he is that silhouetted figure—observing the destruction and desolation, and then turning to the audience with something like a cynical shrug. Meanwhile, in Wagner's music the theme of the Gods' Downfall yields to that of Redemption by Love and the hope of a better world—glorious music that (in Ernest Newman's words) "seems to spread consoling wings over not merely the present scene but the whole stupendous drama."

This is a flip and musically insensitive way to end the cycle—a cop-out solution to what is often considered a problem (though there is no problem in following Wagner's own clear instructions: men and women gaze in awe at the conflagration in the heavens; during the Destruction theme, flames seize on the hall of the gods; the curtain falls while the Redemption theme wells from the orchestra). Lehnhoff doesn't seem to have made up his mind about Loge (who is, admittedly, an elusive figure) and has been variously quoted as calling him "Wotan's Henry Kissinger" and "the god of truth . . . the constantly ringing alarm clock that reminds Wotan of what is morally right." There is fire music, certainly, in the final scene of *Götterdämmerung*: it pictures destructive yet purifying fire, not a clever, tricky commentator who turns to the audience and dismisses the tremendous tragedy with a "So they've all gone up in smoke! What did I tell you?" In fact, there's no warrant, either, for setting Loge apart from the other gods at the close of *Das Rheingold*. Wagner's direction is specific: after wondering whether or not to distance himself, Loge goes nonchalantly to join them.

I had some sharp—amid some appreciative—things to say about the 1983 *Rheingold* and *Walküre*. *Siegfried* last year suggested that Lehnhoff was maturing, had grown bolder, and was readier to free San Francisco's *Ring* from the accretions that have marred modern stagings—readier to look with fresh eyes at the work itself. But now, disappointingly, he has restaged *Das Rheingold* and *Die Walküre* and staged a *Götterdämmerung* crusted with modern clichés. Watching the shows is rather like reading a play whose main text has been larded with glosses, commentary, and criticism. These take the form of added, gratuitous characters and incidents: six fellow-giants for Fafner and Fasolt; Fricka, Donner, and Froh snoozing onstage while Alberich places the curse on the Ring; Wotan in person at the start of *Die Walküre*; a gang of gorilla henchmen around Hunding at each of his entrances; and so on, up to the intrusion of Loge at the end. Or of sport with "parallels": Siegfried falls upon Brünnhilde at the close of *Siegfried* as Siegmund does upon Sieglinde at the close of *Die Walküre*; in both operas the love music is sung with the lovers largely on opposite sides of the stage. Much of what Lehnhoff has taken over or invented is not merely willful but positively undramatic, untheatrical. When Siegmund and Sieglinde have been pawing one another almost from the moment of their meeting, the thrill of their first embrace where Wagner planned it and keyed it into his music is sacrificed. When, in the final scene of *Siegfried*, Siegfried and Brünnhilde are required to scurry and scamper round and round a circular track, as if playing tag, they look silly. Lehnhoff has generally been at pains to avoid too dignified a presentation of gods and heroes. After singing the battle cry, his Brünnhilde gives Wotan a playful poke in the tum with her spear. Kirsten Flagstad's Brünnhilde never did that.

Sword and spear are potent symbols in *The Ring*, potently used. Lehnhoff has clogged their significance with extra business. In his version, the sword that Siegmund draws from the tree has already been waved by Alberich, during his speech about world dominion; has been used by Fafner to kill Fasolt; has been drawn, bloodstained, from the giant's body by Wotan, handed by him to Donner, and passed by Donner to Froh, who holds it on high as he leads the procession into Valhalla. It's true that in 1876 Wagner did instruct his Bayreuth Wotan to brandish a sword when the theme of the "great idea" (later the Sword motif) leaped from the orchestra. It was not altogether a happy notion and did not find its way into the definitive text. If Nothung the Sword is simply a stray bit of booty, dwarf-forged, that the giants overlooked, then Mime's later difficulty in reforging it makes little sense; Mime is the dwarfs' master smith. If Lehnhoff's intention is to spell out that the sword is a tainted weapon, then his visual glosses are both

334

laborious and at odds with the bright ring of the sword music. Again and again, such visual explanations destroy Wagner's ironies, ambiguities, and richness. In *Götterdämmerung,* in the Brünnhilde and Siegfried-as-Gunther encounter Lehnhoff adds a "big moment" of his own devising: Siegfried grabs Brünnhilde's spear from her and snaps it. It is gratuitous and is diminishing of Wagner's big moment: Siegfried's wrenching of the Ring from Brünnhilde's finger. Meanwhile, amid the unnecessary added business and incidents some necessary incidents are omitted. Siegmund's sword, for example, doesn't shatter on Wotan's spear; Siegmund simply tosses it into the wings. Erda doesn't rise, mysterious and awesome, from the depths; both times, she simply walks on. No great door suddenly flies open when Sieglinde and Siegmund avow their love, to flood an imprisoning chamber with spring radiance; the walls of the courtyard they are in slowly retract into the wings. One can't take altogether seriously a *Ring* where big, important things that should happen don't happen. It's rather like leaving out important episodes of the score while writing in new counterpoints and trying out new instrumentation elsewhere. Moreover, modern producers seem unwilling or unable to achieve theatrical effects that used to present no problems: scenic transformations behind banks of cloud or mist (here a black curtain is dropped); Rhinemaidens who swim up and down, to and fro, on a stage apparently filled with flowing water (here, earthbound, they or their evident doubles simply pop up and down behind rocks); a rampart of raging fire fierce enough to daunt any but a hero; a flash of lightning from Wotan's spear when, in the second collision of these two symbols, it is shattered by the sword. Lehnhoff's work isn't unthoughtful or careless, and it's not dull. His basic ideas about *The Ring* as expressed in several interviews are (except for a partial view of Wotan, which closer attention to the music could have amplified) uncontroversial. But in executing them it is as if he had lost his nerve, feared to give himself up to the work, and tried to maintain his independence by scrawling his own little doodles—and some suggested by his immediate predecessors—over Wagner's great design. It's a large-scale, imposing production, but not as accurate or stirring a one as the *Siegfried* had led us to expect.

Musically, the exciting thing about the performance was the emergence of a noble, commanding, and vocally resplendent Wotan—the first I've heard since Hans Hotter resigned the role, and one with a voice more reliably firm than Hotter's was. James Morris studied the part with Hotter, and in places—especially at the close of the second act of *Die Walküre*—their performances were extraordinarily alike. But there was no suggestion in Mr. Morris's of a rote-learned interpretation. He had already sung the *Walküre* Wotan in Baltimore and in Vienna; in San Francisco he added the *Rheingold* role. He was magnificent. His voice rang out with easy, unforced power—the timbre complicated and eloquent, the focus secure—and was equally clear and telling in the quiet confidences of Wotan's long narrative. His presence was godlike. At the end of *Die Walküre,* he lifted Brünnhilde in his arms and carried her upstage to her place of rest. Plainly, as he grows further into the part he will be more moving still. The text was trenchantly pronounced, every word clear, but there was a tendency to emphasize all the words, even all the syllables, too evenly. Insofar as this resulted from an insistence on bel canto line, it was welcome. It was insensitive of him to interrupt Alberich's curse with a peal of loud, contemptuous laughter. I look forward to hearing Mr. Morris again. He seemed to me the Wotan we have long waited for.

The *Siegfried* Wotan was sung by Thomas Stewart, a master of the role, and he was in good voice. The three cycles overlapped, the second and third beginning before the previous one was done, and so some sharing of roles was no doubt a practical necessity. Not just Wotan but Brünnhilde, Erda, and Fricka had two performers. Gwyneth Jones's *Walküre* Brünnhilde was warm, assured, generous, but vocally unruly. Eva Marton's Brünnhilde in *Siegfried* and (her first) in *Götterdämmerung* was powerful in the upper range, but the long notes were often strident and unsteady. Her low notes were weak. She put loudness before expressiveness. Helga Dernesch, who has already sung five roles in *Götterdämmerung*—Brünnhilde, Gutrune, the Second and the Third Norn, and a Rhinemaiden—now added Waltraute and repeated the Second Norn. Earlier in the cycle, she had been the *Walküre* Fricka. She is an incisive, dignified, and vivid artist. I wish she had also sung Erda, for neither Mariana Paunova (the *Rheingold* Erda and also the First Norn) nor Hanna Schwarz (the *Siegfried* Erda and also the *Rheingold* Fricka) was so impressive.

René Kollo is probably the best Siegfried around. The notes are all there, audible, agreeable in tone, if not exactly heroic. He looked good, if rather too tidily coiffed. He tended to bounce around in rather too determinedly boyish a manner, as Set Svanholm and Wolfgang Windgassen used to. He carried it off more credibly than they did, but it made him a less than substantial hero. Jeannine Altmeyer's Sieglinde was bright but could have been more warmly emotional. Peter Hofmann's Siegmund had pitch problems. Helmut Pampuch was a lively, even rather charming little Mime in *Das Rheingold;* in *Siegfried* he seemed to be losing voice. Walter Berry's Alberich was somewhat shabby, hardly formidable enough. William Lewis was dry of tone in Loge's lyrical music. Roland Bracht and James Patterson, as Fasolt and Fafner, looked enormous and sang fairly well. John Tomlinson, the Hunding and the Hagen, is an intelligent, interesting artist with a dark, grainy, but not really imposing bass. Gutrune was directed as a lustrous vamp, ever ready to twine voluptuous arms around both her brother and her half-brother; the traditional straightforward interpretation is more satisfying, and Kathryn Bouleyn's voice seemed small in this cast. She was also the Third Norn. Gunther likewise was made a caricature, but Michael Devlin sang the part admirably. The Freia, Nancy Gustafson, was excellent. The Froh and the Donner, Walter MacNeil and John Del Carlo, were unremarkable. There was a poor, ill-tuned trio of Rhinemaidens and a splendid team of Valkyries. All in all, it was as well cast, as well sung a *Ring* as one is likely to encounter today. The orchestral playing was satisfactory. The conducting was dull. Edo de Waart, who has been in charge of the San Francisco cycle since it began, showed little ability to give true dramatic impulse to the music, to shape its spans, to render it in anything but careful, well-rehearsed prose.

GREAT HANDEL

July 15, 1985

THE Handel opera productions of this tercentenary season have been many and varied. No single one of those I've attended has united all the virtues a Handelian hopes to find, but not one has been without merits; only one (a very feeble *Alexander's Feast*) was I tempted to leave. In general, besides being enjoyable they have taught two linked lessons, one long familiar to all ardent Handelians but still unlearned by some of the big companies, the other more readily demonstrated in the theatre than from the scores: that Handel's operas are not too long to be played without severe abridgment; and that every one of them has its distinctive character and atmosphere—what Verdi called the *tinta* of an opera. The old notion that Handel operas are strings of fine arias—some pathetic, some brilliant—but not true dramatic adventures dies hard. In *Das Orchester* I read of a potted *Agrippina* in Cassel, playing only two and a half hours, in which a third of the music played came from other Handel operas or from other composers. (The death scene from Handel's *Tamerlano,* one of the most specific and carefully placed in all opera, was inserted; one could as decently drop Isolde's death into *The Flying Dutchman* or *The Mastersingers*.) That's an extreme case; but in recent seasons the City Opera's hashing of *Giulio Cesare* and the Met's of *Rinaldo* were severe. The Fort Worth Opera's production of *Agrippina,* in March, offered another approach. I didn't see the show, but this is what Michael Fleming, the music critic of the Fort Worth *Star-Telegram,* wrote:

> Many opera companies, when they stage Baroque works, operate on the assump-
> tions that their general directors learned in Music History 101: that eighteenth-
> century operas were intolerably long, that audiences then attended only for the
> singers' vocal acrobatics anyway, and that audiences now will not attend at all
> unless a Baroque work is cut to the bone musically and gussied up visually.
>
> The Fort Worth Opera gave such conventional wisdom a kick in the pants
> Thursday evening when it presented the U.S. stage premiere of Handel's *Agrippina.*
>
> *Agrippina* was presented virtually intact, in a lively, witty staging by Ken Cazan,
> and it was a grand success.... [The audience] heard some of Handel's freshest
> music and saw a lively tale of intrigue that belied the notion of Baroque opera as
> a concert in costume.
>
> The opera seemed so rich—and in its way, so contemporary—because Handel
> was taken seriously.

All over the country, in cities large and small, one heard and read similar comments about unhashed, unabbreviated—or but slightly shortened—Handel productions. In Carnegie Hall, there were concert presentations of *Orlando, Ariodante, Semele,* and *Alessandro* done complete, planned and cast by Matthew Epstein. Those were performances given with star singers—Marilyn Horne, Kathleen Battle, Ashley Putnam and Gianna Rolandi (as the rival prima donnas of *Alessandro*), Tatiana Troyanos, Jeffrey Gall, Samuel Ramey—famous in our day as Faustina, Cuzzoni, Farinelli, Boschi were in Handel's. But since I—invited to be a critic before rather than after the event—played some part in the preparation of two of the Carnegie shows, I'll say no more about them.

Ariodante appeared again at the Spoleto Festival in Charleston, South Carolina, in May and June. It was slightly shortened—not much. (When Kennedy Center staged *Ariodante* in 1971, several arias were omitted and several were abridged; numbers from *Alessandro, Teseo,* and *Giulio Cesare* were inserted.) The *Ariodante* plot, laid in Scotland, is exceptional both in Handel's œuvre and in the *Orlando Furioso,* from which it is derived: it is not heroic, dynastic, or magical but a direct, human drama, and closer to Shakespearean romance than anything else Handel set. (Shakespeare, indeed, had already treated the matter in the Hero-Claudio part of *Much Ado.*) Ariodante is a magnificent role: welling with happiness in Act I; stricken in Act II when he apparently sees his Ginevra admitting another man to her bedchamber; grieved more deeply still in Act III when he learns that his accusation of her was unjust; finally joyful. Ginevra's music is on the same high level. She, too, passes from deep, loving joy to despair—when, instead of marriage to her beloved, a charge of infidelity which she cannot comprehend confronts her—and thence to happiness. The progress and pattern of the opera is from light to gloomy darkness and emotional bewilderment, and then to light more brilliant still. The prelude to Act II depicts moonrise in the royal garden, in ten magical bars; romance is soon polluted by the machinations of the villain, Polinesso; the act ends with Ginevra exclaiming in a troubled nightmare. Two of Ariodante's most striking airs are the anguished "Cieca notte," in C minor ("The Night's deceitful Shade, A faithless Dress and View, You have a Heart betray'd," in the 1734 translation), and the brilliant "Dopo notte," in D major, after Polinesso's villainy has been exposed ("After a black and stormy Night The Morning breaks more Fair and Bright"). There are four duets, three of them unconventional in structure. The opera, in the words of Burney's *History,* "abounds with beauties and strokes of a great master."

The Spoleto performance—sung in Italian, by and to Americans—was, alas, more decorative than dramatic. Catherine Turocy, the director, had taught her cast period movement but not passionate declamation. In some respects, the production essayed an "authentic" style, with attitudes and gestures based on precepts of the old primers and on contemporary images, but in other respects it was a sorry example of a staging cluttered with trivial and meaningless activity. There are nine and sixty ways of putting Handel operas on the stage, but not every single one of them is right. One right way was shown by Peter Sellars in his direction of the *Orlando* that ran for forty performances at the American Repertory Theatre, in Cambridge, in 1981–82. It was a production filled with movement—movement that at every point mirrored, enhanced, intensified the shapes of Handel's music and gave form to the characters' emotions. It was a dramatic tour de force of a kind only a Sellars could achieve—wonderful, gripping from beginning to end, unforgettable. Another possible, more modest way, it seems to me—and it would be disingenuous of me not to own that it was a way I tried when directing a student production of *Tamerlano* at Bloomington, Indiana, earlier this year—is to let Handel's music, the text he set, and the singers' utterance of it do most of the work and to restrict action to a few simple moves based on the "ground plan" of the arias. Miss Turocy's way was to "animate" the long arias with pointless business. When a singer stopped singing for a moment, she or he might cross the stage to take a flower from a vase and sniff it; or she might cross the stage to pick up a fan and fan herself; or other people might come on, mop and mow, perhaps dance around the singer, and then retire again.

Ariodante was Judith Malafronte, a mezzo with a vivid presence and fluent, direct coloratura. Ginevra was Julianne Baird, a soprano who divides opinion, and who leaves me divided between admiration of her style (she is, as my *Times* colleague put it, "an interesting artist," and "one becomes curious to hear what she will do with the next aria, the next phrase") and dislike of the timbre of high notes that suggest the penetrating, vibratoless ringing of musical glasses. Cynthia Miller was a lively Polinesso. In the smaller roles of Dalinda and Lurcanio, the soprano Ann Monoyios and the tenor Jeffrey Thomas gave much pleasure. The band, the Concert Royal Baroque Orchestra, sounded thin and peaky. James Richman was a trudging conductor, and again and again he seemed to find it hard to bring his players in together. The décor was unattractive. Charleston's Dock Street Theatre, where *Ariodante* was given, purports to be built on eighteenth-century lines, but in fact it has a deep-sunken orchestra pit—a late-nineteenth-century innovation—which inhibits any easy rapport between instrumentalists and singers.

America's best baroque players were evidently engaged elsewhere. The performances of Handel's *Teseo* that I attended at the Boston Early Music Festival in May boasted the finest eighteenth-century band I have ever heard, anywhere. The players of the Boston Early Music Festival Orchestra had been handpicked mainly from Boston, New York, and California, and had been rehearsing together six months before the festival began. The familiar merits of "authentic" orchestras—lithe timbre, lively articulation, limpid texture, easy balance with the voices—were attended by none of the frequent disadvantages: podium plod, out-of-tuneness, seasick string tone, curdled woodwinds, and a general lack of firmness and substance. This was playing to convince skeptics and to delight believers and unbelievers alike—spirited, adept, risk-taking, and beautiful. The band, as in the old days, sat in a long double row at house-floor level, principals facing the singers they accompanied. Nicholas McGegan, at one of two harpsichords, led the performance, with other continuo players—cello, two theorbos, violone—close at hand. The personnel list was a roll call of leading early-music artists. All thirty or so deserve to be named; the particular stars were John Gibbons (second harpsichord), Myron Lutzke (first cello), Dennis Godburn (first bassoon), Paul O'Dette and Jakob Lindberg (theorbos), and, above all, Stephen Hammer (first oboe), in the leading role that Handel wrote for the composer and virtuoso oboist John Ernest Galliard. Mr. Hammer and Mr. Godburn also played a dulcet pair of recorders. The opera is inventively and richly scored, but the orchestra's thus taking pride of place reflects the fact that the singers, who should rightly have held most of our attention, were less accomplished performers than their accompanists.

Teseo, Handel's third opera for London, produced in 1713, remained unrevived in Britain until this year—in Manchester in March, at Covent Garden this month—and in Boston it received its American première. The libretto, by Nicola Haym, is adapted from one Philippe Quinault wrote for Lully. Aegeus and Theseus, father and son, both love the princess Agilea; Agilea and the princess and sorceress Medea, who is betrothed to Aegeus, both love Theseus. Aegeus doesn't know that Theseus is the son he begot years before in Troezen, and he connives with Medea in a plot to poison him. But in the nick of time the youth's identity is revealed. The action is a mixture of familiar legend and extravagant spectacle intended to display the scenic designer's art: "Medea by her Inchantments changes the Scene into a horrid Desart full of frightful Monsters"; "The Furies go off; and the Scene changes into an Inchanted Island"; "Medea in a Chariot drawn by flying Dragons." Medea is a magnificent role, passionate and powerful—one to set beside Handel's Armida and Alcina. Nancy Armstrong didn't seem to feel it, and she gave a rather blowsy performance, lacking in dignity. Agilea, Medea's gentle but far from colorless foil, another fine role, was pallidly played by Judith Nelson. Theseus was the soprano Randall Wong; it is surprising to hear high C-sharps from a male throat, but neither his singing nor his demeanor was heroic. The most stylish performance was Drew Minter's, as Arcanus—a fairly small part, originally taken by the contralto Jane Barbier. The work was sung in (mostly poor) Italian, but a facsimile of the 1713 bilingual libretto was available and there was light to read it by.

The Manchester production of *Teseo,* it seems, was set in a country house serving as a wartime hospital, where nurses tended young officers. When Medea embarked on her horrid enchantments, gas masks were donned, and sentries kept watch on searchlight towers. The Boston performance, given in the Boston College Theatre Arts Center (a six-hundred-seater, acoustically dry), was a historical reconstruction along the lines of the celebrated *Orlando* at Washington University, St. Louis, two years ago. The same team was in charge: Mr. McGegan both musical and stage director, Scott Blake the scenic designer, Kevin Flynn the designer of light simulating that of an eighteenth-century theatre. Bonnie Cutter was the happily named costume designer. Some of the scenery was identical. It was once again fascinating and instructive to see a modern essay in baroque theatre practice. Mr. Blake's inventive décor once again struck me as too "impressionistic" in facture, not definite enough in the drawing or the painting. The frightful monsters and the dragon-drawn chariot were fun. But the cast wasn't strong enough to fill the scenes with pulsing human emotion. Stock settings carried over from opera to opera—an apartment in the royal palace, a smiling grove, the shore (with long painted rollers revolving to counterfeit billows, as in St. Louis and Boston), a horrid cavern—were common in the eighteenth century. Nevertheless, I can't help feeling that Handel, the great dramatist who transcended conventions, deserves better than he got in his day: that, ideally, décor should be specific to the character, the *tinta,* of the opera concerned. (Trying to test such critical notions in practice, I rejected for

Tamerlano a conventional, all-purpose baroque set and proposed instead something Appiesque: tall, stark, simple spaces to house a tragic drama that is unique among Handel's operas in having every scene laid indoors.)

Authenticity, Robert Donington remarks in the closing section of his *A Performer's Guide to Baroque Music,* "is for getting a natural match between the music and its interpretation. It is not history for history's sake. It is history for the music's sake. . . . The only authenticity of primary importance is the authenticity which, without any fuss or need for explanation, gets straight across to the audience." And that's what the orchestral playing in this *Teseo* did. It had "the proficiency and the brilliance, the robustness and vitality" that Donington calls "part of the authenticity."

Teseo, Handel's only five-act opera, is sometimes described as long, but the Boston performance, uncut, ran for less than three and a half hours. There was an intermission between Acts III and IV, and between Acts IV and V an entr'acte in the form of the D-minor Organ Concerto, Opus 7, No. 4, with Mr. Gibbons, still at the harpsichord, as soloist and leader. Handel would play organ concertos between the acts of his oratorios; I know of no precedent for inserting one in an opera. But its presence could hardly be regretted, for Mr. Gibbons is an interpreter of rare intensity. He's not unmannered, but his declamation can hold listeners rapt. Moreover, the two-cello duet at the start of the concerto had the fervor and the fullness that much of the singing lacked. [*More about* Teseo *on p. 344.*]

INFINITE VARIETY

July 29, 1985

THERE are high claims in Donald Grout's *Short History of Opera* which when it appeared, in 1947, before many of Handel's operas had been revived, had to be taken largely on trust. The tercentenary Handel season is providing testimony in sound to their accuracy. Of Handel's expressive arias, Grout said: "The number and variety of these arias is so great, and the power of capturing the most subtle nuances of feeling so astounding, that one is tempted to believe that there is no emotion of which humanity is capable that has not found musical expression somewhere in Handel's operas." Handel's Caesar, Cleopatra, and Bajazet are dramatic creations Grout described as "universal, ideal types of humanity, moving and thinking on a vast scale, the analogue in opera of the great tragic personages of Corneille." Handel by his music brought them to life, transcending the protocol and the conventions of the stock librettos he began with. And the quality that makes his characters great "is more than the reflection of a certain musical style or a consummate technique; it is the direct emanation of Handel's own spirit, expressed in music with an immediacy that has no parallel outside Beethoven. It is the incarnation of a great soul." So Handel keeps company with

Corneille and Beethoven, but other names should be mentioned, too. He is not only grand, noble, and wise. He is witty, funny, and graceful. He delights in pleasures of the senses. His art, "like that of Bach, has the power of glorifying the apparently trivial," says Grout. "The song of the birds [in *Rinaldo*] is a magic window opening on a glimpse of pastoral Eden." He has a Mozartian certainty in dropping notes into exactly the right places, a Schubertian font of never-failing melodic invention (when other men's tunes play in as tributaries, he transmutes them), and a Shavian capacity to treat serious matters in an entertaining manner. Aeschylus, Shakespeare, Monteverdi, Purcell, and Verdi are other big names that are apt to turn up in Handel criticism as being, in one aspect or another, his companions.

In some forty operas and twenty dramatic oratorios, Handel rejoiced in his strengths. *Giulio Cesare,* first heard at the King's Theatre in 1724, is one of the longest and richest of his operas. Six characters—Cleopatra, Caesar, Cornelia, Sextus, Ptolemy, and Achillas—are fully and vividly drawn. The range of emotions spanned in the three carefully controlled acts is vast. The interplay of personalities and political strife is keen. The opera has often been revived with success, but usually in versions that scatter and discolor its rich treasures and distort its psychological subtlety. For many years, a version edited by Oskar Hagen, first performed in 1922, held the stage. It was a pioneering achievement—*Cesare* had been unheard for nearly two centuries—but it inaugurated, and its success perpetuated, unfortunate practices that linger on in some large houses. (As late as 1963, I heard the Hagen *Cesare* in Munich, with Lisa Della Casa, Hermann Prey, and Fritz Wunderlich.) The editor rescored the piece for a romantic orchestra; he abridged it heavily; he set not only heroic Caesar but also the foppish Ptolemy, the boy Sextus, and the eunuch Nirenus growling their music an octave too low. (Winton Dean remarked in *Handel and the Opera Seria* that "a performance of *Giulio Cesare* that sounds like nothing so much as a cross between the St. Matthew Passion and *The Flying Dutchman* does no lasting service to Handel.") In 1927, Smith College introduced *Giulio Cesare* to America in the Hagen version. In 1965, Kansas City produced a *Cesare* that (in Dean's words) "made nonsense of music and drama alike": roles were transposed; the seduction scene of Act II was "enriched" by the prison duet from *Tamerlano*. In 1966, the City Opera staged, and in 1980 it revived, a scrambled, largely transposed version in which only three of thirty-three arias were heard complete. (Yale performed that edition this year, thereby forfeiting, in Handelian eyes, any strong claim to be considered a seat of higher learning.) From the English National Opera production of *Cesare,* which was restaged in San Francisco three years ago, about a third of the score (including ten arias) was missing. The pitches, at least, were more or less right. (Some of the title role was lifted to accommodate Janet Baker in London and Tatiana Troyanos in San Francisco.)

Now, at last, we have had a complete *Giulio Cesare.* It was given eight performances this month as part of the PepsiCo Summerfare festival, at Purchase, New York. It was a production responsive at every point to the seriousness, the splendor, the humors, and the variety of the work, alert at every moment to the movements and the meanings of the music. Peter Sellars was the director and Craig Smith the conductor, working in the harmony that irradiated the *Orlando,* the *Così fan tutte,* and the *Mikado* they did together. (Happy the director and conductor who achieve such concord. In *Teseo,* another Summerfare offering, Nicholas McGegan ensured it by being both musical and stage director of his production.) The show was set in the modern Middle East, but that was unimportant except insofar as it sharpened the audience's sense of watching real characters caught up in real events. Sellars hears Handel's music kinetically and realizes it in stage movement suggested by its flow, its tensions, its melodic, rhythmic, and dynamic shapes. At its best, his "choreography" is as subtle, musical, and revealing as Balanchine's. Sellars's means are eclectic. In *Cesare,* they included baroque sign language inflected with an amusing Egyptian accent, Kabuki enactment of deep, powerful emotions, and pop idioms of our day. Cleopatra sang "Piangerò" prostrate, trussed, blindfolded, writhing in slow shapes that limned and intensified the music. When her ships came home at last, her simile aria ("Da tempeste il legno infranto . . . salvo giunge in porto") found literal representation: gunboats sailed into the harbor. Again and again—alike in moments of stillness (such as Sextus' heart-stopping "Cara speme," one of those *largo* rhapsodies shared between cello and singer which Handel often placed in a first act) and in moments of deliberate, giddy silliness—Sellars created unforgettable imagery. In a program note he wrote of numbers "with clearly discernable comic intent" that "surround, quite unexpectedly, areas of peaceful contentment, maddened anxiety, and mind-bending bloodlust," and commented, "This is brilliant showmanship." So was his. *Cesare* can never have seemed richer, stranger, stronger, more passionate, or more high-spirited than in this presentation by artists aflame with appreciation for the opera as Handel wrote it, seeking not to conventionalize but to illumine its fierce originality.

The show called for, and had, singers of uncommon vocal and physical ability. Susan Larson, the Cleopatra (a role Montserrat Caballé undertook in Rome earlier this year), is a soprano compelling in everything she does, one whose lines are finely and eloquently molded. She caught exactly the infinite variety of the heroine's eight-aria progress from charming frivolity to lambent maturity. If intonation sometimes faltered in "V'adoro, pupille," one could blame it on the difficulty of singing while descending on a wire from the flies: Sellars is prepared to sacrifice vocal comfort to theatrical effect when the balance is dramatic gain. Jeffrey Gall, the Caesar, is a consummate singer unfazed by antics: he carolled a dazzling cadenza while crawling under a table. He gave a brilliant performance as a smiling, smiling statesman ("Va tacito" was a conference-table statement of deadly smoothness), as a lighthearted lover who gets into deeper waters, as a resourceful man of action who snatches victory from setback. Lorraine Hunt, the Sextus, is a discovery—a soprano with wonderful candor and directness in her timbre and her manner, with tones and a temperament that held the house intent. Mary Westbrook-Geha, the Cornelia, was incisive in mourning, in self-defense against importunate lovers, in vindictive triumph; her words were oddly flecked with what sounded like an assumed German accent. Rodney Hardesty, the Ptolemy, was ugly of tone but assured in presentation. James Maddalena, the Achillas—bluff, honest betrayed captain—was moving as he wrestled with problems of loyalty and honor. Cheryl Cobb's Nirena (Handel gave precedent for turning the eunuch into a handmaiden) was piquant, and Herman Hildebrand's Curius—here Caesar's advance man cum bodyguard—was wondrously fleet and nimble.

Some of Smith's tempi at first struck me as—by what might be called absolute standards—slow. The opera lasted four and three-quarters hours—about half an hour longer than the complete *Cesare* done in Birmingham, England, eight years ago. But on Handel tempi there is seldom much agreement, and Smith is not one of those conductors who approach a Handel score with preconceived, "absolute" ideas, determined by notation and convention, and are then unprepared to modify them to match the words of a particular aria, the actions of a particular production, and what most effectively suits a particular singer. Everything he did carried conviction; everything was felt; everything seemed apt. The instruments were modern. The opera was sung in Italian. The "wild beasts" that menace Cornelia became a pair of Doberman patrol dogs, and they raised no textual problems. But it was mildly disconcerting to hear Cleopatra address Nirena as "my faithful [male] companions" and her platoon of troops as "my faithful handmaidens," and to hear submachine guns called "swords."

Teseo—the Boston Early Music Festival production that I wrote about two weeks ago, which was conceived as a historical re-creation, so far as possible, of a performance of Handel's day—came to Summerfare and provided a striking contrast. In Boston, I had missed any strong dramatic presentation of the rival heroines, the sorceress Medea and the princess Agilea. In Purchase, I revelled in the sensuous beauty of the music, so lovingly shaped by Mr. McGegan, his singers, and his peerless band of instrumentalists making the sounds of Handel's day. The sequence that opens Act III is surely as lovely a stretch of composition as exists: Arcanus' slow-rolling arpeggios through a lush web spun by two recorders and five-part strings (divided violas); Clizia's airy two-part invention with a lively cello; Arcanus' fascinating alternation of 3/8 and 3/4 measures, his voice doubled in octaves by recorders and violins; Agilea's love-warm aria lapped by four-part strings and two bassoons. It's a feast of melodies, rhythms, timbres. But one can drop into this early opera almost anywhere and find comparable delights. In the Purchase theatre, more attractive than and acoustically superior to the one in Boston, the opera flowered. The singers made more of the music. Judith Nelson, the Agilea, took on new color. Drew Minter, the Arcanus, is a countertenor whose timbre and line again ravished all ears.

Serse, a late work—Handel's last opera but two—is an engaging and uncharacteristic piece, often revived. The libretto is adapted from one Nicolò Minato wrote for Cavalli, in days (1654) when operatic form was more fluid than it later became. The plot contains two incidents documented by Herodotus (the monarch's extravagant admiration of a plane tree, voiced in "Ombra mai fu," and his bridge of boats over the Hellespont); comic episodes around the Leporello-like servant Elviro; and a main matter sometimes serious, sometimes amusing, often both at once, that has *Twelfth Night*–like intricacies of lovers (two brothers, two sisters, and a third woman, the disguised Amastris) at cross-purposes. Handel responded with a score in which beguiling arias, ariettas, songs, arioso, and recitative mingle in a flexible and masterly way.

A big hit of the London season has been *Xerxes*—*Serse* in a new English translation, by the director of the show, Nicholas Hytner—at the English National Opera, done uncut (and lasting just over three and a half hours), in a sprightly, eclectic staging that ranges freely from Persepolis to Vauxhall Gardens. *Xerxes* at the Juilliard Theater in April, done by the Juilliard American Opera Center in a new English translation by the conductor of the show, Albert Fuller, was cut to shreds and had what *Opera News* not unfairly called "the kind of performance that gives the composer a bad reputation." The staging, by Norman Ayrton, was in the conventional-cute, reach-me-down-Restoration, frilly manner once thought appropriate for "period" pieces, and particularly unsuited to student performance. The décor, by Kenneth Foy, was glittery and gaudy. Mr. Fuller's conducting was dull. The orchestral playing should have brought blushes to Juilliard cheeks. And all that was a pity, for onstage there were some talented young singers. Two mezzos from Peking, Yun Deng and Yan-yu Guo, played Xerxes and his brother Arsamenes; Rebecca Russell was Amastris, a princess dressed as a soldier.

Heroine

August 26, 1985

Bellini's Norma is among the most challenging of operatic roles. The composer himself called it "encyclopedic." The soprano who would essay it needs power, grace, pure, fluent coloratura, tones both violent and tender, force and intensity of verbal declamation, and a regal stage presence. Lilli Lehmann, the first Met Norma (in 1890)—who early in this century made noble records of "Casta diva" and of the heroine's duets with Adalgisa, the seconda donna—sang Clotilde, Norma's handmaiden, in her early Prague years (as Joan Sutherland did, to Maria Callas's Norma, in her early Covent Garden years), and later she sang Adalgisa. But she refused all invitations to tackle Norma until she had mastered Mozart's Donna Anna, Beethoven's Leonore, and Wagner's Isolde; only then did she feel ready to undertake a role she considered "ten times more exacting than Leonore." In her autobiography, Lehmann deplores modern performances of the opera undertaken without due preparation and seriousness: "*Norma* ... should be sung and acted with fanatical consecration, rendered by the chorus and, especially, the orchestra with artistic reverence, and led with authority by the conductor; to every single eighth-note should be given the musical tribute that is its due." Several of the sopranos whose recollections appear in Lanfranco Rasponi's *The Last Prima Donnas* say much the same. Ester Mazzoleni, for example, recalls that in the second and third decades of the century "there were three exceptional Normas: Giannina Russ, Celestina Boninsegna, and myself." (All three can still be heard on records.) The prima donna characterizes them—"Russ was a superb virtuosa but a little cold; Boninsegna's tone was utterly ravishing but a little too sweet," and "Mazzoleni, the critics claimed, combined the bel canto art with much fire"—and continues:

I simply cannot understand what is happening now. They all sing Norma today—the coloraturas, like Sutherland, Deutekom, and Sills; the lyrics, like Maria Luisa Cioni and Scotto; the spintos, like Caballé, whom I admire in certain roles very much. But how can they do justice to this terrifying score? It is an utter travesty of what Bellini wrote, and the audience takes a lot of punishment.

Gina Cigna, the Met's third Norma (in 1936; Lehmann and Rosa Ponselle were her only predecessors there), says:

We did not have the mentality of today's singers, who want to sing everything and, alas, are allowed to do so. We were brought up with a deep reverence for the composer and the librettist. Some years ago I was invited to talk in the intermission at the televised *Norma* from La Scala. I never should have accepted, because I always say what I think. It did not sit well with anyone when I announced that what I was hearing was not Bellini's *Norma*. . . . Caballé has a God-given, beautiful lyric instrument, but she was forced to force all the time, and I use the same verb twice on purpose.

Mazzoleni's Norma and Cigna's Norma—their recordings show it—had power and temperament, but their singing is often strident and unshapely. I prefer the sound of Caballé's. In the *Norma* performances I've heard her give, she varied. Sometimes, indeed, she did force. When she sang within her strengths—which, *pace* Cigna, were considerable—one admired what the Viennese critic Eduard Hanslick admired in Lehmann: "in slow cantilenas the most beautiful portamento and the securest and purest intonation and swelling [also magical floating and fining down] of the high notes." But—as Hanslick also said of Lehmann—"one may conceive of a thunder of passion more imposing, of lightning flashes of jealousy and anger more incendiary." No Norma seems able to compass all aspects of the role. In our day, Maria Callas came closest to doing so. I learned to love the opera in her performances. When she sang, one was caught up in the work itself. Her successors—Sutherland, Caballé, Sills, Shirley Verrett, Grace Bumbry, Scotto, and, most recently, Olivia Stapp—have tended to induce not so much ecstatic absorption in Bellini's drama as cool assessment of the particular soprano's merits and inadequacies in the tremendous leading role.

The first Norma, Giuditta Pasta, in 1831, had earlier that year created the ingénue heroine, Amina, of Bellini's pastoral opera *La sonnambula;* as she was a renowned tragic actress, we should not make too much of the fact. (Callas, too, was a notable Amina.) The success as Norma of Jenny Lind, whose most famous roles were perhaps Amina and Donizetti's Daughter of the Regiment, points more convincingly to the possibility of a lighter, less forceful kind of heroine than we usually hear—one who achieves her effects by accuracy and vividness of presentation. Lind's high A's—prominent notes in "Casta diva" when the aria is sung (as it usually is) transposed down two steps, into F major—were free and brilliant; for the long-drawn middle A that starts the aria she employed, we are told, "a veiled tone of ravishing beauty." A small-scale *Norma* would hardly be the real thing (Toti Dal Monte's record of "Casta diva" suggests a charming, pretty little priestess), but a carefully scaled presentation, matched to the strengths of the protagonist, and beautifully and accurately sung, would surely be less distressing, more enjoyable, and more striking than one in which much of the music is stridently and imprecisely voiced, in a vain attempt to sound grandly heroic.

The City Opera's *Norma,* the first in its history, is a revised edition of a production, directed by Andrei Serban and designed by Michael Yeargan, that was presented by the Welsh National Opera, in Cardiff, earlier this year. It played in Cardiff's New Theatre, which seats a little over a thousand people. The heroine there was Suzanne Murphy, who had been the Welsh National's Elvira in *I puritani*—another Serban-Yeargan show—in 1982. British critics described her as tall, beautiful, and dramatically alert—an imperfect singer but an impressive one. She joins the City Opera *Norma* in November. The City Opera's current heroine, Olivia Stapp, made her State Theater début thirteen years ago, as Carmen, and has sung Lady Macbeth, Elektra, and Tosca at the Met. In *Norma,* she was an imperfect singer—her intonation errant, her coloratura approximate, her tones often unpleasing—and not impressive. Elena Nicolai, an Adalgisa to many Normas, pays tribute (in Rasponi's book) to those of them whose voices "poured out." Miss Stapp's seemed, rather, to be pushed out. Serban's production did not help her to achieve the character that her singing lacked. Most of his operatic work has been done in Britain: *Eugene Onegin, Rodelinda, The Merry Widow,* and the two Bellinis for the Welsh, *Il Trovatore* for Opera North (all designed by Yeargan), *Turandot* for the Royal Opera. I've seen only the *Turandot,* the *Traviata* he staged for the Juilliard, the City Opera's *Alcina,* and now *Norma,* and at all of them have been surprised that a stage director whose work for La Mama has been adventurous can be so untheatrical and imperceptive when dealing with lyric drama.

Bellini gave Norma a grand entrance, in the third scene of the opera—the kind of entrance a prima donna dreams of. The setting is the sacred forest of the Druids: in the center stands Irminsul's great oak tree, the Druidical altar stone before it. It is night. Between the trees we see fires flickering in the distance. In this romantic set we have already heard Oroveso's aria and Pollio's aria. Now Druids, priestesses, warriors, bards, acolytes assemble, awaiting the moonrise and the arrival of their high priestess. They sing the solemn, expectant chorus "Norma viene." (A cancelled page in the autograph score shows how carefully Bellini prepared and timed the heroine's arrival.) Norma appears, her tresses streaming, her brow crowned with verbena, a golden sickle in her hand. She mounts the Druidical stone and gazes around her as if inspired. All are silent—and then Norma breaks into that silence with her opening words, "Sediziose voci."

In the City Opera production, there was a dumpy little woman busily pottering about in the very first scene, in stockinged feet. Her tattered black dress stopped short above her ankles. She wore a golden apron and fancy headgear; a stiff hank of artificial red hair fell down her back; she carried a sickle and a piece of cloth. She looked like a bag lady who'd found some finery, and I assumed she was the Druids' temple cleaner, a new character Serban had invented. She was bustling about again, amid the throng, in the third scene—and then, suddenly, she turned round and sang "Sediziose voci," and I realized she was to be the heroine of the evening. Nicolai's first Adalgisa was to the Norma of Wera Amerighi-Rutili, whom she describes as a Norma "of huge dimensions, but with a nobility that left one in awe." (Her recordings of the role are untidy and overemotional but highly dramatic.) Amerighi-Rutili told her: "The entrance in an opera is of the greatest importance, for you must let the audience know who you are right away. How you walk, hold yourself, the kind of light your eyes give out—this you must never fail to put across the footlights. . . . If they don't notice you when you come in, it will take a long time for them to do so later." It took a long time for a bag lady padding about in her socks to turn into a Norma. Nicolai also recalled, of Gina Cigna's heroine, that "her eyes were fantastic—like stars." Miss Stapp was required to sing several of Norma's phrases with her eyes invisible—behind a mask. A City Opera handout informed us that "masks are worn when the characters are presenting their 'public images' or are performing rituals; masks are removed when they are revealing their true feelings." It's a simplistic idea, inappropriate to the style of this opera and hard on the singers. Serban's main concern seemed to be not with the performers but with what at any moment they wore. Masks, aprons, headgear went on and off. Pollio and Adalgisa's duet, "Viene in Roma," was a striptease in which he pulled off her dress. The defiant martial chorus became a disrobing number in which the Gallic warriors shed their cloaks, and their women scurried on to bundle up the discarded garments and carry them off.

The City Opera is being promoted as a purveyor of opera apprehensible by morons. A page in the *Norma* program book proclaims: "You don't have to read up on the plot in advance. Or be concerned that you won't be able to follow what's going on. You can just sit back and enjoy yourself, the way you do at a movie with subtitles." It's a point of view—opera for tired businessmen—but not one that I share. *Norma* seems to me an opera deserving of some effort on the part of the audience as well as of the performers. The City Opera's claim, it is true, is made specifically in relation to the "supertitles"—a simplified, summary translation of the sung Italian text, phrase by phrase, flashed on a screen above the stage more or less at the time the phrase in question is being sung. "At NY City Opera, we give you 'instant understanding.' " It bears the sort of relation to true understanding that instant coffee does to real, or canned peas do to fresh. Useful commodities all, substitutes for people unprepared to devote time and trouble to art or to food. Serban, in fact, doesn't approve of the mechanical glosses. In a *Times* interview, he said that he was "shaking with horror at the prospect of the subtitles," that he believed in "unconscious, secret, invisible communication," and that in operas "where you really must understand what is being said—well, they should just be done in English!" But in the simplified emphases of his staging—the use of masks, for example—he provided something like a visual analogue of the supertitles. Stage actions and supertitles conspired to present a child's eye view of the rich and subtle work. The overture was treated as an accompaniment to a series of "vignettes," tableaux vivants, of the drama to follow. Into the final scenes Serban had written a prominent new role for Adalgisa (who in Bellini's opera is not present), but he failed to carry his idea through and did not compose anything for Adalgisa to sing. So anyone encountering *Norma* for the first time here gets the impression that Bellini was an incompetent composer and Felice Romani a bungling librettist, who could leave one of their principals mute in the crowning scene of their drama.

Adalgisa was composed for the young soprano Giulia Grisi, who later became a famous Norma herself. In Cardiff, it was sung by a soprano. But mezzo-sopranos have long laid claim to the role, and in the City Opera production Judith Forst, a mezzo-soprano, offered the deftest singing of the evening. She ran about in bare feet and showed her knees a good deal. Two novel features of the Cardiff production were happily dropped in New York: Norma and Adalgisa didn't give the children a bath during the stretta of their "Mira, o Norma," and Adalgisa didn't join Norma on the pyre in the final scene. But "Mira, o Norma" lost its simple poignancy, because Adalgisa neglected the traditional business and the children didn't approach their mother. What should happen—what the text implies—is spelled out, a shade sentimentally, in the scholarly annotated score of *Norma* edited by W. S. Rockstro: "Adalgisa, taking the children, places them on their knees before their mother, and lifts their little hands in a supplicating posture." At the City Opera, the words "ai tuoi ginocchi" were sung but were not enacted or translated; Adalgisa was asked to utter nonsense. The Pollio was Robert Grayson, whose singing was clean but plain, without fire or virtuosity. He suggested a callow NCO rather than the distinguished Roman commander to whom Virgil addressed two Eclogues. William Dansby's Oroveso was not grand. The chorus sounded small. Yeargan's costumes were all black (except for the children, who wore white shifts). His set was a collection of small Roman ruins, disposed in various arrangements against a backcloth lit in different colors. A drift of autumn leaves spanned the front stage in Act I, and in Act II was swept into a heap for the children to play with. Richard Bonynge conducted. Much of the time, he seemed brisk, almost perfunctory. No one since Tullio Serafin has managed the majestic twin climaxes of the finale convincingly: Bonynge simply slammed into low gear at the fortissimo, with jarring results.

Verdi's *Attila* is a difficult opera to bring off. The characters are unpleasant, the dramaturgy is clumsy, and a fair amount of the music is coarse. In the City Opera production—first staged four years ago, revived this season—two of the large scenic effects on which the composer counted are muffed. The second scene, the founding of Venice, errs by omission. Emanuele Muzio, Verdi's companion and amanuensis, described a "villainous" Scala staging in 1846: "The sunrise occurred before it was indicated in the music. The sea, instead of being rough and stormy, was calm and without a single breaker. The hermits had no hovels; the priests had no altars." In the City Opera version, there was no evident sunrise and no sea at all. The scene of the procession from Rome, led by Leo I, that repulses Attila at the gates of the city (overhead he seems to see giant figures of Sts. Peter and Paul with flaming swords) brought no procession: curtains were drawn back to reveal a choral society assembled outside Attila's tent. For the rest, it's a picturesque show, richly costumed by Hal George. Lotfi Mansouri's old-fashioned staging has its ridiculous moments but is confident. I enjoyed the production more in 1981 when Justino Díaz was the Attila, Marilyn Zschau the Odabella, and Sergiu Comissiona the conductor. Samuel Ramey, in the revival, sang the title role very well but was not much of an actor; his Attila was a series of bold postures rather than a character alert to what happened onstage around him. Linda Roark-Strummer, a lyric soprano, was taxed beyond her vocal capacities by the part of Odabella and pushed what might be an attractive voice into edginess and unevenness. She looked good, moved well, and wore her costumes handsomely. Frederick Burchinal sang Aetius in measured, darkly covered tones, without much brio. Jon Fredric West was an energetic little Foresto. The chorus, as in *Norma,* sounded underpowered, and Christopher Keene's conducting was thin-blooded.

Melodious Cats

September 2, 1985

THE ENGLISH CAT is the fifth of Hans Werner Henze's operas to be given its American première by the Santa Fe Opera. (The others were *Boulevard Solitude, The Stag King, The Bassarids,* and *We Come to the River.*) *The English Cat* was some four years in the making. In November 1977, in Paris, Henze saw the Argentine theatre troupe TSE play a dramatization, by Geneviève Serrault, of Balzac's epistolary tale "Heartaches of an English Cat"—his contribution to Grandville's *Scenes from the Private and Public Life of Animals.* (Grandville's images of men and women with animal heads have become newly familiar with their appearance in the columns of the *New York Review.*) The composer was struck with the operatic possibilities of the subject. In April 1978, he invited the playwright Edward Bond, his collaborator on *We Come to the River,* to undertake a libretto:

> What fascinates me is the idea of masks. The story of a country cat married to a rich city cat too old to have fun, then her secret love affair on the London rooftops, and then the intrigue: the officer (a fox), whom she rejects, organizes the assassination of her lover, which is declared a suicide, just as in *Ballo in maschera* or *Rigoletto*—all this smacks of today. These elements alone are so stimulating that already I *hear* everything. It may seem a shade arty, but it isn't. . . .
> I need your arias and duets and recitatives (for dialogue) just as Verdi and Rossini needed their librettists' texts, and with your help my music will become aggressive and alarming beneath its mask of stylization. It will upset all the usual readings that people think they find in the old work. Everything seems to be sweet and charming, and then it is suddenly grim and really terrifying.

Bond produced a schema, on two typewritten pages, in March 1979, in London, on a day of biting cold. A libretto, sent by unregistered mail, reached Henze in Italy in the early days of June. Composition began in March 1980. The opera had its first performance at the Schwetzingen Festival in June 1983, in a German translation. A Paris production, in French, followed in February 1984, at the Opéra-Comique. Last month, Santa Fe gave the original-language première of the work.

Meanwhile, Henze kept a working diary, and his *Die englische Katze: Ein Arbeitstagebuch, 1978–1982,* a four-hundred-page volume published in 1983 by S. Fischer, provides a fascinating and detailed account of the score's genesis. The opera was composed in rapid, exuberant bursts. One marvels at entries for the days on which, after filling many pages with music, Henze had energy left to set down analytical accounts of what he had been doing. The principal cat-music note row receives a move-by-move harmonic and emotional description. (The row is "*Affekt*-laden, like the intervallic system of a keyboard sonata by C. P. E. Bach or Haydn in the emotional vein, but also mysterious and protean, like the inner life of animals"; and Henze cites a line of Hölderlin about animal souls dwelling in men.) The derivation of later movements from the lusty street song of Arnold, the raffish nephew of Lord Puff, the elderly husband, is carefully traced. Thoughts about orchestration are set down as they occur: Tom, the hero of the piece, will have two clarinets, about which Henze, while writing for recorder in his children's opera *Pollicino,* had "begun to dream as a thirsty man dreams of cool beer." Minette, the heroine, will have a zither, and also harp, mandolin, and violins. Should the Royal Society for the Protection of Rats be represented by the piano? "Animal sounds must *not* be imitated, that would be false, but one can try to suggest the fabulous rustle and ripple of fur, the mystery and enigma of animals. Also, what we find funny about them, and they about us. But the arias and ensembles need more substantial material, melodies! And clear rhythmic and harmonic relationships. We'll see." The diary also includes summary accounts of the busy composer's moves and meetings, of concerts heard, of work on other pieces (*Barcarola,* the new scoring of Monteverdi's *Ulisse, Miracle of the Rose, La tempesta*); some reflections on life and art; correspondence between Henze and Bond; and, in facsimile, much annotated, the working draft of the libretto. It is a document of high interest. There is a good deal in print by and about Henze: the diary he kept while composing the ballet *Ondine,* small volumes on *Der Prinz von Homburg* and *El cimarrón,* a source book for the ballet *Orpheus,* volumes of collected essays (one is available in English translation, published by Cornell). The *English Cat* diary is the fullest and frankest of the series: an extended invitation to visit the composer's workshop and observe the workings of his musical mind.

The opera, in two fairly long acts, is cast in the form of forty-one musical numbers, some of them instrumental interludes. At least twelve singers are needed; Santa Fe used fifteen, assigning separate singers to some of the roles Henze suggests may be doubled. There are six principals: Minette (high soprano), her sister Babette (mezzo), Lord Puff (tenor), Arnold (bass), Tom (lyric baritone), and Louise (soprano), a mouse the RSPR has adopted. There is much variety of texture, of form, of instrumental color, and of vocal forces. "Neoclassical" is the aptest catchall epithet for the style, and Hindemith is the composer most often suggested, both by the busy nonconsonant counterpoints and by episodes of fluent but hardly memorable melody. The score is thoroughly and attractively composed. But I can't share Henze's enthusiasm for the dramatic fable. It seems to me uninteresting, arbitrary and unconvincing in its progress, largely pointless. Also heavy in its humor and confusing in its presentations of political argument. (I don't usually think this of Bond, whose humane, exciting, disciplined plays I admire with what some deem extravagance.) In a 1979 letter, Bond wrote, "The play is partly about good luck, chance, hope, charity, opportunism—as opposed to understanding what you are doing and not relying on fortune or accidents (fascism v. socialism)." The "moral" is presumably the one Tom proclaims when he comes to the footlights and sings:

> *While rats depend on cats*
> *There is no hope for rats*
> *Only when rat helps rat*
> *Will rats be free*
> *Till then cats feed on rats*
> *And call it charity.*

Tom, a buoyant and resourceful alley cat, down on his luck, is discovered to be Lord Fairport, lost in infancy, and now "the wealthiest man in England." The members of the RSPR murder him for his money. The last word is left with Louise, the mouse: "O Tom—they have killed him! And he was the best of them! I see they cannot be trusted! One day when they are hungry they will eat me! . . . I have lived with cats and studied their ways!" She steals the contents of the RSPR collection box and sings:

> *I have become a mouse again*
> *I'll steal the milk and rob the grain*
> *My teeth are sharp and I can bite*
> *I'll give the ladies such a fright*
> *They'll stand upon their chairs and yell*
> *I'll be a little fiend from hell*
> *Screech! Screech!*

Well! It may be that in a production more astutely focussed than the very mild one Charles Ludlam presented in Santa Fe *The English Cat* will seem less feeble from a dramatic point of view. It may be that when one can hear the words—few of them were audible in Santa Fe—it will prove more interesting in the theatre. As it was, one watched a cute, charming animal charade while listening to some elegantly wrought music. The strongest performance came from Kurt Link, a vividly feline Arnold. He alone had claws. Inga Nielsen (Minette), Lisa Turetsky (Babette), Kathryn Gamberoni (Louise), Michael Myers (Lord Puff), and Scott Reeve (Tom) weren't bad, but the characterizations lacked precision. Nothing was alarming, suddenly grim, or really terrifying. Steven Rubin's animal costumes were fine; his settings were ugly and ill-proportioned. George Manahan's conducting was neat, respectful, and unadventurous.

Richard Strauss is another composer regularly honored in Santa Fe: nine of his operas have been done there. This year, the 1982 production of *Die Liebe der Danae* was revived. It is Strauss's glowing, gorgeous farewell to the world of not unfruitful, not unrewarding illusion and metaphor in which an opera composer spends his life—a work wise, warm, and beautiful. I've loved *Danae* since its first public performance, at the 1952 Salzburg Festival. The Santa Fe production is hideous to look at and bluntly staged. John Crosby was at best a pedestrian conductor, and the excellent Santa Fe orchestra, sunk in a deep pit, could not bloom in the open-air acoustics. Yet something came across. Ashley Putnam may not have the body and beauty of tone or the full, soaring lines that the title role requires (it's a role in which Leonie Rysanek excelled), but she is a sensitive and attractive artist. Dennis Bailey, the Midas, was a young-heroic tenor back on form—ardent, exact, compelling in all he did. Victor Braun took the immense role of Jupiter—his final monologue perhaps the longest in opera. Jupiter needs to be Hans Sachs and Wotan in one: Hans Hotter sang the role at the 1944 "dress rehearsal" performance, given just before the German theatres were closed, and Paul Schöffler sang it in Salzburg. Braun was not ideal, but he was in fuller voice than he had been three years ago; and although by the end he was tiring, there was emotion and eloquence in his performance.

The other Santa Fe offerings were the première of John Eaton's *The Tempest* (a Shakespeare opera for which I fashioned the libretto), a new production of *The Marriage of Figaro,* and a revival of *Orphée aux enfers.* The *Figaro,* bluntly played in gaunt, ugly sets—bare to the point where Susanna had to use a lapboard to write her letter—was in most ways deplorable. Kevin Langan's polished Bartolo provided the only touch of distinction, and Ruth and Thomas Martin's resourceful English translation was clearly uttered. *Orphée*—sung in French, with Ann Howard, as Public Opinion, vivacious and ever-present as a translating commère—was a big, glitzy show, efficient in its rather low way. The version used treated Offenbach's score in cavalier fashion, and the plot almost disappeared.

"Land of Enchantment" is the legend on New Mexico car license plates, and at each visit to Santa Fe I've found the spell of the place unfading: days under immense skies, walking or riding amid piñon and juniper; evenings at the opera beneath moon and stars, with the noble mountain ranges as backdrop. (One soon forgets the nights when the thunder rolls, cold winds rake the theatre, and rain drowns the music.) The level of performance, as I've suggested above, varies. But always there's a sense of dedication, of seriousness, of caring about opera as something important—more than an entertainment for tired business-men.

The Lake George Opera Festival, another organization with a commitment to contemporary opera, this season presented what was billed as the première of Richard Wargo's *The Seduction of a Lady.* (The piece had a workshop showing at the City Center last year, put on by the National Institute for Music Theater, and has since then received a student production.) The libretto, by the composer, is based on Neil Simon's dramatization of a Chekhov short story. The opera is a light, beguiling piece for three singers (soprano, tenor, and baritone) and three players (violin, cello, and piano). Wargo sets words deftly and melodiously. His score is formally dapper and neatly composed, the jokes are trimly made. *The Seduction of a Lady* was played on a double bill with another one-act, three-singer work after Chekhov—Dominick Argento's *The Boor,* his first opera (1957). The high-spirited piece holds its own against William Walton's more flamboyant setting of the same matter, as *The Bear* (1967). The same three singers—Pamela South, Joseph Evans, and David Barron—played the Wargo and the Argento, and in both they were admirable. Words were clear, characterizations sharp-edged. Dorothy Danner, the director, has a happy touch with comedy; the shows were inventive and exuberant but never gross. Joseph De Rugeriis conducted the orchestra of *The Boor*. James Morgan designed a slight set for the Wargo and a full, witty one for the Argento. The other festival works were Gounod's five-act grand opera *Romeo and Juliet,* Donizetti's *Daughter of the Regiment,* and—"showcase" productions for young singers—*The Beggar's Opera* (in the Britten version) and Tom Johnson's *The Four Note Opera.*

The company plays not beside Lake George but in a school auditorium at Glens Falls, nearby. At Glens Falls—strictly speaking, on an island in the river between Glens Falls and South Glens Falls—is the most famous of all American literary sites: the Hudson cave so picturesquely described in *The Last of the Mohicans,* wherein Cora, Uncas, Hawkeye, and their companions took refuge. Generations of readers—from Schubert onward—have dreamed of visiting this romantic place. Alas, it is inaccessible now except by fence climbing, trespass, and a scramble I found too daunting to venture on. Festival pilgrims must be content with a visit to another shrine—the great soprano Marcella Sembrich's memento-filled studio at Bolton Landing, beside the lake.

PART
III
1985–1986

THE main theme of this year's Edinburgh Festival was the Auld Alliance, between Scotland and France, and French art was prominent in the programs. The principal operas were Marc-Antoine Charpentier's *Actéon,* Rameau's *Anacréon,* Chabrier's *L'Etoile,* and Debussy's *Pelléas et Mélisande. Anacréon* (1757) and *Actéon* (about 1685) were played on a double bill, without an intermission: at the close of the first opera, Anacreon invited his guests to enjoy a divertissement, *Actéon,* prepared for their entertainment, and on we went. The performers were Les Arts Florissants, the Paris-based ensemble, directed by an American, William Christie, that has taken the lead in the revival of French baroque music. It is named after a Charpentier opera it has recorded; its big hit is a recording of Charpentier's opera *Médée,* and it has also recorded *Anacréon* and *Actéon* (all of them on Harmonia Mundi). Records and concerts have made the ensemble famous, but it also gives fully staged performances. The Rameau-Charpentier bill, which opened in Edinburgh, is booked for an extensive European tour, beginning in the theatre at Versailles.

In Charpentier's day, French music was dominated by Lully, who tolerated no rivals, and until recently Charpentier was known by little more than his tuneful, carol-based Messe de Minuit, which has often been recorded. *Médée*—three acts of it were broadcast by the BBC in 1953, with Patricia Neway, Joan Cross, and Richard Lewis in the principal roles, and the following year a disc of excerpts, conducted by Nadia Boulanger, appeared—revealed a composer of greater range. He seemed more passionate and more profound than Lully. But only in the last decade—and largely as a result of Les Arts Florissants' ardent advocacy—has Charpentier, the Italian-trained Frenchman, emerged fully from the shadow of Lully, the Italian who became, in effect, arbiter of music under Louis XIV. In the first edition of Grove (1878–90), Lully warrants a two-page entry and Charpentier no entry at all; in the New Grove, Lully gets fifteen pages, and Charpentier follows close, with thirteen and a half.

French theatre music of the seventeenth and eighteenth centuries can offer two distinct kinds of satisfaction to the modern listener. One is dramatic: the regular operatic excitement of being caught up in characters' plights and being moved by what they feel. Some episodes in Lully's operas and whole acts of Rameau's noble tragédies provide it. The other is more specifically musical: a keen delight in grace, proportion, and felicities of melody, timbre, and harmony. Rameau's music unfailingly provides it. Although several of his stage pieces have but threads of plot—and little action that by conventional canons could be called dramatic—they prove captivating, and even mysteriously stirring, in the theatre.

Anacréon is such a work. It is little more than a declaration, in a convivial setting, that wine and love are not incompatible pleasures and that advancing age should not hinder indulgence in the latter. Cupid and a Priestess of Bacchus turn up at Anacreon's party, which ends with the choral affirmation

> *Tout s'unit pour nous enflammer.*
> *Bacchus ne défend pas d'aimer,*
> *Et l'Amour nous permet de boire!*

The metrical alertness with which the civilized discourse is set, the variety of paces, rhythms, and textures, and many sudden, wonderfully beautiful phrases hold the attention securely. *Actéon* has similar virtues and more drama, for it is a miniature tragédie lyrique. The hero's hushed "sleep" aria and, above all, his recitative and plainte as he is transformed into a stag are episodes of high inspiration.

The performances were given in an intimate, attractive theatre, the Royal Lyceum. The staging, by Pierre Barrat, seemed underrehearsed and will no doubt become more polished; it was on the right lines. The dances that play so large a part in early French opera are always a difficulty. François Raffinot's choreography could be described as tactful, but the dancers—men and women of the Ris et Danceries troupe uniformly dressed in loose off-one-shoulder tunics and with long, lank golden wigs, bare, dirty feet, and impassive modern faces—belonged to a different world from the Louis XV one evoked by the singers. Mr. Christie's band of period instruments, twenty strong, and his company of sixteen singers—who had steady, forward voices and were adept at telling declamation—balanced well. The Actaeon, Dominique Visse, an haute-contre with an eloquent, ductile timbre and a lively stage presence, was the star of the evening.

At an afternoon concert, Les Arts Florissants revealed yet more of Charpentier's achievement, in the long, highly dramatic motet "St. Peter's Denial." The sopranos Agnès Mellon and Jill Feldman (who had been the Diana of *Actéon* and the Priestess of *Anacréon*) vied in moving the audience to ecstasy by their passionate yet disciplined utterance of amorous plaintes by Michel Lambert, Lully's father-in-law. Music like this, which may look plain on the page, becomes powerfully affecting when brought to life by such interpreters. Sacred works by Guillaume Bouzignac and Etienne Moulinié were also vivid.

L'Etoile and *Pelléas* were performed in the pleasing little King's Theatre by the Lyons Opera, whose musical director is the Englishman John Eliot Gardiner. The company has in recent years been acclaimed for its adventurous repertory (it does Charpentier's *Médée*, and next season is to do Jean-Marie Leclair's *Scylla et Glaucus*, commonly held to be the finest of French eighteenth-century operas after Rameau's); for its brilliant international young orchestra, the average age twenty-five; and for its general liveliness. *L'Etoile* is a captivating light opera, very well composed. It is easy to hear why Chabrier has been revered by French musicians (Ravel said that his *Roi malgré lui* changed the whole direction of French harmony), hard to understand why *L'Etoile* was so long neglected, and tempting to predict that the sparkling Lyons production—which has also been seen at the Opéra-Comique, and has been recorded on EMI—may lead to its becoming a repertory piece. The libretto, which includes lyrics by Verlaine, is frothy. The performance, staged by Louis Erlo and conducted by Mr. Gardiner, was witty and elegant. Colette Alliot-Lugaz, in the travesti role of Lazuli, won every heart.

Pelléas was an odd production, staged by Pierre Strosser in a single set of black curtains and a row of tall French windows. A program note suggested that "the central drama of a withdrawn girl marrying a troubled man much older than herself and then becoming involved with his boyish half-brother" has no need of the symbolist imagery in which Maeterlinck clad it: "a realm deep in the mists of chivalric myth, a fairy land forlorn where the casements of the royal castle open on to perilous seas, sunless forests, sinister grottos, uprearing towers, deserted wells." Maybe so: but when a creator employs poetic metaphors his work is seldom improved by having its plain sense recast in prose. (Today, *The Ring* often suffers a similar reduction.) The effect was rather as if the members of a houseparty had decided to go into a big empty room and perform *Pelléas* without costumes or scenery. There were also suggestions that the drama unrolled in Golaud's mind and that what troubled him was more-than-fraternal feelings about Pelléas which two marriages had not quelled. During the scene of his first, forest meeting with Mélisande, he sat in a chair, a broken old man remembering the past, and her voice came from offstage; the butler who led him to bed later played the Shepherd. Pelléas killed himself by running onto Golaud's knife, and died in his brother's passionate embrace while Golaud stroked the boy's long, curly hair. (Mélisande had a short Eton crop.) In the final scene, Mélisande did not die but rose from her chair and walked out into the garden, watched by the others. There was no newborn *petite;* it had been thrown out along with the tower, the tresses, and the rest.

In its perverse way, the production was fascinating. The mismatching of text and action produced its own new crop of veiled, ambiguous half-statements. The performance was subtly and precisely executed, and musically it was on a very high level. Mr. Gardiner had returned to Debussy's first score, whose thin, fine orchestration was in many places thickened and made less strange when the composer revised it. The orchestra was seated as Debussy suggested:

> The strings make not a barrier in front of, but a circle *around,* the other instruments. Scatter the woodwinds: mix the bassoons with the cellos, the clarinets and oboes with the violins, so that their intervention is something other than a "Mayday" distress call [*la chute d'un paquet*].

And the expanded orchestral interludes, which Debussy added to cover slow scene-shifting at the first production, were omitted. The effect was delicate but strong. The music lived along every line, in pure colors. (Debussy said he strove for Mozartian purity, as opposed to Wagnerian richness.) The singers—Diana Montague the Mélisande, François Le Roux the Pelléas, José van Dam the Golaud—had an exquisite command of word and tone. French well sung is the most beautiful of all musical languages.

The orchestra also gave two Usher Hall concerts, one of Mozart, one of

Schumann's *Paradise and the Peri,* which Schumann called "an oratorio—but one for bright, happy people, not for the oratory." He also declared it to be "my greatest work and perhaps my best." It is not that, but it contains much attractive music and forms ideal festival fare. To enter Paradise, the Peri must bring to its gate "the gift dearest to Heaven." She arrives with the last drop of an Indian patriot's blood, and then with the last sigh of a girl who chose to die beside her lover in plague-stricken Egypt, but neither is found adequate. When she arrives from Syria with the tear of a repentant sinner, her entrance is assured. The exotic subject inspired picturesque scoring. Nile spirits, for example, sing over a rippling cello line touched with triangle, pizzicato strings, and woodwind chords, and when the Peri adds the broad, yearning phrase, "Ach Eden, ach Eden," a soft trumpet call accompanies her aspiration. It is an uneven piece, however. The finale, the Peri's jubilant "Freud', ew'ge Freude, mein Werk ist gethan," punctuated by a choral welcome, is square. When the oratorio was introduced to London, in 1856, with Jenny Lind in the title role, the *Times* critic was unappreciative. Schumann, he said, "began nobly, as a critic and general writer upon music. . . . But, unhappily, he began to compose himself." Her Majesty "magnanimously remained until the termination of the *cantata,*" even though "a less 'dainty dish' was assuredly never 'set before the Queen.' " Mr. Gardiner's players were excellently dainty in episodes that called for them to be so. The fine Edinburgh Festival Chorus was impressive. But most of the soloists, who were mainly American—Pamela Coburn the Peri, Brenda Boozer the angel doorkeeper, Neil Rosenshein the narrator, Thomas Hampson the baritone who describes Syria's beauty—lacked legato. Only Catherine Dubosc, as the Egyptian maiden, joined notes into lines.

The festival brought excellent new compositions by Peter Maxwell Davies and Alexander Goehr. Davies's *The Peat Cutters* is a twenty-minute cantata written for the national Youth Brass Band of Scotland and the Scottish National Orchestra Junior Chorus and Youth Chorus. The composer, in a program note, called it "a record of and reflection upon a disastrous hill fire last year on Hoy" (the Orkney island on which he lives). The imagery is vivid: as fire sweeps up a hill, it is as if the sun had descended to become incarnate there, while the earth-hugging heather now aspires skyward in swirls of spark and smoke. Eagles soar aloft in the heat haze, deserting their young; the hare darts from the fire like a living brand. Text (the composer's own) and music have a larger resonance: catastrophe has been sparked by man's carelessness; the natural order is reversed, and an Eden becomes an inferno. The work opens in a sun-drenched stillness and closes in a charred stillness within which new life has just begun to stir. Between comes the fierce, sudden pageant of violence, swift destruction, and horror. The music is wide-ranging, growing from the quiet start through audible transformations, distortions, and destruction. The large forces—eighty players, two hundred singers—are used in sonorities now broad, now furious, often delicate. The young choristers sang with cleanly focussed pitch, and sang their rhythmically difficult music without scores. The young instrumentalists played like virtuosi. Geoffrey Brand conducted.

Goehr's . . . *a musical offering (J.S.B. 1985),* written for the Scottish Chamber Orchestra, is, in its composer's words, "a kind of meditation on the expressive character of polyphonic techniques." There are three movements: Prelude, Ancient Dance Steps, and Ricercar. It is a "learned" composition—in a program note Goehr talked of proportions based on numerical translations of Bach's initials—but with a learning not at all crabbed. Rather, there is a sense of delight in ingenious, smiling, or poignant juxtapositions, metamorphoses, and concinnities. The piece, which lasts about seventeen minutes, is colorful, scored for four contrasting groups: flute with a quintet of upper strings; brass trio; two clarinets and percussion; piano and double-bass. It flows. In the middle movement it dances to the rhythms of Bach's keyboard suites. Through it all there runs, often audibly, a plainchant Alleluia that is sung at the start, in canon, by horn and trombone. It was played at a sunlit morning concert in the Queen's Hall, once a church and now the Scottish Chamber Orchestra's home. Oliver Knussen conducted. The concert ended with Goehr's gentle, carefully wrought, moving Sinfonia, written in Jerusalem in 1980.

BROUGHT TO LIFE

October 14, 1985

IN the 1830s, Donizetti was Europe's leading composer—chief contributor to the stream of new operas that audiences of those days expected. In the mid-forties, after a marvellous final burst of activity, his mind was clouded by madness. Verdi became his successor, and in the decade 1843–53 turned out sixteen operas. By then, Wagner was at work on *The Ring*. People's thinking about opera changed, and Donizetti's reputation did not survive the century. Thirty years ago, he was still held in low esteem. The 1954 Grove summarized current opinion: music written as rapidly as his "can be no more than successful improvisation"; it drew its life from the virtuosi for whom it was composed; "facile, sentimental melodies can no longer sustain the interest or be supposed to represent adequately dramatic action, and Donizetti seldom rises above that standard"; he lacked Rossini's "brilliancy" and Verdi's "earnest sincerity"; "only his delightful comic operas, *L'Elisir d'Amore* and *Don Pasquale,* are still thoroughly alive, while *Lucia* continues to hold the stage in Italy." Then things started to change. That year at La Scala and the following year in Berlin, Herbert von Karajan and Maria Callas joined forces in a *Lucia di Lammermoor* that, preserved on records, can still lead modern doubters of Donizetti's dramatic force to admire him. Two years later, an *Anna Bolena* at La Scala, Callas its heroine, showed that there is more to the serious Donizetti than *Lucia;* in 1960 a Scala *Poliuto,* again with Callas, confirmed it. Meanwhile, in 1959, at Covent Garden—the theatre where in 1925 *Lucia,* revived for the first time since 1909, had been laughed off the stage after one performance—Joan Sutherland and *Lucia* triumphed with public and critics alike. Some years later, at the New York City Opera, Beverly Sills sang in *Lucia,* in her "Tudor trilogy" (*Anna Bolena, Maria Stuarda,* and *Roberto*

Devereux), and then in *Lucrezia Borgia*. Montserrat Caballé took up *Lucrezia, Caterina Cornaro, Gemma di Vergy, Parisina*. Prima donnas were in the van of this Donizetti revival, but not for them alone were his operas staged. In London, I saw productions with less famous singers of *Torquato Tasso, Marin Faliero, Belisario, Poliuto, Linda di Chamounix;* in Italy, of *Pia de' Tolomei, Caterina, Il furioso, Le Duc d'Albe*. The comedies—*Le convenienze ed inconvenienze teatrali, Il campanello, Betly, Rita*—were also revived. *La Fille du régiment* and (a star opera of mezzos) *La Favorite,* two works that, *pace* Grove, had hardly disappeared, were done more frequently. There was lots more. *L'esule di Roma, Maria di Rohan, Maria di Rudenz, Maria Padilla, Fausta* reappeared. Radio stations and recordings, official or pirated, carried the performances to listeners around the world. The newsletters and journals of the flourishing Donizetti Society (its address is 56 Harbut Road, London SW11) provided a forum for Donizetti enthusiasms, and the society reprinted scores that had long been out of print. Musicology kept pace. Congresses were held. Learned papers were published. Donizetti was so prolific—author of some seventy operas—and so ready and practical with revisions and adaptations devised to suit a particular company that Europe's archives hold enough still unexamined material to keep scholars busy for decades.

The first, excited flush of rediscovery has perhaps started to fade. *Anna Bolena, Maria Stuarda,* and *Lucrezia* are again familiar operas. Donizetti virtues long underrated, then reacclaimed, are now taken for granted, and the failings that, perhaps in overcompensation for past injustice, were for a while dismissed too readily are no longer ignored. The new, balanced picture is of a swift, sure composer who chose his subjects with care and sought to give them apt expression; of an inventor in most of whose operas we find striking formal departures from convention; and of a generous, warmhearted, lovable man quick to sympathize with innocence wronged, the pangs of guilty remorse, the hurt of real or apparent betrayal, and steadfastness in the face of suffering brought about by men's cruelty or the turns of a hostile fate. Skillful hand and generous heart conspire, but sometimes haste of execution takes its toll. Sometimes—especially in fast movements—there is too easy a recourse to formula. And on occasion external circumstances have compromised artistic integrity. *Pia de' Tolomei,* one of Donizetti's most profound and poignant operas, is dramatically weakened by the presence of a superfluous principal, a mezzo-soprano *en travesti* forced into the plot, against the composer's better judgment, to provide a role for a protégée of the commissioning theatre's president.

This summer, Donizetti's *Gabriella di Vergy* of 1838—a different opera from his *Gabriella di Vergy* of 1826 and from his *Gemma di Vergy,* of 1834, whose action is set some two centuries later—was brought to the stage for the first time. It was done by Dorset Opera, a British company that mounts a production each year in the hall of Sherborne School. The performance—with young professional soloists, an admirable orchestra drawn largely from the Bournemouth Symphony, and a keen, well-trained young chorus—was at once fresh, urgent, and stylish. The opera dates from one of Donizetti's best periods—that of *Pia, Roberto Devereux,* and *Poliuto*. The earlier *Gabriella*—to an 1816 libretto, written by Andrea Leone Tottola for Michele Carafa—was composed not to commission but, Donizetti said, for his own enjoyment. It has never been performed, and some of its music went into other works. The second *Gabriella,* with a different libretto but the same basic plot, was written for Naples. Some questions about it remain; what seems likely is that Donizetti began the piece, laid it aside for *Poliuto,* then completed it in a hurry when *Poliuto* was banned by royal censorship and he was due to leave for Paris. It was not performed; another *Gabriella,* Mercadante's, was done in its stead, and some of Donizetti's music found its way into *Adelia,* his 1841 opera for Rome. The two *Gabriella* operas became footnotes in musical history. In 1869, a pasticcio *Gabriella,* cobbled from parts of both and from various other Donizetti works, with a new text and new orchestration, was produced, without success, in Naples. Then, a few years ago, Don White and Patric Schmid, the directors of Opera Rara, turned up a manuscript copy of the 1838 *Gabriella* in the Sterling Library of the University of London. (Opera Rara is an organization that edits, performs, and records forgotten works of the nineteenth century. In 1977, it staged the first of Donizetti's "Tudor" operas, *Elisabetta al castello di Kenilworth.* Its record albums are essential, enjoyable listening for all students of the century; the full catalogue is available from 25 Compton Terrace, London N1.) Opera Rara recorded *Gabriella* in 1978, and a concert performance was given in Belfast.

The earlier *Gabriella* may have been undertaken as an exercise in handling the matter of romantic melodrama: its situations adumbrate those of Donizetti's mature operas. The manner, however—to judge by excerpts presented as an appendix to the Opera Rara recording of the 1838 *Gabriella*—is still largely Rossinian, and the hero is a contralto. Donizetti returned to the subject, twelve years later, as a master of the more directly dramatic style established in Bellini's first Milanese operas—the so-called *canto d'azione,* which Donizetti adopted and Verdi developed. *Gabriella* has a simple plot that moves to a gruesome close. The soprano, Gabriella, believing the tenor, Raoul, to be dead, has acquiesced in a loveless marriage to the baritone, Fayel, Count of Vergy. But Raoul turns up, very much alive. In a duet akin to that of Verdi's *Un ballo in maschera,* he wrings from Gabriella an admission that she still loves him, although she is bound by honor and duty to her husband. (The duet was first sung, in its *Adelia* reworking, by Giuseppina Strepponi, Verdi's future wife; *Adelia* is dedicated to Strepponi.) Fayel, finding Raoul at his wife's feet, challenges him to a duel. Fayel wins, and delivers to Gabriella her lover's heart on a platter. She expires of grief. (In earlier, horrider versions of the tale—the ninth novella of the *Decameron's* fourth day is one—he serves her the heart in a stew.) Donizetti's score is compact, swift-moving, and energetic, with forms fashioned to the turns of the action. The departures from convention include cabaletta second verses that are not straight repeats but have counterpoints— commentary and interjections from other characters—written in. Applause after one aria is obviated and dramatic impetus maintained by the device of lapping the subsequent recitative over the instrumental coda. (Mozart did the same thing in *Idomeneo;* Verdi tried it after the Veil Song in *Don Carlos* but then recast the passage to bring the aria to a full stop.) There is a tenor-baritone duet movement in dulcet thirds and sixths, borrowed from the 1826 *Gabriella* and boldly recast for the two male voices in a way to make it a forerunner of Lensky's and Eugene Onegin's tense, lyrical reflections before their duel.

In Dorset, Marie Slorach was a moving Gabriella who produced some finespun cantilena and phrased delicately but was not always pure of tone in outbursts. Justin Lavender's Raoul was honest, assured, and fluent. Best of all was the Fayel of Peter Savidge, a singer with a direct, unforced, unspoiled baritone, a telling stage presence, and a clear, incisive delivery. Robert Glen's staging, in simple, well-devised settings by John Hodgkinson, was straightforward and apt. Patrick Shelley's conducting was sensitive to the grace, the charged emotional content, and the brio of the score. Verve, confidence in the power of the piece, and technical proficiency united to rekindle the elated, almost uncritical response to unfamiliar Donizetti which routine or eccentric revivals had begun to dull.

Donizetti's first opera—composed in 1816, when he was a student at the Bologna lyceum; first performed only in 1960, in Bergamo—was a *Pigmalione,* one of the many pieces based on Rousseau's *Pygmalion.* The philosopher's *scène lyrique*—a spoken monodrama punctuated by musical interludes—appeared in 1770; in various translations, various settings, it quickly made the rounds of Europe. Pygmalion is a powerful myth of artistic creation. It moved Cherubini, whose own music was, and is, often called marmoreal and cold, to give stirring expression to the idea of an artist's being driven to despair and near-madness by his inability to impart warmth, life, and breath to even his greatest work. By Cherubini's *Pimmalione* (1809), it is said, Napoleon was moved to tears.

Bologna's 1985 Feste Musicali—eight September days of music that included Cherubini's Mass for the Coronation of Charles X, Liszt's *Via Crucis,* a program of church music Byzantine and contemporary, and Gluck's *Paride ed Elena*—opened with a double bill of Pygmalion musical dramas after Rousseau: Ferdinando Provesi's (c. 1820) and Gian Battista Cimador's (1790). Provesi was Verdi's early teacher. One of his—and later Verdi's—duties as Busseto's *maestro di musica* was to provide fare for the "academies" of the Busseto Philharmonic Society, whose programs often included short spoken plays. Provesi's *Pigmalione*—spoken, like Rousseau's—evidently gave a chance both to some local actor and to the dilettanti instrumentalists of the Philharmonic. The thirty-two brief musical passages that articulate the monologue (Galatea, when brought to life, has just four exclamations) are nothing special. Most of them sound like aria introductions unfollowed by arias. They are couched in the Rossinian lingua franca of the day. A flute tune over pizzicatos (while Pygmalion reflects that not his statue but an ideal it represents has won his heart) and flute and bassoon solos (to which the statue starts to move) are pretty. Very full wind scoring reflects the composition of the Busseto Philharmonic. A rich Verdi exhibition in the newly restored Ducal Palace at Colorno, near Parma (it runs until early December), included a Philharmonic membership list showing that there were far more wind than string players.

Cimador's *Pimmalione,* a *scena drammatica* that is sung, not spoken, is more substantial and more interesting. It was composed for Matteo Babini, a celebrated tenor with an international career: he sang all over Italy, in Berlin, in

St. Petersburg, in London at the King's Theatre, in Paris in duet with Marie Antoinette. He was one of those who helped to displace the castratos as heroes of the operatic stage. He was admired more for his intelligence, handsome appearance, and dramatic intensity than for vocal prowess. Babini played Cimador's *Pimmalione* widely; the more famous Giovanni David also took it up; as late as 1836 it was still being performed. Cimador himself moves on the fringes of music history: in 1791 he settled in London, where he published much of Mozart's music; with Haydn he visited Bath; *Pimmalione* was sung in London in 1797. The epithet that comes to mind for *Pimmalione* is Mozartian, and it has melodic phrases in common with *Così fan tutte*. Neither work can have influenced the other, however: they appeared on the same day, one in Venice and the other in Vienna. Both composers employed—and Mozart transfigured—the common musical language of the late eighteenth century. Cimador's piece has a character of its own, provided by its unusual formal structure. It is a sequence of orchestrally accompanied recitatives, ariosos, and ariettas, amounting to a half-hour dramatic monologue that arrestingly changes pace, changes mood, pauses for reflection, then moves on again. It is like an eighteenth-century *Erwartung*—an adventurous and unconventional piece. It is tempting to surmise that Donizetti encountered it in his student days and that its example lingered when he composed the vivid scenas—recitative, instrumental solos giving utterance to inner thought, ariosos, arias begun and then cut short—that, even more than the set-piece solo numbers, project the drama of his mature operas. Surprising that so evidently gifted a composer as Cimador wrote so little. His *Ati e Cibele* (Venice, 1789; revived in London in 1795) and *Ratto di Proserpina* (Venice, 1791) have been mislaid. Some songs and a double-bass concerto written for Dragonetti survive.

The performances were given in the Aula Magna of Bologna's Academy of Fine Arts, established by Napoleon in a former church. It is an uncommonly handsome room, designed by Alfonso Torreggiani, the architect responsible for many of Bologna's eighteenth-century splendors. The Academy's plaster casts of masterpieces from the antique to Michelangelo decked it as Pygmalion's studio, and the modern, living Galatea (in Provesi's piece) was as naked as they. Tito Gotti conducted members of the Teatro Comunale orchestra. Giuseppe di Leva directed. Paolo Bessegato, in the Provesi, was a mannered actor; Carlo Gaifa, in the Cimador, sang intelligently and clearly but in a tenor of effective compass even narrower than Babini's. Cimador's *Pimmalione* would lend itself to concert-hall presentation: it needs only a tenor, a chair, and a shapely young woman able to stand still for a long while and then sing a few simple phrases. It's a work that enterprising chamber orchestras and tenors in quest of a tour de force might well revive. I commend it to the planners of the Mostly Mozart festival.

THURSDAY SPLENDOR

October 21, 1985

THE so-called stagione—as opposed to the repertory—way of putting on operas allows a company to focus its forces intently on the polished presentation of just one or two shows at a time. This season, the first six weeks of the New York City Opera, a repertory company, brought ten operas: *The Student Prince, La rondine, Lucia di Lammermoor, Carmen, The Mikado, La Cenerentola, The Daughter of the Regiment, Attila, Norma,* and *I puritani.* The first six weeks of the English National Opera brought three: an elaborately spectacular (but, I thought, heavy and hideous) new production of *Orpheus in the Underworld* and revivals of *Rigoletto* and *Così fan tutte.* The first five days of the Metropolitan season brought four operas: *Tosca, Jenůfa, Falstaff,* and *Der Rosenkavalier.* The first two weeks of the Covent Garden season brought two: Karlheinz Stockhausen's *Donnerstag,* a new production, given six performances, and a revival of *Il barbiere di Siviglia,* done twice. *Donnerstag (Thursday)*—music, libretto, dance, actions, and gestures composed by Stockhausen—is a work that stretches a company's scenic, technical, and organizational resources to the utmost. It lasted about five and a half hours, counting from the brass, piano, and percussion Greeting that welcomed the audience in the foyers of the theatre to a five-trumpet Farewell that at the earlier London performances was played from windows and balconies in the street outside Covent Garden but was then moved into the theatre after protest from wakened residents of the quarter. The work is one "day" of a seven-day opera-in-progress, *Licht,* upon which Stockhausen embarked in 1977. A scene from *Tuesday,* called "The Course of the Years," appeared in Tokyo that year. Scenes from *Thursday* appeared in Donaueschingen (1978), Jerusalem (1979), and Amsterdam (1980); the whole opera was assembled and staged at La Scala in 1981. (A Deutsche Grammophon recording was published in 1983.) During the next three years, parts of *Saturday* appeared in Metz, Assisi, Donaueschingen, and Ann Arbor; the whole opera was assembled and staged by La Scala last year. Stockhausen is now busy with *Monday,* and seriatim premières of its parts have been announced.

The principal characters of *Licht* are Michael, Eve, and Lucifer. *Thursday* is essentially Michael's drama, *Saturday* is Lucifer's, and *Monday* will be Eve's. In 1977, Stockhausen devised a formula—or genetic cell, or microcosmic blueprint—in which Michael's, Eve's, and Lucifer's themes are ranged on three staves, and vertical bars divide the days. The themes are strongly characterized and soon become recognizable. The tonality, pitches, melodies, proportions of *Licht* are derived from this formula. It is reproduced and some of its applications in *Thursday* are lucidly demonstrated in Peter Britton's article "Stockhausen's

Path to Opera," in the September 1985 *Musical Times*. In Mr. Britton's words, "The *Formel* blueprint, in which the groundplan for each opera, each act and each scene is implicit, provides a touchstone of coherence. It will suggest new paths if the imagination falters; it will also adapt itself to unpredictable surges of inspiration, the intuitive 'flashes' that are so vital." The coherence of *Thursday* and, even more, of *Saturday* has, however, been questioned. Act I of *Thursday* is a trio, Act II a trumpet concerto, and Act III something like a scenic oratorio. The circumstances of the commissions that gave rise to each scene have plainly played a part in the shaping of the operas: *Saturday* includes a band episode, composed for the Symphony Band of the University of Michigan (which went on to Milan to take part in the première of the whole opera), while the segment first heard in Assisi is a setting of words of St. Francis. The performers close to Stockhausen have also determined to some extent the forces he employs: his trumpeter son, Markus, is one of the incarnations of Michael, and the clarinettist Suzanne Stephens is one of the incarnations of Eve; *Thursday* also has prominent roles for his pianist daughter, Majella, and his saxophonist son, Simon. Chance events have also played their part: a strike by the Scala chorus which maimed the earlier performances of *Thursday* is echoed in an episode of *Saturday*. The variety of forces, forms, textures, and matter seems to me, however, a strength and a pleasure of *Thursday*. The grand design is flexible enough to admit of incidentals that come along. The somewhat ramshackle construction saves the work from solemn pretentiousness. There is even a playful quality about much of it, although the essential seriousness is not in doubt and inner musical integrity is not compromised.

In *Thursday*, Michael, Eve, and Lucifer are given each a threefold embodiment: by a singer (tenor, soprano, and bass), an instrumentalist (trumpet, basset horn, and trombone), and a mime/dancer. The composer summarizes the plot thus:

Michael is the Creator-Angel of the local universe of which our Earth is a tiny part. He is engaged on the great experiment which is Man, despite the opposition of Lucifer, the purist intellectual. The experiment, in which Eve has taken responsibility for the quality of new human beings, will involve Michael coming to the Earth, experiencing human life and returning to the heavens. During this process we first see Eve as Michael's earthly Mother and as his lover and artistic muse Moon-Eve, and Lucifer as Michael's earthly Father.

Act I, "Michael's Youth," is apparently autobiographical. The boy's mother delights in his skills. His father, a schoolmaster, takes him shooting. His mother is removed to an insane asylum and is there put to death. His father joins the Nazi party and goes to war. In the second scene, Michael meets Moon-Eve, a fantastic bird-woman, playing the basset horn, and "discovers that he can control the creature's music by erotically playing with her body." The third scene is his examination for entrance to the Musikhochschule: as singer, as trumpeter, and as singer, trumpeter, and dancer together he recounts the matter of the previous scenes in three "trial songs" that ensure his enthusiastic admission. The principals perform against the mysterious, fluctuating background of a drone chord (sounding, on trumpet, basset horn, and trombone, the three pitches that open the Thursday segment of the formula) and a distant, invisible choir, both of them on tape. The examination scene is also accompanied by brilliant, quirky music from an onstage piano.

Act II, "Michael's Journey Around the Earth," is a chapter of musical autobiography. The trumpeter Michael plays his call and climbs aboard an immense globe, which rotates through a star-filled sky and brings his music into contact with musics of Germany, New York, Japan, Bali, India, Central Africa, and Jerusalem. It is a stretch of rich, exciting, and very dramatic composition: a concerto for trumpet and chamber orchestra with important, enacted roles for a pair of clarinets, a trombone, a tuba, and a double-bass. Moon-Eve reappears. Slowly, tenderly, trumpet and basset horn learn one another's melodies. The orchestra dissolves into a chromatic shimmer, a soft-sparkling cascade, and (in the words of the libretto) "the sounds of the trumpet (playing the Eve formula . . .) and basset horn (playing the Michael formula . . .) are flying very slowly and peacefully across the sky, revolving around each other, circling around, gliding." The love duet closes on a rapturous unison trill.

In Act III, "Michael's Return Home," the archangel in his triple manifestation, rejected of men, is greeted on high by Eve, in hers. She has arranged a festival of welcome: invisible choirs (on tape) ring the theatre; there are five choirs onstage, and in the pit a full orchestra. It is a glorious flood of sound. Michael is presented with three mystical plants, the significance of whose forms is explained. Three wondrous "compositions of light" appear. Then Lucifer interrupts the proceedings: as dancer, he suddenly emerges from a globe given to Michael as a souvenir of his earthly visit; as trombonist, he tap-dances on and engages the trumpeter Michael in a duel; as bass, he harangues the tenor Michael from the audience. Dancer and trombonist are routed, and the bass retires in disgust; his last words ("You're a fool! a fool! a fool!") circle around the theatre and drift into the distance. E-flat, the final pitch in the Thursday segment of the formula, steals through the house, and the triple Michael turns to the audience: the tenor sings (in slow motion, and on E-flat) the Michael theme; the trumpeter sounds the Lucifer theme in sequences gradually invaded by and taken over by Michael's music; and the dancer mediates between the two. In seven brief shadow plays, episodes from the previous action are reënacted, and their music is recalled, while Michael declares that on earth he experienced

Melodies of childhood . . .
Intensity of love . . .
Chromaticism of the soul . . .
Harmony of languages . . .
Audiogrammar of the emotions . . .
Ecstasy of polyphony . . .
Light of the resurrection . . .

The acrostic is picked out in light. Then "a wonderful arc of light" spans the stage, and Michael sings:

I became man . . .
as child born from a human mother's womb
to grow, to learn, to aspire,

childlike to invent games with sounds
which, even in human form, still move the souls of angels:
that is the meaning of THURSDAY *from* LIGHT.
I became a man . . .
to bring celestial music to humans
and human music to the celestial beings,
so that Man may listen to GOD
and GOD *may hear his children . . .*

The lights fade, and outside the theatre the trumpet calls of Michael's Farewell have started to sound.

In its visionary conception, lush, grandiose imagery, generous rhetoric, and personalized mythology, all this recalls the prophetic books of Blake. With Isaiah in Blake's *Marriage of Heaven and Hell,* Stockhausen might say, "My senses discover'd the infinite in every thing," and with Ezekiel that he was moved by "the desire of raising other men into a perception of the infinite." Blake had asked the Prophets, over dinner, "how they dared so roundly to assert that God spake to them; and whether they did not think at the time that they would be misunderstood." Stockhausen, in a talk before the London première, called Michael, Eve, and Lucifer "living realities," and his opera "nothing but a ritual which tries to evoke them." "I am confident that the angels will be with us tomorrow night," he said. (One critic recalled Hotspur's commonsense retort to Owen Glendower, who boasted that he could call spirits from the vasty deep: "Why, so can I, or so can any man; But will they come when you do call for them?") The composer makes lofty claims, and does so with a confidence that allows his Lucifer, in the final confrontation, to play devil advocate: "Don't you have any sense of humor, little Jupiter? . . . How many more JOURNEYS AROUND THE EARTH does Michael wish to trumpet? How many more FESTIVALS does he wish to have celebrated in his honor?" And Michael himself admits to the audience that "I know many of you will ridicule me when I sing to you." Whether angels wafted with their wings through Covent Garden during the two performances of *Thursday* that I attended, I know not. But I can affirm that hearing and seeing the drama is an engrossing, enjoyable, and elevating adventure. Ear, mind, and spirit are engaged. And, as I suggested, moments of jokiness, naiveté—silliness, even—save the work from being unbearably solemn: Stockhausen-Sarastro has a vein of Papageno in him. There is a great deal to listen to and to watch. Some of the spans, especially in the last scene, are traversed slowly. But things happen; the music doesn't fall into simplistic repetitions or numbing stasis. There are counterpoints to follow. There are supple melodies and rich harmonies. There are wonderful sounds—new and stirring sounds. The score is a culmination of the marvellous musics—in whose making Michael's vision, Lucifer's technical skills, and the inspiration of Eve's love seem to have conspired—that have poured from Stockhausen during the last thirty years. The land of *Licht* is reached after journeys through *Gesang der Jünglinge, Gruppen, Momente, Hymnen, Stimmung, Mantra, Trans, Inori, Sirius.* The mystic, intuitive compositions of *Aus den sieben Tagen* and the small-force music-theatre entertainments were also steps on the way. An approach for London audiences was paved earlier

369

this year by a seven-day Stockhausen retrospective, presented by the BBC, with open rehearsals, films, lectures, and six concerts.

When *Licht* is complete, it will keep analysts busy for decades as they trace and define the musical processes, the symbolism, the mythology, anima and ego aspects of Eve and Lucifer, links between autobiography and imagined events, and the interdependences of all these. (If Stockhausen's wives and companions have kept diaries, they may one day make reading as fascinating as Cosima Wagner's.) But what matters most now is the excitement of entering this huge, ambitious work, responding to the sounds and sights, trying to understand it, and feeling, perhaps, that it is—by intention, at least—something like a Divine Comedy and a Comédie Humaine in one.

The Covent Garden production, designed by Maria Björnson, was less beautiful than—to judge from photographs—the spare, clear Scala première, designed by Gae Aulenti, but it was rich, dramatic, and technically exuberant, with a huge openwork globe, Michael aboard, rotating in Act II, and in Act III a vast wheel capable of many motions and metamorphoses. Chris Ellis's lighting was subtle and bold, by turns stark, lustrous, jewelled. Michael Bogdanov's staging was confident, imaginative, powerful, and concerned to serve the work, not gloss it with directorial effects. (The ethnic vignettes marking the stages of Michael's Journey fell into cliché; that was presumably by intention, but the music could be better matched.) The performers were without exception accomplished and eloquent. Some of them were those of the Scala production: Markus Stockhausen, a shining trumpeter Michael, and Michèle Noiret, his limpid dance incarnation; Annette Meriweather, a warm, radiant soprano, Miss Stephens, a tender, lyrical basset-hornist, and Elisabeth Clarke, a bright dancer, the three Eves; Alain Louafi, a crisply danced and mimed Lucifer; Majella Stockhausen, deft accompanist at the examination; Simon Stockhausen, a burly saxophone-playing seraph; Peter Eötvös, the masterly conductor. Others were new: Julian Pike, admirable as the tenor Michael; the fine young bass Nicholas Isherwood and the vivid trombonist Michael Svoboda, both trenchant Lucifers. Covent Garden orchestra players—Ashley Wall (tuba), John Bakewell (double-bass), James Watson and Peter Reeve (trumpets), and David Petken (trombone)—took the stage with aplomb. Although the word setting ensures that a good deal of the text is audible, and although the singing Eve and Lucifer were American and the singing Michael was British, *Thursday* was done in the original German. Against the loss of direct communicativeness must be placed the fact that Stockhausen often uses vowels and consonants for their sonic effect: "Ein Narr!" cannot be translated to allow a final rolled "r." A bilingual libretto was available. The soloists—singers and instrumentalists—had each an individual microphone, and over forty more microphones were used in the pit and on the stage and the side stages. Loudspeakers ringed the theatre. Stockhausen, with assistants, sat in the center of the house, a thirty-six-channel mixer before him and a twenty-four-channel mixer beside him, to control balances, dynamics, and timbres. The "sound perspectives" were exquisitely fashioned; the only bothering moments came during a stretch in the last act when Miss Meriweather's voice, on the top line of a long, full ensemble, sounded unnaturally boosted. Covent Garden had devoted to *Thursday* the long weeks of concentrated rehearsal that in summers past it used to spend preparing the annual *Ring* cycles. Its production was a high and inspiring achievement.

[*La Scala performed* Monday *in 1988, and* Saturday *is now recorded by DGG.*]

Making Music Theatre

October 28, 1985

We need a term to describe the way that in the opera house the music itself can seem not merely to enhance but to create, even become, the drama. *Dramma per musica,* a phrase from opera's early days, is sometimes used to suggest what happens, but strictly it means no more than a play written to be set to music, a drama for—not "through"—music. The text of Aurelio Aureli's *Erismena* (1655), written for Cavalli, was published as a *drama per musica.* (The spelling with two "m"s was established only later.) Another designation of those days for what we now call a libretto was *dramma musicale;* as such, G. A. Cicognini's texts for Cavalli's *Giasone* and Cesti's *Orontea* (both 1649) were published. In the later nineteenth century, the term was revived (and not only for Wagner's "music dramas") to distinguish from mere "operas" those works all of whose musical, verbal, and scenic elements conspired to create the "drama." Verdi chided an enthusiast transported by the solos and duets of *La forza del destino* for inattention to "the varied, vaster scenes that fill half the opera and constitute the real *dramma musicale.*" The librettos Verdi supervised and set were published with various designations: *dramma lirico, tragedia lirica, melodramma.* (The last does not indicate—as a recent reviewer of *Rigoletto* thought—an opera whose action is melodramatic; it seems to have been used to indicate a libretto with some literary pretension.) More is at issue than nice terminological games: the attempts at definition reflect discernment of particular qualities in particular operas and kinds of opera. "Music theatre" is one phrase that has been much heard in the last twenty years. For the New Grove, I defined it thus:

A catch-phrase that became common in the 1960s, particularly among composers, producers and critics who had artistic or social objections to the cost of traditional grand opera and the conservatism of grand opera companies and their audiences. It was, and is, loosely used in three senses: (1) To designate musical works for small or moderate forces which involve a dramatic element in their presentation. . . . (2) To describe either an opera in which the theatrical element is deemed powerful enough to compensate for an indifferent or insubstantial score . . . or any uncommonly dramatic opera. (3) To describe a manner of opera performance in which the acting and staging are thought to be so vivid as to compensate for mediocre, or complement admirable, singing and playing.

Penderecki's *The Devils* and Felsenstein's carefully acted productions of the traditional repertory are offered as examples of "music theatre" in the second and third senses. I might frame that less tendentiously today. It is hard to find definitions not excluding the proposition that all good operas, well performed, are "music theatre." And if one tries to proceed by elimination—"Fat sopranos and tenors walking about the stage and making loud noises are *not* music theatre"—one is halted by the realization that a loud, true, ringing high C can, in the right context, be excellently dramatic.

The first newsletter of the American Music Theatre Festival, in Philadelphia, begins with a statement by its directors, Eric Salzman and Marjorie Samoff: "Music theatre is the bursting, blooming, burgeoning American art form of the moment. Contemporary music theatre has roots in opera, in musical comedy, in pop and classical music, and in the avant garde. It is both serious and entertaining, a mixture of art, ideas and fun. . . . It is a form in evolution— particularly American, very alive and very much of our time." The program book attempts a definition: "Music theatre is theatre that sings. It's an art form in which music and theatre play equal roles." So is opera (or so it should be), and so is the musical. But "because the traditional institutions of opera and Broadway provide few opportunities for bold and adventurous new work," this annual festival has been brought into being as "a place where a wide range of works and artists can come together during an intensive time period," and "creators, performers and the public can participate in an atmosphere of creative excitement." The 1985 festival, the second, ran for five weeks in September and October. It presented Lee Breuer and Bob Telson's *The Gospel at Colonus;* Zalmen Mlotek and Moishe Rosenfeld's English-Yiddish musical *The Golden Land;* Kirk Nurock and C. J. Ellis's Kipling musical *Mowgli; X,* an opera by Anthony, Thulani, and Christopher Davis; and *Seehear,* a collaborative "performance work" from California. Four theatres of different shapes and sizes were used. After the shows, there was festival cabaret. Some mornings, there were panel discussions. Before considering the two productions I saw—*Seehear* and *X*—let me report that during a short visit I found the directors' hopes fulfilled: Philadelphia was indeed a place where people who care about music and theatre were busily receiving and exchanging ideas.

Seehear is the third panel of the *How Trilogy,* made up of "performance works" directed by George Coates. (The earlier parts are *The Way of How,* which was done at the Brooklyn Academy's 1983 Next Wave festival, and *are/are.*) The music is by Paul Dresher. The work was "conceived through a collaborative process" by Coates, Dresher, the tenor John Duykers, and the scenic designer Jerome Sirlin. Thirteen musicians and their conductor are assembled on the stage, in a pyramidal set. Light plays upon them; they merge into the setting; often it seems as if the décor were making music. The scenes shift constantly, changing color, pattern, and form. An abstract stippled or hatched design becomes a temple, a cathedral, a palace room, a prison, a cityscape. The backcloth becomes a magic casement opening onto strange scenes and images: a giant chess game in the sky is one. Drops go up and down, but most of the transformations are achieved by projection; Jeremy Hamm and Clint Gilbert are the lighting designers. A mime (Soo-Young Chin), a soprano (Thomasa Eckert), and two tenors (Duykers and Rinde Eckert) come and go. The arias are wordless. (In *The Way of How,* "Vesti la giubba" and "Recondita armonia" are sung over accompaniments that Leoncavallo and Puccini would not recognize.) Odd, quaint things happen: principals are transported on and off on dollies ("I always think of opera singers as sort of being these immense MX missiles," Coates has said. "I just think they should be wheeled on, put in place, sing their song, then be wheeled off"); sometimes the conductor is upside down. The music is a fluent, colorful, diatonic, repetitive, and—to my ears—banal minimalist suite. Eighty minutes go by easily enough, and some particularly striking scenic effects—drawing oohs and ahs of delighted surprise from the audience—are held in reserve to recall attention when, having admired the technical invention and ingenuity of the illusions, one starts to think about other things. The piece comes from Berkeley, a place I associate with more rigorous modes of artistic activity.

In the old days, opera composers learned their skills, as a rule, by working in opera companies—as instrumentalists (Beethoven played viola in the Bonn pit), coaches, chorus directors, subconductors, conductors, house composers. Today, when opera companies play more old works than new, and active composers figure seldom on musical staff lists, other ways are found to help beginners over the hurdles on the way to a successful first appearance before the opera public. The first act and part of Act II of *X*, Anthony Davis's first opera, were tried out as a work-in-progress at last year's American Music Theater Festival. In April this year, the Springfield Symphony gave a concert performance of Acts I and II; in May, there was a month-long "workshop" at the Brooklyn Academy of Music during which further work was done on the piece. *X* had its full-length première in Philadelphia this month; but its "official world première" has been billed for the New York City Opera next season. I'm glad the City Opera is taking up the piece. It struck me as not just a stirring and well-fashioned opera—that already is much—but one whose music adds a new, individual voice to those previously heard in our opera houses.

The protagonist is Malcolm X. Act I deals with his childhood and criminal youth; it ends with him in prison, reflecting on the forces that have shaped his life. Act II tells of his conversion to Elijah Muhammad's Nation of Islam and his role as its minister; it ends with his comment on President Kennedy's assassination, "In my view, it's a case of the chickens coming home to roost," and Elijah Muhammad's displeasure thereat. Act III deals with his secession from the Nation, his pilgrimage to Mecca, and his conversion from Elijah Muhammad's theories to a wider vision of an Islamic brotherhood of man; it ends with his assassination, in 1965. Toward the end of his autobiography, Malcolm X remarks that his life "never has stayed fixed in one position for very long," that he has "often known unexpected drastic changes." The autobiography itself is an impressive but disconcerting book. It was related (to Alex Haley) largely before but partly after Malcolm X's pilgrimage to Mecca, and the first sixteen and the last three chapters might almost have been written by different people. (It's rather as if Saul/Paul had written epistles both before and after the Light from Heaven shone round about him as he approached Damascus.) References to the blue-eyed devil white man, contempt for Martin Luther King and the March on Washington ("that 'Farce on Washington,' I call it"), and remarks like "All women, by their nature, are fragile and weak" cadence at last into "I saw all

373

races, all *colors*—blue-eyed blonds to black-skinned Africans—in *true* brotherhood! In unity! Living as one! Worshipping as one!"

This is difficult matter for opera. The dreams and acts of a fiery popular leader, his political and personal development, his effect on public life, the opposition he arouses call for treatment on the scale of Wagner's five-act, six-hour *Rienzi.* *X* is half that length. But then it is not intended to be an epic opera or a full-scale dramatic biography. It is, rather, a dramatic poem, woven from strands in Malcolm X's life, dealing with his personality and with reasons for the influence it exerted. Much is omitted; much is condensed. The various companions of Malcolm's youth in Boston coalesce into Street, his mentor in methods of survival. In Philadelphia, one tenor doubled the role and that of Elijah Muhammad, Malcolm's spiritual mentor. Many other doublings, not random, suggest patterns and recurrent imagery while allowing a company of twenty-three singers and eight figurants to encompass a many-charactered cast. Besides Street and Elijah, the principals around the protagonist are his mother, Louise (soprano), his sister Ella (mezzo-soprano), and his brother Reginald (bass-baritone). The "story" was shaped by Christopher Davis, the composer's brother, a director, actor, and writer. The libretto was written by the poet Thulani Davis, the composer's cousin, and it is very well written—in language direct enough for the stage yet poetically charged, in strong lines that move surely between narrative, reflection, and rhetoric. Anthony Davis, born in 1951, was Yale trained and was then prominent in the New York jazz loft scene. (His work can be heard on the India Navigation and Gramavision labels.) *X* was accompanied initially by his ten-piece group Episteme (Knowledge); the scoring is now for an orchestra of thirty-five. (In Philadelphia, Episteme and the Concerto Soloists of Philadelphia combined.) The score is conveniently described as "third-stream music," which—in the words of Gunther Schuller, who coined the term—"synthesizes the essential characteristics and techniques of contemporary Western art music and various types of ethnic music." Through the Harlem chapters of Malcolm X's autobiography the music of Lionel Hampton and Billie Holiday often rises, and I imagine it is a current in parts of Davis's score. But Davis in his approach disciplines the jazz musician's fondness for extended self-expression. He here makes virtuosity serve specific dramatic ends. His score is constantly impressive for its metric, rhythmic, and harmonic control of structures and pacing. I'm treading unfamiliar ground, diffidently, but will suggest that, just as ears customarily attuned to "Western art music" can respond readily to, say, Thelonious Monk's command of thematic variation and added-note harmonies, and to his feeling for the expressive connotations of intervals, so an "ordinary" operagoer will be able to respond readily to the music of *X.* The vocal lines are eloquent. The choral writing is vivid.

The Philadelphia production was devised and directed by Rhoda Levine, who has been with *X* from the start as "creative consultant." It was a skillful and potent staging, in simple but telling décor by John Conklin. Peter Aaronson was a sure conductor. Avery Brooks was very impressive in the title role, which he had assumed at a few days' notice, when Michael Smartt fell ill. He played with confidence and subtlety. An actor and a pianist as well as an accomplished singer, he was musically trenchant, and he has the ability—which should be commoner than it is—to sing lines with the awareness of their meaning that a keen speaker would give to them. Priscilla Baskerville, the Louise, was a moving actress—except during her long aria in Act I. Then she became something more like an opera singer, pouring out notes that shone beautifully but doing so in a manner unresponsive to Thulani Davis's poetry. Deborah Ford, a young singer of great promise, gave an admirable performance as Malcolm's calm, capable sister—until she reached the big aria in Act III. Then she seemed to be playing Jessye Norman rather than Ella, and projecting her rich, powerful voice as if into the Met rather than into the thousand-seat Walnut Street Theatre. On the other hand, Thomas Young, the Street and the Elijah, made every word tell, added incisiveness of inflection to clear pronunciation, hit words and notes precisely, and didn't break character in either role. In the large cast, there were several other sharply etched performances.

Troubled Times

November 4, 1985

MUSSORGSKY'S *Khovanshchina,* a somber, beautiful opera, has returned to the Met after an absence of thirty-five years. Its matter is the political and religious turmoil in late-seventeenth-century Russia which preceded Peter the Great's assumption of authority. Mussorgsky began the piece after completing *Boris Godunov,* which deals with Russia at the turn of the sixteenth and seventeenth centuries. He contemplated a third historical opera, *Pugachevshchina,* dealing with the late-eighteenth-century peasant revolt led by Emelian Pugachev against Catherine the Great; it was to be tackled once *Khovanshchina* had been finished. But the composer, in his last decade a drunken and disorderly genius, died without finishing *Khovanshchina.* Most of it was set down in piano score; only Martha's song and a chorus in Act III were orchestrated. Rimsky-Korsakov prepared the opera for performance. He supplied the missing conclusions to Acts II and V. He orchestrated the whole in glowing colors. By generous cutting, he tidied up the action. He also tidied up music in which he discerned (as he records in his memoirs, writing of Mussorgsky's manuscript legacy in general) "clumsy, incoherent harmonies, shocking part-writing, amazingly illogical modulations or long stretches without any modulation at all, bad scoring in the works that were scored, in general a bold, self-conceited amateurishness, some moments of technical dexterity and skill but more of technical impotence." Nevertheless, he concluded, the publication of works "so fine, original, and live" was imperative, and what was needed was a practical performing edition "designed for the revelation of Mussorgsky's genius, not the study of his idiosyncrasies and artistic blunders." *Khovanshchina,* reworked by Rimsky, had its première in 1886, five years after Mussorgsky's death, and in that form— particularly after Diaghilev's 1913 production, seen in Paris and London (which

375

had further orchestrations by Ravel and Stravinsky)—the opera made its way around the world. Most people who have examined Mussorgsky's score and Rimsky's recension agree that the latter went too far in regularizing strange originality. But the fact that the examination is possible justifies Rimsky's claim that he destroyed nothing, that he was not like a restorer who paints out old frescoes forever: Mussorgsky's manuscripts remained, and once the music entered the public domain "every publisher will be free to bring out archeologically correct editions." Pavel Lamm brought out an archeologically correct piano score of *Khovanshchina* in 1932, and in 1958 Shostakovich orchestrated it. His score was used for a 1959 film, was performed at the Kirov in 1960, and was published in 1963. Since then, both scores, Rimsky's and Shostakovich's, have been current. In 1950, the Met used Rimsky, and today it uses Shostakovich. In 1963, I heard the Shostakovich version at Covent Garden and, three days later, the Rimsky version in Florence, with Bolshoi singers. As late as 1973, a new edition of the Rimsky version was published in Russia.

The *Khovanshchina* case is not quite parallel to that of *Boris Godunov*, where the choice is effectively between Mussorgsky's own orchestration and Rimsky's rewriting. Some alien hand must intervene before *Khovanshchina* can be played. And Shostakovich did not simply essay Mussorgsky pastiche. He scored in his own manner. (Back in 1940, he had reorchestrated *Boris* and had presented it, as Edward Reilly puts it in his pamphlet tracing the mazes of Mussorgsky editions, "in a new coloristic guise that is as far removed—perhaps even farther—from the composer's own as is that of Rimsky-Korsakov.") But Shostakovich did, for the most part, respect Mussorgsky's idiosyncrasies of melody, harmony, and rhythm, and he didn't cut. He did, however, introduce what the preface to his score calls "minor, purely technical changes, made imperative for the sake of clarity by the considerations of texture or compass," and by those "clarifications" he smoothed some peculiarly plangent part-writing. Until some new orchestrator steeped in Mussorgskian sonorities comes along, the Shostakovich *Khovanshchina* must be counted the closer to the original of the available versions. What the *Boris* and *Khovanshchina* cases do have in common is that the Rimsky recension is easier to bring off successfully—being shorter, dramatically trimmer, more "effectively" scored, and altogether more "practical." The original *Boris* and the Shostakovich *Khovanshchina* offer a greater challenge—and greater rewards when their demands are nobly met.

Boris Godunov, based largely on a play by Pushkin, has a protagonist and a plot. *Khovanshchina* is a set of six tableaux freely fashioned from history by Mussorgsky under the direction of V. V. Stassov, scenarist and mentor to the Russian nationalist composers. The action has a visionary rather than any narrative coherence. Stassov wrote of a drama dominated by "the majestic figure of Dositheus, the head of the Old Believers, a strong, energetic man ... a deep spirit ... who, like a powerful spring, directs the actions of the two princes—Khovansky, who represents ancient, fanatical, deep, dark, unfathomable Russia, and Golitsin, the representative of the West, which some, even in the party of the Princess Sophia [Peter's half-sister, regent during his minority], had begun to understand and value." Stassov proposed contrasts between orderly life in Moscow's German settlement, the home of the Lutheran Pastor and his daughter

Emma, and riotous life in the quarter of the Streltsy, the drunken, savage army led by Khovansky; between the bluff, violent, feudal Khovansky and his foolish, ambitious son, Andrew, consumed with love for Emma; between the urbane Golitsin, Sophia's foreign minister, and the ruthless (but, in the opera, movingly patriotic) Shaklovity, in charge of domestic affairs. (Golitsin seeks alliance with, and Shaklovity is determined to destroy, both Khovansky and the Old Believers.) Stassov supplied the composer with character sketches of the heroine, Martha, of the wily Scribe, of the boastful, handsome young Strelyets Kuzka, and of the bewildered, unhappy people, victims of forces too strong for them. Mussorgsky embraced the subject. The completion of *Boris* had induced in him a state that his biographer M. D. Calvocoressi calls "mystic confidence." The success of *Boris* at the Maryinsky induced what Rimsky-Korsakov, in his memoirs, calls "a certain mysteriousness, even arrogance.... His self-conceit grew enormously, and his obscure, involved manner of expressing himself (which had been characteristic even before) now increased enormously." In 1872, to Stassov, Mussorgsky wrote of the rapture that reading Darwin had brought him; of poetry's two giants, "the crude Homer and the subtle Shakespeare"; of music's two giants, "the meditator Beethoven and the ultra-meditator Berlioz"; of the Russian giants Glinka, Dargomizhsky, Pushkin, Lermontov, Gogol, Gogol, and Gogol again. And he continued:

Darwin has finally confirmed me in my innermost idea (about which I once felt rather foolishly shy), that the artistic representation of mere beauty in its material manifestation is crude, immature, art in an infantile stage. The subtlest traits of human nature, manifest in individuals and in the masses—exploring and conquering these little-known regions—that is the artist's true mission. "To new shores!" [a motto of the Mussorgsky-Stassov creed] Boldly, through storms, shoals, and hidden reefs, to new shores! Man is a social creature and cannot be otherwise; masses, like individuals, always possess subtle, elusive traits that no one has touched upon. To note them, to study them, to read, observe, and conjecture, to dedicate one's entire being to their study, to offer the result to humanity as a nourishing food it has never before tasted—that is the task, the joy of joys! That is what we shall try to do in our *Khovanshchina*—not so, my dear Oracle?

Performers and listeners alike must approach *Khovanshchina* attuned to its composer's lofty aims and tolerant of the fact that by any commonsense canons of dramatic construction the work is a mess. Mussorgsky's almost mystic pursuit of "truth" led him to write wonderfully penetrating, unconventional, uncompromising music—great music that can help modern audiences to understand the motivations of leaders impelled by conflicting ideologies, the tugs of patriotism and lust for personal power, and faith that leads to martyrdom and mass suicide. But the whole opera he and Stassov envisaged was not written. Transcendentalism and what Mussorgsky and his cronies called "to trans-cognac oneself" became confused. Rimsky recalls, "None of us knew the real subject and plan of *Khovanshchina*, and from Mussorgsky's accounts, flowery, affected, and involved (as was his style of expression then), it was hard to grasp the subject as something whole and consecutive.... Flashes of powerful creativeness continued for a long time, but his mental logic was growing dim.... He composed more slowly, by fits and starts, lost the connections between separate movements, and jumped from one subject to another." Between 1874 and his death, in 1881, he worked alternately on *Khovanshchina* and the unfinished Gogol opera *Sorochintsy Fair*. The flashes of powerful creativeness also brought forth *Pictures at an Exhibition* and the song cycles *Sunless* and *Songs and Dances of Death*.

Khovanshchina as we know it has several loose ends. The scene in the German settlement (which Mussorgsky had sketched in a "quasi-Mozartian" style) is missing, and what remains of Emma and of the Pastor is abrupt, oblique, and hard to understand. (The Met, following Rimsky, simply cuts the Pastor scene.) So is what remains of the Old Believer Susanna, who once had a larger role. "In the present version," Rimsky observed, "she is an unnecessary character." (The Met, concurring, removes her altogether.) Yet the grand design can be grasped—just—if one does some homework on Russian history, notes the foreshortening and simplifications of it that Stassov and Mussorgsky introduced, and reads Stassov-Mussorgsky correspondence to discover what they had in mind in addition to what actually got set down. The information in the Met program is not unhelpful; it could be enhanced by the Isaiah Berlin essay on *Khovanshchina* with which Covent Garden and San Francisco introduced their productions of the opera. The Met performance is sung in Russian. An English translation is on sale. Prepared by Christopher Hunt for the San Francisco production, it is incomplete, but it includes some passages that the Met omits. What is needed is an annotated libretto that will explain, for example, what Golitsin and Khovansky refer to when they trade taunts in Act II. *Khovanshchina* is an opera worth taking trouble over.

All this may make *Khovanshchina* sound difficult of access. It's not that, but merely puzzling, and a little drab at times if there are singers without vivid personalities and beautiful voices in long, looping monologues that need to be followed in verbal detail. But the general sense of the scenes is unmistakable; and although the subject matter is unorthodox—an opera without heroes or villains, an impartial yet passionate study of political forces embodied in personalities—Mussorgsky cast the work in grand-opera form. There are arias, duets, big choruses, an incantation scene, a *romanza*, a *preghiera*, a ballet, a spectacular finale during which the heroine, Norma-like, leads her errant lover to the pyre.

Martha is one of opera's great mezzo-soprano roles. In her, all the threads of the drama meet and cross, tearing against the central fact of her life, her love for Prince Andrew. (Mussorgsky intended to end Act II with a quintet for Martha, Golitsin, Shaklovity, Khovansky, and Dositheus.) It is a complex role and—especially in Mussorgsky's and Shostakovich's keys—a very difficult one, calling for stamina and power at the extremes of both contralto and mezzo ranges. Martha is a sorceress, a prophetess, an ardent woman racked by love, jealousy, and religious anguish. She must be Ulrica, Cassandra, and Donna Elvira in one. She is the soul of suffering Russia become incarnate and at the same time an individual. Chaliapin, a famous Dositheus, devotes two pages of his book *Man and Mask* to Martha's song in Act III:

She sings an artless strain . . . and all the time she is thinking not of the past but of the future. . . . Martha's song must be sung so that the listeners can realize her secret soul; they must be aware not of the rosary of her memories but of the underlying emotion that her surface thoughts disguise. . . . If Martha's secret thoughts are not visible, then there will be no Martha on the stage, but a lady of more or less stout proportions who sings more or less adequately words devoid of all meaning.

In Act V, by sheer intensity of will—sensual and sacred emotions fused in ecstasy—she hypnotizes her lover to follow her into the fire. In this great role, Helga Dernesch—replacing the mezzo originally announced—made her Met début. She is an intense, intelligent, dignified, and potent artist—formerly an Isolde and Brünnhilde, now a striking Fricka, Waltraute, and Erda—and her Martha was wonderfully moving, aflame with tenderness, grief, mystic force (in the divination scene), resistless fascination. I have heard more opulent voices in the role, but none more sharply focussed on the sense of the phrases. Chaliapin would surely have approved. One thing I missed, but the fault was mine: Miss Dernesch always makes much effect by her charged utterance of words, and while her Russian may be as fluent as her German and English are, mine isn't.

No one else was quite on this level. Martti Talvela's Dositheus had a generalized solemnity and majesty, but not the variety of inflection that—whether one can understand the words or not—makes one attentive to each phrase. Aage Haugland's Khovansky was big and bold but similarly undetailed. (Is he the first Khovansky who joins in the dance of his Persian slaves? This ballet was lewdly choreographed by David Toguri.) Wieslaw Ochman's Golitsin seemed just to be sung, not subtly felt and enacted. And Allan Monk's Shaklovity did not sustain interest through his long aria of rolling rhetorical questions and supplications. I attended the first night. The performance may by now have gained confidence and character. Neeme Järvi, who conducted altogether too plainly, may now be bringing more fire and life to the music. August Everding's production, in scenery by Ming Cho Lee, was curious. The crowd scenes seemed to be little more than blocking, and there was a good deal of unmotivated activity—people scurrying across the stage for no discernible reason. (It began during the prelude, which was treated as a pantomime, not the gradually brightening dawn picture that the composer specifies.) The scenery is simple, largely colorless, deliberately unromantic; Everding said he wanted no sense of period or pageantry. Golitsin's summer house was so sparsely furnished that his harpsichord had to double as a serving table, and his guests had nowhere to put their drinks but on the floor. A strange trench, serving no apparent purpose, spanned the forestage during the crowd scenes, and people hopped in and out of it.

I found it hard to determine what Everding and his team were aiming at, beyond the removal of all grand-opera allure, and hard to respond very keenly to anything but Miss Dernesch's Martha. It was the sort of modest staging that would perhaps be better served by performance in an English translation. (The Met used English in 1950.) Of course, *Khovanshchina* does sound better in Russian. The paradox of music closely tied to speech inflections—Monteverdi's,

Mussorgsky's, Janáček's—is that the text at once needs to be understood in detail and proves especially resistant to singable translation. (I see no great objection to macaronic performances, in which each artist uses whatever tongue he or she finds most communicative. Amid the conventions that make up opera, one more is easily accepted.) It will be interesting to discover how this *Khovanshchina* develops: whether the missing scenes are restored; whether grand new artists—Yevgeny Nesterenko, as Khovansky, is one I am eager to hear—illumine the drama in different ways.

In a 1988 revival, nobly conducted by James Conlon, missing music was restored, but the cast, again led by Talvela as Dositheus, was unremarkable, and the staging seemed as drab and "curious" as ever.

Birthday Honors

November 11, 1985

The year has brought centenary observance of Thomas Tallis, who died in 1585, and Heinrich Schütz, who was born that year; of Bach, Handel, and Domenico Scarlatti, who were born in 1685; of Alban Berg and—less widely—George Butterworth, Deems Taylor, and Egon Wellesz, who were born in 1885. Handel has held, and holds, the limelight; there was much great music by him, neglected for centuries, waiting to be rediscovered. On Scarlatti's birthday, October 26, Bach and Handel were sung and played in Merkin Hall, by the Sine Nomine Singers and Baroque Orchestra, conducted by Harry Saltzman. The works were two representations of Alcides at the bivium—young Hercules at the point in his life when he had to choose between the paths of pleasure and of virtue. He chose the path of virtue. The edifying scene—with two allegorical figures, one stern and one alluring, vying for the hero's adherence—was often treated by artists and composers. Later in the eighteenth century, Metastasio's *Alcide al bivio,* written for the wedding of the nineteen-year-old Joseph II and Isabella of Parma, in 1760, was much set. Bach's version, *Hercules auf dem Scheidewege: Dramma per Musica* (Cantata No. 213), was first performed in a Leipzig coffee-garden on the eleventh birthday of the Elector of Saxony's son, in 1733. There is a wonderful opening chorus, an extended movement dancing through many harmonic fields. Pleasure, a soprano, lullabies Hercules' conscience with the lovely "Schlafe, mein Liebster," familiar from the Christmas Oratorio, for which Bach reused the cantata. There it is dropped from B-flat to G, the voice is doubled in octaves by a flute, and four oboes—two d'amore and two da caccia—are added to the score. The sound is magical; but the simple string version in *Hercules* is melting, too. In the cantata, oboe timbre is saved for the following numbers. An oboe d'amore as well as a second voice plays echo to answer the questions of Hercules, an alto. (Bach makes one of his rare jokes, when the echo jumps in impetuously to give some decisive answers on notes that Hercules has not yet sounded, taking the words out of his mouth.) And an oboe and a violin second the aspirant exhortations of Virtue, a tenor. Hercules and Virtue embrace in duet. Mercury, a bass, draws the moral—this has been an allegory of Electoral merit—and summons the Muses to sing a final gavotte. If their words scan oddly, it is because the number is adapted from Cantata No. 184.

Handel's *The Choice of Hercules* was first performed at Covent Garden, in 1751, on a bill with *Alexander's Feast*. The score was adapted from incidental music Handel had written for a production of Tobias Smollett's *Alceste* which was planned on a grand scale but didn't come off. Handel took trouble over his contribution, and his music was well worth saving, even though its fit to the new subject is sometimes loose. This musical version of the legend contains two lullabies; in *Alceste* they were alternative settings of an air, "Gentle Morpheus," that Calliope sang over the stricken Admetus. The first of them, recast as "This manly youth's exalted mind," introduces an unusually gentle Virtue, accompanied by rocking figures from flutes and strings. The second, Hercules' "Yet, can I hear that dulcet lay, As sweet as flows the honey dew," while he inclines toward Pleasure, is one of the most tenderly seductive airs that Handel ever wrote. Drama begins with a newly composed trio: the hero's bewildered "Where shall I go?" is answered in different strains by Pleasure's "To yonder breezy plain!" and Virtue's "To yonder lofty fane!" It ends on a half-cadence, Hercules still in doubt; Virtue breaks in briskly and develops her trio theme in an air, "Mount, mount the steep ascent." Hercules makes his decision, and Handel, music's great hymner of sensuous delights, seems almost to regret it, for the hero announces his intention in D minor, adopting the *Alceste* air in which Charon had summoned shades "to Pluto's dreary shore." The chorus lauds the choice in a severe G minor.

Both works reveal their composers in unstrenuous vein. They made a happy pairing. Bach's Hercules was presumably a boy, and Handel's may have been Gaetano Guadagni, Gluck's first Orpheus. The roles were taken by the counter-tenor Jeffrey Dooley; his singing was clean, pointed, and brave, but the timbre in the higher reaches was owly. Bach's Virtue was sung by Frank Hoffmeister, Handel's (a lowish soprano part) by Marianna Busching. Julianne Baird, in both works, embodied Pleasure with a delightful sense of line and a bubbly feel for decoration. No two people agree about baroque tempi nowadays; I found some of Mr. Saltzman's just a bit slow. Happily, he didn't beat time through all continuo-accompanied airs but let singers and players make music together, listening to one another. The oboe d'amore and oboe solos were played by Stephen Hammer, a prince of baroque oboists. The natural horns in the Bach—the parts are fiendishly difficult—emitted some murky sounds. The chorus was alert.

Between the Bach and the Handel, as entr'acte, the harpsichordist of the ensemble, Edward Brewer, played Scarlatti's C-major Sonata, K. 513. Earlier that day, he had played it up at Symphony Space, where Scarlatti's birthday was being celebrated with an eight-hour, free-admission concert. Some ninety of his five hundred and fifty sonatas were played. On the platform, a Steinway was flanked by a fine Franco-Flemish harpsichord built by William Dowd and an Italian harpsichord, tangier in timbre, built by Carl Fudge. Eleven harpsichordists and eight pianists took part. Fernando Valenti, who in the fifties recorded Scarlatti sonatas by the shoal, opened the proceedings on the Dowd. Ivan Davis followed on the Steinway. Then Mr. Brewer took up the Fudge, and so did Colin Tilney. Robert Taub played the Steinway. I stayed for two hours: Symphony Space, like most modern concert halls, has no windows, and it is not agreeable to be in a windowless room for longer than that. Besides, there was a long line of Scarlatti-hungry people on the sidewalk outside, waiting to be served.

Concert-hall performances of Scarlatti played on the piano by Gieseking, Casadesus, Lipatti, Michelangeli, Horowitz have bewitched me, and so I am in no position to deplore the unsuitability of the modern instrument. Nevertheless, ears change, fashions change, and musicological perceptions eventually affect audiences' ways of listening. I doubt whether anyone left Symphony Space unconvinced that the clean, precise harpsichord is the apter machine for the display of Scarlatti's boldness and brightness—other things being equal, of course. But they weren't equal: Mr. Davis's fleet, exhilarating virtuosity and Mr. Taub's poetic intentness—each pianist at one with his instrument while he drew from it Scarlatti's music—were different in kind, one from the other, and both from the harpsichordists' various manners. The concert was a demonstration of creative genius that can bear many kinds of interpretation. Four sonatas were played on a Yamaha synthesizer by John Van Buskirk. Other evidence of adaptability could have been provided by guitar transcriptions (the record catalogues attest to their popularity), or Wendy Carlos's recordings on the Moog. (A harpsichordist friend of mine, on first hearing these, said sadly, "To think that I've spent years and years trying in vain to approach such evenness and accuracy of statement.") At least three of the sonatas were written for the organ; some of them—possibly hundreds, Joel Sheveloff says in the New Grove—may have been intended for the fortepiano.

The party was arranged by Sara Fishko and Teresa Sterne, in association with WNYC, and WNYC broadcast it—four hours live and four delayed by two hours while "A Prairie Home Companion" took over. After the Merkin Hall concert, I caught the final stages over the air. Kenneth Cooper played four sonatas, and then an encore, with such bounding enthusiasm that the audience responded to his strokes with audible delight. What I heard was—the whole event must have been trebly so—a marvellous revelation of Scarlatti's ceaseless inventiveness. There was no question of monotony or of diminishing returns. The performers covered all possible approaches. Some of them played in pretty strict tempo; others were wayward, capricious, flamboyant. Some of them broke sonatas cleanly into two parts across the central double bar, as the old editions do; others observed the elisions that, in over a hundred sonatas, eliminate the barrier. The music was brilliant, poignant, witty, quirky, gentle, delicate, exuberant. This was a splendid display at once of Scarlatti's achievements and of the differing ways in which modern musicians respond to them.

Schütz is a composer whose radiance, nobility, grandeur, directness, dramatic power, and range should be known to the widest possible public. The fifth

Grove had an eloquent essay on his music, by Anthony Lewis. In the New Grove, Joshua Rifkin's biographical section contains the fruit of new research, but Kurt Gudewill's account of the music is plainer than Mr. Lewis's. Colin Timms's, which replaces it in the Grove "offspin" volume *North European Baroque Masters,* is plainer still. Schütz's music doesn't fit easily into the concert scene. It is all for voices, much of it accompanied by instrumental consorts unorthodox today. A good deal was recorded in the fifties and sixties, but the quatercentenary has not brought the flood of polychoral Psalm settings and of Symphoniae Sacrae that might have been expected. Mr. Rifkin's article in the October *Opus,* "Whatever Happened to Heinrich Schütz?," suggests two reasons for this. First: the early-music specialists, most of them active in instrumental fields, have become victims of their popularity; the former pioneers are now much in demand for yet another set of Brandenburgs, yet another *Messiah,* yet another *Four Seasons.* Moreover, as Mozart, then Beethoven fall into their province and become "early music," their forces tend to consolidate as a small string orchestra with a handful of winds, and the seventeenth century stands even less of a chance. This is a very rough summary of Mr. Rifkin's careful arguments as he contemplates "the paradox of how the very success of early music has come by now to narrow its horizons." His second suggestion—that student protest of the seventies led to the rejection of a composer championed by National Socialist musicians and scholars—seems to me less convincing. By that reckoning, Bach and Handel would be similarly tarnished.

"We have no organizations to whom Schütz would come as a natural mandate," Mr. Rifkin says. "In most instances, performing him means assembling the forces pretty much from scratch." I became a Schütz admirer in the 1950s, when recordings appeared of the Musical Exequies, the Seven Last Words, and (vividly sung by Hugues Cuénod, with Vienna instrumentalists conducted by Daniel Pinkham) a collection of Kleine Geistliche Konzerte and Symphoniae Sacrae. I became a Schütz devotee in 1962, at the inaugural concert of such an organization as Mr. Rifkin desiderates. That year, in London, Roger Norrington founded the Heinrich Schütz Chorale, a group of professional singers, and the Heinrich Schütz Choir, an amateur chorus—counterparts of Schütz's *coro favorito* and *capella*—and set St. Bartholomew-the-Great aglow with three masterpieces: the Musical Exequies, the Seven Last Words, and the German Magnificat. In successive years, in various seventeenth-century churches—Wren's St. Andrew-by-the-Wardrobe, which has the general proportions of Schütz's church in Dresden; Wren's St. Stephen, Walbrook with its elaborate disposition of space—Norrington and his artists revealed the richness and variety of Schütz. In America, I've felt Schütz-starved—until last month, when the thirtieth International Heinrich Schütz Festival was held on the campus of the University of Illinois at Urbana-Champaign at about the time of Schütz's birthday (the exact date of which is still in dispute).

The festival was combined with an international conference; some interesting—and one or two challenging—papers were read. There were six concerts in four days. The works spanned Schütz's career: from his Opus 1 (1611), the Italian madrigals he published after his years of study with Giovanni Gabrieli, in Venice, to his Opus Ultimum (1671), a monumental eight-part, double-chorus setting of Psalm 119, followed by Psalm 100 and the Magnificat. (It was published for the first time last year. The six surviving partbooks, thought to have been lost in the Second World War, turned up in Dresden, among some unclassified music of the sixteenth to eighteenth centuries; the editor, Wolfram Steude, has had to reconstruct the treble and tenor lines of the second choir.) Only excerpts were given in Urbana, but the whole work has now been recorded. The University of Illinois Chorale and Concert Choir and an eight-voice chamber choir from the Hanover Musikhochschule took part, but the great performances were those of Alexander Blachly's Pomerium Musices, six finely tempered singers; Les Filles de Sainte-Colombe, four viol players of uncommon accomplishment; and the tenor Paul Elliott. Their account of the Resurrection History was deeply moving. Mr. Norrington conducted. A few hours earlier, one of the scholars had illustrated his paper with excerpts from Norrington's 1970 recording of the work. It seemed wonderful fifteen years ago. Today—as the conductor himself was quick to observe—it sounds too slow and too "thick." Years of exploration have brought great changes in performing style. Other highlights—moments of rare and inspiring beauty—were provided by the tender Annunciation dialogue, swv 333, with Ann Monoyios as the Virgin and Drew Minter as the Angel; by the large-scale setting of Psalm 116, swv 51, with its evocations of despair, salvation, and grateful praise; and by the impassioned monologues "Erbarm dich mein," swv 447, and "Eile, mich, Gott, zu erretten," swv 282, sung by Peter Stewart and Mr. Elliott, respectively. One small reproach and one disappointment must be recorded. At several of the concerts, the program books contained no texts but only translations; Schütz's word-setting is one of his glories. And, in a town not without churches, all the performances were given in campus concert halls, none of them both acoustically and architecturally apt for Schütz. Otherwise, nothing but gratitude for days of marvellous music, sung and played with fervent, subtle artistry.

VOICES OF TODAY

November 18, 1985

A SEVENTIETH-BIRTHDAY concert for George Perle, in Merkin Hall last month, brought the première of his Wind Quintet No. 4 and the American première of his Six New Etudes, for piano. The quintet, written for the Dorian Wind Quintet, is a happy piece. It is in four movements—Invention, Scherzo, Pastorale, Finale—and lasts about eighteen minutes. One of the pleasures Perle's music affords is meeting themes that behave like characters who become more engaging the more we get to know them. They pass through many moods in the course of a work, change aspect, sometimes peek out behind disguises, then step forth, smiling and confident, *en clair*. They don't outstay their welcome. They aren't forced through paces by a puppetmaster but seem to live their own lives. They enter and move through classical forms with the ease of people entering and moving through shapely rooms chosen or designed to suit them well. If the description suggests something neoclassical, that is not inappropriate, provided any implications of dryness are avoided. Portraits of ancestors and honored friends hanging in those rooms probably show Debussy, Bartók, Berg, and the late Stravinsky—not Hindemith or the middle Stravinsky. But Perle has developed his own language. By what technical process his harmony functions I don't know. (A program note spoke of "the utilization of the totality of relations inherent in the chromatic continuum" and of "a new concept of musical space, in which coherence in progression and the establishment of tonal centricity are realized to a degree unknown since the major-minor scale.") That it does function well is apparent to the ear.

Grace, wit, an unaffected elegance are qualities regularly discerned in Perle's compositions. There is also a vein of emotion, which rises closest to the surface in the third movement of Serenade III (1983), in the Cello Sonata (1985), and in some of the Six New Etudes. The first set of Six Etudes (1976), written as if by some late-twentieth-century Chopin, soon became popular. (They are recorded by Bradford Gowen on New World.) The new set, which might, rather, be ascribed to some late-twentieth-century Schumann, will surely do so, too. The first study, "Praeludium," makes play with one of Perle's characteristic rising themes. "Gigue" is a light, heady whirl of dancing cross rhythms. "Papillons" flutters by in four-against-three. So far, the music is essentially in Perle's favored two-part texture—though a line is often colored by, as it were, underlining in the form of a second, simultaneous note. The fourth study, "Romance," employs richer sonorities, shining through delicate clouds of carefully indicated pedal. "Variations" is perhaps the most demanding piece of the set: a study in constantly changing meter, sudden dynamic contrast, and abrupt shifts of register. The final "Perpetuum Mobile" is a piano-solo version of the exhilarating fourth movement of Serenade III—the instrumental parts here condensed into a single left-hand line. Six New Etudes, commissioned by the United States Information Agency, was given its first performance in China, in May, by Shirley Anne Seguin. In New York, it was played by Michael Boriskin—a gifted and sensitive young American pianist so far better known in Europe than here. He met the successive challenges, both technical and expressive, with eagerness, warmth, and dexterity. He has recorded the set, along with Perle's *Pantomime, Interlude, and Fugue*, Short Sonata, Fantasy Variations, and Suite in C, for New World.

The concert—the first of the season in Merkin Hall's Music Today series—began with Serenade I (1962), for solo viola and ten players (eight winds, double-bass, and percussion), and ended with Serenade III, for solo piano and ten players (seven winds, violin, cello, and percussion). Both were conducted by Gunther Schuller. The early Serenade, with its dedicatee, Walter Trampler, as soloist, sounded underrehearsed, balanced with less than chamber-music precision. Serenade III, with Seymour Lipkin as soloist, went better. The Cello Sonata completed the program. André Emelianoff, to whom it is dedicated, and who introduced it, in Merkin Hall, earlier this year, and Mr. Boriskin gave a noble, impassioned account of the rich piece.

The second Music Today concert, three weeks later, conducted by Gerard Schwarz, offered an international program at once varied and satisfying. Menahem Avidom's *Enigma* (1962), for woodwind quintet, percussion, and piano, is a cluster of five carefully wrought little pieces. Karl Amadeus Hartmann's Concerto for Viola and Piano (1955) is a masterwork. Hartmann, much admired in the fifties, is little heard now, and audiences are the poorer. The concerto has the energy, the economy, the intellectual toughness and emotional fire that mark all his best music. The scoring is unorthodox—three each of flutes, clarinets, bassoons, trumpets, and trombones; six percussion players—but so skillfully handled that the soloists (who in this performance were Sol Greitzer and John Van Buskirk) are not drowned. The two pieces, one from Israel, the other from Germany (where Hartmann's music was silenced from 1933 to 1945), were American premières. There followed two New York premières.

Ellen Taaffe Zwilich's Chamber Concerto (1984), for trumpet and five players, was commissioned by the National Endowment for the Arts for performance by new-music ensembles in Pittsburgh, Boston, and San Diego. It is short, cheerful, and confident—undemanding of its listeners, though difficult to play. A *Petrushka*-like call runs through the three movements. The scoring (flute, clarinet, percussion, double-bass, and piano) is subtle and engaging; Zwilich has a fresh, lively ear. The soloist must be able to hit spot-on high notes, for this is a virtuoso trumpet piece. Neil Balm smudged some of them.

Bernard Rands's song cycle to poems about the sun, *Canti del sole,* had its première as a work for tenor and orchestra, at the Philharmonic's Horizons '83 Festival. (The following year, it was awarded the Pulitzer Prize for Music.) Like Rands's companion cycle of moon poems, *Canti lunatici,* for soprano and orchestra (which was done at the London Proms this year), it exists also in a version for singer and chamber ensemble. This ended the Merkin concert. The soloist, as at the Horizons event, was Paul Sperry, a careful and intelligent artist who makes the most of modest vocal equipment. I'm not sure whether the music does more than drape charged poems with apt, evocative sounds. Perhaps that's enough. The Baudelaire setting, "Harmonie du soir," sounded ravishing in this chamber version.

The first half of the New Music Consort's concert in Carnegie Recital Hall last week was attractive. The program began with Henry Cowell's *Pulse* (1939), for six percussionists. It is brief, bright, and engaging. The textures are thin and definite, the musical arguments lucid. The players were William Trigg, Joseph Grable, Kory Grossman, Michael Pugliese, Frank Cassara, and Dominic Donato—a keen, precise team. Then there was Joan Tower's *Wings* (1981), for solo clarinet—a graphic and beautiful piece. The image behind it, the composer says in a program note, "is one of a large bird (perhaps a falcon) that at times flies very high and very slowly and at other times builds up tremendous speeds that result in elaborate downward (or upward) flying patterns." It is a work in the genre of George Benjamin's *Flight,* for solo flute, and Peter Maxwell Davies's *Sea Eagle,* for solo horn. Charles Neidich was its poetic interpreter. There followed Elliott Carter's Elizabeth Bishop song cycle *A Mirror on Which to Dwell* (1976), for soprano and nine players. The singer was Carmen Pelton. Given that her words were mostly inaudible and that her tone grew impure above the staff—it's a lot to give—it was an impressive performance. Her feeling for line, for the movement, shapes, and stresses of Carter's lyrical phrases, was sure. What a wonderful composition this is—so rich, intense, and delicate in emotion! (There is a fine recording by the first performers, Susan Davenny Wyner and Speculum Musicae, on CBS.) Verbal obscurity during performance is partly the fault of the composer's setting: he wrote for a listener who has a text sheet before him. The Consort provided one, but not enough light to make it legible at a glance. I go on about this matter of light, I know, but still can't understand the thinking of an organization that distributes texts, acknowledging their importance, and then makes them not easily usable. Few people can memorize six difficult poems before the lights go down. Even the singer of *Mirror* hadn't memorized words and music; in the modern manner, she sang from a score. Bishop's and Carter's jokes passed apparently uncomprehended.

Avian imagery was provided here by the stuttering, piping oboe (played by Wesley Nichols) of the sandpiper, running "finical, awkward, in a state of controlled panic" along the water's marge. Birds in song, in flight, or (like Ravel's kingfisher) in stillness have ever been composers' inspiration. Long before Messiaen's ornithological exactitude, Handel's warbling turtles and nightingales seconded a heroine's plaints. As a flute, the lark flutters through poor Ophelia's mad musings in Ambroise Thomas's *Hamlet;* as a violin, it soars through Vaughan Williams's *The Lark Ascending,* to become "an ecstasy to music turned." In Carter's Symphony of Three Orchestras, a trumpet plays Hart Crane's gull "shedding white wings of tumult, building high over the chained bay waters Liberty." Last spring, an American composer living in Tuscany wrote to me of the nightingale song that rings through the valleys there, turning the dark to music: he felt awed, humbled, exalted by the birds' command of melodic variation, expressive timbre, and antiphonies. Musicians who live always in cities, unawakened by a dawn chorus, uninspired by nature's song, lose touch with living springs of their art. They may count to twelve in many cunning fashions, and pattern strains and pangs of urban life in careful, elegant constructions, but through the music of the composers who stir listeners most deeply there seem to run deeper patterns: birdsong, the rhythms of wave and water, the mystery and majesty of stars in their courses, the surge of the seasons. Among living composers—anyone can draw his own long list from the past—there come to mind creators as diverse as Carter, Davies, Henze, Messiaen, Stockhausen, Tippett.

The second half of the Consort's program contained Olly Wilson's Piece for Four (1966), John Cage's Music for 5, and Charles Wuorinen's Trio for Bass Instruments (1981). The first movement of Wilson's quartet (trumpet, flute, double-bass, and piano) seemed crabbed and arid; lyricism broke through with the double-bass solo of the second movement and the trumpet tunes (inspired by Miles Davis) of the third. The bassist was Joseph Tamosaitis, the trumpeter Christopher Gekker. The Cage piece presented an aspect of his *Music for . . . ,* a work in progress consisting of parts that may be used alone, in ad lib combinations, or along with other scores. Ten individual parts have been written so far, and, in a spoken introduction, the composer suggested that in time a work for conductorless full orchestra might result. The title varies according to the forces chosen. For this concert, flute, cello, piano, and two percussion parts were used. It seemed rather like ear-training—listen attentively, and make what sense you can of it all—and it went on for a long time. I recalled Bayan Northcott's passing remark about Cage, Feldman, and Glass in an article about Stefan Wolpe: "Once their basic—often simplistic—premises are swallowed, their actual music proceeds to offer no radical challenge in itself whatever (except perhaps tedium)." But the performance did bring an acoustic surprise. While onstage the percussionists and pianist thumped, scraped, rattled, and tinkled away—pots and pans were among their paraphernalia; sometimes one blew a conch or a penny whistle; sometimes they cried aloud—the flutist and the cellist (Rachel Rudich and Madeleine Shapiro) played at the back of the hall, one in the balcony, the other beneath it. And the sound—at any rate, to someone seated on the main floor—was so vivid and intimate as to suggest that artists might do well to station themselves there regularly, rather than up on the curtained platform. Wuorinen's trio is for bass trombone, tuba, and double-bass—a gruff combination. He writes for it with wit and vivacity, and the performers—David Taylor, David Braynard, and Mr. Tamosaitis—were deft.

HANDEL IN MARYLAND

November 25, 1985

THE Maryland Handel Festival—now four, previously three, days of concerts and international conference—flourishes. Its directors are the conductor Paul Traver and the scholar Howard Serwer. The principal site is the College Park campus of the University of Maryland. At the first festival, in 1981, *Messiah* was the main work performed—a conservative choice, but controversially presented. Then a chronological progress through the oratorios began: *Esther* in 1982, *Deborah* in 1983. Last year brought a bicentennial diversion—a monster *Messiah* in Washington Cathedral, based on the 1784 commemorative jamboree in Westminster Abbey. But this year things got back on course, with *Athalia,* and *Saul* is due next year.

In Winton Dean's great book on Handel's dramatic oratorios, chapters on the early works begin with magisterial verdicts: "*Esther* is one of those works, like the operas of Glinka and Dargomijsky, whose historical importance exceeds their aesthetic value." "*Deborah* is a failure." "*Athalia* is the first great English oratorio." But Maryland showed that *Esther,* like Glinka's operas, is well worth getting to know. It lightened the sentence on poor *Deborah,* which holds some marvellous music and some stirring scenes. This year, it confirmed the judgment on *Athalia. Athalia,* like *Esther,* is based on a drama by Racine. *Athalie* (1691) was his last play. Like his *Esther,* it was written for the demoiselles of Saint-Cyr.

388

Voltaire declared that if Racine's *Iphigénie* was "the masterwork of the classic stage," his *Athalie* was "the masterwork of the human spirit." A. W. Schlegel disputed the former opinion but endorsed the second in an enthusiastic page of his *Lectures on Dramatic Literature:*

> In *Athalie* ... the poet exhibited himself for the last time, before taking leave of poetry and the world, in his whole strength. It is not only his most finished work, but, I have no hesitation in declaring it to be, of all French tragedies the one which, free from all mannerism, approaches the nearest to the grand style of the Greeks. The chorus is conceived fully in the ancient sense. . . . The scene has all the majesty of a public action. Expectation, emotion, and keen agitation succeed each other, and continually rise with the progress of the drama: with a severe abstinence from all foreign matter, there is still a display of the richest variety, sometimes of sweetness, but more frequently of majesty and grandeur. . . . Its import is exactly what that of a religious drama ought to be: on earth, the struggle between good and evil; and in heaven the wakeful eye of providence beaming, from unapproachable glory, rays of constancy and resolution.

What Schlegel says of the drama is true of Handel's music drama. The librettist, Samuel Humphreys, made a decent job of translating and adapting the play for Handel's use. Some of his lines are memorable. *Athalia* is not Handel's greatest oratorio; the Aeschylean *Saul,* which followed, soars higher, and plumbs more deeply the sources of human character and action. So do *Samson, Belshazzar, Theodora,* and *Jephtha.* But already the themes of national destiny, individual rulers' cares, opposed creeds, oppression bravely borne and heroically resisted are woven in a work that has the grandeur, mounting tension, and variety that Schlegel admired in Racine. It touched its listeners' lives. Handel throws the choral cry "Bless the true Church, and save the King" into prominence; both Jacobites and Georgians in his audience could respond with fervor. Modern audiences find their own analogues. *Athalia* was first performed in the Sheldonian Theatre, Oxford, in 1733, and is on occasion revived there. I had never heard it anywhere else until the Maryland performance, which was given in the Memorial Chapel at College Park. For the first time, the festival had engaged a dramatic director—Nicholas Deutsch, whose "semistaged" presentation of *Belshazzar* in Tully Hall last March [see p. 285] was so impressive. *Athalia* wasn't staged, either, but again, with carefully timed entrances and exits and carefully planned platform stationing, the patterns of the drama were revealed. By simple means—the chorus parted in homage as the treble soloist ascended the steep chorus risers and turned at the top to dominate the scene—Racine's big tableau, of the boy king enthroned and the baffled Athalia below, was potently suggested. It wasn't quite as remarkable as the *Belshazzar:* the singers held scores; the chapel's lighting resources were less than Tully's; and Mr. Deutsch overused an effect that in *Belshazzar* had been striking. There, the monarch seemed to quail before the chorus's massed accusatory glance; here, when the choristers intently followed stichomythic dispute, swivelling their gazes as one, the result tended to suggest a slow-motion Wimbledon. But the artists all knew what the work was about, and their singing took fire therefrom. Handel composed *Athalia* in cumulative scenes and acts, not in numbers. Many of the movements are short, and often they are broken into by the chorus; the extended airs are few and are strategically placed. The Maryland presentation conveyed a strong sense of a single day's action—a day of crisis that has been long preparing. It is the festival of Shavuot; the celebration, interrupted, can resume at the end with unforeseen extra cause for rejoicing. Racine laid all the action in the Temple. Humphreys and Handel moved one scene to the royal palace, where in anguished, startling music Athalia, tyrannical regent of Judah, recounts her foreboding dream. (It began with a minatory visit from the shade of her mother, Jezebel, and passed to a fearful vision of Jezebel's death, as she is torn apart by dogs.) In contrast, her courtiers try vainly to cheer her in some of Handel's most seductively lovely strains. (The "voluptuous beauty of heathendom" was the apt phrase of R. A. Streatfeild, Samuel Butler's friend and executor, and a perceptive Handel commentator.) No one tells us just what scene from *Athalia* it was that Berlioz performed at the Opéra in 1840. I like to think it was this one, which has Berliozian graphicness.

Linda Mabbs did not have the temperament for the formidable, Clytemnestralike role—"the lonely towering figure of Athalia," as Dean puts it. (Joan Sutherland recently recorded it, for Oiseau-Lyre.) Theatrically, she had softened what could be a proud royal profile with a housewifely hairstyle, and this seemed to reflect a reluctance to give full dramatic value to the part. But she had got a good deal of the way, and her singing was assured. Judith Nelson was well suited by the music of the anxious, gentle, loving Josabeth—quietly steadfast in her opposition to Athalia, and in dynastic analogy perhaps a Church of England Mary or Anne with no wish to see her Roman Catholic parent on the throne. Miss Nelson's voice moved fluently and truly through Handel's music, and shone as it rose. (Josabeth is, in fact, the prima donna role; it was composed for Anna Strada, who remained loyal to Handel when his other Italians deserted to the rival Opera of the Nobility.) Joad, the High Priest of Judah, Josabeth's husband, was sung by Derek Lee Ragin, an American countertenor who has made a European reputation. His voice is well formed and of agreeable quality. His line was flexible and cleanly drawn. There is something not yet quite right, but it's hard to define: a touch of preciousness, perhaps. I was reminded of the early, Alfred Deller days of the countertenor revival. Ragin seemed a shade too smilingly anxious to please; he lacked the assurance of manner with which a Drew Minter or Jeffrey Gall deploys the countertenor as one among the many voices that can delight us. But he is very promising. Maybe he just needs more stage experience. The boy king Joas was touchingly sung by Christopher Pittenger, whose treble rang out with sweetness and sincerity. It broke just once, and not inappropriately for the characterization of a seven-year-old boy who suddenly learns that he must now be a king. Abner, the Judaic general, was resonantly sung by Gordon Hawkins, a gifted young baritone, but one who showed signs of aspiring to bawl Verdi or Gershwin into America's oversized opera houses. If he wants to be a Handelian, he must learn to lighten and refine his tones and achieve a more forward focus.

The foundation on which the Handel Festival is built is the University of Maryland Chorus—an ensemble of lithe, fresh, responsive young voices—and its founder and conductor, Mr. Traver. The chorus is, as Dean says, "the real hero and hub of *Athalia*." The Maryland chorus sang precisely, brightly, trenchantly—sensuously as Athalia's Baalites, fervently and grandly as the people of Judah. Mr. Traver commands light-stepping, dancing baroque gaits and achieves grandeur without heaviness. Once or twice, I thought his tempi a little slow. Sometimes there were delayed cadences where Handel, surely, intended a springboard into what follows. The Smithsonian Chamber Players, mustered at strength (the score calls for four-part violins, solo cello, horns, trumpets, recorders, a theorbo), played well. The orchestra was so seated that many of the players could see the singers.

The festival began with Handel's masque *Acis and Galatea,* given a concert performance in the chapel. Unstaged, it can be done with just eleven performers: five singers—a soprano, three tenors, and a bass—and six instrumentalists, provided the oboists double on recorders. The soloists join as the chorus, and it's a long sing for the Galatea, the Acis, and the Polypheme. In Maryland, there were twelve performers. (First oboe and first recorder were taken by different players.) The piece was unconducted, and it seemed to me underrehearsed: an able account by an assemblage of proficient artists, but one without much character or liveliness. The individual contributions of Ann Monoyios, a limpid Galatea, and of Patrick Romano, verbally and musically incisive in the small role of Damon, gave much pleasure. Other festival pleasures were provided by Miss Nelson and Mr. Ragin in vocal chamber music (especially the duet setting, in Italian, of Horace's "Beatus ille," composed in 1742, the year of *Messiah*), and by a concert in the Library of Congress auditorium at which Mr. Traver conducted his choir in radiant Schütz performances, and the Smithsonian players in a graceful, high-spirited account of the *Water Music.*

College Park seems short of restaurants. (Each day, Howard Johnson's was a scene of high-powered scholarly discussion.) Otherwise, it's a good place for Handelian activity. The university has a Center for Renaissance and Baroque Studies. The university library houses the collection of the Handelian scholar J. M. Coopersmith. The Library of Congress, the Smithsonian Players, and the Washington Friends of Handel make their contribution. Famous Handelians are invited from round the world. It was at the 1982 festival that plans were mooted for a new, Anglo-American Handel edition, corrective to the snail-progress and what Grove gently calls the "varying standard of reliability" of the Handel edition coming from Halle. (If Prince Charles were to be patron of such a venture, the old connection between Handel and the House of Hanover would be renewed.) Possible rivalry was resolved in cooperation: Halle, thus challenged, reorganized its editorial policy and promised to pull up its socks. Notable among the papers delivered this year were Robert Hume's questions about some biographical facts that should have caused scholars more surprise; John Roberts's demonstration of Handel's covering his tracks when, putting on Vinci's *Didone abbandonata* with his company, he carefully recomposed passages he'd earlier borrowed from it for use in his own operas; and Dean's demonstration, centered on *Ottone,* of the care Handel took to get his operas right.

An American Handel Society, based in College Park, has been founded. Its address is Department of Music, University of Maryland, College Park, Maryland 20742.

Good reports have been coming from Milwaukee about the work there of the Skylight Comic Opera. A visit to the company's production of *Serse,* which was given a run of twelve performances last month, proved them accurate. The show was serious, stylish, and entertaining—conceived with high intelligence and executed with enthusiasm. *Serse,* which Handel completed in 1738, the year he composed *Saul,* is a late opera, and freer in form than its predecessors. The libretto was originally written for Cavalli, eighty years before, when opera was still young and the da capo and exit-air conventions had not been codified. *Serse* mingles—sometimes in the same scene—profound emotion and merry observation of life's more absurd aspects. It has been well called Mozartian in tone—by, among others, Dean, who in the New Grove writes, "This comprehensiveness of mood and dramatic approach gives [Handel's] operas a depth seldom attained in the history of art." He continues, "But their quality can emerge only from productions based on a complete understanding of the convention." Stephen Wadsworth, the director of the Skylight *Serse,* and his cast showed such an understanding. Among the many productions of a Handel-rich year, this one holds a high place. It was neither an eighteenth-century "reconstruction" nor an updated version. The setting, although described as "an imagined England, 1730s," was a simple seven-arched arcade, the arches filled with rich Persian hangings that could be drawn in different patterns—a practicable and attractive décor, designed by Thomas Lynch. The Skylight Theatre, which is small (it seats two hundred and fifty), was ingeniously and intimately used. All moves had a purpose. Each number—in what the program note rightly called a "story of love, growth, and self-knowledge"—made its points precisely and movingly.

The outstanding performers were Lynnen Yakes, in the title role, and Wendy Hill, as Romilda. Miss Yakes's delivery of "Più che penso"—the monarch at once majestic, voluptuous, and ironically self-aware—goes on delighting memory's ear and eye. She has a wonderful stage face, with speaking eyes, eloquent frowns and smiles. Her performance was gleaming, wholehearted, various, and disciplined. Miss Hill sparkled, charmed, and was affecting. Donna Stephenson's Arsamenes was precise and moving in song and action. John Kuether's Elviro was trimly and amusingly sung; his stage movement was a bit loose and wild. Michael Pisani, at the harpsichord, directed a small, alert band; the string playing could with advantage have been lighter and thinner at times. Cutting was gentle: only four of the forty airs, ariosos, or ariettas, and two brief choruses. Mr. Wadsworth had made a crisp, sensitive new English translation.

A HAPPY, EASY FEELING

December 2, 1985

AARON COPLAND was eighty-five on November 14, and he was at Avery Fisher Hall that evening—smiling, lovable of presence as ever—to be greeted and acclaimed by the audience. The Philharmonic played an all-Copland program: *Fanfare for the Common Man* (1943), *Letter from Home* (1944), *John Henry* (1940), the Piano Concerto (1927), *Proclamation for Orchestra* (the première of an orchestration, by Phillip Ramey, of *Proclamation for Piano,* sketched in 1973 and completed in 1982), *Prairie Journal* (1937), and the First Symphony (in its 1928 scoring, without organ). Sixty years of achievement was being celebrated: the Philharmonic gave the symphony its first performance, in the original version, in 1925. The orchestra is playing much Copland this season, avoiding the works most often heard—*Appalachian Spring, Quiet City, Lincoln Portrait*— and reviving others from the extensive catalogue. *Letter from Home, John Henry,* and *Prairie Journal*—all new to the Philharmonic—date from the days when American radio stations still maintained orchestras and commissioned music for them to play. All three are short, poetic, and high-spirited, in Copland's uncontroversially masterly and winning manner. The *Fanfare* was conducted by Leonard Bernstein, in a fervent, full-hearted, full-throated reading. The other performances, conducted by Zubin Mehta, seemed to me empty, inflated, noisy, with little of the easy, natural gait and inflections that should mark Copland in either his prairie-boy or his emphatic vein. Bennett Lerner, however, was a good soloist in the concerto.

The next night, at the Henry Street Settlement Theatre, on Grand Street, I heard a stylish, exhilarating, and moving performance of music by Copland. The piece was his "play-opera for high-school performance," *The Second Hurricane* (1937). The plot is simple. Six children—four boys and two girls—eager for adventure, set out to help with flood relief and are marooned themselves. They quarrel, part, come together again, and, while they await rescue, learn the value of mutual support:

> We got an idea of what life could be like
> With everybody pulling together,
> If each wasn't trying to get ahead of all the rest.
> What it's like when you feel you belong together
> With a sort of love, making you feel easy . . .
> A happy, easy feeling,
> Like freedom, like real freedom.

393

There are choruses of parents, high-school children, and younger children. All join in an affirmative march theme: "That's the idea of freedom, it's feeling equality; It's all men feeling free and equal." Before it can become pompous, Copland dissolves the march into a happy, rangy dance tune. The libretto, written with a sure touch, is by Edwin Denby, who wasn't afraid of sentiment or naiveté but didn't become mawkish. *The Second Hurricane,* contemporary with Marc Blitzstein's *The Cradle Will Rock,* is a socially committed work of art that has dated not at all. William Schuman—contributing to the valuable, very readable autobiography-cum-biography *Copland: 1900 Through 1942,* on which the composer and Vivian Perlis collaborated—remarks, "Because of his agreeable disposition, Aaron is never thought of as being exacting, and this does him an injustice." But his exacting standards in matters moral and political as well as musical have never been in doubt. Of being questioned by Senator Joseph McCarthy I've heard him give a hilarious account—yet with sternness and censure unconcealed. His music, in whatever vein, seems to reflect an innate, uncompromising *goodness,* coupled with clear-eyed good humor, quiet assurance, and zest. The score of *The Second Hurricane* is beautifully spare: reduced sometimes to two lines, or to ostinatos cunningly not quite regular, or to chord alternations so placed and spaced, in register and time, that by simple means they make a great effect.

The 1937 production, given in the same theatre, was conducted by Lehman Engel (who had earlier conducted Kurt Weill's *Der Jasager* at the Settlement) and directed by Orson Welles, assisted by Hiram Sherman. The staging, one reads, was simple: bare playhouse walls, bleachers left and right for the choruses, a platform at the back for the orchestra. The reviews were mixed. In *Modern Music,* Virgil Thomson wrote, "The music is vigorous and noble. The libretto is fresh and is permeated with a great sweetness. Linguistically it is the finest English libretto in some years." But he felt that the end was too easily achieved, "the plot falling to pieces at the very moment when our anxiety is greatest about the fate of the characters," and it is possible to agree with him. A few critics were unenthusiastic. The *Times* called it "pretty dull fare." Denby was away, in Haiti; Copland sent him the reviews, reminding him that an opera sometimes takes fifty years to catch on. He replied, "I have to laugh when I think of how when we're eighty the Metropolitan will give it with Martinelli as Gyp and Flagstad as Queenie, and everybody will be completely serious about it."

I'd be serious about such a production, but perhaps less appreciative than I am of the Henry Street Settlement revival. It's given in a gem of a theatre, built in 1915, and ideal in every way but one for operas on a small or moderate scale. The stage is deeper and wider than that of most small houses. The capacity is three hundred and fifty. The acoustics are warm and true. The sole drawback seems to be the depth of the orchestra pit, which sinks back under the stage instead of stationing the players in close relationship to those they accompany. In *The Second Hurricane,* the disadvantages of this Wagnerian arrangement were largely overcome—by raising a few instrumentalists on platforms, by placing the important piano (crisply played by Paul Sportelli) on the main house level—but some of the instrumental colors were muted. Everything else was vivid. There was no stage bareness this time: Steve Saklad was the set designer, and a galaxy of artists had contributed elements of his décor, among them Elaine and Willem de Kooning, Red Grooms, Larry Rivers, Robert Wilson, and John Cage. The cast of thirty, their ages ranging from eight to twenty-three, had been brilliantly directed and choreographed by Tazewell Thompson. It was an elaborate, animated, and carefully disciplined show—emotionally precise, and more spirited than anything else I've seen on the New York opera stage this season. The solo singing was true, unaffected, and unforced. The choruses were clean and punchy. Charles Barker conducted alertly.

The Second Hurricane did not have to wait fifty years for recognition. (Nor as long as Britten's *Paul Bunyan,* unheard from 1941 to 1976.) The piece had several productions. In 1960, Leonard Bernstein conducted it at a Philharmonic Young People's Concert, with students of the High School of Music and Art. Denby reported to Copland that "Lenny played it for drama, as you would expect, a trifle extra fast and extra slow if one knows the piece." He also said, "Musically it was immeasurably better than any performance ever, and the beautiful freshness of the music is ravishing." The performance—the spoken dialogue much abridged, the score slightly cut, with Fat's song about being lonely and scared the main casualty—was recorded.

The American Composers Orchestra concert in Carnegie Hall last week began with Copland's *Statements* (1935) and continued with William Schuman's Symphony for Strings (1943). The performances, conducted by Paul Dunkel, were uninspired—plain, proficient executions by a band of able professionals. At the start of the concert, David Diamond was presented with the $50,000 William Schuman Award. (It was established in 1981, at Columbia's School of the Arts, by the Bydale Foundation, to honor Schuman's seventieth birthday, and to celebrate "a lifetime achievement in American musical composition." Schuman himself was the first recipient. Diamond receives it in his seventieth-birthday year.) As the second part of the concert, Diamond's Ninth Symphony had its first performance. This Ninth, dedicated to the memory of the conductor Dimitri Mitropoulos, is a magniloquent forty-minute, two-movement work for large orchestra, begun in the early sixties and completed this year. It incorporates settings of powerful, unhappy lines by Michelangelo: "Enemy of myself, I shed my sighs and tears, but uselessly"; "I make my peace with death, since I am tired and near the end of speech"; "Sweet is my sleep—but more to be mere stone so long as ruin and dishonor reign." It is richly and fully scored, insistently rhetorical, gestural in manner, with sudden silences. Much of it seems to be unhappy, but the second movement contains some consolatory gleams. David Arnold sang the baritone solos clearly, if without fervor. Bernstein conducted an impassioned, emotional performance, and the orchestra was transformed, playing with real tone and with dramatic force.

There have been several Casanova operas and operettas, the most successful of them being Ralph Benatzky's spectacular revue-operetta *Casanova,* made from melodies by Johann Strauss II. It opened in Berlin in 1928, with Michael Bohnen and Anni Frind as the stars. (Miss Frind's record of the Nuns' Chorus remains popular.) Last April, two more appeared: Dominick Argento's *Casanova's Homecoming,* at the Ordway Music Theater, in St. Paul, and Girolamo

Arrigo's *Il ritorno di Casanova,* at the Grand Théâtre in Geneva. Both start where Casanova's memoirs break off: at his return to Venice in 1774. Arrigo's piece, which has a libretto by Giuseppe di Leva, is based on Arthur Schnitzler's novella *Casanova's Homecoming.* Argento's, which has a libretto by the composer, ingeniously refashions earlier incidents from the memoirs into a week of Venetian carnival adventure during which—Argento suggests— Casanova makes another kind of return: to being his true self again after a period of proper behavior enjoined on him as a condition of his being allowed to return to Venice. (In life, he became a spy for the Inquisition.) Toward the end of the opera, he sings the irresponsible credo with which nearly a quarter- century later he introduced his memoirs: "My system, if it can be called a system, has been to glide unconcernedly on the stream of life, trusting to the wind wherever it led."

The work, commissioned by the Minnesota Opera for the opening of the Ordway Theatre, was presented there by the company and the St. Paul Chamber Orchestra. This month—the title shortened to *Casanova*—it came to the City Opera for three performances, and it was warmly received. After the ambition shown by Argento's earlier full-length operas *The Voyage of Edgar Allan Poe* (1976) and *Miss Havisham's Fire* (1979), I found *Casanova* somewhat disappointing—unchallenging, and even a shade philistine. But a respected colleague, Peter G. Davis, found "marvelous music, a delightful and masterly- crafted entertainment," "an irrepressible ebullience that bubbles to the surface in every scene," and "the same heart-catching joviality that courses through Verdi's *Falstaff.*"

Act I concerns Casanova's seduction of a castrato in female guise. (She turns out to be a woman after all, pretending for reasons of career to be a castrato.) In Act II, he plays upon the credulity of a rich, foolish old woman in order to steal from her. In Act III, we learn, amid callous jokes, that he has caused her death. He escapes from a murder charge by declaring that for amorous reasons the crazy old woman ventured with him in secret on the lagoon, and produces a small part of her money as proof that she paid him for his service to her. The rest he has spent on a dowry and wedding for his pretty godchild, who proves to be his illegitimate daughter. As related in Casanova's memoirs, his gulling and fleecing of Mme d'Urfé is elaborate, extended, fantastic, and funny. As potted in the opera, into one unkind prank, it seemed to me more distasteful than hilarious. In the memoirs, Casanova's conventual escapades are related in elegant, almost innocently intricate detail. In the opera, there is a "one-liner" for the audience to snigger at: "I can hardly bear to leave you—but my Mother Superior will be wondering," spoken by the first of three women who scuttle from behind the hero's bed curtains at the start of Act III. Argento, it appears, began with a genuine attempt to capture the tone of the memoirs and the "zest for life" for which they and their author have been admired; and ideas of Guardi's Venice, the city's carnival, ridottos, and operatic glitter (one scene is set in the opera house, during an opera seria) evidently excited him. But in the execution the tone has been coarsened and cheapened, for a popular success too easily won.

Casanova is an efficient piece of opera-making. The principals are neatly worked into the various escapades. The music is eclectic, shot through with memories of Puccini and, more nearly, Britten—well-woven shoddy. The City Opera performance (directed by Arthur Masella, designed by Franco Colavecchia, conducted by Scott Bergeson) was efficient, too, in a superficial, conventionally "operatic" way. One performer created a character: Carol Gutknecht, as Giulietta, Casanova's former mistress, had wit and charm, and she sang well. The others (Timothy Nolen in the title role, Susanne Marsee as the faux castrato, Michele McBride as the goddaughter, Joyce Castle as a cackling Mme d'Urfé, Melissa Fogarty as Marcantonio, an urchin who becomes Casanova's apprentice) were bright and obvious. Some of the voices—but not that of David Hamilton, as the young Lorenzo Da Ponte—sounded a bit frazzled at the top. The words were often hard to catch. In abridgment, they were projected onto a screen above the stage.

Flutes, and Figaro

December 9, 1985

Wendy Rolfe gave a pleasant flutes recital in Merkin Hall last month: music by Handel, Telemann, and Bach on a boxwood, one-keyed baroque flute; by J. P. Pixis and Mozart on an 1818 crystal flute; and by Frank Martin, Harvey Sollberger, and Francis Poulenc on a modern metal instrument. *Die Zauberflöte* has now been recorded with a baroque flute in the title role—an Erato/RCA set, conducted by Ton Koopman, recorded live in the Royal Theatre in The Hague, with the Amsterdam Baroque Orchestra (largely British strings and European winds). The spoken dialogue is omitted, which makes for some jarring juxtapositions. It's a fresh, urgent performance, with light, forward voices and instruments that Mozart would have recognized; the Tamino, Guy de Mey, is outstanding, for perfectly focussed tones and beautifully distinct words. But the magic flute itself sounds feeble. Tamino's comment after its first strains—"Wie stark ist nicht dein Zauberton"—seems quite inappropriate, and through the trials by fire and water it proves but a faltering guide. This may, however, have something to do with microphone placing and the position of a stage flute, for the orchestra flutes sound fine. And Miss Rolfe's baroque flute—made two years ago, by Catherine Folkers, on the model of one by G.-A. Rottenburgh, whose flutes were famous—was clear, limpid, and lovely in tone. Its intonation, in fact, was purer than that of the nineteenth-century seven-keyed crystal flute, by Claude Laurent, on which she chose to play Mozart. The piece was the arrangement for flute, in D, of the C-major Rondo for violin and orchestra, K. 373; the fourth note of the rondo theme, an A, tended to sag.

In the mid–nineteenth century, Theobald Boehm redesigned the flute, making it into the modern instrument that can be kept in tune in all dynamics, at all ranges. When Miss Rolfe returned after the intermission to play a Boehm flute, the sound was shocking at first—full, fat, and furry after the more delicate boxwood and crystal notes. But soon, of course, one's modern ears adjusted to the familiar instrument and heard delicacy in music that had been written for it. Sollberger's *Riding the Wind II,* for solo flute, exploits the sonic possibilities of the modern instrument beyond what its inventor intended, with a noisy clicking and clacking of its keys such as flute students learn to avoid, with breathiness, with broken notes, chords, and counterpoints that form no natural part of the instrument's utterance. It's an exciting piece, and Miss Rolfe's account of it was arresting.

In Richard Strauss's opera *Intermezzo,* the hero defends his wife's abrasive, extravagant behavior by declaring that she puts some gunpowder in him. Sollberger's *Riding the Wind II* put some gunpowder in Miss Rolfe. Elsewhere, I felt, she had charm, poetry, sensitivity, and rare technical ability—it was certainly an enjoyable recital—but perhaps not the fire that makes one go away with the memory of how certain phrases were delivered singing on in one's mind. She played everything with her eyes glued to the score. That's not important unless it also *sounds.* When I tried listening without looking, I thought that it did sound: that even from a recording of the recital a listener might deduce that she was playing from the page—not addressing her audience with full, free mastery, responding to its responses. (Contrariwise, that *Zauberflöte* recording can fill even a solitary listener with the sense that artists and audience are together bringing the work to life, with mutual, spontaneous rapture.) Miss Rolfe played Telemann's A-minor Fantasy for solo flute, I felt, with insufficient fantasy and boldness—not ending a thought decisively before embarking on the next. Notions of toying with the music and teasing the audience—in Handel, Mozart, Poulenc—were missing. But there was grace in her phrasing. A Romance by Pixis (a composer best remembered as a contributor, along with Liszt and Chopin, to the *Hexameron*), Martin's Ballade, and the central movement of Poulenc's Sonata were lyrically handled.

The baroque flute was accompanied in Handel and Bach by a gamba and a harpsichord, played by Alice Robbins and Wendy Young. The crystal flute was accompanied by a fortepiano, played by John Van Buskirk, who played a Steinway in the Martin and Poulenc works. The platform dispositions were for soloist with accompaniment, not for players making chamber music together— Miss Rolfe turned her back on the harpsichord—but in fact the ensemble throughout the evening was amiable and well balanced.

An authentic-instrument *Così fan tutte* has also arrived on record, from Oiseau-Lyre. Arnold Östman conducts the Drottningholm Court Theatre Orchestra, which has some members in common with the Amsterdam ensemble. (The string first desks contain the Salomon Quartet, which opened Merkin Hall's On Original Instruments series this season.) It's a frank, forthright performance, and on that count likable. There are some pleasantly strong and decisive utterances in the recitatives. The wind players are expert, and their sextet-serenade that opens the garden scene of Act II is beguiling in timbre. But Mr. Östman is often brisk or square to the point of roughness; again and again he leaves no time or space for the singers and the players to shape their phrases carefully, to sound the marvels of the music. Moreover, the men—Gösta Winbergh as Ferrando, the veterans Tom Krause and Carlos Feller as Guglielmo and Don Alfonso—sing in the standard international Mozart style of our day, and none too well at that. Unlike the new *Flute* recording, the new *Così* is not a fresh, careful essay in the re-creation of a Mozartian performance in all its details. The text is an odd mixture of modern barbarisms (in the form of blunt, repeated-note phrase endings) and accuracy. The set can be prized instrumentally, and dramatically for some vivid points made by Rachel Yakar's Fiordiligi in recitatives (the arias tax her) and by Alicia Nafé's Dorabella in both recitatives and arias. Otherwise, it demonstrates that using the right instruments is not in itself enough; there's more of the essential *Così* in the old, unauthentic recordings conducted by Fritz Busch and Karl Böhm. Unlike them, however, this new version is complete. And Guglielmo's rejected aria "Rivolgete a lui lo sguardo" is included as an appendix.

Many of the world's operatic cities have a *Nozze di Figaro* directed and designed by Jean-Pierre Ponnelle. New York's version arrived last month, at the Metropolitan Opera. It is a polished and precise execution, as one would expect from someone whose staging of the opera has been through so many "editions." In some ways, however, the drama is overdirected and is weakened by elaboration. Mr. Ponnelle can seldom resist adding to the original stage pictures. Mozart began his Act II with the Countess alone onstage—all the other characters have been introduced in lively dialogue—reflecting on her emotion-ally lonely life. It's a striking image. Mr. Ponnelle adds Susanna to the scene. Elsewhere, there are similar excrescences: a chorus appears at the end of the Count's aria, for example.

The basic set is a three-bay triumphal arch whose stuccoed surface is peeling and decrepit; in several places the interior brickwork shows through. Perhaps it proclaims that the world is built of bricks and that the aristocrats' elegant plastered façade will soon disappear altogether. Behind the arch, the various rooms of the first three acts take shape. The outer bays hold doors in Acts I and II; in Act III, the palace throne room, they become gun-filled niches; and in Act IV they are spanned by garden gates. It's a handsome décor, executed in tasteful shades of brown and gray, with some white and some black costumes, and with touches of color provided by Cherubino's blue breeches, Dr. Bartolo's blue coat, Marcellina's purplish-brown bustle, and the battered red carnation that Antonio brings into the second-act finale. Some of the costuming is odd. Cherubino enters as a modern rock star, with a huge tangled mane, an extravagantly frilly blouse, skintight satin breeches, and bare feet. The Countess wears a Fortuny nightdress, and she walks through the palace corridor wearing it. In Acts III and IV, she wears a hat. Susanna, in the Act II cabinet (and, in terms of the plot, alone there), manages to lace herself into a wedding dress that surely must require a dresser's assistance. The Countess makes her last entrance—for the episode that Joseph Kerman called "the most beautiful thing in the opera"—still wearing Susanna's short skirt, and loses dignity thereby.

Possible architectural symbolism apart, little attention is paid to the opera's revolutionary content. But then this was a curiously bland *Figaro* from every dramatic point of view. There was little menace in Figaro's defiance of his master, and any danger in the Count was suggested not by Thomas Allen's delivery of the fierce, vindictive aria but by a stagy lighting effect: a lamp beside the prompter's box came on and cast a giant shadow on the wall behind the singer. The class war and the sex war are far from being the whole of *Figaro*, but an audience should share emotions that are strong, deep, and sometimes painful. This performance remained on a decorative level. It was as if the drama had been composed by Paisiello, not by Mozart. The setting did nothing to combat the house's unsuitability for Mozart. Carol Vaness, the Countess, was way upstage at the start of "Porgi amor"—far from the orchestra, even farther from the audience.

James Levine conducted the overture fast—too fast for the notes to tell. Nearly a century ago, Bernard Shaw said, "If you want to ascertain whether a musician is hopelessly belated, benighted, out of date, and behind his time, ask him how this overture should be played. If he replies 'In three and a half minutes,' away with him at once; he is guilty." On the first night, Mr. Levine certainly seemed guilty, and in textual matters he and his cast were certainly benighted and out of date. One doesn't expect—wouldn't want—to hear authentic instruments in a Met *Figaro* but does expect to find an educated approach to eighteenth-century musical notation. This performance had dozens, perhaps hundreds, of wrong notes in the form of missing appoggiaturas, and all Mozart's invitations to gracing and to cadenzas were gracelessly declined. In Shaw's day, singers still knew about such things. (I didn't in fact mind the shocking hole Miss Vaness left in the middle of "Dove sono," for she used it to dramatic—to shock—effect.) On the other hand, after the initial misjudgment Mr. Levine led a beautifully rehearsed, loving, and expertly played performance, which held many passages of musical delight. Mr. Ponnelle's production contains some ensemble episodes where the singers "freeze" and, eyes on the conductor, concentrate on balance, tuning, and rhythmic exactitude. All these were good to hear.

Kathleen Battle was the Susanna. She has Elisabeth Schumann's secret of being sparkly and melting at once. (Schumann had left the stage in the years when I heard her, but to the end she retained what Desmond Shawe-Taylor, in the New Grove, calls "a beautifully controlled high soprano of delicate, ringing timbre and of crystalline purity," and in her recitals it was easy to discern still the "charming stage presence, especially in demure, mischievous parts"—qualities that in combination "made her ravishing as Susanna." She recorded Susanna's two arias.) Great singers sometimes utter a word or two in a way that listeners never forget. Years after he heard it, Verdi recalled the way Adelina Patti sang Gilda's "Io l'amo," in the last act of *Rigoletto:* "No expression can express the sublime effect of this word as she uttered it," he told Giulio Ricordi. Bellini was transported by the way Maria Malibran sang Amina's phrase "Ah, m'abbraccia," in the finale of *La sonnambula*. (In fact, she sang "Ah, embrace me," for this was at a Drury Lane performance in Sir Henry Bishop's English version.) I'll not forget the way Maria Callas sang Norma's "Son io," in the last act of Bellini's *Norma*. Or the way Elisabeth Schwarzkopf (modelling herself on Melba) sang the single word "Bada," in Mimì's farewell. Or the way Miss Battle (modelling herself on Schumann, perhaps) sang the single word "Bravo" in Susanna's first aria. Just two notes, a drop from G to D—but struck with a certainty, sounded in a timbre, and joined by a subtle portamento that gave exquisite pleasure. The arcs of the second aria were traced in tones of crystalline purity. Miss Battle's stage motion was not always quite so sure; she tended to wave her arms about. I'd like to hear her in an intimate house and in a more intimate kind of production.

Miss Vaness's Countess was promising, but there were problems of scale. This is a big voice. When Miss Vaness essayed, commendably, to draw it down to a very fine line, that line sometimes faltered. And there were moments of stage gaucheness in a generally graceful portrayal. Frederica von Stade's Cherubino is familiar; she was in the last Met production of the opera, ten years ago. Her singing has become almost too smooth; runs that Mozart slurred in paired notes were so evenly emitted that something of the youth's impetuosity was lost. Ruggero Raimondi was an excellent—if perhaps too consistently amiable—Figaro. The production makes the hero rather more of a peasant, less of a gentleman's gentleman, than usual. Mr. Allen's Count seemed small-scale in the Met; neither the voice nor the personality told strongly in that enormous space.

At the New York Flute Club concert in CAMI Hall last week, Judith Pearce played an instrument made by Albert Cooper—a modern flutemaker who has added refinement, in the matter of exactly where the holes should be placed, to Boehm's design. Miss Pearce was once the flutist of the Fires of London—she can be heard on the Unicorn recordings of Peter Maxwell Davies's *Eight Songs for a Mad King* and *Vesalii Icones*—and now lives in New York. Several composers have written for her; two of them were represented on this program. Nicholas Maw's *Night Thoughts* (1982), for solo flute, is ten minutes of ardent but disciplined lyricism. Davies's *The Kestrel Paced Round the Sun* (1975) is five minutes of graphic, inspired imagery; it stands high in the catalogue of "bird" compositions for solo wind which I wrote about last month. The title comes from the Orkney poet George Mackay Brown.

Miss Pearce is a pleasing player. Perfect intonation makes a good start. Her tone is strong, firm, and full—never bloated, and free from the wobble that disfigures (except when a composer calls for it) much flute playing. It's an individual, subtly inflected voice. But, like Miss Rolfe, Miss Pearce performed everything from the page, even the works that were written for her. She suggested a flute-playing Alice—well-mannered, sweetly reasonable, logical and imaginative at once. Alice is adorable. W. H. Auden found her "an adequate symbol for what every human being should try to be like." But a public performer should have a touch of flamboyance as well, in certain works. The finale of Spohr's E-flat Sonata, Opus 113, for flute and harp, needs more "presentation" than Miss Pearce gave it; it needs to be phrased with a smile. Perhaps the sober mien—unlike the usual infectious panache of Fires players—was adopted specially for this concert given not so much for the general public as for the specialist audience of the Flute Club. The ear could discover both a master of the instrument and a cogent, gleaming, poetic artist. The accompanists were Elizabeth DiFelice, piano, in Charles Koechlin's Fourteen Pieces and Carl Reinecke's *Undine* sonata, and Kathleen Bride, harp, in the Spohr and in William Alwyn's *Naiades*. At a time when several American soloists have moved to London, Miss Pearce adds something to New York's musical life.

NIGHTINGALES AND EAGLES

December 16, 1985

IN the three days after Thanksgiving, the Fires of London, conducted by Peter Maxwell Davies, gave five concerts—well, five music-theatre performances—in Alice Tully Hall. I'll wait to write about them till after Davies's latest opera, *The No. 11 Bus,* has had its American première (in Stamford, Connecticut, the next stop on the Fires' American tour). Meanwhile, let me worry at a question put to me by a young American composer at one of the Fires events: "Why do we not have in America a group that plays as well as the Fires?" The question, I think, is fair. The simple retort, "But we do, and more than one: Speculum Musicae and the Da Capo Chamber Players, for a start," covers the plain fact that, player for player, America's best instrumentalists are not less able than Britain's. I've heard peerless performances from those ensembles. But there is a difference.

Had the question been "Why do we have nothing like the Fires (or, for that matter, the London Sinfonietta, or IRCAM's Ensemble InterContemporain, or the BBC Symphony, or the Proms)?" answers would have to be sought in the economics of the music business, the level of music education in public schools, the extent of government support for the nation's creators and their interpreters, and the lack of a national, coördinated radio system providing employment, enjoyment, and education in a systematic, not a haphazard, way. Reasons for a difference in the kind of playing are more simply found. For one thing, the Fires work together constantly, giving about fifty concerts a year. (Speculum has only six New York concerts this season and four or five outside New York; Da Capo has four in New York and six elsewhere. The Fires have played Elliott Carter's Triple Duo in public about twenty times; Speculum has played it four times.) So, of course, they become an ensemble finely tuned one to another, bringing music to life in the light of full familiarity with it and in the knowledge of what happens during performances. That's different from giving just one or two accounts of a difficult new work, however careful the rehearsals may have been.

Second—and as a consequence—being a member of the Fires is likely to be a musician's main occupation, whatever his or her other engagements. Being a member of one of New York's contemporary-music ensembles, on the other hand, can hardly be a first occupation. These ensembles (among them the Contemporary Chamber Ensemble, Da Capo, the Group for Contemporary Music, the League/ISCM Chamber Players, Merkin Hall's Music Today ensemble, Musical Elements, the New Music Consort, the New York New Music Ensemble, Parnassus, and Speculum) draw largely from the same pool of Manhattan free-lance instrumentalists—marvellous players—who must be here today, somewhere else tomorrow. I see and hear them night after night under different banners, in orchestras and in ensembles. Their work is always proficient. Sometimes it is eloquent, dedicated, and thoroughly rehearsed. But sometimes the result is kin to American opera performance as Sarah Caldwell described it recently: opera performers in this country, she said, "never really have enough time anywhere—*anywhere*—to rehearse, and they become facile. They learn how to learn music rapidly, and they learn how to sometimes look like they're acting in a production—how to adapt quickly when there isn't time. And so, because you're the sum product of your experiences, you develop a kind of artistry that is a product of this. And, we are all capable of a much higher level of artistry."

A third answer to that questioner is that the Fires are stoked by a great composer, one who provides them with a large part—though by no means all—of their repertory, who writes for their special strengths, who lives with them in a relationship of mutual inspiration, learning from their work and moving them to new achievement. Haydn had this accord with his Esterházy players and singers, and Rossini and Donizetti with their Neapolitan companies. Britten had it with the English Opera Group, and Stockhausen has it with his performing "family" of daughter, sons, and companions. The nearest New York equivalent is probably the Group for Contemporary Music, founded by Charles Wuorinen and Harvey Sollberger, but those composers don't have year-round day-to-day contact with their interpreters. (My arguing is, inevitably, Manhattan-based; I don't know the work of, for example, the Chicago Contemporary Chamber Players, founded and directed by the composer Ralph Shapey, well enough to take it into account.) The relationship is not necessary for great composition—neither Mozart nor Schubert directed a regular company or ensemble; Elliott Carter doesn't—but a company or ensemble thus directed is privileged.

Musical Elements, directed by Daniel Asia and Robert Beaser, is giving three concerts this season, in the Great Hall at Cooper Union. The sound there is bright and immediate, but occasionally some piece of machinery joins in with a soft low boom. I try not to miss Elements concerts. Contemporary-music events are sometimes solemn, gritty affairs; Mr. Asia and Mr. Beaser have a gift for choosing works that combine charm and grace with challenge. They are composers in their own right but bill their own works seldom. Their programs usually combine music from abroad (I recall with pleasure works by Henze, Hans Abrahamsen, Robert Saxton, Jonathan Lloyd first met at Cooper Union), new American works, and works from the recent past worth hearing again. The first concert of the season, last month, began with Ellen Taaffe Zwilich's Chamber Symphony (1979), scored for the "*Pierrot* quintet" and a viola; Mr. Beaser conducted a tense, passionate, and moving performance. There followed Stephen Albert's Joyce song cycle *To Wake the Dead* (1978), for soprano and the "*Pierrot* quintet," plus an "assistant" who helps to stop or pluck piano strings and, in the last song, holds sustained chords on a harmonium. (Elements used a small synthesizer.) The piece has become fairly well known. There are two recordings, on CRI and in the Smithsonian Collection series, and the score is published by Carl Fischer. This performance was sung by Carmen Pelton in a limpid, beautiful soprano and was conducted by Mr. Asia. The concert ended—I pass over, here and later, pieces that left no strong impression—with the American première of Hans Abrahamsen's *Märchenbilder,* for a chamber orchestra of fourteen players. Everything of Abrahamsen's I have heard has proved captivating. *Märchenbilder,* which he composed last year for the London Sinfonietta, is a twelve-minute work of flickering enchantment, tiny pastorals, sudden alarming or blissful visions. It is busily but exquisitely written, with the lightest of touches, and the forms are cunningly shaped. Mr. Beaser conducted.

Elements sometimes tackles works that, it proves, there has not been rehearsal time enough to bring to fully polished and precise performance, but I have not heard the ensemble give a sloppy, uncaring, or dry performance, or misrepresent the spirit of a composition. The playing is warm, eager, and communicative, and the individual instrumentalists are expert.

Parnassus, directed by Anthony Korf, has two Merkin Hall concerts this season; and the Winds of Parnassus blow in Tully Hall in February. I've sometimes teased the group in print for its earnestness, for its appearing to regard music-making as a grimly serious matter, without a playful side. Unlike Wilde's Algernon, it can seem to rate accuracy above "wonderful expression." But I have thrilled to Parnassus performances of Varèse, Stravinsky, Schoenberg, Stefan Wolpe, Wuorinen that were both fervent and precise. The first concert of the season, last month, began with an unrelaxed, unwinning account of Copland's Duo for flute (Keith Underwood) and piano (Edmund Niemann). But it also brought the American première of Abrahamsen's Six Pieces, for violin, horn, and piano, lightly and wittily played by Cyrus Stevens, David Wakefield, and Mr. Niemann. The six sharply characterized miniatures are entitled "Serenade," "Arabesque," "Blues," "Marcia Funebre," "Scherzo Misterioso," and "For the Children." It was pleasing to find merry Abrahamsen granted admission to Parnassus's bracing heights. His work was commissioned (by the Danish Radio) to be done on a program with Ligeti's Horn Trio, and is drawn, with sharpened contours, from his Ten Studies for Piano.

The concert included a strongly colored, thoughtful, and full-toned account of Carter's *Canon for 4,* played by Mr. Underwood, Anand Devendra (bass clarinet), Mr. Stevens, and Chris Finckel (cello), and it ended with Stockhausen's early *Kontra-Punkte* (1953), for piano (Mr. Niemann) with nine other instruments. *Kontra-Punkte* is a fiendish piece to play—a metrical maze in which almost every note has its own dynamic indication. I think it was pretty accurately done. (That's only an impression, strengthened by trust in Parnassian punctiliousness.) But it didn't take off. The tempo keeps changing; *Kontra-Punkte* needs elegant, careful conducting. Mr. Korf, beating out a conscientious three (occasionally five) to a bar through five hundred and thirty bars of 3/8, at tempos ranging from an indicated eighth-note = 120 to eighth-note = 200, controlled the heady dance of contrapuntal lines, and the work lasted a third as long again as the duration suggested in the score.

I missed Speculum's first concert of the season, given in Merkin Hall in October, but have caught up with it on tape—a tape clear and vivid enough to show that Berg's Chamber Concerto, for violin, piano, and thirteen winds, had a stunning performance. A quarter-century ago, the work seemed problematical, difficult to balance, even graceless. (More so, no doubt, in 1927, when it had its first performance.) The epithets will surprise young people who learn it in performances as confident, as graceful, as romantic as Speculum's—or the Group for Contemporary Music's in 1981, with Benjamin Hudson the violinist, Robert Black the pianist, and Mr. Sollberger the conductor. For Speculum, Mr. Hudson was again the violinist, Aleck Karis was the pianist, and Mr. Black conducted. The program was historical: before the Berg, two early works of Stockhausen, *Kreuzspiel* (1951) and *Zeitmasze* (1956), divided by one of his "intuitive" compositions from the sixties—*Interval*, from the *For Times to Come* series. *Kreuzspiel*, for piano (here Mr. Karis) with oboe, bass clarinet, and the three percussionists, caused an uproar at its first performance; it has become a classic. Again, I remember early, anxious accounts in which the "line" of the piece was hard to follow. Not so here. *Zeitmasze*, a woodwind quintet, needs to be seen as well as heard: it is plotted partly by measured pulses, partly by "subjective" ones ("as fast/slow as possible"), and the composer wants the players' demeanor to mirror the plot. *Interval*, for two pianists, has six strophes of verbal instruction as its score and is more interesting to perform than it is to listen to.

Changes of personnel and of typical repertory have made Speculum hard to characterize, but the ensemble seems to be in buoyant form. In a fifteenth-anniversary tribute, Wuorinen hails musicians who bring to contemporary music the flair of virtuosi and love that goes "beyond the requirements of the merely professional." The tribute appears in a Speculum booklet planned to be at once a companion to the season's programs and "a forum for debate." The first issue contains an essay by David Schiff, "Toward Virtuosity," urging listeners to play a "heroic role" as "we compose the pieces we hear along with the composer" and "perform them along with the performers." The next concert consists of Henze's *El cimarrón*. A fifteenth-birthday concert in May promises what one thinks of as distinctive Speculum fare: Wuorinen, Carter, Mario Davidovsky, and Milton Babbitt.

Da Capo might be called the poets of the contemporary-music scene. The basic ensemble is a "*Pierrot* quintet": Patricia Spencer (flute), Laura Flax (clarinet), Joel Lester (violin), André Emelianoff (cello), and, new this season, Sarah Rothenberg (piano). Assemblage for rehearsals must be easier and less costly than with the larger groups. In the musical-chairs melee of bringing new music to performance, rehearsal time can be—and often is—saved by employing a conductor to lay out a work that the instrumentalists have not yet learned so well as to be able to play it as chamber music. (The Fires do Carter's Triple Duo, Davies's *Ave Maris Stella* and *Image, Reflection, Shadow* as chamber music; American performances I've heard of those works have used a conductor.) Da Capo, a week after the Elements' conducted performance of Albert's *To Wake the Dead*, gave a chamber-music account of the cycle, in Symphony Space. It had the intentness, delicacy of balance, and fineness of detail that result from each player's knowing the whole piece intimately, not just his or her own line. I had admired the work before but now felt I was hearing it fully for the first time. Lucy Shelton, as on the Smithsonian recording, was the soprano, and she was in beautiful voice. At the heart of the cycle lies the magical Humpty-Dumpty song from the page of *Finnegans Wake* that breaks into musical notation. Albert raises

Joyce's tune at its first appearance, by a tenth; Miss Shelton sang it with high, crystalline purity and shaped every word clearly. The concert began with James Greeson's Fantasy for Five Players (1984), written for Da Capo. It seemed to be a piece both intelligent and imaginative, but not concise. There were two lively, lyrical performances of Carter's *Canon for 4*, one before and one after a trenchant, sharp-cut account of Wolpe's exuberant Trio in Two Parts (1963), for flute, cello, and piano.

By calling the Da Capo players "poets" I mean to suggest that their virtuosity is of a thoughtful, satisfying kind, that there is no "automatic" glitter—dazzle for dazzle's sake—in their playing (although there is swift, sure brilliance whenever the music calls for it), that their phrasing is warmly eloquent, that their performances excite the imagination as well as admiration. ("That's a great deal to make one word mean," as Alice said to Humpty-Dumpty.) The next Da Capo Concert is a "da capo" program—new hearings of works composed for the group over the years.

UNHAPPY QUEEN AND HAPPY PRINCE

December 23, 1985

OXFORD has launched a new series of musicological monographs, Studies in Musical Genesis and Structure, edited by Lewis Lockwood. Each volume is to deal with "an individual work by an important composer." Philip Gossett was invited to contribute an account of Beethoven's "Pastoral" Symphony. (He is the author of an important study on the sketches for the first movement.) Instead, he elected to write about a Donizetti opera, and his *Anna Bolena and the Artistic Maturity of Gaetano Donizetti* inaugurates the series. Beethoven and Donizetti used some of the same singers: Carolina Ungher, the alto of the Ninth Symphony and the Missa Solemnis, was Donizetti's Parisina, his Antonina in *Belisario*, his Maria di Rudenz; Domenico Donzelli, the tenor of Beethoven's trio "Tremate, empi, tremate" in 1824, had earlier that year created the role of Almuzir in *Zoraida di Granata*, Donizetti's first success, and was later Ugo, Conte di Parigi, and Ruiz in *Maria Padilla*. (Bellini also composed for Ungher and for Donzelli.) Not until recently, however, has Donizetti been reckoned a respectable topic for musicological research of the kind to which Beethoven has long been subject.

Mr. Gossett's book will prove enthralling to everyone who has been stirred by *Anna Bolena*—as thousands of people have been since Maria Callas, at La Scala in 1957, restored the once-popular opera to the international repertory. Many revivals followed. After citing the accepted view—that in *Anna Bolena*, the thirtieth of Donizetti's seventy-odd operas and his first international success, the composer for the first time broke the Rossinian molds and found his personal style—the author declares it to be an assertion often made, often repeated, but hitherto unsupported by much evidence. So he tests it, and after a careful examination of the composer's autograph he establishes its "essential truth." Donizetti made many changes, large and small, as he composed *Anna Bolena,* and he rewrote the important soprano-tenor duet altogether, in a form that limns the characters more sharply but taxes the singers severely; a strenuous finale follows. (The alternative duet was published separately from the rest of the opera; Eve Queler revived it in the *Anna Bolena* she conducted in San Diego two years ago.) In a chapter on this duet, Mr. Gossett says: "All the examples of changes in detail and melodic variation present in *Anna Bolena* and other scores of Donizetti very nearly find in this first section of the new Duetto for Anna and Percy their quintessential exemplification. The composer transforms the rather formal encounter of the archetypical Rossinian duet into a confrontation of characters burning with passion." And his conclusion is that as we catch the composer "in the act of making compositional decisions: decisions affecting phrases, periods, entire sections; decisions concerning details, proportion, continuity, and large-scale structure" we find that while his first instinct is to follow Rossinian precedent, his alterations "express impatience with these models," and "we can watch Donizetti tentatively pressing against his boundaries." The book is generously illustrated with music type: we can, indeed, watch the composer at work. And Mr. Gossett doesn't simply set out facts. He speculates on reasons for the changes. He assesses their dramatic effectiveness, and not all of them are approved. This is humane musicology—musicology-as-criticism. The reader becomes a sharper and more responsive listener to *Anna Bolena,* has a keener understanding of the way Donizetti's mind worked and of what he endeavored to do.

The author has deliberately addressed himself to testing, in the common assertion about the opera, only one proposition: that in *Anna Bolena* Donizetti broke the Rossinian molds (of which Mr. Gossett, editor-in-chief of the new Rossini edition, has a knowledge unparalleled). To what extent Donizetti had been doing this in his previous operas is left to later studies. Another study—I commend it to graduates in quest of a Ph.D. topic—could profitably be made of *Anna Bolena* and Bellini's *Beatrice di Tenda.* The two operas have the same basic plot: Beatrice, Agnese, Orombello, and Visconti are a second Anne Boleyn, Jane Seymour, Percy, and Henry VIII. The main difference is that the ambitious mezzo, wooed by the amorous, tyrant bass, also loves the tenor. (In other words, Agnese is a Jane Seymour with a strong dash of Princess Eboli.) Otherwise, the situations are similar and give rise to encounters carrying the same formal imperatives. Felice Romani (the librettist of both operas) and Bellini were well aware of this, and they strove to avoid copycat charges. Such a study could open out to illumine the way that Bellini and Donizetti against the background of the Code Rossini—like Haydn and Mozart against the background of eighteenth-century common practice—inspired one another, turn and turn about. Bellini in his early operas did much to initiate *canto d'azione,* of ferocious declamation, which Donizetti then adopted (and which Verdi later developed from Donizetti), while Bellini himself became more "mellifluous." In 1830–31 (with *Anna Bolena* and *La sonnambula* at the Teatro Carcano) and again in 1831–32 (with *Norma* and *Ugo, conte di Parigi* at La Scala), the two composers were set in competition. Bellini evaded the first challenge, by dropping his *Ernani* and answering the dramatic *Anna Bolena* with the pastoral *Sonnambula*. When *Norma* had triumphed over *Ugo*, he was ready, in *Beatrice,* to take up the challenge of *Anna Bolena*. (His melodic manner, incidentally, became more Donizettian.) In 1835, there was another "confrontation," with *I puritani* and *Marino Faliero* at the Théâtre-Italien, written—as *Norma* and *Ugo* had been—for the same four principals. (In fairness to the generous-minded Donizetti, it should be added that it was only Bellini—and a public eager to play favorites—who treated the paired commissions as competition bouts.) Later that year, Donizetti capped Bellini's *I puritani* with *Lucia di Lammermoor*—similarly structured, similar in subject matter—even rewriting one of its melodies in a more interesting and affecting form. Bellini died three days before *Lucia* reached the stage; Donizetti's next opera, *Belisario,* seems to pay tribute to him.

I'm making unsupported assertions comparable to those which Mr. Gossett deplores in critics of *Anna Bolena* from 1830 to the present day. If life were longer, if many centuries of music did not claim listeners' attention, and if newspapers and magazines ran regularly to pages of music type, critics could perhaps demonstrate their points to musicologists' satisfaction. (I shored up the Bellini-Donizetti observations years ago in the medium of radio, which allows listeners to hear the evidence.) It is good that Mr. Gossett has discovered, weighed, and printed so much detailed evidence for the "essential truth" of what people for over a century have been saying about *Anna Bolena,* and that in doing so he has made possible a nicer, fuller appreciation of the work.

When Callas first sang Anna, enraptured listeners didn't bother about the many cuts that had been made in Donizetti's work; there was so much else to discover and admire. But the performance prompted study of the score. When the opera was staged later with the same disfiguring cuts but in lesser productions than Luchino Visconti's and with heroines less spellbinding than Callas had been, it was hard to condone the butchery. It was impossible to condone butchery even more severe in New York's latest revival of *Anna Bolena,* a concert performance given in Avery Fisher Hall last month and carried across the country by television. Joan Sutherland was the star, and her husband, Richard Bonynge, conducted. Will Dame Joan become an Angelica Catalani of our day? Catalani was a prodigiously gifted prima donna of the early nineteenth century who arranged works around her own appearances in them (to an extent that, as the fifth Grove puts it, "destroyed opera" at the King's and later at the Théâtre-Italien while she reigned at those theatres). Her proud husband defined the style: "Ma femme et quatre ou cinq poupées—voilà tout ce qu'il faut." The best of the *poupées* in the Fisher Hall *Bolena* was Cynthia Clarey, as Smeaton (a role Janet Baker sang in New York nineteen years ago): she lost half her romanza and all her cavatina.

Dame Joan had a public triumph and was applauded to the skies. For thirty-three years I've admired her, in a variety of roles—among them Frasquita in *Carmen,* Aida, Agathe, Amelia in *Ballo,* Eva, and Pamina. At the age of fifty-nine, she retains plenty of voice and uncommon agility. The lower notes have faded—they were never strong—and some important recitative moments were pushed up an octave. Edward Dent may have exaggerated when, thirty years ago, he said that "the grandeur and genuine passion of *Anna Bolena* and other operas of that type lies not in the arias, but in the force and rapidity of the dialogue," yet without forceful, passionate declamation a soprano can hardly be a convincing Anna. Dame Joan's timbre was often clouded. Still, in its way this was an impressive performance. And there is ample precedent for tailoring a role to display the strengths and mask the weaknesses of a prima donna. Other things were more distressing: above all, the snipping away of two, four, eight, eighty bars all over the place, in a manner suggesting contempt for Donizetti's periods and proportions (Mr. Gossett's chapters "The Search for Continuity" and "Problems of Balance and Proportion" demonstrate the care the composer took with these), and contempt for musical syntax beyond that of immediate chord sequence. (If a reader cuts from the first "in" of this paragraph to the "in" of the sentence before this parenthesis, the result is still "grammatical," but it hardly expresses my meaning.)

Judith Forst was a blowsy Jane Seymour. (For convenience, I called this a mezzo role, since mezzos usually tackle it today, but in fact it was written—like Adalgisa in *Norma*—for a young soprano.) Jerry Hadley, once so promising, gave charm and elegance to a few of Percy's phrases, but much of the time he bawled in the modern manner. "Honeyed elegance" was Henry Chorley's phrase for Giovanni Battista Rubini, the first Percy. Gregory Yurisich, an Australian bass-baritone, has a strong, grainy voice; he planted his feet and belted out Henry's music at a monotonous forte, without expression. Mr. Bonynge's conducting was brisk and coarse. It was the sort of performance in which the artists stop singing as the end of a number approaches, gathering strength to scream out unwritten high notes, regardless of harmony, through the final tonic-and-dominant cadences.

Donizetti was better served by the Vineyard Opera Shop's presentation of his next opera, *Gianni di Parigi,* in its American première. ("Probably his next opera," I should say: the autograph is undated, but the circumstantial evidence is strong.) An avowal that I spent the evening in a state of euphoric delight does not mean that I think the Vineyard singers should forthwith replace Dame Joan and the others on the world's stages. The performance was on a tiny scale: it was given in the Susan Bloch Theatre, on West Twenty-sixth Street, which holds 137 people; it was accompanied by an ensemble of piano, flute, clarinet, and bassoon (the work had been deftly rescored by the music director, James Kurtz); and it had a male-voice chorus of three (Gregory Gunder, Paul Shipper, and John Tarr). But there was an imaginative matching of resources to requirements (the three-man representation of a long regal procession was an entertaining tour de force) which brought pleasure in its own right. The singing was perfectly scaled to the space, and therefore made the impact that big voices make in a big house only when they are unforced. (In any case, purity and projection matter more than size: Kirsten Flagstad did not shatter the hundred-seat Mermaid Theatre, and Kathleen Battle fills the four-thousand-seat Met with sweet, true tone.) Not a note of the published vocal score was cut. (I put it that way, cautiously, because *Gianni*—like every Donizetti opera—has its textual problems, and I've done no research on it; for all I know, the published score is accurate.) So one heard Donizetti's carefully balanced periods as he planned them. Above all, there was the sustained enchantment of listening—intently, intimately—to a masterly

Donizetti composition for the first time. If *Gianni di Parigi* were as familiar as *L'elisir d'amore* and *Don Pasquale,* one would probably rate it below them. It holds less of the rich human comedy that (except in performance by buffoons) shines in those works. *Gianni* is a divertissement—but a captivating one.

Donizetti wrote it for Rubini and gave it to him to take to Paris and London as something to sing on a benefit night. In Naples, Rubini had already been the hero of Donizetti's *Gianni di Calais,* another romantic comedy based on a French original, and had sung in Francesco Morlacchi's *Gianni di Parigi.* Donizetti reset the Morlacchi libretto, which is by Romani, based on Boieldieu's *Jean de Paris.* Johnny from Paris is in fact the French Dauphin in disguise as a rich commoner. He has come (like Don Carlos at the start of Verdi's opera) to make advance observation of his destined bride, the Princess of Navarre. She recognizes him at once, doesn't let on, and plays along to the point of responding to Johnny's amorous advances. Consternation on the Dauphin's part yields to mirth and general rejoicing when the Princess reveals that she knew all along who he was. The setting is a hostelry. The innkeeper is a rich buffo role. His pretty daughter, the second soprano, flirts merrily with Johnny's page, Oliviero, a mezzo-en-travesti role. The Princess's very proper seneschal, shocked by his mistress's readiness to be familiar with a commoner, completes the cast. He's a fussy buffo, the landlord is a jolly one, and the two have a delightful duet. It is a neat and witty libretto. The Vineyard company sang the piece in Italian, and although much of it was badly pronounced, all of it was clear. The company *used* the text and made much of it. Another factor contributing to euphoria was the pleasure of hearing a libretto unread in advance—a libretto by Romani, that most graceful of all opera poets—unfold so clearly and intelligibly.

The work to which *Gianni di Parigi* is closest in spirit, musically and dramatically, is Rossini's bewitching late comedy *Le Comte Ory.* I have been unable to establish positively that Donizetti knew it. His Neapolitan company did *Ory* while he was in Milan, for *Anna Bolena.* On the journey north, he left Rome just before *Ory* was given there (it may have been in rehearsal), and the first Milan run of the piece was over before his arrival in the city. But the score was published, and the opera was making the Italian rounds. (Giuditta Pasta, the first Anna, had already sung in it.) The evidence of one's ears declares that Donizetti knew *Ory.* He didn't simply "copy"; but, for example, the shaping of the soprano-tenor duet, the melodic contours, and the way the voices enter suggest that it inspired him. Bellini was also in his ears; a lovely D-flat period in that duet is in purest Bellinian vein.

The Vineyard has done enjoyable Donizetti before: *Betly* and *Il giovedì grasso.* *Gianni di Parigi* reached a new level. As the Princess, Ilya Speranza ran through roulades with delicate precision; she shaped and timed phrases, lyrical and brilliant, in a way that made one listen. In the title role, Richard Slade tackled high Rubini tessitura without straining and made it sound easy. He sang gracefully. He was not much of an actor; neither, by all accounts, was Rubini, who, Chorley said, "rarely tried to act.... The voice and the expression were, with him, to 'do it all.'" Cynthia Reynolds was the innkeeper's daughter, Alice Lowenhaupt was the page, Wilbur Lewis was the innkeeper, and Peter Ludwig was the seneschal. All had been stylishly prepared by Mr. Kurtz and by Joseph

LoSchiavo, the stage director. Whereas the artists of the concert *Anna Bolena* handled Donizetti's work in a largely self-serving fashion, the Vineyard artists, intent on serving the composer, served him well.

Rubini never sang this *Gianni di Parigi*. It reached La Scala, in a production unauthorized by the composer, only in 1839 (the year before Verdi's comedy *Un giorno di regno,* composed for the same soprano, tenor, and primo buffo). It was heard in Naples in 1846, and the vocal score was published in Italy and France. It seems not to have been heard again until the Vineyard production—difficult to understand why.

TUNEFUL CHOIRS

December 30, 1985

THE New Amsterdam Singers, conducted by Clara Longstreth, gave two performances this month of a wide-ranging Heinrich Schütz program; it included many of Schütz's better-known compositions, from the madrigal "Dunque addio" of Opus 1 to the big German Magnificat of the "Swansong" collection. The first concert was sung in Immanuel Lutheran Church, the second in St. Ignatius, on West Eighty-seventh Street—a 1902 Episcopal church by Charles Haight, lofty, Gothic, and interestingly shaped (a Latin cross ingeniously condensed onto a rectangular site), where Mass is chanted partly in Latin. The chorus is sixty strong. A semichorus of nineteen emerged from it to sing the smaller compositions. Two violins, a cello, and organ provided instrumental parts. The church was packed.

The chorus has good intonation. The balance was excellent. And the rhythmic mazes of such a piece as the six-part "Ich bin eine rufende Stimme" (John the Baptist's "I am the voice of one crying in the wilderness") were surely trod. But right from the start—as the choir sang "Cantate domino canticum novum" without clearly struck "c"s, "t"s, and "d"—there was something missing: a strong response to the sound and shape of words. Miss Longstreth's admirable program notes referred often to the vividness of Schütz's text settings. She pointed out that in the Lord's Prayer he declaimed "Give us this day our daily bread" in a way to suggest petition by people who, during the Thirty Years War, had known famine. And her singers plainly understood what they were singing about. In "Ad dominum cum tribularer" they voiced the sobbing semitone descents of the phrase eloquently. But they didn't use the four consonant attacks and the four vowel colors of "tribularer" to make vivid the phrase. In fact, their declamation was sometimes so mealy—lips and tongues so lazy—that even as one followed the texts in the program book it was hard to know which line had been reached. It's no good singing in Latin and in German if one doesn't use the sounds of those languages for communication. (Perhaps in this country Schütz should be sung in English; he himself gave precedent for translation, in many pieces that have come down to us with both Latin and vernacular texts.) Words were mushed for the maintenance of full, "rounded," agreeable tone. I wish Miss Longstreth had urged her chorus to use harder, brighter, more forward sound, and her sopranos to emulate boys with open, uncovered timbre. When Schütz's lines broke, as often they do, into eighth-note exuberance, the riffs were not revelled in. This is a good choir, and it does adventurous programs. It was an enjoyable concert. A sharper dramatic focus on the text of each piece would have made it more enjoyable still.

New York's Sunday-afternoon church concerts are a reason for not leaving the city at weekends. On the last Sunday of November, the Classical Quartet and the oboist Stephen Hammer were playing Haydn, Mozart, Boccherini, and Beethoven in Corpus Christi's Music Before 1800 series. Only something very special could induce one to miss that, and something there was: in Fifth Avenue Presbyterian Church, Pomerium Musices (fourteen singers, including their director, Alexander Blachly), the New York Consort of Viols (four players, including their director, Judith Davidoff), and the harpsichordist Charles Sherman joined in a program of music from sixteenth-century Naples. It was not all sacred. It included a setting by Lodovico Agostini (made long after the event) of the canzona that welcomed Lucrezia Borgia to Naples as the bride of Alfonso of Aragon, madrigals, villanescas, and dances. The performers, solo and in varying ensemble combinations, presented a captivating picture of the musics that flourished in the restless, excitable city. The Spaniard Diego Ortiz and the Fleming Giovanni de Macque were directors of the viceregal cappella; the latter, at the close of the century, increased the musical forces until they rivalled those of St. Mark's in Venice. Naples was also a center of keyboard activity. In Gesualdo, sixty miles to the east, the Prince of Venosa, whose father had been served by Macque and by Pomponio Nenna, devoted himself to composition. At this concert, music by all these men and several others was performed with rapt, eager artistry. Gesualdo's "Ave, dulcissima Maria" made a wonderful close. Stravinsky, writing in a preface to Glenn Watkins's book about Gesualdo, feared that modern singers, busied in a breadwinning round of taping commercials and "disposing of seasonal oratorios," had no time to "achieve the blends, the exactness of intonation, the diction and articulation that the Prince's singers would have had to master." But the Pomerium singers were masterly.

Judas Maccabaeus is a Chanukkah oratorio: in Act III, the Feast of Lights, inaugurated to celebrate Judas's victory over the Syrians, is solemnized. (The saga of the Maccabee brothers was continued in Handel's next oratorio, *Alexander Balus,* which had what may have been its American première in Washington last year.) Handel wrote the work to celebrate the Duke of Cumberland's defeat of the Young Pretender, at the Battle of Culloden. It is an oratorio that has long been popular. Hermann Albert, Mozart's biographer, praised its depiction of a military leader "who performed famous deeds thanks to his own great heart and strong arm, as only Germany's chivalry has done," and thought that Handel intended a "subtle criticism of the British character." (Later, in Nazi Germany, the libretto was recast as *Wilhelm von Nassau.*) The action is all offstage. The mood alternates between dismay and jubilation, and the sad pieces are the more stirring: the magnificent choruses of mourning for Mattathias—Judas, Simon, and Jonathan's heroic father—at the start; the despairing "Ah! wretched, wretched Israel!," for cello, soprano, and chorus, in Act II. Jonathan Keates, in his *Handel: The Man and His Music*—an enthusiastic "layman" study combining attention to recent research with discerning personal appraisals—defends *Judas* and its enduring popularity, despite the "occasionally rather coarse appeal to communal sentiment": the "very absence of local, individualized drama" led to the "universal expressions of happiness, freedom and religious devotion."

Two Chanukkah performances of the oratorio were given at the 92nd Street Y by the Y Chorale and the Y Chamber Symphony, conducted by Gerard Schwarz. (I heard the second.) The chorus, thirty strong, trained by Amy Kaiser, was first-rate—firm tone, clear words, energetic delivery, expressive phrasing—and in "Sing unto God" it produced coloratura of startling distinctness and brilliance. Benita Valente, as the Israelitish Woman, and André Emelianoff, the solo cellist, were eloquent in "Ah! wretched, wretched Israel!" Kristina Carlson was the Israelitish Man (her New York début). This is the role in which Caterina Galli, at the first *Judas*, in 1747, made her name and, as Burney reports, "became an important personage among singers." She specialized in breeches parts; Handel went on to write Alexander Balus and Solomon for her. (She lived on into the nineteenth century, and made some Covent Garden appearances in her mid-seventies.) Today, with increasing frequency, countertenors take over these transvestite roles. Miss Carlson struck no convincing blow for restoring them to her sex: her ample voice was often untidy, not finely and keenly focussed; her words were not beautifully pronounced. But Burney's phrase for Galli "there was something spirited and interesting in her manner" could be applied to a few passages where Miss Carlson dug arrestingly into chest voice. Rockwell Blake's Judas was fluent but unattractive in timbre. Jan Opalach, as Simon, was poised, polished, and vigorous. His bold, clear divisions in "The Lord worketh wonders" lent animation to an undistinguished bravura aria. (A week later, he could be heard as a rather impressive baritone soloist in Vaughan Williams's *Sea Symphony*—a St. Louis performance, spaciously conducted by Leonard Slatkin, broadcast by WNYC.) But he must conquer a tendency toward what Plunket Greene (in *Interpretation in Song*) calls "clergyman's" English—the plummy delivery that "converts the manly English pronunciation of 'God' into a compromise between 'Guard' and 'Gurd.' " Mr. Schwarz's rhythms were sometimes alert, sometimes a bit ploddy. After each number, and even between each recitative and its ensuant aria or ensemble, he made a long, awkward pause (while the chorus rose or sat and the soloists shifted their stations). This had an unhappy effect on the sweep and surge of Handel's long sequences.

The next day, I went to the first of Musica Sacra's two Advent *Messiah*s, conducted by Richard Westenburg, in Avery Fisher Hall. This was very differently paced: close-knit, with crunched recitative cadences acting as springboards into aria or chorus. There were no holes, but there was no hustle, either; it was a balanced, beautifully shaped and proportioned account of the work. Charles Jennens, who compiled the text for Handel, called *Messiah* a "fine Entertainment," and its early London performances were given—many considered this scandalous—in theatres. Of course, it's also a sublime entertainment, and for modern listeners it carries emotional resonances that cannot be escaped. But the most moving—the most spiritually moving, I'd say—performances are those that, like Mr. Westenburg's, are essentially buoyant while being, in the Passion sequence, intensely dramatic. Part I deals with the Prophecies, the Annunciation, the Nativity, the Adoration of the Shepherds; Part II with the Passion, the Resurrection, the Ascension, Pentecost, and the establishment of the Church. Part III is a Last Judgment that has lost its terrors, since death has been defeated, the Judge is on our side, and the very Prosecutor "makes intercession for us." There are episodes of mystery, awe, pain, tenderness, splendor, but in sum *Messiah* is a joyful piece. Handel himself associated it with Easter celebration; to Christmastide it is also appropriate. Handelians have long complained, and with justice, that the immense popularity of the work eclipsed a fuller knowledge of the composer's range and distorted the common view of him. What should they know of Handel who only the one oratorio know? In the long run, however, public opinion tends to be right—right in its assessments, although wrong in the narrowness of its pursuits. After the manifold and various adventures of this Handel tercentenary year, I found this Musica Sacra *Messiah* the most stirring adventure of them all.

Mr. Westenburg used a small, expert professional chorus of twenty-nine—eight sopranos, seven each of altos, tenors, and basses—and a basic band of nineteen strings, two oboes, and a single bassoon (plus trumpets and drums where called for), which he directed from the harpsichord, sharing the continuo role with an organist. It was hardly an "authentic" Handelian balance. Handel's timbre (after the strings-only Dublin version, with just one trumpet appearance) would have been reedier; at a Foundling Hospital *Messiah* in 1758, he had four oboes and four bassoons with twenty strings, a pair of horns doubling the trumpets, and a chorus of seventeen, with boy sopranos. (His soloists—there were six of them—probably joined in the choruses. The Musica Sacra soloists didn't, except in the "Hallelujah" Chorus.) But Fisher Hall is perhaps ten times the size of the Foundling Hospital chapel, and the Musica Sacra instruments are modern. This was not a "reconstruction," such as can successfully be attempted only in a small hall, but a sensitive re-creation with modern materials. Musica Sacra does *Messiah* each year, and each year—it's an inexhaustible work from many viewpoints—aims to do something new. Sometimes it's an unexpected textual choice from the score's many alternatives. This year, the principal innovation was long stretches of nonvibrato string playing. It's a modern trick—olde-worlde appliqué, not authentic baroque practice. Sustained non-vibrato, by all the accounts, is as alien to eighteenth-century string playing as is "rich" modern vibrato. (A gentle, unobtrusive vibrato was cultivated, amplified at moments as an expressive ornament.) But it's a trick that works: Richard Bradshaw used it to electrifying effect for the death scene of the *Tamerlano* he conducted in Bloomington earlier this year. It drains the fatness from tense, modern, steel-strung violins. It enforces delicacy and care about intonation. (A cynic might add that by emphasizing any deviations from exact pitch it suggests the out-of-tune sound of some of our old-instrument bands; I'd rather not pursue that one.) To the *pifa* pastorale before "There were shepherds abiding in the field" it lent a rustic charm, suggesting the wheezy drone of the shepherds' pipes. And it lent plangency to the long notes of "And with his stripes we are healed," producing what Robert Donington (in his treatise *String Playing in Baroque Music*) calls "some quite special and rather theatrical effect." It's a trick that loses its attractiveness if tried too often.

Handel divided the solo numbers among five or more singers when he performed *Messiah*. Mr. Westenburg used just four. Sylvia McNair, the soprano, was a shade reticent in the Christmas sequence, a shade too well mannered. In "Rejoice greatly" she sacrificed the "r" and the "j"—likewise the "b" and the "h" of "Behold"—to smoothness. But she sang "I know that my redeemer liveth" fully, fervently, and fearlessly, with tone that glowed the brighter as it rose. This is a beautiful young voice. To the alto part Michael Chance brought clarity, intelligence, impeccably clear words, and well-formed tone. On the long E-flat of "grief," in "He was despised," he produced a wonderful *messa di voce* (a swelling of the tone from soft to loud and then a fining down to soft again). One looked forward to admiring it again in the da capo. Mr. Chance, an artist and stylist, did something different: he now hit the word hard, with strong attack on the "gr," and then slowly, with perfect control, keeping the vowel pure, he diminished the note until it disappeared in a whispered "f." Both times, differently each time, the word was given potent expression. (At the first *Messiah* performance, after Mrs. Cibber—who had emerged from retirement after a messy divorce case—sang "He was despised," the Reverend Dr. Delany rose to his feet and cried, "Woman, for this be all thy sins forgiven thee!")

David Gordon, the tenor, essayed some overambitious and disfiguring decoration in his first number, making plain places rough. But he sang the recitatives and air of Part II with noble emotion, and was especially poignant in "Thy rebuke hath broken his heart" and "Behold, and see." David Evitts was a strong, agile bass with sharp-focussed coloratura. The chorus achieved grandeur without portentousness, lightness without frivolity, and all it did was vivid. In modern *Messiah*s, "All we like sheep have gone astray" sometimes sounds positively giddy and gleeful; in this performance—as light and fleet as any—there was a hint in the timbre of regret for the errancy.

FLAMES

January 6, 1986

THERE were two performances of Schoenberg's monodrama *Erwartung* in Carnegie Hall last year. Phyllis Bryn-Julson sang it in March with the Cincinnati Symphony, conducted by Michael Gielen; Anja Silja sang it last month with the Cleveland Orchestra, conducted by Christoph von Dohnányi. The opera is one of the marvels of our century, poured out in seventeen days of 1909—the year that brought also the Three Piano Pieces, Opus 11, and the Five Orchestral

Pieces—and still a work that holds listeners intent on each turn of its progress of thoughts, fears, and memories (as the heroine presses through a wood now dark, now lit by shafts of moonlight, which is also a psychological metaphor), of marvellous sounds from a very large orchestra handled with the utmost delicacy, and of post-*Tristan* tonality taken to the brink of dissolution. Miss Silja and Mr. Dohnányi recorded *Erwartung* four years ago (on London, with the Vienna Philharmonic), but she wasn't singing as well then as she sings now: twenty-five years of pushing the bright, clear soprano through a wide variety of roles (the Queen of Night, Lady Macbeth, Fiordiligi, Isolde, Zerbinetta, Brünnhilde, Rosina, Turandot) with unstinting dramatic concern for each of them seemed to have taken a toll; wildness and wobble disturbed the flame of her singing. But in the Carnegie *Erwartung* that flame burned bright and true. The voice was newly fresh, focussed, and disciplined. Whatever Miss Silja touches she brings to life, and this was a marvellous performance—accurate, shining, verbally incisive. It made one eager to hear the soprano again in the theatre; her last Met engagement was in 1980. [*Later in 1986, she appeared in Boston as the heroine of Janáček's* The Makropulos Affair.] Mr. Dohnányi's conducting was masterly, and the orchestra played with great beauty and expression.

The Met has been having a success with triple bills: Stravinsky's *Rite, Nightingale,* and *Oedipus,* and now the "Parade" of works by Satie, Poulenc, and Ravel. Perhaps it should next put on a Schoenberg triple bill, of *Erwartung* (a neurotic tragedy), *Die glückliche Hand* (an allegory of felicitous artistic creation), and *Von Heute auf Morgen* (a blithe marital comedy)—as *Expectation, The Happy Touch,* and *From One Day to the Next.* James Levine's orchestra could do them justice. [Erwartung, *on a double-bill with Bartók's* Bluebeard's Castle, *appeared at the Met in 1989.*]

At the Philharmonic last month, Leonard Bernstein conducted the third symphonies of three American composers: Roy Harris, William Schuman, and Aaron Copland. The works are about forty years old—the span that divides *Norma* from *The Magic Flute, Pelléas* from *La forza del destino,* Berlioz's *Symphonie Fantastique* from Haydn's late symphonies—and none of them seemed as "modern" as the seventy-five-year-old *Erwartung.* Music history moves in no steady stream but, like an Elliott Carter composition, in many tempos at once. I found it hard to recapture responses I once had to each symphony—the Harris first met on the Koussevitzky recording, the Copland conducted by Adrian Boult and by Jascha Horenstein. We've lately been hearing many Copland works in less portentous veins; after them, the Third Symphony can seem a strained piece of construction, its opening movement suggesting dance paragraphs slowed down and overscored. Virgil Thomson found "something false" and unspontaneous about the piece. The composer himself (in a conversation reported on the cover of his CBS recording of the symphony) said, "Before the Third Symphony, my so-called grand-manner music was what might be termed lean-grand. The Symphony tends more toward the fat-grand side." It's become a classic. There have been at least five recordings so far, and the Philharmonic concert was recorded to make a sixth. (The audience was invited to help itself to cough tablets from dispensers on the grand promenade and the second tier. There were still plenty of noisy feet scuffing or stamping on Fisher Hall's resonant wooden floor: the audience noise level there is higher than anywhere else I know.)

Mr. Bernstein's conducting of all three works was large and impassioned. The orchestra glowed for him. Swiftly, he fanned the glow to a blaze. In fact, there were passages where I felt that he raised the temperature too soon—especially in the Schuman. The opening passacaglia soon reached such a peak of intensity that it could mount no further as the movement progressed. The week before, Mr. Bernstein and the Philharmonic did Mahler's Seventh Symphony, and it was a magnificent performance. The first movement seems to bring the modern world before us. (The work was composed in 1904–05.) In the two Nachtmusik movements, there was reticence, delicacy, and great tenderness. The scherzo was alarming in its contrasts of spectral dance and fierce sarcasm. The finale is beastly racket in almost any performance, and there's nothing much to be done about it except to play the music—as Bernstein and the orchestra did—with wholehearted enthusiasm.

Last June, David Del Tredici's *March to Tonality,* composed for the Chicago Symphony, had its première: ambiguous chordal progressions discover a home base in D-flat major, proclaim it, and after any excursions inexorably return there. Michael Torke's *Bright Blue Music,* which had its première at a New York Youth Symphony concert, conducted by David Alan Miller, in Carnegie Hall in November, is a *marche sur place*—twelve minutes of marking time with a good deal of energy and activity but no progressions. The work begins, stays, and ends in D major. Wittgenstein, the composer says in a program note, is responsible: "Inspired by Wittgenstein's idea that meaning is not in words themselves but in the grammar of words used, I conceived of a parallel in musical terms: harmonies in themselves do not contain any meaning. . . . Harmonic language is then, in a sense, inconsequential. If the choice of harmony is arbitrary, why not then use tonic and dominant chords—the simplest, most direct, and—for me—the most pleasurable?" E major was blue for Rimsky-Korsakov, as F-sharp major was for Scriabin. For Wagner, on the evidence of *Lohengrin,* A major was blue. But D major, says Torke, "has been the color blue for me since I was five years old." (He is now twenty-four.) *Bright Blue Music* makes an effect very different from the jazzy minimalism of Torke's *Vanada,* which was played at last year's ISCM Festival, in Amsterdam, or the rhythmic jitters of his *Ecstatic Orange,* which the Brooklyn Philharmonic and Lukas Foss did last May. It is busily and fully written for a large orchestra—the pages of the score present a dense dance of notes—in 9/8, animato. What sounds like scraps of waltz tune drift through the D-major glitter. The work is at once absurd and attractive. Torke casually jettisons centuries of harmonic endeavor; Gesualdo, Wagner, Schoenberg have lived in vain. A few chromatic notes intrude, but they are soon resolved. It's a happy piece. And observing someone exuberantly at play usually gives pleasure—for a while, at least.

Bright Blue Music was the latest in the Youth Symphony's series of First Music commissions, for large-orchestra works from young composers. Last season brought David Lang's *Flaming Youth,* Aaron Jay Kernis's *Mirror of Heat and*

Light, and Ronald Caltabiano's *Poplars.* It's a valuable series. Composer and orchestra come together for a ten-week rehearsal period. Mr. Miller's orchestra, a hundred strong, with an average age of fifteen and a half, plays warmly and ably, and his programs are usually adventurous. *Bright Blue Music* was preceded by Dvořák's *Othello* overture and followed by Mendelssohn's "Reformation" Symphony. Mendelssohn was twenty when he wrote it; the contrast between his earnest, aspirant mastery and Torke's insouciant bravado was striking.

Richard Strauss's second opera, *Feuersnot,* was given its New York première last month by the Manhattan School of Music—the first American production, it seems, since the American première, in Philadelphia in 1927, with Nelson Eddy in the cast. The title is untranslatable: "Fire-Dearth" has been suggested, but the word can also mean "conflagration" or "the crisis produced by a conflagration." Strauss wrote the piece as, he said, "a little revenge on my dear native city [Munich], which thirty years before had accorded no friendly welcome to the great Richard, and then accorded no more to the little Richard." In 1895, his first opera, *Guntram* (the short score of which he closed with the inscription "Deo Gratia! Und dem heiligen Wagner"), was dropped by the Munich Opera after a single performance. Discouraged from composing for the theatre (although ever active as a conductor there), for five years he wrote tone-poems—*Till Eulenspiegel, Also sprach Zarathustra, Don Quixote,* and *Ein Heldenleben.* In 1898, he left the Munich Opera for the Berlin Court Opera. In 1900, he embarked on *Feuersnot.* The librettist was Ernst von Wolzogen, of whose Überbrettl cabaret theatre Schoenberg was soon to become musical director.

The setting is medieval Munich. The burghers are suspicious and unappreciative of Kunrad, a young wizard settled in their midst. It is Midsummer Eve. Children are singing and playing. The high-spirited Kunrad kisses Diemut, the town beauty, the mayor's daughter, full on the lips, in public. Offended, she takes revenge: inviting Kunrad to join her on her balcony, she hoists him up toward it in a basket but leaves him suspended halfway, to be jeered at by the populace. He invokes the arts of his great master, Reichhart, and at a stroke extinguishes all fire and light in the city. He reaches the balcony and, lit by a shaft of moonlight, lectures the awed townsfolk: once they drove away the wagoner, the daring one ("den Wagner"), who wanted to put their life on wheels; now a successor has come to renew the strife ("zum Strauss"). (Themes from *The Ring, The Flying Dutchman,* and *Guntram* point the puns.) The girl he chose has mocked his warm love in a show of virtue; for virtue of that kind he has no use. And now, he concludes, "only from a warm, young maiden's body" ("aus heiss-jung-fraulichem Leibe") can Munich's fire be restored. Diemut draws him into her room. There follows the lush Liebesszene, which Beecham used to do as a concert piece. At the moment of Kunrad and Diemut's union, there is an instant of silence; then orchestra, lights, and fires blaze forth again, and the people rejoice.

Feuersnot is an uneven work, but it contains much attractive and skillful music, blending tuneful, pretty comedy, especially in the children's songs, with soaring love music. It's worth seeing once or twice in one's life, even though its best passages the composer bettered elsewhere. I first encountered the opera in

Munich, in 1958, in a production conducted by Rudolf Kempe. (It was on a double bill with *Josephslegende;* the opera, in one act, lasts about ninety minutes.) The Manhattan presentation was strongest from an orchestral point of view. John Crosby, a devoted Straussian, drew warm, beautiful playing from his young, large orchestra. The staging, by Lou Galterio, was extravagant and cluttered. Instead of the single street scene before the town gate, there were rickety scaffolding constructions, by David Sumner, in ceaseless motion, with people clambering up and down and through them. The libretto suggests a hint of grotesque exaggeration in both architecture and costumes; Dona Granata's costumes were a wild carnival gallimaufry. With so much costuming, so many people, and so much movement packed onto the small stage, the singers had little chance to act or to express—perhaps even to consider—what they were singing about. *Feuersnot* is already a challenging work for students to perform; this tastelessly overelaborated version of it would have taxed any professional company. The show was dramatically blunt. The words (those of the English translation, by the composer William Wallace, that Beecham used for the London première of the opera, in 1910) were largely inaudible. Lauren Wagner, the Diemut, deployed a bright but somewhat edgy and charmless soprano. Cheyne Davidson, the Kunrad, looked handsome and sang strongly in a bald, unimaginative way. The sense of the piece came across hardly at all. Strauss would have been better served by something simpler, wittier, more thoughtful and poetic, with detail in the individual performances. Onstage, it was an ambitious but tacky romp. There was poetry in the orchestra.

ACTIONS OF MAGNITUDE

January 13, 1986

SINCE Beethoven's day, the symphony has been regarded as the "highest and most exalted form" of orchestral music. The phrase is from the preamble to the long, admirable New Grove essay on the subject, in which three authors trace developments of the form through three centuries. In the previous Grove, Frank Henry Shera began a long essay on "symphony" by suggesting analogies with Aristotle's definition of tragedy, the highest form of poetic composition: "an imitation of an action that is serious, complete, and of a certain magnitude; in language embellished with each kind of artistic ornament, the several kinds being found in separate parts of the play; in the form of action, not of narrative; through pity and fear effecting the proper purgation of these emotions." A symphony, too, is "a high argument treated as a unity," adopting different manners for its different movements; Tovey's insistence that a great symphony is a dramatic action is recalled; and "the effect of the whole on the observer should be to make him forget his own petty concerns and live for the time being on a plane of universal experience." Since Beethoven's day, "Whither, symphony?" has been a question often asked and variously answered. Composers content to work within traditional forms have produced dozens, perhaps hundreds, of symphonies well worth hearing. ("A sense of beauty is not a thing to be despised," Tovey wrote, "even in pseudo-classical art; and neither the many beautiful, if mannered, works of Spohr, which disguise one stereotyped form in a bewildering variety of instrumental and literary externals, nor the far more important and essentially varied works of Mendelssohn deserve the contempt which has been the modern correction for their high position in their day.") Other composers have attached the title "Symphony" to works that are symphonies only in name. Yet others have striven to rethink and by their music redefine the formal structure and the "essence" that together make a large orchestral piece recognizably a new symphony in the grand tradition. Peter Maxwell Davies's Third Symphony, a fifty-minute span of rich, engrossing, difficult music, confirms what its two predecessors had foretold: that in the late twentieth century there is a composer striding forward to lead listeners further along the symphonic highroad that Beethoven, Schubert, Brahms, Mahler, and Sibelius trod—a composer not marking time, not cutting attractive capers down side paths, not dancing neoclassical variations or loitering in neoromantic nostalgic dreams, but, strong with cumulate strength and wisdom learned of the old symphonic masters, and armed, too, with the new sound arrangements that our century has discovered, moving purposefully onward.

Davies, like Brahms, came late to the symphony, not before establishing mastery in many other genres and training symphonic muscles by other large-scale orchestra endeavors—notably, in Davies's case, the Second Taverner Fantasia (1964) and *Worldes Blis* (1966–69), a forty-minute "motet for orchestra." His First Symphony was begun in 1973, completed in 1976, and first played in 1978. (It was recorded by Decca.) The Second, commissioned by the Boston Symphony, appeared in 1981. The Third, commissioned by the BBC for the fiftieth anniversary of its Manchester-based orchestra, the BBC Philharmonic, had its first performance in Manchester (Davies's native city) last February; radio and then television carried it through the country. The London première was at last year's Proms, where I heard it for the first time. (Again it was widely broadcast.) Now a recording is available, on the BBC Artium label. All these performances were given by the BBC Philharmonic, conducted by Edward Downes (who conducted Davies's opera *Taverner* at its Covent Garden pre-mière, in 1972, and returned to conduct its revival there in 1983).

The form of the Third Symphony—a first movement that begins slowly and accelerates, two scherzos, and a slow finale—recalls that of Mahler's Ninth. (Mahler's first movement, however, is an andante with allegro elements.) The second scherzo stops to admit "windows" looking toward the finale—a device that Davies in his program note calls "shamelessly borrowed" from the corresponding Mahler movement. At a first hearing, the symphony is very easy to enjoy, for (as in Mahler's symphonies) there is much picturesque music. There are evocations of spacious landscape, of swelling seascape, of high, clear skies with birds wheeling overhead; a sudden, close flurry of birdsong ends the first movement. There are perky clarinet tunes, poignant flute tunes, stirring brass salvos, solemn drumbeats. But listening on this level does not conceal a challenge unmet. The symphony is also architecture, built on or of harmonies. It's like a great, intricate, beautiful building that the listener explores. The composer uses the image in his program note. The paired scherzos are likened to two viewings of a Renaissance church interior, the first from a central point, "with all the proportions revealed," the second as if from a side arcade, with everything skewed. The symphony, "throughout its four movements, articulates the same architectural outline," and the slow finale is a "double" (in the eighteenth-century sense) of the first, "giving the material time, now, to breathe and expand to its full expressive potential, and resolving the long-range harmonic tensions set up so far." The symphony does not, of course, "represent" a church; but "the theories of Brunelleschi, Alberti, Piero della Francesca, and Leonardo ... together with a lot of time spent experiencing the buildings themselves, have influenced the tonal-modal thinking." The listener need hardly concern himself with the technical details. (One doesn't take a tape measure to San Lorenzo or to the Santa Maria Novella façade; Roy Howat's recent demonstration that Debussy probably constructed *La Mer*—and much else—precisely to golden-section proportions scarcely affects one's valuation, or perhaps even one's perception, of the music.) What matters is that the symphony seems, "feels," sounds shapely, and that at each hearing the details of its form and their relationships can be more clearly discovered. It's a symphony in D, with a "dominant" on G-sharp; the harmonic perspectives are further defined by the minor thirds, F and B, that divide the tritones D–G-sharp–D. (These are also the harmonic regions of the two previous symphonies, in F and in B, respectively, and both also with tritone "dominants.") The tonality is spelled out clearly in the opening and closing pages. The final tonic is not sounded but is pointed to, plotted, like an unstated but all-important Renaissance vanishing point, by the notes that are there.

Davies is a fecund composer. Almost each month seems to bring a première. And for this he has been chided by those subscribing to what Henry Chorley called the "huge and untenable fallacy" that incessant production necessarily compromises quality. Chorley was writing in defense of Donizetti—measured defense, to be sure, for he deemed Donizetti "essentially a second-rate composer"—but he extended the principle to embrace greater men: "With few exceptions, all the great musical composers have been fertile when once educated, and capable of writing with as much rapidity as ease. Bach, Handel (whose *Israel* was completed in three weeks), Haydn (more of whose compositions are lost than live), Mozart—all men remarkable as *discoverers,* and renowned as classic authors—held the pens of ready writers." And such composers' "fancies are strengthened by the very process and passion of pouring them forth." It takes the resources of two publishing houses, Boosey & Hawkes and J. & W. Chester, to keep pace with Davies's output. The phonograph helps interested listeners to keep up. *Into the Labyrinth* and the Sinfonietta Accademica—two of three chamber-orchestra works that appeared in 1983, pointing a way toward the new "architectural" clarity of the Third Symphony— are now available on a Unicorn record. The long, powerful Piano Sonata (1981), which has so far not been played in New York, is recorded by its dedicatee, Stephen Pruslin, on Auracle. The incantatory *Runes from a Holy Island* (1977) and the beautiful *Image, Reflection, Shadow* (1982), which have been played here, have also appeared on Unicorn.

Unicorn recordings of *Vesalii Icones* (*Images of Vesalius*) and *Eight Songs for a Mad King*—two of four music-theatre pieces that Davies's ensemble, the Fires of London, brought to Alice Tully Hall in November and December—have long been available. The recordings are important, for in stage performances of these works it is very easy to devote too much attention to the actor protagonist—a dancer in *Vesalius,* a baritone in the *Eight Songs*—and miss the full drama that is being enacted by the six instruments. Both pieces in their day—they appeared in 1969—were expressionist shockers: on the simplest level because a dancer, moving through the Stations of the Cross, appeared for a moment seemingly naked on the stage of the Queen Elizabeth Hall, and a baritone converted "Comfort ye, my people," from *Messiah,* into a foxtrot; and on deeper levels because the scores challenged, tested, and taxed listeners' stock responses to familiar strains and "signifiers." Neither score has dated in the least; passing years and varied productions bring enhanced admiration for constructional strengths and richly wrought details. Both dramas are searing. If in the Tully Hall performances they proved less painful than usual, it was partly because the new George III, Andrew Gallacher, was the most lyrical and "musical" interpreter— the best *singer*—of the cycle I have yet heard, and the new *Vesalius* dancer, Mark Wraith, was less agonized than his predecessors had been; and partly, I suppose, because I was deliberately focussing on the musical discourse rather than the flamboyant theatrical surface. The Fires instrumentalists seemed to me to play the pieces more incisively and expressively than ever before. The players were Madeleine Mitchell (violin, viola), Helen Keen (flute), David Campbell (clarinet), Jonathan Williams (cello), Mr. Pruslin (piano, harpsichord), and Mark Glentworth (percussion). The first two and the last are new to the ensemble this season.

The other music-theatre pieces done were *Miss Donnithorne's Maggot* (1974) and *Le Jongleur de Notre Dame* (1978). Mary Thomas, who has been the Fires soprano since the ensemble's foundation, in 1967 (as the Pierrot Players), was in brilliant form as the mad, exuberantly moody Miss Donnithorne. (Her bridegroom jilted her on her wedding day, in 1856; she spent the remaining thirty years of her life in her wedding dress, a moldering wedding breakfast uncleared from her tables. Her only consolation was books; one of them may well have been *Great Expectations,* published in 1861.) And I admired the *Jongleur* more than before—perhaps because, discounting the weakness of the dramatic presentation (which used to bother me), I listened intently to the purely musical content, which is not at all weak but athletic and inspired. Mr. Campbell's clarinet solo was especially notable.

In Tully Hall, the Fires also gave three performances of Davies's opera *The Lighthouse.* This was the New York première. First performed at the 1980 Edinburgh Festival, *The Lighthouse* has been perhaps the most successful of recent operas, played widely in Europe, and in this country in Boston and Philadelphia; a San Diego production is due soon. The Fires sextet is here increased to an ensemble of twelve (horn, trumpet, trombone, viola, double-bass, and guitar are added), and there are three singers: tenor, baritone, and bass.

Three lighthouse keepers, *à huis clos,* battered by sea and storm—the relief ship long overdue—and pressed by ghosts from guilt-racked memories, succumb to hallucinations, are seized by mutual hysteria, and become savage beasts. I described the action after the stunning Boston production [see p. 70], directed by Peter Sellars—a production in which staging and music became one. (The work's "most exhilarating and terrifying moments," Mr. Sellars wrote in a program note, "are driven by a Stravinskian precision and resource within a tightly organized structure.") The Fires production, conducted by the composer, was instrumentally even more vivid but theatrically feeble. Neil Mackie, who in 1980 sang the role of Sandy naturally and easily, with winning Scots vowels, had acquired a prim English elocution; lines like "Come on, Firebrand, we need a change of tack," tricky to bring off at the best of times, sounded faintly ridiculous. Christopher Keyte, the Blazes, was an improbable former Glasgow thug. And Mr. Gallacher lacked the coarse, gravelly bass-trombone force that Arthur must have. The music, however, and the wonderfully cogent instrumental playing carried the day.

It was disconcerting at all these Fires performances to find musical execution on the highest virtuoso and expressive level linked with amateurish theatrical presentation. Some excuses are easy to find: the limitations imposed by touring; too little rehearsal time in Tully Hall, perhaps; and the drawbacks of the place itself, too big for intimate performer-audience contact, and with dead (though clear) acoustics. But the Fires—a touring music-theatre ensemble—should have learned how to deal with these things. Davies, like other composers, has no doubt suffered from stage directors who treat dramas as raw material for their own extravagant fancies, and don't listen to what the music says and does. But he and the players were not well served by direction as meekly respectful, as colorless, as fuzzy in detail as Brenda McLean's. (Miss Keen's portrayal of a frightened bullfinch, in the *Eight Songs,* was one of the few pieces of vivid acting.) The lighting was inept. The Tully platform was shrouded in fusty black curtains; last year's *Belshazzar* and a semistaging of Virgil Thomson's *Lord Byron* shortly after the Fires' visit showed how much more theatrical the space is when, simply, the tall stage portals are thrown open as a set of receding wings. The organ pipes that provided a glinting backdrop for *Belshazzar* could have done the same for the *Jongleur* and the *Eight Songs.* Last time the Fires visited New York, they played Symphony Space, and the place was packed. Lincoln Center's high prices—*Lighthouse* seats twenty-five dollars, the others twenty—must surely have deterred many young people who would otherwise have come.

Davies is busy with a large opera, *Resurrection,* for Darmstadt. It is tempting to think that in his latest music-theatre piece, *The No. 11 Bus,* he was gathering forces for it, retesting the ideas, devices, and techniques of the early expressionist dramas, refining or reforging them in the light of what he has done since. *Bus* had its première in London in 1984, and most of the critics were dismissive. ("I could easily have mistaken it for an end-of-term lark by a group of precocious fourth-formers": the *Financial Times*.) The American première—a single Fires performance brought to the Palace Theatre, Stamford, last month for the Stamford Center for the Arts—made a rather different impression.

The No. 11 bus route traverses London. From its eastern terminus, at Liverpool Street, it passes the Bank of England, St. Paul's, the Houses of Parliament, Westminster Abbey; along the King's Road it reaches—and manages to go beyond—World's End, to arrive at a western terminus in Hammersmith. Glories of Church and State pass in review. Moreover, passengers can take the bus for destinations in Paradise Walk, Harper Road, and St. Peter's Grove; also Houndsditch, Burnfoot Avenue, and Fetter Lane. Field trips on the real bus suggested to the composer the characters of his allegorical drama. Readings of the tarot suggested the sequence of its episodes. Traversals of a "magic square" (a block of figures all of whose columns, vertical and horizontal, yield the same sum) guided the musical transformations of the sixteen sections. The "compositional aids," of course, are no more important to the listener than Bach's or Berg's numerology, or Harrison Birtwistle's sheets of computer-generated random numbers. *The No. 11 Bus*—the score bears the dates November 1983, at the start, and January 14, 1984, at the close—seems to have been composed in a sustained, exuberant burst of inspiration.

The pianist is the driver of the bus, the percussionist is the bus conductor, and the four other instrumentalists are passengers. The musical conductor is a policeman on his podium. Three singers (mezzo-soprano, tenor, and baritone), two dancers, and a mime play many roles along the route. All Davies's preoccupations and obsessions come crowding in: the use of magic squares, the tarot, plainchant, hymnody, and parody as compositional tools; the sounds of exotic or homely percussion (rubber plunger and plastic bucket); thoughts of materialism, violence, evil, Antichrist, the Pope, aspects of the Church that have long called forth some of Davies's fiercest, bitterest music; compassion for simple, suffering people leading simple, ordinary lives; the schoolboy humors of such a piece as his *Cinderella*. It's a bewildering and uncomfortable work; so much anger and so many jokes cannot comfortably be packed into its fifty or so minutes. It calls for quicksilver responsiveness on the listeners' part: invitations to laughter are followed by assaults. Davies's transformation techniques move at their swiftest pace. Mr. Pruslin, who knows Davies's music from the inside, said before the London première that *Bus* was "technically and musically even harder than the Piano Sonata or the Second Symphony." I believe it. There was more than could be taken in at a single, excited hearing.

TAKING THE LEAD

January 20, 1986

MUSICAL performance is the result of cooperation between composers and their interpreters. In opera, the most elaborate of musical arts, perfectly balanced cooperation is especially hard to attain: singing, acting, and instrumental playing are combined; scenery, lighting, and, often, dancing have their parts; and responsibility for preparing the different ingredients is usually shared by several people. In 1871, Verdi (who had been reading Wagner) prescribed for his mature operas "one superior intelligence to take charge of the costumes, the scenery, the props, the stage direction, etc., in addition to an exceptional musical interpretation." In 1852, Wagner deplored conductors who pay little heed to the staging of operas they conduct—concentration on the score alone leads to "capricious, purely musical interpretation," with wrong tempi and wrong expression—and he deplored stage directors who pay little heed to the orchestra and as a result are "urged to caprices of another sort." The practice produces a breed of "mere opera singers," content to get up the notes of their roles at the piano and "pick up the dramatic by-play in a few stage rehearsals . . . in whatever fashion may be directed by operatic routine and certain fixed suggestions of the director for their comings and goings." Wagner's concern was mainly with his own operas—the remarks form the preamble of his pamphlet "On the Performance of *Tannhäuser*"—but "it is equally certain that even the sickliest of modern Italian operas would gain immeasurably in representation were due heed paid to the coherence that subsists even in them."

The first rehearsals for an opera, Wagner proposed, should be without music, just spoken—the whole company, including conductor and chorus, present, the stage director in charge. "The singer incapable of reciting his part as a play role, with an expression answering to the *poet*'s aim, will certainly be incapable of singing it in accordance with the *composer*'s aim." When the play has been mastered, musical rehearsals can begin, and the conductor "has gained a fresh, an essentially heightened viewpoint for his labors." There are companies today who do work in that way, insofar as rehearsal schedules allow. But there are few singers today equipped to take—and, perhaps, few conductors prepared to countenance—the next step that Wagner recommends: the gradual assumption by the singer of the main interpretative responsibility for the performance. A singer, he declares, should first learn the music in tempo, but, once that has been done, "then at last I urge an almost entire abandonment of the rigor of the musical beat, which was up to then a mere mechanical aid to agreement between composer and singer, but which with the complete attainment of that agreement is to be thrown aside. . . . From the moment when the singer has taken into his fullest knowledge my intentions for the rendering, let him give the freest play to his natural sensibility, nay, even to the physical necessities of his breath in the more agitated passages; and the more creative he can become, the more he will earn my delighted thanks. The conductor will then only have to follow the singer, to keep unbroken the bond between vocal rendering and orchestral accompaniment."

Wagner was writing in days before the orchestra sat in a sunken pit: the players could hear the singers more easily; many of the players, looking past the conductor (who then usually stood by the prompter's box) toward the stage, could see the singers. Even so, Wagner realized, much rehearsal would be needed to give the instrumentalists "exactest knowledge of the vocal phrasing," and the vocal lines, words and music, should be copied into the players' parts (as

425

in old instrumental parts they often are). He distinguished, of course, between a conductor who is a "co-creative artist" and one who merely serves "prima donnas' wayward whims, as their heedful, cringing lackey." But the surest sign of a conductor's having accomplished his task, he said, "would be the ultimate experience, at the production, that his active lead is scarcely noticeable."

I have lately heard two performances of Verdi's *Rigoletto* in which the conductor's active lead was not at all unnoticeable. One was presented in Carnegie Hall earlier this season by the Philadelphia Orchestra, conducted by Riccardo Muti; the other is a Philips recording of the opera, conducted by Giuseppe Sinopoli. Concert or recording-studio performance focusses attention on the relations between composer, conductor, singers, and players, undisturbed by considerations of scenery and staging. It cannot provide a whole performance of an opera, but it can be dramatic. (Long before I'd seen *Rigoletto* in the theatre, I knew it as a drama from the old Columbia recording eloquently conducted by Lorenzo Molajoli, Riccardo Stracciari its protagonist.) Neither "Muti's *Rigoletto*" nor "Sinopoli's *Rigoletto*" proved dramatic: the fact that one can refer to the performances in that way indicates, in part, what was wrong. Both conductors were dictating. Neither had accomplished his task of inspiring the singers to take charge, while he accompanied. The conductors must not be blamed too severely, however. Modern singers tend to be reliant, passive interpreters—instruments of a conductor's (and in their acting of a stage director's) will, executants of his ideas about phrasing and tempo. "Co-creation" of the kind that Maria Callas and Tullio Serafin, Callas and Tito Gobbi and Victor de Sabata, Callas and Herbert von Karajan, Renata Tebaldi and Karajan practiced has become rare.

Muti conducted the New York première of the new *Rigoletto* score, edited by Martin Chusid, published by the University of Chicago Press and Casa Ricordi, which is the first volume of the new Verdi edition; and Sinopoli adopted several of its readings. The need for new Verdi scores, closer to what the composer wrote in details of phrasing, dynamics, accentuation, sometimes orchestration, occasionally notes and words, has long been recognized; I have often written about it. Verdi orchestrated swiftly, commonly indicating dynamics on just one or two of the instrumental lines, slurring and accenting inconsistently, and writing out apparently identical passages with differences. Generations of Ricordi copy editors have amplified and tidied his scores—not unnecessarily, and not unmusically, but typographically in ways that make it impossible to distinguish between what he wrote and what they contributed. In general, they have regularized what was inconsistent and have proposed simple, surefire solutions to tricky performing problems. Nearly thirty years ago, the conductor Denis Vaughan challenged the standard Verdi performing material. He had detected more than twenty-seven thousand differences between the autograph of *Falstaff* (which has been published in facsimile) and the current Ricordi score of the opera. He suggested that the composer may not always have intended phrases built on the same notes to be delivered each time in exactly the same way. He speculated whether when in a tutti passage the composer did not mark all the instruments with exactly the same dynamic he may have wanted certain tone colors to predominate. He questioned whether when woodwinds and strings play a phrase in unison they must necessarily observe identical phrasing and articulation if the composer has indicated different ones. A fine old brouhaha resulted, with a 1962 public debate, or "confrontation," in Milan at which the Italian Radio Symphony demonstrated Vaughan's points and a jury including the conductors Antonino Votto, Gabriele Santini, and Carlo Maria Giulini rejected them. But in the long run Vaughan, abetted by conductors and scholars who believe that Verdi, at least some of the time, may have meant exactly what he wrote, has won the day. The new Verdi edition prints what Verdi wrote. It also prints a great deal more, but by various typographical devices distinguishes between the composer's and the editor's ideas.

All the same, this new *Rigoletto* score is in my view somewhat overedited. In the prefatory material, four pages of the autograph are reproduced in facsimile. One of them shows the orchestral start of "La donna è mobile." In the new printed score, these eight bars alone contain some sixty indications—for dynamics, accents, slurs—that Verdi didn't write. All that the composer supplied in the way of dynamics was an initial *pp* for the cimbasso (presumably to keep the oom-pah-pah accompaniment from becoming a beery OOM-pah-pah) and a *p* for the cellos at the sixth bar. Chusid adds *pp* to all the instruments that play the accompaniment (to the pah-pahs as well as to the ooms) and assigns a gratuitous *f* to all the instruments that play the tune. Since this tune sails out four octaves deep—on cellos, bassoon, divided first violins, clarinet, oboe, flute, and piccolo—it hardly needs that *f* to make it tell. The result strikes me as ill balanced and overemphatic. It struck me that way in Muti's performance. (Muti subscribed to pretty well all Chusid's ideas about the interpretation of *Rigoletto* and treated the heavily edited text as gospel.) At the start, Chusid changes Verdi's accents on the first three notes of the tune, ∧ ∧ ∧, to > > >. At the sixth bar (corresponding to the words "muta d'accento"), he extends the cellos' *p* to all the instruments playing the tune, reinforcing a "one phrase loud, one phrase soft" approach. The previous Ricordi score, edited in 1964 by Mario Parenti and reprinted in 1980, presents a reading that is in fact slightly closer to the autograph—but with the important difference that Parenti's added marks are not typographically distinguished from Verdi's marks, whereas Chusid's are. They are, that is, in the full score, but in the new orchestral parts the editorial additions and alterations are not shown as such. Chusid's decisions are all perfectly reasonable, and the thinking behind them is clearly set out in a companion volume of critical commentary. A conductor has the evidence before him and can make up his own mind. But if he decides on an airier, less strenuous approach to "La donna è mobile," quarts of white-out on the parts will be needed. It is easier to pencil markings into instrumental parts than to alter markings already printed. Examination of other passages yields similar results. There has been much regularizing, and where Verdi left dynamics unstated—left them, perhaps, to be determined by the conductor in relation to the particular cast, perhaps even at the particular performance—*some* dynamic has been firmly supplied.

A good deal of attention was drawn to the absence in Muti's performance of the traditional interpolated high notes; but this has nothing to do with the new edition. The notes have never been printed. (Renato Bruson, the Rigoletto, seemed to miss them: at "È follia!," "Un vindice avrai!," and "All'onda!" he pushed on the lower, printed notes until they shook.) The only note changes that are significantly audible are monotone B's for Gilda's dreamy murmuring of "Gualtier Maldè," toward the close of the aria (instead of a rise to E), and repeated D-flats at the top of Rigoletto's "Miei Signori, perdono, pietate" (with the cresting over to an E-flat reserved for the repeat of the phrase). The first of these readings has already been widely adopted. The second comes as no surprise to users of the Novello or the Boosey *Rigoletto* score; the passage has always been right there. (And it's sung that way on several early recordings.) The noticeable word change is the Duke's order to Sparafucile, in the last act, for "Tua sorella e del vino." The old reading, "Una stanza e del vino," never made sense. Twenty years ago, suspecting that a censor's prudish hand had intervened here, I reinstated (from the Hugo play) that order for "your sister" into my English translation; and I'm delighted to discover that that is what Verdi originally wrote.

It was sensible to start the new edition with a relatively unproblematical opera. *Rigoletto* is one of the few works that Verdi did not revise. The score may bring few major "revelations" in the form of big, striking changes, but in hundreds—in thousands—of small ways it does present a sharper image of the opera that Verdi composed. And they are cumulative. The stage directions, for the first time, are set above the bars during which Verdi intended them to be enacted. David Lawton, who has conducted *Macbeth, Aida, La traviata,* and *Il trovatore* from scores newly edited from the autographs, writes (in an *Opera Quarterly* article), "Differences in sound are subtle but profound, and result from the accumulation of hundreds of details. In every case, restoration of the autograph reading significantly reinforces a musical or dramatic idea. Audiences do and will respond to these details, even if they are not aware of their exact nature." His performances, and Muti's, have proved it.

In one respect, Muti's reading—otherwise so keenly and lovingly focussed on the score and what it means—was as cavalier in approach as that of any despised "traditional" conductor. He paid small attention to the metronome markings. His pulses were generally faster than those indicated, but that of the finale was much slower. Sinopoli observed the markings rather more nearly—just about exactly in "Parmi veder le lagrime," "Tutte le feste," and the Quartet. But this is a big subject. One day I must return to it.

MEDIEVAL AND MODERN

January 27, 1986

THE Mannes Camerata, directed by Paul Echols, this month put on an ambitious, accomplished, and remarkable double bill of medieval music dramas: *The Play of Robin and Marion* and *The City of Ladies. Robin and Marion* is the first comic opera, written by Adam de la Halle late in the thirteenth century for the diversion of the Angevin court in Naples. It is a famous piece, charming, funny, and tuneful, about a shepherdess who resists the advances of an amorous knight and remains faithful to her simple Robin. His stalwart cousins Gautier and Baudon and her friend Peronnelle complete the cast, and the evening ends with country games. The work was given a bright, clear performance, distinguished by many subtle touches, but never arty in ways to obscure the essential freshness and directness. Alexandra Montano and John Collis were Marion and Robin. William Hooven was the knight. Tom Zajac and Grant Herreid were the cousins, and Susan Bess Reit was Peronnelle; these three also played a variety of medieval instruments. The work was sung and spoken in Old French, inflected (the program said) with a Picard accent, and the actors had learned how to use—not just how to pronounce—the language.

The City of Ladies was a more elaborate affair. It was a dramatization by Mr. Echols of Christine de Pisan's *Livre de la cité des dames* (1405). Christine, born in Venice in 1365, married at fifteen to an official of Charles V of France's court, was widowed young, with three small children to support. She turned to letters—to such effect that in time both Henry IV of England and Gian Galeazzo Visconti of Milan invited her to grace their courts. She preferred to stay in France, and, after Agincourt, retired into a convent and into silence, breaking the silence only to write, in 1429, a hymn honoring Joan of Arc. Christine wrote books about women's roles in society. She attacked the celebrated *Romance of the Rose* as being insulting to women, and defended her attack in disputes with famous scholars. She wrote a treatise on military strategy which Henry VII had translated for the instruction of his army. And in *The City of Ladies* (Persea publishes a paperback translation) she set forth a vision of an ideal society founded on and regulated by feminine intellect, valor, fortitude, and good sense. The Mannes dramatization showed Reason, Rectitude, and Justice visiting Christine to rouse her from despondency to action. To assist her in the endeavor, they summoned in turn Sappho, the Cumaean, Erythraean, and Tiburtine sibyls, the martial queens Thamiris and Semiramis, the constant Hero, Penelope, and Thisbe, and, at last, the Queen of Heaven, who consented to rule the city. (Christine's book holds a much longer catalogue of heroines; Mr. Echols had to make a choice.) While the company of women grew, their city shaped itself before our eyes. The audience was banked down the two long sides of the concert room at Mannes College. In the bare field between them, a mystic ground plan was suddenly revealed; cornerstones rose, then walls; and at the close a glittering, diaphanous roof swelled and spread to shelter the melodious choir of citizens.

In previous Mannes Camerata productions (Peri's *Euridice,* Gagliano's *Dafne,* Vittori's *Galatea,* put on in Ralph Adams Cram's picturesque Christ Church), Mr. Echols displayed a flair for using available space imaginatively, to provide sounds and spectacle that, without compromise of musicological virtue, re-create for a modern audience the excitement that spectators of early music drama must have felt. This show in Mannes itself combined a sense of courtly entertainment with the ringside intimacy of a production like Grotowski's *Constant Prince.* The music for *The City of Ladies* was compiled from compositions by Christine's contemporaries: all male, alas, but including Gilles Binchois (who set Christine's poems), Baude Cordier, Johannes Ciconia, and Guillaume Dufay. Some complicated compositions were chosen, and it was a measure of how far and how fast the Camerata has grown that they were sung—onstage, without book, without conductor—with pure intonation and lively rhythms. Singer after singer appeared with clear, unforced, steady tone and telling words: among them Evelyn Simon (Christine), Mimi Kate Munroe (Reason), Sheila Burke (Rectitude), Margaret Southwell (Justice), Katherine Galvin, Bettina Reinke, and Deborah Miller (the three sibyls), Ema Bustos-Vale (Hero), Alexandra Visconti-McAdoo (Penelope), and Johanna Maria Rose (Thisbe). The scenic designs were by Bob Phillips and Edmond Ramage. The costume designs, which recalled the illuminations in the British Library manuscript of the *Cité des dames,* were by Susan Douglas. The lighting was by Eric Cornwell. Dorothy Olsson Rubin devised the dances. The three instrumentalists of *Robin* played again, joined by four others, among whom Patricia Neely, on vielle, was outstanding.

The principals and the choristers of the Metropolitan Opera's revival of Gounod's *Roméo et Juliette,* staged by Fabrizio Melano after Paul-Emile Deiber's 1967 production, could with advantage have learned from the Mannes show how to wear medieval dress convincingly, how to paint their faces, comb their hair or wigs, arrange their features, and move their bodies so as to suggest Montagues and Capulets. The disparity between Rolf Gérard's simple, patrician designs and company demeanor that ranged from modern jock (Tybalt, Paris, Mercutio) to opera stock (Lord Capulet, Friar Laurence, the Duke of Verona) was disconcerting. The show was saved—and lifted to an enjoyable level—by its Juliet and by the conductor. Catherine Malfitano, the Juliet, is a serious and dedicated artist. Her voice ran fluently through the intricacies of the famous role. Her trill was plausible. Her coloratura was accurate. The sound was clear and pure, and it filled the big house. She has youth, charm, and also the determination that a Juliet needs. She moved gracefully, winningly, eloquently both as an actress and as a singer, timing and inflecting Gounod's phrases in ways that made one listen. She reinstated Juliet's dramatic potion monologue at the close of the bedroom scene (corresponding to Shakespeare's "I have a faint cold fear thrills through my veins.... How if, when I am laid into the tomb, I wake before the time that Romeo come to redeem me? ... O! if I wake, shall I not be distraught? ... Romeo, I come! this do I drink to thee"), which had probably not been heard before at the Met. Its omission was practiced even during the first run of the opera, at the Théâtre-Lyrique in 1867. Adelina Patti seems to have sung it upon occasion in London (my evidence is a libretto now in the New York Public Library, annotated by a former owner with details of an 1875 Covent Garden performance); but the revised score published in 1888 to conform with the Opéra première of *Roméo* has the unequivocal footnote "A l'Opéra on passe cet Aria." Patti made her Opéra début in the 1888 production, stepping in at short notice when Hariclea Darclée, later the first Tosca, found the role beyond her. The Met program note was misleading on the point, and the

Times critic described the aria as "cooked up" for Patti in 1888. It was part of Gounod's opera from the start; and Miss Malfitano made much of it.

Of *Roméo,* as of most operas, there is no "definitive" version, and it is hard to get things straight. A glance at six scores in the Public Library revealed different music in each of them; my own score, representing the Opéra-Comique version of 1873, is different again. In brief, the long opera was revised during its initial run at the Théâtre-Lyrique (1867–68, ninety performances), revised and abridged for its Opéra-Comique production (1873–87, nearly three hundred performances), and amplified again when it was transferred to the Opéra (1888–1958, six hundred and twenty performances). And at each stage Gounod's publisher, Choudens, without changing the plate number (A.C. 1411), changed the plates and the pagination. Gounod seems to have added the *Idomeneo*-like chorus "O jour de deuil" to the fourth-act finale in 1873; and in 1888, for Jean de Reszke's Romeo, he reworked the number again. At the Met, the big divertissement scene of Juliet's wedding to Paris (played at the Théâtre-Lyrique and at the Opéra but not, it seems, at the Opéra-Comique) is omitted (all but its final pages, Juliet's apparent death, which are tacked on to the preceding scene). At the start of Act V, the little exchange between Friars Laurence and John, explaining how the former's letter to Romeo went astray, is omitted. (I've never heard it in the theatre.) A ballet is danced in the first act. Acts II and III are played without an intermission; so are Acts IV and V. It is a well-devised performance text, preserving the scale of a grand-opera *Roméo.*

The conductor was Sylvain Cambreling, music director of the Brussels Opera, principal guest conductor of Boulez's Ensemble InterContemporain, and conductor last year of Berio's *La vera storia* at the Opéra. I praised him four years ago for a superlative account of Charpentier's *Louise* at the English National Opera. Distinguished conductors seldom come to the Met, so Mr. Cambreling—making his début here—was doubly welcome. Earnest musicians often have mixed feelings about Gounod; Martin Cooper's essay in the New Grove is brief and not unsevere. There was nothing patronizing in Mr. Cambreling's approach. He seemed to have fallen under what Bernard Shaw—reviewing an 1889 *Roméo* with de Reszke and Melba—called "the spell of the heavenly melody, of the exquisite orchestral web of sound colors, of the unfailing dignity and delicacy of accent and rhythm." He was quick to all Gounod's virtues, and re-created the spell for his listeners.

Romeo is an important role. Jussi Bjoerling used to sing it at the Met. A 1947 performance was recorded there and has been published on the Met's own label. Conrad Osborne, reviewing the album in the December 1984 *Opus,* hailed it as a demonstration that sometimes in this world perfection can be attained and that "it is possible for a person to act in a way that is at once perfectly harmonious, fully committed, and quite unfettered." He likened Bjoerling's tone to "an interstreaking of silver and gold, tinted by emerald and ruby. . . . Listening to it is the equivalent of peering deep into a crystal of perfect form and beauty that is turning in the light, so that it is a prism that flashes to us the spectrum in all its variety, yet always in harmony. And along with these sensory affects, it has emotive properties, the power to sadden or to thrill. It has this power in and of itself, independent of the meanings of words (though not of their sounds)." The tone "nevertheless bears the word's encoding, which rides within it like a written scroll embedded in richest amber, and sends its messages therefrom with an aesthetic lift and finish it could not otherwise know." It would be idiotic to chide the Met's new Romeo, Neil Shicoff, for being no Bjoerling, but it would be wrong not to chide him for not trying harder, for not seeking at once to refine and to enlarge his art, for being apparently content—as Placido Domingo and Luciano Pavarotti are apparently content—to make unfailingly decent tenor sound and do little more. Mr. Shicoff displayed a well-trained and well-formed tenor, but he was no Romeo. His "acting" was a handful of arm-waving mannerisms; the least Romeo-like gesture was pressing his fingertips together and then raising them to his nose—like a schoolmaster pondering his acid comment on a schoolboy's misconstruction. (Does he find it necessary to "pop his ears" before any important entry?) Operatic acting is a mystery of its own. In 1889, the *Star* sent its drama critic, "Spectator," to Covent Garden's *Traviata,* Emma Albani the heroine. And Shaw, the music critic of the *Star,* later reported, "He spoke of the whole performance with unqualified contempt, and positively refused to take our eminent lyric *tragédienne* seriously as an actress. What is more—and I recommend this point to all who are interested in opera— Spectator was right. . . . There is no denying that the sort of thing that Madame Albani and her colleagues do at the Opera is beneath the notice of any intelligent student of dramatic art." When I heard Bjoerling sing Rodolfo at Covent Garden, in 1960, his demeanor was that of a dignified Swedish ambassador. He did not scrabble on the floor in the search for Mimì's key; the Mimì—Rosanna Carteri, down on her knees—had to raise a hand to the tabletop so that Rodolfo could grasp it and exclaim at its coldness. [*A reader chided me for these remarks: did I not know that Bjoerling suffered great physical pain in his last years? I didn't. I let the sentence stand because of what immediately follows.*] But by tones and by phrasing Bjoerling gave a vivid impersonation of the ardent young poet. Mr. Shicoff's tones and phrasing seemed to come straight from a vocal studio. He was unspontaneous, unconvincing, monotonous—voicing Romeo's music with fine technical control but without "the power to sadden or to thrill." Against Miss Malfitano's Juliet, alive at every instant, this Romeo was a tenor going through movements. One wouldn't bother to complain did Mr. Shicoff not seem to be potentially a valuable artist, capable of better things, and endowed with a voice that could be used for the creation of characters. Perhaps all he needs is acting lessons—of the kind that fire an artist's imagination to vivid, communicative, apparently spontaneous utterance. I'd like to hear him in a production that had been rehearsed by Peter Hall, Peter Brook, Frank Corsaro.

The Boston Early Music Festival Orchestra—star of the 1985 Festival, and America's answer to the contemporary eighteenth-century orchestras long established in Europe—came to New York this month to give a concert in Alice Tully Hall. Gustav Leonhardt conducted a program of Zelenka, Muffat, Bach, and Rameau. He conducted in the twentieth-century manner, standing in front of the band. The sounds were not as bold, joyous, and free as those Nicholas McGegan, seated at a harpsichord, drew from the orchestra in the Boston production of

Handel's *Teseo* last year, but they were elegant, well shaped, and pleasing. There was pretty interplay, in Zelenka's Sinfonia a 8 Concertanti, between violin and oboe, and violin, oboe, and bassoon, but also a smudge or two, unexpected from such virtuoso instrumentalists as Daniel Stepner, Stephen Hammer, and Dennis Godburn. Mr. Leonhardt holds his executants on a tight rein. His ideas are firmly shaped, individual, often piquant. The Rameau was a long suite of bewitching instrumental numbers drawn from the heroic pastoral *Zaïs*, starting with that extraordinary overture representative of Chaos broken into clashing elements and then arranged into order.

The orchestra is a band of choice players, mainly from Boston, New York, and California, and for the New York concert it was reassembled without change of personnel. After *Teseo*, I declared it the finest baroque band I'd ever heard. (Winton Dean said the same, in the *Musical Times*.) This concert, the second in a Lincoln Center Great Performers series on original instruments, didn't quite confirm that first impression; but then Tully Hall—a bleak place, acoustically and visually—may have taken a toll. Friends seated toward the back told me that fine detail was not reaching them.

Thomas Gallant gave a short, lively recital entitled "The New Oboe" in Carnegie Recital Hall this month. The new oboe is not the plangent, pastoral instrument heard piping its slow ditty in the country scene of Berlioz's Fantastic Symphony. It chirps and chatters, bubbles and bounces. It's the instrument Elliott Carter wrote for in the "Sandpiper" song of his Elizabeth Bishop cycle. Mr. Gallant's program began with Heinz Holliger's Study II (1982), which opens on one of the oboe's highest notes, drops to the lowest, and runs the range of new, "unnatural" sounds, undreamed of by those who designed the instrument, which modern players have learned to coax from it. In Harvey Sollberger's *Two Oboes Troping* (1963), Mr. Gallant was joined by Claudia Coonce, and the pair suggested two birds pecking and chortling merrily over a basket of delicious nuts. Gilbert Amy's *Jeux* (1970), for one to four oboes, was done in a three-oboe version—Marilyn Coyne joined the ensemble—and the trio became the *Macbeth* witches in unmalicious vein, cackling and gossiping volubly over each subject that came up. There was both brilliance and lyricism in Luciano Berio's *Sequenza VII* (1969), for solo oboe against a pedal B (supplied from the wings by Miss Coonce and Miss Coyne). Berio uses "multiphonics"—those faint chordal squawks whose pitches seldom sound convinced—in a musing, poetical manner. Eleven strings from the Group for Contemporary Music, conducted by Anthony Korf, then joined Mr. Gallant for Berio's *Chemins IV on Sequenza VII* (1975)—the earlier solo cradled in an intricate web of string counterpoints. Krzysztof Penderecki's *Capriccio* (1965), also for oboe and eleven strings, is a work of sixties avant-garde which has stayed fresh. Mr. Gallant is a player who unites technical mastery with intentness, charm, and wit. This was an unusual and attractive recital.

February 10, 1986

THE Metropolitan Opera's revival of *Idomeneo* last month had merits—most of them provided by Frederica von Stade, as Idamantes. It was good to hear and see her right back on form, finding again the forward, direct quality of tone which evokes an instant response in the listener, giving a fearless yet touching portrayal of a young prince with nerves close to the surface. The Ilia, Electra, and Idomeneus were new to the production. Carol Vaness's Electra was striking, but her timbre was sometimes opaque, covered—not fresh and bright—and Jean-Pierre Ponnelle's production keeps Electra on the verge of caricature. Linda Zoghby's Ilia seemed workaday until she reached the third aria, "Zeffiretti lusinghieri," through which her voice moved firmly and well. The new, slim, boyish David Rendall took the tragic title role. He looked too young for the part and did not sing brilliantly enough to justify the instatement of the long version of the bravura aria "Fuor del mar."

Mr. Ponnelle's sepia stage pictures are handsome. His production, staged now by Lesley Koenig, retains all its tiresomeness. At every mention of Neptune or the *implacabili dei*—who are mentioned often in *Idomeneo*—a giant, glowering mask of Neptune lights up in the background. Miss Zoghby suffers most from Mr. Ponnelle's insistence on filling the stage with unwanted extra characters. She sings her first aria in competition with cross-stage dumb show behind her from Miss Vaness and Miss von Stade. Her second is "prompted" by Miss von Stade, playing peekaboo from behind a pillar. ("Try another verse, dear, and see if Dad won't relent.") In the third, a soliloquy if ever there was one (the recitative begins "Solitudini amiche"), she shares the scene with Miss von Stade. The opening words of Act II, Idomeneus' to Arbaces, are "Siam soli"; the Met curtain goes up on a stage dressed with supers, who have to be waved off before the act can begin. Miss von Stade presents a living, breathing character. The others suggest singers going through moves that Mr. Ponnelle prescribed for them.

Jeffrey Tate's conducting was balanced and careful; some of the numbers seemed to move rather slowly. Many necessary appoggiaturas were missing. The harpsichord accompaniment to the recitatives, played by Dan Saunders, was as laggard as it had been in *Figaro,* and arpeggios went rolling on well after any occasion for them had passed. Surely among the Met comprimari and choristers it should be possible to find four well-matched, agreeable young voices to sing the duet and quartet episodes of the first-act choruses.

In Carnegie Hall last month, the Philadelphia Orchestra, conducted by Charles Dutoit, gave a glowing account of Bartók's opera *Duke Bluebeard's Castle*. The bard who speaks the prologue—it was omitted in this concert performance—suggests that the stage on which the action unfolds may well be one of the mind. *Bluebeard* can be overwhelming in the theatre, but it is hardly less impressive when the orchestra alone depicts the gloomy, menacing castle hall, the shafts of light streaming in as each door in turn is opened, the scenes revealed behind them: a ghastly, bleeding torture chamber; high-heaped, sparkling jewels; a broad domain of "silken meadows, velvet forests, tranquil streams of winding silver"; a lake of tears; the pale presences of Bluebeard's former wives. Some performances of *Bluebeard* use the score for a display of high-powered orchestral virtuosity. This Philadelphia performance, played with great warmth and beauty of tone, was subtle and moving. The emotions of the drama and its mysterious psychological symbolism took first place. The Judith was Sylvia Sass, and she was surprising. At the Met she has sung Tosca, at Covent Garden Norma, in Turin Lady Macbeth; but for Judith she found a thin, quietly telling, poignant timbre. Her performance was gentle, delicate, lyrical, and loving. The Bluebeard was Aage Haugland; he was noble and affecting. The work was sung in the original Hungarian and is best listened to that way, for the trochaic tetrameters of Béla Balázs's libretto sung in English or in German, taking heavy tonic accents, in a metre never varied, always sound like *Hiawatha*—whereas in Hungarian they flow more freely, and the singers break almost automatically, it seems, from exact, pedantic adherence to the written note values.

The Philadelphians' visits to Carnegie Hall are usually high points of New York's busy orchestral scene. At this concert, *Bluebeard* was preceded by an account of Sibelius's Violin Concerto in which Young Uck Kim and Mr. Dutoit conspired in a rapturous, sometimes almost febrile interpretation. It was unconventional but gripping.

Two weeks later, the orchestra returned, under its music director, Riccardo Muti. The concert began with three pieces by Giuseppe Martucci, a contemporary of Leoncavallo and an Italian composer who wrote not operas but instrumental music. As a conductor, Martucci was important: he introduced *Tristan* to Italy (in 1888); he championed the music of Brahms, of Sullivan, Stanford, and Parry. As a composer, he seems small beer, on the evidence of the three works Mr. Muti presented. They were the Notturno and Novelletta that Toscanini used to play, and a Giga—all three of them orchestrations of piano pieces. Perhaps there is more to Martucci. Elgar's stature is hardly revealed by *Salut d'amour,* or Dvořák's by the Humoresque.

Richard Wernick's Violin Concerto followed—a New York première, a few days after the world première, in Philadelphia. I'd like to write about it with enthusiasm, for Wernick's earlier music—there is a fair amount of it on record—has been arresting. But of this concerto I retain an impression only of a carefully wrought structure, a few striking passages, uninspired thematic material, and clean, confident playing by the soloist, Gregory Fulkerson. Dvořák's Fifth Symphony, in F, completed the program. Mr. Muti's approach was not lighthearted. (In a playful—but appreciative—essay on the symphony Tovey called it "naughtily Dvořáky," suggested that by *grandioso* Dvořák meant "the grandeur of a Christmas tree," and likened the thematic combinations of the slow movement to the Dormouse's way of continuing to murmur "Twinkle,

twinkle" until pinched or put into the teapot.) But the playing was exquisite, with lovely timbres and translucent textures.

The Cracow Philharmonic, conducted by Krzysztof Penderecki, gave two Carnegie Hall concerts last month. The first brought the New York première of Penderecki's Second Cello Concerto, the second (which I missed) that of his Polish Requiem. The concerto—first played by Mstislav Rostropovich, three years ago—is an effective piece. Penderecki's music is always "effective." He's an odd composer, difficult to assess. Honest emotion and aspiration are not in doubt. The working is skillful. But the musical ideas can be banal, and when they are piled up to make grandiose statements about subjects of great significance a listener feels uneasy. The new concerto is not grandiose, however. I'm unsure whether it is a glittering addition to the cello repertory or just a cunning, elaborate construction. Yo-Yo Ma was a brilliant and impassioned soloist.

The concert began with Penderecki's *Jacob's Awakening,* which exploits the eerie, elusive sound of twelve ocarinas, and it ended with Shostakovich's Sixth Symphony. Penderecki is a first-rate conductor, clear, incisive, and thoughtful, and the Cracow Philharmonic is an excellent orchestra. The lean, athletic string tone, the shapely wind phrasing, the general sense of expressiveness without fatness were striking. Shostakovich's Sixth is a defiantly personal work: a long, slow tragic first movement followed by what the program note called "a bright, mischievous scherzo" and "an amusing rondo." I hear no mischief or mirth in those movements (or in the outwardly "bright" movements of the Ninth, which is in some ways a successor of the Sixth). Nor, it seemed, does Penderecki, for in this Polish performance they took on a chilling quality of animation without gaiety. Themes kin to those of Prokofiev in his most buoyant, perky vein carried overtones of bitterness, smart, and anger.

The latest of the movie palaces now become home to a symphony orchestra is the Fox in San Diego—built in 1929, bought in 1984 by the San Diego Symphony, and reopened this season as Symphony Hall. Like Powell Hall in St. Louis, Heinz Hall in Pittsburgh, the Paramount in Oakland, and the Orpheum in Vancouver, the building welcomes concert audiences into romantic, picturesque, and opulently decorated spaces. The San Diego Fox—unlike its contemporary homonyms in Atlanta, St. Louis, and Detroit (all newly restored to splendor) and in San Francisco (razed)—was not built on a Babylonian scale. The architects were William Templeton Johnson and William Day. The style is what is loosely called Spanish Renaissance—not the stern grandeur of the Escorial or Charles V's Granada palace but the later exuberance of Santiago de Compostela and Toledo Cathedral, recaptured in San Diego by the buildings of the 1915–16 Panama-California Exposition, which still stand in Balboa Park. Johnson and Day went further, gave free rein to their fancy, added memories of Loire châteaux and of Hampton Court to their Spanish capriccio, and produced an eclectic Xanadu. Like many other picture palaces, this Fox is a curious and attractive mixture of gimcrack pretension and real grandeur—an evocation in plaster of what the old craftsmen carved in stone. It lacks the distinction of work by Thomas W. Lamb, Timothy Pflueger, George L. and C. W. Rapp, John Eberson,

C. Howard Crane—architects of America's most notable popular cathedrals. But it is a building that disposes listeners to pleasure as they enter it and promises them something unusual, lifted above the daily round.

Like most of the picture palaces converted into concert halls, the Fox is not intimate, either visually or acoustically. It now seats twenty-two hundred and fifty people; the rows are widely spaced, and the aisles are generous. Early reports on the acoustics were mixed, and work is still being done with arrangements of the acoustic rig on and above the platform. When I visited the hall last month, I sat in the first of its two balconies and found the results pleasing. Ideally, I would ask for slightly longer reverberation, for chords to go ringing on for just a moment after the singers and players sounding them have stopped. But the sounds that reached me were true. The hall's profusion of balustrades, bosses, and bas-reliefs, pilasters, coffering ensures a proper dispersal of timbres throughout the range.

The program, admittedly, was not that of a standard symphony concert. David Atherton, a founder of the London Sinfonietta, is the music director of the San Diego Symphony, and its programs are seldom commonplace. This was a Stravinsky double bill: the Mass, for chorus and ten instrumentalists, and *The Soldier's Tale,* for three actors (who were amplified), a dancer, and seven instrumentalists. The conductor was Michael Lankester, conductor-in-residence of the Pittsburgh Symphony. He gave an excellently poised account of the Mass, combining lapidary strength with elegant phrasing. The San Diego Master Chorale sang surely. (The opening clause of the Credo was for some reason not chanted; the movement began in mid-sentence.) *The Soldier's Tale* was given in a crisp, clear production, directed by Jack O'Brien (who is the artistic director of San Diego's Old Globe Theatre). Robert Foxworth, the narrator, and Gary Dontzig, the Devil, were masters of tone, timing, and inflection. Andrés Cárdenes, the orchestra's concertmaster, was trim in the important violin part, and all the instrumentalists were expert, Peter Rofé playing a strikingly melodious double-bass.

FROM HIGHEST GLORY FALL'N

February 17, 1986

WHEN Covent Garden, a year ago, staged its new production of Handel's dramatic oratorio *Samson,* the result was greeted with a chorus of disapproval and dismay. The show was a joint venture of Covent Garden, the Lyric Opera of Chicago, and the Metropolitan Opera. *Samson* went on to Chicago, and last week it reached the Met—a solemn, splendid tombstone laid on a year of bright Handelian adventures. Handel first performed *Samson* at Covent Garden, in 1743, and he revived it there in eight further seasons (and once at the King's). The work returned in 1958, staged by Herbert Graf in rich scenery, by Oliver

Messel, that suggested Tiepolo Biblical tableaux brought to life; Jon Vickers was the hero, and Joan Sutherland sang "Let the bright Seraphims." Nearly thirty years later, Mr. Vickers is again the protagonist, and the new production has been built around his weighty, powerful, pious representation of the remorseful hero.

Handel's drama has three sources: the Book of Judges; Milton's long, noble tragedy after the manner of the Ancients, *Samson Agonistes;* and Newburgh Hamilton's reworking of the tragedy (which was intended for the study, not the stage) as a libretto, leavened by lyrics adapted from earlier Milton poems. Hamilton brought in the Philistines, with their exuberant revels. He omitted Puritan propaganda, such as passages in praise of temperance. He softened the characterization of Dalila (Milton's and his spelling). Something of Milton's bitter misogyny survives: Micah sings of women that "so much Self-love does rule the Sex, They nothing else love long," and the chorus adds, "To Man God's universal Law Gave Pow'r to keep the Wife in awe." (But at the Met both Micah's air and the chorus are deleted.) As first composed, the oratorio ended in Miltonic vein, with "peace and consolation ... And calm of mind all passion spent." But before the first performance both the opening scene of Philistine celebration and the close were expanded: the opening with airs and a choral refrain adapted from Milton's Psalm 81, the close with the Israelites' jubilant "Let the bright Seraphims" and a choral "endless Blaze of Light."

The new production is designed, by Timothy O'Brien, in black and white, varied by a ragged gray robe for Samson, a touch of blue in Dalila's bodice, and a red uniform for Harapha, the Philistine captain. The chorus costumes are eighteenth-century—black with white ruffles and white cravats. The women wear white housemaids' caps, and the Philistine women carry fans that they flutter and snap more or less in time to the music. The Jewish men wear tricornes; the Philistine men wear curled white wigs and white gloves. Elijah Moshinsky's production is in the modish manner of Luca Ronconi, with formal groupings (some of them impressive, others affected) amid big chunks of scenery that are trundled into various positions: a white arch, after Wren; two black columns; tall bookshelves; and, in the final act, a towering portal. Samson is wheeled about on a large dolly. Harapha is confined to an elevated white playpen on wheels. During the Samson-Harapha duet, the two vehicles lock and, like bumper cars, go round and round. Micah (a part that Gaetano Guadagni sang in some of Handel's revivals) is for some reason dressed as a woman, his role changed from Israelite chorus-leader to that of, apparently, Samson's housekeeper. In general, this is a serious and thoughtful—if misconceived—production spoiled by episodes of miscalculation and silliness. Handel composed *Samson* for the theatre but not for the stage. It is not easy, here or in the other dramatic oratorios, to find apt visual representation for action conceived as if for an ideal theatre—one in which elaborately decked scenes can change in the twinkling of a cadence, crowds muster or disperse in an instant, and the "focus" change with cinematic swiftness from mass tableau to intimate close-up. The mannered Augustan imagery of Mr. Moshinsky's production, the avoidance of realism, the execution in diagrammatic monochrome represent a considered approach to the difficulties, but the direct impact of Handel's drama is reduced.

Handel's music seems to tell of actions more vivid, picturesque, and spontaneous. Like many other directors of the opera and oratorios, Mr. Moshinsky has decided—mistakenly, in my view—to put a distancing "frame" between the work and its modern audience. The result is, in his own words (as reported in a *Times* interview), "like a play within a play, the eighteenth century putting on a play about the Biblical Samson."

Mr. Vickers as Samson could hardly be contained by any frame, however robust. He wallows in the role. It is a self-indulgent performance, without subtlety—violent and extreme. He roars, snarls, croons, moans. He tears Handel's passions to tatters, o'erdoing Termagant. One can think it a tremendous performance or an unbearable one, or both. The recitatives are delivered very slowly, with big pauses and sledgehammer emphases. The rhythm of the airs is pulled out of shape. The powerful, unwieldy, heroic voice is forced through the notes. The singer, it is plain, is moved by fierce identification with Samson's blinded suffering, humiliation, and shame, his self-reproach for sensual weakness, and his anger at his traitress wife. Beyond that, Mr. Vickers seeks fervently to convey a sense of spiritual light beginning to shine through the blighted hero's moral and physical darkness. The image does run through the oratorio: Samson's last song, "Thus when the Sun from's wat'ry Bed, All curtain'd with a cloudy Red," is a sunrise air. *Samson*, like *Samson Agonistes*, is the tragedy of a strong, proud man brought low by his own fault and rallying to compass one mighty deed before his death. Yet in none of the versions is the Samson story a conventionally edifying one. The Biblical Samson is an amorous folk hero, and cruel to animals. (He ties lighted brands to foxes' tails.) In the words of the Old Testament scholar Stanley Arthur Cook, "He is inspired by no serious religious or patriotic purpose, and becomes the enemy of the Philistines only from personal motives of revenge, the one passion which is stronger in him than the love of women." Milton gives him grandeur, but the play is veiled autobiography, moving in its lamentation of blindness, less so in its railing against Dalila, and ennobled and raised to sublimity by the poet's command of language. Handel's version, as Winton Dean remarks in his great book on the oratorios, "is little concerned with religion and philosophy." ("That does not diminish its artistic stature," he adds.) *Samson* is not *Parsifal*. Like *Messiah*, it was devised as a fine entertainment, albeit one on a grand and elevated level. The Met production, taking its tone from the protagonist's approach, gives it a heavier charge of solemnity, morality, and preachiness than it can decently bear, and, by a familiar paradox—the weakening effect of *underlining* all important statements—lessens the Aristotelian catharsis that more directly Handelian performances of *Samson* achieve.

Heaviness reigns. Droning organ accompaniment dulls many passages that in Handel's day would have been declaimed over fleeting harpsichord chords. The composer wrote Dalila's role for a soubrette, Kitty Clive, a famous Polly in *The Beggar's Opera,* celebrated for her impersonations of country girls, hoydens and dowdies, superannuated beauties, viragos and for her parodies of Italian divas. (Dr. Johnson called her "a better romp than any I ever saw in nature.") Kathleen Battle could recreate the role in that spirit; at the Met, Leona Mitchell turned Dalila into a majestic matron. She was beautiful to look at, and her tones were voluptuous—Samson's infatuation was understandable—but she was hardly the Dalila implied by the score. The song for the Philistine Woman, which opens the drama, and the song for the Israelitish Woman, which ends it, were both composed for Christina Maria Avoglio (who at the first performance also sang the turtledove air, "With plaintive Notes," that in later revivals—and in the Met production—was taken by Dalila). Avoglio must have been a light, bright soprano; the Nativity scene of *Messiah* and Iris in *Semele* were other parts she created. Carol Vaness, who in London last year was the Dalila, sang the pieces strongly but with sound that was rich rather than bright and forward, and she swallowed the words. In "Let the bright Seraphims" a scene change behind her competed for the audience's attention. Sarah Walker, as the female Micah, was gravely eloquent, although the voice seemed a little small for the Met. She used the text expressively. John Macurdy, as Manoah, Samson's father, produced deep tones of beautiful quality, but he did not sing in tune. Paul Plishka's Harapha blustered boldly. Enrico Di Giuseppe, the Philistine Man, was feeble. The chorus was sometimes weak, sometimes very strong—depending, it seemed, on where the singers were placed and which way they faced.

Julius Rudel conducted, as in London. There the critics cast him as the villain of the evening. "Julius Rudel's view of the score revives all the worst excesses of the old tradition, with sagging rhythms, romantic rubatos and rallentandos, recitatives after the manner of church responses, and a grossly unstylistic treatment of the organ" (Winton Dean in the *Times Literary Supplement*). "The articulation was heavy and airless" (Stanley Sadie in *Opera*). "Rhythmic lifelessness and rhythmic insecurity (sometimes both at once)" (Max Loppert in the *Financial Times*). I feel slightly more kindly, and anyway Mr. Rudel has since conducted both the London and the Chicago runs of the piece, and found possible ways of executing a score written for a small theatre in ever larger theatres. At the Met, the final (Samson-less) scene moved surely, I thought: the Dead March was the more moving for being restrained, almost understated; the entries of the threnody "Glorious Hero" were well placed. Otherwise, it was a performance deliberately geared to the eccentricities of Mr. Vickers' craggy, intractable Samson. There is not much any conductor can do except go along with them, and reconcile the rest in a manner that will not seem stylistically quite incompatible.

The Met sells a libretto reproduced from the old Handel Society edition, with its misreadings of Handel's autograph uncorrected: Samson deplores the "gratuity" (read "garrulity") that led him impiously to "blast" (read "blab") God's counsel to his wife.

The City Opera has announced new productions of *Don Quichotte* and *Werther* for its 1986 season, and a revival of *Cendrillon,* but in general the Massenet high tides of a few years ago have receded. People curious to hear *Grisélidis, Ariane, Bacchus, Cléopâtre, Amadis* are still waiting. This month, however, Bel Canto—the company that gave us *Esclarmonde* before the Met did—put on a double bill of the one-act *Le Portrait de Manon* (1894) and the two-act *Thérèse* (1907). *Le Portrait de Manon*—which was given a concert performance at Hunter College eight years ago—is sentimental and slight: a four-character opera in which the aging Chevalier des Grieux (now a baritone) forbids his ward Jean (a *travesti* role) to marry the penniless Aurore but relents when struck by Aurore's resemblance to Manon. Aurore—as des Grieux's friend Tiberge reveals—is Manon's niece. The score is a potpourri of themes from *Manon*.

Thérèse—of which a London recording appeared a few years ago—is a three-character opera, with a few minor roles and a small part for chorus. Act I is set in 1792, Act II a year later. André Thorel, a Girondin leader, son of the steward on the Clerval estate, has bought the château and secretly, like a loyal retainer, holds it in trust so that in calmer times he can restore it to his childhood friend Armand de Clerval. His wife, Thérèse, in days before the Revolution loved Armand. Armand turns up, and André hides him in the château. Thérèse is torn between love and matrimonial duty. When the Girondins fall, and from the window she sees André being led to the guillotine, she cries "Vive le Roi!" to the mob below and thus condemns herself to join her husband on the scaffold. It's not a serious political drama—less so, even, than Giordano's *Andrea Chénier,* which reached Paris in 1905 and no doubt gave Massenet some ideas. Other sources of inspiration, he recounts in his memoirs, were the brave death of Lucile Desmoulins; a visit to Bagatelle, an Artois house in the Bois de Boulogne both before and after the Revolution, later bought by Richard Wallace (of the Wallace Collection); and, perhaps most of all, the singer Lucy Arbell, Massenet's muse at the time and, it seems, a Wallace herself. (One consults Grove in vain for information about this important dramatic mezzo, who created roles in six Massenet operas and after his death kept two more—*Cléopâtre* and *Amadis*—off the stage for years while she laid claim to them.) The composer and his librettist, Jules Claretie, spun an effective sequence of duets, monologues, and a trio, reaching its climax in a Bernhardt-like speech for Thérèse that is dramatically declaimed, the tempo but not the pitches indicated. (As an appendix, the score has an alternative version, with notes, for heroines who prefer to sing the scene.) *Thérèse* is a domestic drama about a wife's dilemma, lent a touch of excitement by the Revolutionary background and a touch of ancien-régime elegance as Thérèse and Armand recall days before the Revolution. Their memories of a ball at Versailles are accompanied by a harpsichord minuet, offstage; at the first performance it was played by the famous pianist Louis Diémer.

The 1954 Grove declared in its article on Massenet that "to have heard *Manon* is to have heard the whole of him." Not so—as performances of the grand operas *Le Cid* and *Esclarmonde,* the fairy-tale *Cendrillon,* the ambitiously picturesque *Hérodiade* and *Thaïs,* the warmhearted *Le Jongleur* and *Don Quichotte* have now shown. One could fairly rephrase the remark, however, as "to have heard *Manon* and *Werther* is to have heard the *best* of him," for in those two works the level of invention is consistently high. Every number pleases. *Thérèse* belongs, rather, with *La Navarraise* and *Sapho* as a drama effectively set to music, not an opera with numbers whose music one remembers.

The Bel Canto productions, given in the Joan of Arc Junior High School Theatre, straightforwardly staged by Cynthia Edwards, in simple settings by Dain Marcus, were good enough to "reveal" the works. In *Le Portrait,* Debra Kitabjian was a poised young Jean. To the title role of *Thérèse* Tamara Mitchel brought admirable dramatic presence and sure musical instincts; although her voice was not purely focussed, she was a striking performer. Johannes Somary conducted rather stodgily, without much grace. The instrument used for the minuet made a tin-tack sound. The minuet returns in delicate orchestral garb as a prelude to Act II; the first oboe seemed unaware that the solo here once moved Massenet to mime, with delight, the plucking and smelling of a spring flower. The operas were essayed in French. Only Miss Kitabjian and Miss Mitchel were generally intelligible, and no one laughed at the jokes in *Le Portrait*.

SCENES WITHOUT SETTINGS

February 24, 1986

IT has been a busy season for concert opera. *Anna Bolena* in Avery Fisher Hall and *Rigoletto* and *Duke Bluebeard's Castle* in Carnegie Hall have already been noted. This month, the American Symphony, conducted by John Mauceri, performed the second act of *Parsifal* in Carnegie Hall. Mr. Mauceri is a thoughtful conductor, concerned to discover what composers intended—what they wanted to hear—rather than simply to conform to current practice. In England and Italy last year, he conducted accounts of *Rigoletto* heedful of the metronome markings in Verdi's score, and this *Parsifal* moves at gaits influenced by those of the old conductors—Carl Muck, Siegfried Wagner—who made *Parsifal* records. The platform disposition—with a double-bass foundation laid out across the back wall, not off center on the right—was unusual. I'd like to call the result a revelation, but it wasn't. The tone of the orchestra was not broad or beautiful enough. The strings didn't sing. On a Carnegie platform narrowed by bevies of flowermaidens at either side, the sound seemed cramped. *Parsifal* needs plenty of space; outside Bayreuth, the acoustically most impressive performance I've heard was in the Albert Hall.

Gary Bachlund, a tenor from Los Angeles and a winner of the Frank Sinatra Auditions, took the title role. He is a find, for he has a strong, easily produced, young-heroic voice of agreeable quality. The Kundry was Gail Gilmore, a beautiful woman, a "presence," and a singer with some lovely sounds in her voice but no sure, even control of them through wide-ranging phrases. Eric Halfvarson was a fierce Klingsor. Reginald Goodall, who in London is preparing *Parsifal* for the English National Opera's Easter production, asked for his principal flowermaiden to be taken out of all other roles during the rehearsal and the run, lest her voice lose its finest bloom. Private enterprise cannot afford such care. Mr. Mauceri's principal flowermaiden, Dawn Upshaw, had been singing Schubert up in Symphony Space two days earlier, and she was due to appear the following day in the première of the Met *Samson*. (In the event, she withdrew from it, indisposed.) The solo flowermaidens were not a particularly

442

seductive sextet; the choral ones, drawn from the Dessoff Choirs, the Mannes College Chorus, and the Y Chorale, were assured but lacked fragrance of timbre and rhythmic beguilement.

The American Symphony seems to be in an unsettled state. Its January concert—Mahler's Ninth Symphony, conducted by Benjamin Zander—sounded underrehearsed and was not well played. Before the *Parsifal* act, however, Mr. Mauceri conducted a noble Sibelius Seventh: excellently paced, and rendered with bold, full, yet sensitively shaded orchestral colors.

On New Year's Eve, and four times again last month, in Fisher Hall, the Philharmonic played a Wagner program: the overture and bacchanale from *Tannhäuser,* the prelude and Liebestod from *Tristan,* the *Siegfried Idyll,* and the finale of *Götterdämmerung.* Edo de Waart conducted, deputizing for Klaus Tennstedt. His work was much like that in the San Francisco *Ring*—episodes of nicely planned and neatly executed detail, but no long line, no inevitable-seeming flow. The orchestral sound was not ample and glowing, and the brass produced some raucous climaxes. Ute Vinzing was the Isolde and the Brünnhilde. She has won some renown as a Wagnerian heroic soprano, and one heard why: the high notes rang out clearly, narrow in timbre but brightly and forcefully projected. Her chest register was also telling. But there were some harsh mid-phrase transitions, and the faces Miss Vinzing pulled while she sang seemed to reflect a strenuous, uneasy method.

The Opera Orchestra of New York, directed by Eve Queler, began its Carnegie series last month with *I lombardi*—Verdi's fourth opera and second great success. This was the first opera I heard Miss Queler conduct, twelve years ago, when her cast was Renata Scotto (who sang her role with flashing energy), José Carreras, and Paul Plishka. Mr. Plishka returned for the revival, Aprile Millo was the soprano, and Carlo Bergonzi the tenor. I had not heard Miss Millo before but had read praise of her Met appearances last season in second casts of *Simon Boccanegra* and *Ernani.* It is easy to be moved to critical overenthusiasm by the excitement of hearing a fine young artist for the first time. Let me say, temperately, that Miss Millo struck me as being superior to most of the Verdi heroines active today, and the equal of any. For a start, she had the whole voice under control, through all the registers. She filled the long, arching spans. She sang accurate and brilliant coloratura. Of both dramatic declamation and lyrical cantilena she had an easy command. She never pushed her voice into edginess or impurity but let it pour out, shining and true. Beyond that, she showed keen musical and dramatic instincts, timing phrases and uttering words in ways that made one listen. Before the performance, it was announced that she was indisposed yet would sing all the same. She began cautiously and appeared somewhat ill at ease in Act I; thereafter, nothing noticeably dimmed a performance at once disciplined and generous, technically and emotionally secure.

Mr. Bergonzi is perhaps the last big tenor left who is able to turn a melting phrase. He spoiled things at times by grunting before an attack, by hanging on to his best notes for as long as they would last—whether or not the sense called for it—and by pushing swelled notes to a grunted cutoff. Those failings apart, he remains an artist with a rare feeling for phrase and line, and—at sixty-one—retains a timbre both virile and liquid. Mr. Plishka was in the imposing form he seems regularly to find for Carnegie Hall appearances. The other important tenor role was bravely sung by Dino Di Domenico. Miss Queler's conducting was urgent and committed.

Earlier in the season, Verdi's *Giovanna d'Arco,* his seventh opera, was performed in Fisher Hall with an eminent cast: Margaret Price, Mr. Bergonzi, and Sherrill Milnes. Miss Price has a real Verdi voice, full, unforced, and beautiful except when it loses purity above the staff. She is not an impetuous artist, does not take chances or yield to the inspiration of the moment. In recitatives, she tended to prolong penultimate notes, like an old-style oratorio singer. The soprano role of *Giovanna,* like that of *I lombardi,* was written for Erminia Frezzolini—whose voice, Verdi's amanuensis, Emanuele Muzio, said, was like Jenny Lind's in its ability to sustain even, flexible phrases—and it is almost equally demanding. Miss Price had worked out an interpretation that matched its demands to her own considerable abilities. It was not an ample, fiery account of Verdi's Joan that she offered, but it was an accomplished and satisfying one.

Mr. Milnes was in good voice. The baritone's first aria is marked *grandioso declamato.* The second rises to a *grandioso,* but it also has phrases marked *piano,* which Mr. Milnes sang loudly, and it should close with a *pianissimo* F-sharp on the staff, not a bellowed one an octave higher. Few baritones are prepared to trust Verdi and try for the excitement of very soft, charged, intense singing of vigorous passages—an effect he often called for and counted on—with volume held in reserve for the opening-out moments.

Richard Bradshaw conducted, making his New York début. His merits as a Verdian are receiving ever wider recognition; reviews of a *Falstaff* he conducted in San Francisco this season were enthusiastic. *Giovanna,* one of Verdi's shortest scores, was cruelly abridged. (Miss Queler's account of the much longer *I lombardi* was almost uncut.) But Verdi himself—in practice, though not in principle—tailored scores to the circumstances of a particular performance. In a Seattle *Forza* that Mr. Bradshaw conducted and I directed, we did likewise. A spell in the theatre, "dirtying my hands" with matters I usually just write about, persuaded me that a shortened version may sometimes be preferable to an underrehearsed full one. Peter Brook in *The Empty Space* argues cogently that "the more the critic becomes an insider, the better," and that "a closer relation with the work will in no way put the critic into the position of connivance with the people he has got to know." At the worst, "a tiny social problem—how does a critic talk to someone whom he has just damned in print?" may arise. It is an argument sometimes contested in this country. So, since I "got to know" Mr. Bradshaw while working with him, let me mute my admiration for his prowess in *Giovanna* by saying simply that he seconded the strengths of his cast, of the Orchestra of St. Luke's, and of the New York Choral Artists in ways that made "a work of brilliant patches" (Julian Budden's phrase for the opera, in his Verdi monograph) consistently exciting; and—since a critic's final concern is with a result, not the reasons for it—reiterate that extensive cuts in a high-priced, metropolitan performance of a rare Verdi opera are unacceptable.

Carnegie Hall's own annual series of opera presentations, in cooperation with Columbia Artists, devised and supervised by Matthew Epstein, aims at the ideal and, by careful casting and long, careful rehearsals, seeks to reach it without corner-cutting. Three Rossini operas were done in 1982–83: *La donna del lago, Semiramide,* and *Tancredi,* with Marilyn Horne the hero in each. In 1983–84, there were three opéras comiques, with Frederica von Stade: Offenbach's *La Périchole,* Massenet's *Chérubin,* and Ambroise Thomas's *Mignon.* The next season brought Handel: *Orlando, Ariodante,* and *Semele* (plus a fourth opera, *Alessandro,* from the Kennedy Center Handel Festival). This year, it is Richard Strauss: *Capriccio, Intermezzo,* and *Daphne.*

The *Capriccio,* last month, hardly fell into the category of concert opera. It was costumed, fully acted, imaginatively lit, and laid out in a furnished stage space much as a theatre performance might be. The only, not unimportant differences from a stage presentation were that there was no surrounding décor—beyond Carnegie Hall's own architecture—to house the scene, and that the orchestra was onstage with the singers. John Cox, who directed Glyndebourne's *Capriccio* in 1973, was again in charge.

Capriccio, a civilized and constantly engaging piece, closed the long line of autobiographical works in which Strauss considered, and demonstrated, what it means to be a composer. As a young man, he had composed *Feuersnot,* a lively, ardent challenge to the conservatism of opera publics. In 1940, when he composed *Capriccio,* he was wise, like Hans Sachs, to what was valuable in the old traditions, yet was still as spontaneous and lyrical a creator as Walther von Stolzing. Onto the stage of *Capriccio* he brings a poet, Olivier, and a composer, Flamand, who are both idealists (like the Composer in his *Ariadne auf Naxos*); an impresario, La Roche, who asserts that, above all, the public must be pleased; the famous actress Clairon; ballet dancers; Italian singers. The year is about 1775; at the Opéra, Gluck's reforms are under way. The cast has gathered in the salon of Countess Madeleine, near Paris, to discuss plans for honoring her birthday. Both the poet and the composer are in love with her. Olivier has written a sonnet for her; Flamand sets it to music. The piece wins her heart, but which of its creators does she love? Words or music, which is more important? The opera ends with the question—although a radiant orchestral interlude introducing the finale has already provided an answer. Meanwhile, the subject has been discussed from every angle. La Roche has announced his plans for a grand theatrical spectacle, all stage effects, and has been howled down by the two young men. In reply, he delivers a magnificent monologue justifying the ways of theatrical managers to creative artists. Eventually, it is decided that the day's events shall be made the subject of a new opera, in which they will play themselves.

That isn't all. Besides the words-or-music argument and its parallel in the poet-composer rivalry, emotional crosscurrents arise from the fact that Olivier was once Clairon's lover and that the Count, Madeleine's brother, is now flirting with her. There is a servants' chorus, as in *Don Pasquale;* a mysterious and touching scene in which the prompter, M. Taupe, who has fallen asleep, emerges to find himself alone in the darkened theatre and reflects on the stage's reality and the illusions of real life; a brief dance divertissement; an Italian duet.

The opera is bubbling with ideas, and although the people do nothing but talk, it seems to be filled with movement. There are teasing, brilliant allusions—to Gluck, to opera buffa, to Strauss's own works. The overture is a string sextet composed by Flamand, and when the curtain goes up the company is listening to it—or in La Roche's case sleeping through it. The intellectual content of the discussions is not profound, but Strauss gives distinction and subtlety to familiar observations by making the points directly in music. More than most operas, *Capriccio* demands quicksilver, attentive following of words and music at once. It is an excellently planned piece—rich, various, and concise. In Grove, Michael Kennedy remarks rightly that none of Strauss's earlier opera scores "is more refined, more translucent, more elegant, more varied and none ends so magically." He compares it to Verdi's *Falstaff*.

The Carnegie performance was given in German, which must to some extent have lessened the enjoyment of anyone unversed in that language. (A bilingual libretto was provided, but close attention to that would distract eyes from the actors.) The cast caught the spirit of the piece, played as a fine-tuned ensemble, and at the same time created individual characters. In 1973, Mr. Cox used the décor of Glyndebourne's earlier production but redecorated the eighteenth-century room in a more modern style, matched to the score rather than to the text. The Countess had Braques and Marie Laurencins on her walls. A young Cocteau and Poulenc might have been vying for her affections. The references to Gluck, to meeting Goldoni "last night," to horse-drawn carriages were retained; a piquant "double focus," inherent in the conception of the opera, proved undisturbing. There was a pleasant sense of continuity, of being still concerned with matters that the eighteenth century debated with similar eagerness. In Carnegie, the time was the present. The "triple focus" was somewhat less readily convincing. Felicity Lott, in her American opera début, sang the Countess. She is an intelligent, cultivated artist, with a clear, easy soprano, who moves many people to high enthusiasm. I find something bland—perhaps the word is "English"—about her performances, which keeps my admiration from being wholehearted. Thomas Stewart was a powerful La Roche. (It was his début role, thirty-two years ago, in the American première of *Capriccio,* at the Juilliard.) Richard Stilwell's Olivier has matured from the shy, constrained poet at Glyndebourne in 1973 into a darkly passionate yet controlled portrayal. Jerry Hadley's Flamand was less polished, and he sometimes sang too loudly; in this company he seemed callow. The cast included Evelyn Lear (Clairon), Walton Grönroos (the Count), Reri Grist and Chris Merritt (the Italian singers), and Hugues Cuénod (at eighty-three, still a delicate and excellently audible M. Taupe). Jeffrey Tate's conducting was poised, and there were fine details in the playing of the Orchestra of St. Luke's. The "magical" passages one looks forward to in *Capriccio* made rather less than their wonted effect, and the platform disposition—inevitably, when one stage holds both actors and orchestra—often precluded intimate, spur-of-the-moment, blink-of-the-eye adjustments.

Virgil Thomson's opera *Lord Byron* was given a "staged concert performance" in Alice Tully Hall in December, by the New York Opera Repertory Theatre. *Lord Byron* is also, in essence, a "conversation piece" (Strauss's term for *Capriccio*).

I wrote about it at length nine years ago, after a broadcast of the first performance, at the Juilliard in 1972 [*Music of Three Seasons,* pp. 482–86]. There have been no other productions. In brief, it is a work decorously controlled but also lively, distinguished by a remarkable ear for the interplay of verbal and musical rhythms, and for poetic inflections transformed into attractive melodies, simple yet subtle. The Tully Hall performance was disappointing, in that it did not proceed from the words. These were largely inaudible. The singers rendered the notes; they didn't bring Thomson's phrases to life. Karen Beardsley (Augusta Leigh), Donna Stephenson (Lady Byron), and Frances Ginsberg (the Countess Guiccoli) were partial exceptions in a large cast that otherwise seemed unable to make sense of its native tongue. The considerable merits of *Lord Byron* have still to be revealed.

Likely a piece more a matter of luck than judgment

PRODIGAL

March 3, 1986

BOHUSLAV MARTINŮ is not an easy composer to assess, and his reputation has never been settled; as the 1954 Grove remarked, "Martinů's music has been pronounced outstandingly good by some and outrageously bad by others." He was immensely prolific. Someone who would bill a work of his hardly knows where to start; in his lifetime, it may have seemed easier simply to commission a new piece. His death, in 1959, was followed by a partial eclipse of his music. Now, it seems, there is reawakened interest in it. In his native Czechoslovakia (which he left in 1923), his orchestral music is played and his operas are staged. In Britain, the Paris-period opera *Julietta* (1937) and the late opera *The Greek Passion* (1959) have been taken up by major companies. In this country, Indiana University has mounted *The Greek Passion,* and brought it to the Met in 1981. Attention seems to be settling on his six symphonies. Václav Neumann and the Czech Philharmonic have recorded them all (Supraphon). In London in 1984, Christopher Adey conducted them in a five-concert cycle. In Moscow last year, Gennady Rozhdestvensky billed all six. The Sixth Symphony ("Fantaisies Symphoniques") has been heard widely in recent years—most often as the score for the last act of Kenneth MacMillan's ballet *Anastasia.* Earlier this year, two of the symphonies were played in New York: the First by the New York City Symphony, conducted by Richard Fletcher, in Alice Tully Hall, and the Fourth by the Philharmonic, conducted by Erich Leinsdorf, in Avery Fisher Hall.

Martinů's music, the annals suggest, once held a commanding place in America's symphonic life. He came to this country in 1941, and from 1942 to 1946 composed a symphony annually—Nos. 1 to 5. Four of the five had prominent premières. The First Symphony and the Third were introduced by the Boston Symphony and Serge Koussevitzky; the Second was introduced by the Cleveland Orchestra and Leinsdorf, the Fourth by the Philadelphia Orchestra and Eugene Ormandy. (The Fifth, composed for the Czech Philharmonic, reached New York in 1948, in a NBC performance conducted by Ernest Ansermet.) Then there was a gap, until the very successful Sixth, introduced by the Boston Symphony and Charles Munch in 1955, crowned Martinů's American career. In 1956, he returned to Europe. During the years in America, he had also composed a much-played two-piano concerto, a piano concerto for Mischa Elman, a violin-and-piano concerto, a viola concerto, a cello concerto, the *Memorial to Lidice,* four operas, a ballet for Martha Graham, a good deal of chamber music, and much else.

Virgil Thomson hailed the First Symphony (when Boston brought it to Carnegie Hall, soon after the première) as "a beaut," and went on to explain why it was one, in a review headed "Smetana's Heir": the symphony is "wholly lovely"; it "shimmers"; and "it is like Smetana because the shining sounds of it sing as well as shine." But Martinů is not performer-proof. The New York City Symphony's performance of the First, in January, was spirited, but it was thick-textured, sometimes lumpy. My faith in the work was restored when I listened to the Neumann recording, in which it not only shines and sings but also dances. Similarly with the Fourth. Mr. Leinsdorf has long been a champion of this symphony: he conducted it with the Rochester Philharmonic back in 1948 and has done it more recently with the Chicago Symphony and the San Francisco Symphony. He did not get the Philharmonic to make of it "a delight to the ear, weightless and iridescent, as of light shining through powdered crystal" (Thomson's phrase when Philadelphia brought it to Carnegie Hall, soon after the première). The performance was drab, not captivating.

The unevenness of Martinů's works has long been stressed. The effect of unevenness, I am sure, has been exaggerated by the unevenness of the performances they receive. Not only can one work sound like a masterpiece and the next self-indulgent, unlicked; the same work can in two different performances leave impressions no less contradictory. Toward the end of his life, the composer said to his biographer Miloš Šafránek, "My whole life has moved concurrently along two opposing lines: between a kind of innate and genuine naivety ... and the other pole of consciousness, knowledge, and intelligence taught me by life." And he added, "My conclusions and thoughts are, I think and hope, right and clear, but my intuitive life is like a boy's.... My view is that art is just when those two opposites meet." Like Berlioz, Martinů, largely self-taught, was intransigent and impatient of discipline. The influences on him, he said in 1942, were many, and the main ones were Czech national music, Debussy, and the English madrigalists. Piquant combination! Like Berlioz, Martinů made himself a master of large forms that defied accepted wisdom and disturbed any conventional expectations. Like Berlioz—I'm suggesting only likeness, not parity—he found his way, attentive to what he admired but not to regular procedures. His music sounds ill-made when it is badly performed. It sounds fresh, exhilarating, and unlike any other when it is brought to life by champions who follow along his paths with something of his own elation, boyish enthusiasm, and springiness, united to refined, subtle execution. In an age when much of the music offered to us is underpinned by formulas, Martinů's unconstrained, instinctive utterance makes a welcome change.

Three Madrigals (1947), for violin and viola, which were memorably recorded by Joseph and Lillian Fuchs—for whom they were written—provide an introduction to Martinů's chamber music at its most inventive, individual, and beautiful; in their long, elegant structures the composer's admiration of Debussy and the English madrigalists can be traced. The Hungarian cellist Csaba Onczay, with the pianist Márta Gulyás, made his New York début last month at a Frick Collection Sunday-afternoon recital and played Martinů's Variations on a Slovak Folk Song. This is a late piece (1959)—his last chamber composition—and is engaging, poetic, generous. Mr. Onczay has a big (but not fat) tone and a romantic (but not flashy) style. The Variations were good to hear. So were Schumann's Adagio and Allegro, Brahms's F-major Sonata, and the *Fifthmusic,* for solo cello, of Kamilló Lendvay, one of the contemporary Hungarian composers (he was born in 1928) whom we read about more often than hear. Carl Nielsen, in an essay enjoining reverence and respect for simple intervals (which "should be to our art what corn and bread and holy water were to the people of the Old Testament"), described a fifth as "the supreme bliss." Fifths are points of departure and arrival in Lendvay's piece, which was composed (in 1979) for Mr. Onczay. The journeys between them are surprising, imaginative, sometimes dizzying in their virtuoso progress. This is an exciting piece.

Frick recitals are packed. Would it be unbearably élitist to suggest that they would be more enjoyable still if the director removed a row or two of chairs, instead of sardining as many listeners as possible into the intimate music room?

Michael Gielen's six seasons as music director of the Cincinnati Symphony are coming to a close; later this year, he goes to Baden-Baden as chief conductor of the Southwest German Radio Orchestra. He will be missed here. For his last Manhattan concert with the orchestra as its music director, in February, Carnegie Hall was filled, and the applause was loud. The program was characteristically bold: just two big works in D minor, written by composers in their twenties— Schoenberg's symphonic poem *Pelléas and Mélisande* and Brahms's First Piano Concerto. *Pelléas* is a dense score, an exuberant web of close motivic working, but Mr. Gielen is a great clarifier. Peter Serkin was the soloist in the concerto. The performance was laid out broadly and clearly. One had the feeling that conductor and pianist had come to full agreement in advance about the interpretation and had left little room for sudden impulses, unforeseen inspirations that might arise during the performance itself. In fact, Mr. Serkin finished one or two phrases a hairline ahead of the orchestral entries. The effect was as of catches not exactly dropped but grabbed, rather than of the ball's falling precisely, after its flight, into poised, waiting hands. In the second subject of the finale, Mr. Serkin flicked the grace notes, as modern singers do in comparable passages—did not give them melodic value. (His father does the same in the famous recording with George Szell.) But his playing was energetic, lyrical, and vital. All in all, it was a noble, slightly severe, and satisfying performance.

Mr. Gielen does not give the impression of being a spontaneous conductor. He doesn't take chances, "go for broke." That may be one reason that he has not, until recently, been acclaimed as one of the world's most distinguished conductors. Vogue epithets such as "charismatic," "glamorous," "sexy" could not be applied to him. He does not lack passion—a passion for getting things right. (It came as a shock when the orchestra closed the Adagio of the concerto with an ill-tuned chord.) Nor does he lack a spirit of adventure. His other post is artistic director of the Frankfurt Opera, and that company under Gielen has been likened to Berlin's legendary Kroll Oper under Otto Klemperer. In my personal annals, Gielen's performances of Schoenberg's *Moses und Aron*, Bernd Alois Zimmermann's *Die Soldaten*, Luigi Nono's *Al gran sole carico d'amore*, and, with the Cincinnati orchestra, Elliott Carter's Variations for Orchestra and Piano Concerto loom large. Mr. Gielen has brought the Cincinnati orchestra to a level of excellence it may not have known since the years (1922–31) when Fritz Reiner was conductor there.

Cincinnati's excellent program notes for the whole season, written by the composer Jonathan Kramer, are collected into a book that is available at the start of the season. Listeners have time to study and digest them in advance. An admirable practice. In the Carnegie program booklet Mr. Kramer's introductory remarks about the two works concerned were reproduced, but his essays were cut short at the point where they began to deal with the music.

Barbara Kolb's *Millefoglie,* commissioned by IRCAM and first performed there last year, had its American première at the second concert this season of Merkin Hall's Music Today series, in December. It is a challenging, attractive, and exhilarating composition, scored for oboe, clarinet, bass clarinet, trombone, two percussionists, harp, cello, and computer-generated tape. It lasts about nineteen minutes. The title refers to the superimposition of layer upon layer of rhythmic and harmonic structures. The work made a favorable first impression; I have delayed a review until now for two reasons. Years ago—at the 1960 ISCM Festival, in Cologne, when new musics of many exciting kinds (by Berio, Boulez, Ligeti, Nono, Sessions, Stockhausen, Stravinsky, Zimmermann) were clamoring for critical attention—that subtle, stimulating musician the late Hans Keller advised me when in doubt to fall back on "intuition." By that he meant "Concentrate on the works that give you the impression that there's something there worth getting to know; and get to know it." Intuition is a fallible and imprecise critical tool, but it does provide a possible starting point. The alternative, when one is attracted yet baffled by some difficult, elusive new strains, is fudging. (Milton Babbitt's Piano Concerto, played at January's American Composers Orchestra concert, in Carnegie Hall, is obviously an important new piece, but it baffled me, and anything I might try to write about it before hearing it again would be fudge.) The other reason is that the Merkin Hall performance of *Millefoglie* provided no fair basis for assessing the work: the computer tape's important contributions to the music were abruptly interrupted by a loose electrical connection. From Kolb's publishers, Boosey & Hawkes, I was able to borrow a tape recording of the IRCAM première and a copy of the score. It would be presumptuous to say that I now know the work, but at least I now know my way around it. And at each hearing of *Millefoglie* I have liked it more.

Marimba, vibraphone, and amplified harp give a precise but mellow definition to the timbres, which at times have almost gamelanlike sonorities. There are five distinct episodes, and they form a varied but shapely discourse. The first of them is rhythmic: developing variations on a phrase of crisp, arresting outline, announced at the start. A computer solo—the instrument treated romantically, singing to its own accompaniment—and a trio for marimba, vibraphone, and harp follow. The oboe begins piping a Morse code–like pattern, which initiates what might be thought of as a modern analogue of a Rossini crescendo, increasing in density of texture, in volume, in harmonic richness, in rhythmic intricacy; one of the percussionists moves to a jazz drum set. Suddenly, the movement subsides into a dreamy final section, a tranquil flow of quietly glowing lyrical thoughts, through which the computer, whispering in a high register, sounds like a voice singing words that one can't quite catch. This final section reminds me of Martinů's *Julietta*—not musically but by its evocation of a mysterious world where memories of events that may or may not have happened are lapped in enchanted layers. Many of the scores coming from IRCAM are experimental—essays, often of great interest and promise, in means or methods. *Millefoglie* is achieved. The Music Today performance was conducted by Gerard Schwarz. How accurate it was I have no idea; it certainly made beautiful sounds.

The concert was also notable for two gleaming vocal performances. Cynthia Munzer—an Amneris, Maddalena, and Carmen—made something very striking of Jacob Druckman's early (1962) psalm sequence *Dark upon the Harp,* for mezzo-soprano, brass quintet, and percussion. She was flamboyant as she recalled strong bulls of Bashan opening wide their mouths like a ravening and a roaring lion; she shivered deliciously when her mourning was turned into dancing. Carmen Pelton—celebrated as Susan B. Anthony in Thomson's *Mother of Us All* and as Lady Billows in Britten's *Albert Herring*—revived George Crumb's *Ancient Voices of Children* (1970) in a performance at once emotional, tender, and pure-toned. How often the vocalists at new-music concerts seem content simply to render composers' notes accurately. One wants to press on them Lotte Lehmann's little book *More Than Singing* (which has just been reprinted as a Dover paperback):

> Not only your voice sings—no, you must sing with your whole being—from head to toe. . . . Your eyes sing, your body, animated by the rhythm of the music, sings, your hands sing. How great is the power of expression conveyed by the eyes and the hands! . . . You must feel what you sing with your whole being, from head to toe, then your eyes *cannot* be cold and lifeless—they will also have to sing, as an essential part of one complete harmony.

It was in this spirit that Miss Munzer and Miss Pelton sang Druckman's and Crumb's music.

SOUL-ANIMATING STRAINS

March 10, 1986

THE Sine Nomine Singers' February concert in Merkin Hall was dedicated to the memory of that elegant, subtle scholar Edward Lowinsky, who died last year. Harry Saltzman, the Singers' conductor, was a Lowinsky pupil at Berkeley. In 1971, the Singers sang for the great Josquin Festival-Conference in New York, which Lowinsky organized; at the 1976 Titian conference at Columbia they sang Lowinsky's realization of the canon that appears in Titian's "Bacchanal of the Andrians." The main work on the Merkin program was a piece of music especially dear to Lowinsky: Nicolas Gombert's Mass "Je suis desheritée." It was published in 1951 in the first of eleven *Corpus Mensurabilis Musicae* volumes devoted to Gombert. Reviewing it in the *Musical Quarterly,* Lowinsky praised "the inexhaustible richness and subtlety of [Gombert's] rhythm and the vitality of his melodic lines." He urged study of "one of the most genuine expressions of true contrapuntal thinking"; and of "Je suis desheritée" in particular he wrote, "Let it be said at once and without blushing that reading this Mass was a case of love at first sight." He called it "one of the rarest gems of six-teenth-century music," a work "of an unparalleled melodic beauty, a haunting, melancholy expression of the greatest intimacy."

Gombert was a composer and choirmaster to the Emperor Charles V. (He wrote a motet for the birth of Philip II.) Contemporaries revered him, and in later centuries he has not lacked champions. Monteverdi found Gombert's works in the ducal library at Mantua, and based his 1610 Mass on a Gombert motet. Dr. Burney discovered Gombert when scoring the various exequies composed for Josquin Desprez (one of Burney's heroes). Although he called it a "tedious task" and accorded Gombert no more than a passing reference in the second book of the famous *History,* a few years later he made amends in the third book: distinguished Gombert among the composers by the dozen who flourished in the mid-sixteenth century, apologized for having mentioned him before "not with sufficient respect," and said that "in scoring more of his numerous works, I find him a great master of harmony, and a disciple worthy of his illustrious master [Josquin]." In earlier Groves—whose essays on composers often make readers eager to hear for themselves music about which New Grove authors are sometimes content to relate plain facts—J. R. Sterndale Bennett was eloquent about Gombert's "power of description" and "the wonderful manner in which the noble music blends itself with the ideas the words convey." ("Facts in themselves are meaningless and uninteresting," Lowinsky once wrote. "Caution and factuality *are* scholarly virtues, but without imagination they are like wingless birds, unable to soar aloft and command vaster views of land and

452

sea.") Lowinsky's declaration of love set a scholarly seal on Gombert's reputation. Yet we seldom hear his music. The current Schwann catalogue lists but one recording, against some twenty devoted to Josquin.

On the page, Gombert's music looks dense—dense in the way that Schoenberg's *Transfigured Night* and *Pelléas and Mélisande* are, with close motivic working and few air holes: when a voice completes a phrase, it must prepare at once for the next entry. (And, as in Schoenberg, the rigorously linear thinking can lead to startling harmonies.) On the page, the skill of the facture and the rhythmic subtlety that mocks a modern editor's bar lines are readily apparent. But then one wants to hear the music sounding through space and time, carried by real, not imagined, voices. The Sine Nomine performance was loving. It was carefully tuned and balanced. It moved well. The choir, being a modern mixed-voice group (twelve women, twelve men), with a repertory spanning the ages, does not cultivate the specialist, sharp-focus timbre of the specifically early-music ensembles. One could imagine a performance of the Mass which, as it were, pressed on the ear a little more keenly, and had a texture in which each individual strand was more sharply apparent.

The concert began with settings—for four, three, and two voices—of the chanson that provided Gombert with his tunes: "I am cast off, for I have lost my friend. . . . Nightingale of the lovely wood, without delay go tell my friend that because of him I am tormented." The second half was chansons by Guillaume Costeley, Clément Janequin, and Orlande de Lassus (all to Ronsard poems) and by Hindemith (settings of Rilke) and Debussy (settings of Charles d'Orléans). Solo lines were taken by Alexandra Montano, a limpid, steady mezzo, the Marion of Mannes's recent *Robin et Marion*. It was an evening of interesting, varied, and beautiful music.

In Lent last year, in Corpus Christi Church, Music Before 1800 presented Alessandro Stradella's oratorio *Ester*. This year, it did his more famous *San Giovanni Battista,* in what was billed as its American première. The first performance was in Rome, in 1675. In a 1949 revival, in Perugia, Maria Callas sang Salome, and Cesare Siepi was Herod. The plot is that of Strauss's *Salome.* If Stradella's version were to be staged, the heroine would have to sing and dance at once, for Part II begins with a lilting dance aria: "Even in the sky the pretty, twinkling stars are always dancing, but they don't outdo me." The dramatic strokes in *San Giovanni Battista* are famous. Burney, who owned a score, devoted nearly five pages of his *History* to them: "Stradella has introduced a greater variety of movement and contrivance in his oratorio, than I ever saw in any drama, sacred or secular, of the same period." When Salome, taking Herod up on the promise to give her whatever she asks for, unto the half of his kingdom, asks for the head of the Baptist, Herod in his consternation leaps right out of key—just as Strauss's Herod does when exclaiming "What, he wakes the dead!" The oratorio ends with a duet of opposed emotions—Salome in ecstasy, Herod filled with gloomy foreboding. Their music is different—hers again lilting, his based on descending scales like those of Wotan in dejection. But their texts coincide on the rhetorical question "Why, tell me why?" And with that question the music suddenly breaks off on the dominant. The effect is startling—so much so that one would suspect a final page had been lost did not all early copies of the work have this abrupt close.

Ester revealed a composer adept at tense dramatic exchanges—confrontations, quarrels—and vivid introspective monologues. (Haman's last one is Macbeth-like.) There are several of these in *San Giovanni Battista,* too. The drama moves swiftly. In the opening scene, John bids farewell to the smiling countryside, while his disciples try to dissuade him from going to court to denounce Herod's marriage to a sister-in-law. At court, a counsellor and Salome urge Herod to lay cares of state aside. John's accusatory voice (like Monterone's in *Rigoletto*) cuts across their revels; in an angry aria with cabaletta Herod orders the prophet's imprisonment. Part II is Herod's birthday party. In effusive arioso, he makes his offer to Salome. The Baptist's voice—as it were, from his prison—rings out, and Herodias tells her daughter what to ask for. Before the execution, Salome and John sing an elaborate duet.

Ester was continuo-accompanied. (If once there were string parts, they have not survived.) In *San Giovanni Battista,* the accompaniments vary from plain continuo to double instrumental ensemble—a concertino and a concerto-grosso group, used both individually and together. In 1675, Stradella had twenty-seven players. (Corelli was probably one of the violinists.) Louise Basbas, the music director and organist of the Corpus Christi performance, had only nine. Even so, the performance lacked the tightness and dramatic urgency of last year's *Ester*. There were laggard moments in arias that should dance; continuo chords were sometimes slow to strike in and impel the dialogue; the little organ that was used had a rather thick timbre. Ill fortune had deprived the enterprise of its intended Salome, Cheryl Bensman (last year's Esther), and that doubtless upset the pacing. At short notice, Mary Ann Hart, the Herodias, undertook the daughter's role as well, and she gave an intelligent, sensitive reading, truly and clearly voiced. But as Herodias she was twice as vivid: of the Queen's short solo she gave not a reading but a free, fully realized performance. Andrea von Ramm took the title role. Usually, she is a marvellously brave, arresting singer who throws her voice out into the spaces of an auditorium. On this occasion, she seemed score-bound—an oddly constrained, though technically accomplished, interpreter of the fiery, fearless prophet. Robert Kuehn, the Herod, and Michael Brown, the counsellor, sang well. The edition used was that of David Wilder Daniels, prepared as his 1963 doctoral thesis. Even if the performance was not all one might have hoped for, it was enjoyable, and it gave a clear impression of how excellently inventive a composer Stradella is. *San Giovanni,* legend had it, was a work whose beauty caused two assassins, set on Stradella by the nobleman with whose mistress he had eloped, to relent and (in Burney's words) "to think that it would be a pity to take away the life of a man whose genius and abilities were the delight of all Italy." Perhaps our chamber companies should be looking at his operas. It would be good to hear his oratorio *Susanna* in Corpus Christi next Lent. [*We did hear it there in 1988, and the next year his* Santa Pelagia.]

St. Ann's (formerly Holy Trinity), one of Minard Lafever's two churches in Brooklyn Heights, has become a busy and important center for music and drama. This month, among other events, Christopher Hogwood's Academy of

Ancient Music and the Chamber Music Society of Lincoln Center play there, and the St. Ann's Chamber Orchestra, conducted by Fred Sherry, joins the Bread and Puppet troupe to present Bach's Cantata No. 4. The church, close to the Borough Hall station, is a brief, easy subway ride from Manhattan, and it offers richer architecture—with a splendor of William Bolton windows—and warmer acoustics than do the Lincoln Center halls. Last month, I attended the third concert there in a Saturday-evening new-music series. The series had been launched by three of New York's best players: the pianist Alan Feinberg, the violinist Rolf Schulte, and Mr. Sherry on cello, with a program including works by Elliott Carter and Charles Wuorinen. The second concert starred the saxophonist Earl Howard. The third brought Halsey Stevens's crisply made Trumpet Sonata (1956), with Stephen Burns the trumpeter and John Van Buskirk the pianist, and, before it, the first performance of Somei Satoh's *Hikari* (*Light*), for trumpet and piano. Mr. Burns and St. Ann's commissioned this after admiring *Journey Through Sacred Time,* an anthology of Satoh compositions "enacted" in St. Ann's last year. A press release declared that Satoh's music "combines lush romanticism and beauty with a Western minimalism." Lushness and minimalism were apparent in *Hikari,* and beauty was provided by the sound of Mr. Burns's trumpet. He is a player on whose lips the instrument becomes a voice that can not only with loud clangor excite us to arms but also sing, murmur, charm, and rival the amorous flute that in dying notes discovers the woes of hapless lovers.

Karlheinz Stockhausen is the twentieth-century composer who has brought the expressive qualities of the trumpet to the fore, with his trumpeter son Markus (who was in the audience at St. Ann's) as principal executor. The second part of the concert was a Stockhausen "suite," consisting of "Eingang und Formel," from Act II of the opera *Donnerstag;* "Aries," the trumpet solo from *Sirius;* "Taurus," "Gemini," and "Leo" from *Tierkreis;* and "Donnerstags-Abschied," the farewell fanfares at the close of *Donnerstag.* This anthology was also called *Leben: A multimedia performance in progress,* conceived and directed by Mr. Burns and Damon Santostefano, with choreography by Felix Blaska. What we saw was the Creation myth reënacted, with Mr. Burns and his trumpet as Adam, Jean Kopperud and her clarinet as Eve, John Rojak and his trombone as Satan, and, stationed on high, Mr. Van Buskirk at the electronic synthesizer as God, supplying a sonic background to the solo events below. To someone who in the theatre has thrilled to *Donnerstag,* where the trumpeter is not Adam but Michael, an archangel who has put on mortality, this was disconcerting. Clarinet or basset horn as woman (mother, sister, goddess) and trombone as Lucifer (father, rival, tyrant) are established in Stockhausen's hierarchy; in this *Leben* the trumpet seemed to play a different role. Yet the musical enactments, if disconcerting, were also eloquent and moving—evidence of great music's being able to support more than the specific meaning a composer put on it. Maybe this was a gloss, of the kind a choreographer imposes when he uses a score to second a scenario of his own devising, different from any the composer imagined. But it was not a trivialization—as, for example, Jean-Pierre Ponnelle's reworking of Wagner's *Flying Dutchman* is. It dealt with high things in a high, serious manner. In these pages, Miss Kopperud in her danced-and-played presentation of Stockhausen's *Harlekin* and Mr. Burns in his of the "Abschied" have already been admired; Mr. Rojak showed himself a performer of their quality. The big Stockhausen works are neglected in this country; no opera company has announced a production of *Donnerstag* or *Samstag,* the two days of the seven-day *Licht* so far completed. These episodes were welcome, and I hope there will be more. Act II of *Donnerstag* contains a rapturous basset-horn-and-trumpet duet that I long to hear again, sounding through space, and not just (in the Deutsche Grammophon recording of the opera) from my loudspeakers. The church acoustics were generously responsive to the three wind instruments; the spaces seemed to come to life with sound. The costumes were by Kew O'Donnel, and the lighting was by Susan Greenbaum. Stephanie Gelsen created the synthesizer sounds.

Romantic Warrior

March 31, 1986

HANS WERNER HENZE will be sixty in July, and through the world his music is being heard even more often than usual. Last month, in Merkin Hall, Speculum Musicae revived *El cimarrón,* the work in which Henze's musical manner—innately lyrical, picturesque, and sensuously beautiful—joined forces with the Marxist thinking that had colored the matter of his compositions for some years. *El cimarrón* was first performed at the 1970 Aldeburgh Festival. The year before, Henze's violent, abrasive *Essay on Pigs,* for baritone declaimer and chamber orchestra, had appeared—a manifesto with musical underlining. It had been written swiftly, in response to the riot that prevented the performance of his oratorio *The Raft of the Medusa* in Hamburg the previous year. (Steelhelmeted police troopers had marched into the hall and scooped up student demonstrators.) The text of the *Essay,* by the Chilean poet Gastón Salvatore, urged an artist to stop arranging thoughts and dreams into sensitive, beautiful patterns, and to act. Two years later, Salvatore and Henze returned to the subject, in *The Tedious Trip to Natascha Ungeheuer's Place,* a "show" for baritone, percussionist, "Pierrot" quintet ("meant to symbolize the old, sick bourgeoisie," the composer said in a note), brass quintet (the voice of repressive authority), and jazz quintet (escapism). Natascha's cajolements trickle honey-sweet from a tape; in the words of a note by Salvatore, "she promises the leftist bourgeois a new kind of security, which will allow him to keep a revolutionary 'clear conscience' without taking an active part in the class struggle." Salvatore observes that his protagonist, although he has stopped short of joining Natascha, has not yet found the way to the Revolution. "He must retrace his path and begin again."

Henze was—and is—too sensible, honest, and musical a musician to scrap all previous achievement and start again from scratch. In a large body of works, he has—with a born composer's need to transmute experience into music—written

456

his intellectual and emotional biography, responded to the musical developments of nearly half a century, and wrestled hard with the hard questions of art's and an artist's role in an unjust and ever-changing society. He has consolidated, transformed, reconciled. Because his works have run through my own life and—like those of Stockhausen and Boulez, near-contemporaries of Henze, and the slightly younger Peter Maxwell Davies—have, one by one as they appeared, wound themselves into my mental autobiography, I can hardly hear them with the objective, contemporary ear one brings to, say, compositions by Nicolas Gombert or Alessandro Stradella. When *El cimarrón* had its première, America was in Vietnam. Nixon was President. In Britain, Edward Heath and his Tories had, three days earlier, replaced the Labour Government. Stockhausen was in Osaka, performing "intuitive" music with his ensemble (earlier that year, the BBC Symphony had given a less than convinced account of his *Set Sail for the Sun,* its "score" not notes but two inspirational sentences), but he was already composing *Mantra,* that clear, beautiful masterpiece which leads to *Licht.* Davies was also at a turning point: the searing *Eight Songs for a Mad King* and *Vesalii Icones* had appeared the previous year; 1971 brought the first Orkney composition, *From Stone to Thorn.*

Henze composed *El cimarrón* in Cuba. In 1963, the Cuban writer Miguel Barnet had come across the 102-year-old Esteban Montejo, living in a Havana home for ex-servicemen, and published his memories of being a slave; a runaway slave (*cimarrón*), living alone in the forests for ten years; a plantation worker again, after the abolition of slavery; and a fighter in the 1895 war of independence. *The Autobiography of a Runaway Slave* is a remarkable book. History, social history, folklore, superstitions, tales, sudden vivid memories of particular people and scenes mingle in its pages. The effect it makes—whatever it may owe to Barnet's art—seems real. The poet Hans Magnus Enzensberger shaped fifteen episodes from it as Henze's text. Henze set them for baritone, flute, guitar, and percussion—specifically, for the American baritone William Pearson, the German flutist Karlheinz Zöller (longtime first flute of the Berlin Philharmonic), the Cuban guitarist and composer Leo Brouwer, and the electrifying Japanese percussionist Stomu Yamash'ta (composer-director of the Red Buddha Theatre). Henze's body of works also limns the features of several individual performers whose art and personalities have left a mark on twentieth-century musical history. *El cimarrón* was a tale to captivate both the old, romantic and the new, revolutionary composer. The forest scenes with exotic birds, mysterious trees, and spirit presences are kin to those of his opera *König Hirsch.* Esteban's final speech—"And that's why I don't want to die, so I can fight in all the battles to come"—rings as a centenarian's chime to the fierce close of the *Essay on Pigs.* And in *El cimarrón* Henze found at last the simplicity, the directness, the freedom from self-indulgent elaboration which had long been his declared aim. He achieved them without sacrificing fineness of musical temper, charm of sound, eloquence of musical idea, or sureness of structure.

The Speculum performance was different in tone from that of 1970: less exuberant, romantic, and lyrical, but musically very strong. Although the four performers were, more or less, costumed—in garb less formal than that customary at New York concerts—the music-theatre aspects of the work were played down. JoAnne Akalaitis, the stage director originally billed, had with-drawn. The platform lighting was plain and unvaried. The scores, and the players' attention to them, were much in evidence. There was little movement. (In 1970, Stomu Yamash'ta, prowling and pouncing through the shadows of his percussion battery, evoked images of field, forest, factory, scrimmage.) The Speculum players scarcely related one to another dramatically. But Jonathan Sprague (who has played Johnny in Krenek's *Johnny Strikes Up* for Britain's Opera North, and Porgy at Radio City Music Hall) gave a masterly account of the central role: alert, strongly projected, verbally incisive, and always intelligi-ble. (Christopher Keene's English translation was used.) And the three in-strumentalists—Susan Palma, flute, David Starobin, guitar, and Joseph Passaro, percussion—made wonderfully expressive sounds, through a score that holds echoes of Ravel's *Chansons madécasses* and of Bartókian night music; gay moments of Afro-Cuban rhythm; bright birdcalls; husky murmurs (from bass flute) stealing through silences; eerie, enchanted tinkling; ferocious climaxes. Speculum should do *El cimarrón* again, soon, and build an evening of potent music theatre on this secure musical foundation.

Alexander Dargomyzhsky's *The Stone Guest* (1865–69), a famous but rather dull opera—recorded, quite often broadcast, seldom staged—received what was billed as its American stage première last month, from the Chamber Opera Theatre of New York, in the delightful little Marymount Manhattan Theatre, on East Seventy-first Street. The text is Pushkin's version of the Don Juan story, one of his four "little tragedies" of 1830. (The others were *Mozart and Salieri,* later set to music by Rimsky-Korsakov; *A Feast During the Plague,* later set to music by César Cui; and *The Miserly Knight,* later set to music by Rachmaninoff.) The recitatives of Dargomyzhsky's previous opera, *Rusalka,* had met with approval; he set *The Stone Guest* in a manner often described as continuous recitative and more precisely termed, by Cui, "melodic recitative," in which "even without the text each musical phrase possesses its own beauty and meaning, but in the overall view and in their ordering there are no absolute musical connections, no abstract musico-logical developments." In other words, there are no musical forms or structures (except for one song set into the action). Lyric declamation proceeds on its way, phrase by phrase, in proportions determined by the length of Pushkin's speeches. *The Stone Guest* was a pioneering work, written without key signatures, with whole-tone harmonies in episodes associated with the titular statue, and in flexible meters. Tchaikovsky called it "the sorry fruit of a dry inventive process." But Rimsky-Korsakov, in his memoirs, tells of the excitement with which each scene was tried out as soon as it had been written, at St. Petersburg soirées where the composer sang Don Juan, Mussorgsky sang Leporello, and Rimsky's future wife played the piano. Dargomyzhsky died before the opera was finished. Cui supplied a missing passage, and Rimsky orchestrated the whole. Some years later, he reorchestrated it, "softening here and there the extreme harshness and harmonic follies of the original."

The ear of faith tells me that with gleaming interpreters, offering subtly and richly voiced performances, and alert to the psychological intricacies of Pushkin's play, *The Stone Guest* might yet prove gripping. The Chamber Opera

Theatre presentation was handsomely housed, in smart, simple, high-gloss scenery designed by Beni Montresor. But it was too plainly sung. Thaddeus Motyka's staging included an orgy and a large white bed (it looked like a water bed), centerstage, that at the first-act curtain held Don Juan, his mistress Laura, and the fresh-killed corpse of Don Carlos, Laura's new lover and Donna Anna's brother. The principals were Ron Gentry (Don Juan), Nicole Philibosian (Laura), Sally Stevens (Donna Anna), Randolph Messing (Don Carlos), and Philip Cokorinos (doubling as Leporello and the Commander, who in Pushkin's version is Donna Anna's husband, not her father). Vladimir Kin conducted. The opera was sung in an English translation by Mr. Motyka and Richard Taruskin.

Gounod's *Mireille* is a charming opera, tender, unpretentious, delicate in its workings, conceived and executed in happiness and high spirits. Gounod composed it in the Provençal landscapes of the action, walking some of them with the poet Mistral, whose *Mirèio* provided the plot. The settings range from a smiling farm to the savage grandeur of the Val d'Enfer. (There, after a three-star dinner at the Baumanière, I once saw *Mireille* staged in spectacular fashion, covering acres, it seemed, of that deep romantic chasm; but the sound was horrid, pushed from loudspeakers at an unremitting forte.) "Provence" is a charged word in Western culture. I write it, and sights, scents, feelings flood me; even someone who has not been there must know the spell if he has looked at Gauguin and van Gogh, read Jean Giono and Roy Campbell, heard a stylish performance of *Mireille*. Gounod's letters and reminiscences of the time he spent in Provence composing *Mireille* sound a familiar note of ecstasy: "I was literally drunk with joy. Ideas came into my head like butterflies in flight; I had only to stretch out my hand to grasp them."

The Juilliard American Opera Center presented *Mireille*—the first New York performance in nine years—last month. As stage director it had engaged Bernard Lefort, who was for eight years the director of the Aix-en-Provence Festival. He should have been able to instill into his young cast some feeling for place and atmosphere. But he didn't succeed in doing so. The show lacked specific character. Maroun Azouri's décor might have come from a warehouse. Jungwon Park, the first-night Mireille, looked exquisite and voiced the notes accurately, but she gave them little expression. Ruben Broitman, the first-night Vincent, sang firmly and well but in the manner of a Rodolfo. A symbolic Death figure had been added to the cast—a tall, black-veiled dancer who stalked the lovers through a tableau vivant gratuitously illustrating the prelude (the spectator's heart sank as he saw it) and made several later appearances. The opera was essayed in French, some of it delivered in a way hard to understand. The use of French no doubt served a pedagogical purpose, for singers must learn to communicate in many languages. But these singers might have learned a more valuable lesson—how to bring sung music to life before an audience— had Hugh Macdonald's new English translation been chosen. Anton Coppola's conducting lacked grace.

Mireille was mutilated from the start by the meddling of its first heroine, Marie Miolan Carvalho, and her husband, Léon Carvalho, the director of the Théâtre Lyrique (where the opera had its first performance, in 1864). Tampering

459

continued when the piece entered the Opéra-Comique repertory, in 1874. No two editions of the score agree. Sometimes Mireille, instead of succumbing to sunstroke and dying in Vincent's arms, recovers from it and marries him. In 1939, Henri Büsser and Reynaldo Hahn attempted a reconstruction of Gounod's original opera; Büsser reorchestrated what he could find only in piano score, and Hahn conducted the result at the Opéra-Comique. This version (heard at the Juilliard) is in general use today, and it must serve until scholars begin to do for Gounod—whose *Faust* and *Roméo* are also badly in need of honest editing—what is being done for Rossini, Berlioz, and Verdi.

Donizetti's *Le convenienze ed inconvenienze teatrali*—its subject the rehearsal of an opera seria—is an amusing romp in the line of Mozart's *Der Schauspieldirektor* and Lortzing's *Die Opernprobe*. The title is tricky to translate: *convenienze* means not only "conveniences, advantages" but also the operatic "conventions" governing such things as the distribution of roles and the relative prominence given to prima donna, primo tenore, etc. Modern versions of the piece have been put on as *Upstage and Downstage, Viva la Mamma!*, and *The Prima Donna's Mother Is a Drag*. The Opera Ensemble of New York, which staged the work last month in the Lillie Blake School auditorium, on West Eighty-first Street, used William Ashbrook's title, *The Unconventional Rehearsal*, and his English translation—revised, adapted, and not improved in a performing edition by Michael Kaye.

Modern revivals of the piece tend to fall into two traps. The first is low, gross clowning, made easy by the fact that the principal role, a formidable stage mother, was composed for a baritone. Mamm'Agata bursts into the rehearsal demanding that her daughter, the seconda donna, be given more to do in the forthcoming opera; when the prima donna sweeps out in a pet, Mamma blithely announces that she herself is quite capable of undertaking the part, and offers a sample of her prowess. The Opera Ensemble production was not gross, but it was not much fun, either. Richard Michael Slater, the Agata, was simply a baritone in wig and skirt, performing without much wit or comic accomplishment. The second trap, which was not avoided, is to suggest that inadequate, approximate singing is funny in itself. Donizetti makes merry with inappropriate trills, extravagant cadenzas, and overdone expression; it needs singers who can trill, sing cadenzas, and be expressive to realize the jokes. The performing edition didn't help. The *convenienze*—which Donizetti observed even while he mocked them—were disregarded. Numbers were displaced, omitted, added. There can be no objection to such procedures—Donizetti himself gave precedent—if the result works well, but this comedy was rambling and shapeless. The addition of Arsaces's long aria "Ah, quel giorno," from Rossini's *Semiramide*, piano-accompanied and very modestly sung, made no point at all. Michael Recchiuti was the conductor, and John Sheehan the director.

SERIOUS, STIRRING

April 7, 1986

SERGEI TANEYEV—a pupil of Tchaikovsky, a teacher of Rachmaninoff, Scriabin, and many others—is a satisfying composer. He stands apart from the Russian nationalists: his invention is less colorful, individual, and exotic than theirs. "The Russian Brahms" is his common label; although musically misleading—one can hardly mistake Taneyev's music for Brahms's—it does suggest his concern with ways that music works on purely musical levels rather than with illustration or with subscription to any literary program. His only opera, an *Oresteia,* has no vivid personal characterizations or graphic depiction of events—it is very different from Mussorgsky's *Boris*—but it does have Aeschylean grandeur and nobility. In Taneyev's music one finds a reflection of the honest, upright character that won the admiration and affection of men whose musical aims were very different from his. He lived frugally. He was a friend of Tolstoy. Unlike most Russian composers, he didn't drink. In 1905, he resigned his post at the Moscow Conservatory in sympathy with revolutionary students who he felt were being unjustly disciplined.

For many people, a first encounter with Taneyev outside the pages of music histories was probably effected by David Oistrakh's championship, in concert and on disk, of the Concert Suite for violin and orchestra. Oistrakh's record of the Suite is no longer in print here, but there is a good version, with Christian Altenburger the violinist and Yuri Ahronovich the conductor, on the Pro Arte label. Ahronovich's performance of Taneyev's impressive, lovable C-minor Symphony is also available, on Arabesque. Other recordings of his music—including an *Oresteia* on Deutsche Grammophon—have come and gone. One of them was an Angel/Melodiya disk of choral music which included five of the twelve Yakov Polonsky settings, for unaccompanied chorus, that make up Taneyev's Opus 27. Ten of the twelve—a thirty-five-minute stretch of rich and beautiful music—were sung last month by the Dessoff Choirs, conducted by Amy Kaiser, in a Merkin Hall concert.

Taneyev was soaked in Bach, and in Ockeghem, Josquin, and Lassus. He wrote a treatise, *Invertible Counterpoint in the Strict Style.* His writing in the Polonsky settings is thoroughly, but not dryly or academically, contrapuntal. The lines lead through adventurous harmonies. The false relations are bold. The chromatic themes, with uninhibited tritone leaps, must be hard to pitch accurately. The canons are flexible. Taneyev's scoring for voices is masterly; varied accentuations and attacks and unconventional spacing produce an almost "orchestral" range of timbres and textures. The songs have the careful, scrupulous finish of all his music. They are at once elegantly wrought and unconventional, unpredictable.

Composed in 1909 and dedicated to the chorus of a Moscow School for Workers, they may not have been intended to be performed as a cycle. (The two that the Dessoff omitted—one with the promising title "Music suddenly sounded from eternity"—were dropped from printings of Opus 27 after the first edition.) But they made an excellent sequence, varied in motion, manner, and mood, which proceeded from lyricism to a central double climax ("On the Ship," a tempest scene with shipwreck narrowly escaped, and a defiant "Prometheus") and closed with scenes of stillness broken by some stormy episodes. Four four-part songs are followed by two in five parts, one in seven, one in six, and, finally, two in eight parts, treated as a double chorus. The poems use symbolist imagery—wave, bird, vessel, rock—in an almost Mallarméan way. The Dessoff performance was given in an English translation, by Miss Kaiser, that sang well. (It was startling to find a raven, not an eagle, sent to rend Prometheus.) The choir, sixty-five strong, produced a fine range of tone colors and dynamics, and was supple in rhythm and rubato, generally very true of pitch, and quick to retune into consonance if a chord reached by tortuous chromatic paths was not quite truly struck.

The Taneyev ended the concert. It began with part-songs by Bartók and Kodály, duets by Dvořák and Brahms (sung by Elizabeth Pruett and Lynn Beckstrom), and Brahms's anodyne Four Songs for Women's Chorus, Two Horns, and a Harp. Daniel Pincus, a lively and engaging tenor, joined Miss Pruett and Miss Beckstrom in a group from Shostakovich's "From Jewish Folk Poetry."

I Cantori di New York, eighteen strong, conducted by Bart Folse, gave a concert in CAMI Hall last week with the title "Laments and Mad Scenes." It began with two Petrarch settings, Monteverdi's "Zefiro torna" and Marenzio's "Solo e pensoso," and continued with the madrigal version of Monteverdi's "Lamento d'Arianna." The program included another setting of "Solo e pensoso," by James Wagoner—born in 1955, four hundred years after Marenzio. This was poignant, and sensitive to the words, but not as vivid as Marenzio's brief "tone-poem," with its slow, lonely path traced by the soprano, its clustering final bars as the poet reflects that he can find no paths so rough and wild that Love does not "ever come communing with me, and I with him." A pity that Giaches de Wert's extravagantly graphic setting of the same sonnet was not also sung. The only mad scene was Jacob Avshalomov's Tom o' Bedlam (1953), for chorus, oboe, jingles, and tabor. Two other pieces for chorus and oboe had been written for the concert. Wagoner's The Falcon is a direct, skillful setting of the Corpus Christi Carol. Frank Russo's The Dakota, a setting of lines by Amy Clampitt, is a shadowy, layered piece—a dark, sad scene evoked by oboe (David Rowland), solo tenor (Jeffrey Sweetland), and a chorus of ghostly voices. The Cantori cultivate a smooth, refined tone; some passages called for harder, tangier sound and a crying out, rather than merely neat pronunciation, of the words.

The Met's revival of Aida last month was almost without merit: a brainless and boring presentation of the opera, undercast, and enacted without drama in ugly and ineffective scenery. Anna Tomowa-Sintow, a good, plain soprano, had neither the fullness nor the beauty of tone for the title role. Fiorenza Cossotto, a veteran Amneris, still has authority, but her voice was hard and unalluring.

Luciano Pavarotti, doing his first Radamès here, looked like a great gilded tent with a whiskered head on top, and sang without light and shade. Matteo Manuguerra was a low-powered Amonasro. Dimitri Kavrakos's Ramfis, smoothly and cleanly sung, in shaped phrases, lent a touch of distinction to the evening. James Levine conducted. The production was credited to John Dexter, and David Sell was the stage director.

The Met's new production of *Carmen* was quite different—presented as if to an intelligent audience appreciative of opera as something more than singers moving around and making loud noises. As Carmen, Maria Ewing gave an electric performance. She employed an uncommonly large range of vocal devices, from richly throbbing vibrato to bleached, desolate tone, from faint (but always audible) murmuring to full-throated cries. She phrased with the verbal incisiveness and subtlety of a cabaret singer. (After her Glyndebourne Carmen last year, at least two critics drew parallels with Edith Piaf.) She closed Act I with a daring bel-canto *messa di voce*, on the sustained F of the final "Prends garde à toi," which was at once highly dramatic—a last insolent challenge flung at Zuniga—and vocally ravishing. The grace notes, mordents, and small, flickering roulades of the role were all distinctly sounded, not slighted, and they were given meaning. Miss Ewing's kaleidoscopic approach to the role displeased some people, but I thought I had never heard Bizet's music brought to life with so much variety, intensity, and detail. A music critic is exposed often to *Carmen*. I have seen most of the eminent interpreters of the title role in the last four decades (not yet Agnes Baltsa, who comes to the Met production next season). Miss Ewing joins the short list of those who have left an indelible impression.

The production, directed by Peter Hall and designed by John Bury, derives from Glyndebourne's. For the Met version, Mr. Bury has cunningly made the huge stage seem quite crowded and cluttered: the piece was composed for the Opéra-Comique, and this is in effect an intimate *Carmen*. It is done with the spoken dialogue (much more of which than usual is included), and it has the "tightness" that the composer aimed at. The visual conception is somewhat too persistently somber for my taste; Bizet said that his *Carmen* would be "a gay thing," by which he no doubt meant that the tragedy would be set amid scenes of sun-drenched brilliance. In this staging, the Act I sky is black, and the Act IV sky part blue and part black; the dragoons—the *canaris*—wear subfusc, not yellow, uniforms. Mr. Bury's buildings sometimes rest unconvincingly on large stages, and his first act is as architecturally uneasy, in matters of proportion and perspective, as was his *Macbeth* décor. (What happens on those two windowless stories of the cigarette factory?) Act III has become a snow scene: in a production whose idiom is essentially realistic, it looks odd when Carmen deals cards onto the snow and when people sit about casually on what fluttering paper flakes have established as snow-covered ground or rocks. That's not real-life behavior. Sir Peter, however, has a gift for making "operatic" behavior seem real and natural, and most of the time it is splendidly displayed here. The transitions from speech to song are as deftly handled as those from recitative to aria in his Mozart productions. His only stagy mannerism—it was obtrusive, too, in the Bayreuth *Ring*—is to put characters down on their knees for important numbers. (Micaëla knelt in the snow to sing her aria.) The chorus looked as if it needed more rehearsal to complete its transformation from stock choristers into living people. But, in general, this *Carmen* has the freshness that distinguishes all Sir Peter's work. There is no forced search for something new and different but, rather, keen, intelligent, fresh-eyed observation of what is there.

In the first two performances, Luis Lima was the Don José. I saw the third performance, at which Placido Domingo took over. He has long been a notable José. Although he looked and sounded somewhat mature to be the ideal match for Miss Ewing's mercurial Carmen, and although he has long since renounced the use of melting soft tones, he gave an impressive performance, and he was impassioned in the finale. Catherine Malfitano's raven-haired Micaëla was lively and was purely sung, if a little fiercely at the climax of the aria. Michael Devlin's Escamillo was hardly dashing. The smaller parts were well played, fluently spoken, and—apart from an edgy Frasquita and Mercédès—decently sung. James Levine, conducting, was in top form. Whereas *Aida* had found him in his blow-the-brasses, bang-the-drums vein, this *Carmen* combined delicacy with brightness, and force with fineness. His accompanying was sensitive to the heroine's lightest breath and slightest inflection. The three entr'actes were exquisitely played; they became visions of an ideal, unsullied world of grace and beauty, and, as such, increased the tensions and contrasts of this most "objective" of all musical tragedies. Bizet advised his pupil Edmond Galabert to make Mozart's operas his constant inspiration. Good advice, too, for Bizet's interpreters.

Smetana's *Libuše*—less an opera than a series of national, patriotic tableaux—is a noble and stirring score. Eve Queler, her Opera Orchestra of New York, and the New York Choral Society gave a generous, stirring account of it in Carnegie Hall last month. *Libuše* opened the Prague National Theatre, in 1881, and reopened it in 1983, after a six-year restoration and stage rebuilding. The two principals of that production (which has been recorded on Supraphon) also sang in the Carnegie performance: Gabriela Beňačková, as the Princess Libuše, and Václav Zítek, as Přemysl, the farmer she chooses to share her throne. Miss Beňačková brings power, passion, and majesty to the role. The sound is lustrous. She is not strident and squally, as Marie Podvalová and Naděžda Kniplová, her predecessors, were. Mr. Zítek has a well-formed baritone but was slightly bland in Přemysl's moving farewell to his fields, his plow, his farmhands. Miss Queler tends to encourage flat-out singing. Her Krasava and Radmila, Linda Roark-Strummer and Barbara Schramm, both screamed disagreeably. Her Chrudoš and St'áhlav, Paul Plishka and Allan Glassman, belted at full power most of the time but stopped short of forcing their tones into coarseness. The grandeur and beauty of the work proved irresistible.

RESPONDING

April 14, 1986

PIERRE BOULEZ's *Répons,* for chamber orchestra, six soloists, and an array of electro-acoustic equipment, had its first performance at the 1981 Donau-eschingen festival. In an essay entitled "Making Musical History," the *Observer* music critic Peter Heyworth told of a work that struck like lightning. The *Sunday Times* critic David Cairns described the sense of joyful expectancy which fills the opening section, until, at the entry of the soloists,

> their arpeggios, taken up and transmuted electronically, echo and re-echo round the hall, encompassing the listener in an enchanted jangle of overlapping and intermingling timbres—piano, harp, vibraphone, xylophone, cimbalom—impossible to describe. It is as though we were suddenly standing on the threshold of some fabulous underground cavern where row upon row of stalactites threw back myriad patterns of light; but the effect is also of slow-motion waterfalls of sound.

There follow, in Mr. Cairns's words, a "dance of delight," "a moment of intense stillness," and, finally, "a solemnly jubilant ritual of celebration which rises to a massive, richly coloured climax, then sinks down again into a magical stillness, full of trills."

A tape of the Donaueschingen performance reached me, and even though it could not capture the important elements of space, it was more than enough to confirm the exuberance, the freshness, and the beauty of Boulez's inventions. A New York performance of *Répons,* I knew, was being planned, else I would have been off to Paris, London, or Turin to hear one of the later performances. The New York *Répons* happened last month, played by the Ensemble InterContem-porain, conducted by the composer, in the Columbia University Gymnasium, as part of a festival, Boulez Is Back!, presented by the New York Philharmonic. This brought Boulez's first appearances here since he left the Philharmonic, in 1978. Other events were two Fisher Hall concerts by the Ensemble, conducted by Boulez, one of them including his *Dérive* (1984); a Philharmonic program, played four times, including his *Rituel* conducted by Zubin Mehta; a Philhar-monic program, played four times, including his three *Improvisations sur Mallarmé,* conducted by the composer; a *Soldier's Tale* suite conducted by Boulez at a New York Philharmonic Ensembles concert; and "A Conversation with Pierre Boulez" up at Symphony Space. The festival formed the climax of the Ensemble InterContemporain's American tour, during which it played *Répons* also in Los Angeles (twice), San Francisco, Chicago, and Boston (twice).

Was Boulez pleased to be back in the city whose musical life he once hoped to transform? He can have found little altered: perhaps only a hardening of the general public's complacent rejection of any challenging new music, and a deeper incuriosity about what goes on in the rest of the world. Although the Columbia gym was packed for *Répons,* there were rows of empty seats at the first of the Ensemble's Fisher Hall concerts. Some of the Philharmonic audience, the *Times* music critic Donal Henahan reported, booed *Rituel,* while he found it to be "Pierre Boulez's homage to catatonia" and undeserving of so vigorous a response. As for *Répons,* it was, he said, "completely predictable and monotonous" and "simply went on and on to no purpose that I could discover." Mr. Henahan returned to the subject in a Sunday essay:

> For all its heady promise, what did *Répons* turn out to offer, beyond a demonstration of how far Mr. Boulez has progressed in learning to program and manipulate Ircam's electronic Cuisinart? A tired set of ideas in a shiny new box. . . . The results differed little, except in electronic sophistication, from what Edgard Varèse achieved with his *Déserts* in 1954 and *Poème electronique* for Brussels World Fair in 1958.

Others since that Donaueschingen première have been less than overcome by *Répons.* Nicholas Kenyon, writing in *The New Yorker* after a 1981 Paris performance, said:

> The music itself . . . made little impact. The cleverness of the means only served to emphasize the thinness of the result. Instead of overwhelming us with its originality and power, as Boulez's greatest pieces do, *Répons* remained a static, unmoving display of skillful technique.

Dominic Gill, after a 1984 Paris performance, questioned the contributions of the elaborate electronic apparatus: "I doubt, even granted some of the very interesting transformations it had wrought earlier on the soloists' material, whether its role was ever *musically* fundamental: ever more than expensive icing on a masterly traditional recipe." It is easy to be put off by hype, by accounts of expensive technological marvels brought to bear on the creation of a work of art (*Répons* uses Giuseppe di Giugno's 4X computer, developed at IRCAM, which can manage "two hundred million operations a second" and instantaneously produce or transform sounds as a composer wishes, and also uses Hans Peter Haller's Halaphone, to mix and move sounds; at least six sound technicians are kept busy during the performance), and by such claims as that in Paul Griffiths's program note on *Répons:* "It is Boulez's response to the task he had implicitly set himself as soon as he accepted the directorship of the future IRCAM. Sooner or later he would have to compose an electronic masterpiece: this is it."

Répons in New York was not easy or comfortable listening. The gym was hot, crowded, and smelly—not conducive to the keenly focussed attention the piece requires, and airless in a way that seemed to oppress the music as well as its listeners. Moreover, *Répons* was played only once. At earlier presentations, between two performances Boulez had talked about his composition and demonstrated aspects of its workings. "The examples he provided were

466

extremely useful," a London colleague reported after a 1982 performance there; "on a repeat hearing elements of the work's syntax could be grasped, some of the building blocks of its construction glimpsed." (On the American tour, *Répons* was preceded by Boulez's latest composition, *Dialogue de l'ombre double,* for solo clarinet in converse with his prerecorded shadow.) By way of introduction to the New York performance, there were two good essays by Mr. Griffiths in the substantial program book: one about the aims and achievements of the Institut de Recherche et de Coordination Acoustique/Musique (IRCAM); the other a summary of ways that composers in this century—John Cage, Otto Luening, Varèse, Milton Babbitt, Stockhausen, Berio—have used electronics to make music.

Back in Monteverdi's day, Francis Bacon, in *The New Atlantis,* described the resources now available in our computer-equipped music studios: the absolute control of pitch, volume, timbres, velocity, disposition in space; the simulation of speech or instruments; the creation of sounds never heard before. (The passage is quoted on p. 167.) A fair amount of music made at IRCAM using some or all of the devices Bacon described—works by York Höller, Roger Reynolds, Tod Machover, Jean-Claude Risset, Morton Subotnick, Barbara Kolb, Conrad Cummings—has been heard here. Many of the pieces combined electronics with live performers. Peter Manning, the Senior Experimental Officer in Music at Durham University, notes at the end of his useful *Electronic and Computer Music* that while some composers remain committed to working solely with synthetic sounds, "the majority have come to place a higher priority on the refinement of links between the synthetic and natural sound-worlds, seeking a language which is common to both." And Mr. Griffiths, in the program book, said that "the most productive aspect of electronic music is not what Varèse and the young Stockhausen first supposed—its freedom from past limitations—but rather its capacity to contrast and interact with the known world of musical sounds." *Répons* is Boulez's response—the response of a great composer and one of the keenest musical minds of our day—to the new possibilities. His concern with electronics goes back to 1948, when he worked for a while in Pierre Schaeffer's musique-concrète studio. His Etudes of 1952—one of them has been recorded—stripped musique-concrète of evocative and picturesque connotations and essayed "pure" composition. But his *Poésie pour pouvoir,* for tape and orchestra, first heard at Donaueschingen in 1958, was withdrawn after that single performance: the tape element did not satisfy him. He shunned electronics for years, and returned to them only with . . . *explosante-fixe . . . ,* for chamber ensemble and a wondrous machine, which New York heard in 1973; the piece is due to be recast more precisely, with the more wondrous machines now developed at IRCAM. *Répons* is not an experimental work but an achieved masterwork, sprung from, standing on, and dominating the latest expanse of "fruitful land" (a favorite Boulez image, Klee-derived) into which music and technology have now marched hand in hand. Like the Second Piano Sonata, *Structures, Le Marteau sans maître, Pli selon Pli,* and *Rituel, Répons* is a monument of its time. Like them, I believe, it will stand firm, to be excitedly reëxplored in each succeeding decade.

On a platform in the center of the gym there was a chamber orchestra of eight strings, nine woodwinds, and seven brasses. The audience surrounded the players on three sides; behind them the electronic machines and their manipulators were stationed. In each corner of the room and at the center of each long side there sat, aloft on an eminence, a soloist: playing piano, piano, harp, cimbalom, xylophone, and vibraphone. The six soloists also had both adjunct instruments (celesta; electric organ; another harp, differently tuned; further percussion) and tape machines charged with what Boulez calls "musical wallpaper," generated in advance by the 4X computer, which they could unroll as required to form a background. Batteries of loudspeakers hung overhead.

Répons begins with a sudden, jagged arpeggio—as if the work were set in motion, Boulez has suggested, by the figure of a lightning flash. There are further flashes, and then the basic motif is revealed as a deep rising arpeggio topped by a trill or a sustained call. A maze of trills creates a feeling of tense expectancy. (It's a Beethoven device writ large.) A trumpet fanfare and a tattoo of *col legno* strings herald the entry of the soloists. Suddenly, wave upon wave of twinkling, glittering sound pours in from every side. At the same time, the hall, lit until now only on the platform, is flooded with light. The shimmer glows to an intoxicating jangle and then fades into silence. (The "movements" of *Répons* are clearly articulated.) There follows a scherzo with a chunky theme of neoclassical cut. As soloists and orchestra answer one another, the texture thickens into a long, dense section pierced from time to time by a low brass note that booms out, foghornlike, to provide a point of stability, a tonal anchor. One might be lost in a swirl of fog banks, which part often to reveal the bright, busy dance of the stars above. Gradually, the music subsides onto one sustained call.

And there, in 1981, *Répons* ended, after twenty minutes. But more had already been planned, and further installments were added successively at performances in London in 1982, in Turin in 1984, and at these American performances. *Répons* has now more than doubled its length, to forty-five minutes, and it has become a more demanding work. At a first hearing of this fuller version, my own responsiveness grew a shade less keen during the next two sections, for they have a static, time-suspended quality—many incidents but little apparent progress. Subsequent hearings, however, even though only in the spatially restricted medium of tape, revealed their variety and proportion. The first of them seems like a new view of the previous section, but rendered in lighter textures, with riffs on the tuned percussions and more exotic transmutations of the soloists' timbres. Woodwind lines through a gamelanlike patter lead into the next section, which is punctuated with the pipping of Morse-code signals and shot through with long, swooping shafts of melody. Then there is a change of gait, into an episode built from big surges of sound, each followed by ripples or stillnesses. Another change introduces a passage of airy textures, trills, and playful solos, invaded by an insistent marchlike rhythm; Boulez seems to be smiling here, even joking. Woodwind runs lead it to a close. The coda is a series of sweeping rhetorical arpeggios, each differently colored, voiced, and spaced. Each is differently answered: by reverberations into silence, echoes of various strange kinds, sudden flurries as of startled birds, or showers of small, bright flakes. The distance between the arpeggios grows greater. One of them remains unanswered except by a long silence, and *Répons* is over.

468

Mr. Henahan began his essay on *Répons* with the reflection that for Beethoven when giving voice to his last, most adventurous musical thoughts a medium of four conventional string instruments sufficed. Busoni, after hearing of Thaddeus Cahill's two-hundred-ton Dynamiphone, or Telharmonium, which by electrical means could generate sounds of any timbre and pitch, wrote—in his *Sketch for a New Aesthetic of Music,* of 1907—"In what direction does the next step lead? To abstract sound, to unhampered technique, to unlimited tonal material." But in 1922 he asked, "Should not music . . . try to express only what is most important with a few notes, set down in a masterly fashion? Does my *Brautwahl* with its full score of seven hundred pages achieve more than *Figaro* with its six accompanying wind instruments?" The sheer cost of *Répons*—created with the resources of the lavishly subsidized IRCAM, executed by a crack orchestra maintained by the French government solely for the presentation of modern music—and the elaboration of apparatus and the amount of rehearsal needed for its performance inevitably raise questions about means and end. I cannot answer such questions except as a listener. Both economy and copiousness can be artistic virtues: there is room in the world for Mozart and Mahler, for Webern and Wagner, for Schubert and the Stockhausen of *Licht.* It is not a matter of exclusive alternatives. Boulez's *Dialogue de l'ombre double* is written, as I said, for just one player and tape, and his *Dérive* is a brief sextet. The Ensemble also performed Elliott Carter's new *Penthode,* which is for twenty instruments played traditionally, without electronics.

Busoni once likened music to a garden in which each composer, however mighty, can "survey, handle, and display only a fraction of the complete flora of the earth, a tiny fragment of that paradise-garden which covers the planets." *Répons* fills a larger plot of that garden than most works do, but it did not strike me as an extravaganza—excessive or unwarranted in its demands. On the contrary, it is precise, disciplined, and logical. I can understand people's disliking or resenting Boulez, for tracts of music's garden which many hold dear he dismisses as rank or withered weeds and tramples underfoot with disdain. But throughout my life since my first, dazzled encounter with *Le Marteau sans maître* at the 1958 Aix-en-Provence festival, he has in work after work shaken any easy, comfortable assumptions and compelled listeners to think afresh; has seized on whatever he finds significant in each wave of new discoveries or inventions and distilled from it something pure and keen; and then, with creative passion, has composed a series of—the word is inescapable—masterpieces. *Répons* is the latest of them.

ONLY CONNECT

April 21, 1986

HANS WERNER HENZE's music—poured from a generous, abundant creator, flowing into every available channel, from intimate miniature to grand opera and monster oratorio, and marked always by prodigious technical skill, coupled with personal poetic vision—has at once illumined and contributed to modern history. Since the Speculum Musicae performance of *El cimarrón*, which I wrote about last month, there has been something like a small Henze festival in New York. Works of nearly four decades were heard. What was called Henze Week up at the Manhattan School of Music brought three performances of his opera *The English Cat*, a chamber-orchestra concert, a recital devoted to his music for guitar, and a public discussion with the composer. On the night of the concert—unfortunate coincidence of events for anyone eager to catch up with Henze's later music—the Concord Quartet, at a League of Composers–ISCM concert in Merkin Hall, played his Third, Fourth, and Fifth String Quartets.

Kammermusik 1958 belongs in time and in spirit with Henze's Kleist opera *The Prince of Homburg*, in which a romantic German prince, in a world of Prussian militarism, is lost in gentle classical dreams. It preceded Henze's outpouring of love music—*Ariosi, Being Beauteous*, the *Cantata della fiaba estrema*—of the sixties, and is a small, lovely manifestation of the encounters between Northern artists and Mediterranean antiquity which have inspired so much art from Goethe onward. The title continues, "on Friedrich Hölderlin's hymn *In lieblicher Bläue*," and the text is from Wilhelm Waiblinger's novel *Phaeton*, which has a protagonist based on Hölderlin and incorporates, it seems likely, fragmentary poems that Waiblinger received from Hölderlin during the poet's years of madness. *Kammermusik* has twelve related movements—and a summatory epilogue, added in 1963—for combinations of tenor, guitar, and instrumental octet (clarinet, bassoon, horn, and string quintet). It is dedicated to Benjamin Britten (whose *Peter Grimes*, heard by Henze in Mannheim in 1946, was an early influence on him); at the first performances, Peter Pears was the singer and Julian Bream the guitarist. The octet plays a Preface, a Sonata, a Cadenza, and the Epilogue; there are six vocal movements, three accompanied by all the instruments, three by the guitar; and there are three Tentos (Portuguese for "ricercari") for solo guitar. The guitar solos and the guitar-accompanied songs have been extracted for independent performance, as *Three Tentos* (which several guitarists have recorded) and *Three Fragments after Hölderlin*. These began the Manhattan School recital. Kristinn Arnason played the *Tentos*, and Peter Thomas Collins, accompanied by Robert Rawdon, sang the *Fragments*. The music is exquisitely fashioned. The pieces ravish the ear and stir the imagination. They also leave one eager to rehear a complete performance of *Kammermusik*, a mysterious and moving work. There some images appear first glimmering, as it were in the depths, imperfectly perceived, and only in later movements take on clear shape. Sometimes, as in the second Tento, single ideas are picked up and, like some lovingly handled object, turned in the light to be raptly observed from many aspects. The variety of textures and colors reflects Henze's responses to Hölderlin's responses to a landscape that he had seen only with imagination's eye. "I can feel this link to the ancient world," Henze wrote in a note about his composition. "In our eyes, our landscapes are transformed and take on Hellenic features." He began work on *Kammermusik* in Greece. Oedipus and Hercules stride through the final song. My own responses to the score are probably colored by memories of standing at the trivium where

Oedipus slew Laius, of walking from Tiryns to Nemea, Lerna, Stymphalia. The Greek light that plays upon high Western art (beside Lake Stymphalia, I watched it burn antelucan vapors into brightness) shines in *Kammermusik.*

The sound of the guitar has run through much of Henze's music. In a 1979 letter—reprinted in the collection *Music and Politics*—he wrote of the instrument: "In *König Hirsch,* at the start of my life in Italy [1953], the guitar was for me like a gate through which one can reach the beginnings of music, a remnant from a bygone age that still lives on, deep in the consciousness of the people." In *Kammermusik,* its tones were invoked "to convey the German soul of the present to the land of our origins." A guitarist is one of the four actors in the dramatic narrative of *El cimarrón.* In the ballet *Orpheus* (which the Stuttgart Ballet brought to the Met in 1979), the rich flow of the music is "determined by the sound of the guitar. All Orpheus' arias begin with its tones. It is the jangling and whining of nerve ends; it is a hundred different hues: dark, shadowy, silvery, weeping, the hollow calls of nocturnal animals; and it is the echo-sounder of history."

The Manhattan recital continued with the two guitar sonatas entitled *Royal Winter Music I* and *II* (1976 and 1979)—works in which the expressive powers of the instrument are put to their fullest use. They were composed for Julian Bream, who brought the first of them to Town Hall in 1976 but declared the second to be unplayable; Reinbert Evers gave the first performance in Brussels in 1980, and David Tanenbaum played the American première in Houston three years later. In a prefatory note to the first sonata, Henze writes of the guitar as "a 'knowing' instrument, reaching back far into our past, into our history—one with many limitations but also many unexplored breadths and depths, one possessing a wealth of timbres which can compass all those available to a modern instrumentarium. To realize this one has only to enter silence, wait, and completely shut out all noise." In an age of racket—electric amplification, background music, streets loud with sirens and brutish honking, opera singers who bawl, conductors who urge the brasses to bray—the strains of the guitar, like those of the clavichord, are balm to musical ears. Even at their loudest, these instruments hurt not. In the Manhattan School's Pforzheimer Hall, where the guitar recital was given, the air was unsullied by the electronic bourdon (from a ventilation system) that fills the Juilliard classrooms I know, and even in some New York concert halls adds its pedal points or washes of "white noise" to the soft passages.

The *Royal Winter Music* sonatas are also suites based on Shakespeare personages. I wrote about the first of them after New York performances by Mr. Bream and Mr. Tanenbaum [*Music of Three Seasons,* pp. 431–32]. The characters of the second are Sir Andrew Aguecheek, Bottom, and Lady Macbeth. In a prefatory note to the score, Henze discloses that the first and last movements, at least, are inspired not only by Shakespeare but also by particular actors. Sir Andrew is an unexpected choice from the long gallery of Shakespeare portraits. When Henze, aged seventeen, was a music student in Brunswick, he missed no performance of a *Twelfth Night* there with a captivating Sir Andrew, played as someone who has "a tenderness about him, and a sadness like that emanating from a wilted meadow-saffron. He is on his way to the flowers to become a flower himself, a thistle probably. . . . He smells of flowers and combs his long, golden English hair." The Lady Macbeth movement, "Mad Lady Macbeth," enshrines a memory of Maria Callas as the heroine of Verdi's opera. So behind a performance of it lie Shakespeare; Carlo Rusconi, who translated the play, and A. W. Schlegel, whose commentary, prefaced to the translation, influenced Verdi's reading of it; the genius of Callas, the director Carl Ebert, and the conductor Victor de Sabata, collaborators in the 1952 Scala production of *Macbeth;* Henze; and then the particular guitarist, faced with music so difficult that he is "likely to approach it with fear and trembling—just as we would not care to cross the path of Lady Macbeth." This "impurity" in Henze's music—its relations and connections to so many other things—is part of its fascination. "Bottom's Dream," the central movement, tells of a man who thinks himself once again young, slim, handsome, and sweet-smelling, and, "in the arms of the gorgeous Titania," has no wish to wake. It is a small, touching pastoral, in the vein of the dream episode in Elgar's *Falstaff.*

The sonatas were played by Mark Delpriora (who gave the New York première of the second in Merkin Hall last year). His performances were intent, poetic, and carefully scaled. The recital ended with *Carillon, Recitative, Masque* (1974), for guitar, mandolin, and harp—an elegant, enchanting piece, but on this occasion imperfectly rendered.

The Manhattan School orchestral concert began with a marimba solo, *Five Scenes from the Snow Country,* composed in 1978 for Michiko Takahashi. Then there was *Apollo and Hyacinth,* an early piece (1949) and an important one in Henze's oeuvre. It is at once a miniature harpsichord concerto (the "orchestra" being a wind quartet and a string quartet) and a small tone-poem about the god's accidental killing of the youth he loved. In the last movement, an alto sings an autumnal threnody by Georg Trakl, a poet whose works accompanied Henze in his school and his soldier years. In *Apollo* Henze found his way from the spikiness of his earlier compositions—Chamber Concerto, First Symphony, First String Quartet—into lyricism, and also mastered serial technique as a personal means: "At the beginning of the piece, I imagined how Apollo appeared in an ancient grove. The beating of his wings, the suddenly darkening sky, and then the great luminous silence of grace, accompanied by the strange, gentle, sensuous excitement of all men and animals, were to be depicted by such abstract means as a harpsichord and eight chamber instruments."

In the Spring 1985 issue of *19th Century Music,* Owen Jander proposed for the Andante of Beethoven's Fourth Piano Concerto not just the usual likening of it to Orpheus' taming of the wild beasts but a theme-by-theme, incident-by-incident program—based on the Orpheus operas of Gluck, J. G. Naumann, and F. A. Kanne, and on Virgil and Ovid—which tells of Orpheus' taming of the Furies, his rescue of Eurydice, and Eurydice's second death. (Mr. Jander stressed that his program is speculative: "Lacking the composer's own definitive explanation, we cannot presume to have unveiled Beethoven's plan.") The hybrid form of concerto and tone-poem is one that Henze has returned to often since *Apollo*—in his cello concerto *Ode to the West Wind* (1953); Second Piano Concerto (1967), its finale based on Shakespeare's Sonnet No. 129; Second Violin Concerto (1971); *Tristan* (1973). He is writing a guitar concerto for Mr.

Tanenbaum, due at the Lucerne Festival in August, based on Mörike's "An eine Äolsharfe." *The Miracle of the Rose,* which ended the Manhattan School concert, is at once a clarinet concerto, a suite of seven dances, and a tone-poem whose program is the vision toward the close of Jean Genet's *Miracle de la rose.* Four men in black—judge, lawyer, chaplain, and executioner—enter the cell of a young murderer on the morning of his execution. He becomes a prince in splendor; they shrink to the size of bedbugs, scuttle up his body, enter it—two by the mouth, two by the ears—and, through a series of strange, charmed landscapes, search for his heart. Its beating sounds toward the end of the fifth movement and through the sixth. The intruders come upon a dazzling red rose, and, in the finale, tear it to pieces.

David Hamilton, reviewing Henze's *Tristan* in *High Fidelity,* wrote of the way "we are expected to apprehend [the piece] not only with our ears, but in the triple framework of the composer's intellectual life, the technical and musical resources at his command, and a 'story line' that is imparted to us before we hear the music." The story line of *The Miracle* was not vouchsafed to the Manhattan School audience; the program leaflet did not even list the movements. Just as "pure music," the score should have made a considerable effect, for it is tautly constructed, graphic in its gestures, vivid in its carefully laid-out rhythms, and bewitching in its instrumentation. I did not hear the concert (I was at the string quartets) but attended the final rehearsal: the performance, conducted by George Manahan, with Mark Spuria as the clarinet soloist, promised to be a fine one. This was the New York première. The piece was commissioned by the London Sinfonietta and was first played, in London, in 1982; Antony Pay was the soloist, and Henze conducted.

Henze's first two string quartets were written in 1947 and 1952. They are dense, rhythmically complex pieces. He returned to the medium only in 1975, at the invitation of the Concord Quartet, and embarked on a set of three quartets. No. 3 was played by the Concord at the 1976 Berlin Festival, and Nos. 4 and 5 the following year at the Schwetzingen Festival. In 1978 the Arditti Quartet (which has recorded all five of Henze's quartets, for Wergo) played Nos. 3–5 as a set, in London. They are memorial pieces, dedicated to the composer's mother, the Chilean musician Victor Jara, and Benjamin Britten. No. 3 is a single movement of tense, eloquent counterpoint—a sustained ricercare that ends with a beautiful viola solo. No. 4, composed while Henze's opera *We Come to the River* was in rehearsal at Covent Garden, is a freer, more theatrical sort of piece. A different player takes the lead in each of the four movements. The Adagio, a musing on a Byrd pavane, with the viola as soloist, is gently eloquent. There is much unmeasured writing; sometimes the score bursts into graphic squiggles; the finale, a "rondo improvvisato," is made of "cells," which, under the general guidance of the first violin, the players assemble as they choose. No. 5, in six movements, was begun at the same time as No. 4 but pondered longer. In a program note Henze remarks that it "seems to move away from the spectacular, to remember the historical concept of the String Quartet as a place of inward intensification, of maximum concentration, of contemplation." But because "in my opinion musical ideas always come from our feelings and adventures," and "life and artistic work are one and the same thing," the quartet seems also to have an emotional program, verbally identified only by the appearance in instrumental guise of the madmen's madrigal from *We Come to the River* and by the composer's assurance that "the piece ends with a representation of the light of the new day, where the creatures and fears of night, scared back to their dismal dens, are dissolved, become invisible and unimaginable, as if they had never existed." The Concord performance of these three quartets provided an evening of memorable and satisfying music.

The English Cat is harder to enjoy wholeheartedly. There is ingenious, stimulating, and attractive music in it. The Manhattan School production, conducted by David Gilbert and directed by Lou Galterio, was neater and crisper than Santa Fe's last summer. There was some accomplished singing. But Edward Bond's libretto seems to me feeble, carelessly wrought, unfunny in its jokes, and fumbling in its satire.

DISCOURSE MOST ELOQUENT

April 28, 1986

ELLIOTT CARTER's *Penthode,* for an orchestra of twenty soloists, was completed in June last year. It is dedicated to Pierre Boulez and the Ensemble InterContemporain, who first played it in London, in July, at the Proms, and played it in New York, in Avery Fisher Hall, last month. The title is a scholar's version of "pentode," or "five-way." Carter's Third String Quartet was a double duo. He has composed a Symphony of Three Orchestras, and a Triple Duo. *Penthode* is a quintuple quartet. The orchestra is divided into five groups of four players: trumpet, trombone, harp, and violin; flute, horn, marimba, and double-bass; oboe, tuba, violin, and cello; clarinet, bass clarinet, trumpet, and vibraphone; and bassoon, piano, percussion, and viola. The slightly odd array was presumably influenced by the constitution of the Ensemble. Carter thrives on challenges, delights in handling new instrumental combinations, and in this work, without ever calling for outré methods of playing, makes new sounds. His note on the music is short: "*Penthode* is concerned with experiences of connectedness and isolation. Twenty players are divided into five groups of four, each group comprising instruments of different types. However, each group has its own repertory of expressive characters embodied in its own special field of speeds and musical intervals. How each of these five groups combines with or opposes the others is the gist of the score."

The piece begins with a long viola melody, "tranquillo, quasi improvvisando, un poco espressivo," unaccompanied except for some points of harmony touched in by members of the viola's own group or by others. It is as if someone unemphatically but eloquently proposed an idea, began a discourse that gradually caught the attention of a large company, provoking assents, riders, qualifications, denials. Soon everyone is talking, but not all at once, for this is a civilized company. One speaker—flute, tuba, harp—has only to raise a voice and the others listen attentively, or utter no more than murmurs of approval or dissension. Then someone else takes up the statement, to extend, modify, or politely question it. The sense of five different groups—as in an after-dinner drawing room—clustered by common interests yet attentive to whatever arresting is being said is strong. Sometimes the commentary remains within the groups. Sometimes other affinities produce new groupings, as when the string instruments, from four different quartets, join together as a string quintet. I must not make *Penthode* sound like an any-day country-house conversation. It is more like conversation at All Souls on a night when the country's best brains are there: awesome in its intelligence, confidence, preciseness, and readiness, yet at the same time winning, welcoming, and unpretentious.

The simile merely suggests a first impression, and it breaks down when musical form is considered. *Penthode,* which lasts eighteen minutes, mounts to a formidable climax that is not at all conversational but is a powerful outcome of what has gone before. The new element in this piece is a "connectedness" more evident and more frequent than in the earlier group-against-group, speed-against-speed compositions. Instruments from different groups sometimes join in a unison line, or one may double just parts of another's melody. Carter's three song cycles—*A Mirror on Which to Dwell* (1975), *Syringa* (1978), and *In Sleep, in Thunder* (1981)—seem to have influenced his instrumental writing to a greater lyricism, and *Penthode* is even more melodious than the Triple Duo. And it is colorful: tuba tunes, a rippling harp, streaks from the piccolo, and positively romantic violin writing sound in its pages.

Penthode was played on a program with Franco Donatoni's new *Tema,* a flickering, busy piece recognizably by the author of *Puppenspiel* (1961); with York Höller's *Résonance* (1981), for orchestra surrounded by sparky tape sounds; and with György Ligeti's Chamber Concerto (1970), a contemporary classic. Amid so much glitter and twitter, trillings and chirrupings, *Penthode* made an almost sober effect, but a substantial one. Its energy of thought was apparent at once. Repeated hearings reveal its elegance, lightness, and charm. The Ensemble performances were masterly.

György Kurtág was sixty in February. Today, his name would probably figure on any short list of the world's most distinguished living composers, but only in recent years has his music been widely heard. His Opus 1, a string quartet, was played at the 1964 ISCM Festival. *The Sayings of Péter Bornemisza,* Opus 7, a long "concerto for soprano and piano," was heard at Darmstadt. But the work that brought him to general attention was the song cycle for soprano and chamber orchestra *Messages of the Late R. V. Trussova,* Opus 17. It was performed first in Paris, by the Ensemble InterContemporain, in 1981, and later that year in London, by the London Sinfonietta. In 1982, it was heard at the Proms. Adrienne Csengery (the soprano of those performances), Boulez, and the Ensemble InterContemporain have recorded the piece on Erato. In this country, it was heard last year at Tanglewood, sung by three sopranos (a different one in each movement) and conducted by Kent Nagano; and in Ithaca, sung by Christine Schadeberg, with the Cornell Contemporary Ensemble, conducted by Fred Cohen. This year it was done in February in San Francisco, and this month in New York, presented by the Brooklyn Philharmonic in a Meet the Moderns program. "Few works of the past five years have achieved a firm place in the contemporary repertory more surely," the critic Andrew Clements wrote after a 1984 London performance.

Everyone I know who has heard *Messages* has been bowled over by it—by the intensity, directness, and beauty of its images, by the sense of spontaneity mingled with exact, intricate working, by the encounter with a distinctive, individual musical voice. Kurtág, like Ligeti, studied at the Budapest Academy with Sándor Veress and Ferenc Farkas. His early works (some of which are published, without opus numbers) are said to be, like Ligeti's early works, Bartók-influenced. In 1956, Ligeti left Hungary, and in 1961 *Atmospheres,* played in Donaueschingen, brought him the international prominence he has enjoyed ever since. In 1957, Kurtág went to Paris, studied with Marianne Stein, attended classes by Milhaud and Messiaen, and heard Boulez's Domaine Musical concerts. He returned to Budapest in 1958, composed the Opus 1 quartet, and has followed it with hardly more than a handful of works, most of them for small forces. Points of reference in describing his style are Webern, for economy and precision of statement (what Schoenberg, in a preface to Webern's Six Bagatelles, called the ability "to express a novel in a single gesture, joy in a single breath"); Berg, for the urgency of emotion in the lines; and Bartók, for a way of building movements from small, charged cells. But the sound of Kurtág's music is all his own. A recurrent element is the cimbalom: it plays in several of his compositions; in others, its figurations, textures, and strangely glinting, dusky timbres are suggested. Easy first steps into Kurtág's musical world are provided by his *Játékok* (*Games*), four books of piano pieces for children. The title combines senses of "play" as in playing games and playing an instrument; the miniatures relate to Kurtág's larger works rather as Beethoven's late bagatelles do to his late sonatas.

Messages of the Late R. V. Trusova is a setting of twenty-one brief poems by Rimma Dalos, a Russian poet who lives in Hungary. The number of poems chosen, the varied instrumentation of each song, and the occasional use of *Sprechgesang* suggest a link with *Pierrot Lunaire.* The subject matter suggests a modern *Frauenliebe und -leben,* but with a deserted, not a widowed, protagonist; Schoenberg's *Erwartung* and Poulenc's *La Voix humaine* also come to mind. The three parts are subtitled "Loneliness," "A Little Erotic" ("little" is meiosis; the four songs of this section are fiercely, uninhibitedly erotic), and "Bitter Experience—Delight and Grief." The third, longest part begins:

> You took my heart
> on the palm of your hand,
> which you then carefully turned upside down.

The Russian original has eight fewer words. Most of the Dalos poems are Tacitean, aphoristic, haiku-like three-liners, Akhmatova-like in the force and poignancy of their statements. For each poem, Kurtág finds a keen musical image. "Heat," the first of the erotic songs, begins from a small, bright flame—a

476

rapid semitone oscillation on the first word, "zhar." It expands, grows to a consuming fire, and breaks into wild arpeggios that reach at last to the Queen of the Night's F; the song dies away in an ecstatic, whispered shudder. In "Autumn Flowers Fading," the voice part is unpitched, except approximately by the slant at which the words are printed through the staff; "mewing" is the instruction to the singer. Lapped descending scales, chromatic or whole-tone, fall very softly from celesta, harp, and piano, while other scales rise more slowly on celesta, piano, and cimbalom; when the cimbalom has reached its highest note it exchanges roles with the harp. Oboe, clarinet, and horn touch in soft harmonies; isolated harmonics from violin, viola, and double-bass gleam like distant points of light; four gongs and a tam-tam beat out a slow, soft ostinato. Any summary description of Kurtág's procedures makes them seem schematic. Performance reveals music that has been delicately "heard" in all its details, music in which the abundant ideas of a teeming imagination have been refined until every note, every sound tells. Kurtág composes slowly. Part of the "compositional act" that produced *Messages* is the ordering of the twenty-one brief songs into a telling sequence. Fifteen more Dalos settings make up a later cycle, *Scenes from a Novel*, Opus 19, for soprano, violin, cimbalom, and double-bass.

In Europe, Kurtág's music has been sung most often, through country after country, by Miss Csengery, a Fiordiligi and Lulu, a Glyndebourne Susanna and Zerlina. The New York soloist was Miss Schadeberg, and she was admirable—pure, passionate (if not as passionate as Miss Csengery), and various, compassing in brilliant fashion the extended vocal and emotional requirements. I hope she is already preparing *Scenes from a Novel*, the *Attila József Fragments*, Opus 20, for solo soprano, and the *Songs of Amy Karolyi*, Opus 22, for soprano and cimbalom, none of which New York has yet heard. Eight of Kurtág's twenty-odd works are cycles for soprano. He has provided a modern concert repertory for our bright young divas—Kathleen Battle, Judith Bettina, Beverly Morgan, Lucy Shelton, Carmen Pelton, Sylvia McNair, Julianne Baird—to shine in. Lukas Foss conducted members of the Brooklyn Philharmonic—sensitive virtuoso players, responsive to the inventions of the score. But there was some corner-cutting (and so *Messages* still awaits its "real" New York première). The band lacked a cimbalom, whose timbre gives much of the music its essential colors; a piano with metal chains lying on its strings was a sorry makeshift. The song "A slender needle of suffering" begins with an extraordinary sound, potently affecting on the record. The score reveals it to be Bartók snap pizzicatos on violin and viola, the cimbalom struck with metal beaters, a stroke on the glass chimes, and "the breaking of a glass." It didn't sound right at the Brooklyn performance: the glass was muted in a paper bag, and instead of splintery glass chimes there was a dry clatter of bamboo chimes.

Nevertheless, this New York première of Kurtág's *Messages* was a high point in a rich season. It crowned an unusually interesting and attractive program: another hearing of Boulez's *Dérive*, and the New York premières of Robert Saxton's *Processions and Dances* and Per Nørgård's *Prelude and Ant Fugue* (*with a Crab Canon*). *Dérive*, like Elliott Carter's *Canon for 4*, was composed to honor Sir William Glock and his achievements, on his retirement from the Bath

Festival (where in 1984 Kurtág was much played). It had its first—and at once its second—performance in 1985, by the London Sinfonietta, conducted by Oliver Knussen. (The audience called for, and was granted, an encore.) The Ensemble InterContemporain introduced it to New York last month. *Dérive* is an eight-minute sextet for flute and clarinet, violin and cello, and vibraphone and piano. In French, the title retains its etymological connotation: "from the shore." The music "drifts" on an enchanted tide of trills, tremolos, and richly decorated chords, but Boulez remains master of its fate. *Dérive,* rhapsody and carefully shaped discourse in one, might be called latter-day Delius—or, as Desmond Shawe-Taylor proposed, "a modern equivalent of late Debussy." I like his suggestion that this short, seductive score "will perhaps one day qualify for inclusion in what the record world would call 'Boulez's Greatest Hits.'"

Saxton's *Processions and Dances,* which was conducted by Steven Mercurio, is a twelve-minute octet, for flute, oboe, clarinet, string trio, harp, and percussion. The initial inspiration, the composer says in a program note, came from "a poster of a snowbound funeral in an East European village entitled 'The Last Jews of Radauti.'" Like other Saxton pieces, it combines disciplined harmonic progress, lively rhythmic incident, and pungent timbres. It dates from 1981, and Saxton has written more important works since then: *The Ring of Eternity,* the Concerto for Orchestra, *The Sentinel of the Rainbow.* His latest work, the chamber symphony *The Circles of Light,* was introduced last month by the London Sinfonietta and Esa-Pekka Salonen. The title refers to Canto 28 of the *Paradiso.* This is the boldest and freest of Saxton's mystic, visionary compositions. I know it only from tape and score, and look forward to a public performance.

Nørgård's Prelude and Fugue (1982), for flute, clarinet, guitar, mandolin, violin, double-bass, and percussion, is a playful piece. The prelude is the first of Bach's Forty-eight transcribed with extensions, octave transpositions, and other devices. The fugue is a "false" one, likened by the composer to those sleight-of-hand trick-perspective drawings that seem to be obeying the rules until one finds water that flows uphill or an ascending stair that leads to a level lower than where it started. It is a deceptive and amusing fugue. Nørgård's music is always ingeniously fashioned. Sometimes it is poetic, too: earlier this season, the guitarist David Starobin opened his recital at the Y with *Returns* (1976), a work both playful and captivating.

This Brooklyn Philharmonic program, which should have drawn crowds, was played twice, on consecutive days in the Great Hall at Cooper Union and in the Playhouse of the Brooklyn Academy. I attended the second, and at the start counted perhaps fifty people there. A choice program had been assembled. The artists had worked hard. The performances were accomplished. But the presentation was poor. The stage of the Playhouse was swathed in black. During the first half, the houselights were turned out; through a long wait before each piece the audience sat in gloomy darkness, unable to read the program notes, and talking in hushed tones, as if at a funeral. There was no clamor for an encore of *Dérive.* For the Kurtág, there was a glimmer of light—not enough to follow with any ease the translation sheet, in small type, that had been provided.

May 5, 1986

MESSIAEN'S *Saint François d'Assise,* commissioned for the Paris Opéra by Rolf Liebermann in 1975, was brought to performance there in November 1983. It is a set of eight tableaux in the life of the saint, enacted to music in the composer's familiar manner, in which slow, emphatic, repetitive melodic declamation is punctuated by bursts of "birdsong"—avian calls transcribed for gigantic instrumental forces, squawked, screeched, hammered out by brasses, woodwinds, a battery of percussion, and the electronic caterwaul of the Ondes Martenot. Before saying more, let me own that in the past I have been prepared to genuflect before some big Messiaen scores (*Chronochromie, Seven Haiku, Colors of the Celestial City, Et exspecto resurrectionem mortuorum*), to be stirred by the play of sounds and colors, to find radiance in the timbres, strength in the heavy, insistent rhythms (based on classical meters and Indian talas), and, even, passion in the succulent added-note harmonies. The works for smaller forces (the long *Catalogue of Birds,* for piano solo; the *Awakening Birds* and *Exotic Birds,* for moderate orchestras) could be enjoyed with fewer qualms. In 1969, Messiaen added a huge choir to his huge orchestra and brought out, in Lisbon, *The Transfiguration of Our Lord Jesus Christ,* which lasted over a hundred minutes. I began a review of it respectfully:

> Olivier Messiaen, who had, like Berlioz, a Dauphiné boyhood, has always been concerned with high mountains, with the dazzle and splendor of sun on snow, with glacier and fell. He has hymned radiance and tried to find sounds for the splendor. In what he himself has likened to mescaline-induced ecstasy, sights and sounds, colors and timbres, have combined in one rapturous vision, and his big works have been sustained outpourings of love: love between man and woman, which found its fullest expression in the *Turangalîla* symphony, and love of God for man and of man for God, given expression in a series of works that includes the apocalyptic dazzle of the *Colors of the Celestial City,* the Resurrection glories and terrors of *Et exspecto* (first played in the Sainte-Chapelle while morning sun fired the windows), and now, largest and longest of all, *The Transfiguration.*

In a program note, the composer told of a day in his life when, gazing at the Jungfrau and at Mont Blanc, he understood the difference between the sun's and the snow's splendor, and imagined how terrible the Transfiguration must have been. His score was a Jungfrau piled upon Mont Blanc. It was tremendous. It was almost unbearable. One surrendered—bashed into submission, perhaps, by the numerous gong strokes—or stoutly resisted. *Saint Francis* now adds the Himalaya to the pile. I did not go to Paris for the première. All of the work that

I have heard live is three of the eight tableaux, brought to Carnegie Hall last month by the Boston Symphony and the Tanglewood Festival Chorus, conducted by Seiji Ozawa: the third, "Saint Francis Kisses the Leper," and the seventh and eighth (which make up the third act of the opera), "The Stigmata" and "Death and New Life."

When George Crumb, in his *Star-Child,* used the small, fine formulas that had produced his delicate chamber music to create a long work for large forces, the result was coarse and displeasing. The parallel with *Saint Francis* is not precise, but part of the way it holds. The work has been composed by formulas that worked well before but are now overextended. The composer proceeds like an organist intoxicated—inspired, if you like—by the power that can be his at the touch of a button and is now holding forth, for much longer than ever before, on an instrument much larger than any he has used before. "What I tell you three times is true" sufficed for the Bellman; "Let me cry it *nine* times" seems to be Messiaen's decision, "and who will dare disbelieve?" The simpleminded, heavy repetitiousness in the score of *Saint Francis* makes minimalist music seem positively Carterian. Litaneutical forcefulness moves into longueur. One seeks relief in flippancy: a critic of the Paris première remarked that "the incessant interruptions by twittering woodwind nearly had me reaching for my shotgun."

In the last paragraph of a program note, the composer admits to an uneasiness lest listeners find all his racket and all his apparatus ill matched to a work about the saint of the Little Flowers, one who "invoked Lady Poverty and her sister Holy Humility." His answer is that St. Francis was "rich in the sun, in the moon, in the colors of the sky, of clouds, of trees, of grass, of flowers, in the sounds of the wind, in the power of the fire, and in the clarity of water," and that therefore "a music high in colors of timbres, of durations, of sound complexes, seems to me to be perfectly in harmony with his true interior nature." Messiaen's aims, honesty, piety, and fervor are not in doubt. I know La Verna, high on its mountain above the Arno, the setting of the seventh tableau, where Francis received the stigmata; have succumbed to its numinous spell, which not throngs of tourists and pilgrims can mar. Most summers I visit it, walk in the calm of the woods above, listen to the birds that sing there. I can understand Messiaen's wish to pour out devotional feeling, uninhibitedly, by pulling out every stop in sight. But I think also of the chaste Andrea della Robbia altars at La Verna: ecstasy distilled, disciplined, unassertive, occupying little space. Made of snow and sky they are, said Vittorio Emanuele Orlando, once Italy's prime minister. (His remark opens John Pope-Hennessy's monograph on Luca della Robbia.) I have no quarrel with anyone who is overwhelmed by *Saint Francis*. I wanted to be. But I find it an unseemly, self-indulgent, bombastic work—musically unchaste, indecent in a way that David Del Tredici's monster *Alice* pieces are. The composer has discovered for himself, it seems, motifs such as Puccini used in *Tosca* and *Turandot* and chord alternations such as open Wagner's *Siegfried,* and he plugs them as if they were new and fresh. A listener cannot hear them that way. The opening of the seventh tableau is punctuated by "the sinister howling of the screech owl," magnified to an earsplitting screech from the Ondes Martenot. Horrid machine, whether it is oozing sweetness (as when Francis kisses the leper) or (in the C-major final roar) cutting through the loudest noises everyone else can make! Messiaen uses *three* Ondes Martenot in *Saint Francis.*

The performance was as good as can be. Mr. Ozawa, who conducted the Paris première, is a complete master of the score. From that production he brought José van Dam, in the title role, and Kenneth Riegel, as the Leper. Kathleen Battle, as the Angel, who melts the Leper's resentment against life and later welcomes the saint into eternity, sang from on high in tones of angelic purity.

As Juvenal said, *rara est adeo concordia formae atque pudicitiae.* Lilla, the heroine of Vicente Martín y Soler and Lorenzo Da Ponte's *Una cosa rara,* is that rare thing: a woman as chaste as she is fair. Although she is pursued by the Prince of Spain both before and after her betrothal to the shepherd Lubino, and by the local Podestà (whom her brother wishes her to marry), and by a court chamberlain, and although she is sore tried by the hot-tempered Lubino's jealous rages, her sweet constancy never falters. *Una cosa rara,* which appeared at the Vienna Burgtheater six months after *Le nozze de Figaro,* in 1786, is probably the most Mozartian of all operas not by Mozart. The first cast included Mozart's Susanna, Nancy Storace (as Lilla), his Countess, Cherubino, Figaro, Count, and Curzio, and his future Ferrando (as the Prince). Within a few years, the opera had been heard all over Europe. What was described as its professional début in the United States was given last month by the Vineyard Theater. One stretch of the score, played by Don Giovanni's supper band, has long been familiar. ("What do you think of this music?" Giovanni asks. "It's what you deserve," Leporello replies.) More of it went into Stephen Storace's very successful composite opera *The Siege of Belgrade* (1791), which reached New York in 1796 and was revived here as late as 1840.

Martín was not Mozart. Had he been, *Una cosa rara* could hardly have become so popular in an age that found Mozart's music too elaborate. The score is simpler than that of *Figaro,* with more songs, fewer ensembles, few developed episodes. It is less demanding of performers and listeners alike. Martín's characters are charmingly and aptly characterized but are not drawn in depth. The comedy, unlike that of *Figaro* or *Così,* is untouched by the possibility of tragedy. But the emotional temper rises in the scenes with Lilla and Lubino. His angry "Vo' dall'infame viscere" has a fierceness to match Count Almaviva's. (Stefano Mandini created both roles.) Her "Consola le pene" is one of the loveliest arias of the period. Their duet of reconciliation, "Pace, caro mio sposo," is deliciously swaying and voluptuous—dangerous stuff for young people to hear, Count Zinzendorf wrote in his diary. (The Emperor himself, Da Ponte says in his memoirs, led the demand for an encore.) There are measures and motifs that Martín and Mozart have in common: some are commonplaces of eighteenth-century opera, and others suggest a closer relationship. The Prince's graceful "Più bianca del giglio" could be sung by Ferrando. Ghita's Despina-like advice to her friend Lilla, "Colla flemma," is couched in Despina's musical accents. (Dorothea Bussani created both roles.) *Una cosa rara* also has a vein not explored by Mozart—pastoral, rustic, ethnic. The scene is the Spanish mountains, whither Queen Isabella has come to slay a boar that has been terrifying her people. She is a gracious queen, who sings a delightful, friendly trio with Lilla

481

and Ghita, and, in a fine florid aria, "Ah, perchè formar non lice," declares that she would gladly exchange the throne for simple, honest country life. (Isabella was one of Josephine Barstow's early roles.) The Prince sings a serenade in syncopated three-bar phrases which sounds piquantly Spanish. The finale includes a pretty seguidilla, danced and sung by the girls in honor of their sovereign. For the first performance, the Spanish ambassadress, Martín's patron, helped to provide authentic costumes (and the opera set a fashion for Spanish dress, Da Ponte says).

The Vineyard performance, directed by Joseph LoSchiavo and conducted by James Kurtz, was scrupulously prepared. The manuscript in the Austrian National Library provided the main text, and in the program book twelve other libraries were thanked for "making available research materials vital to this production." The only cutting was in recitatives. The orchestra was slightly reduced (by second oboe, second horn, and viola). There were single strings (in the tiny theatre more are hardly needed), and there was no double-bass. Mr. LoSchiavo's staging was apt, simple, and direct. Susan May, as Lilla, sang appealingly, at times limpidly. Karen Grahn was a merry Ghita, and Karen Van Poznak an attractive Queen. Robert Osborne's Lubino sounded both the Ford-like fury and the amorous episodes of the role in well-focussed tones. Richard Slade's Prince, however, was a stick. In general, I would have welcomed, as usual, a lighter, more forward sort of voice production, closer to proficient pop singing, livelier words (the piece was essayed in Italian), and recitative nearer to nimble speech. Dozens of appoggiaturas struck on the lower fourth were prolonged.

The audience had more fun at the last *Cosa rara* I attended, in London eighteen years ago, which was done in Roy Jesson's deft English translation. In its own day, the opera swept Europe in German, Russian, Danish, Polish, and French translations. The Italian-language productions were mostly in Italy: in Bologna and Bergamo, Crema and Cremona, Florence and Faenza, Leghorn, Lodi, and Lucca, Parma, Pavia, and Pistoia, Turin and Trieste, Udine and Urbino, Vercelli and Verona, Genoa, Milan. In those days, a successful opera "played" as a successful movie does now. It seems to me crazy for an all-American cast, in an intimate theatre where every word is audible, to be performing an unfamiliar comedy in a foreign language—and much of it ill pronounced. (The Met, with its international artists playing, for the most part, in standard repertory, is another matter.) The Public Theatre might as plausibly do its Ibsen in Norwegian, its Molière in parley-voo. The result embodies a misconception of the nature and purpose of opera. Nevertheless, anyone who commands Italian was able, after some aural "deciphering," to follow the Vineyard artists' words, and to others the vague, general sense of what was being sung was apprehensible.

Stanisław Moniuszko's *Straszny Dwór, The Haunted Manor,* is (as I wrote after a Detroit production four years ago: *Musical Events: 1980–1983,* pp. 350–51) a delightful opera, brimming with good tunes, and every number a winner. Although the plot is slight, the emotional tone is moving. After the Warsaw risings and massacres of the 1860s, Moniuszko sought to console his countrymen, oppressed by Russian tyranny, with a bright picture of Polish chivalry, Polish high spirits, Polish particularities. Again and again, a stirring patriotic note rises through the romantic comedy. (After the first three performances, in 1865, the Russian authorities banned the opera.) Bel Canto Opera, which staged Moniuszko's *Halka* in 1983, last month produced *The Haunted Manor,* for three performances (in English), in the Joan of Arc School theatre. It was not a wholly satisfactory revival. The stage direction was unfocussed and cliché-ridden. The conducting was precise, metronomical—every beat beaten out—and often at odds with the singers, who phrased more musically. The orchestral timbre was dense—not transparent, elegant, and sensitively matched at each moment to whoever was singing. Anyone to whom *The Haunted Manor* was new may not have placed its composer in a world that Rossini, Smetana, and Sullivan also inhabit, where beguiling melodies flow freely and the musical touch is light. But there were rewards. The four principals—two sisters and two brothers who pass through misunderstandings to betrothal—were fairly good. Mary Lynne Bird, the Hanna, might be called Bel Canto's prima donna; her coloratura runs fleetly, sweetly, and (if not all the time) truly. Debra Kitabjian, the Jadwiga, has an attractive timbre and an intricate, attractive stage personality. John Daniecki, the Stefan, is a singer we may be hearing more of. The timbre is a shade metallic, but his tenor is free, virile, and unforced. He doesn't push, and he gives to each vowel its distinct, proper color. To fulfill his promise, which seems to be for young-heroic roles, he must learn to invest a consistently bland stage presence with some dramatic variety. Henry Lackowski was a pleasant Zbigniew.

NURSTLING OF THE GRACES

May 12, 1986

GIOVANNI BATTISTA PERGOLESI, who died at the age of twenty-six, two hundred and fifty years ago, had a modest six-year career during which he composed six operas—four serious, two comic—and two intermezzos, all but one of them for Naples. Later, he became internationally famous. His Stabat Mater, first printed in London in 1749, was the work most often published in the eighteenth century; Bach was among those who made new arrangements of it. Pergolesi's two-character intermezzo *La serva padrona* was carried throughout Europe by touring Italian troupes. Played by one of them at the Paris Opéra in 1752, between the acts of Lully's *Acis et Galatée,* it lit the fuse for the celebrated Querelle des Bouffons: an argument about Italian opera versus French, about easy entertainment versus artistic earnestness, about (if that formulation seems tendentious) the superiority of natural, heart-easing lyric song to elaborate, aspiring, difficult music. The war was waged fiercely, and hundreds of sharp-tongued polemical pamphlets were discharged before French opera, both serious and comic, carried the field when Rameau's *Castor et Pollux* and *Platée* were revived, in 1754, and the Italian troupe departed. Today, the Querelle des Bouffons is sometimes dismissed as shrill Parisian intellectual cackle, which could have been resolved with the sensible observation that the world has room for more than one kind of music. But some of the grounds on which the disputants took their stand are still in dispute. Although the nationalistic issues have long since faded, echoes of the Querelle sound on when champions of a contemporary music that presents to the public no problems of first-time understanding (say, David Del Tredici's, Olivier Messiaen's) decry the practice of composers more challenging (Elliott Carter, Pierre Boulez).

Pergolesi's posthumous reputation grew swiftly. Back in 1742, the year of *Messiah,* when Thomas Gray attended the opera *Olimpiade* at the King's "two nights did I enjoy it all alone, snugg in a Nook in the Gallery, but found no one in those regions had ever heard of Pergolesi." By 1760, Oliver Goldsmith could write that "musicians seem agreed in making only three principal schools in music; namely, the schools of Pergolese in Italy, of Lully in France, and of Handel in England." Stefano Arteaga, in his famous history (1785), called Pergolesi "the Raphael and Virgil of music." Burney devoted pages of his famous history (1789) to this "child of taste and elegance, and nurstling of the Graces," who "had perhaps more energy of genius, and a finer *tact,* than any of his predecessors," who wrote works "in which the clearness, simplicity, truth, and sweetness of expression, justly entitle him to supremacy over all his predecessors and contemporary rivals," who was "the principal polisher of a style of composition both for the church and stage which has been constantly cultivated by his successors, and which, at the distance of half a century from the short period in which he flourished, still reigns throughout Europe." That year, Grétry exclaimed in his memoirs, "Pergolesi was born, and the truth became known." There was a demand for more of his music. Publishers and copyists met it by affixing his name to the music of others. Burney had already questioned the authorship of some trio sonatas ascribed to Pergolesi. About half the melodies Stravinsky used in his ballet "after Pergolesi," *Pulcinella,* have now been assigned to other composers; so have the well-loved, oft-recorded arias "Se tu m'ami" and "Tre giorni son che Nina." A Pergolesi Opera Omnia appeared in 1939–42; in its twenty-six volumes more than twenty different composers are represented, and about one work in five is by Pergolesi. The libraries of the world contain about three hundred and thirty compositions attributed to Pergolesi; some thirty-six of them are by, or possibly by, Pergolesi. I draw these figures—and the Arteaga and Grétry quotations—from Barry Brook's article on the composer in the March *Musical Times.* Nine years ago, a Pergolesi Research Center, directed by Professor Brook, was founded at the Graduate Center of the City University of New York. Its linked aims are research, promotion of performances, and publication. The first volume of a new Complete Works, containing the opera seria *Adriano in Siria,* edited by Dale Monson, has appeared, and *Adriano,* along with its original intermezzo, *Livietta e Tracollo,* was staged last year at the Florence Maggio Musicale. Ingenious, elegant techniques have been devised for distinguishing the genuine from the misattributed, autographs from copies, and the genealogy of copies descended from copies. The proceedings of a conference held in 1983 in Jesi, the composer's birthplace, have been published as the first number of *Studi Pergolesiani/ Pergolesi Studies.* (Mr. Monson's contributions range beyond Pergolesi and have a general bearing on the performance of eighteenth-century recitative.) The second number is to contain the proceedings of a busy two-day Pergolesi conference held at the City University last month.

A composer whose record has been so thoroughly ravelled offers plenty of scope for scholarly lint-picking. At the conference, Evan Owens distinguished nicely between seven different English reworkings of *La serva padrona* played in London between 1758 and 1783, to which Stephen Storace, Charles Dibdin, and Samuel Arnold made contributions. But there is still plenty to learn about Pergolesi himself. Francesco Degrada's confrontation of the Stabat Mater with Bach's "parody" thereof, as a setting of Psalm 51, shed light on both composers. Now that the winnowing has been done, we must hear more of Pergolesi's music and discover whether the eighteenth century rated him rightly, and whether—like the composers Leonardo Vinci and Antonio Caldara—he has something individual and valuable to offer late-twentieth-century listeners. Only the Stabat Mater and *La serva padrona* are at all familiar. (A recording of *Adriano,* in a maimed text, with a baritone in the soprano title role, taken from a 1980 French Radio performance, is available on the Voce label; it has its high moments.) A Pergolesi concert given during the New York conference, and directed by Albert Fuller, presented an attractive violin sonata, a more arresting cello sonata, the cantata *Segreto tormento,* and two pieces that Burney singled out: the Salve Regina and the "celebrated cantata of Orpheus and Euridice." The soprano, Rachel Rosales, had a pleasing, steady voice but was insufficiently communicative. She didn't address the words, urgently, to her small audience, or sing reprises with free, spontaneous inventions. But there was beauty in the Salve Regina and, in the Orpheus cantata, drama of a kind that made one eager to hear the opere serie.

A League-ISCM concert in Symphony Space earlier this season began with Judith Weir's *King Harald's Saga* (1979), a three-act grand opera in miniature, with nine characters, which includes narratives, recitatives, five arias, a duet, and a chorus, and is written to be dispatched by a single soprano, unaccompanied, in ten minutes or so. It is a witty and brilliant piece of compression, a tour de force on the composer's part which can also be one for the interpreter. Jane Manning, for whom it was written, sang it in Symphony Space three years ago. At the League concert, the soloist was Christine Schadeberg, and I thought her even more vivid and various. She took rather more time over it than the composer suggests—about seventeen minutes rather than "just under ten"— and that enabled the taut, striking little numbers to be shaped surely.

Eliza Garth and Jonathan Haas played David Chaitkin's *Scattering Dark and Bright* (1979), for piano and percussion—a lushly attractive and vital work, with long lines of melody that sweep through rippling textures. Miss Garth introduced George Benjamin's *Sortilèges* (1981) to New York. This two-movement piano fantasy casts its spells securely—Messiaenic magic without the insistent, repetitive emphases of the older master. It is fresh, beautifully constructed, harmonically bewitching, and sensitively written for the instrument.

Criticism is a parasitical profession, but some parasites are not solely harmful. An enthusiast flourishing, like mistletoe, on some life-giving branch, new or old, of music's great tree may help to draw the public's attention to sustenance it would otherwise miss. In less metaphorical terms: one joy of a critic's life is being able to follow—with the intentness possible to someone whose job it is to attend concerts by night and study music by day—the progress of composers who mean much to him. Benjamin's music is a new, exhilarating addition to life. That of Alexander Goehr, now professor of music at Cambridge University (where he taught Benjamin), has accompanied me for many years. Goehr's works have been slow to cross the Atlantic; it is fourteen years since I heard the noble Piano Concerto, commissioned by the Koussevitzky Foundation for Daniel Barenboim to play, and twenty-four since I heard the adventurous Violin Concerto; I have not heard his latest opera, *Behold the Sun,* produced last year by the Deutsche Oper am Rhein. Goehr was nursery-soaked in Schoenberg and exposed early to Messiaen and Boulez. He found his own way by the strong light of Beethoven. He has never been a splashy composer. His works have evinced a care for traditional formal decency that tempers and toughens any extravagant lyrical impulses. Unbridled music can be exciting but is satisfying only when a genius has let go the reins. Disciplined music like Goehr's, with passion unconcealed but distilled, lasts well.

Miss Garth shared a recital in Merkin Hall in February with three string players: Cyrus Stevens, violin; Lois Martin, viola; and Sarah Carter, cello. The big works were Brahms's C-minor Piano Quartet and Goehr's Piano Trio, Opus 20, first heard at the 1966 Bath Festival. The trio is one of Goehr's high achievements—a work of charged forms, taut harmony, and precise, intimate utterance. The first movement is a set of variations, each of them (as the composer says in a program note) "a little character piece on its own," which form a coherent, logical, and exciting sequence. The second movement is a slow, rapt aria in which the melody passes from voice to voice, delicately accompanied, and the three players seem to be joined in one long, beautiful thought. The trio prepared the way for Goehr's Second String Quartet, Opus 23 (1967), which begins with even richer variations and ends with a *Heiliger Dankgesang.*

David Froom's Piano Quartet, dedicated to Miss Garth, had its first performance. It is an engaging piece—well planned, succinct, warmly felt, and decisively written. Mario Davidovsky's elegantly wrought Chacona (1973), for piano trio—fascinating, difficult, widely spaced music (there is a good CRI recording)—completed a program of excellent, varied chamber music, played with ardor, intelligence, and fine technical accomplishment.

Spectrum, a distinguished contemporary-music ensemble from Europe, conducted by Guy Protheroe, made its first New York appearance last month, at the Cathedral of St. John the Divine. The concert was part of a short American tour (Hartford, New York, Buffalo, and Albany). It began with Elliott Carter's

Riconoscenza, played by Irvine Arditti, the leader of the Arditti Quartet (which, as a component of Spectrum, was also making its New York début; three days before the Hartford concert, the Arditti had played Carter's three string quartets in London). In the resonant spaces of St. John the Divine, the five minutes of violin rhapsody soared and sang. John Marlow Rhys, whose *Two Portraits* followed, is a young British composer, whose music I had read about but not heard. The portraits are contrasted: animus and anima, yang and yin—one assertive, the other gentle and winning. The first movement begins with violent piano writing; the second unfolds in soft, trilling textures. The forces are flute, clarinet, string quartet, and piano. Anthony Payne's *The Song Streams in the Firmament*, composed for the Spectrum tour, is a sixteen-minute song for clarinet, accompanied by string quartet and double-bass. The song—the composer explained—pours without constraint as if from someone who knows that death is near. It is an ecstatic, lyrical composition, but not formless. The work begins *misterioso* and moves to an *alla danza* section; then the first song returns in an extended, wilder, more passionate form. David Campbell, an eloquent clarinettist, brought a wonderful range of timbres and dynamics to this unusual piece. Iannis Xenakis is a specialty of the Arditti Quartet, which has made a dazzling record of his string compositions (RCA)—music I don't understand but find exciting. Part of the excitement comes from hearing the players meet apparently impossible technical demands. The first part of the Spectrum concert closed with Xenakis's string trio *Ikhoor* (ichor, the fluid that runs in godly veins); in a live performance the virtuoso physical impact of the piece was even more striking.

The second half consisted of two American works, also written specially for the tour: Michael Gordon's *Acid Rain* and James Sellars's *Return of the Comet*, both of them for flute, clarinet, string quartet, double-bass, and electronic keyboard (played by Yvar Mikhashoff). There is a kind of modern music, unintellectual, diatonic, repetitive, busily figured, that means little to me. Gordon's piece was, however, less brutal, less primitive, and more concise than his *Thou Shalt/Thou Shalt Not*. Sellars's piece was looser, rambling: it included episodes in Mendelssohnian, English-pastoral (or wandering-woodwind-solo), and Sousa veins.

The cathedral was an odd venue for such a concert. About fifty people clustered beneath the crossing, in the largest Gothic church in the world. It was very cold. Mr. Campbell's clarinet tones took wing, as Mr. Arditti's violin tones had done, but the Gordon and Sellars works lost any punchiness.

THE New York Youth Symphony's First Music series in Carnegie Hall—of short full-orchestra works by young American composers, resulting from the city's only regular orchestral-commissioning scheme—enables young instrumentalists to work with new music by a living composer, and young composers to write for a large orchestra in the assurance of abundant rehearsals and a public hearing. Michael Torke's *Bright Blue Music* [see p. 417] has been taken up by the Baltimore Symphony and the Detroit Symphony (and his *Vanada* has been played in the BBC's Music in Our Time series). Kamran Ince's *Infrared Only*, which the Youth Orchestra played in February, is a strong, striking, sometimes almost aggressive composition. Ince's Piano Concerto, of 1984 (which I have heard on tape), could be described in the same way, but its exuberantly eclectic manner, in which sounds and harmonies reminiscent of early Strauss and early Stravinsky or Prokofiev mingle with exotic episodes, is not free of youthful brashness. Ince was already twenty-four when he wrote it—by which age Strauss had embarked on *Don Juan* and *Death and Transfiguration* and had had his F-minor Symphony played in New York by the Philharmonic, and Schubert had composed seven symphonies. American musicians often start their careers late, lingering on campuses, becoming "doctors," while their European contemporaries are out in the world learning their trade and earning their living before the public. Ince is still a doctoral student at the Eastman School of Music. But he is maturing fast. The Piano Concerto revealed a confident, individual, arresting voice; in *Infrared Only* it is heard through a succinct, tautly shaped score, which covers a good deal of ground in ten minutes. If I describe the piece as suggesting Varèse imposed on Mahler, that may seem an odd combination. But *Infrared Only* is an odd—and fascinating—composition. The Varèse sounds are not the sustained "solid objects" of *Octandre* but similar noises hammered out in repeated chords. There is something here of Bernd Alois Zimmermann's way of bringing extremes into a confrontation where pretenses and politeness are dropped, and naked declarations embarrassing to a gentle-minded listener force him to consider and to take sides. I resisted the work initially, but about halfway through was won. In further hearings it has continued to fascinate me. (But each time the final chord—in a work of powerful harmonic impulse—has seemed to me more asserted than honestly earned.) Kamran Ince is a name to watch for.

One can't have a winner every time. Scott Lindroth's *Two-Part Invention,* the latest work in the Youth Symphony's First Music series, proved dry and dislikable. Lindroth, born in 1958, is a composer-in-residence at the American Academy in Rome. The two parts of his invention are a jittery rhythmic pattern and what in a program note he calls "a rambunctious, disjunct melody," adding, "I use this term optimistically." The optimism is unjustified: a listener's ear can hardly construe the isolated blurts from various parts of the orchestra as a "melody." But Lindroth does achieve his avowed intention of "creating an effect similar to driving a car on a bumpy road" whereon "the stretches of rough terrain gradually became longer and longer." It's not an agreeable ride.

David Alan Miller, the conductor of the Youth Symphony, is just twenty-five. He preceded the *Two-Part Invention* with an account of Beethoven's *Leonore* No. 3 which was broadly and bravely planned and admirably executed—a performance in which instinct and good technique were combined. He didn't chuck himself about, crouch, squirm, shimmy, jump in the air to signify climaxes. He directed the music with the tip of his baton, in the tradition of Nikisch, Richter, and Sir Adrian Boult.

Three years ago, Mr. Miller and the Youth Orchestra gave the New York première of Schubert's Seventh Symphony, with its orchestration completed by Brian Newbould. (In Schubert's autograph full score, after 110 fully written measures only the main lines are filled in.) Schubert's Tenth Symphony was given its New York première last week, in Carnegie Hall, by Neville Marriner and the Minnesota Orchestra. Its existence was unknown until, in preparation for the Schubert 1978 celebrations, a sheaf of D-major symphonic sketches in Vienna was reëxamined with the aid of modern graphological, rastrological, and papyrological techniques, and what was formerly considered a series of starts—nine different movements—for a D-major symphony was determined to consist of material for three different unfinished D-major symphonies, dating from 1818, 1820–21, and 1828. The first two are bold, experimental pieces: the second subject of the 1820–21 work begins not in A but in A-flat; Schubert anticipates Peter Maxwell Davies's symphonies with a "tritone dominant." These substantial fragments, which Schubert sketched in two-stave particella, are well worth hearing. Newbould scored them, and they can be heard, along with Symphonies Nos. 1 to 10 (No. 7 in Newbould's scoring; No. 8, the "Unfinished," finished by Newbould's completion of the scherzo and the *Rosamunde* B-minor entr'acte as finale; and No. 10 in Newbould's performing version), on a seven-disc Philips album, or six little compact discs, played by the Academy of St. Martin-in-the-Fields, conducted by Sir Neville. For the 1828 work, something like a complete symphony survived.

Schubert's last symphony, written three years after the Great C Major! A musician's heart leaps at the prospect. The works of Schubert's last year—Book II of *Winterreise, Schwanengesang,* the late piano sonatas, the C-major Quintet, the E-flat Piano Trio—are among those the world holds most dear: fashioned by that marvellous mind which, as if aware of death's approach, hastened to lead listeners into new realms of beauty and sorrow, of peace after strife and order after anguish. In his last symphony, Schubert did new things. In mid-movement, he slowed the second subject from allegro maestoso to andante and darkened it from A major to B-flat minor. For the B-minor slow movement he conceived a melody and countermelody, over a stark pizzicato tread, that anticipate Mahler at his most plangent. As finale, he drafted a scherzo that in formal ambition out-Beethovens the scherzo of Beethoven's Seventh: a sonata-rondo as scherzo-finale, charged with the contrapuntal energy of the finale of Mozart's last symphony. Death intervened before the work was done. But enough had been set down, Newbould decided, to provide the material for a performable symphony.

The sketches for this Tenth Symphony, which have been published in facsimile by Bärenreiter, are difficult to read. Schubert jumps pages, and one must thread a maze of crossings-out and hastily jotted from-here-to-here connective signs. Comparison of the sketches with Newbould's score fills one with admiration for his skill and perspicacity. But much of his work—as the preface to his score freely reveals—is inevitably conjectural: not only in instrumentation and harmonic detail (almost all of which has to be supplied) but also in large structural matters. Of the first movement, for example, we have the exposition (two versions, in fact, with different first subjects) and the andante episode mentioned above. This is presumably the start of the development; but it leads to a tonic presto, which is presumably the coda. Newbould has constructed development and recapitulation sections "in the belief that Schubert formulated in his mind an ultimate plan for the movement . . . but did not indicate it as it required no further material and he would work out its detail later." So Newbould had to deduce a possible "ultimate plan" and then work out the detail for himself.

That devoted Schubertian the late Maurice J. E. Brown, writing of J. F. Barnett's and Felix Weingartner's versions of the Seventh Symphony (which is at least structurally complete, and unequivocal in its instrumental indications, so far as they go), did not regret that neither version had joined the repertory: "Schubert has clearly indicated the form of his movements and his melodies, but harmonic details, accompaniment figures and cadences, are anything but clearly indicated and it is in these essential features that Schubert's magic chiefly lies. . . . At this crux or that the solution of one or the other is admirable. But each version is inevitably a distorted or at least a partial Schubert, and better no Schubert at all than that." I cannot agree. Nor can anyone who has been stirred by the inventions of the Seventh Symphony (available now in Newbould's more sensitively Schubertian version), by the striking fragments of the abandoned 1818 and 1820–21 symphonies (abandoned, it may be, because they contained ideas almost too bold to be carried through), and by the Tenth Symphony. No one seeks to claim this Tenth as fully "authentic." Had death not intervened, dissatisfaction might well have caused large changes. (High strokes in the Great C Major resulted, we know, from the composer's new thoughts as he wrote out his full score in all its details.) But even in this conjectural form the Tenth Symphony is rich in wonderful Schubert melodies, characteristic, breathtaking harmonic shifts, captivating thematic combinations, subtly molded, irregular periods—in Schubertian felicities of all kinds, including formal audacities not merely presumed from but present in the sketches. There are also things that seem lame: melodic turns that the composer would surely have strengthened, halting transitions, bald patches that seem to call for more figuration or harmonic enrichment, and too flighty an ending. Schubert is not diminished by them: these were his first, rapid thoughts, material to be reworked in the light of the whole. Nor is Newbould to be chided for scrupling to alter—to "strengthen"—what Schubert himself set down. Other realizations have been essayed (Peter Gülke's lusher treatment of the Mahlerian slow movement was heard at the 1978 Schubert conference in Detroit), and no doubt more will be essayed. Newbould's interpretation seems to me most of the time uncommonly convincing, and the melodically "weak" moments that I have checked against the sketches are present there, too. Schubert's Tenth—unlike Mahler's Tenth, which was left more nearly completed, more nearly completable—may not be, in its imperfect state, the crown of his symphonic career, but more than enough of it survives to provide radiant glimpses of what that crown might have been. Better this than no Schubert Tenth at all.

The Minnesota Orchestra's performance was neat, poised, and spirited. Sir Neville is seldom a conductor who goes into things deeply. He did not seem to feel the poignancy of some harmonic events or the smiling, shaft-of-sunlight quality that illumines others. Everything slipped by rather too easily. The first performance of the symphony, which was given by the BBC Welsh Orchestra, conducted by Bryden Thomson, in 1983, was more ardent, if less polished; it "placed" the great phrases more tellingly. I have not heard the recording (on Ricercar) by the Liège Philharmonic, in which the Newbould score has been retouched by the conductor, Pierre Bartholomée, or Gülke's recording (on Eterna) of his own reconstruction.

MUSICAL ELEMENTS

May 26, 1986

THE score of Jacob Druckman's *Athanor* bears the completion date "2 May 1986." Six days later, the Philharmonic, to which Druckman is composer-in-residence, gave the work its first performance; Zubin Mehta conducted. The athanor, the composer reveals in a program note, was "the cosmic furnace of the alchemists"; he tells of an occult hill, mist-shrouded on three sides, clear on the fourth, where are a well from which azure vapor ascends, a basin filled with clear fire, and two reservoirs of black stone, containing the wind and the rain. The four movements of the work are named for the elements. Familiar musical analogues are used in their depiction: although the Philharmonic follows the strange American practice of printing movement headings and program notes on different pages of its program book, a listener did not need to page to and fro to discover which element was being treated. The unexpectedly deep and solid brass tones heard in "Fire," along with sparky woodwinds and strings' clear shine, presumably picture the fire's deep source.

Athanor lasted about twenty-four minutes. For some years, Druckman has been composing works in which form is defined, for the most part, by timbres and textures rather than by any sustained thematic discourse. (The Viola Concerto, of 1978, is an exception.) No harm in that, as an admirer of Varèse and early Ligeti must readily admit. What matters is the quality of imagination and invention. In *Athanor,* short-breathed inventions and dense polytonal harmonies produced a somewhat conventional effect, and even the sounds were less surprising and new than one expects from Druckman. I'm reporting first impressions; it may well be that subtler, more picturesquely colored—and longer-rehearsed—performances will bring *Athanor* to light and life. The Philharmonic's first, ill-formed account of Druckman's *Windows,* in 1975, gave little idea of that work's merit. It would be good to hear, consecutively, the orchestral cycle that began with *Windows* and has continued through *Mirage, Chiaroscuro, Aureole, Prism,* and now *Athanor.* Some orchestra should at once start planning such a bill; it could well celebrate Druckman's sixtieth birthday, in 1988. [*There was no such birthday bill in 1988, but several of the pieces had individual revivals.*]

Peter Maxwell Davies's opera [see pp. 70–72] *The Lighthouse* has elemental and alchemical strands woven into it. Three men, called Sandy, Blazes, and Arthur, are pent in a lonely lighthouse: earth, fire, and air are isolated and are surrounded by water. ("Arthur" presumably has a Joycean link with "aether"; perhaps Davies also recalls the medieval use of the name for the star Arcturus.) While Sandy and Blazes play cribbage, Arthur, his voice become the mysterious Voice of the Tarot, intones from aloft a vision of the Fool in Triumph bestriding the world, and he evokes the elements:

> *Black legs rooted deep in earth*
> *His fish-scales skim the water.*
> *The devil's bat-wings beat the air,*
> *His face flames crooked laughter.*

Not everything about *The Lighthouse* is clear and pat. There are inconsistencies, moral ambiguities, puzzles. Davies's fierce hatred of joy-denying, guilt-inducing fanaticism, which makes the sanctimonious Arthur an agent of evil, is given strong expression—as strong as that of the cry Verdi gave to Amneris: "Empia razza! anatéma su voi!" The situation is explosive, and Arthur is the catalyst, but in the catastrophe that he induces retribution is not altogether unmerited: Blazes has been a casual murderer; Sandy betrayed and denied his love when the cock crew. Like many dramas in which not all is explained, *The Lighthouse* has attracted numerous and varied productions. Robert Carsen's vision of the piece, revealed this month at the Guelph Spring Festival, in Ontario, was individual, precise, and arresting. It goes on to the Canada Pavilion of Expo '86, in Vancouver.

The central metaphor of the lighthouse itself—sending its warning out into the world, yet in the keepers' crazed minds seeming to draw up past and present evil from the depths with its bellowing foghorn and dazzling beam—was powerfully realized. Michael Eagan's set, crisply constructed, responsive to the events of the drama, was at once the keepers' quarters and the lantern room. At the height of the mad scene, the men entered into the lantern itself—became part of it, their features bestially distorted by the revolving lenses. It was a memorable image. So was the "opening shot" after the prologue: three men, penned within the confining lighthouse walls, trying to stay each as far from the two others as possible, as if resisting, instinctively, a destructive conjoining of earth, air, and fire. The characters and the tensions between them were sharply defined. About Arthur, as played by Christopher Cameron, there was something of Melville's Claggart: fine-cut, raven-haired, pale-faced, mild-mannered until unholy ecstasy seizes him. Cornelis Opthof was the coarse, companionable Blazes, living easy with murders on his conscience until Arthur sets it churning. Ben Heppner gave a sensitive, sterling performance as Sandy, a burly young Scot unable quite to repress the bewildering memory of his boyhood romance. All three sang well. Steuart Bedford conducted with a masterly control of both formal progress and dramatic coloring. The playing of the Canadian Chamber Ensemble—the professional core of the Kitchener-Waterloo Symphony—was admirable. From twelve instrumentalists Davies has conjured a marvellous range of sounds, and his music reveals new subtleties at each hearing. Its secrets can be studied in the pocket full score of *The Lighthouse*, just published by Chester.

Richard Strauss's *Daphne*, unheard in New York since the Little Orchestra Society's semistaging in Avery Fisher Hall eleven years ago, was given a concert performance in Carnegie Hall last week—a concert performance lightly and deftly dramatized by entrances and exits, sensitive lighting (by Tom Hennes), and a simple, effective enactment of the heroine's final metamorphosis into a laurel tree. *Daphne,* like *Friedenstag,* is a stage tone-poem. (The two operas were planned and performed as a double bill.) Most of Strauss's later works return, in ways, to his earlier successes from *Salome* through *Ariadne auf Naxos. Arabella* returns to *Der Rosenkavalier,* and *Capriccio* to the *Ariadne* prologue. *Die ägyptische Helena,* with its action unfolding swiftly around a single woman and culminating in her triumph, has something in common with *Elektra.* Strauss made the comparison, and Hofmannsthal qualified it: "If one likens *Elektra* to a taut chain of gloomy, massy iron links, then *Helena* is a festoon of intertwined lyrically drawn garlands.... In Act II the flowery chain must be as *taut* as the iron chain was." In these returns, however, there is not mere repetition but an exploration of veins far from completely mined, and new refining. In 1923, Strauss begged Hofmannsthal for "a second *Rosenkavalier* without its flaws and longueurs," since "I've not said my last word in that genre." The late one-acters *Friedenstag* and *Daphne* return to the form of *Salome* and *Elektra* but treat a new kind of subject matter. We miss the flare of youthful forgetive genius that made those scores so exciting. The stream of invention flows more calmly but perhaps more beautifully, and it does not flag. *Friedenstag* and *Daphne* were composed in 1935–37, when the world around the composer grew dark. The first hymns peace and the brotherhood of man. The second has a heroine who shrinks from the touch of the rude world, seeks refuge in idealism, and learns, too late, that nonengagement is in itself an action that can bring suffering to others. That is not all *Daphne* is about. Rather as Hofmannsthal used once to lecture Strauss, Strauss now lectured his new librettist, Joseph Gregor: "You see, it must all be psychologically far more subtle and intricate." Unknowing, Daphne must in some sense be in love with both her suitors, Leucippus and Apollo—stirred by both Dionysian and Apollonian love. Although her parents, Peneus and Gaea, are in this version mortals, something of the divinity they have in the original myth—as river god and earth goddess—invests them still, and Strauss gives them the accents of Wotan and Erda. *Daphne* is the fullest statement of the German composer's loving reverence for classical antiquity. Strauss would ask Gregor now for greater clarity, then for everything to be bathed in twilit ambiguity. (It's surprising the libretto turned out so well.) And, independently of the text, *Daphne* can be listened to as a pastoral tone poem—an extended lyrical song for soloists, orchestra, and chorus, in well-defined and well-varied strophes.

The opera is hard to cast. The first Daphne, in Dresden in 1938, was Margarete Teschemacher, a soprano of Pamina-to-Sieglinde weight. Her recording of the final scenes—with Torsten Ralf, the original Apollo—reveals a voice at once silvery and substantial. At the Scala première, in 1942, the role was taken by Gina Cigna, a famous Turandot—powerful, passionate, but not a classically delicate vocalist. My first Daphne in the theatre—in Munich in 1964—was Ingrid Bjoner, a shining Leonore who reached to Brünnhilde. Rose Bampton, who began as a mezzo and carried rich mezzo color up into her soprano roles, was the first American Daphne, in Buenos Aires in 1948. (The performance, which was conducted by Erich Kleiber, has circulated on pirate labels.) Gloria Davy, a lustrous Aida, gave the New York première of the opera, in Town Hall in 1960. Yet on record the successful Daphnes have been much lighter sopranos— Sophies, not Marschallins: Hilde Gueden (on Deutsche Grammophon) and Lucia Popp (on Angel). The role is evidently one that, like Butterfly, lends itself to diverse vocal interpretations, by both Sophies and Sieglindes. Catherine Malfitano, the Carnegie Daphne, was not at her best. Although she tackled the part with her wonted artistic seriousness, she strained at it, pushed until the timbre became tense. Daphne's innocence, gentleness, simplicity in the earlier scenes were not sounded, and there was little change of color—of heart—after Leucippus' death. At the same time, Gregor and Strauss's text was mushed: consonants were blurred, and vowel values were sacrificed to vocal convenience. Miss Malfitano, the program announced, will be singing Daphne in a new Munich production of the opera. If she relaxes into the role, allows song to flow from her as truly and beautifully as possible, and concentrates on the shape and sense of the words, she should be a remarkable interpreter.

Apollo is a Wagnerian role—taken by Ralf, by Set Svanholm in Buenos Aires, by James King and Reiner Goldberg in the recordings. It needs to be sung lyrically, with godlike ease, from strength. In Carnegie Hall, Jon Fredric West tackled it *tutta forza*. Leucippus is a role for a lyrical hero—one in which Anton Dermota, Fritz Wunderlich, and Peter Schreier have excelled. Chris Merritt, the Carnegie Leucippus, had the voice for it but not the style. The most convincing Straussians in the cast were Ortrun Wenkel, the Gaea, whose words were telling and whose tones compassed the low E-flats of the part, and Victor Braun, the Peneus. The two maids and four shepherds were cast at strength: Tracy Dahl, Joanne Kolomyjec, Gaetan Laperriere, Keith Olsen, John Fanning, and Christopher Cameron (all but Mr. Olsen Canadian). The orchestra was the Toronto Symphony, conducted by Andrew Davis, and two Toronto performances had preceded the Carnegie one. Mr. Davis has done a good deal of Strauss. His strength is a feeling for long, smooth, flowing line, his weakness an occasional failure to secure telling individual details of phrase along the way.

The final concert of the season in Merkin Hall's On Original Instruments series, last week, brought a program of Beethoven, Haydn, and Mozart. Arleen Augér sang. Malcolm Bilson played a fortepiano built by Philip Belt in 1970, after the 1795 instrument in the Smithsonian. Stanley Ritchie played a violin built this year by Samuel Zygmuntiwicz, after a 1737 Giuseppe Guarnieri ("del Gesù") instrument. It was an evening of bliss without alloy: of great music, in which charm, humor, passion, and wit were present, sung and played with the highest accomplishment, in a well-lit, intimate setting, before an attentive audience. Miss Augér, Los Angeles–born, made her name in Europe (nearly twenty years ago she sang the Queen of the Night at the Vienna State Opera) but has lately become more active here. I have long admired her, and I admired her more than ever at this recital, where her tone had a beauty, freshness, and purity to dissolve listeners into an ecstasy of delight. Vocal sound of this quality is rare today, and the usual epithets of approval seem inadequate. Let me relate, to suggest my enthusiasm, that at the start of the intermission, after Miss Augér's Haydn group, I telephoned to friends within reach urging them to drop whatever they were doing and hasten to Merkin Hall (where there were one or two seats still empty) to hear Miss Augér sing Mozart. Description of voices is most readily achieved by comparison and contrast. Another soprano with tone that in itself provides delight is Kathleen Battle. Miss Augér's voice has a slightly fuller quality (and it flows from her without the face-pulling that seems inherent in Miss Battle's method). It does not have the sparkle and liveliness that often bring references to Elisabeth Schumann into accounts of Miss Battle's singing. Miss Augér recalls, rather, the young Lisa Della Casa at her most limpid, or the young Irmgard Seefried, who sang Mozart songs with similar clarity and candor.

No texts were supplied, and—provided listeners understood German, the language of the Mozart group—none were needed, for Miss Augér's words were excellently clear. She did not *use* them in quite the magical way Schumann would: with her shaping of the word "concealment" in Haydn's "She never told her love," and of the phrase "und der Vorhang rollt herab" in Mozart's "Abendempfindung," she did not touch on responsive nerves in the listener in the keen way Schumann did. On the whole, the first-person songs were more vividly presented than the narratives. Miss Augér fell into slinky lorelei poses and gave siren oeillades as she sang "The Mermaid's Song"—not quite what Haydn intended, perhaps, but alluring. Of the scena "Als Luise die Briefe ihres ungetreuen Liebhabers verbrannte" she gave a particularly poignant performance. There was an initial gesture of casting the perfidious letters into the flames, and later there were glances at them as they burned. It might be said that a line between overacting, with gestures apter to the stage, and underacting, with insufficient use of eyes, hands, and posture to enhance the presentation of a song, was not surely held. But this is hypercriticism. The directness of Miss Augér's singing, the beauty of her timbre, and the grace of her phrasing conspired to make this the finest lieder singing I have heard in years. The fortepiano, which can be played loudly and bravely without swamping a singer, provided ideal support, and Mr. Bilson was an ideal partner. Haydn's English canzonets are charming; Mozart's best songs, performed like this, have the vividness of Hugo Wolf's.

The evening began with Beethoven's "Spring" Sonata and ended with Mozart's D-major Violin Sonata, K. 306. Mr. Ritchie and Mr. Bilson were in free, bold form. The latter has a wonderfully beguiling fashion of easing into a melody, and of giving life to the simplest oom-pa-pa-pa accompaniment, in ways unachievable on a modern grand piano.

CHILD MABEL

June 16, 1986

DURING the last eighteen years, David Del Tredici has composed nearly six hours of music inspired by *Alice's Adventures in Wonderland* and *Through the Looking-Glass:* from *Pop-Pourri*, of 1968, to *Haddocks' Eyes*, which had its première in Purchase last month and then came to New York. A listing of the *Alice* works (with place and date of first performance, and approximate duration) may be helpful, since people find it hard to remember which of them they have heard and which not:

1. *Pop-Pourri* (La Jolla, 1968; 28′).

2. *Lobster Quadrille* (London, 1969; 13′).

3. *Adventures Underground* (Buffalo, 1975; 23′).

4. *Vintage Alice* (Saratoga, California, 1972; 28′).

5. *An Alice Symphony,* so far unperformed as an entity, comprising: *In Wonderland,* incorporating No. 2 (Aspen, 1975; 24′), and *Illustrated Alice* (San Francisco, 1976: 17′).

6. *Final Alice* (Chicago, 1976; 64′).

7. *Child Alice* (New York, 1986; 137′), comprising: *In Memory of a Summer Day* (St. Louis, 1980; 63′), *Quaint Events* (Buffalo, 1981; 25′), *Happy Voices* (San Francisco, 1980; 17′), and *All in the Golden Afternoon* (Philadelphia, 1981; 32′).

8. *Haddocks' Eyes* (Purchase, 1986; 15′).

The earlier fits of this *Alicead* were performed widely, but not in New York until in 1977 the Philharmonic played No. 6, *Final Alice*—a work that proved to be as little final as Ned Rorem's *Final Diary*. Nos. 1 to 6 had been a series of pieces for amplified soprano, "folk group" (saxophones, mandolin, banjo, and accordion) or (in No. 1, which also uses a chorus) rock group, and orchestra. Del Tredici then turned to the group of pieces making up the evening-filling No. 7, in which an amplified soprano is pitted against a more-than-Mahlerian orchestra. No. 8, which is for amplified soprano and ten players, could well be the start of a new chamber cycle, for there is plenty of *Alice* and *Alice*–related material still unset by Del Tredici, including the earlier version of the Mouse's Tale; "You are old, Father William" (and the Southey poem it parodies); the Humpty-Dumpty and the Lion-and-the-Unicorn scenes; and the Wasp episode from *Through the Looking-Glass,* which Carroll deleted in proof and which has been newly recovered. *Haddocks' Eyes*—its text the White Knight's song and Tom Moore's "My Heart and Lute"—could easily be made five times as long by settings of Carroll's first version of the song, "Upon the Lonely Moor," and of "Resolution and Independence," Wordsworth's poem about the leech gatherer, which it parodies.

The earlier works in the series were concerned, for the most part, with Alice's adventures. Then, in *Final Alice,* Del Tredici turned to speculation about real-life feelings that Charles Dodgson (alias Lewis Carroll) might have had for the ten-year-old Alice Liddell, to whom the tales were first told. As if peeling through layers of reticence to a love that the author hardly dared avow, Del Tredici set, in turn, the White Rabbit's "They told me you had been to her," Carroll's earlier version thereof, which begins "She's all my fancy painted him," and William Mee's sentimental ballad "Alice Gray," which underlies it:

> *She's all my fancy painted her,*
> *She's lovely, she's divine. . . .*
> *O, my heart, my heart is breaking*
> *For the love of Alice Gray.*

In *Child Alice,* Alice's adventures are also left behind, and Dodgson, contemplating Alice, is the protagonist. Part I is a double setting of the prefatory poem to *Through the Looking-Glass,* and Part II a double setting of the prefatory poem to *Alice in Wonderland.* The first setting of each poem, the composer says in a program note, is "pure, innocent," and the second is "rapturous, impassioned, even tortured": charged with "the passion Carroll dared not express (or perhaps even feel) waking ... here given full, romantic rein, as might happen in a dream—Carroll's dream of love of Alice." The songs are framed by lush orchestral movements, two of them intended to suggest tales that didn't get written down—"as it were, chapters from *Alice's Adventures in Wonderland* that got away." *Child Alice* was brought out—as the table above shows—in four separate installments but was planned as a single piece. The chance to assess it as such came at an American Symphony Orchestra concert in Carnegie Hall in April, when John Mauceri conducted the world première of the whole thing.

A creative artist is not called upon to be a scrupulous biographer. Handel's *Giulio Cesare,* Spontini's *Milton,* and Verdi's *Don Carlos* are not damned for a want of historical accuracy; Del Tredici could be forgiven his heated fantasies about the gentle Oxford mathematician and the Dean of Christ Church's well-mannered little daughter had an enthralling work of art resulted. Yet it does seem to matter that his *Alice* pieces sail under false colors; that Alice's tones are not heard in them, and those of Lewis Carroll heard but seldom; that he has laid an insensitive hand on and grossly glossed a text whose influence on the thought and conduct of English-speaking peoples can hardly be overrated. Alice has been likened to Beatrice and to Laura. "The question for an adult reader of Lewis Carroll," W. H. Auden wrote in a 1962 essay, "is not the author's psychological peculiarities, but the validity of his heroine. Is Alice, that is to say, an adequate symbol for what every human being should try to be like? I am inclined to answer yes." In a world of ill-mannered, bossy, bewildering people, Alice remains courteous, curious, truthful, sweetly reasonable, and tidy-minded. But Del Tredici has given to her and to her creator rackety, repetitious music—more bombastic and noisier than the finales of Mahler's Second and Seventh Symphonies or Strauss's *Thus Spoke Zarathustra*. To make themselves heard above the orchestral din, they must bawl at the top of their voices. The program note to *Child Alice* contains these sentences: "With the clanging of an anvil, the listener may think he is at the sonic peak, but a succession of climaxes leading at length to a screaming siren (marked *Climax of Climaxes* in the score) will prove otherwise"; "As Carroll warms to his task of story telling, the music picks up speed, becoming increasingly grandiose—trumpets blaze, a siren wails" [this in the "pure, innocent" setting of "All in the golden afternoon"]; "Forces again quickly gather, and, borne by the largest crescendo of the piece thus far, we arrive at the *Quodlibet,* presented thunderously by the whole orchestra." A listener is tempted to imitate Alice when, as the Lion and the Unicorn were drummed out of town, she "put her hands over her ears, vainly trying to shut out the dreadful uproar." In another essay, Auden divided writers ("except the supreme masters who transcend all systems of classification") into Alices and Mabels. (Mabel is the girl living in a poky little house and knowing such a very little who Alice, during her identity crisis in Chapter II of *Wonderland,* hopes she isn't.) Among Auden's paired examples are:

Alice	*Mabel*
Montaigne	Pascal
Jane Austen	Dickens
Turgenev	Dostoyevski
Virginia Woolf	Joyce
E. M. Forster	Lawrence

By those fastidious lights, Del Tredici is among composers clearly a Mabel, not an Alice; and he is becoming ever more Mabeline. The earlier *Alice* pieces contained ingenious juxtapositions of music in various manners, reflecting disarray and order, originals and parodies, different views of the same event, and contrasts of character. But with *Child Alice* Del Tredici collapsed into simple-minded Victorian diatonicism, melodic banality, and excess. The first part of his piece is based on a quite pretty flute tune. When it is sung as "Child of the pure unclouded brow," the words fit awkwardly and prove unintelligible. When it is blared out by the full orchestra, the result is horrid. The second part is based on a jerky, jaunty tune unsuited to the lines "All in the golden afternoon Full leisurely we glide." No golden afternoon here, no gliding, no easy pull from Oxford to Godstow while tales are told, but a trip that starts choppily and runs into tempests that would wreck a liner. Even the gentle close is accompanied by the wailing of a wind machine. The piece is self-indulgent, uncontrolled, orgiastic.

In the Carnegie Hall performance, the soprano role, which spans an extravagantly wide range and, much of the time, lies uncomfortably high, was shared by three singers: Tracy Dahl, high soprano; Dawn Upshaw, lyric soprano; and Victoria Livengood, mezzo-soprano. (Although Alice Liddell's sisters, Lorina, Charlotte and Edith, did accompany her on that 1862 excursion when *Alice in Wonderland* was first improvised, these three singers, lined up before their microphones, suggested, rather, the Andrews Sisters.) The electronic amplification of the soprano voice into a super-Brünnhilde power instrument, screaming out above a huge orchestra in full cry, is an unattractive feature of the *Alice* works, and the combination of loudspeaker blast, crude word setting, and high tessitura ensures that very little of the text can be understood. Mr. Mauceri conducted an enthusiastic and full-blooded performance, often jumping into the air in his endeavor to obtain ever louder sounds from his players.

The White Knight scene is one of the most memorable in *Alice:*

> Of all the strange things that Alice saw in her journey Through the Looking-Glass, this was the one that she always remembered most clearly. Years afterwards she could bring the whole scene back again, as if it had been only yesterday—the mild blue eyes and kindly smile of the Knight—the setting sun gleaming through his hair, and shining on his armour in a blaze of light that quite dazzled her—the horse quietly moving about, with the reins hanging loose on his neck, cropping the grass at her feet—and the black shadows of the forest behind—all this she took in like a picture, as, with one hand shading her eyes, she leant against a tree, watching the strange pair, and listening, in a half-dream, to the melancholy music of the song.

The Knight has often been considered a gentle self-portrait of Carroll himself— mild, affectionate, dreamy, inventive, and concerned with metalinguistic niceties. The tune of the song, the Knight claims, is his own invention, but Alice recognizes it as that of Moore's "My Heart and Lute." It is an amiable tune, to which "A-Sitting on a Gate" can agreeably be sung. (A copy in the New York Public Library has simple cadenzas pencilled in by a former owner.)

Del Tredici views the scene quite differently. He hears the Knight's words "spilling out with increasing frenzy," he writes in a program note. "The musical setting is meant to be at once funny, brusque, and breathless—a kind of infernal *perpetuum mobile* machine ever in danger of flying apart." The words are gabbled to a little tag of tune unrelated to their natural rhythms and inflections. No attempt is made to distinguish between the singer as narrator, the singer as interrogator, and the old man answering. At the climax of the song, *fff marcato*—on "I weep, for it reminds me so Of that old man I used to know"—piccolo and clarinet shriek in octaves, trumpet and horn bray, the piano is hammered hard, and the soprano voice bellows from loudspeakers. Between two settings of "A-Sitting on a Gate," there is a setting of "My Heart and Lute," to a four-notes-up, four-notes-down tune in even eighth-notes unmatched to the rhythm of the lines.

Haddocks' Eyes was commissioned and performed by the Chamber Music Society of Lincoln Center. Phyllis Bryn-Julson, long associated with the *Alice* pieces (she sang in the premières of *Pop-Pourri* and *In Memory of a Summer Day*), was the soprano. The composer conducted. Whoever commissions the next installment of the *Alicead* should stipulate a work for just singer and guitar, unamplified. An inventive and generous composer has splashed and wallowed long enough.

Del Tredici used to be a composer of finer mettle. The early (1964), delicate James Joyce setting "I Hear an Army," for soprano and string quartet, is proof enough of that. It is dedicated to Miss Bryn-Julson and has been recorded by her, on CRI. In April, it was revived at a Symphony Space concert given by the Queens College Contemporary Players, directed by Ralph Shapey, with Elsa Charlston as the soloist. The program was for the most part historical—Ruth Crawford Seeger's Suite for Wind Quintet, Varèse's *Octandre,* Schoenberg's First Chamber Symphony—but included the New York première of Philip Fried's *Meditations and Satires,* a cycle of apothegms translated from the Chinese and the Latin, set for soprano and instrumental ensemble. The texts are plainly important, and they were printed in the program, but since the houselights were turned off there was nothing much to be made of the piece.

The concert was one of several by university-based ensembles which were heard in New York this spring. *Octandre* had also been played the day before, by the Stony Brook Contemporary Music Ensemble, directed by Arthur Weisberg, in the McMillin Theatre of Columbia University. The program continued with Miriam Gideon's gravely beautiful cycle for tenor (here Gary Glaze) and instruments, *The Resounding Lyre* (1979), which is also recorded on CRI, and Elliott Carter's Brass Quintet. The second part was the New York deuxième of Hans Werner Henze's *The Miracle of the Rose* (1981), with Evan Spritzer, clarinet, a buoyant soloist.

In Alice Tully Hall, the Percussion Group/Cincinnati, a trio-in-residence at the University of Cincinnati College–Conservatory of Music, gave the New York première of Mark Saya's *From the Book of Imaginary Beings.* Unable to attend the concert, I caught up with the work on tape, and discovered an engaging new composer with a voice of his own. Saya has built four witty, poetic structures inspired by creatures in Borges's *Book of Imaginary Beings.* The movements are "Bahamut" (the immense fish, of terrifying beauty, on which the universe ultimately rests), "The Lamed Wufniks" (the thirty-six righteous men for whose sake God spares the world), "A Bao A Qu" (which accompanies human souls on their quest for Nirvana, and suffers greatly when they fail), and "The Fauna of Mirrors" (who will one day cease to mimic the images of our world, and appear in their own shapes and colors). Borges's inventions lend themselves to music: Bahamut, a program note explains, is "both comprehensible and incomprehensible" and "fades in and out of focus in the human mind"; the loud wailing of the A Bao A Qu "is to us only a whisper, like the rustling of silk"; and when the

Fauna of Mirrors prepare to invade the world, "from the depths of the shiny surfaces will come the faint clatter of weapons." Composers for percussion are tempted toward excess: by the sheer variety of instruments available, by the showers of notes that the -phones and the -spiels can so easily provide, and by the sheer racket so readily obtainable from gongs, cymbals, and drums. But Saya is economical. He makes his effects by a few well-chosen timbres deployed in space and across silence with a precise control of rhythmic eloquence and of small but telling color changes. None of the movements outstays its welcome. The three Cincinnati players—Allen Otte, Jack Brennan, and James Culley—are master musicians.

The Peabody Percussion Ensemble (from the Peabody Institute of Johns Hopkins), directed by Jonathan Haas, joined with the American Saxophone Quartet for a performance in Symphony Space of Bernard Hoffer's *The River,* a symphony for saxophone quartet and large percussion array. It is a picturesque piece, telling of the seasons of the Nile: "In the Dry Season" (Bartókian rustlings and tappings), "The River Rises" (the sound swells, the patterns grow fuller), "The River Overflows Its Banks" (timpani break into exuberant, generous song), and "The River Nourishes the Land" (the four saxophones spin wave patterns rather like those of *Das Rheingold*). The program began with Dean Drummond's *Dirty Ferdie,* whose sounds were clean, light, and attractive, and continued with Bernard Heiden's neat, sturdily Hindemithian Variations for Timpani and Saxophone Quartet, and Morton Subotnick's energetic but, it seemed, rather coarsely scored *The Key to Songs,* in which the Peabody Computer Music Consort joined the Percussion Ensemble.

The New Jersey Percussion Ensemble (in residence at William Paterson College, Wayne), directed by Raymond Des Roches, came fourteen strong to the McMillin Theatre last month and offered what, by the time the evening was done, proved to be a surfeit of tinklings, tappings, jingles, chimes, and thumps. I enjoyed the pretty timbres of Jeffrey Kresky's *Bell Music* (1975), for four players, and the ingenuities of Mario Davidovsky's *Synchronism No. 5* (1969), for five players and tape; and admired the aplomb with which the expert, enthusiastic ensemble traversed the rhythmic thickets of Matthias Kriesberg's *State of Siege* (1976), for twelve players plus piano, which was receiving its belated première.

A fortnight later, Carter's famous *Three Pieces for Four Timpani* (1966), in a poised, thoughtful performance by Daniel Druckman, demonstrated—with even greater economy of means than Saya employed—how rich music can be made from simple strokes set out with delicacy and skill. This opened a satisfying and varied program given by the New York New Music Ensemble in Carnegie Recital Hall: George Crumb's *Makrokosmos IV,* for piano duet; Boulez's captivating *Dérive,* for flute, clarinet, violin, cello, percussion, and piano; and the first performance of Nicholas Thorne's earnest *Songs from the Mountains,* for tenor (Paul Sperry) and the same instruments.

ANOTHER ORPHEUS SINGS

THE composers Harrison Birtwistle, Peter Maxwell Davies, and Alexander Goehr, the pianist John Ogdon, and the trumpeter and conductor Elgar Howarth, students together at the Royal Manchester College of Music in the early fifties, for a while made up what was called the Manchester Group, whose contribution to the music of our day has been large. The composers soon pursued separate paths. Music has many mansions; there is no call to play favorites. But many people—increasingly many since the Birtwistle fiftieth-birthday concerts and the appearance of the orchestral piece *Secret Theatre,* in 1984—agree with Stephen Walsh's estimate of Birtwistle in the New Grove: "the most forceful and uncompromisingly original British composer of his generation." Pierre Boulez has ever been his champion, in New York, London, and Paris. Birtwistle's orchestral piece *Earth Dances,* given its first performance by the BBC Symphony earlier this year, was hailed as a new *Rite of Spring.* His opera *The Mask of Orpheus,* given its first performance last month by the English National Opera, was called by the critic of the London *Times* the second "perfectly satisfactory reinvention of opera since Stravinsky"—the first being Birtwistle's earlier opera, *Punch and Judy.* His third opera, *Yan Tan Tethera,* a pastoral tale (its title "one two three" in Pennine shepherds' numbering of their sheep), is to be produced in London in August. *The Mask of Orpheus,* billed for eight performances and a BBC broadcast, has been drawing full houses.

Birtwistle's music is not easy to describe. Varèse and Stravinsky are early influences on it, and then it goes its own way, owing nothing to exemplars or schools. Among its features are a fondness for monody, for a strong single line of discourse generating its particular harmonies and lending a protagonist-with-chorus aspect to many passages; a "gestural" kind of utterance which suggests sounds turned into shapes; and unhurried, deliberate progress that calls for long-span listening and gives a processional quality to several of the scores. But against the image of a score moving past the listener must be set that of a listener moving through the score. Some Birtwistle compositions are likened to landscapes, fixed in their features but revealing different views to the beholder-listener as he traverses them by different routes. Titles such as *An Imaginary Landscape, The Fields of Sorrow,* and *Silbury Air* emphasize this analogy, and the composer has often invoked it when talking about his work. (Davies has talked about "laying out" the proportions of a work-in-progress across a real landscape; Boulez has likened scores of his to city maps: one can make very different traversals of a city that itself remains unchanged.) Above all, there is a concern for structure which places Birtwistle among the least "self-expressive" and most rational and objective of composers. He would probably assent to a Pythagorean view of music as numbers made manifest; numbers play a part in forming the features of many of his works. This does not mean that the music is schematic, or predictable in its progress. In Paul Griffiths's *New Sounds, New Personalities*—conversations with twenty British composers of the 1980s—Birtwistle says:

> For *Secret Theatre* I draw up a lot of pre-compositional ideas about how things could progress, how they could get from point to point; I constructed a whole map, as it were. But then in the process of composition, in the journey, I went other ways.

Similarly, in an interview that closes Michael Hall's monograph *Harrison Birtwistle* the composer says:

> You can create a formal position before the event, an elaborate schemata, and that you can call your idea. That's what you're trying to express. You have a duty to that schemata, a duty to that initial idea. But in the process of composition you make contexts which are not necessarily concerned with it. Other things are thrown up which have a life of their own and are just as important. You now have a duty to two things.

He tells of starting a work in a playful, improvisatory way: "That's how most of my pieces begin. I indulge my fantasies: I allow intuition to take over. . . . But intuition only takes you so far. After that you need a method of working which enables you to manipulate the material." He stresses a composer's responsibility to his material; likens himself to a dry-stone waller, finding the exact, fitting place for each piece of material that comes to hand, and to a medieval carver: "I carve the stone or the piece of wood to make the object I want, but there are elements in the material beyond my control. So the essential nature of the stone or the wood remains inviolate. It has a life of its own."

One more significant quotation: "Everything I've written is a multiple object. What is shown at any one time can only be a facet of it. I can never show its entirety." For further discussion of layers and levels, of pulses, of timbre, of fixed points and freedoms, and of the elusive notion of an "ideal" work whose features can be discovered and revealed only a few at a time, I recommend Mr. Hall's book. But words alone cannot suggest what makes Birtwistle's music an adventure different in kind from any other. One must hear it. A fair amount has been recorded over the years.

Orpheus is the incarnation of music's power over the souls and actions of men. The first operas, Peri's *Euridice* and Caccini's *Euridice,* and the first great opera, Monteverdi's *Orfeo,* told of him. When opera was in need of reform, of a return to first principles, Gluck retold the tale. Wagner gave Orphean attributes to two of his heroes, Tannhäuser and Walther von Stolzing. Stravinsky, Hans Werner Henze, and Elliott Carter are among the many later composers who have been inspired by thoughts of Orpheus. Like Apollo and Dionysus, whose myths are linked with his, he moves through Western music: a divinely inspired musician so eloquent and persuasive that none can resist him, yet a fallible mortal, unable to achieve his goal. The artist triumphs; the man falters, and loses his Eurydice. Faust, another type figure of Western art, embodies ambitious, aspirant man. But Orpheus—Apollo's son, by some accounts—is a mediator between gods and men, and the founder of a religion whose followers called themselves children of the starry heavens and the fruitful earth.

When Peter Hall, due to become the artistic co-director of Covent Garden, approached Birtwistle about an opera, in 1970, the composer at first considered a *Faust*. He was already at work with Hall on an *Orpheus* for London Weekend Television, and this then became the subject of the new opera. In a series of *Orpheus*-related works—notably *Nenia: The Death of Orpheus* (1970), *Meridian* (1970–71), and *The Fields of Sorrow* (1971), a setting of Ausonius' lines about lovers wandering in Avernus—he moved toward the opera, discovering methods, testing preoccupations, laying foundations. The first two acts of *The Mask of Orpheus* were composed in 1973–75, when Birtwistle was in America, teaching at Swarthmore College and then at the State University of New York, Buffalo. Covent Garden dropped the piece (Hall never took up his appointment there); Glyndebourne dallied with it; and Birtwistle resumed work on it only in 1981, when the English National Opera, fortified by a generous gift from an anonymous American donor, promised a production. Act III was composed in 1981–83. (It was preceded by *On the Sheer Threshold of the Night,* a madrigal setting of Boethius' verses about Orpheus and Eurydice.) Meanwhile, Birtwistle had been since 1975 the music director of the National Theatre. His major National Theatre scores are the music in Hall's production of the *Oresteia* and the music-theatre piece *Bow Down;* and his most widely heard score must be the incidental music for Peter Shaffer's play *Amadeus.*

The libretto of *The Mask of Orpheus* is by Peter Zinovieff, who both as a writer and as the creator of an electronic studio has worked with several composers. (The text of *Nenia* and the electronic realization of Birtwistle's *Chronometer* are by him; Henze's *Tristan* is dedicated to him.) The word "Mask" suggests at once a connection with "masque"—a symbolic enactment in song, dance, and spectacle—and a sense of deeper meanings beneath any surface. The work, Zinovieff explains in a preface to the libretto, "tends to the Aristotelian view that Orpheus did not exist as an individual but is a collective inheritance"—which "enables any aspect of the diverse mythology to be treated as equally possible." The grand progression is linear—from the birth of Orpheus and his mastering of speech, then song, to the silencing, by Apollo, of Orpheus' singing skull, which after his death continued as an oracle. But within the opera time moves at different paces, leaps episodes, doubles back. We see several times the first death of Eurydice (once in alternative versions simultaneously, as, on one bank of a river fleeing from and on the other yielding to Aristaeus, she is bitten by the serpent); several times her second death, when Orpheus turns to look at her; and several times the various deaths of Orpheus recounted in different legends: by suicide, felled by a thunderbolt from angry Zeus, dismembered by maenads.

The structure of the opera is intricate. Act II—Orpheus' dream of his descent to and return from the Underworld—has an "imaginary construction" (not represented on the stage) of a seventeen-arch viaduct, bearing a flow from the mountainside of the dead to that of the living. Each arch opens onto a different landscape, associated with different objects and different emotions. Act III has an underlying form of (imagined) tides advancing and receding on a beach, covering or revealing (imagined) symbolic objects. A superimposed structure is that of a three-part Orphic ceremony—a Marriage and a Funeral in Act I, a Sacrifice in Act III—which suggests that all the rest may be parts of the same Orphic ritual presented in other than ceremonial modes. Six times, moreover, the action of the opera "freezes" while a troupe of mimes, to electronic music, enters to enact a tale. Three of the tales are violent and deal with Dionysus: the Titans' dismemberment of the god and his reconstitution by Rhea; the death of Lycurgus; and the death of Pentheus. (These, we are told, reflect the murder of Orpheus.) Three are lyrical metamorphoses: Adonis and the anemone; Hyacinth; and Dryope and the lotus. (These reflect Orpheus' love for Eurydice.) The three-hour opera is divided into three (unequal) acts—summer, winter, and spring—of three scenes each. There are 126 named "events" in the action, three of each kind: Three Arias of Prophecy, Three Screams of Passion, Three Poems of Reminiscence, etc. The three principals (Orpheus, Eurydice, and Aristaeus) are given each a threefold representation: by a singer, a mime, and a puppet. Much of Act III is uttered in an invented language, built from phonemes in the names Orpheus and Eurydice. The libretto includes a glossary and brief syntax. All in all, it is a formidable document, packed with charts, tables, diagrams, drawings, timings. It resembles a film script as much as a conventional libretto. From my brief characterization of Birtwistle's music one important twentieth-century influence, that of film, was omitted. Elliott Carter has told how the general plan of his First String Quartet was suggested by Cocteau's film *Le Sang d'un poète,* which is punctuated by slow-motion sequences of a dynamited chimney—images of "interrupted continuity" establishing "the difference between external time . . . and internal dream time." Michael Hall quotes a passage from Ralph Stevenson and J. R. Debrix's *The Cinema as Art* most relevant to *The Mask of Orpheus* if for "the cinema" we read "music," and "stage" for "screen":

> The cinema can either imitate exactly the time of the physical world, or can modify it radically. By modifying it, the cinema can, as Robbe-Grillet suggests, assemble on the screen, by various means, but principally by montage, something more like the time of our mental than our physical life—a mixture of future, past, and present, passing over some events in a flash, dwelling on others, returning to others. Something less continuous, less predictable, less inflexible than the time of the physical world.

Birtwistle has long been a master of time slowed, time speeded, time stopped, time passing at various speeds. Wagner, with his anticipations, recapitulations, and retraversals of events and his montages of motifs, was another: Wotan's narration in *Die Walküre* and the Norns scene of *Götterdämmerung* are also "a mixture of future, past, and present, passing over some events in a flash, dwelling on others." In most respects, the two composers are very different, but they share a fundamental seriousness about musical theatre, and share, too, a way of transforming and compounding basic myths to make the spectators participants in a dramatic confrontation: between an individual and what might be called the accumulated weight of history, tradition, or, even, the collective unconscious. Wagner did so by nineteenth-century and Birtwistle does so by twentieth-century means.

The Mask of Orpheus starts slowly, and the music is slow to form. It becomes richer and richer. Act II mounts to a boisterous climax. Act III opens—and continues—with exuberantly theatrical strains that, wise after the event, we can link with the composer's adventures in the National Theatre. The orchestra employed is large: no strings, but four each of flutes, oboes, clarinets, bassoons, horns, and trumpets; three saxophones; six trombones; two tubas; mandolin, guitar, bass guitar, and three harps, all amplified; seven percussionists. The electronic music, composed at IRCAM (with the composer Barry Anderson as a collaborator), is very important, and of three kinds. The Voice of Apollo, created on IRCAM's Chant program, rings out with tremendous divine imperatives. "Aura" sounds, evoking the music of winds and tides and the buzz of Aristaeus' bees, provide "subliminal" backgrounds. The accompaniments to the metamorphosis episodes—sharp, clean, exquisitely controlled episodes, created from computer-analyzed and synthesized harp notes, set apart from the rest—have justly been hailed as some of the most exciting electronic compositions to have come from IRCAM.

The first page of the English National Opera program book pictures a Tibetan ceremonial dance, high peaks in the background, and carries a sentence from Zinovieff's preface:

> Plato, in *Epinomis,* wrote: 'I confidently assert, both in jest and in all seriousness, that such a play will, from the many senses it has now, possess a uniform body, and become one from many and will give happiness.' This is the difficult task we have given to the producer [director] and designer of our piece.

(Let it pass that the *Epinomis* is assigned to the Plato apocrypha.) David Freeman, the director of *The Mask of Orpheus,* and Jocelyn Herbert, the designer, have fulfilled the difficult task with high accomplishment. Many of the elaborate stage directions in the libretto, the preface says, "while seeming very precise, are allegorical." Others are "symbols, hints, and clues . . . not production or design instructions." And the staging "need not be lavish." We read of in the libretto but do not see onstage the Golden Carriage of Mirrors that bears Orpheus on his journey to and from the Underworld; see sketched in the libretto but do not see onstage—for, like the arches and the tides, they are "metaphorical"—the various two-dimensional and three-dimensional frames within which the metamorphosis episodes are enacted. I praised Mr. Freeman's 1981 production, for the English National, of Monteverdi's *Orfeo* for its intelligence, directness, and force. He writes about it in the Cambridge Opera Handbook devoted to *Orfeo,* calling it not "an interpretation" but "an attempt to tell the story in as allusive, tangible, ambivalent and unsentimental a way as possible." Mr. Freeman's production of *The Mask of Orpheus* was similarly intelligent and direct—uncluttered by directorial frills or fancies, lucid, strong. Miss Herbert's designs were likewise clear and concise. For first encounters with a work in which there is so much to attend to, this presentation was ideal.

Mr. Freeman excels in inspiring singers with a total eloquence in which physical and vocal presence conspire. Philip Langridge, the singing Orpheus, was as vivid a mime during the long, seventeen-strophe aria that makes up most of Act II as was the mime Orpheus, Graham Walters. Mr. Langridge sang nobly, tirelessly, proudly, tenderly. It was a remarkable performance. Jean Rigby, the principal Eurydice, and Tom McDonnell, the principal Aristaeus, were first-rate. The singers of the three roles in puppet incarnation, Nigel Robson, Ethna Robinson, and Rodney Macann, should also be praised. The other main soloist is the Oracle of the Dead, a frenzied high soprano; her music was sung with startling brilliance by Marie Angel. Elgar Howarth, with Paul Daniel his associate in layered passages, conducted what seemed to be a splendidly secure performance. Mr. Anderson and five assistants controlled the electronics, amplification, and sound diffusion. Once again, the English National—which on the day before the première had given a stunning performance of Busoni's *Doctor Faust,* another serious, important opera—showed itself to be the model of a modern opera company.

Uplifting, Entertaining

June 30, 1986

Busoni believed that opera was the supreme musical form. "Music, which makes the unspoken eloquent and transports human cares from the depths aloft to the imagination, finds in opera principally the creative space for its expansion." The domain of opera extends from simple ballads and dance tunes to the densest counterpoint, comprehends both singing and orchestral music, both the worldly and the spiritual. Moreover, opera "demands more intensive expression, a more tensely strung bow, a more powerful diction" than does concert music. Busoni's view of opera was a high one. He deplored pieces that were mere entertainments or mere plays set to music, such as *La traviata* and *Tosca.* (*Otello,* because it contains a drinking song, a mandolin-accompanied chorus, the Willow Song, and an evening prayer, "becomes nearly an opera.") "Taking its cue from the old mystery plays, opera should be cast in the form of a ceremony—unconventional, half-religious, uplifting but also stimulating and entertaining."

> *Such plays of unreality require*
> *The help of Music, for she stands remote*
> *From all that's common,*

he wrote in the spoken Prologue to his opera *Doctor Faust.* (The other quotations are from his 1921 essay "Observations on the Possibilities of Opera.") Among old operas, *The Magic Flute* came closest to Busoni's ideal. Harrison Birtwistle's *The Mask of Orpheus* is a new opera that fulfills it. Busoni's own exemplification was his magnum opus *Doctor Faust,* of which the English

507

National Opera gave the British stage première a few weeks before it mounted *The Mask of Orpheus*. The two operas, a half-century apart, have things in common besides nonnaturalistic action. In each, the choice of the particular subject seemed less important than the necessity of finding one that would provide a structure for the sorts of music the composer wanted to write: Busoni contemplated Leonardo da Vinci, Merlin, and Don Juan before he decided on Faust; Birtwistle contemplated Faust before he decided on Orpheus. In each opera, musical forms take precedence of pacing determined only by the dramatic action. Each opera was long in the making: Busoni drafted his libretto in 1910, wrote it fully in 1914, and composed the music from 1917 until his death in 1924; Birtwistle composed two acts in 1973–75, the third in 1981–83. Each opera was preceded by many "satellite" concert works: Birtwistle's were an exploration of musics and methods for the forthcoming theatre score, Busoni's were sketches and even complete movements for it. There are sonic similarities: a fondness for "bell" harmonies, with their irrational but stirring overtones; contrasts of lucid, sharp-cut music and deliberate, mysterious blurring and dissolution of rhythmic or harmonic detail.

Doctor Faust has long seemed to me one of the great twentieth-century operas. I have seen three productions: the Wuppertal Opera's in the sixties; a fine one in Bloomington, Indiana, directed by Hans Busch (whose father, Fritz Busch, conducted the world première, in 1925; in Bloomington, a third-generation Fritz played the youth, Faust's son, who strides off into the future); and now the English National's. And have heard the piece several times more, for the BBC has ever been its champion, presenting concert performances—conducted by Adrian Boult, John Pritchard, and Michael Gielen—and relaying foreign performances. Deutsche Grammophon recorded a Munich radio production with Dietrich Fischer-Dieskau in the title role. Successive encounters bring not the second thoughts that sometimes temper first-hearing enthusiasm for an ambitious, unusual work but reinforcement of belief in its importance, beauty, and profundity. I recall that Harold Schonberg after the Bloomington performance urged the City Opera or the Met to acquire the production without delay. A company with the resources for *Doctor Faust* which prefers first to exhume *Adriana Lecouvreur, Francesca da Rimini, Esclarmonde* forfeits much claim to be taken seriously.

Perhaps managements fear that the opera is too "intellectual" for the public. "It moves on a plane of spiritual experience far beyond that of even the greatest of musical works for the stage," Edward Dent wrote in his Busoni monograph. The listener, Edward Sackville-West wrote, is "enthralled by an intellectual power, a spiritual magnificence, and an austere yet luminous beauty that are found together only in Bach and the great polyphonic masters of the sixteenth century." Yet on the simplest theatrical levels the opera also works splendidly. The London performances were packed. David Pountney, the director, ensured a popular success with a spectacular, controversial, somewhat flashy production. Faust was an atom scientist dreaming of power. (The program book included a brief biography of Edward Teller.) Mephistopheles was a Jungian shadow. (The program book quoted Jung's "A man can be as high-minded as Faust and as devilish as Mephistopheles if he is able to split his personality into two halves, and only then is he capable of feeling 'six thousand feet beyond good and evil.'") In the Parma scene, he wore a spangled bra and skirt. Helen, Busoni's "unattainable ideal of beauty," shimmied on as a floozy. There were other cheap or irrelevant touches. But it was a fundamentally serious performance, and it was executed with the utmost accomplishment. Thomas Allen was a noble, moving Faust. Graham Clark was a glittering, persuasive Mephistopheles. Eilene Hannan was a glowing Duchess of Parma (but her high notes were frayed at one of the two performances I heard).

Busoni died before he had completed the first Helen episode and the important final scene; his pupil Philipp Jarnach supplied what was missing. Now Antony Beaumont (whose *Busoni the Composer* is a thorough and excellent study), working from sketches unavailable at the time to Jarnach, has been able to reconstruct these scenes in a form closer to Busoni's intentions. (The details are set out in an article by Mr. Beaumont in the April *Musical Times.*) Mr. Beaumont conducted the first of the performances I heard. I found it an overwhelming evening in the theatre, and responded even more ardently to another performance, heard over the air as a BBC relay, which was conducted by Mark Elder. The mind's eye could now discount all but the high, apt strokes of the staging. The ear was bewitched by the shapes and colors of the music, realized by Mr. Elder, his cast, and his players with passionate conviction. The score was not uncut but was more nearly complete than in other postwar performances. Dent's English translation, revised by Mr. Beaumont, was used.

Three other recent productions have brought reassurance that grand opera can still be a living art. Janáček's *The Makropulos Affair* is based on a play, Karel Čapek's—a cold, cruel play refuting Shaw's suggestion in *Back to Methuselah* that mankind if given sufficient longevity would learn from its mistakes—but is more than a play set to music. There is a supernatural element that Busoni might approve: the time is Čapek's present, 1922; the action passes in a lawyer's office, backstage at the opera, and in a Prague hotel; but Elina Makropulos has lived for more than three centuries, thanks to an elixir administered to her at the court of Emperor Rudolph II. Death approaches, and can be stayed only by a new infusion of the elixir, its formula mislaid among the documents of a lawsuit that has dragged on for generations. Čapek warned Janáček that his play—he called it a comedy—was unpoetic and garrulous. Janáček cut it skillfully and filled it with the strong, strange poetry of his music, transforming cynicism and irony into compassion for the aged, terrified, still beautiful, still brilliant heroine. His previous opera, *The Cunning Little Vixen,* had celebrated the renewal and recreation of Nature; in the final scene the aging Forester, amid the springing new life of the forest, is at peace. The music is serene, consoling. *The Makropulos Affair* is a tragedy; in the final scene Emilia Marty (as the heroine now calls herself—latest in the long series of names, their initials always E.M., which she has used through the centuries) renounces immortality in a bout of drunken desperation. The music is harsh, searing.

Much of the time, the orchestra carries the musical burden while the characters converse in prosaic utterance; then key phrases break into moments of impassioned song. A little heraldic motif—a distant strain from the past, an echo from Rudolph's day—hints at the mystery surrounding the modern woman. One can analyze Janáček's use of telling motifs and piquant harmonies, describe his precise, sharp or sensuous timbres, examine his abrupt, wayward rhythms, but it is hard to explain why the music strikes so deep and sounds so true. Janáček himself said, in his last year, "I penetrate because there is truth in my work, truth to its very limit. Truth does not exclude beauty."

The Opera Company of Boston production of *The Makropulos Affair* last month, directed and conducted by Sarah Caldwell, was penetrating, beautiful, and true. The principal role was played by Anja Silja, a great soprano at her prime. Čapek's stage direction for the heroine's entrance is "Emilia Marty sweeps grandly into the office—a tall, strangely beautiful woman. What so many lesser actresses try to be, she is: cold but dazzling, unique, impelling, mysterious, and always at ease." Some interpreters of the role, like some of Tosca, take too strenuously flamboyant an approach to it and overplay the prima donna. And Miss Silja herself in the past has been on occasion an artist flamboyant but vocally ill-disciplined. As Emilia Marty she was gleaming and controlled—the voice strong, sure, and steady, the presence now lustrous, now opaline with the shades of weariness, disillusion, and fear. It was a keen, subtle, intricate performance of great range, from numbed understatement to fiery outbursts— never exaggerated, and touched at times with mordant humor. There is a moving interlude with violin solo in Act III during which, as Michael Ewans puts it in his book on Janáček's tragic operas, "an adolescent girl, buried for three hundred years by science, is reborn." Marty has been carried offstage; when she returns, "Elina Makropulos stands before us, like a shade or phantom, but unmistakably herself; for in succumbing to age she has regained her youth." Miss Silja's assumption of, at once, a vulnerable, virginal quality and a harsh, tormented awareness of cruelty done to her, and then by her, across the centuries was an extraordinary feat. The final monologue is a flood of melody at last, voice and orchestra conjoined (Janáček rhythmically reshaped Čapek's prose), and the audience is pulled into the action: Janáček directed that greenish light should flood both stage and auditorium; the choric interjections of the others onstage are taken up by an offstage chorus singing, as it were, for the spectators. The drama comes to an overwhelming climax.

There are seven other principals: sharply defined characters, a cross-section of humanity, each of them intensified and ignited—played upon as if a burning- glass—by their encounters with Marty. In Boston, the roles were vividly taken. The young couple were Cynthia Clarey (Christa, a budding singer, dazzled by Marty's art) and Jon David Gruett (Janek Prus, who kills himself when he learns that his father is the successful rival for Marty's love). Prus, a precursor of Dr. Schön in Berg's *Lulu*, was powerfully played and sung by Chester Ludgin. William Cochran (the accomplished Mephistopheles of the Deutsche Grammo- phon recording of *Doctor Faust*) was an admirable Gregor, Marty's great- great-great-great-grandson, in love with her as his ancestor had been. (How many "great"s is unclear; Marty in her drunkenness stammers out six, but "Do I know how many thousands of my brats are scampering round the world?") John Lankston was touching as Hauk-Šendorf, the senile aristocrat who in his youth loved one Eugenia Montez and rediscovers her in Emilia Marty. (Beno

Blachut, the leading Czech tenor of the forties and fifties, sings the role in a London recording of the opera, which has Elisabeth Söderström as its heroine.) Richard Fredricks was the insistent, formidable lawyer Kolenatý. Noel Velasco was the charmingly fussy law clerk Vítek. Janáček gave life and individuality—through characteristic utterance—to even the smallest parts, and the adept, lively, but not overemphatic cameo performances of Mary Westbrook-Geha (a theatre cleaner), James Billings (a stagehand), and Pamela Gailey (a chambermaid) should not go unmentioned.

All in all, this *Makropulos* showed the Boston company at full strength, presenting an opera that matters, and in a way to bring to life what matters about it most. Miss Caldwell's inspired dramatic and musical direction combined insight with instinct. The first productions of *The Makropulos Affair*, in Brno (1926) and Prague (1928), were designed—by Josef Čapek, the playwright's brother—in elegant Jugendstil. So was Boston's—handsomely, almost too eye-catchingly so—with scenery by Helen Pond and Herbert Senn, and costumes by Fiandaca. The piece was sung in English.

The Welsh National Opera (whose *Makropulos*, part of a complete Janáček cycle, I reviewed eight years ago) is a year-round company with a strong team of resident singers, a fine orchestra, and a repertory that extends from a touring *Così* scaled for the smallest theatres to *The Ring* (which it brings to Covent Garden this September), *Tristan*, and *Parsifal* (both of which it has recorded, on London and Angel respectively). *The Trojans*, a joint venture with Scottish Opera and Opera North, is in preparation. The home base is the New Theatre in Cardiff, which seats twelve hundred people; grand opera there has a directness and impact unattainable in America's large houses. The company has always welcomed the stimulus provided by guest directors. James Levine conducted *Aida* for it in 1970, the year before he first came to the Met. Joachim Herz, Harry Kupfer, Ruth Berghaus, Lucian Pintilie, and Andrei Serban have staged operas there. And on a two-day visit to Cardiff last month I saw an *Otello* directed by Peter Stein and a *Wozzeck* directed by Liviu Ciulei.

The engagement of Stein, the famous director of the Berlin Schaubühne, was a coup for the company. At his first incursion into opera—a *Rheingold* for the Paris Opera ten years ago, start of a cycle that was never completed—Stein burned his fingers. While planning *Otello*, he studied the Welsh company for two years, on and off, and then he rehearsed with it for months. Some of my British colleagues, I think, slightly overpraised the show. In *Opera*, for example, Max Loppert wrote: "Stein's reputation as an absolute master of stagecraft was borne out in every production detail down to the smallest." But community copulation in the piazza, in celebration of Othello's victory, seemed to me a vulgar modernism, and Othello and Desdemona's rolling on the ground at the end of the act (instead of Verdi's slow, loving exit to the castle, prescribed to the very beat) a misreading of the music. On the night I attended, Othello in Act II backed toward a sheaf of lilies obviously waiting there to be used as a prop in "Ora e per sempre" and in Act III clawed at a red curtain in ways that were more stagy than spontaneous. The fourth-act curtain opened too early, to the detriment of Verdi's music. But in general it was an energetic, exciting, and intense presentation of the drama, in simple, striking scenery, by Lucio Fanti, that had a Piero-like exactness of placing and perspective. There were many memorable images. The chorus was dynamic, its role in the drama sharply defined. In a program article, Stein said that one thing that drew him to *Otello* was the chorus, Verdi and Boito's addition to the Shakespeare play: "The chorus themselves create the space for the protagonists to act in." Stein worked in full knowledge of, without slavishly following, the Verdi-Boito production book, compiled by Giulio Ricordi. The solo singing—Jeffrey Lawton as Othello, Helen Field as Desdemona, Donald Maxwell as Iago—was able but not "world class" (though one often hears worse at the Met). It was alive, intelligent, engrossing. Richard Armstrong, the musical director of the Welsh National since 1973, conducted magnificently. This was something different from seeing and hearing, let's say, Mr. Domingo, Dame Kiri, and Mr. Milnes doing their thing amid opulent, decorative scenery. (If those artists could work for months with Stein and Armstrong, in a small theatre, something even finer might result.) " 'Why can't we have such things at Covent Garden?' was the war-cry afterwards," Mr. Loppert reported. And answered, " 'Such things' require the basis of a company, a real company; the widely-gathered ingredients of international opera seldom allow for such carefully adjusted combinations." This Welsh *Otello* is likely to be remembered as Felsenstein's for the Berlin Comic Opera is. The only curious decision was to sing it in a foreign language.

Armstrong's conducting—the detail, force, and eloquence of the orchestral playing—was the great merit of *Wozzeck* (which was performed in English). Ciulei played fast and loose with Berg's careful dramatic construction. "It was the function of the composer to solve the problems of an ideal stage director," Berg once wrote, and so from Büchner's "twenty-six loosely constructed, sometimes fragmentary scenes" he selected fifteen and shaped them into acts that would allow "the laws of musical structure" to operate. Ciulei blurred the definition, turned the interludes into pantomimes, brought characters on and off at will (Marie appeared during the Doctor's examination of Wozzeck), ignored Berg's dramatic images, and added others of his own. As a version of Büchner's play, spoken, this staging might have been effective. As a version of Berg's opera it seemed tin-eared. Stein's *Otello* focussed all attention on the work and the actors. In Ciulei's *Wozzeck*, the director held the limelight.

PERSPECTIVES

July 7, 1986

HORIZONS, the New York Philharmonic's summer festival of new music—directed by Jacob Druckman, the orchestra's composer-in-residence—began promisingly, in 1983. The festival theme, "Since 1968, a New Romanticism?," was challenging. In a program essay, Druckman suggested that the tide had turned against "the music of Boulez, Babbitt, Xenakis, and Carter," that "sensuality, mystery, nostalgia, ecstasy, transcendency" were now in favor. His programs addressed themselves to something real and disturbing in American musical life; it could also be called the capitulation of many once rigorous and exploratory composers to the tastes of a public that likes what it knows. In the first concert, Peter Maxwell Davies's taut, beautiful *Ave Maris Stella* was contrasted with David Del Tredici's *Alice* piece *All in the Golden Afternoon;* in the second, Donald Martino's knotty Triple Concerto with John Harbison's Violin Concerto; in the third, Barbara Kolb's Chromatic Fantasy with John Adams's banal *Grand Pianola Music.* Seven concerts—one of them an open rehearsal of new works by young composers—along with five symposia and six "Meet the Composers" sessions, brought much to think about and a good deal of music interesting to hear. For two weeks, at least, the Philharmonic was not what Virgil Thomson, in 1952, called the Met: "not a part of New York's intellectual life."

Horizons '84 was even better. The theme, "The New Romanticism—A Broader View," admitted compositions by Boulez, Babbitt, Xenakis, and Carter. There were big new works by Charles Wuorinen and Roger Reynolds. In ten days, there were ten concerts and twelve public discussions. Many electronic and computer pieces were played. Virtuoso "performance artists"—Joan La Barbara, Diamánda Galás, Robert Dick—appeared. All in all, it was as stimulating a contemporary-music festival as any I've attended. Last year, there was no Horizons; the orchestra had gone off on tour. This year, Horizons dwindled to just seven concerts, spread across a May–June fortnight, without any related events except a "preview party." Attendance dwindled, too. There was no special festival program book. Music publishers set up no booths. The coffee stall was closed. (Tower Records, that unofficial but lively component of Lincoln Center, did better, putting on display the large part of the Horizons repertory which was already available on disk.) Some good music, some important pieces were played. But there was little festival feel. Twenty-three works were done, by nineteen composers; seven of them were works of the 1980s.

British critics who care about contemporary music sometimes remark that "they order this matter better in France"—especially since the establishment of IRCAM and its Ensemble InterContemporain. I can't help contrasting the Horizons '86 program with that of the Almeida Festival under way at the moment in London: seventy events in the space of four June–July weeks, achieved on a budget reported as about $200,000 (Horizons cost over $800,000), and held in an intimate theatre (whose restaurant, the brochure says, is recommended by good-food guides) and a nearby chapel. Horizons had a performance of Arvo Pärt's *Tabula Rasa;* Almeida had Pärt in person, *Tabula Rasa,* and thirteen other Pärt compositions, including some of the choral pieces he has been writing since he left Russia, in 1980. Horizons included Toru Takemitsu's *Rain Tree;* Almeida had Takemitsu in person, *Rain Tree,* and some thirty other Takemitsu works, set in the context of a dozen concerts presenting contemporary music from Japan. Horizons included Steve Reich's *Music for Eighteen Musicians;* Almeida had Reich talking, twenty Reich compositions, and two films, in the space of two days—a fiftieth-birthday celebration, the main concerts of which the BBC is also broadcasting. Ten further Almeida concerts brought new music from Spain. Individual concerts or clutches of concerts were devoted to Giacinto

Scelsi (thirteen compositions), Sylvano Bussotti (sixteen), Chris Dench, Michael Rosenzweig, Jonathan Lloyd, James Wood. There were premières of works by Peter Maxwell Davies and Oliver Knussen, local premières of works by Hans Werner Henze, Peter Lieberson, Richard Felciano, John Cage, György Ligeti. And much else. Far more than a single person could take in, or want to. Programs that allow one to indulge special interests, discover new ones, and then pursue them intensively.

The theme of Horizons '86 was "Music as Theatre." Promising notion: I looked forward to New York performances of Harrison Birtwistle's *Secret Theatre* and John Buller's *The Theatre of Memory* (which has just been recorded on Unicorn-Kanchana); a revival, perhaps, of George Rochberg's chamber symphony *Music for the Magic Theatre;* another hearing of Henze's *Miracle of the Rose,* subtitled "Imaginary Theatre II," in a repeat performance by either of the two New York ensembles that have played it recently. None of those happened, but six of the seven programs included a work or works in whose presentation an element of staging was involved. The first concert was devoted to excerpts from Ligeti's opera *Le Grand Macabre* and a staging of his *Aventures* and *Nouvelles Aventures.* The second was a mixed bag. The third brought the belated American première of Stockhausen's *Trans.* For years—for fifteen years, ever since the première, in Donaueschingen—I had been looking forward to a live production of *Trans.* The recurrent descriptions of it were fascinating. The Deutsche Grammophon recording—one side of the disk the première, which was greeted with both cheers and jeers, and the other a studio performance—was impressive.

Trans came to Stockhausen in a dream. Bathed in an eerie violet-red glow, a double row of string players spans the stage. They are all but motionless. Only the bows move, very, very slowly, as dense cluster-chords, underpinned by an electronic organ, weave a kind of sonic curtain. Behind it, invisible, there are four wind ensembles—four flutes with bass clarinet and celesta; four oboes with trombone; four clarinets with bassoon and double-bassoon; four trumpets with tuba—each group accompanied by a percussionist. They play elaborate, brilliant music. Every twenty seconds or so, the sound of a giant wooden shuttle (recorded) clacks from side to side of the hall, and each time the composition of the string chord—and the picture it makes—is subtly altered. Four exuberant solo incidents, or "scenes," are set into this frame, involving a violist, a cellist, a violinist, and a trumpeter. It is a rich, strange composition—not "dreamy" in the usual sense of the word but at once hallucinatory and very active.

The Philharmonic production was disappointing. For one thing, most of the music had been prerecorded, by the South German Radio Orchestra, conducted by Peter Eötvös. The Philharmonic, conducted by Gunther Schuller, added only the "curtain" chords and the solo episodes. A program note described this mostly-on-tape presentation as "now the authorized version" but continued with statements from the composer about the importance of live players' being present: "That makes the decisive difference." In any event, the sound reproduction seemed rudimentary. The score gives instructions for plotting the music through twelve carefully placed loudspeakers; where I sat, everything appeared to come from one big loudspeaker. Perspectives were flattened. There was no sense of mysterious distance.

Trans was preceded by Stockhausen's *The Little Harlequin,* a captivating clarinet solo to be both played and danced. Jean Kopperud, who has played and danced Stockhausen's big, forty-five-minute *Harlequin* so well, in Symphony Space, was a winning interpreter, but the choreography prescribed in the score had been cheapened into cutesy capering around an unresponding male mannequin. The concert began with the New York première of Louis Andriessen's *De Staat, The Republic*—thirty-five minutes of earnest minimalism which Andriessen composed, he says, "as a contribution to the discussion about the place of music in politics." Repetitive patterns are executed in bold, solid colors: the orchestra is four each of oboes, horns, trumpets, and trombones, along with electric guitars, pianos, harps, and four violas. From time to time, a quartet of amplified mezzo-sopranos cries lines derived from Plato's *Republic*—the language unidentifiable in the Horizons performance, as also in the Composers' Voice recording of the piece. Andriessen's sections are shorter than those of Glass or Reich, but there is one particularly tiresome stretch of five-note ostinato not made more interesting by the phase-shifts of its accompaniment. In a program note, Andriessen wrote that "a good composer poses like an actor." Bach enhanced the rhetorical gestures of his music by his physical appearance, for he "dressed in wig and knee-breeches." And: "Stravinsky is our best actor. Every musical gesture he makes is a quotation of a historical musical formula; but since he is a good player, one immediately recognizes it as *his* gesture." There were gestures in *De Staat* that one immediately recognized as Stravinsky's—borrowed from *Petrushka* and *Sacre,* simplified, "tested" in the modern world. *De Staat* won UNESCO's Rostrum prize in 1977; the recording was made at the 1978 Holland Festival. There is a fair amount of Dutch music, I find—thoughtful, carefully fashioned, energetic and even adventurous music— that doesn't last well or travel well, although in context, performed for and eagerly discussed by a public concerned with contemporary music and its social role, it may once have made a considerable impression and have seemed important. The young Danes make their points with a lighter touch.

The fourth Horizons program, also conducted by Mr. Schuller, contained Pärt's *Tabula Rasa.* Pärt is another kind of minimalist; he makes a little go a long way with such economy and precision of placing that one hangs on his utterances. *Tabula Rasa* is a two-violin concerto. The first movement suggests a Vivaldi concerto slightly off-centered, which keeps stopping and starting over again; the second is a very beautiful sequence that flows and flows until it dissolves into silence. The Philharmonic soloists, Kerry McDermott and Marina Kruglikov, played with a radiance almost equal to that of Gidon Kremer and Tatjana Grindenko on the ECM recording (which has the composer Alfred Schnittke at the prepared piano). Pärt's music is at once puzzling and pleasing— unlike any other, and very pure. He is a composer-in-residence at the Cabrillo Festival, in Santa Cruz, later this month. [More about him on pp. 535–36.] The Horizons concert began with Hale Smith's *Ritual and Incantations* (1974), which sounded like movie music; included a new piece by Morton Feldman,

515

Coptic Light, which I found tedious, and Takemitsu's slight, pretty percussion trio *Rain Tree;* and ended with Witold Lutoslawski's well-known *Three Poems of Henri Michaux* (1963), admirably performed by the Gregg Smith Singers.

The fifth concert consisted of Luciano Berio's *A-Ronne* and *Laborintus II,* two works that are always good to hear. They were brilliantly performed by the Electric Phoenix, a British vocal group, with Speculum Musicae players and the composer as conductor in *Laborintus.* The sixth concert was devoted to American minimalism: an act of Paul Dresher's opera *Slow Fire* and Reich's *Music for Eighteen Musicians.* Dresher seems to have relaxed into a soggy world of soft-rock schlock. *Slow Fire* showed easy attractiveness, muddled aspiration, and a lack of intellectual rigor—a combination one is tempted to describe as Californian. Reich's compositions hardly bear listening to more than once, and *Music for Eighteen Musicians* (1976) has been much played.

The final concert began with the New York première of *Le Tambourin,* by Bernard Rands, once an astringent, now a picturesque and still able composer. It continued with the *Three Hallucinations* of John Corigliano, who thinks, according to the program note, "it is the job of every composer to reach out to his audience with all means at his disposal" (secondhand *Sacre* here being one of those means). The work derives from a movie score. These were conducted by Leonard Slatkin. The festival ended with two works by Druckman himself. *Animus II* (1968), a music-theatre trio, was alluringly sung by Kimball Wheeler and was deftly played but too mildly enacted by Daniel Druckman and Gordon Gottlieb, as the percussionists beguiled and excited by the heroine's siren song. Of the concert scena *Lamia* (1974–75) Jan DeGaetani, for whom it was composed, gave a tremendous performance. The soloist is an enchantress, and the scena ranges from naive folk spells—girls of Poitiers asking to see their future husbands—to Medea's dark conjuration and Isolde's commands to wind and wave. Years ago, the Metropolitan Opera—which has produced no new work since Marvin David Levy's *Mourning Becomes Elektra,* in 1967— commissioned operas from Corigliano and Druckman. Corigliano's *A Figaro for Antonia* has been announced for performance in 1990–91. The Druckman opera has now been abandoned, but Tony Harrison's libretto, *Medea: A Sex-War Opera,* appears in his *Dramatic Verse 1973–1985.*

The second Horizons concert included Poul Ruders's *Corpus cum figuris.* Ruders is a Danish composer (born in 1949) quite often heard abroad and beginning to be known in this country: his *Manhattan Abstraction* (1982) comes to Tanglewood next month; Delores Stevens played his Second Piano Sonata (1982) in New York earlier this year. In a 1983 essay, Oliver Knussen (who conducted the Horizons concert) described him as "not only a leading figure in an exceptionally promising generation of Danish composers, but . . . surely one of the most strikingly individual voices to have emerged anywhere in recent years." The two pieces of his I've heard (the other is the chamber concerto *Four Compositions,* of 1980, which has been recorded by the London Sinfonietta and Knussen, on the Paula label) confirm it. With his compatriot Hans Abrahamsen, Ruders shares easy, smiling confidence. Even at its most elaborated, his music never sounds labored. It flows. The current has been fed, I guess, by Stravinsky, Britten, Peter Maxwell Davies; it runs into fresh, unpredictable channels. (*Four*

Compositions reaches its climax on an exuberant misquotation of the opening horn call of *Der Rosenkavalier.*) *Corpus cum figuris* (1984), a twenty-minute piece for twenty players, which was commissioned by IRCAM's Ensemble InterContemporain and the Danish Radio, opens as a slow, somber march. The "figures" of the title invade it, and they start to take over as the pace quickens, with sudden jerks into faster motions. New, unexpected thoughts appear: waltz strains, and what the composer, in a program note, calls "views from the Middle Ages." The details on the large acoustic canvas, he says, may be "alien and weird," and he proposes an analogy: "You climb a mountain and beyond the peak you see a new world, completely different from what was expected." The companion with whom I listened found that final prospect bleak and terrifying. I didn't agree with her; it seemed to me merely surprising. (The composer calls it "a terminal scream.") But we were both held intent on the musical progress.

I hope that the Philharmonic, now that it knows *Corpus cum figuris,* will continue to play it. And take some more Ruders—and some Abrahamsen—into its repertory. Druckman evidently believes in Ruders: in November, he conducts *Corpus cum figuris* with the St. Paul Chamber Orchestra.

Let's Make an Opera

July 14, 1986

Recently, I wrote about two operas—Busoni's *Doctor Faust* and Harrison Birtwistle's *The Mask of Orpheus*—whose composers reworked archetypal myths in exciting contemporary music. This review is of three new, less ambitious operas—two with action set in the past, sixty to seventy years ago, and one with action set in the present—fashioned to more conventional formulas.

William Mayer's *A Death in the Family,* which was performed last month by the Opera Theatre of St. Louis, is based on James Agee's book and on the play, *All the Way Home,* that Tad Mosel drew from it. It is unpromising matter for a musical drama, though not for music: Samuel Barber's concert scena *Knoxville: Summer of 1915* captures at once the cadences of Agee's elaborately wrought prose and the "feel" of his work—the re-creation of time, place, and emotions through a carefully chosen, carefully arranged catalogue of memories. The book also re-creates characters: the boy Rufus, at the center, and many members of his family, stretching back through three generations (through five in an episode where he is taken to meet his great-great-grandmother). One merit of Agee's work is its reflection of the way, in life, one gets to know and understand people: observing behavior, hearing sudden revelations, piecing together past and present, sometimes realizing the import of scenes only years after they happen. The quiet, slow autobiographical novel is a subtle and tender piece of work. A balance between the boy's perceptions and the adult narration is finely held.

In a dramatization, that merit is lost. Things move now at stage time. Dialogue must replace catalogue, description, and accounts of what people think and feel.

Abridgment that retains only the most striking phrases and incidents distorts them: their context is destroyed. The book moves on two time scales, one spanning days, the other years. The action is the death—"offstage," in a motor accident, unobserved even by the narrator—of Rufus's father, Jay; the effect of it on the family; and his funeral. But there are important scenes outside that foreground span—Rufus's memories of earlier years—which Agee's editors placed in italics after Part I and Part II of the main narration. (*A Death in the Family* was posthumously published.) Both play and opera (Mayer was his own librettist) collapse Agee's two time schemes into one, cram the events of years into a few overfilled days, and thus introduce further distortion. Rufus is sometimes six, sometimes three or four. His little sister Catherine, his companion in the principal action, is dispensed with: she can hardly be at once unborn and an important presence. All that remains of Agee is incidents. And what might be called the ground bass of his work, the conflict of religious faith and unbelief, is unsounded.

There is music in the book—actual music, beyond the melody of Agee's prose. Jay sings to Rufus, and so does Mary, his mother—song after song after song. Some of the songs appear in the opera, but not as they do in the book; if they did, operatic action would have to stop for a solo recital lasting "nearly an hour" while Jay comforts his son after a nightmare. In one of Agee's memorable scenes, Catherine watches her grandmother, after the funeral, apparently playing her piano but in fact only pressing down the keys silently; and there is no place in opera for silent scenes. I can imagine an evening of music in the theatre—it might be called *Scenes from "A Death in the Family"*—that would include something like Barber's *Knoxville*, Jay's song recital to his son, the Charon-like scene in which Jay and his car are ferried across the river, Uncle Andrew's account of the funeral (a butterfly lighted on the coffin, rested there, and then flew up into the sun), Rufus's careful listening to his parents' singing of "Swing low, sweet chariot":

> When she sang the second "Swing" she just sang "swing low," on two notes, in a simple, clear voice, but he sang "swing" on two notes, sliding from the note above to the one she sang, and blurring his voice and making it more forceful on the first note, and springing it, dark and blurry, off the "l" in "low," with a rhythm that made his son's body stir. And when he came to "Tell all my friends I'm coming too," he started four full notes above her, and slowed up a little, and sort of dreamed his way down among several extra notes she didn't sing, and some of these notes were a kind of blur, like hitting a black note and the next white one at the same time on Grandma's piano.

Such a work might capture the essence of Agee's book more faithfully than any attempt to wrest from it a conventionally well-made opera. In Mayer's version, the bar to which Jay takes Rufus ("There was no music: only the density of bodies ... only the thick quietude of crumpled talk") becomes a singing saloon, and is then invaded by a comic posse of Temperance Ladies with cornet and drum. Many operas include a reflective ensemble, a largo concertato. It was an element of the operatic form within which Verdi worked, and so the slow ensembles launched by Macbeth, Violetta, Amonasro, Desdemona seem musically essential and dramatically natural. Janáček, in later life, feared he had sacrificed dramatic verity to musical form by including the largo concertato "Every couple has troubles to overcome" in *Jenůfa*. His fears were groundless; the ensemble bothers only directors who would stage an opera as if it were a spoken play. But in Mayer's opera the ensemble "Who shall tell the sorrow of being on this earth?" sounds like a number contrived so that, somewhere, there will be the traditional ensemble. Similarly with the flashy "Hallelujah!" production number that ends Act II, when Great-Aunt Hannah buys Rufus a flashy cap; it's out of scale, and too evident a bid for brightness.

Opera composers, it is often said, must "rape" their source material to produce vital offspring. But there is no such violence—rather, loving cooperation—in Verdi's handling of Shakespeare, Berg's of Büchner and Wedekind, Britten's of Melville and Henry James. The operas rise to their subjects. Only trash—which Agee's *A Death in the Family* is not—needs transfiguration. Metaphors aside, let me suggest that if Mayer's music were stronger, it might conquer objections to his libretto. But his music is for the most part trite. The Tennessee songs are deftly but glibly harmonized, as if for a campus glee club. The score follows and illustrates the situations and the text, whereas in admirable operas the text and the situations can seem, albeit paradoxically, to have been determined by the score.

The opera, the composer said in a program note, went through "an extended workshop" in Minneapolis. It was first performed in 1983, by the Minnesota Opera, and was revised for this St. Louis production. No composer could hope for a better presentation of a work. Jake Gardner, as Jay, and Dawn Upshaw, as Mary, gave beautifully precise and freshly, admirably sung performances. Young Jeremy Cummins, as Rufus, was a star who put not a foot wrong. The large cast, Rhoda Levine's direction, Bruce Ferden's conducting, and John Conklin's décor did everything possible for the piece.

William Neil's *The Guilt of Lillian Sloan,* which was produced by the Lyric Opera of Chicago last month, is based on the 1922 murder trial of Edith Thompson and Frederick Bywaters. Edgar Lustgarten, in *Verdict in Dispute,* says of it:

> Few are unfamiliar with the outline of a tragedy that cast a City bookkeeper and Ilford housewife for a rôle befitting Bernhardt or Réjane. Beneath a commonplace plot of jealousy and intrigue lay hidden a drama of such spiritual intensity that it fascinates even those most repelled by crime.

The acts of the crime are not in dispute. Mr. and Mrs. Thompson, he thirty-two and she twenty-eight, were walking home after a visit to the theatre (to see Cyril Maude in *The Dippers*) when Bywaters, Mrs. Thompson's twenty-year-old sailor lover, appeared, thrust her aside, and confronted her husband. In the words of Bywaters's statement, "I said to him, 'You have got to separate from your wife.' He said, 'No.' . . . We struggled. I took my knife from my pocket and we fought and he got the worst of it. . . . I loved her and could not go on seeing her leading that life. I did not intend to kill him. I only meant to injure him." Mrs. Thompson was heard to cry out, "Oh don't, oh don't," and she ran off to summon help.

Bywaters maintained steadfastly that she had had no hand in the murder. But among his belongings the police found sixty-five letters that she had written to him during the year since their meeting. They proved fatal to her.

The letters give the case its lasting interest. Edith Thompson, a reader of romances, was living a romance of her own. Amid accounts of her daily life, she poured out her love:

> I'll always love you—if you are dead—if you have left me—even if you don't still love me. . . . I shall always have this past year to look back upon and feel that "Then I lived."

Sometimes she reproached Bywaters for not thinking about her, for not writing to her for at least five minutes a day while he was on his voyages. She reflected on the difference in their ages: "Shall I always be able to keep you? Eight years is such a long time—it's not now—it's later—when I'm Joan and you're not grown old enough to be Darby." She talked about books in a way disturbing to anyone who tends to escape from life into literature:

> Aren't books a consolation and a solace? We ourselves die and live in the books we read while we are reading them and then when we have finished, the books die and we live—or exist—just drag on through years and years, until when?. . . We are not the shapers of our destinies.

In another letter she wrote, "The endings are not the story. . . . Do as I do. Forget the end, lose yourself in the characters and the story, and in your own mind make your own end." And in some letters she described attempts to murder her husband by putting ground glass in his food, poison in his tea. Modern commentators tend to agree with her statement in court that these were fantasies, not facts: "I wanted him [Bywaters] to think that I would do anything for him to keep him to me." Thompson's body, exhumed, showed no traces of glass or poison. But the 1922 jury decided that the lovers had planned the murder together. Edith Thompson and Bywaters were both hanged.

Is this matter for a musical drama? I hesitate to say no, for Janáček might have made much of it. His *Kát'a Kabanová* deals with a woman in a somewhat comparable plight. The Neil opera, which has a libretto by Frank Galati and the composer, is tame and ordinary—cast as a trial scene with flashbacks. The characters are puppet: out through their paces. The music never takes command but flows on drably, undramatically, in arioso unrelieved by vivid word setting. There is a moment right at the end where Lillian (as the protagonist is renamed) breaks into a passionate, Turandot-like phrase, "Turn your eyes as I do." One expects an aria or duet to ensue, but nothing happens. Neil has been composer-in-residence at the Lyric for three years. He contemplated an Anne Frank opera, but someone else had the rights. He began *The Devil's Stocking,* after the Nelson Algren novel based on the Hurricane Carter murder trial, and the first scene had a workshop performance in 1984. But again there was a rights difficulty, and he turned to *Lillian Sloan.* Five scenes had a workshop performance last year. Both works-in-progress were chewed over by panels; after one or the other, the composers Stephen Paulus, Gunther Schuller, and

Dominick Argento, the librettist and director Stephen Wadsworth, the conductor Bruno Bartoletti, the scholar Philip Gossett, the Chicago *Tribune* critic John von Rhein said their say. I don't know what advice they gave, or whether Neil took it.

The performance, put on in a campus theatre by the Lyric Opera Center for American Artists in conjunction with the Northwestern University Theatre and Interpretation Center, was unimpressive. The librettist directed. The cast barely acted and seemed to have no idea that dramatic singing lives in the way words are uttered. Only those of the tenor Donald Kasch, in the Bywaters role, were consistently audible.

Chester Biscardi's *Tight-Rope,* which was produced last October by the University of Wisconsin–Madison, has an original libretto, by Henry Butler (the librettist of Marvin David Levy's *Mourning Becomes Elektra*). A film is being made about Luther Dane, "poet and cult hero," who disappeared and is presumed dead. The actor playing Dane jibs at speaking lines he feels ring false. Dane, alive after all, steps forward and declares that he might well have written them. The actor protests:

> *I will not lie!...*
> *We walk a tight-rope:*
> *one false step, one dishonest word,*
> *and we fall ... we deserve to fall.*

Dane, dropping into the blank verse in which much of the libretto is written, replies:

> *I had forgotten such sincerity.*
> *Then let me help ... my memory is good.*

He takes the actor back through some "memory scenes," on a living visit to Kathryn, a woman he loved, and to a statue of himself erected in a public park:

> *Go back to work. You know me now ...*
> *dreamer, scoundrel, lover, bastard, saint.*

And the actor does go back to work on the film, reciting with new confidence the lines

> *I must live with my many selves:*
> *lover, striving saint, drunken comrade,*
> *and above all, the fool ...*
> *until the fabric is worn thin*
> *and can no longer safely hold my heart.*

The libretto is soft-edged and arty. (There is one good idea: in one "memory scene," the actor's quick identification with Dane enables him to take over the poet's part.) Biscardi described his music, in an interview, as "someplace between Sondheim, Puccini, Gershwin, and me." Of the "me" who composed *At the Still Point,* in 1977, there is little trace. Biscardi spoke of breaking free from

Schoenberg and Babbitt, of relaxing into triads and tunes. The result resembles cocktail-lounge music—bland, innocuously amiable.

The opera was commissioned by the Music School of the University of Wisconsin–Madison (where Biscardi once studied) to celebrate the reopening of the Music Hall, an agreeable Victorian Gothic building dedicated (as the university Assembly Hall) in 1880. The scale is right for chamber opera, but the pit is deep, preventing the direct communication between singers and instrumentalists that chamber opera requires. Ten performances of *Tight-Rope* were given, with two casts. The first cast included John Reardon, accomplished veteran of many premières, as Dane, and Adria Firestone, as a gleaming Kathryn.

None of these operas was of musical interest. Mayer's had what might be called vision; the others seemed like exercises in opera-making. All three conformed to some lowest-common-denominator view of what the public expects opera to be. Not that opera *is* any single thing. A short list of contemporary operas worth listening to (and not requiring large-company resources) would include works as diverse as Birtwistle's *Punch and Judy,* Davies's *The Lighthouse,* John Eaton's *The Cry of Clytaemnestra,* John Harbison's *Full Moon in March,* Henze's *Elegy for Young Lovers,* Argento's *Postcard from Morocco,* and, by older composers, Stravinsky's *The Rake's Progress,* Britten's chamber operas, Tippett's *King Priam* and *The Knot Garden.* Do they have anything in common? Perhaps this: each is a strong musical construction, not just a play set to music.

At a Sunday-afternoon recital in Merkin Hall, the pianist Samuel Viviano devoted the first half of the program to George Crumb's *Makrokosmos II.* An infant in the hall set up a rival performance—*Modern Voices of Children?*—adding gentle wails to eleven of the twelve pieces and using the last of them to accompany his toddling processional exit up one of the aisles, parents in attendance. The result was piquant, Ivesian, but not really helpful to a composition in which Crumb has already worked out, with delicacy, ingenuity, and thoroughness, all the effects he needs (including some cries from the pianist). Mr. Viviano is an able performer—sure fingers, clever timing, large-scale control—but sometimes I found his musical presentation a little too smoothly, almost glibly accomplished. In the second half, he played the Alcotts movement of Ives's "Concord" Sonata; John Anthony Lennon's rhapsodic but also effusive, slack-limbed *Death Angel,* a New York première; and the first performance of a ballade by Don Freund entitled *Feux d'Artifice—Tombeau* *("Shuttle Explodes; Seven Feared Dead").*

Two days later, again in Merkin, the clarinettist William Powell gave a glittering recital. He is a performer who catches a listener's attention with the first phrase and continues to hold it, in the way great singers once did, by precision of timing, variety of attacks, and masterly, imaginative molding both of single notes and of melodic strands. He played Joji Yuasa's *Clarinet Solitude* (1980), an elegiac span of long, affecting melodies. With Virko Baley as pianist, he played Kathleen St. John's *The Sacrifice of Iphigenia* (1978), a suite of thirteen movements with titles like "Agamemnon with Clytemnestra," "Artemis' Revenge," "Iphigenia's Transport to Tauris." Mr. Powell's artistry lifted the work above the obvious. Baley's own *Sculptured Birds*—the first movement, "The

Jurassic Bird," composed in 1979; "Eagle," "Bird in Glide," and "The Chinese Nightingale" added in 1984, for Mr. Powell—struck deeper. The imagery was keen, the musical thought original. Again and again, Mr. Powell touched a nerve of pleasure with a clarinet specialty: a note stealing gently from silence. His timbres were protean. Even to a city that houses many fine clarinettists Mr. Powell—who is Juilliard-trained but now lives and works in the West—is a remarkable visitor. I'd love to hear him and a Don Alvaro of comparable magnetism collaborate in a performance of *La forza del destino*, with its important clarinet solos. Mr. Baley began the recital with the Second Piano Sonata (1975) of Valentin Silvestrov, one of Russia's better-known serialists—a gently poetic but slightly wan piece.

High Time

July 21, 1986

On May 10, Milton Byron Babbitt was seventy, and that month the first all-Babbitt record appeared: Harmonia Mundi HM 5160, a piano recital played by Robert Taub. The program spans nearly forty years of Babbitt's music, from the *Three Compositions* of 1947–48 to *Lagniappe*—a "gift thrown in"—which was composed last year specially for the record. The piece is dedicated to René Goiffon and Robina Young, directors of American Harmonia Mundi. The piano writing limns the particular virtues of its interpreter in a way that may enable music historians centuries hence to discern features of Mr. Taub's artistic personality, rather as music historians today reconstruct the art of Handel's favorite interpreters by studying the airs that Handel composed for them. The disk also includes *Canonical Form*, composed for and dedicated to Mr. Taub. Future historians will, of course, have the advantage, denied to Handel historians, of being able to hear the interpreters in question perform the music written for them. Four days after Babbitt's birthday, Mr. Taub played much of the program in public, in Alice Tully Hall; he framed the Babbitt pieces with Bach, Brahms, Ravel, Scarlatti, and Liszt, placing Babbitt firmly in the great keyboard tradition. Earlier this season, in October, also in Tully Hall, he played Babbitt's *Tableaux* in a setting of Mozart, Bartók, and Chopin.

In April, at a Group for Contemporary Music recital at the 92nd Street Y, Alan Feinberg placed Babbitt in a specifically twentieth-century pianistic frame: his program included Rachmaninoff preludes (1910), a Debussy study (1915), the Busoni Toccata (1920), and pieces by George Edwards, Charles Wuorinen, and György Ligeti. The Babbitt was the New York première of *Time Series*, a diptych of *Playing for Time* (1977) and *About Time*, which is dedicated to and was composed for Mr. Feinberg, in 1982. Earlier this year, in Carnegie Hall, Mr. Feinberg was the soloist in the first performance of Babbitt's Piano Concerto, commissioned for and dedicated to the American Composers Orchestra. The piano writing of *About Time* and of the concerto pictures Mr. Feinberg's art as that of *Canonical Form* and *Lagniappe* does Mr. Taub's. I have written before of Mr. Feinberg's prowess in Babbitt, Wuorinen, and Ravel. In the concerto, Babbitt makes unstinting use of that strength, stamina, and commanding artistic presence.

America has many fine pianists. Ursula Oppens, Charles Rosen, and the others must forgive me if, with thoughts on Babbitt, I suggest that Mr. Taub and Mr. Feinberg have been the piano stars of the particular New York season now ending. How should one describe them? Lamb and lion could serve as a caricature characterization, but it is misleading, for the lamb can be formidable and fierce when the music requires, and the lion can purr winningly. Poet and prophet? That comes closer, provided one adds that in Taub the poet there can be a vein of crackling fire, and in Feinberg the fiery prophet a streak of tender lyricism. Anyway, it is a matter not of competitive rating but of rejoicing that there are two virtuosi who play Babbitt's music so well. The only Babbitt I have heard both of them do is *Partitions* (1957). Differences between them are suggested above; they share technical mastery, command of form, and a zest for the music which proves infectious.

Earlier Babbitt pianists were also named Robert: the composer Robert Helps, for whom *Partitions, Post-Partitions* (1966), and *Tableaux* (1973) were written, and the late Robert Miller, for whom *Reflections* (1974), for piano and tape, was written. Mr. Helps recorded *Partitions* (for CRI), and Mr. Miller recorded *Post-Partitions* and *Reflections* (for New World). It is fascinating to compare the Taub recording of those pieces with the earlier versions; and Mr. Taub's Harmonia Mundi *Three Compositions* with the version he recorded five years ago for CRI; and his *Tableaux* and *Reflections* with memories—and, more precisely, in these days of copious "sound documentation," with tapes—of New York performances of *Tableaux* by Matthias Kriesberg and of *Reflections* by Aleck Karis. Again, it is not a matter of competitive rating. Rather, it is a recognition that Babbitt's piano music has become a part of the modern repertory, and that—like Chopin's, Debussy's, Ravel's—it can bear many different approaches. The varied performances are complementary.

Mr. Taub brings to this music something not heard—or not heard so regularly—in earlier performances: the full range of tonal colors that the piano can compass. When compared with his versions, others sound monochrome—scrupulous in their attention to the dynamic indications that mark almost every note in a Babbitt piece but executed in a single, bright, "modern" timbre. Mr. Taub's performances are opaline, iridescent. His piano is the instrument of Ravel's *Gaspard de la nuit,* not simply the wide-ranging machine that, more efficiently than any other controlled merely by human muscles, can execute a score's precise instructions about pitch, timing, and dynamics. In a program note for the May recital Mr. Taub wrote, "The music of Milton Babbitt must be played from the heart. The dazzling, highly imaginative pianism—enormous registral leaps, juxtaposition of dynamic extremes, highly complicated rhythms, innovative pedal techniques—always serves an intensely musical end, which, as in all great works, should be so completely mastered that the music is free to soar in performance." And, in a birthday interview, the composer said of Mr. Taub,

"When I write a piece, I have a mental image of a perfect performance. When Bob plays it, he gives me precisely what is in my mind."

Babbitt's music is not easy. He is a self-professed "maximalist": in 1975 he wrote, "I have presumed to pursue the goal of attempting to make music as much as it might be." Anyone who acquires the Harmonia Mundi disk should perhaps listen first to the three pieces that begin the recital—*Three Compositions, Duet,* and *Semi-Simple Variations*—and then jump at once to *Canonical Form,* a set of twice-twelve variations, its paragraphs defined by cadences and fermatas. It is a work of uncommon energy, brilliance, and charm—tense in its thought but set out with elegant spareness and clarity. Some variations concentrate on a particular region of the keyboard; others claim all seven octaves as their territory. *Lagniappe* follows, and this, too, is a work in distinct sections—a suite of lively ideas. When these two pieces have been apprehended, the longer paragraphs of the other works present less difficulty. Then *Lagniappe* can be heard again, as a summation-coda for the whole recital: its sections are—in ways that analysts will no doubt soon be demonstrating—new reflections of ideas first proposed in the earlier pieces. It is, in the words of the essay that accompanies the record, "a distillation and synthesis of the many diverse styles of Milton Babbitt's piano writing."

In Mr. Feinberg's program note for a 1983 Merkin Hall recital at which he played Babbitt's *Partitions, My Complements to Roger* (one of several pieces in which Babbitt celebrated Sessions birthdays), and *Playing for Time* he remarked that "these Babbitt works have all the exhilaration of virtuoso études together with a kind of Dixieland freshness." In a note for the April recital at which *Playing for Time* was joined with *About Time* he said of the latter piece, "Astaire & Rogers have been often in my mind while practicing it, especially in places where the melodies seem to hold hands on one pitch and then (in mirror fashion) step out and away from each other; swivel or plié and then return." His performances have a kind of dancing quality—a rhythmic exuberance that brings the jazz vein in Babbitt closer to the surface than it is when Mr. Taub plays. *Playing for Time* and *About Time* are a stunning pair of pieces—two-part inventions, largely, of limpid counterpoint, often audible canons, and sudden surprises. *Playing for Time* ends with a tune in octaves and an F-major cadence.

New World has recorded the Piano Concerto, coupled with the virtuoso song cycle *The Head of the Bed.* The concerto, in a single movement, lasts twenty-two minutes. The pianist plays almost all the time; there is just one episode, of about fifty bars, toward the end, for orchestra only, and otherwise the soloist appears to determine and direct the musical progress. It is an immensely challenging piece: for the listener, for the orchestral players, and, above all, for the soloist. Mr. Feinberg and the American Composers Orchestra, conducted by Mr. Wuorinen, rose nobly to the occasion. At the performance, I was excited but baffled. Many hearings later, I am just beginning to get my bearings. It is a work of big gestures, glittering sounds, long spans of carefully controlled tension. It calls for quicksilver attentiveness.

A good deal has been written about Babbitt. The principal collection of essays and articles is a 1976 double issue of *Perspectives of New Music,* which marked his sixtieth birthday. [*A seventieth-birthday tribute appeared in two 1986 numbers of* Perspectives.] The analytical articles there are tough going. There are also less formal observations. The composer recalls the moment when, playing clarinet in the Jackson, Mississippi, Boys' Band, he realized that the melodious second subject of the *Oberon* overture crests (with other notes in between) on the three notes of Oberon's magic horn call, in transposition, and glimpsed something about "the perplexing question of musical order and reference." (In that 1975 statement Babbitt said, "For some three and a half decades, a central, pervasive notion of musical relations appears determinative in all my compositions.") Elliott Carter writes of the "Rameaulike contribution of Milton Babbitt to the clarification and ordering of the twelve-note method" but also of "rational order based on a realistic consideration of the process of listening with its memory accumulations rather than on abstract number patterns." Bethany Beardslee, the leading Babbitt singer (she has recorded *Du, Vision and Prayer, Philomel,* and *A Solo Requiem*), says, "It's the rhythm in Milton's music that is the hardest thing to get, because you have to be precise in the ensemble. Yet, because he has such close relations to jazz, the music always has to be loose and not metronomic." It is hard to find a mean between rebarbative analysis and simple assertions that the music is enjoyable. Analysis can support the claim that this is "a kind of music in which everything is form, in which every line, every chord, every rhythm is justified within a strongly determined polyphony." That is Paul Griffiths's summary in his book *The String Quartet.* But he also writes of Babbitt's "mobile jazzy feel, good humour," and "rhythmic bounce." The most eloquent advocates are the interpreters: champions such as Mr. Taub and Mr. Feinberg.

PARNASSIAN PEAKS

July 28, 1986

ANTHONY KORF's *Symphony in the Twilight* had its first performance in March, played in Carnegie Hall by the American Composers Orchestra, which had commissioned it, and conducted by Paul Dunkel. It is a substantial two-movement piece, lasting about twenty-six minutes. The movements have titles: "Twilight and Troubled Dreams" and "Into the Horizon." From the program note we learn that Korf thinks of the piece "as like a Freudian *Heldenleben*"; that the first movement ends in a mood "sort of lonely, leaving-you-off-at-the-train-station-in-the-middle-of-the-night"; that the second sets out from a place "very hazy, lost, moody, distant, trying to reach for something and get something going," until in the final section it is "reaching up the mountain." No further personal program is revealed; in fact, we are told that "the work was generated by formal principles and is not a tone poem." But the chief formal principle invoked is that of altering one element of a gesture or a thematic complex so that it takes on a different aspect, and this, too, is intended to carry programmatic connotations: "just like in life certain things that are demons are terrifying to us, but if we look at them or take a different attitude, we can deal with them and live our lives."

Plainly, something autobiographical is going on here. Yet what I like about the symphony is not so much the story it tells as the sounds it makes and the structures it builds. Korf, born in 1951, and trained at the Manhattan School as a percussionist, professes to be a composer largely self-taught—and taught most by his work as director and conductor of the ensemble Parnassus. Parnassus specialties are the works of Milton Babbitt and Stefan Wolpe; there is nothing Babbitty or Wolpine about the symphony, however. It is grounded in harmony: chords, clashes, confrontations. The upward drift of thirds from the *Tristan* Act III prelude appears, not as a citation but, it seems, as something newly discovered—a natural, inevitable musical emanation from "troubled dreams." I was reminded at times of Michael Tippett by the sonorities; by episodes of buoyant, unlabored counterpoint; by construction in juxtaposed sections, not with transitions; and by a lively, dancing lyricism that animates the lines and the play of line upon line. I don't suppose there was any direct influence; it seems to be a case, rather, of two minds moving forward in similar ways. The piece is beautifully scored, with much feeling for consorts of woodwinds and of brasses. There are some unconventional, exquisite combinations. Korf has found and mastered his own voice more surely than in earlier works. The symphony should win favor with conductors—and audiences—who are in quest of something new but are glutted with secondhand, second-rate neoromanticism, are bored with minimalist mechanics, and are chary of tackling such technically difficult pieces as, say, Babbitt's Piano Concerto. The Composers Orchestra performance had excellent things in it but also some errant moments. In one or two passages, the argument seemed to hang fire, the tension to slacken; that might not happen in a completely assured performance.

In April, in Merkin Hall, Parnassus and Mr. Korf gave the first performance of John Watrous's Chamber Symphony, which was commissioned by and is dedicated to them. Watrous was a name new to me, and the program booklet vouchsafed nothing about him. (I learned subsequently that he was born in 1955, studied with Donald Martino, and lives in Massachusetts.) I enjoyed his piece: a clean-edged, confident, eventful work. It is for ten players, is in three movements (sonata form, scherzo and trio, and variations expanding into a finale), and lasts about nineteen minutes. Ancestors are evidently Schoenberg's and Webern's works in symphonic mold; the instrumental disposition is close to that of Webern's Concerto, Opus 24. But the symphony is a fresh creation, not an exercise. It is a work of dashing rhythmic impulses, with energetic solo writing (episodes executed by Stephen Taylor, oboe, and Eliza Garth, piano, were particularly striking), mercurial changes of mood and gait, and concerto-grosso contrasts between small chamber combinations and the full ensemble.

Watrous's Chamber Symphony was the centerpiece of a distinguished program executed with high accomplishment. It began with Stravinsky's Septet (1953), that dazzling contrapuntal display of melodious tonal serialism—composed while Bach looked over one shoulder and Webern over the other. It ended with Wolpe's Piece in Two Parts for Six Players (1962), which crackles with electric energy of invention. The three big pieces were separated by two lightweight intermezzi: Donald Martino's *Canzone e tarantella sul nome Petrassi* (1984), for clarinet and cello, composed as an eightieth-birthday card for the composer Goffredo Petrassi (a *Traviata* medley forms part of it); and Fred Lerdahl's Waltzes (1981), for violin, viola, cello, and double-bass. All the players, assembled in various configurations for the different pieces, deserve mention. They were Laura Conwesser (flute), Stephen Taylor (oboe), Alan Kay or Dennis Smylie (clarinet), Lauren Goldstein (bassoon), David Wakefield or Scott Temple (horn), Raymond Mase (trumpet), David Braynard (tuba), Cyrus Stevens (violin), Maureen Gallagher or Lois Martin (viola), Chris Finckel or Jonathan Spitz (cello), Donald Palma (double-bass), Eliza Garth or Edmund Niemann (piano), and Barbara Allen (harp). This was one of Mr. Korf's and Parnassus's high evenings.

Song recitals of the season included four given by good baritones. In November, William Parker, with Dalton Baldwin as his pianist, sang a French recital—Debussy, Ibert, Jacques Leguerney, and Poulenc—in a cultivated style and in tones that were mostly beautiful but sometimes opened up too eagerly. In February, Jan Opalach, with Ted Taylor as his pianist, sang Ives, Schumann's Eichendorff cycle, and French and modern American groups. He has intelligence and aplomb, but affects an oracular utterance—plummy pronunciation, "rich," backward tone—that lends a slightly pompous, parsonical touch to his performances. Orpheus with his lute, in William Schuman's song, moved lugubriously; Miriam Gideon's gentle Herrick setting, "To Music," was heavily handled.

Christopher Trakas, the winner of the 1985 Naumburg International Vocal Competition, is readier to bring words and tone forward onto the lips. In April, with Steven Blier as his pianist, he sang Ravel, Mahler, Poulenc, George Butterworth's *Shropshire Lad* cycle, and some modern American songs. Larry Alan Smith's *All Good Men,* written for Mr. Trakas, had its first performance. Horn, clarinet, and piano join the voice in a setting of "Now is the time for all good men to come to the aid of their country" (Mr. Smith's note calls it a "well-known phrase"; it is perhaps better known in a less patriotic version—". . . of the party"—as a typewriter-testing sentence), Melville's "The March into Virginia," and Wilfred Owen's "Dulce et decorum est." It is a strong, moving piece—a classier companion to Al Piantadosi's equally affecting "I didn't raise my boy to be a soldier," which Marilyn Horne recently recorded. Mr. Trakas is promising, but does not yet give to each song its full, distinct character.

These three artists were all handicapped by performing in Alice Tully Hall, which is too large to allow intimate communication between a singer and his audience, and whose acoustics are not warm. None of them struck an easy mean between confiding, with a glance and a murmur, and singing out into the large, unresponsive space. Thomas Hampson, for his New York début, in April, chose Town Hall, a happier setting for a song recital. With Armen Guzelimian as his pianist, he sang Wolf, Debussy, Samuel Barber's Joyce trilogy, and Richard Strauss. Mr. Hampson, well known on the stages of Europe, appears at the Met next season as the Count in *Figaro*. He has a smooth, beautiful baritone, clear words, and a ready, winning manner. But—there's a "but" in each of these accounts—there was a lack of energy, of bite, in the interpretations. After a while, everything began to sound much the same—consistently agreeable, but bland.

Fundamentals

August 11, 1986

THE June *Musical Times* has an arresting essay, by the Wagner biographer Barry Millington, entitled "Saucepans of Spaghetti: A Semiology of Opera Criticism." Mr. Millington's starting point is London critics' mockery of the English National Opera's new production of *Parsifal,* directed by Joachim Herz, and the Royal Opera's of *The Flying Dutchman,* directed by Mike Ashman. He calls much of what they wrote "thoughtless jibes," "abusive superficial description." Wolf Münzner's design for Act II of *Parsifal,* which they described as "a bowl of pink rags," "a basket of jelly babies," to him "brilliantly suggested an artificial paradise, set apart from the world," which Parsifal could step outside "in a striking visualization of the character's mental torment as he struggles to free himself from the temptations of Kundry." The critics, he complains, didn't wonder *why* Herz and his designer had made the enchanted flower garden so ugly. (I, who didn't see the show, wonder why, if the garden was so ugly, Parsifal should have found it tempting.) Mr. Millington's general points about "fidelity to the composer" and his claim that "the modern producer who brings his or her conception to the fore is acting in full accordance with the principle of music drama" set me thinking, and, even, examining my conscience. I have been reproached for critical inconsistency: for lauding productions by Wieland Wagner, Peter Sellars, David Pountney that departed far from the composer's stage directions, and deploring productions by Patrice Chéreau, Jean-Pierre Ponnelle, Andrei Serban, Liviu Ciulei that did the same. But there are distinctions to be made. Not all "modern" stagings use the same tactics. Not all classics are equally amenable to updating. Mr. Millington charges music critics with "a hankering after literalism," with wanting "respectful, neutral stagings." That wasn't what I had in mind when I called Ciulei's production of *Wozzeck,* for the Welsh National Opera, "tin-eared." In similar vein, the London critic Max Loppert wrote after Covent Garden's recent *Fidelio,* directed by Serban, "I would say that the man who produced this *Fidelio* is deaf to the music, to its workings and meanings."

Fidelity to a creator and to his work when that work must be brought to life before a contemporary audience is a difficult concept. It was raised in acute form by two shows at PepsiCo Summerfare, at Purchase, which has become New York's most vital summer festival. Both were eighteenth-century classics: Schiller's *Die Räuber* (1780), which is perhaps the most influential play ever written, and Mozart's *Così fan tutte* (1790). Both were performed in stagings that would have astonished their creators. *Die Räuber* has been a test piece for an ancient work's "relevance" ever since Erwin Piscator's celebrated 1926 production. Schiller's play was much cut and radically refocussed, and some critics thought Piscator was on the wrong track: "One cannot deep-freeze warm classics as Piscator has done; what is required is not variants of Coriolanus and Karl Moor [Schiller's protagonist], altered in form and content until they are aesthetically unrecognizable, but quite simply new plays from new authors" (Bernhard Diebold). But Piscator drew up six Fundamental Principles for the revitalization of classical drama, "which will enable us to face the future unresigned and full of hope." No. 3 states that a director "cannot be a mere 'servant of the work,' since the work itself is not something rigid and final." He must be "the servant and exponent of his times," and find a point of view determined neither by "gratuitous cleverness" nor willfully. No. 4 states that, while a director's standpoint may be either artistically or ideologically determined, an artistic standpoint will be "purely external" and "lose itself in a myriad of fortuitous combinations." These are defined in No. 5 as originating in "speculation on financial success, on public recognition, on personal originality," and in "a retreat into 'solutions' that are mere nuances." Without subscribing in full to Piscator's arguments, a critic can join him in denouncing updated productions of the classics which are merely clever, ingenious, novel, and must deplore those which may be honestly but are not intelligently or perceptively conceived. "Let's set it in Little Italy/in modern Greece/on the moon" and "Let's pretend it was all Tamino's/Violetta's/the Steersman's dream" are not recipes for automatic revitalization. They are, however, devices that—when the work permits—a director may well use to further his deeper aim.

Thirty-one years later, in Mannheim, Piscator directed *Die Räuber* again—this time, we are told, with special emphasis on the long monologues that in 1926 he had shredded. Then, in 1963, in Florence, he directed *I masnadieri*, the opera that Andrea Maffei and Verdi made from *Die Räuber*. It wasn't good. It taught lessons about differences between a spoken play and a music drama which many directors have still to learn. Paul Walter, the designer, had repeated the empty stage and the three tall, steep staircases of the Mannheim production: bare scaffolding amid hints of trees for the robbers, formal steps for the Moor castle, a towering central flight for Karl's spectacular entrance. Up and down the singers went. The audience felt uneasy, and the soprano, Margherita Roberti, seemed uneasy as, in a long dress, she negotiated at once very difficult music and precipitous unrailed steps. In 1926, according to a contemporary review, Piscator's robbers "erupted onto the stage to pulsing jazz rhythms, punctuated by the 'Internationale,'" and their "disciplined tumult . . . had the audience on the edge of their seats, exhilarated, involved." In Florence, during Verdi's bandit choruses they marked time to the music with an effect more comic than stirring—especially when the music slipped into waltz time.

A great dramatic composer is likely to be to some extent his own stage director. He determines tone and timing, prescribes the inflections and emphases of the drama. A Verdi, a Wagner, a Berg has also visualized the stage actions and on occasion set them to music so precisely that making a wrong move or making the right move at the wrong moment will be as noticeable as singing a wrong note or making a wrong vocal entry. A director who works within such a composer's prescriptions should feel no more "inhibited" than does the singer who sings the right notes, adding her own musical inventions only in places where the composer invites her to do so. The director has greater—but not limitless—freedom.

The Purchase *Räuber* was played by the troupe of the Bochum Schauspielhaus, directed by Alfred Kirchner. About half of Schiller's text was used. (The show, with one intermission, ran for three and a half hours; for America it had been somewhat shortened. Piscator's 1926 production ran for only two hours.) The tumid rhetoric, the pages-long monologues were abbreviated or omitted. Delivery was clipped, emphatic, incisive; there were no rolling, relished periods. Athletic pantomimes were inserted; Mahler, Beethoven, Brahms, and Philip Glass were drawn on for incidental music. The heroine, Amalia, was played by a young man. Period ranged freely between the eighteenth and twentieth centuries: white wigs popped on and off; the robbers went raiding in a beat-up truck. It was a stunningly efficient, if at times modish, evening of theatre, and it set one thinking about the violent play that once inflamed Europe. (I first encountered *Die Räuber* in Chapter 28 of *Jane Eyre,* where Diana and Mary thrill to the sound of it, although they need a German dictionary to puzzle out its sense. Purchase considerately provided a simultaneous translation through headphones.) Much more could be said. A music critic's point is that the lively Bochum approach could not successfully be taken to Verdi's opera. On the simplest level, no young man, however gifted a falsettist, could compass music that Verdi composed for Jenny Lind. More generally, a spoken text can sustain transformations that would destroy a music drama already embodying the composer's particular, personal interpretation of the play. The point should be obvious. It will need making so long as eminent directors (Chéreau with the Bayreuth *Ring,* Ciulei with the Welsh *Wozzeck*) direct, however brilliantly, just the librettos of operas, and not the operas themselves.

"Deeds of music made visible," Wagner's phrase for his music dramas, is a good phrase, too, for Peter Sellars's operatic productions. In the Purchase *Così,* his performers gave convincing physical shape to the phrases of Mozart's score, creating solo and ensemble imagery that was appropriate and beautiful. The donnée of Mozart's plot—that two young women don't recognize their lovers when they come wooing in false whiskers and Albanian costume—had been scrapped. The mysterious ambiguities of the opera—its intricate play of make-believe and utter seriousness—yielded to a clear, unambiguous presentation of emotional quicksands. An invented Alfonso-Despina relationship figured largely in Sellars's plot. Dorabella's flighty "È amore un ladroncello" was replaced by the poignant "Vado, ma dove?" (which Mozart composed for Louise Villeneuve, the first Dorabella, to sing in a Martín opera); the character was deepened, altered. There were many good jokes—some intrinsic, others springing incidentally from the setting in Despina's diner-by-the-sea—but the emotional tension was constantly high, and as a result the affective peaks of the opera ("Fra gli amplessi," the Fiordiligi-Ferrando duet, for one) had less than their usual prominence. This was a *Così* that kept its listeners on the heights—

caught up in each turn of the plot, rapt in the revelations of the score. Sellars had directed the score rather than the libretto. He brought onto the stage—"underlined" is perhaps not too strong—all the marvels that he found there; left nothing unexplained; tweaked and twisted the plain sense of the words when it didn't match his perceptions of the music. I can understand resistance to this *Così* as easily as my surrender to it. In any event, it was opera on a level of seriousness, intensity, and passionate, spirited achievement very different from the New York norm—long and lovingly rehearsed, expertly designed (setting by Adrianne Lobel, costumes by Dunya Ramicova) and lit (by James Ingalls). It played in a 670-seat theatre.

The production was based on and developed from the one in Castle Hill two years ago [p. 192], and, in the director's words, it "goes much further." Susan Larson (Fiordiligi), Sue Ellen Kuzma (Despina), James Maddalena (Guglielmo), and Sanford Sylvan (Don Alfonso) played their roles even more vividly than before. There was a warm, winning new Dorabella, Janice Felty, and a clear, stylish, ardent Ferrando, Frank Kelley. (In a deliberately tendentious program note, Sellars observed that "the baldness of the composer's own tortured self-portrait as Ferrando makes one wonder what combination of desperation and coldness and dread it must have taken to invite his wife to the premiere.") The band was the Boston Early Music Festival Orchestra, which played beautifully, on period instruments: Sellars described "the darker, clearer aspects of the new staging" as "consonant with the darkling, awake and gritty colorations of our new orchestra." Craig Smith was a devoted—but once or twice too lingering—conductor.

Besides *Die Räuber* and *Così,* PepsiCo Summerfare presented theatre troupes from Cracow (directed by Andrzej Wajda), Mexico City, Minneapolis (directed by Ciulei), and Galway; five dance companies; and copious, carefully planned concerts of Haydn's music. Six theatres and halls on the SUNY campus, where the festival is held, were kept busy.

APPROXIMATIONS

September 8, 1986

SEVERAL operas have been made from Goethe's novel-in-letters *The Sufferings of Young Werther.* The latest of them is Hans-Jürgen von Bose's, performed at the Schwetzingen Festival in April and due in Hamburg next year. The most famous of them, Massenet's *Werther,* rejoined the City Opera repertory in July, in a new production, directed by Lotfi Mansouri and conducted by Sergiu Comissiona, the company's music director–elect. The opera was presented in "picture-book" fashion. Acts began with a frozen tableau, behind gauze, within a painted frame. Thierry Bosquet's décor was influenced—according to a company handout—by impressionism and "the warm hues of Renoir's paintings," but the execution was in insipid pastel shades. (Werther lost his famous yellow waistcoat.) The effect was pallid, not passionate. Mr. Mansouri has the reputation of being a "traffic cop" director, not one who reveals the poignancy or the power of a work, and he sustained it by parading the principals and the chorus in dullest textbook fashion. His chief innovation was a bad one: treating Act IV, Scene 1—Massenet's "Nuit de Noël," a bird's-eye view of the little town of Wetzlar in the moonlight, snow falling, lights twinkling in the windows—as a pantomime of Werther's suicide.

Jerry Hadley sang his first Werther. This rising young tenor has been accused recently of bawling: as Percy to Joan Sutherland's Anna Bolena, as Flamand in the Carnegie Hall *Capriccio.* In an *Opera News* interview before *Werther,* he suggested that tenors like Alfredo Kraus (not, say, Placido Domingo) would henceforth be his model. He should aim higher—should listen to the records of Werther's music made by Edmond Clément, Fernando De Lucia, Tito Schipa. His performance was careful but monochrome, uninflected, rhythmically plain, not caressing, and his climaxes tended to blare in a way that suggested attention to vocal "method" rather than an access of romantic ardor. He has still to take the step from placing notes conscientiously to being a dramatic character. Charlotte is a role compassable by both sopranos and mezzos: Emma Eames first sang it at the Met; Ninon Vallin and Lotte Lehmann left famous recordings. The City Opera Charlotte was Wendy White, a mezzo, making her company début. For two acts, she played Charlotte, unaccountably, as a flighty soubrette (more of one, indeed, than Charlotte's young sister Sophie, the soubrette role, to which Claudette Peterson lent a plumply mature aspect). In Act III, which contains the Air des Lettres and the Air des Larmes, Miss White came closer to the character—without, however, giving to the words their full expressive power. William Stone was a decent, sober Albert. Mr. Comissiona's conducting, warm but not graceful or aristocratic, emphasized Massenet's debt to Wagner and his influence on Puccini's *Tosca.*

Two of the company's three new opera productions this season are of Massenet: *Werther* was followed, last month, by *Don Quichotte.* Along with revivals of Massenet's *Cendrillon,* of Bizet's *Pêcheurs de Perles* and *Carmen,* and of *Faust,* they make up what is billed as a Festival of French Opera. The works are sung, more or less, in French, while "supertitles"—phrases of an abridged English translation—are flashed onto a screen above the stage for the benefit of those who don't understand the language or can't catch what the American singers are saying.

Don Quichotte, which appeared in 1910, first in Monte Carlo and then in Paris, is one of those late Massenet operas infused with a warmth, geniality, and humor seldom found in earlier pieces. It is dedicated to Lucien Fugère, the first Paris Sancho Panza, whose recordings tell of a generous and lovable personality. In five acts we see Don Quixote serenade Dulcinea (here no simple country girl but a glittering contralto courtesan); tilt at the windmills; retrieve—by simple sweetness of character—Dulcinea's necklace from a band of rough brigands; return it to her in a scene where her heart is touched for a moment, and his is broken; and die, with his faithful Sancho beside him. Don Quixote is absurd but pure and good: the brigands recognize it; Dulcinea does;

and Sancho brings Act IV to a powerful close as he rounds on the company that has been mocking his beloved master. Massenet based his score on a few telling melodies, economically handled, but the most touching moments are phrases of recitative which the singers must bring to life. In the final scene, Don Quixote, lucid at last, tells Sancho that although he had promised him castles, even a fertile island, he can now bequeath to him only the Island of Dreams. Sancho interjects into the speech "C'était un simple îlot que je voulais avoir!" Vanni Marcoux, the first Paris Don Quixote (who left a wonderful record of the scene), once told a friend of mine that Fugère's utterance of the simple phrase would sometimes move him so deeply that he found it difficult to continue the opera. That kind of detailed verbal inflection was missing in the City Opera performance. Samuel Ramey, the Don Quixote, lacked presence and personality, although his voice was admirable. To suggest the character, he adopted a backward-leaning pose, moved like a windup toy, and kept his features impassive except when baring his teeth in a careful smile. Joseph McKee's Sancho had more vitality. Victoria Vergara, tall and beautiful, played Dulcinea with cool composure but with strident coloratura. Mario Bernardi's conducting was straightforward, not especially elegant.

A company handout described the production, directed by John Copley, as "a sophisticated 'storybook' presentation." During the brief prelude, the troupe assembled and, taking costumes from hampers, prepared to play or to sit around watching a Don Quixote drama. Robin Don's set was a black box with giant enlargements of the famous Gustave Doré illustrations, in monochrome—one for each scene—hung slantwise at the back. From two of them a practicable staircase popped out. It was a conventionally arty approach, not helpful to the emotions of the piece. The windmills episode was feebly achieved. The moving final image—the Knight asleep and dreaming aloud, then dying, on his feet, standing propped against a tree trunk—was lost: the set had no tree.

These presentations of *Werther* and *Don Quichotte* were generalized, approximate. They made the operas seem hardly worth doing. There was superficial, cosmetic adornment, but the essentials—subtle, intense, engrossing individual performances—were missing. I prefer to hear Massenet in the original French, but—witness De Lucia's and Schipa's recordings in Italian, Lehmann's in German—the language chosen is less important than vivid projection of whatever words are sung. In both shows, the actors, women and men alike, were got up as painted dolls. Charlotte had heavy eye makeup and false eyelashes, and bright patches of rouge on her cheeks. (Whoever supervises the City Opera makeup seems to have forgotten that it should be unnoticed by the audience.) A small point, but indicative of a disregard for period and style, of a large carelessness about the way specific characters should look, move, and deliver their lines. Massenet's Werther is not Goethe's and his Don Quixote not Cervantes's, but something of the original feeling survives in both operas. Little survived in the City Opera presentations; nor was there much feeling for Massenet's own precise, delicate charm. By contrast with, say, the *Makropulos Affair* that Sarah Caldwell directed in Boston or the *Così fan tutte* that Peter Sellars directed in Purchase, these were hardly serious performances. They offered entertainment, nothing more.

534

FESTIVALS

October 13, 1986

ONE of America's most adventurous and attractive festivals, the Cabrillo Music Festival, began in 1961, when the composer Lou Harrison organized some chamber-music concerts in a roadhouse at Aptos, outside Santa Cruz. It grew under the sponsorship of Cabrillo College. This year, it moved from the college's auditorium to a tent, seating nine hundred, on the Santa Cruz campus of the University of California, high above the town. It's a wonderful site. The campus, once a ranch, is a place of rolling cow pastures, redwood forests, romantic ravines. The festival tent, with attendant pavilions for food and drink, is pitched on a plateau, wide pastures falling all around. The sweep of Monterey Bay lies far below, a crescent of twinkling light as the evening darkens. For thirteen years, Dennis Russell Davies has been the music director. Last year's composers-in-residence were Charles Wuorinen and Elliott Carter; this year's were William Bolcom and Arvo Pärt. Two Thursday-to-Sunday weekends of music were given. Attending the first, I enjoyed six Pärt compositions, from the piano miniature *Für Alina,* of 1976, to the three-choir Te Deum, of 1984, and the Stabat Mater, composed last year. Pärt is a curious composer—a "mystic minimalist." In these later works, there's not a sharp or flat in sight (after the key signature), unless a Bach theme or the B-A-C-H theme is around. But it is not mindless, busy, mechanical minimalism—chaste, reverent economy, rather, with a strong feeling for pure or passingly troubled consonance and a Carl Nielsen–like freshness of response to the adventure of simple melodic steps. Pärt is like a musical Nazarene. The serialism, rhythmic mazes, and elaborate orchestration of his earlier pieces have been not so much forgotten as pared down to essentials. The precise spacing of triads, careful dynamic gradations, rhythmic order emphasized by its occasional disturbance, and subtle balance of periods are his concerns. The first movement of *Had Bach Been a Beekeeper* gradually builds up, over a steady pulse, a B-A-C-H fantasy—from murmurs to a ferocious buzzing climax, from limpidity to rhythmic and chromatic density. The second movement is a span of radiant, untroubled polyphony, swelling from the start of the B-minor Prelude in the first book of Bach's Forty-eight: after the swarming and stings, sweetest honey.

For one day, the festival moves to San Juan Bautista, an unspoiled little country town some miles inland. Populace and visitors picnic on the grassy plaza, three sides flanked by the mission church, its convent, and other old buildings; the fourth, dropping into the San Andreas Fault, open to a wide view of plain and hills. The big adobe church, built in 1803–12, is the most romantic and, though restored, least manicured of the California missions I know. It has luminous

535

acoustics, with a depth of bass response rare in concert halls. At an afternoon concert, the A-minor sequence of Pärt's Stabat Mater, for vocal trio and string trio, stole through the spaces, and the big sonorities of his *Arbos*—composed in 1977 for recorders and triangles but rescored now for brasses, bells, and gongs—set them ringing. Stravinsky's Symphonies of Wind Instruments ended the program. Pärt's Te Deum, heard that evening, begins with a marvellous, mysterious deep pedal tone, derived from a recording of a wind harp, which filled the church like a sound of nature—elemental, stirring, beautiful. The three choirs and a string band exchanged chants and refrains in D minor and D major, clashing tonalities in two episodes. The solemnity of Orthodox ritual recreated in a Spanish-colonial outpost (still the parish church) brought powerful extramusical associations. The other work on the program was Harrison's *La Koro Sutro*, a Buddhist text sung in Esperanto, accompanied by a sonorous "American gamelan" including aluminum tubes, billycans, trash cans, and oxygen cylinders sawn to pitch. Pärt's hard-won simplicity and Harrison's easy, relaxed, generous music were in piquant contrast.

Bolcom pieces at Cabrillo included the Piano Concerto, Piano Etudes, and (but after I'd gone) the Third Symphony, the Second Violin Sonata, and the Fantasia Concertante, first heard at Salzburg earlier this year. Bolcom is an arresting composer, Ives-open to American music of all kinds. The third featured composer was Ravel: orchestral, chamber, solo, and vocal music. There was an evening of American popular song (Joan Morris and Mr. Bolcom), an afternoon of operetta (Renate Gola and Daniel Parkerson, accompanied by Mr. Davies), a concert of music about trains (from Hans Christian Lumbye, through Honegger and Villa-Lobos, to Duke Ellington and Robert Hughes), and one of music for computers and instruments. The Cabrillo Festival Orchestra, drawn from all over the country, played for Mr. Davies with enthusiasm and brilliance. There were two exceptional young soloists: Milagro Vargas, a lustrous, exciting mezzo in Ravel's *Shéhérazade,* and the pianist Marc-André Hamelin, who won Carnegie Hall's American Music competition last year. In performances of Bolcom and Ravel he united big technique, poetry of tone, and supple beauty of phrasing.

About forty miles down the coast, at Carmel-by-the-Sea, the Carmel Bach Festival—directed and conducted for thirty-one years by Sandor Salgo—presented three weeks of concerts and recitals (one week of programs, twice repeated). A big Bach work, an opera, and a candlelit concert, with processions, in the Carmel mission church have become regular. The opera this year was *Figaro,* with an engaging cast of, mainly, San Francisco Opera cadet singers. Ruth Ann Swenson's "Deh vieni" was exquisite. Jacob Will's Figaro was lively. Mark Delavan's Count revealed a promising young baritone with voice, presence, and (pleasing to the author of the translation used) an incisive way with words. The Bach was the St. John Passion, Karl Markus the Evangelist. I missed that but caught Mr. Markus's keen, dramatic Bach singing in a Bach-Mendelssohn program. Most concerts are given in the Sunset Center Theatre, a tall Gothic auditorium, once a school's, seating a few over seven hundred. By contrast with the casual dress, bold programs, airy setting, and youthful spirit of Cabrillo, these Carmel events seemed staid, conservative. The performances were "traditional," scarce touched by the new baroque concerns of our day. But great music of the past was lovingly and decently performed.

The new opera at Santa Fe this year was Aulis Sallinen's *Kuningas Lähtee Ranskaan* (*The King Goes Forth to France*)—a joint commission from the Savonlinna Opera Festival (in Finland), Covent Garden, and the BBC. The première was given at Savonlinna two years ago; a Covent Garden production is due in April. Critics at Savonlinna suggested that Kalle Holmberg's staging there, while theatrically spectacular, was unhelpful to the piece. In Santa Fe, where the opera had a plain, trim staging, directed by Alfred Kirchner, in a standard black-box set, by John Conklin, I felt that some spectacular effects would have been welcome: the music and text weren't enough to hold one's interest. Paavo Haavikko's plot—originally a radio play—tells of England's King in some future Ice Age who frivolously embarks on an invasion of France. His route follows Edward III's. The centuries mingle. The chronicler Froissart reappears. "People harnessed horses to their cars and took out the engines.... The automobile developed into a vehicle that was fast, versatile, and cheap." The libretto, allusive, elliptical, jerky in its satire, does not make connected sense. A listener inevitably misses many points and may well think others too obvious to be worth making.

Sallinen's score is eclectic. It opens with a chorus in Carl Orff's monumental declamatory style. The King's potential brides—two called Caroline, two called Anne—enter to perky neoclassical strains. Act II has a sequence of a lushly romantic aria for a Caroline, speech over sound effects for Froissart, a Prime Minister's address in Weillish cabaret vein, a Dessau-like duet for King and Minister, a rousing Weill chorus for Genoese bowmen. The Battle of Crécy is again narrative over sound effects: massed whistling from the male chorus imitates the flight of arrows. An English bowman's arioso recalls strains of "God Save the King" and "John Brown's Body." In Act III, the Burghers of Calais break into Latin-American rhythms. (The distasteful episode burlesques the Flemish-deputies scene in *Don Carlos;* in Santa Fe the burghers wore formal attire but were trouserless.) The opera comes to a climax in Prokofiev's epic, *War and Peace* choral manner, but a big affirmation—"To Paris! Hark to the beating of great birds' wings!"—then fades before the bleak whine of a wind machine. A candid essay, by Hannu-Ilari Lampila, in the Santa Fe program book suggested, rightly, that "Sallinen's principle was to follow the libretto so closely that in places he attempts to subordinate his music to it completely," and that "film music may well give us the right basis for studying the artistic principles of Sallinen's score." *The King Goes Forth to France* didn't amount to much: a long, not particularly entertaining evening of big issues handled fliply, or tritely, with smart, self-defeating obliquity. In comparisons with Weill's *Mahagonny*, Henze's *We Come to the River* (which Santa Fe did in 1984), or—the closest parallel—Ligeti's *Le Grand Macabre, The King Goes Forth* paled.

Santa Fe did pretty well by the piece. Richard Buckley's conducting was secure. The Danish baritone Mikael Melbye was a confident King, forthright in tone, lacking only clear English pronunciation. (The opera was sung in an English translation by Stephen Oliver and Erkki Arni.) James Ramlet's Prime

Minister was trenchant. Stephanie Sundine, Emily Golden, Melanie Helton, and Joyce Castle were the Carolines and Annes. The actor David Garrison, as Froissart, gripped attention at all appearances: so much so as to suggest that the whole thing might have been more effective—and more seemly—as a crisp spoken drama larded with musical numbers.

The heart of the Tanglewood festival is a week of contemporary music performed, for the most part, by the Fellows of the Tanglewood Music Center—young instrumentalists, singers, conductors, and composers learning their craft. Leon Fleisher directs the Center; this year's programs were arranged and, largely, conducted by Oliver Knussen, a Tanglewood Fellow in 1970, when he was eighteen, and this year's composer-in-residence. The week began with Knussen's *Fanfares for Tanglewood,* completed the day before—bright calls for three brass groups, with bells and gongs. A deuxième, and Knussen's *Coursing,* followed the première. A fair amount of British music was done during the week. Jonathan Lloyd's lively miniature *Feuding Fiddles,* composed as if for two country fiddlers who also know the Berg concerto, was a shade too politely performed by Marta Szlubowska and Sara Parkins. In Robert Saxton's Concerto for Orchestra, the young Tanglewood players sounded more of the fine detail in its waves of "mystic radiance" than the BBC Symphony had managed at the Prom première, two years ago. In Simon Bainbridge's fizzy *Concertante in Moto Perpetuo,* the virtuoso oboe part was bravely tackled by Alexa Zirbel. Britten's Third String Quartet was gently and movingly played by the Cassatt Quartet. Jonathan Harvey's *Mortuos plango, vivos voco* (its title the inscription on a Winchester Cathedral bell that, together with a treble voice, provided the sonic material of the piece) was a hit of three electro-acoustic recitals that gathered work from the IRCAM, Columbia-Princeton, Stanford, and MIT studios.

Danish "new simplicity"—less primitive, more fanciful in its procedures than American minimalism—was happily represented by Hans Abrahamsen's *Märchenbilder* and Poul Ruders's *Manhattan Abstraction*. Louis Andriessen's Symphony for Open Strings produced remarkable new sounds and effects from the limited means defined in its title. Toru Takemitsu was prominent; his *Rocking Mirror Daybreak, Water-Ways, Dream/Window,* and *From Far Beyond Chrysanthemums and November Fog* were done. It's impossible to dislike but hard to feel strongly in any way about these delicate, wispy "intuitive" scores. In strong contrast, on a bill with *Water-Ways,* was Henze's new *Fandango sopra un basso del Padre Soler,* first played in Paris earlier this year—an exuberant, exhilarating big-orchestra piece, destined for popularity.

Michael Torke, born in Milwaukee in 1961 (and a Tanglewood Fellow in 1982 and 1983), was the only young composer—under thirty—performed by the orchestra. His *Ecstatic Orange,* first done last year by the Brooklyn Philharmonic, is twelve minutes of moto perpetuo in E, based on a single bright tune that dances through the glittering texture, breaking into little motifs and sparkling little canons, while the music passes through kaleidoscopic episodes with color headings: "Absinthe and apricot," "Terra cotta," "Unripe pumpkin." Torke is an original. He's puzzling, rather as Lloyd and Pärt are, to any listener who, bored by minimalism and glutted with neoromantic nostalgia, can yet find himself

538

charmed or stirred by modern music as bravely untroubled in its harmonic innocence as *Ecstatic Orange* (or, for that matter, Henze's fandango). Among the senior American composers represented were Stefan Wolpe, Elliott Carter (by *Penthode,* whose high challenge was confidently met), George Perle (by the elegant, intelligent Fourth Woodwind Quintet, this year's Pulitzer Prize winner), Milton Babbitt (by tape pieces), Gunther Schuller, Morton Feldman, and Yehudi Wyner (by the glowing, poetic song cycle *On This Most Voluptuous Night*). There were two premières besides Knussen's fanfares: *Cinq Visages de LaForgue,* by Alan Stout (born in 1932), for soprano and small orchestra, is a set of five short, delicate slow movements, meticulously worked; the Double Concerto of Deborah Drattell (born in 1954), for violin, cello, and an ensemble of nine, consists of three intense, somewhat overwrought slow movements.

The policy of "compartmentalizing" contemporary music is sometimes questioned. (Through Tanglewood's thirty mass-audience weekend programs in the big Shed, just Bernstein's Serenade, Knussen's *Music for a Puppet Court,* and Pärt's *Collage on the Theme B-A-C-H* were scattered.) But there is much to be said for playing such programs to an alert, eager, interested audience—listeners who have gathered to hear the new music, not to sit through it for the sake of familiar fare or a famous soloist in the rest of the program. These new-music concerts, given in the thousand-seat Theater–Concert Hall, were well attended— by hundreds, if not by the thousands who throng the Shed and the lawns around it. The atmosphere was lively, inspiriting. After the last orchestra concert (Torke, Saxton, Takemitsu, Ruders), the Tanglewood players set up a cheer of their own—"Ol-ly! Ol-ly!"—for their inspiring young composer-conductor.

INDEX

Compositions reviewed are indexed under their composers. Boldface figures indicate extended discussion or, in long entries, distinguish reviews of the work or the performer in question from passing references. Musical organizations outside New York based in a particular city are generally listed under that city (e.g., Boston, Opera Company of).

541

542

543

566